THE SHORT OXFORD HISTORY
OF THE MODERN WORLD

General Editor: J. M. ROBERTS

THE SHORT OXFORD HISTORY OF THE MODERN WORLD

General Editor: J. M. ROBERTS

BARRICADES AND BORDERS

═══

EUROPE 1800–1914

═══

SECOND EDITION

ROBERT GILDEA

OXFORD
UNIVERSITY PRESS

Oxford University Press, Great Clarendon Street, Oxford OX2 6DP

Oxford New York
Athens Auckland Bangkok Bogotá Beunos Aires Calcutta
Cape Town Chennai Dar es Salaam Delhi Florence Hong Kong Istanbul
Karachi Kuala Lumpur Madrid Melbourne Mexico City Mumbai
Nairobi Paris São Paulo Singapore Taipei Tokyo Toronto Warsaw

with associated companies in
Berlin Ibadan

Oxford is a registered trade mark of Oxford University Press

Published in the United States
by Oxford University Press Inc., New York

First published 1987
Second edition 1996
Paperback first published 1996

British Library Cataloguing in Publication Data

Data available

Library of Congress Cataloging in Publication Data
Gildea, Robert.
Barricades and borders.
(Short Oxford history of the modern world)
Bibliography: p.
Includes index.
1. Europe—History—1789–1900. 2. Europe—
History—1871–1918. I. Title. II. Series.
D358.G55 1987 940.2 86-28577

ISBN 0–19–820625–9

5 7 9 10 8 6 4

Printed in Great Britain
on acid-free paper by
Biddles Ltd, www.biddles.co.uk

TO MY PARENTS

PREFACE

Were I asked to write this book today, I should probably decline the honour. It is a rash enterprise to attempt a 'total history' of nineteenth-century Europe while being able to consult only a fraction of the literature. Some aspects inevitably proved more interesting than others. Students at King's College, London, on whom I inflicted my first lectures inspired by this brief, complained that I was obsessed by nationalism and had too much to say about 'little countries' in eastern Europe. One afternoon, researching the niceties of Swedish banking history, doubts of my own about the wisdom of the project almost got the better of my patience. There is no pretence here to originality: at best, the book is intended as a humane synthesis of new and not-so-new writing on nineteenth-century Europe and aimed at the student of the 1980s. I am indebted to the resources of the Bodleian and British Libraries. Among those who gave me crucial advice I would like to thank Jeremy Black, Tim Blanning, Peter Dickson, Robert Evans, Anne Hardy, Derek McKay, Tony Nicholls, Andy Pitt, Mike Rosen, Hamish Scott, Liam Smith, Nigel Smith, and Andrew Wathey. Philip Waller read painstakingly through the first draft of the manuscript, and saved me from too many errors in British history. John Roberts has been a model editor, and repeatedly sent me back to the drawing-board to mend my text. The typists who have tried to cope with my handwriting are too numerous to mention, but in particular I am grateful to Gil Dixon and Belinda Timlin. The unfailing scepticism of my students in both London and Oxford has forced me to clarify my ideas, and to reject many of them, but their enthusiasm has always come up with others to take their place.

R.N.G.

Merton College, Oxford
January 1986

PREFACE TO SECOND EDITION

This book has been substantially revised for the second edition, both to take into account the shifts of recent research, and to clarify the text in the light of teaching experience. The most drastic revisions have been to sections dealing with the middle classes, religion, socialism, and nationalism; there is also an entirely new section on feminism. I hope that the student of the 1990s will find that the work has acquired something in the way of a new lease of life.

R.N.G.

Oxford
July 1995

CONTENTS

MAPS

TABLES

PART I

Europe 1800–1850

I

THE QUICKENING PACE

Demographic Revolution

In the *Essay on the Principle of Population*, first published in 1798 and substantially revised in 1803, Thomas Robert Malthus, a Surrey curate and Fellow of Jesus College, Cambridge, issued a gloomy forecast for the nineteenth century. Population, he argued, had a constant tendency to increase geometrically, doubling in size every twenty-five years. But the resources necessary to sustain that increase could be multiplied only arithmetically, adding only a fixed amount every year. Individuals had therefore to impose a 'preventive check' on the natural growth of the population by postponing marriage until they were in a position to maintain a family, and to abstain from sex in the meantime. If they did not, the population would be reduced to the level that resources could maintain by means of 'positive checks' in the shape of war, famine, disease, and the fourth Rider of the Apocalypse who would always be with them, death.

As an analysis of conditions prevailing at the end of the eighteenth century, Malthus's study was remarkably shrewd. The population of Europe had been growing rapidly since about 1750. But closer inspection shows that the rate of growth was not the same in all countries, and the growth-rates before and after 1800 often varied considerably. The population of Spain and Portugal grew steadily between 1750 and 1800, and that of Ireland and Hungary increased dramatically. But in all four cases the growth-rate declined after 1800. In the Scandinavian countries a moderate growth-rate before 1800 improved to a good growth-rate after 1800. The performance of France was disappointing. The increase in her growth-rate was only marginal. Most remarkable, however, was the achievement of England, Wales, and Scotland, where the growth-rate doubled after 1800.

A population explosion might seem logically to be the result of more births, but from the end of the eighteenth century in western Europe the birth-rate was in fact declining. Between 1790 and 1850 it fell in Germany from 40 per thousand of the population to 36.1 per thousand, in Great Britain from 35.4 per thousand to 32.6 per thousand and in France from 32.5 per thousand to the very low figure of 26.7 per thousand. What really mattered was that the death-rate was falling, so that people were living longer. In the same period the death-rate fell from 29 per thousand to 26.8 per thousand in Germany, from 23.1 per thousand to 22.4 per thousand in Britain and from 27 to 23.8 per thousand in France. The conquest of major epidemic diseases

TABLE 1. *The population of European countries, c.1750–1851*

	Population (m.)		Average annual rate of growth (%)	Population 1851	Average annual rate of growth (%)
	1750	1801			
England & Wales	6.140[a]	8.893	0.7	17.928	1.3
Scotland	1.265[b]	1.608	0.6	2.889	1.2
France	20.000[c]	27.349	0.5	35.783	0.6
Ireland	3.191[d]	4.753[g]	1.0	6.552	0.6
Hungary	3.000[d]	8.500[h]	3.0	13.192	0.7
Spain	9.160[e]	10.541[i]	0.5	15.455[j]	0.4
Portugal	2.410[e]	2.932	0.6	3.844[k]	0.5
Denmark	0.798[f]	0.929	0.5	1.415	0.8
Norway	0.671[b]	0.883	0.6	1.490[l]	0.9
Sweden	1.781	2.347	0.6	3.471	0.8

[a] 1751.   [b] 1755.   [c] 1740.   [d] 1754.   [e] 1768.   [f] 1769.   [g] 1791.   [h] 1789.
[i] 1797.   [j] 1857.   [k] 1854.   [l] 1855.

such as the plague and smallpox was an important contribution, but vulnerability to disease had persisted as a result of poor health. The main reason for the general improvement in health was a marked increase in the food supply.

Whereas before 1740 population increases had been regularly cut back by massive subsistence crises which killed off the surplus by starvation and disease, the increase in food supply after 1740 muffled the effects of Malthus's 'positive checks' and permitted sustained population growth. It has been suggested that the last great European famine took place in 1816–17, when volcanic dust in the atmosphere caused by an eruption in Indonesia inflicted a very cold summer and failure of the harvest. Countries bordering the North Sea and the Baltic, such as Great Britain, Belgium, the Netherlands, Prussia, and Scandinavia escaped with lower grain prices and lower mortality than southern and western Germany, Switzerland, the Habsburg lands, the Balkans, and Spain, where hunger and disease took a heavy toll. Later subsistence crises, as in 1831–2 or 1846–7, were less severe or confined to regions that were hampered by agricultural backwardness and isolated from supply routes, and therefore relief, should their own harvest fail. In general this meant parts of southern and eastern Europe such as Spain, which suffered a major subsistence crisis in 1856–7, or Russia, which was struck by famine in 1891–2. The death-rate in these countries remain over 30 per thousand and the pace of population growth that had been signalled in the later eighteenth century was not sustained into the nineteenth.

There were basically two ways in which the food supply could be stepped up: the conquest and improvement of marginal land, bringing forest, moorland, and fen under cultivation; and the elimination of fallow land. It is clear that what was deemed 'wasteland' in one respect might be economically

viable in another, such as the marshes of the Po delta which provided employment for fowlers and fishermen, or the oak forests of Serbia which offered
rough grazing for pigs. But whereas in eastern Europe, where the population
was not too dense, it was still possible to practise a primitive field-grass husbandry—ploughing up new land, cropping it to exhaustion, and then moving
on—in western Europe the pressure of numbers meant that the land had to
be reclaimed once and for all and put to the most productive use. The danger
there was that agriculture was based on cereal production, especially cash
crops like wheat, which drained the soil of goodness and subjected it what the
English farmer Arthur Young called the 'thraldom of regular fallows'. As
late as 1848 a quarter of arable land in Bohemia, the most advanced part of
the Austrian Monarchy, was under fallow. The way out of the 'infernal circle'
of cropping to exhaustion and leaving fallow was to cultivate new crops, such
as maize in southern France and the Danubian Principalities, or potatoes on
the North European Plain from Ireland to White Russia. Potatoes had the
advantage of producing three times as much food per acre as grain. Another
solution was to perfect the rotation of crops. Artificial grasses like clover
rotated with cereals eliminated fallow by restoring nitrogen rapidly to the
soil, while rotation with root-crops like turnips both improved the soil and
provided winter feed for animals. Whereas the extensive farming of eastern
Europe was widely given up to livestock, in western Europe the tyranny of
cereals meant that livestock was ignored, with the exception of draught animals, sheep on the uplands of Spain and Italy, and a few mangy beasts turned
loose on the stubble after the harvest. Too often cattle were regarded as
rivals for food, and yet animals provided manure which (before the importation of Peruvian guano after 1840) was the only fertilizer which could enrich
the soil and increase the yield of grain. A balanced animal and arable husbandry was practised only in parts of the British Isles, Denmark, Flanders,
and the Swiss cantons, which were oriented towards the market.

To increase the food supply was the main way to stave off a Malthusian
'positive check' so that the population could increase. Another way was to
increase the volume of employment outside agriculture. But this was conditional on two factors: that agricultural productivity was high enough to feed
a non-agricultural population; and that there was sufficient demand for manufactured goods to support those engaged in making them. Much of Europe
was still confined to a subsistence economy, with local communities not only
growing and consuming their own food but making their own clothes, shoes,
and tools as well. However, the impact of a wider demand was beginning to
make itself felt in 1800, whether it was the wartime demand for iron cannon
and timbered ships, the demand for cheap cotton textiles in foreign markets,
or the demand for beer and spirits at home. It was this demand that fuelled
the beginnings of the industrial revolution in Europe. By about 1850 the
proportion of the active population engaged in manufacturing, mining or

TABLE 2. *Structure of the active population in Europe, c.1850 (%)*

	Agriculture, forestry, fishing	Manufacturing, mining, building	Trade, banking, transport	Services, armed forces	Activity not adequately described
Great Britain 1851	21.9	48.1	5.8	18.4	5.5
Belgium 1856	46.8	37.4	4.9	10.9	—
France 1856	51.7	26.9	6.8	14.6	—
Ireland 1851	48.4	25.1	5.0	10.9	10.6
Netherlands 1849	44.2	24.1	10.9	18.1	2.7
Denmark 1850	49.4	21.9	4.3	7.4	17.0
Austria 1857	52.3	17.6	1.6	10.0	18.5
Hungary 1857	56.1	10.1	1.7	13.3	18.9

Source: P. Bairoch, *La Population active et sa structure* (Brussels, 1968).

building had reached 17 per cent in France, 37 per cent in Belgium, and 48 per cent in Britain. On the other hand the map of industrialized Europe was very patchy: the regions around Glasgow and Belfast, the Midlands, North of England, northern France, and Belgium, Alsace, Rhineland-Westphalia, Saxony, Silesia, and Bohemia, with Catalonia and Lombardy the only possible contenders in Mediterranean Europe. They were islands in an agricultural sea. Over half the active population was still engaged in agriculture in France and Austria in 1850, with 62 per cent in Italy and a much higher proportion in eastern Europe. The very low level of agricultural productivity kept the vast majority of the population in these countries locked into the countryside in order to ensure their subsistence. The shallowness of rural demand was scarcely adequate to sustain industrial production at the best of times; when the harvest failed, the results could be disastrous. For the first two-thirds of the nineteenth century bad harvests were the single most important cause of industrial depression. And when the urban populations starved, revolution never seemed very far away.

The consequence of minimal industrialization was the congestion of the countryside as a growing population fought for the same amount of land. Plots were infinitely subdivided in many parts of France, northern Spain, southern Germany, and Sweden. In Ireland the growth of the potato made possible a greater fragmentation than would have been possible under grain, the availability of plots encouraged early marriage and the population supported by them doubled between 1781 and 1841 from four to eight millions. In the early period of the industrial revolution it is true that most industry was based not in the towns but in the countryside, and provided ancillary occupations for rural inhabitants, which might enable them to make ends meet. In the textile industry much spinning was for long done by peasant-women at home with their spinning-wheels. When this became mechanized the factory-spun yarn was 'put out' by merchants to peasant-weavers from Lancashire to Silesia. From the Pyrenees to the Urals, the iron industry prospered near forests which provided charcoal to smelt the ore and fast-flowing rivers to work its tilt hammers. Coal-mining, brewing, and distilling were usually undertaken on the estates of large landowners. Fishing provided an additional resource for the peasantry of the Atlantic and Mediterranean coastlines. But the subdivision of the land still left a growing mass of landless labourers, who were fully employed only during the harvest season and whose very mass pushed down the level of the wages they were paid. In times of hardship they might form bands of brigands in order to terrorize landowners. Even in England, where a system of parish relief existed after 1795, agricultural labourers rose in revolt across the southern counties in 1830.

In many cases the rural surplus, unable to survive in the countryside, moved off to the towns in search of work. In addition charity, both lay and ecclesiastical, was town-based. The early part of the nineteenth century was one of rapid urbanization. A quarter of a million people moved into London in the 1840s, so that its population reached one million by 1850, including an Irish-born colony of 109,000. At that date Paris had over half a million people, Vienna and Moscow nearly that. Whether the immigrants would find employment was another matter. For the typical large European town in this period was still not a mushrooming mill or mining town but a city dominated by a princely court (numerous in Germany and Italy), the Church with its cathedrals and convents, the army with its garrisons, and the magistracy with its train of legal officials and litigants. Their growth was generated by state-building, but they were parasitic on the economy of the surrounding countryside. A second kind of town was commercial, and these expanded more or less rapidly according to patterns of trade. Thus towns involved in the booming Atlantic trade, such as London, Paris, Rotterdam, and Antwerp, grew rapidly in the period 1800–50, while those involved in the declining Baltic or Mediterranean trades, such as Stockholm, Copenhagen, Amsterdam, Lisbon, Genoa, and Venice, grew rather slowly. Even in the industrial towns, the structure of employment was not congenial to the immigrant worker. Large-scale industry was to be found in the suburbs or in single-industry towns away from the capital. The skilled trades were dominated by craft guilds which imposed strict limitations on entry in order to guarantee their market. Often there was little alternative to finding casual and irregular employment in street trades, sweated workshops, domestic service, on the building sites, or waterfront, or as a last resort in the army, crime, or prostitution. In the 1840s, a decade in which doctors and social reformers for the first time took stock of the misery of these populations, the term 'proletariat' meant not so much industrial wage-workers as this strange race, savage and apart. The conditions they lived in were atrocious: overcrowded lodging houses, cellars, and garrets, shanty towns in the insalubrious districts beyond the town walls.

TABLE 3. *Proportion of population living in cities of over 100,000 inhabitants*

	c.1800	c.1850
England and Wales	9.7	22.6
Scotland	—	16.9
Denmark	10.9	9.6
Netherlands	11.5	7.3
Portugal	9.5	7.2
Belgium	—	6.8
Italy	4.4	6.0
France	2.8	4.6
Spain	1.4	4.4
Ireland	3.1	3.9
Prussia	1.8	3.1
Austria	2.6	2.8
Russia	1.4	1.6

Source: A. F. Weber, *The Growth of Cities in the Nineteenth Century* (1899; Cornell, 1963), pp. 144–5.

Disease in them was rife and when cholera swept across Europe in 1832, it took an especially heavy toll in the working-class ghettoes. Figures for Sweden in the period 1816–40 show that the death-rate was 22.3 per thousand among the rural population, 34.4 per thousand among the urban population and 45.1 per thousand in Stockholm. Towns everywhere were death-traps in which growth was maintained only by a constant supply of recruits from the countryside. Cut off from the countryside, they would have wasted to nothing.

The one safety-valve for over-population was emigration. Clearly it did not attain in this period the proportions it reached later in the century. Emigrants from Europe averaged about 110,000 a year in 1821–50 as against 900,000 a year in 1881–1915. The first burst of emigration dated from the aftermath of the Napoleonic Wars, when agricultural depression and urban unemployment made an alternative existence in North America or the colonies seem extremely attractive. In 1830 Edward Gibbon Wakefield founded the National Colonization Society to promote British settlement. But the main zones of emigration were those like Ireland and South Germany where the parcellization of properties had reduced the peasantry to a marginal existence which made them extremely vulnerable at times of agrarian crisis. In Europe the harvest of 1846–7 was bad, and in Ireland the failure of the potato crop was catastrophic. On the other hand the cost of transatlantic fares fell by 75 per cent between 1815 and 1840. Between 1847 and 1854 about 935,000 people emigrated from Germany and 1,629,000 from Ireland, travelling steerage from Rotterdam, Antwerp, and Liverpool.

The Expansion of the Market

Though rising agricultural and industrial production was necessary to avert the 'positive checks' on the growth of population described by Malthus, a growing population was also an element of the expanding market which was a pre-condition of agricultural and industrial revolution. But given the shallowness of the domestic market, and its vulnerability to harvest failure, foreign markets played a leading role in the stimulation of economic growth. This gave an immediate advantage to western European countries with a seaboard, colonies, and fleets and confined those countries of eastern Europe that were to all intents and purposes land-locked to a sluggish economic development. In 1800 the import of spices and coffee from the East Indies, the shipping of slaves from Africa to the West Indian plantations, and the import of sugar and cotton from the West Indies for re-export to other parts of Europe accounted for the prosperity of Glasgow, Liverpool, Bristol, Nantes, Bordeaux, and Barcelona. In addition, Great Britain was fast becoming the workshop of the world, exporting almost as much cotton cloth as long-established woollen cloth, together with hardware, to Europe, the United States, and beyond.

The economic issue rapidly resolved itself into a military issue. Sea-power was required to secure colonies and control foreign markets, and in turn the possession of colonies and foreign markets promoted industrial and thus military power. Great Britain, for example, depended on her former colonies in America and on the Baltic for the importation of 'naval stores', timber, tar, and hemp, without which her fighting fleet could not sail. After 1795 she used her sea-power to cut off France and her European allies from their colonies and export outlets and to confiscate or destroy their shipping. But the triumph of Napoleon on the Continent presented a severe threat to British trade. After his defeat of Prussia in 1806 and of Russia in 1807, and following the French seizure of power in Spain and bullying of Portugal, Napoleon managed to force every state on the northern coasts of Europe, with the sole exception of Sweden, into a Continental Blockade to shut the British out of European markets. In the first instance it was simple economic warfare, to throw the British economy into chaos by depriving her of outlets for her surplus products and to make the import of essential raws, foodstuffs, and semi-finished goods extremely difficult and a drain on her resources, since she would have to pay in bullion. In addition, it was part of a grand design whereby France would be able to catch up and even overtake Great Britain as the leading European industrial and military power. The Napoleonic land-empire was to be made into a zone protected artificially against cheap British textiles and hardware, and France would be compensated for the loss of her colonies by markets of replacement on the European mainland, harnessed to her own economy by means of preferential treaties and the monopoly of some markets, as in Italy.

There is no doubt that the Continental System had a profound effect not only on the French economy but also on other economies in Europe. Protected against cheap British imports yet provided with the whole French Empire as an internal market, the Continental textile industry flourished. The Norman woollen towns which had suffered under the treaty with Britain in 1786 now revived, as did the woollen industry at Aachen and Verviers in Belgium, which was mechanized by an expatriate manufacturer of jennies from Lancashire, William Cockerill. Cotton manufacture, importing the raw material from the Levant, took off in Normandy, Alsace, in Flanders at Roubaix and Ghent, and in Saxony. The silk industry expanded in Lyons, drawing on the raw silk cultivation of Lombardy, and at Krefeld, on the left bank of the Rhine, while linen did well at Elberfeld and Barmen on its right bank, and in Silesia. Again in Belgium, at Liège, the traditional iron industry based on the charcoal-furnaces and water-power of the Ardennes was developed under the eye of William Cockerill into a modern ironworks, with puddling furnace and rolling-mill, to cast cannon and build machines. However, the British economy was not brought to its knees, thanks to the supremacy of British sea-power. The Orders-in-Council of the British government in November 1807 replied to Napoleon's boycott by blockading the ports of France and her allies, allowing them to trade with each other and with neutral countries only if they did so via Britain. Steps were taken to ensure that the United States never became part of Napoleon's system, a development that might have been disastrous. Britain attacked French, Dutch, and Spanish colonies, inflicting terrible damage on the Catalan cotton industry. Then, after the occupation of Spain by France in 1808, the Spanish American colonies revolted. Britain penetrated the newly liberated Latin American markets, while the shift of French troops from northern Europe to the Iberian peninsula meant that henceforth the boycott of British trade could only be ineffectively enforced.

If the Napoleonic Empire was a common market, it was of the 'one-way' variety, subordinated to the economic interests of France. Nevertheless, the period after 1815 represented a step backwards, for the fragmentation of Europe into little states led to the multiplication of customs barriers along state boundaries and tolls on important rivers such as those at the mouth of the Rhine imposed by the Dutch. Imposed by war-ravaged states burdened by debt in order to raise revenue, these barriers severely restricted trade between European states. As far as wider trading relations were concerned, the aftermath of the Napoleonic Wars was similarly disastrous. The dismantling of the system of blockade and counter-blockade which had provided an artificial protective tariff for Continental Europe now exposed it again to the competition of cheap British textiles. The textile industry suffered (notably the linen manufacture of Flanders and Silesia which could not withstand the competition of cheap cotton goods) and governments were pressed to protect native industries by the establishment of import duties. On the agricultural front, the end of the war led to the flooding of the European grain market with Russian grain, which was cultivated on a growing scale by serf labour in the black-earth provinces above Odessa. Since 1750 prices had been rising but this period came brutally to an end with a depression lasting from 1818 to 1830. In Prussia, hitherto a leading exporter of grain to countries like Britain, the Junkers tried to weather the depression by switching to other enterprises, such as sugar-beet, distilling, or sheep-farming for the wool market, but they were racked by debt. In Great Britain the landowning aristocracy sought to protect itself by having the government pass protective 'Corn Laws' which kept out cheap foreign grain for the benefit of home producers.

Such defensive measures were understandable. But they restricted markets even further and could only hamper economic growth. In response, lobbies appeared which favoured the dismantlement of all obstacles in restraint of free trade. They drew their basic principles from Adam Smith, who had argued that each country should invest its capital in what it produced most efficiently, so that its products would have the maximum exchangeable value. The corollary of this was that a 'vent for surplus' must exist, that surplus produce must be exchanged in foreign markets without official let or hindrance. As a result the volume of the export market would stimulate greater productive powers at home in the form of an increased division of labour, and wealth would multiply. Spokesmen for the manufacturing interest like David Ricardo, whose *Principles of Political Economy and Taxation* was published in 1817, proposed that the Corn Laws should be abolished and cheap foreign grain accepted if agrarian countries in turn accepted British manufactures. Cheap bread would permit manufacturers to lower wages, increase profits, and attract more capital investment, while the lower costs of production would enable them to undercut all other rivals in the world market for ironware and textiles. For their part the Prussian Junkers, faced by Corn Laws in Britain, the Netherlands (which included Belgium between 1815 and 1830), and elsewhere, were prepared to accept foreign manufactured goods if manufacturing nations would accept their grain, wool, and timber.

Some progress was made towards the establishment of free trade by 1830, but not without squeals of protest from the protectionists. In Great Britain the government of the Duke of Wellington converted the blank prohibition of the Corn Laws in 1828 into a sliding scale whereby duties fell as the price of grain at home rose. However it was influenced more by the need to safeguard food supplies in years of scarcity than by Ricardo's advocacy of maximum industrialization. Curiously enough, the first parts of Europe really to profit from free trade were the Danubian Principalities. Entirely subordinate to the Ottoman Empire until 1829, they could send their wheat, timber, and livestock only to Constantinople, where the price was artificially low. But a Russian victory over the Turks in that year opened wide markets in the west to the Principalities; prices rose and production was stimulated. Prussia was likewise anxious to find outlets, and was the driving force behind the abolition of high tariffs between states or groups of states in Germany and the foundation of a Zollverein, or customs union. The south German states (Bavaria, Württemberg, Hesse-Darmstadt) joined the Prussian system by 1831, and gained considerably from the ability to export their foodstuffs and raw materials to North Germany. But the main attraction of Prussia's customs union was the foreign outlets it was able to negotiate for German products. In 1831, for example, Prussia concluded a Rhine Navigation Act with the Netherlands, freeing that waterway of all tolls. This attracted the central German states, including Saxony with its growing cotton industry, into the Zollverein, which was fully constituted in 1834. Subsequently, the Zollverein negotiated commercial treaties with the Netherlands (1839), Britain (1841), and Belgium (1844). But while this satisfied the Junker landowners and exporters such as Rudolf Camphausen, who founded a steamship company at Cologne in 1844, and David Hansemann, who promoted the Cologne to Antwerp railway, it did nothing to placate the industrialists of the Rhineland. In return for trading outlets these manufacturers had to suffer competition from Dutch refined sugar, British textiles, and Belgian cast-iron, rails, and rolling stock produced by John Cockerill at the vast ironworks at Seraing, near Liège. The protectionist manufacturers of Germany found an influential mouthpiece in Friedrich List, former professor of political economy at Tübingen. His *National System of Political Economy* (1841) pointed out that Smith's vision of an universal economy, in which each country would produce what it was best suited for, was only a camouflage. It meant that all countries would be subjected to the industrial hegemony of Great Britain, in return for which France, Spain, and Portugal would provide Britain with wines and Germany deliver 'toys for children, wooden clocks [and] philological writings'.[1] But this made sense only in a Utopian world of universal peace. In order to catch up, other nations must protect their infant industries by artificial means, as Britain had herself done at an earlier period by mercantilism. Trade was subordinate to politics. Free trade without equality of industrial development was imperialism.

British manufacturers continued the campaign for free trade, conceding cheap grain imports as the price for wider export markets. The Anti-Corn Law League was set up in 1838 by Richard Cobden and John Bright to expound their views. This 'Manchester school' of political economy refuted old Malthusian arguments that massive industrialization would only produce a glut and fall in profits, and denounced the Corn Laws as a rampart of aristocratic privilege. The triumph of the Conservative party against a Whig-Radical alliance in the elections of 1841 seemed to safeguard the Corn Laws,

---

[1] F. List, *National System of Political Economy* (tr. Philadelphia, 1865), 207.

but the Prime Minister, Robert Peel, managed to get the Commons to agree to their repeal in 1846, albeit at the sacrifice of his own career. It was noted that the Corn Laws had done nothing to maintain prices in the period of glut that followed the Napoleonic Wars. In 1845 famine struck in Ireland and only the import of vast quantities of foreign grain could limit the extent of the disaster. Without the protection of the Corn Laws, landowners would need to improve their estates, switch to mixed husbandry or cattle-farming, and look to the growing demands of urban markets.

Free trade only became an issue as improving communications, the vehicle of import and export, broke up the honeycomb pattern of local economies and unified them into a wider market. The central problem in the early nineteenth century was how bulk goods could be transported. Roads built privately by turnpike trusts were fast: coaches travelled from London to Manchester or Paris to Rouen (half as far) in a day in the 1780s, but were for passengers. Governments were interested in roads only for strategic reasons—to carry armies—whether the military roads built in Scotland by British engineers or the roads built by Napoleon from Paris to the counter-revolutionary Vendée, to the Rhineland, across the Alps, and down to Illyria on the Adriatic coast.

Waterways were far more significant for the carriage of bulk, the cost of which on navigable river or canal was between a half and a quarter of the cost by road. The deepening of rivers, cutting of canals, and building of deep-water harbours extended the range of sea-borne commerce without difficulty into the low-lying countryside of Britain, northern France, Belgium, and the Netherlands. Under the auspices of Prussia much was done to improve navigation along the Rhine and the Rhine was linked to the Danube in 1845. But just as the roads of eastern Europe were uniformly bad, so the Danube remained intractable for both natural and political reasons, and faced the wrong way. In Russia, similarly, many rivers turned towards land-locked seas, and raw materials and fuel might be situated hundreds of miles apart. Prussia was not much better off, for the Vistula, Oder, Elbe, and Rhine flowed from south to north, while after the acquisition of the Rhineland in 1815 the country was oriented politically east-west. Grain, timber, and wool were exported to Great Britain from Danzig or Königsberg, and woollen and cotton yarns imported at Hamburg or up the Rhine, but there was no direct communication in Prussia between the agricultural east and the industrial centre of Rhineland-Westphalia.

A revolution in transport was made possible by steam. On the waterways steamboats plied across the Channel after 1821, on the Rhine after 1824, on the Danube after 1831, and on the Volga after 1843 but they were viable only on such short hauls. Fuel was heavy and expensive, and over long distances steam was no faster than sail. China was opened up by an armed steamship, *Nemesis*, in the Opium War of 1841, but it was the sailing-ships, not the paddle-boats, that brought back silk from Bengal or tea from China. The major impact of steam was made through the classic achievement of nineteenth-century transport: the railways. In the first quarter of the century, railways were already transporting coal from the pithead to the nearest canal, or port, whether in Northumberland, South Wales, or the coal basin of Saint-Etienne. As such, they were only an adjunct of the waterway system. It was the perfection of the steam engine by George Stephenson in 1825 that converted the railway into a means of transporting heavy goods which would replace both road and canal. By 1835 it was being adopted in Belgium and Germany; the railway linking Antwerp, Liège, and Cologne was finished by 1844, and the connections across Germany from Cassel in the west to Leipzig and Warsaw in the east were completed by 1850. Much more than the Zollverein, the railway made Germany into an economic unit. In addition, the railway transformed the course of the industrial revolution in Europe. The first industrial revolution, that of textiles, had been dependent on consumer demand for stimulus, and had been financed on a shoe-string. The second, that of coal and iron, was provoked uniquely by the railway mania of the 1840s, and demanded real capital investment.

Capitalist Practices: Agriculture

Backwardness may have been the characteristic of agriculture in many parts of Europe in 1800, looked at from the economic point of view. But in a social sense agriculture was at the service of the peasant community, and the communal and collective patterns that were imposed on agriculture, though they might not be the most efficient in terms of production, were often in the best interests of that community. The woodland and waste that lay beyond the cultivated land was common land, which provided timber for fuel and building, and rough pasture for cattle, sheep, and goats. On the arable land a system of three-field rotation prevailed, the third lying fallow. In the *bocage* regions of Europe, from Brittany and Westphalia to Bavaria and parts of the Hungarian Plain, where isolated farmsteads were dotted among little fields surrounded by hedges, the peasants could farm their plots with relative independence. But in the open fields of the North European Plain, from northern France and Germany to Denmark, southern Sweden, Poland, and Russia, the ownership by one peasant of strips in many different fields required the collective regulation of ploughing, sowing, and harvesting. This was especially so in Poland and Russia where the strips were periodically redistributed by the peasant commune among the households according to their needs and to ensure that no family obtained a monopoly of the best land. After the harvest the peasants enjoyed the collective right to glean and to graze livestock on the stubble. The simple technology in these villages kept social stratification to a minimum. Use was made of the light *araire* or *sokha*, instead of the heavy plough. It did not cut very deep, but on the other hand it was ideal for thin, sandy soils. It was cheap, and could be drawn by a nag instead of several pairs of oxen. The heavy plough and the ox-teams only served to differentiate between the rich peasants who owned them and the landless labourers who were employed as ploughmen.

The peasant community was concerned essentially with subsistence agriculture. For this reason the rapid rise in agricultural prices between 1750 and 1815 which favoured a capitalist and market-oriented approach to agriculture threatened the traditional peasant community. In some cases capitalist farming could still operate within its constraints. For instance, seigneurs exploited their privileges to drive their flocks and herds on to the common land. The response of poor peasants in France was to demand the equal division of the common land, something that was conceded by the Revolutionary government of 1793, should a third of the village community request it. In Spain the peasants profited from the anarchy of the War of Independence to occupy communal and uncultivated lands. In 1813 and 1820 liberal regimes in Spain authorized the distribution of half these lands to veterans of the war and destitute families, and the sale of the other half on the open market, but these measures were annulled by the absolute monarchy.

In general, however, capitalist farming methods involved the destruction of communal and collective traditions. The pre-condition of progress was seen by both agrarians and agronomes to be enclosure. The enclosure of common land permitted the systematic exploitation of timber or its improvement as arable land to meet the rising demand for grain. The enclosure of open-field permitted the consolidation of strips, the adoption of new crop courses with grasses and roots to eliminate the fallow, the breeding of pedigree stock, fenced off from inferior species, and the abolition of the peasants' tiresome rights of access for gleaning and pasture. Enclosure made viable the introduction of new agricultural machinery and created a more numerous agricultural proletariat to work it. From the end of the eighteenth century the enclosure movement spread from England to the Netherlands and Denmark, to France, and to north-west Germany with the improvement of Lüneburg heath in Hanover after 1802, to Prussia under an ordinance of 1821, to Sweden under decrees of 1803 and 1807 and to the Baltic provinces. From there the movement spread southwards to south-west Germany, the Alpine regions, and Italy, although the bulk of the enclosure of common land in Spain did not take place until after 1855.

Enclosure meant the assertion of private property rights against communal custom, and invariably told against the rural poor. In Cologne Karl Marx, writing for the *Rheinische Zeitung* in 1842, noted that peasants who until now had been guaranteed traditional rights to gather dead wood in the forests were now being prosecuted for theft, while landlords who had an interest in selling timber to building contractors and ship-yards in a rising market had their claims supported in the Rhineland parliament. The defence of common

rights in woodland and waste against usurpation by landowners and speculators often led to violence. It came to a head in the turbulent years 1848–9
when peasants in South Germany, the Alpine region, including south-east
France, and Sicily took up arms in defence of their customary rights and
invaded common land which had been appropriated.

'The division of the open fields', ran a Prussian saying, 'makes a nobleman
out of the big peasant and a beggar out of the cotter.'[2] A second effect of
enclosure was to accentuate sharply social stratification in the countryside.
Those who gained were the landlords, whether the entrepreneurial lords of
the manor east of the Elbe who undertook the direct exploitation of their
estates, or the *rentiers* of western Europe who let out enclosed land to large
tenant-farmers at twice the rent that could be had for open-field. Those who
lost out were the small tenants or cottagers who might receive some compensation for the loss of a strip in a consolidated field but nothing for the loss of
customary rights on the common land. The army of landless labourers grew
thicker, but remained for the most part in the countryside because reclamation and intensive farming required much labour, and because the low level
of industrialization in many countries meant that they had nowhere else to go.

Social stratification was pronounced in the countryside of Europe even
before the enclosure movement. There was a hierarchy among the peasants
themselves, with 'large' peasants who owned plough-teams and hired additional labour to work their fields, 'small' peasants who had insufficient land
to support a family and were obliged to hire out their own labour, and 'middle' peasants who owned or rented just enough land to meet the subsistence
needs of the peasant-family and could make do with the labour of the family
to cultivate the land. But although peasants farmed all the land in 1800, they
often owned less than half of it. The rest was in the hands of the Church and
nobility, protected against sale by entail or mortmain, or owned by urban
corporations, or bourgeois landowners. During the French Revolution most
Church lands and some noble properties were sold off. But the only peasants
who benefited were those who were already substantial tenants or owners,
for the aim of the Revolutionary government was not to help the poor but to
reduce the burden of government debt; land was sold to the highest bidder.
Those who did best were bourgeois land-buyers, though they did not so much
eclipse the landed nobility as combine with them in a single *rentier* class, part
noble and part bourgeois. The sale of Church lands was undertaken by the
Napoleonic regimes in Italy, yet there again the buyers were not peasants but
existing landowners, speculators, army contractors, merchants, and the
administrators, magistrates, and lawyers who supported the rule of the
French. No rural society was more stratified than that of Spain, especially in
the south, where one of the results of the *Reconquista* had been the grant of

---

[2] Quoted by Jerome Blum, *The End of the Old Order in Rural Europe* (Princeton, 1978),
270.

vast estates to the Church, military orders, and nobility. Whole tracts of these latifundia lay uncultivated and derelict, while the mass of the peasants, without land of their own, had no choice but to labour on those parts of the estates that were tilled. In 1797 landowners formed 8.0 per cent of the rural population in southern Spain, while 17.7 per cent were tenants and 74.3 per cent were landless labourers. Some attempt was made to dissolve the religious orders and sell off their properties by both the Napoleonic regime in 1808–9, and the liberals in 1812–13 and 1820, but the brisk trade in Church lands and breaking of noble entails had to await the triumph of the Progressive party in 1836–7. Even then, no threat was posed to the larger nobles, whose estates were viable, and the purchase of available property by the newly-rich bourgeoisie only served to strengthen latifundism, the system of large estates.

In eastern Europe, where serfdom still existed in 1800, the peasants did not even have full ownership of their own allotments. Serfs did not own their plots of land but rather occupied them and worked them in return for dues paid to the lord in money, or kind, or unpaid labour service performed on his estate. Where the territory had been colonized relatively late, where labour was scarce and markets distant, landlords tended to exploit their estates directly, exacting labour services, called *Robot* in German-speaking countries and *barshchina* in Russia, from their peasants. Prussia, Poland, the Austrian provinces of Bohemia, Moravia, and Galicia, much of Hungary, and Transylvania, the Danubian Principalities, and southern Russia, fell into this category. On the other hand, where the population was denser and local markets stimulated peasants to produce a surplus, landlords preferred to let out their estates and live on the rents, commuting labour services into the payment of seigneurial dues. This was the normal pre-Revolutionary pattern in France, western and central Germany, and the Alpine region including parts of Austria. Either system was oppressive, but the serf was not free to sell up and move on; he was not in a market situation. For the other face of serfdom was coercion by non-economic means. The serf was subjected to a hereditary personal servitude which denied him the right to inherit or dispose of land, of money, marry, leave the manor, or take up other employment without the lord's consent. The serf was beyond the reach of the ordinary courts of law and all disputes on the manor were settled in the seigneurial court, which was staffed by the lord's men. In France, personal servitude was to be found only in the eastern provinces and the serfs there were emancipated in 1789. But the abolition of dues and services that derived from occupation of an allotment was conditional on the landlord being compensated by the peasant. In the event peasant revolt and the abolition of seigneurial justice made it impossible to impose such compensation, and all traces of feudal dues were eliminated by the Jacobins in 1793. The destruction of feudal dues and seigneurial justice was carried out beyond the borders of France by the Revolutionary and Napoleonic armies, from Savoy in 1792 to the left bank of the Rhine and Switzerland in 1798, the Kingdom of Naples in 1806, and West-phalia in 1807, Spain in 1808, and the Hanseatic states in 1811. The campaign was largely political, to break the back of those aristocracies that opposed French rule and to impose the equal subjection of all citizens to the French state. The abolition of feudalism to strengthen the modern state was also attempted by Prussia after her defeat at the hands of France in 1806. But there were also economic reasons for the abolition of serfdom. In particular, until 1818, rising farm prices encouraged landlords both to increase the pro-portion of their estates under direct exploitation and to do away with what was considered an inefficient form of rural labour. These goals could be achieved by the abolition of serfdom.

The Prussian case is instructive. Hereditary servitude was abolished in 1807 to appease a peasantry in revolt although seigneurial jurisdiction and police powers remained intact. In 1811 labour services and dues were abol-ished, but peasants had to indemnify their lords for this loss by surrendering between a third and a half of their allotments. If they were in debt or had insufficient land to support their families, they were now obliged to sell their labour to the lord as the only possible employer. By 1815 the Junker aristoc-racy was back in the saddle and concessions became even more restricted. Those eligible to redeem labour services and dues were limited in 1816 to large peasants who owned a plough-team. This meant that the mass of poor serfs had to continue to perform labour services or, in the case of Silesian serf-weavers, to pay dues. In many cases they were better off abandoning their plots, burdened with obligations as they were, and hiring themselves out as free wage-labourers. However, what tended to happen was that the lord did not pay wages but allowed the labourer a small shack, garden, and some pay in kind. In return he would continue to work on the lord's estate, on a short contract, and vulnerable to eviction at short notice. For with the abo-lition of serfdom went the abolition of *Bauernschutz*, the obligation of the lord to protect his serfs.

As a result of emancipation Prussian landlords increased their holdings of agricultural land by about six per cent, and the number of landless labourers increased. In the Baltic provinces of Estonia, Livonia, and Courland, which were within the Russian Empire but dominated by German landlords, the serfs were emancipated even more cynically in 1816–19, without any land at all. In the main part of Russia, where Napoleon had not seen fit to declare the serfs free in 1812, nothing was done to improve the lot of the peasants, except on state lands, because of the dependence of the state on the nobility. In Sweden, where serfdom did not exist, enterprising landlords nevertheless responded to rising markets by taking direct control of their estates and replacing the small tenant-farmers and crofters who worked them by landless labourers.

It was not however the view of all East European landlords that serfdom was an unviable proposition, and the trend to emancipation was not uniform. In some areas the possibilities of the market actually resulted in an intensification of forced labour. In the Ottoman Empire Turkish fief-holders either exacted a tribute of one-tenth of the peasant's produce if they were absentee, or required forced labour services if they or their stewards ran the estates, as in Bulgaria. In Serbia the payment of dues to Turkish overlords came to an end as a result of insurrections against Turkish rule in 1804 and 1815, and no hereditary Serbian landlord class was set up in their place. In Greece, after the revolt against the Turks, Turkish lands were taken over by the new state in 1831, although the Greek peasants enjoyed squatters' rights on them until being granted full property rights in 1871. In the Danubian Principalities, the defeat of the Turks by Russia in 1829 resulted in a redefinition of labour services in the Danubian Principalities under the Organic Regulation of 1831. Though carried out under the auspices of a conquering Russian general it was dictated by boyars avid to take advantage of the new markets in Europe that had opened to them. By various insidious means, the amount of labour service due fixed at twelve days a year was indefinitely extended, so that Marx reported one boyar to have exclaimed, 'the twelve corvée days of the Organic Regulation amount to 365 days in the year!'[3]

While the screw was tightening on the serfs in the Danubian Principalities there was no sign that it was being relaxed over the Carpathians in the Austrian Monarchy. In Bohemia and Moravia 156 days a year of unpaid labour were demanded of peasants with a full holding, and the situation was even worse in Galicia. In the Monarchy emancipation did in fact have a clear political sense: it could be used in order to undermine the Polish gentry of Galicia and the Magyar gentry of Hungary who were asserting themselves against Vienna. When the Polish gentry rose in revolt in Galicia in 1846, the serfs did not follow them, for their enemy was the serfowner, not the Emperor. The Monarchy did not at once learn its lesson, and little was done to relieve the plight of the peasantry. As a result there were peasant strikes in both Slav and German provinces in 1847, demanding the abolition of servile obligations without compensation to landlords, and in the spring of 1848 the serfs were up in arms. The Hungarian Diet at Pressburg, dominated by the Magyar gentry, voted the emancipation of the serfs on 14 March in order to keep them on their side. In the Austrian part of the Monarchy, emancipation was ratified by the Constituent Assembly on 7 September. The problem of the indemnification or otherwise of landlords remained as a thorny problem, and one that was not truly resolved until the land settlements of 1851–4, after the revolutionary turbulence had died down. As so often happened in these cases, the degree to which the landlords were compensated by the peasantry for the loss of dues and services depended above all on the light in which the government viewed those landlords. In the German part of the Monarchy,

[3] Marx, *Capital* i (Harmondsworth, 1982), p. 348.

peasants were required to pay some redemption; in Galicia and Hungary, where the gentry had risen against the Crown, no compensation by peasants was demanded.

Capitalist Practices: Industry

In 1800 the European economy was for the most part local and cellular. Artisans sold the products they made and knew their customers. Trades were under the control of craft guilds which claimed a monopoly to exercise that trade in a given town or district. This was partly to maintain standards in the craft but more especially to maintain prices and profits by limiting competition. The guilds could tailor supply to suit demand, restrict the number of apprentices and journeymen who might be taken on by each master, and bar outsiders from practising the trade. In Germany, which had about a million craft-masters in 1800, there were *Freimeister* and *Dorfmeister* who were authorized by the state authorities to practise outside the guilds, notably in the villages. On the great noble estates of central and eastern Europe, noblemen were occasionally granted privileges to exploit mines and iron deposits, to manufacture woollen cloth, or distil spirits, for the military needs of the state. But it was the guilds rather than the 'manufactories' that were the norm.

This restrictive and monopolistic system was subjected to powerful disruptive forces. New trade routes from the Americas to the East Indies and China, together with the expanding population at home, created wide new markets for commodities like textiles which the craft-guilds were ill-equipped to supply. The expanding population and the emancipation of the serfs pushed migrants towards the small towns and cities in search of employment, whether inside or outside the guilds. Of course the guild system had been partly eroded already. It had long been dismantled in Great Britain and its last vestiges, the apprenticeship clauses of the 1563 Artificers' Act, were repealed in 1814. In France the guilds had been abolished for a short time in 1776, then swept away at the Revolution. The Napoleonic armies abolished them in annexed territories such as the Rhineland and the Kingdom of Westphalia, and ensured that they were weakened in satellite states like Bavaria. Prussia abolished the guilds in 1810–11 and the Spanish Cortes followed suit in 1813. The intention was both to increase the power of the state at the expense of local communities and institutions, and to facilitate the mobilization of labour and sale of goods within the new Common Market. After 1830 the guilds managed to recover much control over their trades in German states such as Bavaria (1834), Württemberg (1838), Saxony (1840), and Prussia (1845). The pressure to open up trades to all-comers was increasing and masters were gradually forced to take on more apprentices and artisans. But whereas previously the journeyman might expect to complete his years of tramping and become a master, husband, and citizen by the age of thirty, now the upward path was blocked. There grew up a pariah class of wage-earning journeymen, often only seasonally employed, condemned to poverty if they married, at odds with the craft-masters and with the guild system itself, who contributed to the labour movement after 1830.

A positive response to the revolution in market conditions came not from guilds but from the entrepreneur. The entrepreneur was first and foremost a merchant with knowledge of markets. He was able to import from and export to distant places. He was sensitive to changes in fashion and fluctuations in demand from one year to the next. He was ready to switch his resources to cope with the eventualities of war or peace, free trade or protection. The entrepreneur was not conservative, like the guild-master. Instead of seeking to restrict competition to keep prices up he accepted the challenge of competition among sellers and sought to maximize sales by minimizing costs. Under the new system there was a separation between production and marketing. The entrepreneur bought up stocks of raw or half-finished materials, put them out to artisans who made them into the finished product, and then collected the finished product for sale.

The entrepreneurs were the shock troops of early European industrialization. They were new men. Very often they had started off as merchants, but as cloth-merchants or even small tradesmen rather than the elegant colonial merchants who had grown rich on the colonial trade in slaves and sugar. Many were called in those turbulent times but few were chosen. The rate of failure was great but some did well, and in textile towns like Rouen or Verviers there arose in time an aristocracy of manufacturers. Further east, in Saxony, Bohemia, Silesia, and Russia, it was the noble estate-owners who became the entrepreneurs. There were cases at Linz in Upper Austria or at Ivanovo, east of Moscow, of serfs running the enterprises of their noble overlords. Successful ones might buy their liberty and then lease back the enterprise on their own account.

The industrial revolution implied a revolution in technology. In the textile industry spinning, done hitherto on a distaff or spinning-wheel, was transformed by the invention in England of the jenny (1765) for the weft, the water-frame (1769), for the warp, and for both warp and weft the mule (1779). These machines could make more, and better quality, yarn than the hand-spinner, and could be harnessed to water-power or steam, although before 1800 the main function of steam-engines was to pump mines dry. Mechanized spinning made its impact in Lancashire and Scotland in the 1780s, in France just before the Revolution, in the Rhineland and Saxony in the 1790s. In 1801 Lievin Bauwens, a Flemish merchant who had made a fortune supplying the French armies and farming their taxes, managed to smuggle a mule and steam-engine out of England and set up the first Belgian cotton mill at Ghent.

Though entrepreneurs like Bauwens had a taste for technical innovation, the technology of the early industrial revolution remained fairly simple. Paradoxically, the multifold increase in machine-spun yarn called into existence armies of weavers who were still using hand-looms, which reached a peak of 250,000 in Great Britain in the mid-1820s. The power-loom, though invented in 1787, was bedevilled by technical problems, and it was not until 1826 that power-looms began to displace hand-loom weavers in the British cotton industry. It did not affect the cotton industry in Belgium, Alsace, and Catalonia until after 1830, in Switzerland until after 1840, in French Flanders until 1850, and in Normandy until 1860. In Bavaria the invasion of the power-loom was a major grievance in 1848. Moreover, the woollen industry remained a long way behind the cotton industry in this respect, for the power-loom did not mechanize the weaving of wool in Great Britain until the late 1830s, or in France and Belgium until the 1840s.

Industry in the early nineteenth century was labour-intensive rather than capital-intensive. More important than technological change was therefore the ability of the entrepreneurs to mobilize large quantities of labour, to confront mass demand with mass production. The first development was that independent artisans, who had hitherto owned their own tools and sold their own products to customers, now became dependent on the entrepreneur who controlled supplies and outlets. Sometimes they continued to own their own tools or looms; in other cases they were obliged to rent from the entrepreneur, who added profits earned from trading looms to his other gains. Artisans were reduced to piece-work for the capitalist, and came into conflict with him over the rates due to them. In Lyons, the silk weavers had become accustomed to a traditional price for their finished cloth, which was enforced under the First Empire but subsequently ignored by the silk merchants. In November 1831 they staged a strike against their employers and took control of the city for over a week.

In industries where labour added relatively little value to each product, entrepreneurs required unskilled rather than skilled labour. Ever sensitive to the commands of the market, they had to be able to take on labour and lay it off, at the shortest notice, as the market dictated. Frequently entrepreneurs relied on middlemen who subcontracted work in boom periods, finding the necessary labour for the job. Because neither wanted to waste capital on building, rent, heat, or lighting, they put out work to a labour-force that worked at home, either in their cottages or in the cellars, garrets, and suburban slums of the large towns. Naturally there were some trades which required a high level of skill that were organized in trade or friendly societies, could enforce apprenticeship, and ensure a good price for their labour. This included, in particular, the skilled metalworking and engineering trades thrown up by the industrial revolution. But in many other trades there grew up a tension between the skilled craftsmen making quality goods for the luxury end of the market, and the unskilled workers brought in by entrepreneurs and speculators to produce standardized, ready-to-use items for the mass market. In the years after 1800 the demand for boots and shoes encouraged London contractors to undercut militant London shoemakers by employing cheap, unorganized labour in and around Northampton. In 1811–12 the stockingers of Leicestershire smashed the machines on which unskilled labour was making an inferior hose on broad frames, for later cutting up and stitching. The official response to 'Luddism' was to make frame-breaking a capital felony. In the Rhineland town of Solingen the skilled cutters reacted in a similar way to intimidate the cheap labour that was being employed to flood the market with low-grade scissors. Bespoke tailors suffered from the expansion of the ready-made clothing industry. In Paris in the 1840s large-scale drapers employed on average ten times as many workers as master-tailors, setting them to work at home for a totally new form of outlet, the department store.

The industrial labour force was recruited from a number of sources. One of the most important was female labour. In the early stages of the industrial revolution women worked in their cottages under the 'put-out system', making lace or spinning linen, wool, or cotton. When mechanization destroyed hand-spinning, the younger, unmarried women were drafted into the factories to work the spinning machines. Once silk-throwing was mech-anized at Lyons, vast mills were set up where girls from the surrounding countryside boarded and worked fourteen or sixteen hours a day. In Great Britain in 1844, women provided 56 per cent of the labour in cotton mills, and 70 per cent of that in woollen, linen, and flax mills. Female labour was cheaper (or rather was paid at half the wage), and was considered by employers to be more docile. The resistance of male handloom weavers to change was a principal reason for the relative lateness of the mechanization of weaving. Once men did move into the factories, however, they reinforced the gendered division of labour, seeing to the machines and overseeing the female millworkers. Married women tended to prefer occupations where the division between home and work was not so pronounced, such as farm-ing, laundering, or dressmaking, sometimes in their own homes, sometimes in sweatshops. Among Paris clothing workers in the 1840s, 60 per cent were female.

It would be wrong to imagine that even the textile industry was fully mech-anized and urbanized by 1850. At that date, in Germany, there were only 600,000 workers in factories and mining, as against 1.5 million in the put-out system and 1.7 million in handicrafts. Many of those working in urban indus-tries were temporary migrants from the countryside. Others were enabled to remain in the countryside because they obtained a supplementary income from industry which allowed the rural economy to survive. Thus poor farm-ers in Belgium worked part-time in rural industry, while rich farmers in Hol-land remained wedded to agriculture alone. Some peasants remained tied to

the land as serfs. Yet serfdom and industrialization were far from incompatible, as illustrated by the case of the serf-weavers of Bohemia and Silesia.

That said, in the long run mechanization created its own supplies of labour.
The power-loom, by destroying the livelihood of the hand-loom weavers,
gave rise to a surplus population that was available for factory work. The
removal in 1824 of protective duties which exposed the Irish linen industry to
a flood of cheap cotton imports from Britain released a labour force from
Ulster and Connaught for the textile mills of Manchester and Glasgow. In
Belgium, the destruction of the rural linen industry of west Flanders after
1830 by the mechanized cotton industries of Ghent and Lancashire liberated
vast numbers of Flemish peasants for the textile mills of Ghent, Lille,
Roubaix, and Tourcoing, or for the expanding coal industry of the Sambre–
Meuse valley, at Mons, Charleroi, and Liège. In Silesia, the serf-weavers
were driven into ever more frightful poverty by the influx of cheap textiles
from northern Europe. They had no alternative but to rise in revolt. For
Marx the explosion of June 1844 was the first concrete example of the existence of a new phenomenon: the class-conscious proletariat.

The Problem of Capital

The early industrial revolution in Europe was based on textiles, and the capital needs of the textile industry were not very great. In 1792 a forty-spindle
jenny cost £6, less than a hand-loom at £7.10s., although in the 1820s a thou-
sand-spindle mule that could be harnessed to water- or steam-power might
cost over £1,000. Workshops were expensive to build or rent, but the enormous multi-storey textile mills at Manchester or Roubaix were not typical.
Yet the frequent destruction of mills by fire and bankruptcy of firms in an
environment of white-hot competition made the textile industry an unattrac-
tive proposition to investors. For their part, entrepreneurs had no wish to be
enslaved to banks. With a few exceptions, such as the Swiss merchant-
bankers who channelled some funds into the cotton industry of Alsace, the
divorce between industry and the capital market in the early nineteenth century was complete.

The key to entrepreneurship was the family. The initial capital was usually
saved within the family, and the family was the organizing nucleus of the firm.
Resources could be multiplied by strategic marriages, with the result that the
mill-owning families of textile conurbations like Lille–Roubaix–Tourcoing
were all interrelated, bearing double-barrelled names such as Motte-
Bredart, Bossut-Grimonprez and Motte-Bossut. Outside the family circle,
another way of finding capital was from members of the same church or sect.
Nonconformists were prominent among successful business families in England. In Germany, one sample suggests that 74 per cent of entrepreneurs in
this period were Protestant, 16 per cent Catholic, and 7 per cent Jewish. The
argument that Protestants made good businessmen because they had to

prove their election by labouring to the greater glory of God on earth cannot provide all the answers, for the mill-owners of Lille, Roubaix, and Tourcoing were vigorously Catholic. Many of these mill-owners were immigrants from Belgian Flanders into much less Catholic France, so another explanation might be that entrepreneurs were outsiders who had to work together in order to survive. This would account for the leading role among Russian entrepreneurs of the Old Believers, a sect which had resisted reform in the Orthodox Church in the 1660s and was subsequently penalized and persecuted. Gathered into tight-knit communities around Moscow and along the Volga, it was they who imported yarn and equipment through Bremen for the Russian textile industry.

After the initial outlay, the new industries financed themselves from profits which, because so little capital had been accumulated in those industries, might run at fifteen or twenty per cent a year. The new entrepreneurs were frugal and parsimonious and diligently reinvested their profits instead of consuming them idly, like the privileged classes. But the extraction of profits from industry required entrepreneurs to perfect a number of business practices. The length of the working day was extended as much as possible, so that after earning their own subsistence, the workers spent the rest of the time creating a clear profit for the entrepreneur. Social reformers were not particularly concerned with what went on in domestic industry, where parents were assumed to retain some control, but when legislation in Great Britain (1833) and France (1841) limited the number of hours a day that children could work in factories, entrepreneurs had an additional incentive to introduce new machines. Within the confines of a set working day mechanization made it possible to produce more goods in the same time, and leave the capitalist with the same profit. The shadow of self-finance, in the early period of industrialization, was the exploitation of labour.

The problem was that although plenty of capital was being accumulated from the land, from colonial trade, or from financial speculation, too much was being consumed, conspicuously or otherwise. Not enough was invested— 13.8 per cent of the gross national product in Great Britain between 1811 and 1850, 10.6 per cent of that of France. Moreover, when capital was reinvested, the system of priorities was the inverse of what would have stimulated rapid industrial expansion. In Britain it is true that London coal-merchants invested in Northumberland and Durham collieries, and Bristol iron-merchants invested in the South Wales iron industry. But much greater quantities of capital were absorbed by urban development, canal-building which became a mania in 1788–96 and the enclosure movement, which reached a peak in 1802–15. Of the capital invested in Prussia between 1816 and 1831, 69 per cent went into agriculture, 21 per cent into building, 7 per cent into transport, and a mere 3 per cent into industry. The banks played their part in this for in many countries they would only lend money on the security of real estate, that is, offer mortgages. Even in Lombardy, which was undergoing something of a commercial revolution, commercial houses had to keep half their capital in land or houses in order to finance their trade.

Land was the first home of investment in the early nineteenth century. Governments which were deeply in debt as a result of war, notably in Revolutionary France, Napoleonic Italy, and Restoration Spain, sold off large quantities of Church land and even Crown lands in order to raise funds. Trade was greatly disrupted as a result of Napoleon's Continental Blockade and the British Orders-in-Council. After France's loss of her colonial empire the merchants of Nantes and Bordeaux sank their capital in the arable land and vineyards of the hinterland. Until 1818 land values and rents rose with agricultural prices, especially where the land was enclosed, making it a wise investment. Falling grain prices after 1818 dealt a particularly severe blow to the Prussian *Junkers*, whose estates were virtually inalienable under Prussian law. However since 1794 the *Landschaften* or local assemblies of land-owners were authorized to issue mortgage debentures on the security of indebted properties. These debentures were extremely popular with the investing public and helped to shore up a hard-pressed squirearchy, but it did nothing to help capital-starved sectors of industry like the linen manufactures of Silesia.

A second magnet for funds was government bonds. The Revolutionary–Napoleonic period was an expensive time for governments. Austria was engaged in a twenty-year war with French aggression. The British government paid out £50m. between 1805 and 1816 to subsidize other countries' soldiers to fight its battles and another £80m. between 1808 and 1816 to finance Wellington's army alone. France, exhausted by war, was obliged after 1815 to support an army of occupation and to pay an indemnity of 700m. francs to the Allies. Spanish governments were faced not only by Napoleon's invasion but also by wars of independence in the Latin-American colonies and by counter-revolutionary struggles after 1833. Government revenues were too inelastic and totally inadequate to finance expenditure on this scale. Following the collapse of trade with the Americas, Spanish customs revenues fell by 60 per cent between the 1790s and 1830s, and treasury income as a whole by a third. In Prussia, indirect revenues were limited by the Zollverein and direct revenues limited by the government's aversion to calling the Diet and the refusal of the landed classes to shoulder a great proportion of taxes. The only answer was for governments to borrow, and that on the security of taxes they might never raise. The British national debt at current prices stood at £244m. in 1790, £443m. in 1800 and £838m. in 1821. The Austrian national debt in gulden rose from 372m. in 1790 to 658m. in 1800 and 1,011m. in 1821. It was only about one-tenth of the British national debt in 1815, but then Austrian revenues were only one-tenth of British revenues. Even a small country like Denmark faced financial problems. Between 1800 and 1814 its national debt in rix dollars rose from 28m. to 126m.

Government loans were raised through the *haute banque*, those private merchant-bankers who had amassed capital from international trade and had moved into finance primarily to oil the wheels of that trade by discounting bills of exchange and providing short-term loans. The world of international finance was small and interconnected. It included families like Hope of Amsterdam, or Baring of London, and Jewish families like Rothschild of Frankfurt, or Hambro of Copenhagen, who were able to place government loans in a network of financial centres. They mobilized the capital of a rich clientele and created a new class of fund-holders who drew a large part of their unearned income from the interest on government bonds. Nathan Rothschild, one of five sons of Meyer Amschel Rothschild of Frankfurt, who settled in London in 1804, was able to raise specie on the European money-markets—including Paris—in order to pay British troops in Spain. James Rothschild, his brother, arrived in Paris in 1811 and helped finance the restoration of the Bourbon monarchy. Alexander Baring managed the loan required by the new French Government to pay its indemnity to the Allies. A third Rothschild brother, Solomon, arrived in Vienna in 1820 and sent a fourth, Charles, to Naples in 1821 to raise funds for the suppression of the Neapolitan revolt and the restoration of the Bourbons of Naples. By managing the affairs of influential princes, Jewish families like the Rothschilds achieved security and recognition. An Austrian decree of 1822 conferred the title of baron on all the brothers and their legitimate descendants.

It took the railway age in the 1840s to transform the European money-markets and begin a flow of capital towards industry. Railways required an investment in fixed capital—bridges, tunnels, rails, and locomotives—which far surpassed the bales of cotton and few looms necessary to launch a textile enterprise. The family firm was too puny and capital had to be drawn from a whole new stratum of middle-class investors through the joint-stock company. But it caught the imagination of that public, especially in Britain, and seemed, unlike other industries, to be a safe investment. The breakthrough did not take place at once. For some time Leeds out-classed London in the busy sale of railway securities. In Belgium early railway-building was undertaken by the government, and much of the capital between 1836 and 1840 was raised by the Rothschilds on the London money-market. British capital played an important part in funding the Belgian and French railway companies: the Chemin de Fer du Nord, formed in 1845, was headed by a Rothschild and included eight English directors, two of them Barings. In Prussia the private Cologne bank of Oppenheim sold shares on behalf of the Cologne–Aachen railway in the later 1830s, but capital was lacking and the Prussian railways were built essentially by the State, not least for military purposes. One major consequence of railway-building was the demand for

coal and iron. But it was only in Belgium that before 1850 there emerged
joint-stock banks like the Société Générale and Banque de Belgique, which
capitalized the mining and metallurgical industry of the Meuse valley. The
link between banking and heavy industry had yet to be forged.

Crisis in the Élite

The beginnings of capital accumulation in the early nineteenth century were
of vital importance in an economic sense. Socially, however, status was determined according to the society of orders, headed by the nobility and clergy,
where it still existed, or by the values of the nobility and their landed estates,
where it did not. This was particularly true in eastern Europe where the small
bourgeoisie that existed was regarded as a parasitic growth on manorial society. The merchants of Moscow, squeezed into the society of orders (nobles,
clergy, and peasantry) by membership of privileged guilds and eligibility
after 1832 for the title of honoured citizen, nevertheless, felt the need to extol
their peasant origins. They were 'nothing but trading *muzhiks*, the highest
stratum of the thrifty Russia *muzhiks*'[4] and expressed this through their
patriarchal families, Asiatic dress, and devotion to the Orthodox faith. In
Hungary the trading population was half Jewish, not least because Jews
were barred from holding land. Excluded from citizens' rights, they serviced
the rural economy by exporting grain and cattle, lending money, and retail-
ing wines and spirits. In Serbia the towns were dominated by Turkish garrisons, and the artisans and traders imitated Turkish costumes and customs.
In Transylvania the towns were populated by 'Saxon' burghers, German-
speaking immigrants who were sandwiched between the Magyar gentry and
the Romanian-speaking peasantry. Elsewhere in the Ottoman Empire, the
merchants were not Turks but Greeks, scattered in a diaspora around the
Aegean and Black Seas, and Armenians who plied their trade as far as
St Petersburg.

In western Europe the pre-Revolutionary system of estates had been abolished, but nobilities still enjoyed certain privileges, and the bourgeoisie of
commerce and finance was keen to assimilate the values and life-style of the
aristocracy. The mercantile patriciates of Amsterdam or Lisbon, Hamburg
or Liverpool, Geneva or Milan, who invested in urban property or land outside the town, acquired municipal office, ran chambers of commerce, patronized churches, and gave richly to charity, were second to none in distinction
and were often nobles in their own right. The poet Carlo Cattaneo described
Milan as 'a city where many of the traders themselves have hardly any respect
for a trader except in so far as he is not a trader'.[5] Cities like Madrid, Rome,

---

[4] Cited by Thomas C. Owen, *Capitalism and Politics in Russia: A Social History of the
Moscow Merchants, 1855–1905* (Cambridge, 1981), 9. *Muzhik* means peasant.
[5] Cited by K. R. Greenfield, *Economics and Liberalism in the Risorgimento* (Baltimore,
1965), 130.

and Paris, French provincial centres such as Rennes, Dijon, and Grenoble, and the capitals of the numerous German states were dominated not by the merchants but by the courts, the Churches, the garrisons of the military, the law-courts of the magistrates, and a long train of officials and professional men. Surveying Angoulême at the Restoration, Balzac described the commercial suburb of l'Houmeau which 'envied the higher town where the government, the bishop's palace, justice and the aristocracy were perched. Nobility and Power above, Commerce and Money below.'[6]

Despite the industrial revolution, or perhaps because of it, the new entrepreneurs were denied social status to match their material wealth. In Rouen, the cotton merchants and manufacturers were considered parvenus by the landowners, magistrates, and lawyers among the bourgeoisie. In Bradford, the woollen manufacturers were immigrants, self-made men, and Nonconformists, and frowned upon by the town's Anglican establishment. In the Rhineland town of Barmen the business community was itself split into two, and the merchant oligarchy with its sense of civic responsibility looked askance at the pushy new entrepreneurs who sought only private profit. As elsewhere in Germany, the business community was isolated not only from courtly and aristocratic circles but also from the *Gebildeten*, the university-educated officials, clergy, professors, and jurists who prided themselves on their guardianship of *Bildung*, or disinterested culture.

The bourgeoisie of the early nineteenth century was less a bourgeoisie of affairs than a bourgeoisie of office. One way of making money respectable was to turn it into landed estate; another way was to acquire a university education and establish a career as a lawyer or public servant. Universities like Oxford and Cambridge remained select and expensive. They recruited from the families of landowners, clergy, and professional men, admitted only Anglicans and saw their main task as the preparation of ordinands for the established Church. Barristers and doctors were recruited by apprenticeship through the Inns of Court and London teaching hospitals. Lawyers, doctors, and clergy then shared the spoils of office, pension, and sinecure with the peerage. It was not until 1825 that Benthamite reformers founded University College London, the first college of the University of London, which itself was incorporated in 1836. Cheap, open to Dissenters and empowered to grant medical degrees, the new university broke the monopoly of the hereditary establishment. The German experience was quite different. The German university population doubled between 1817 and 1831, and at the University of Halle in 1832 41 per cent of students were from groups: lower officials, artisans, and farmers. Universities were set up and closely controlled by state governments in order to train their bureaucracies. The legal, medical, clerical, and academic professions in Germany, far from

---

[6] Honoré de Balzac, *Les Illusions perdues* in *La Comédie Humaine* (Paris, 1977), v. 151.

being liberal, were modelled on the bureaucracy, tightly regulated and often salaried by the state. Russia closely followed the example of Germany. Its bureaucracy expanded from 38,000 officials in 1800 to 113,900 in 1856. Former military men who were usually noble were replaced by career bureaucrats who were usually non-noble, and whereas in the 1800s only 14 per cent of high officials in Russia had received a university education, by the 1840s the figure was 80 per cent.

In France, the faculties of law, medicine, letters, and theology which had been organized by the Catholic Church before the Revolution now came under the control of the state. The state theology faculties were effectively boycotted by the Catholic hierarchy, which was allowed by Napoleon to train priests in its own seminaries. Parallel with the faculties was a system of *grandes écoles*, headed by the École Polytechnique which was set up in 1794. The task of these schools was to train military engineers for fortifications, artillery, and the equipment of the fleet, and civil engineers for the building of roads, and bridges, and the exploitation of mines. This élite of engineers was highly accomplished in mathematics and dedicated to the service of the state. Its members did not go into the world of industry. For trained engineers, industry had to await the foundation of the École Centrale des Manufactures in 1829.

The training of technocrats in schools that were entirely separate from the traditional faculties was taken up readily in Germany. Its first *Technische Hochschule* was founded at Karlsruhe in 1825. Others followed at Munich in 1825, Nuremberg in 1829, Dresden in 1828, Stuttgart in 1829, Cassel in 1830, Hanover in 1831, Augsburg in 1833, Brunswick in 1835. In addition Justus von Liebig, who had worked in Paris at the École Polytechnique, set up a chemistry laboratory in the University of Giessen in the 1830s, the first modern centre of chemical research. England lagged behind informal instruction. Its pale imitation of Giessen was the Royal College of Chemistry which opened in London in 1845 under the patronage of the Prince Consort.

The great expansion of higher education in the early nineteenth century was not without risk, especially in the more backward countries. There it was not just social prejudice that deterred anyone with an education from entering trade; the low level of economic development meant that such opportunities simply did not exist. One alternative was a career in the Church. In Germany the calling of pastor was still a respectable option for a middle-class student, while in England nearly two-thirds of Church livings were in the gift of the aristocracy and gentry in 1831, and provided maintenance for their younger sons. In France, on the other hand, the middle classes scorned the priesthood after the Revolution, and the Church became an escape-route for peasants with a little Latin. This only served to increase the pressure of the educated classes on office and the liberal professions. In Spain, where the passion for office was particularly rife, aspirants for office were given the collective name of *pretendientes*. They swelled the junior ranks of the ill-paid military and were given to launching periodic revolutions in the provinces as the best way to create jobs. In Prussia it was fairly easy to pass the first state examination to become a probationary jurist, but because the higher posts were occupied the lower ranks became clogged by untenured trainees who were unable to obtain promotion. All over Europe the liberal professions became overcrowded with barristers without cases and doctors without clients. In the French medical profession there was a move in the 1840s to end this overcrowding at a stroke by abolishing the lower grade of the profession, the health officers, but it came to nothing. Tension increased in the universities where students saw their prospects of a career dwindle.

As a result there grew up an intellectual proletariat that could not afford professional training or found the road ahead barred. It took to the world of letters, doing private tutoring, translations, annotations, reviews, or articles as a way of continuing an intellectual activity and earning a meagre living. Journalism was not a career in an established sense but the resort of people who had failed in other careers. The political consequences were very significant. In England, perhaps, where Parliament was an unmatched political forum and politicians were largely bred in the Inns of Court, the political journalist was modest. In Germany or Austria, where the blue pencil of the censor was impossible to avoid, politics was conducted in newspapers through literary allusions. But in France journalists were the party-politicians *par excellence* and journalism became a quick track to office. Adolphe Thiers, a Marseilles lawyer who founded the *National* newspaper in 1829, carved out a ministerial career for himself under the July Monarchy. In 1848, the 'revolution of the intellectuals', the provisional government in France was composed of the editorial boards of the *National* and *Réforme* newspapers.

Political power in the early nineteenth century was still in the hands of the European nobilities. High office and command were a privilege of noble estates or *Stände*. But nobilities certainly had to demonstrate their resilience in this period, because privileges were being shaken down, birth was being challenged by merit, and landed property was never secure.

The size and wealth of nobilities differed greatly from one European country to another. Much depended on the nature of the law of succession. In Prussia, or Spain before 1836, perpetual entails prevented the break-up of large estates. In theory this guaranteed the maintenance of the nobility, but in practice these estates, insulated from the market, tended to lose their value and lie uncultivated. On the other hand the absence of entail, combined with the abolition in Revolutionary and Napoleonic Europe of the privilege of the first-born in favour of the equal inheritance of all heirs, resulted in the fragmentation of estates. This was certainly the danger in France, or in Spain after 1836. Where the noble title passed to all heirs there multiplied vast, impoverished, rural nobilities. In the 1820s four per cent of the Magyar population were nobles. The majority of these were extremely poor, and variously called the 'sandalled' nobility because they could afford no boots, or the 'seven plum-tree' nobility because they owned no land. Indeed, apart from having exemption from taxation and the obligation to perform public works, they were virtually indistinguishable from the peasantry and often just as ignorant. The situation was probably even worse in Poland, where 300,000 people or seven per cent of the population claimed membership of *szlachta* or nobility in 1810. Of these, those who could claim the labour services of a single serf family could count themselves lucky; others took to begging, brigandage, the Church, or fighting in the armies of Europe. In Prussia the entailing of estates combined with the inheritance of the title by all nobles' sons, gave rise to a surplus of landless nobles looking for careers in the army or bureaucracy. The best compromise existed in Great Britain. There it was primogeniture rather than equal inheritance that prevailed. Under the strict settlement the estates of the nobility could not be broken up for three generations, to guard against spendthrifts. But in practice they were renegotiated every generation to provide adequate maintenance for widows, dowries for daughters, and capital for younger sons who went into the Church, army or the City of London.

The privileges held by nobles usually included tax exemptions, the right to sit in estates of nobles, and the exercise of seigneurial justice. The British peerage had long given up manorial courts but instead dominated (with the gentry) the country magistracy. They had no tax exemptions but they wielded massive influence in the House of Lords, even if the more numerous Scottish and Irish peers had to be content with sending only representatives. Feudalism had been eradicated in Great Britain; in Russia it had never existed. The *dvoryanstvo* or Russian nobility had no charter of privileges until 1785. This gave them the right to elect provincial and district assemblies, but these rarely met and were quite powerless. In France noble privileges were all swept away in 1789 and hereditary nobility itself was abolished in 1790. Napoleon resurrected the nobility when he founded the Empire, but without the tax exemptions. At the Restoration in 1814 a Chamber of Peers was established, to seat both the Bourbon and imperial nobilities, and though no more hereditary peers were created after 1831, in 1840 only 37 of the 311 peers in the Chamber had no title of nobility. In Prussia the noble *Stand* was abolished in 1808. But a status-group founded on birth was replaced by professional status-groups such as the officer corps, or the Prussian civil service, the *Beamtenstand*, the privileges of which were enshrined in the General Legal Code of 1794.

It is clear that by the early nineteenth century the nobilities of Europe had weathered important changes. The ancient feudal nobility, which held land in return for military service performed during the Middle Ages, was no more than a myth. Nobility was granted in return for service, in order to consolidate political support, and the lineage of most nobles was measured in decades or generations rather than centuries. In Russia the equation of nobility and service was quite explicit: after 1722 nobility was only acquired by service in the army or bureaucracy. Until 1845 commoners were ennobled on reaching the eighth rank in the Table of Ranks; after 1845 they had to reach the fifth rank and in 1856 the fourth rank before nobility was conferred. Even in *ancien régime* France the nobility was basically one of service, acquired by promotion in the army, magistracy, or administration. Napoleon took the matter to extremes. Less than a quarter of the imperial nobles were in fact Bourbon nobles who had rallied to his cause; 59 per cent of his nobles were sabre-rattling soldiers and another 22 per cent high civil servants. The Restoration changed relatively little. The Chamber of Peers in 1840 was packed with marshals, generals, admirals, ambassadors, state councillors, prefects, magistrates, and academics, 44 per cent of whom held current posts and the rest of whom had served previous regimes. In Spain, Queen Isabella ennobled thirty-one military men, many of whom were leading political figures. Great Britain, with its minimal bureaucracy and splendid isolation, might be considered an exception to this rule, but even there the character of the peerage was changing. In the eighteenth century peerages had been given above all to great landlords, but between 1801 and 1830, partly because of the Napoleonic Wars, half the new peers created were in reward for military, official, or diplomatic services, and most of these continued to pursue their careers. John Scott, the son of a Newcastle coal-factor who rose to become Chancellor of England (1801–27) as Lord Eldon, was not an isolated success story. Naturally, the older nobilities tried to set themselves apart from the newer blood. Marquisates were almost unknown in England before Pitt's time but were then sought after to achieve superiority over common-or-garden earls, and twenty-three could be counted in 1837. In Prussia, the *Landadel* which derived its social influence from its estates looked down on the *Dienstadel* which had been ennobled as a result of service. Similarly in Russia the old nobles who had built up vast estates, married into the best families, and provided the close advisers of the Tsar, set themselves apart from the nobles whose families had worked their way up through the Table of Ranks and possessed few serfs or none at all. Even so the real influence lay with the servants of the Crown, not with the rural nobility and gentry, however eminent they may be.

2

NAPOLEONIC EUROPE

France: Revolution from Above

On 18 *brumaire* Year VIII of the Revolutionary calendar (9 November 1799) Napoleon Bonaparte, a young general in the armies of the French Republic, seized power by *coup d'état*, laid the foundations of a military dictatorship and gave a word to the language of political mythology—*brumaire*. The Directory he overthrew was an oligarchy of republican officials which was suffering defeat abroad and lacked wide support in the country. Not only *émigrés* and armed counter-revolutionaries but a large proportion of the social élite regretted the abolition of the monarchy in 1792. On three occasions, in 1795, 1797, and earlier in 1799, royalist majorities in parliament were prevented only by military coups, and on the first it had been Bonaparte's 'whiff of grapeshot' that helped to secure the Republic. The oligarchy which ruled the Republic was also threatened by Jacobins in parliament, the clubs, administration, and army. They wanted to introduce the democratic Constitution of 1793, which had remained on paper because of the Terror, and to make popular sovereignty a reality. The *coup d'état* of 18 *brumaire* was an insurance against both Jacobin revolution and royalist restoration.

Napoleon was not just another despot, enlightened or otherwise. He was not an arbitrary ruler in the strict sense, for he issued constitutions. He claimed legitimacy not only by the grace of God, like the Bourbon kings, but also, like the revolutionary governments, by the will of the people. But he had no time for the endless deliberations of constituent assemblies and submitted ready-made constitutions directly to the people for ratification by plebiscite. The Constitution of the Year VIII (February 1800) provided for three consuls, with a First Consul, elected for ten years, having power to override the other two. It was approved by 3,011,007 votes to 1,562, but the army was not polled because of its Jacobinism, there were massive abstentions in the royalist west, south, and annexed Belgium, and there is evidence that the other figures were 'cooked' by the Ministry of the Interior. In response to more royalist and Jacobin plots a second constitution was devised in May 1802 and ratified by a similar majority. Napoleon now became Consul for life, with almost dictatorial powers. But his position was still not secure. War broke out with England in 1803, which encouraged royalist conspiracy, and in 1804 Napoleon felt obliged to have the Duc d'Enghien, a young *émigré* and prince of the blood, shot, and to poll the people once more on the foundation of a hereditary Empire. This was the last time before 1815 that the mass of French citizens were consulted by plebiscite. On 2 December 1804 Napoleon crowned himself Emperor in Notre Dame Cathedral, in the presence of Pope Pius VII.

The French Revolution had swept away the corporate privileges of orders, provinces, and corporations that stood between the king and his individual subjects and circumscribed his power. The privileges of the nobility—tax exemptions and the right to sit as an order in the estates, seigneurial dues and jurisdictions, primogeniture, and hereditary nobility—were abolished in 1790–1. Equality meant the equal subjection of every citizen to the state-power which was clarified by Napoleon in the Civil Code that he issued in 1804. He was far more powerful than a monarch of the *ancien régime*. On the other hand some of his subjects were more equal than others. The word of employers was always preferred to that of workers in labour disputes. Under the Civil Code a woman who married lost control of her property to her husband, was deemed incapable of making contracts and could not sue her husband for divorce on grounds for which he could sue her. The Concordat between Paris and Rome, concluded in 1801 and published in 1802, recognized Catholicism as the religion of 'the great majority' of French people, if not all of them. Napoleon was cynical about the re-establishment of the Catholic Church. 'In religion', he said, 'I do not see the mystery of the Incarnation but the mystery of the social order.' Moreover the Catholic Church was not the powerful landowning corporation it had been before the Revolution. Its land had been confiscated and sold and Napoleon decided that those who had bought confiscated Church lands were to be secure in their possession. In return bishops and *curés* would receive government stipends.

Apart from equality before the law, indeed, the Napoleonic regime made few concessions to equality. The consecration of the sale of Church property was integral to Napoleon's desire to consolidate a ruling class based on landownership which was both noble and non-noble, a single propertied class of 'notables'. Of course wealth was being made rapidly in other ways in the Napoleonic period. Tax collection was improved but syndicates of financiers were still called upon to advance cash on the security of those taxes. Suppliers of military goods for the insatiable armies of the Empire could make huge profits. The property market was fluid and open to speculation. Most wealth, however, had a tendency to settle in land and that stability was what the regime needed. This is reflected in the fact that representation was on the basis of landownership. Elections were indirect, and membership of electoral colleges at *arrondissement* level required a minimum of 150 francs a year income from property or real estate. Electoral colleges at the *département* level were drawn from the six hundred highest-taxed proprietors in the *département*, and three-quarters of direct taxes came from the land tax. It is therefore not surprising that of nearly 70,000 electors at both levels in 1810, 24.6 per cent were *rentier* landlords, 8.2 per cent landowners who farmed their own properties, and 18.1 per cent mayors or local officials who were invariably landowners. Clergy made up only 1.2 per cent of the notables, military men 2.4 per cent. Far more significant was the weight of civil servants (15.8 per cent), the liberal professions, including barristers, notaries, doctors, and academics (14.4 per cent), and merchants and tradesmen (10.8 per cent).

One of Napoleon's aims was to organize a professional bureaucracy, dedicated to public service, which could guarantee the order, justice, and revenues of the Empire. The purchase of office that prevailed in the *ancien régime* had been abolished and fees were replaced by salaries. Careers were open to talent and a more regular hierarchy of grades was established. Family connections and patronage still counted for much in recruitment and promotion. But the sweeping away of old dynasties of magistrates and the expansion of the administration and judiciary in the Revolutionary–Napoleonic period, not least in the Empire, created opportunities for lower officials and the liberal professions, especially lawyers, who provided 44 per cent of Napoleon's magistrates and half of his administrative officials. The most brilliant careers were made in the army. Despite the long service of noble officers in the armies of the Republic, half the generals in 1805 had begun their careers after 1792. Promotion to the officer corps was possible through the military schools such as Saint-Cyr (1808) or the École Polytechnique, through training units for a social élite destined for the Imperial Guard, from foreign units, and by the promotion of NCOs on the battlefield, to replace casualties among subaltern officers. This last route became increasingly common after 1809.

It was to reward bravery on the battlefield that Napoleon founded the Legion of Honour in 1802, the first step towards reconstituting the nobility. Between 1804 and 1815 some 40,000 awards were made, although the price of bravery meant that only 25,000 were still alive in 1815. In 1804 eighteen marshals were created, including Joachim Murat, the son of an innkeeper, and the titles of prince and duke followed. In 1808 the imperial nobility was completed with the ranks of count, baron, and chevalier, all of them hereditary. Large incomes were required before titles were awarded, but fiefs and landgrants were carved out of conquered territories in order to endow the new titles. This looked like the 'refeudalization' of France, but in fact 80 per cent of ennoblements were for military or bureaucratic service. The privileges of the *ancien régime* nobility were not reinstated. Napoleon was anxious to make it possible for old nobles to rally to the imperial court, but only 22.5 per cent of the imperial nobles owed their original titles to the monarchy and 80 per cent of Bourbon nobles refused to serve Napoleon.

Napoleon did very little for representative government. His constitutions included a Legislative Body, elected by the colleges, which could vote on legislation but not debate. The Tribunate, a sort of brains' trust, could debate but not vote—but the liberal opposition of *idéologues* like Benjamin Constant was too much for Napoleon, and the Tribunate was purged in 1802 and finally abolished in 1807. And the Senate which was first appointed, then co-opted, was an alternative organ through which the Emperor could legislate. The hub of the system was the Council of State, a body of appointed jurists which prepared all the legislation, and was attended by many future prefects as part of their training.

What characterized the Napoleonic regime above all was the strong executive, under the control of a single charismatic figure who appointed and dismissed ministers, generals, prefects, and bishops, commanded armies, directed foreign policy, saw to the codification of the laws, and reorganized the systems of education, worship, and administration. Whereas in the Revolutionary period administration had been the function of committees, now it was the function of all-powerful individuals. In the *départements* the administrations were replaced by prefects who were directly responsible to the Ministry of the Interior and in their turn appointed mayors in all the communes. General councils at *département* level and municipal councils represented the propertied classes, but carried little weight. Bishops were far more powerful than under the *ancien régime*, for cathedral chapters had been abolished and Napoleon refused to authorize any but a few charitable or teaching orders, mainly of women. The bishops were overseen by the Ministry of Worship which authorized the seminaries they set up to restock a priesthood that had been depleted by the revolutionary years and confirmed the clerical appointments that they made. The Catholic Church became the ecclesiastical arm of the state-power and the bishops 'prefects in purple'. Finally it was under Napoleon that the police was fully developed. Fouché, a former agent of the Terror who became Minister of Police just before the *coup d'état* and indeed helped to organize it, established a prefect of police in Paris and general *commissaires* of police in the large towns, especially at the ports and frontiers, who took over police powers from the prefects. He was also responsible for a secret police that was as active abroad as it was in France. Jacobin and royalist subversion was kept under control, albeit by irregular methods. 'Special courts' were set up in 1801 to deal with suspects, which were staffed by army officers as well as magistrates, and dispensed summary justice without jury and without appeal. A network of prisons was set up in 1808 and a decree of 1810 enabled the government to imprison arbitrarily suspects who could not for political reasons conveniently be brought to trial. This was nothing less than the old *lettre de cachet*, but the Napoleonic police-state introduced a new efficiency into its methods. Moreover, ordinary French people were increasingly forced to reckon with the police-force. Smuggling, the evasion of conscription, and desertion were all forms of popular resistance to the regime which reached epidemic proportions in the early years of the Empire. However, by 1810–11 a professional and disciplined police-force, through the use of spies, garrisons, and terror, managed to bring this resistance under control and made possible the mass conscription of the final years of the Empire.

The Hegemony of Napoleon

According to the *Memorial of Saint Helena*, a lengthy piece of self-justification taken down from the Emperor's table-talk to create a Napoleonic legend, the Emperor was a liberator and defender of nationalities. Speaking of the French, Italians, Germans, and Spaniards, he is recorded as having in mind 'the agglomeration, the concentration of peoples geographically one, but dissolved and fragmented by revolutions and politics'. 'I would have liked', he is quoted, 'to make of each of these peoples a single and united national body', bringing them together subsequently in the harmony of a 'great European family', along the lines of the United States of America.[1] Fifteen years later his nephew, Louis-Napoleon, reasserted the view that the Emperor was 'the messiah of new ideas' who had liberated peoples from feudalism, monasticism and corrupt dynasties and cherished a 'grand design' to gather them into a 'European Confederation'.[2]

In fact Napoleon had no such ambitions. These were myths created by succeeding generations of Bonapartists for their own political ends. The European strategy of Napoleon, devised in conjunction with his brilliant Minister of Foreign Affairs, Talleyrand, was to ensure the hegemony of France. Peoples would be grouped *ad hoc* into states which were entrusted according to dynastic principles to Napoleon's brothers or generals, and used like pieces on a vast chess board in a game to checkmate the powers that contested his supremacy, Austria, Prussia, Russia and Great Britain.

Napoleon's reputation as a liberator of peoples originated in the Italian campaign of 1796 when, as a general of the Directory, he 'freed' Lombardy from Austrian domination and established the Cisalpine Republic, based on Milan. In 1797 he put an end to the old Venetian Republic, but it became clear that he was interested not in Italian unification but in the Adriatic empire of Venice, including Istria, Dalmatia, and the Ionian Islands, the last of which were seized by the French as stepping-stones to the Levant and Egypt. At the Peace of Campo Formio in October 1797 France was happy to surrender Venetia to Austria if in return she could secure her position in the Adriatic, while in 1798 France invaded Switzerland to strengthen her position in the Alps. The same year Napoleon led an expedition to Egypt in an attempt to cut off British trade routes to India, but instead the British destroyed the French fleet at Aboukir Bay. At the beginning of 1799 French armies, having annexed Piedmont and Tuscany, and established republics in

---

[1] Comte de Las Cases, *La Mémorial de Sainte-Hélène* (London, 1823), iv, 125–6.
[2] Louis-Napoleon Bonaparte, *Des Idées napoléoniennes* (London, 1839), 15, 141, 164.

Rome and Naples, controlled the whole of the Italian peninsula except Venetia and the islands. But the Directory did nothing to unite Italy, as the Italian Jacobins desired, for fear of creating a potential rival on the other side of the Alps. Soon the moment had gone, as a Second European coalition, including Austria, Russia, Britain, and Turkey formed against France, driving her out of Italy and the Ionian Islands, which became a Russian protectorate.

Napoleon now seized power from the bankrupt Directory and directed foreign policy as First Consul as well as general. In 1800 he sent one army across the Rhine into Bavaria and led another across the Alps into Italy. Defeats were inflicted upon the Austrians at Marengo and Hohenlinden. Peace was made with the Austrians at Lunéville in 1801 and with the British at Amiens in 1802. But still Napoleon had no plans to create an Italian nation-state. For strategic reasons Piedmont was annexed directly to France in 1802 and the Ligurian Republic, centred on Genoa, suffered the same fate in 1805. A second Cisalpine Republic was set up as a buffer-state against Austria, and Napoleon even allowed it to be called the Italian Republic in 1802, but Venetia remained outside it. Little more was done to 'liberate' Germany. The left bank of the Rhine was annexed by France in 1797, and between 1801 and 1803 German princes of the Holy Roman Empire met French representatives in Regensburg to discuss compensation for territorial losses on the Rhine. As a result all the imperial knights and almost all the ecclesiastical princes and free cities lost their sovereign rights. South German states such as the Landgraviate of Hesse-Darmstadt, the Margraviate of Baden, the Duchy of Württemberg and the Electorate of Bavaria were correspondingly enlarged. However, there was no question of creating a single German state. On the contrary, the south German states now served as a third force in alliance with France to counterbalance the pretensions of Austria and Prussia.

Napoleon's domination of Germany, Italy, Switzerland, the left bank of the Rhine, and the Low Countries, together with his continuing colonial ambitions, unsettled his European rivals and made a lasting peace impossible. Friedrich von Gentz, a Prussian Protestant who transferred to the service of Austria in 1802, in that year published an important survey of the *Political State of Europe before and after the French Revolution*. In this he argued that French Revolutionary expansion had destroyed the balance of power in Europe, that Prussia and Austria should sink their traditional differences and become the axis of an anti-French coalition of powers, and that the 'ancient ramparts' against France in the Austrian Netherlands, Holland, the left bank of the Rhine, Switzerland, Savoy, Piedmont, and Italy should be restored to their original defensive purpose. In the long-term this book anticipated the way France would be dealt with at the Congress of Vienna. In the short-term it was a call to arms of the Third European coalition against

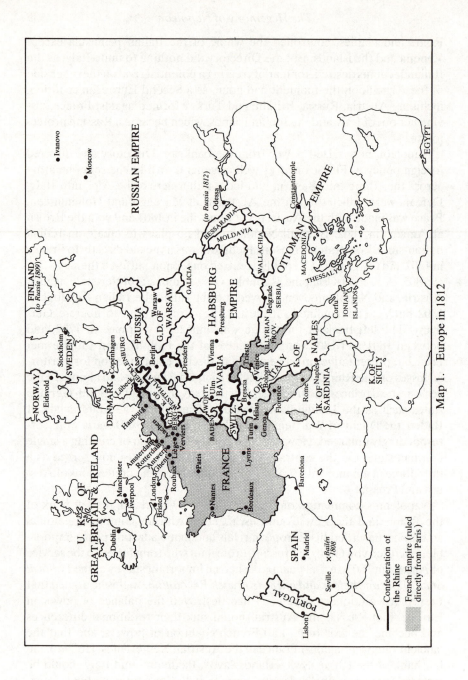

Map 1. Europe in 1812

Legend:
—— Confederation of
the Rhine
French Empire (ruled
directly from Paris)

RUSSIAN EMPIRE

Ivanovo
Moscow

FINLAND
(to Russia 1809)

BESSARABIA
(to Russia 1812)
Odessa

MOLDAVIA

WALLACHIA

GALICIA

HABSBURG
EMPIRE

SERBIA
Belgrade
ILLYRIAN
PROV.

OTTOMAN
EMPIRE

Constantinople

MACEDONIA

THESSALY

EGYPT

Corfu
IONIAN
ISLANDS

NORWAY

SWEDEN
Stockholm
Eidsvold

DENMARK
Copenhagen
Lübeck
MECKLENBURG

PRUSSIA
Berlin
Warsaw
G.D. OF
WARSAW

Pressburg
Vienna

Dresden

K. OF
WESTPHALIA

Hamburg

BADEN
WÜRTT.
Ulm

BAVARIA

SWITZ.

Trieste
Venice
Bologna
K. OF
ITALY

Brescia
Milan
Turin
Florence
Genoa

K. OF
SARDINIA

K. OF
NAPLES
Naples
K. OF
Naples

Rome

K. OF
SICILY

U. K. OF
GREAT BRITAIN & IRELAND

Manchester
Liverpool
Dublin
Bristol
London

Amsterdam
Rotterdam
Antwerp
Ghent
Liège
Aachen
Verviers
BERG
G.D. OF
Roubaix
Cologne

FRANCE
Paris
Lyons
Nantes
Bordeaux

SPAIN
Madrid
× Bailén
1808
Barcelona
Seville

PORTUGAL
Lisbon

France which took shape in 1803–5. The architect of that coalition was Alexander I, Tsar of Russia from 1801, who concluded treaties with Austria, Prussia, Sweden, and Great Britain. The First four powers provided men; Britain provided ships and, as the 'banker of the coalition', money.

Disaster struck the Coalition almost at once. The French and Spanish fleets were defeated at Trafalgar on 19 October 1805, but the next day the Austrian army surrendered at Ulm in Bavaria. The Prussians made a truce and the Austrians and Russians, eager to give battle, were smashed at Austerlitz on 2 December 1805, the anniversary of Napoleon's coronation. By the Treaty of Pressburg, signed on the 26 December 1805, Austria surrendered the Tyrol to Bavaria which became a monarchy and the following month Bavaria, Württemberg, and Baden signed a secret federative pact with France. The Grand Duchy of Berg was created in March 1806 from territories belonging to Bavaria and Prussia and entrusted to Joachim Murat. Berg and the southern states of Germany formed as it were the stalk and body of the pear-shaped Confederation of the Rhine, which was set up in July 1806 under the protection of Napoleon to serve as a barrier between France and Prussian and Austrian power. By this act, the German states abjured their allegiance to the Holy Roman Emperor, and on 6 August 1806 the Emperor Francis II, who had already proclaimed himself Emperor Francis I of Austria, dissolved the Holy Roman Empire which had ceased to have any meaning. Under the Treaty of Pressburg, France finally obtained Venetia, which was incorporated into the Kingdom of Italy (as the Italian Republic became in 1805), together with Istria and Dalmatia on the Adriatic coast. After the failure of an Anglo-Russian invasion of Naples in 1805–6, Naples was set up as a separate kingdom under Napoleon's brother, Joseph, instead of being integrated into the Kingdom of Italy.

Napoleon was now supreme in Central Europe. Russia replied by opening up a new theatre of war in the Balkans. In September 1805 Great Britain managed to negotiate a treaty between Turkey and Russia, which permitted the Russian fleet to sail through the Straits and reinforce its position in the Ionian Islands. But the Balkans were stirring in revolt. The attempt of Sultan Selim III to centralize the administration of provincial governors and create a modern, disciplined army had only antagonized the traditional janissary corps and the provincial governors or pashas, who had appropriated their fiefs and built up private armies like so many warlords. These pashas—Mohammed Ali of Egypt, Ali Pasha of Janina in Epirus and Albania, and Pasvanoglu Osman Pasha of Bulgaria—received some support from the French. In 1801 janissaries in league with Pasvanoglu seized Belgrade and the terror that followed provoked a rising of Serbs in February 1804 led by Karageorge (Black George), a cattle-merchant who had seen service in the Habsburg armies. The Serbs received support against Pasvanoglu from Constantine Ypsilantis, the Hospodar or Governor of Wallachia. Though the

Danubian Principalities were under Ottoman suzerainty, they had also been a Russian protectorate since 1774. When therefore the Sultan dismissed Ypsilantis, Russia invaded the Principalities (1806). Prince Adam Czartoryski, Alexander's close adviser on foreign affairs, was already dreaming of a federation of Slav states in the Balkans under Russian protection. Further south, the tyranny of Ali Pasha was provoking resistance among the Greek *klephts* or mountain brigands in Thessaly and Macedonia and among the Italian-speaking aristocracy of the Ionian Islands, led by John Capodistrias. In the summer of 1807 Capodistrias, with the support of the mainland rebels and Russia, launched a campaign against Ali Pasha which might be described as the first manifestation of Greek nationalism.

Russia was nevertheless soon forced to come to terms with France. Prussia was defeated by France at Jena and Auerstädt on 14 October 1806 and the French occupied Berlin, Warsaw, and the Hanseatic towns. Russian forces held Napoleon to a bloody draw at Eylau on 7 February 1807 but were defeated at Friedland in June. On 8 July Napoleon and Alexander confronted each other on the river Niemen and arranged the Treaty of Tilsit. Napoleon's priority was to reduce Prussia to a shadow of its former self. The Kingdom of Westphalia was carved out of Prussian territory, Hesse-Cassel, Brunswick, and southern Hanover, to reinforce the Confederation of the Rhine against Prussia, and entrusted to Napoleon's brother, Jérôme. A Polish state was created from the Polish lands annexed by Prussia under the Partitions, although it was an insult to Polish nationalism. It included none of the Polish territory appropriated by Russia under the Partitions, was called the Grand Duchy of Warsaw, and was ruled by the King of Saxony. Russia paid for the truce by ceding the Ionian Islands to France but as compensation was able to turn against its erstwhile ally, Sweden, in February 1808, and deprive her of Finland.

After the conclusion of the Franco-Russian alliance only Great Britain stood in the way of Napoleon's European supremacy. The French navy was in ruins, but the British economy was dependent on the possibility of exporting textiles and metal wares to Europe, and of importing naval stores from the Baltic and Russia, and cereals through Hamburg and Danzig. On 21 November 1806 the French issued decrees from Berlin ordering the closure of European ports to British vessels and founding what became known as the Continental System. British trade found a loophole in Denmark, and France and Russia combined to put pressure on Denmark to force her into the Continental System. The British demanded the surrender of the Danish navy, and then bombarded Copenhagen until they did so. This only drove Denmark firmly into a French alliance. Sweden under Gustav IV Adolf held onto the British alliance and its funds, but found itself at war with Russia, Denmark, and France, whose forces invaded under General Bernadotte. The pro-French party overthrew Gustav in 1809 in favour of the senile and childless Charles XIII. Sweden made peace with Russia and joined the Continental System. The Riksdag or parliament then elected Bernadotte Crown Prince in the hope that, in the long term, Sweden would recover Finland.

One yawning gap remained in the Continental System: the Iberian peninsula. King Charles IV of Spain counted for little and affairs were managed by Godoy, a Guards' officer and the Queen's lover. Godoy brought Spain into the Continental System in February 1807. The French government then required Portugal to close her ports to British shipping and to declare war on Great Britain. When Portugal refused, France and Spain agreed to partition Portugal (27 October 1807), French troops invaded the country, and the royal house of Bragança fled to its colony, Brazil. But Godoy had now become extremely unpopular in Spain. The Madrid mob, supported by discontented nobles and army officers, overthrew him on 17 March 1808. Charles IV had no choice but to abdicate in favour of his son, Ferdinand, Prince of Asturias, 'the Desired One'. However, the military presence of the French at Madrid, under Murat, made itself increasingly felt, and a popular revolt against the French occupation on 2 May 1808 was put down with great savagery. Napoleon now invited both Charles IV and Ferdinand to Bayonne, where he was stationed with the main French army, and obliged them to renounce their rights in favour of Joseph Bonaparte, King of Naples. It was this act that triggered off the Spanish War of Independence. At the end of 1807 the British had responded to Napoleon's Continental System by Orders-in-Council blockading the ports of France and her allies. Now Britain answered the appeals of the Portuguese provisional junta and landed her own troops under Sir Arthur Wellesley in August 1808, in order to recapture Lisbon. The Peninsular War had begun.

The outbreak of war and revolution in Spain dramatically exposed the vulnerability of Napoleon's Empire. Troops had to be moved *en masse* from northern to southern Europe. In the summer of 1808 the Prussian Chief Minister, Karl vom Stein, devised a plan to combine a war of liberation with sweeping reforms. In the event Austria was the first defeated power to contest French hegemony, by launching attacks in April 1809 on French positions in Bavaria, the Tyrol, Venetia, and the Adriatic. Napoleon, who had annexed the Papal Legations in 1803, and Umbria and the Marches in April 1808, consolidated his defences by absorbing the rest of the Papal States into the Kingdom of Italy in May 1809, taking Pope Pius VII prisoner, and beat the Austrian forces decisively at Wagram on 5 July 1809. Under the Treaty of Schönbrunn on 14 October 1809 the French now gained the Austrian port of Trieste, which was still trading with Britain, much of the Slovene provinces of Carinthia, Styria, and Carniola, and parts of Croatia, including the Military Border with the Ottoman Empire. These were now forged into the Illyrian Provinces, which had purely strategic significance and were in no sense intended to encourage Slovene, Serbo-Croat, or South Slav nationalism.

Neither did Napoleon mean to help the Serbs. If anything, he would have handed them over to Austria, for his policy now was to conclude an alliance with that country, prepared in March 1810 by his marriage to the Emperor's daughter, Marie-Louise.

The Continental System was becoming increasingly porous. Trade with Great Britain continued through Amsterdam and the Hanseatic ports of Bremen, Hamburg, and Lübeck. In 1810 Napoleon acted decisively. Holland, since 1806 a satellite state under his brother Louis, was annexed directly to the Empire in June. The whole of the north coast of Germany, including Hanover both within and outside the Kingdom of Westphalia, followed in December. Russia, smarting from the humiliation of Tilsit, hostile to the French presence in the Grand Duchy of Warsaw, and finding its trade strangled, effectively withdrew from the Continental System at the end of 1810. In order to save the Continental System, Napoleon was obliged to launch an invasion of Russia. His right flank was secured by an alliance with Austria in December 1811. Austria would surrender Galicia in order to build the Grand Duchy of Warsaw into a stronger buffer-state against Russia, to be further enlarged by Lithuania and White Russia, and would herself recover the Illyrian Provinces at the end of the war. King Frederick William III of Prussia was bullied—on pain of losing his crown and the complete dismemberment of his state—into an alliance with France in February 1812. On 24 June 1812 the French armies invaded Russia.

Russia however was not unprepared. Napoleon had greatly angered his former general, Bernadotte, by his occupation of Swedish Pomerania in January 1812, and Bernadotte had his own dynastic ambitions. In April Alexander was able to bring Sweden into an alliance. In May he concluded a truce with the Turks at Bucharest and closed the Balkan theatre, sacrificing as he did the hopes of the Serb rebels. The French campaign was a disaster in which 400,000 troops were lost, and on 13 January 1813 Tsar Alexander recrossed the Niemen at the head of his victorious forces.

The Prussian minister, Stein, had been at the Russian Court since early in 1812, and in February 1813 an alliance was signed between Russia and Prussia. Stein's ambition was to provoke a national insurrection in Germany which would shatter Napoleon's creature, the Confederation of the Rhine, and make way for a united German Reich under Prussian leadership. To Metternich, who became Chancellor of Austria in October in 1809, and his grey eminence, Gentz, such ideas were anathema. The patronage of revolution by Russia and Prussia had to be stopped. Metternich made clear his opinion of German nationalism by arresting Baron Hormayer, who had formed an Alpine League to raise revolt against France and Bavaria in the Tyrol and Illyrian Provinces. On 8 August 1813 Metternich was still trying to avoid war by getting Napoleon to renounce his protectorate of the Confederation of the Rhine. When Austria did go to war alongside Prussia and

Russia on 12 August it was emphasized that this was not for the German nation but in order to maintain the balance of power in Europe. After the battle of Leipzig, Metternich set to work to bring Bavaria, Hanover, and the other German states into the alliance, offering them guarantees of sovereignty and territorial integrity. Unlike Stein's vision of a revolutionary, unitary Reich under Prussian hegemony, this was the sober construction of a conservative, federal Germany under the control of Austria. For the time being, Metternich's strategy prevailed.

Assault on the ancien régime

The impact of Napoleon on the political and social structure of Europe was not everywhere the same. It was greater in territories that were annexed than in satellite states, and greater in satellite states than in those which were occupied only with difficulty and by force of arms. Where French Revolutionary armies had passed before, overturning feudal and ecclesiastical institutions, there Napoleonic rule had a firmer grip. French military support for local rulers enabled them to undertake by 'revolution from above' what as minor enlightened despots in the eighteenth century they had failed to achieve. But Napoleon was above all a dynast and conqueror: what he required from subject territories was men and money. If they could be provided without administrative reforms, so much the better. Some states which remained sovereign imitated Napoleon's methods in order to weaken traditional élites or to strengthen state-power. Far more common however was resistance to Napoleon, whether blind peasant hostility to taxes and conscription, the defence of aristocratic, ecclesiastical, and corporative privileges, or liberal opposition to arbitrary, bureaucratic, and foreign rule.

Belgium, or the Austrian Netherlands, was annexed in 1795, divided into departments and placed under French prefects and judges. The French encountered the hostility of a nobility and Catholic Church which still looked towards Austria, and proceeded to dissolve the monasteries and persecute the secular clergy. The introduction of conscription in September 1798, as in France, provoked a widespread peasant revolt, which had to be put down by force. Those who gained from French rule were above all the middle classes who bought Church lands, and enjoyed the abolition of the guilds and wide, protected markets in France.

The left bank of the Rhine was occupied in 1792 and again after 1794. The great prince-bishoprics of Trier and Mainz were swept away and Jacobin ideas seduced Rhenish democrats. With some support from the French General Hoche they declared an independent republic on the left bank in September 1797. But Hoche died almost at once and the Directory annexed the Rhineland and subjected it to a military dictatorship. It was not until 1800 that the Rhineland was organized into departments on the French model. As in Belgium, it was the bourgeoisie which did best, notably the merchants and manufacturers of Aachen, Krefeld, and Cologne who became mayors, municipal councillors, and presidents of electoral colleges, together with the educated class which was prepared to serve in the administration under French prefects.

Propaganda from the French Revolutionary armies found more fertile soil in Piedmont. The king was forced to flee from Turin to Sardinia, and Jacobins from the towns, dreaming of a united, democratic Italy, were put in charge of the towns. The Austro-Russian invasion of 1798 returned royalists to power, and when the Directory held a plebiscite in February 1799 on the question of the annexation of Piedmont to France, there was a massive insurrection against it. After 1800 Piedmont and Tuscany were firmly integrated into the French administrative system. In 1805 and 1808 respectively, Turin and Florence were given princely courts, but they were purely decorative and in no sense autonomous governments. Though some noble families, such as the Cavours or Balbos, grew rich on church lands, others looked nostalgically towards the exiled royal house in Sardinia.

When the Cisalpine Republic was recovered in 1800 it was treated as a conquered province. A provisional government was maintained there by force for two years. There could be no question of a plebiscite on a constitution, after what had happened in Piedmont, and Napoleon was not one to waste time with constituent assemblies. At Christmas in 1801 he summoned an assembly of Italian notables to cross the Alps to Lyons, where they received a constitution from his hands and acclaimed him President of what he agreed to call the Italian Republic. A representative of the wealthy Milan patriciate, Melzi d'Eril, was appointed Vice-President.

Melzi was anxious to break all ties with the first Cisalpine, which had been far too revolutionary; although he could not call upon the imperial nobility of the former duchy of Milan, which was too Austrian, he wanted the Republic to be founded on landed wealth, whether old or new, and disagreed with Napoleon who wished also to bind the commercial and educated bourgeoisie to the Republic. The electoral colleges for the legislative body therefore included 200 merchants, meeting at Brescia, 200 professional men, meeting at Bologna, and 300 landowners, meeting at Milan. Most of the landowners were nobles: 77 per cent in Lombardy, 89 per cent in Venetia when it was added to the Kingdom of Italy in 1805. Napoleon naturally became King of Italy. His son-in-law, Eugène de Beauharnais, became Viceroy in March 1805 and presided over the establishment of an Italian nobility in 1808.

The tradition of the vigorous self-governing Italian commune fitted ill with the centralized system of French administration. But a rising in Bologna in 1802 provoked Melzi to carve the Italian Republic into departments and impose prefects. His inclination was to favour nobles as prefects, but they were poor administrators. After 1806 Lombardy was ruled by Venetian prefects, who were all noble, while Venetia was ruled by Lombards. Only when

France went to war with Austria in 1809 were more servants of the first Cisalpine appointed as prefects, and the prefectoral corps came to look something like a professional bureaucracy.

Like the Italian Republic, the Kingdoms of Westphalia and Bavaria, and the Grand Duchy of Warsaw were all satellite states. Jérôme received a constitution for Westphalia in an envelope from Napoleon, which attacked the privileges of the (largely Hanoverian) nobility along with those of provinces, towns, and guilds, in two ways. First, the Civil Code and a system of bureaucratic centralization was introduced. Second, in the parliament, which in the event met only twice, representation of orders—nobility, clergy, and cities—gave way to the representation of wealth in the shape of seventy landowners, fifteen merchants or manufacturers, and fifteen professional men or bureaucrats. The only compensation for the nobility was that serfs lost only their personal servitude, gained no land, and had to continue providing dues and services unless they redeemed them.

In Bavaria the support of the French army permitted the Chief Minister, Count Maximilien von Montgelas, to smash the privileges of the nobles who dominated the estates, of the cities, and of the Church, which was particularly troublesome in the Tyrol, taken over from the Austrians in 1805. A constitution was promulgated in 1808, providing for electoral colleges in each of fifteen administrative circles drawn from the 400 most-taxed landowners, merchants or industrialists. As it happened the parliament did not meet before 1818 but the circles were admirably governed by French-style prefects and the old collegiate system of central government, in which decisions were reached by majority, was replaced by departmental ministries. To compensate the nobility, the Civil Code was only partially applied and nobles could resist the redemption of lucrative seigneurial obligations.

The Grand Duchy of Warsaw was another artificial creation. When Alexander I turned down the offer it was entrusted to Frederick Augustus, King of Saxony, and equipped with a constitution issued by Napoleon in July 1807 from Dresden. The Civil Code was introduced. The lesser nobles who had fought in Polish Legions alongside the French were suspected of Jacobinism. Moreover, Napoleon was now in alliance with Alexander I and it was therefore the Polish magnates around the Tsar's adviser, Prince Adam Czartoryski, who dominated the regime. Serfdom was abolished, but if a serf left his master he left his land, horse, and plough behind also. If he stayed, labour services were required until he redeemed them. Napoleon was impatient with the Polish nobles' cherished Sejm or parliament. 'As for their deliberating assemblies', he said, 'their *liberum veto*, their diets on horseback with drawn swords, I want nothing of that.... I want Poland only as a disciplined force, to furnish a battlefield.'[3]

[3] Quoted by André Fugier, *La Révolution française et l' Empire napoléonien* (Paris, 1954), 265.

In 1798 Holland and Switzerland had both become unitary and democratic republics, the Batavian and the Helvetic, under the patronage of the Directory. In Switzerland the new order was in the interests of the lesser burghers and officials, and of districts like the Vaud and Argovie, which had been subject to the urban patriciate of Berne. Napoleon on the other hand favoured the urban patriciates, who recovered power under the constitution of 1803, promulgated in Paris, which restored cantonal sovereignty and the federal diet, but refused the Swiss a common army. In the Batavian Republic the National Assembly, dominated by radicals, finally agreed on a unitary constitution in April 1798. But the traditional ruling élites with their local power-bases recovered power two months later. The following year the British attempted a landing in Holland and Napoleon decided that he could take no chances. The National Assembly was broken up by a *coup d'état* in September 1801 and replaced by a Regency of State which represented the urban patriciate of Amsterdam and the landowners of the inland provinces, some of whom were partisans of the deposed House of Orange. When full-scale war broke out with Great Britain, Napoleon entrusted Dutch affairs to a single Grand Pensionary (1805) and then made Holland a kingdom under his brother Louis (1806). Louis Bonaparte was far from being a subservient tool and paid for his independence dearly in 1810, when Holland was annexed directly to the French Empire.

Outside these satellite states French power was much less firmly consolidated, and rested first and foremost on superior military force. The French had been ejected from Naples in 1799 by Russian and Turkish troops, the British navy, and a peasant rising organized by Catholic clergy into the Sanfedists or Army of the Holy Faith. In February 1806 the French re-occupied Naples and obliged King Ferdinand to flee to Sicily, where he was supported by British money and sea-power. French requisitions immediately provoked another rising in Calabria, and though it was suppressed, brigandage remain endemic. Joseph Bonaparte set about attacking the power of the Neapolitan barons whose fiefs gave them tax exemptions, a noble chamber in the estates, seigneurial dues and monopolies, and their own baronial courts to enforce them. A law of August 1806 abolished feudalism but it remained a dead letter until 1808, when Joseph moved to take the throne of Spain and was replaced in Naples by the Grand Duke of Berg, Joachim Murat. Baronial jurisdiction was abolished, as was personal servitude, but dues and services attached to land tenure remained unless they were redeemed. Moreover the division of common land and the sale of monastic lands enabled the nobility, as well as their bailiffs and the *gabelotti* who sublet their estates, to enlarge their landholdings. A constitution drawn up for Naples was never implemented. Intendants like French prefects were put in charge of the administration but were not as important as the regional military commanders who commanded an army 40,000 strong. Murat however was clever enough to promote Neapolitans into the army, bureaucracy, and ministries. These Neapolitans became influenced by Carbonarist ideas of a united, democratic Italy which were introduced into Naples by the French after 1807. When Napoleon allied with Austria in 1809 Murat began to contemplate turning against the emperor with his new power-base. In Sicily, the British minister, Lord William Bentinck, tried to build a bridge to Murat as the 'Italian Bernadotte' by forcing a British-style constitution on the hapless King Ferdinand in 1812.

Napoleon was no more successful in his dealings with the Bourbons of Spain. Their deposition on 10 May 1808 sparked off an insurrection of the Madrid mob and peasants along the Mediterranean coast, both against the French and against the collaborating Spanish authorities. The movement was taken over by the notables—local gentry, clergy, and officials—as the only way to control it. Provincial juntas were elected to organize the apocalypse, each with its own guerilla army, and on 19 July that of Seville defeated the French army at Bailén. The regular Spanish army which at first had offered no resistance to Murat gradually came over to the cause. Provincial juntas sent delegates to a central junta at Aranjuez. Composed of grandees and prelates, it swore to preserve 'our rights, *fueros*, lands and customs, and especially the succession in the reigning family'.[4] Joseph Bonaparte was now in retreat. At the end of July 1808 he was forced to abandon Madrid. His regime was based on a minority of *afrancesados*, notably bureaucrats who saw a chance to complete the enlightened reforms of Charles III. But these reforms consisted mainly of persecuting monks and priests who were seen to be stirring the ignorant peasants into rebellion. A constitution drafted at Bayonne was never promulgated. Spain was divided into departments but prefects were never appointed; French rule was that of the military governors.

Within the forces of resistance a struggle now developed between the generals and the provincial juntas, some of which they considered to be 'republican'. An attempt was made to smooth over the differences in September 1810 by calling a Constituent Cortes to Cadiz. But this only highlighted the tension between the 'two Spains'. The Cortes was dominated by liberals who enacted a constitution in 1812 which divided legislative power between the king and Cortes and abolished the *señorios* or jurisdictions of the nobility. The nobles, clergy, and constituted bodies had their revenge in the ordinary Cortes elected in 1813. To be rid of the liberals they were prepared to invite back Ferdinand VII, 'the Desired One', on any terms.

At the other end of Europe the Prussian state was all but destroyed after its defeat by the French, huge reparations were imposed, and in October 1807 Frederick William III was virtually obliged to hand over the government to a team of reforming ministers led by Stein and Hardenberg. Stein

---

had plans to limit the personal rule of the king by a Council of State and collective ministerial responsibility but his attack on economic and social reform was more ambitious still than his political reforms. In order to head off peasant revolt, serfdom was abolished in October 1807. The nobles who had performed so lamentably in battle suffered the consequences. The nobility ceased to be a privileged order in 1807. From 1808 noble birth was no longer a guarantee of promotion in the Prussian officer corps. *Rittergüter*, or noble estates which carried tax exemption and a seat (should they meet again) in the provincial diets, were made available to non-noble buyers. Stein realized that Prussia would have to become not only less privileged but also more liberal if she were to survive. In the summer of 1808 he tried to persuade the king not to accept French reparation demands but to authorize a national insurrection and grant a 'free constitution'. In this way the patriotic energies of the people would be mobilized behind the state. Yet all that Stein could achieve was municipal self-government, and reactionary aristocrats at Court ensured that peace was made with France and Stein dismissed from office (November 1808) before he could do too much damage. After 1810 Hardenberg tried further to increase the powers of the state at the expense of the Prussian nobility. But the Assembly of Notables which he summoned in 1811 refused to countenance the taxation of noble estates without the recall of the provincial estates, and the national assembly of noble, town, and peasant representatives that met in 1812 was the tool of the nobility rather than of the government. Hardenberg's 'Gendarmerie Edict' of 1812 which proposed to abolish the patrimonial jurisdiction of the Junkers and replace the elected noble *Landrat* in the provinces by a centrally appointed bureaucrat was also defeated by the nobility, intent on safeguarding the society of orders against both bureaucrats and the populus.

Austria and Russia were also given cause to reflect by defeat at the hands of Napoleon, but few reforms were carried out. In neither country were the serfs emancipated. Austria failed to develop a ministerial system that corrected the delays of collegiate administration on the one hand and the arbitrariness of the personal rule of Francis I on the other. The Hungarian Diet was the only representative institution in the Habsburg Monarchy, dominated by nobles, and only agreed to vote men and supplies when the French were at the gates of Vienna. After Austerlitz Count Philipp Stadion and the Archduke Charles relaxed censorship in order to mobilize opinion for revenge against France and built up *Landwehr* and volunteer battalions. But after a second defeat at Wagram in 1809 Metternich became Chancellor and put an end to such foolish experiments.

In Russia the traditional representative institutions of Poland were destroyed after its annexation was completed in 1795, and replaced by military rule. The constitution of Finland, on the other hand, was endorsed by Alexander I before the Finnish diet in 1809, although another diet was not summoned until 1863. After Tilsit, Alexander's brilliant Chief Minister, Speransky, pushed through a programme of reforms in Russia proper. A Council of State on the Napoleonic model was introduced to draft decrees and control ministers, who replaced the collegiate system. The Senate lost its administrative responsibilities, but remained the highest court of appeal. A Civil Code was published in 1812, and meritocracy introduced into the civil service, ending the monopoly of the nobles. However, Speransky's bold plan for a state Duma came to nothing, and a pincer movement by Alexander and the nobility drove him out of office when Napoleon invaded.

Even the Scandinavian countries were affected by the hegemony of Napoleon. Under the patronage of the Emperor the Danish king, Frederick VI, was able to integrate the Duchy of Holstein into the Danish Commonwealth, attack the privileges of its German nobility, and in 1810 require the use of Danish in the administration, law courts, and schools. In Sweden Gustav IV Adolf had ruled without the Riksdag since 1792, but in March 1809 he was overthrown by a group of high officials and army officers. The Riksdag was called and the constitution of 1809 enshrined the privileges of the nobility in the traditional four-chamber system of estates: nobles, clergy, townsmen, and peasants. Bernadotte cemented an alliance with Russia and Great Britain against Napoleon and defeated Denmark on the way towards Paris. He received from Denmark its dependency of Norway in January 1814. But the Norwegians called a Constituent Assembly at Eidsvold in April 1814, drew up a constitution which provided for a Storting or parliament, elected on a low property franchise and elected the Danish prince Christian Frederick their king. As a result, Bernadotte invaded Norway, and obliged the Storting to accept a union with Sweden and elect Charles XIII of Sweden as king. In return for this, Bernadotte guaranteed the Norwegians their constitution. In Norway at least, liberalism triumphed against absolutism, bureaucracy, and privilege.

The Generation of Nationalism

Nationalism is the feeling that belonging to a nation is more important than belonging to a town, province, class, social order, or religious group, and the struggle for a state to defend the interests and identity of that nation. The period of the Revolutionary and Napoleonic wars witnessed the first upsurge of nationalism in European history, partly under the inspiration of the French armies and their message of liberation, partly in reaction against those armies and the realities of occupation and oppression. The term 'nationalism' first appeared in the writings of the Jesuit Abbé Barruel in 1798, to describe hatred of the foreigner, not love for him.

The different meanings of nationalism broadly reflect different meanings of the term 'nation'. For the French Revolutionaries, the Nation was a body of free and equal citizens. They were free because they had asserted their claim to be a sovereign people, with authority to make laws for themselves, at the expense of the arbitrary and God-given powers of the monarch. They were equal because they were equally subject to those laws, against which no privilege of town, province, order, or religious group could stand. The Revolution made France into a *patrie*, not in the old sense of place of origin, but in the new sense of a land of liberty, freed from oppression. To defend that *patrie* against foreign tyrants, revolutionary armies were formed after 1791, composed of Frenchmen instead of Swiss or German mercenaries, and citizens rather than professional soldiers. The volunteers of 1791 and 1792 were drawn from the bourgeois militia or National Guard; the *levée en masse* of 1793–4 created a people's army one million strong.

The French Revolutionary armies saw themselves not as conquerors but as liberators, at the service of a universal ideal of liberty, equality, and fraternity. Their mission was to free subject-peoples from tyranny, aristocracy, and fanaticism, and to create a brotherhood of nations. They were received with enthusiasm by Jacobin patriots in the Rhineland, the Netherlands, and northern Italy. The Piedmontese poet Count Vittorio Alfieri renounced his status as a subject of Piedmont, with the consequent loss of his nobility, and called upon his fellow writers to 'seek liberty wherever it is to be found'.[5] Polish legionaries who fought in Bonaparte's armies against the Austrians in 1800 carried on their shoulder-flashes the motto 'free men are brothers'.[6]

French armies certainly dealt a blow to the monarchical, aristocratic and ecclesiastical state-system of Europe. As late as 1806, on the eve of the battle of Jena, the philosopher Hegel praised Napoleon for doing away with the mass of petty states that secured only the private interests of their rulers, and replacing them with larger, bureaucratic states which were governed in the general interest. 'This world soul … dominating the entire world from horseback', proclaimed Hegel. 'It is impossible not to admire him.'[7] The notion that these new states were governed in the general interest, however, was not widely shared. Neither was the idea that French armies had come to liberate the peoples of Europe, rather than to oppress them. The victorious French imposed massive indemnities on defeated states. They requisitioned supplies, confiscated lands, imposed taxes, and conscripted troops in enormous numbers. The number of Italians under arms rose from 22,000 in 1804 to 71,000 in 1812. There were 90,000 Poles in the Grand Army which invaded Russia in 1812. On that occasion, only 200,000 of the 600,000 troops were French, 100,000 were drawn from annexed territories, and the rest from satellite states or allies. The satellite states were no more than vehicles for making foreigners pay for and fight Napoleon's wars. No wonder that Alfieri

    [5] Adrian Lyttelton, 'The National Question in Italy', in M. Teich and R. Porter, *The National Question in Europe in Historical Context* (Cambridge, 1993), 63.
    [6] Quoted by Norman Davies, *God's Playground: A History of Poland* (Oxford, 1981), ii, 295.
    [7] Quoted by S. Avineri, *Hegel's Theory of the Modern State* (Cambridge, 1972), 63.

changed his mind in 1804, publishing a tract entitled *Misogallo*, in which he urged fellow Italians to hate 'with an implacable and mortal loathing those barbarians from across the mountains' as 'the single and fundamental basis of your political existence'.[8]

Given the collapse of established states, or the fact that many rulers meekly accepted the demands of Napoleon and passed them on to their subjects, it is no surprise that the most dramatic challenge to French rule was popular insurrection. There were popular revolts in Belgium in 1798, Italy in 1799 and 1806, and of course Spain in 1808. The Spanish insurrection became a sustained people's war, fought by irregular volunteers who were in fact paid more than the regular forces by the juntas. It was fought for two irreconcilable ideals, the one a liberal constitution, enacted in 1812, which proclaimed the sovereignty of the people, the other *La Religión, el Rey y la Patria*, which sought to restore King Ferdinand and the Spanish Inquisition, and for which the regular army ultimately deserted.

The elaboration of a coherent alternative vision of the nation took place not in Spain but in Germany. The dissolution of the Holy Roman Empire, the collaboration of the states of south and west Germany with Napoleon in the Confederation of the Rhine, and the supine behaviour of the Prussian state, enabled the educated middle classes to seize the initiative and lay the foundations of a German national revival. Johann Gottlieb Fichte, who in 1799 had lost his post as professor of philosophy at Jena for espousing the principles of the French Revolution, delivered a series of *Addresses to the German Nation* in 1807–8 in which he argued that France now represented despotism, not liberty, and that the cause of freedom had now fallen to the German nation. He took up the teaching of Herder that the nation was identified not with the state, an artificial body, but with the organic body of the *Volk*, the people. Like Herder he rejected the French idea that Enlightenment was universal, and argued that each nation had its own language and culture, and that this language and culture expressed the soul of the *Volk*. The poet Ernst Moritz Arndt, asking where the German nation was in 1813, answered that 'As far as the German tongue rings | And to God in heaven Lieder sings | That's where it should be | That, bold German, pertains to thee.'[9] The consequence of this was that if a state were necessary to defend the values and interests of the German nation, it would not be Prussia or Austria or Bavaria but the state of a united German people.

In the years before the War of Liberation many organizations were set up by the educated middle classes both to train for battle and to develop a civic virtue that would equip them for participating in the free institutions of the

---

[8] Quoted by Derek Beales, *The Risorgimento and the Unification of Italy* (London, 1971), 110.

[9] Hagen Schulze, *The Course of German Nationalism. From Frederick the Great to Bismarck, 1763–1867* (Cambridge, 1991), 34.

new Germany. The Tugendbund, or Society for the Practice of Public Virtue, was set up in Königsberg in 1808, and soon had branches across Germany. The Berlin academic Friedrich Jahn set up a Deutsche Bund in 1810 to draw together like-minded nationalists across Germany, and in 1811 founded a Turngesellschaft or Gymnastics Society to train the physique and character for the coming struggle. Frederick William III gave Napoleon 20,000 men for the invasion of Russia, but when Napoleon beat a retreat he issued a patriotic address to the German nation in March 1813 to rise up against the French. Stein returned to office and with General Scharnhorst mobilized *Landwehr* militia, *Jäger* and *Freikorps* volunteers, which were predominantly middle class, and *Landsturm* home guards, to serve alongside the regular army.

The states which resumed the struggle against Napoleon had to tread a difficult path between the need to mobilize mass patriotic forces and the need to avoid endangering the position of monarchs and nobilities by being forced to make political concessions. By and large, they succeeded in this enterprise. When Austria went to war with France in 1809, and experimented with militias and volunteers, the *Appeal to the German Nation* of Archduke Charles, penned by the romantic writer Friedrich Schlegel, declared that Austrian armies would not annihilate the laws and customs of the various German states, or overturn any thrones, but only release them from dependence on France and restore the autonomy of the Habsburg Monarchy. The rising of the Tyrolese, seeking release from their incorporation into French-dominated Bavaria, was not encouraged by the Austrian government, and the execution of its leader, Andreas Hofer, by the French, was not unduly bemoaned by them. The Russian state managed to call on militias, Cossacks, partisans, and peasants to drive out the French at the cost of 1.5 million lives, without proclaiming the emancipation of the serfs, largely by whipping up enthusiasm for the Tsar and Orthodox Church. After Napoleon confiscated the Black Virgin of Smolensk, Alexander was able to denounce him as the catspaw of Moslems and Jews, while General Kutuzov told his troops on the eve of Borodino that they were protected by the Black Virgin. During the invasion scare of 1803–5 the British government recruited over 200,000 volunteers to supplement the regular army. They avoided appeals to patriotism, which carried powerful connotations of political radicalism, and called for loyalty to George III, who enjoyed a revival of popularity. The union of King and people was symbolized by the review of 27,000 volunteers by George III in Hyde Park in October 1803. British nationalism was as opposed to French anarchy as it was to French tyranny, and set the defence of the monarchy and Protestant Church above the widening of the citizen body, at least in the short term. The lesson of the Napoleonic wars in the long term, however, was that nationalism was a revolutionary force that would not always do the bidding of governments.

3

METTERNICH'S EUROPE

The Vienna Settlement

The European peace settlement of 1814–15 was ultimately directed against revolution and therefore against nationalism, which was seen to be a revolutionary force. Immediately, it was directed against France, the revolutionary power *par excellence*, which had been responsible for a generation of turmoil in Europe. Until the end of 1815, the anti-revolutionary purposes of the Coalition were sublimated into debate on the restrictions that would have to be imposed on France in the interests of the balance of power. After 1815, by a curious twist of emphasis, those anti-revolutionary purposes became more explicit, but in fact concealed a preoccupation with the balance of power that would be upset if any of the major states made use of revolution in any country to extend its hegemony.

The balance of power established in 1814–15 had five main principles. The first was that the great powers fighting Napoleon stuck together rather than competed with each other, in the general interest of lasting peace among the powers collectively rather than in the short-term, selfish interest of any one of them. The undermining of the Coalitions first by one power, then by another, leaving to do a separate deal with France, had allowed the French to divide and rule, at the cost of twenty-five years of war and five million lives. But under the Treaty of Chaumont in March 1814 Great Britain, Austria, Prussia, and Russia agreed not to make a separate peace with Napoleon and joined forces in a Quadruple Alliance. The success of the negotiations depended on the co-operation of the British Foreign Minister, Castlereagh, the Austrian Foreign Minister Metternich, Tsar Alexander of Russia, Frederick William III of Prussia, and later the French Foreign Minister Talleyrand.

The second principle was that while Napoleon had to be deposed and the Bourbon monarchy restored in France, France should retain the territorial integrity it had enjoyed before it went to war in 1792 and the independence of a great power. The Allies entered Paris at the end of March 1814, Napoleon abdicated in April and was exiled to the Mediterranean island of Elba, and Louis XVIII returned to Paris in May. The Peace of Paris on 31 May 1814 gave France slightly more than her frontiers of 1792, but rebuilt the 'ancient ramparts' of which Gentz had spoken more sturdily than ever. In the north, the Kingdom of the Netherlands was extended to include Belgium, occupied by the French for the last twenty years, and Antwerp was reopened, though purely as a commercial port, in consideration of Britain's naval

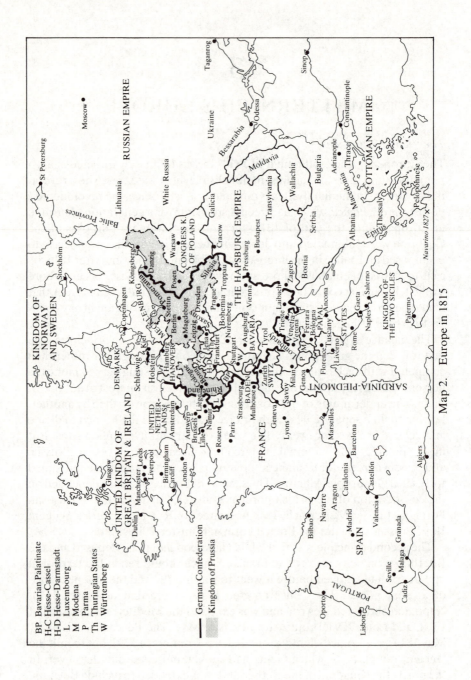

BP Bavarian Palatinate
H-C Hesse-Cassel
H-D Hesse-Darmstadt
L Luxembourg
M Modena
P Parma
Th Thuringian States
W Württemberg

German Confederation

Kingdom of Prussia

RUSSIAN EMPIRE

Moscow

St Petersburg

KINGDOM OF
NORWAY
AND SWEDEN

Stockholm

Copenhagen

DENMARK

Baltic Provinces

Lithuania

White Russia

Ukraine

Odessa

Taganrog

Bessarabia

Moldavia

Wallachia

Bulgaria

Serbia

Bosnia

Transylvania

Budapest

Pressburg

THE HAPSBURG EMPIRE

Vienna

Prague

Bohemia

Troppau

Galicia

Cracow

CONGRESS K.
OF POLAND

Warsaw

Posen

Silesia

Danzig

Königsberg

Pomerania

MECKLENBURG

Stettin

Berlin

Magdeburg

Hamburg

Leipzig

Dresden

Meissen

Frankfurt

Nuremberg

Augsburg

BAVARIA

Stuttgart

W

Zagreb

Laibach

Trieste

Venetia

Verona

Lombardy

Milan

Genoa

SARDINIA-PIEDMONT

Savoy

Geneva

SWITZ.

Zurich

BADEN

Mulhouse

Strasbourg

Lyons

Marseilles

Paris

Rouen

FRANCE

Lille

Brussels

Namur

Liège

Antwerp

Amsterdam

UNITED
NETHER-
LANDS

Cologne

Rhineland

L

H-D

BP

H-C

Th

Schleswig

Holstein

HANOVER

Hamburg

UNITED KINGDOM OF
GREAT BRITAIN & IRELAND

Dublin

Glasgow

Cardiff

Liverpool

Manchester

Leeds

Birmingham

London

SPAIN

Madrid

Navarre

Aragon

Catalonia

Barcelona

Castellón

Valencia

Bilbao

Granada

Malaga

Seville

Cadiz

PORTUGAL

Oporto

Lisbon

Algiers

Florence

Tuscany

Livorno

Bologna

Ferrara

PAPAL
STATES

Ancona

Rome

Gaeta

Salerno

Naples

KINGDOM OF
THE TWO SICILIES

Palermo

Tyrol

Spezzia

Albania

Macedonia

Thrace

Epirus

Thessaly

Peloponnese

Adrianople

Constantinople

Sinope

OTTOMAN EMPIRE

Navarino 1827 ×

Map 2. Europe in 1815

interests. In the east, the cantons of Switzerland, in a state of near anarchy, were reorganized under a new Federal Pact. In the south, the Kingdom of Sardinia-Piedmont recovered its integrity, including Savoy, and gained Nice and the port of Genoa.

The third principle was that the legitimate rights of monarchs were to be upheld, not the rights of nations to self-determination, which would have been an endorsement of revolution. The Bourbon dynasty was restored not only to the throne of France, but to that of Spain, in the person of Ferdinand VII, and to that of the Two Sicilies. The British, who had sheltered King Ferdinand on Sicily, were keen to return him to Naples as well, even though the Austrians had allied with Joachim Murat, King of Naples, in January 1814, against Eugène Beauharnais, the Viceroy of Napoleon's Kingdom of Italy. Similarly, Talleyrand was insistent that the King of Saxony should not lose his throne, even though he had fought alongside Napoleon in 1813, since to depose one German monarch was to place all the others at risk.

This related to a fourth principle, that the cannibalism that had character-ized the balance of power in the eighteenth century, when the gains by one ally had to be compensated by the gains of another, and states like Poland had simply disappeared from the map, would not be allowed to recur in the nine-teenth century. It seemed that it might recur, when Alexander proclaimed the liberation of Poland, ending the Partitions, with himself as king, and allowed Frederick William of Prussia to take possession of Saxony. This suggested that France was not the only danger to European stability, and that Russia, whose armies had driven across Europe to Paris, was also a potential menace. To counter the threat, Talleyrand orchestrated a secret pact between Great Britain, Austria, and France (January 1815) in order to regulate and limit the Russo-Prussian deal. As a result, Poland was resurrected as a 'Congress Kingdom', but remained only two-thirds of the size of the Grand Duchy of Warsaw, with a population of three million. Its king was the Tsar of Russia, and as the Partitions effectively stood, most Poles continued to live under Russian rule in Lithuania, White Russia, and the Ukraine, under Austrian rule in Galicia, or under Prussian rule in Posen. Prussia gained about two-fifths of Saxony, but was compensated much further west, receiving most of the Kingdom of Westphalia and the left bank of the Rhine.

The last principle was that while not all powers could be equal under the balance of power, the hegemony of the great powers had to balance against the right of small states to independence and security. This was ensured in Germany by building up states such as Saxony, Hanover, and Bavaria into substantial kingdoms, then inviting the thirty-nine German states to send government representatives to a Diet at Frankfurt, which became the central organ of the German Confederation. This was the brainchild of Metternich, who brushed aside Stein's dream of a unitary Reich and Hardenberg's plan for a more federal Germany. Since Austria and Prussia were partly within and partly outside the Confederation, they were entitled to send representatives, and Austria indeed held the chair, but the influence of Prussia in north Germany, balancing that of Austria in south Germany, effectively gave the states of the 'third Germany' a considerable degree of independence. In Italy, Austria recovered the provinces of Lombardy and Venetia, of which the Austrian Emperor became king, Habsburg princes returned to the duchies of Tuscany and Modena, while Princess Marie-Louise, the Austrian Emperor's daughter and Napoleon's estranged wife, became duchess of Parma. In March 1815, Murat marched north and issued a proclamation to the Italian people, calling on them to liberate themselves from foreigners and set up an independent state, but the great powers combined against him and Ferdinand of Naples had the pleasure of having him shot. Austrian influence in the peninsula was limited by the restoration of the Kingdom of the Two Sicilies, of the Papal States, to which Austria had to surrender the Marches and Legations or Romagna, centred on Bologna, and of Sardinia-Piedmont. Metternich had ambitions to set up an Italian Confederation on the model of the German, but this was strenuously resisted not only by the other Italian states but also by powers such as Britain, France, and Russia, which wanted to preserve a balance between the influence of great powers and the independence of small states in Italy. In the Balkans, finally, the consensus was that the influence of the great powers should take precedence over the demand of emerging nationalities for statehood. At Vienna, Castlereagh refused to receive Serbian delegates no less than six times. The Serbs staged a revolt in 1815 under their new ruler, Miloš Obrenović, and the Ottoman Empire conceded them internal autonomy for fear of provoking intervention by Russia. On the other hand Capodistrias, now one of Tsar Alexander's secretaries of state, failed to secure independence for the Ionian Islands, which in November 1815 became a British protectorate.

The unexpected return of Napoleon from Elba and Hundred Day rule only served to excite the other powers into putting the finishing touches to the European settlement. The Final Act of the Congress of Vienna was signed on 9 June 1815, a few days before Waterloo. It renewed Quadruple Alliance and provided for future congresses of monarchs or their ministers to promote the peace and prosperity of Europe. In September 1815, Tsar Alexander, Francis I, and Frederick William III signed a Holy Alliance, to deal with each other and other peoples on the basis of the Christian gospel. For Alexander some dialogue between princes and peoples was intended, but Metternich insisted that the Alliance must be only between princes and against the demand of peoples for constitutions and reforms. Castlereagh saw it as absurd, but had no objection to the Prince Regent signing it personally, as a way of restraining Russia, Prussia, and Austria. After Waterloo, France was shorn of more territory, had to pay an indemnity and suffer an army of occupation for five years. But the skill of her ministers was such that in 1818, at the Conference of Aix-la-Chapelle, the indemnity was revised, the occupation was ended, and France was invited to join the Concert of European powers.

The Revolutionary Tradition

From exile during the Revolutionary and Napoleonic period nobles and clergy who had defended their privileges against enlightened despotism before 1789 now saw things in a different light. They still dreamed of a decentralized provincial order in which the privileges of the ancient estates would be cocooned, but now the monarchy was seen not as the enemy of that order but as its guarantor. Unfortunately for them, Napoleon had taught the crowned heads of Europe a few lessons, and they were not prepared to break up the shiny apparatus of centralized administration and ministerial power in order to humour the defenders of privilege. On the other hand the revolutionary aspirations of the last twenty-five years did not dutifully lie down in 1815 as monarchs took up their old stations. Liberals insisted on the rule of law under a constitution. If the power of the state had increased, then ministers must be made responsible to elective assemblies, a free press must articulate and educate public opinion and legal proceedings must be free of administrative interference, open to the public, and conducted before juries. In parliament, representation of nobles, clergy, and urban communities should be replaced by the representation of individual citizens, or at least by those who owned property and paid taxes.

After the defeat of Napoleon at Waterloo, vengeance was wreaked on Bonapartist notables during the White Terror in the south of France and the ultra-royalists won a landslide victory to the 'Matchless Parliament' of August 1815. But ministerial and bureaucratic authority remained in the hands of moderates who fought this *frondeur* nobility all the way and kept a tight rein on the Catholic Church and education. Neither could Louis XVIII ignore liberal opinion and he had granted a constitutional Charter in June 1814, while maintaining the fiction that it was a gift of his regal generosity; there was no truck with plebiscites. An electorate of 100,000 property-owners elected the Chamber of Deputies while appointed peers sat in the upper house. These concessions were insufficient for such liberals as Benjamin Constant, editor of the *Mercure* after 1817 and then a deputy, who insisted on the acknowledgement of ministerial responsibility to parliament, a free press, and trial by jury instead of the arbitrary provostal courts. A revolutionary fringe among students, officers on half pay, and some of the 300,000 demobbed soldiers went so far as to incite mutiny in the garrisons along the eastern frontier in 1821–2, but the leaders were caught and executed.

Louis XVIII's brother, Charles X, succeeded to the throne in 1824, and restored influence to the nobility and clergy. His reign saw the growth of a moderate liberalism which was happy with constitutional monarchy and forgot the republic. But Charles X had no great respect for constitutions. When the liberals triumphed in the elections of June–July 1830 he issued three edicts which imposed press censorship, dissolved the Chamber before it met, and quartered the electoral body in preparation for new elections. Barricades were thrown up in the streets of Paris and the army was sent in to restore order. As it happened, most of the best troops were conquering Algeria and low pay and liberal ideas combined to lower morale among the remainder. Three regiments deserted, Charles X was forced to flee, and power passed to moderate, propertied liberals who formed a National Guard to control the mob. The Chamber of Deputies revised the Charter, and offered the crown to Louis-Philippe, the Duke of Orleans, only on condition that he endorse it. Louis-Philippe became King of the French, a genuine constitutional monarch.

French armies did not move beyond the frontiers in 1830 as in 1792, but the trails blazed by Revolutionary and Napoleonic armies in the past might easily be rekindled. In the United Netherlands the regime of the Orange monarch, William I, was absolutist, run by Dutch officials using the Dutch language and, if it was not overtly Calvinist, certainly kept the Catholic Church firmly under State control. Opposition built up in the Belgian half of the monarchy, both among the Catholics who predominated there and among French-speaking liberals. In 1828 liberals and Catholics sank their differences and joined constitutional associations to force William to give ground. William agreed to call the States General but then made the fatal mistake of sending royal troops to take control of Brussels. Barricades went up on 23 September 1830, volunteers arrived from other towns to reinforce what now became a national uprising, and a provisional government declared Belgium an independent state on 4 October 1830. William asked for the armed intervention of the great powers, but the French intervened to support the Belgian rebels, and the main concern of the British Foreign Secretary, Palmerston, was that Belgium should not once again fall under French influence. The matter was settled by the powers meeting in conference in London. Belgium was declared neutral, under the collective guarantees of the powers and placed under a monarch who belonged to none of the major ruling houses. A Belgian national congress was called, and elected one of the sons of Louis-Philippe king, but the British insisted that they think again, and Leopold of Saxe-Coburg was elected instead.

In the Restoration period Great Britain was already firmly established as a constitutional monarchy, although the Union with Ireland in 1800 involved the abolition of the Irish parliament in Dublin. Irish constituencies now sent their representatives to Westminster. Insulated from Napoleonic Europe, Britain did not take the same road towards administrative centralization. County magistracies were in the hands of the local aristocracy, gentry, and clergy and the modest central administration in London was also colonized by landed families. In Parliament the House of Lords was dominated by the landed aristocracy and the landed gentry, often related to the peerage, held sway in the House of Commons. Even during the Napoleonic Wars opposition had been growing to an aristocratic system that was seen to result in bad government, pensions for the rich, and taxes for the poor. The constitutional opposition was led by the patrician radical Sir Francis Burdett, elected to Parliament in 1807. The mass, revolutionary opposition was led by 'Orator' Henry Hunt, whose rally at Spa Fields in 1816 led to an attack on the Tower of London, while that at St Peter's Fields outside Manchester in 1819 provoked brutal repression by the local yeomanry and regular troops, known as the Peterloo massacre.

Considerable pressure for reform came from Ireland, where three-quarters of the population was Catholic yet denied office, and the vote controlled by an Ascendancy of Protestant landlords. A Catholic Association of small gentry, merchants, lawyers, and journalists was organized by Daniel O'Connell who also used the Catholic clergy to break the Irish tenantry away from the landlords. O'Connell was elected for County Clare in 1828 and forced Catholic emancipation from Wellington's government in 1829 as the only way to prevent social war. He then went on to attack the Anglican Church in Ireland and to campaign for the repeal of the Act of Union. In England an agricultural labourers' revolt and cotton-spinners' strike, together with the organization of political unions by merchants, manufacturers, and tradesmen in large towns like Birmingham convinced the Whigs, who formed a government in November 1830, that concessions would have to be made to reform in order to head off revolution. The Reform Bill of 1832 redistributed seats from rotten boroughs to populous towns and counties and increased the electorate from 478,000 to 814,000. The propertied, manufacturing, and educated middle classes were 'hitched to the constitution' alongside the landed interest as the best way to reinforce it.

In Central Europe an uneasy balance was maintained between royal absolutism, impatient of any constitutional restraints, the bureaucratic centralism beloved of ministers dedicated to state-building, aristocratic reaction which wanted to restore a society of orders, and liberal ideas generated by the War of Liberation. In the German universities students and young academics, many of whom had fought as volunteers in the national uprising of 1813 and dreamed of a free, united Germany, formed *Burschenschaften*, or fraternities, which were inspired by these views. On 18 October 1817, the 300th anniversary of Luther's Ninety-Five Theses and the fourth anniversary of the battle of Leipzig, the *Burschenschaften* organized a massive festival at Wartburg Castle, outside Jena. Gentz told Metternich in 1818 that 'of all the evils affecting Germany today, even including the licentiousness of the press, this student nuisance is the greatest, the most urgent and the most threatening'.[1] When August von Kotzebue, a reactionary playwright, was murdered by a theology student from Jena who considered him a Russian agent, Metternich seized the opportunity to convoke the representatives of ten German governments to Karlsbad in Bohemia. They drew up decrees to close student fraternities, tighten press censorship, and organize police surveillance in universities, which were adopted by the Federal Diet in September 1819.

Metternich, who became Austrian Chancellor in 1821, ran the Habsburg Monarchy as a bureaucratic police-state. No constitutions were granted, and representative institutions existed only as a façade, to placate the various nobilities. The Polish nobility of the Galician estates met in 1817 for the first time since 1782, and the constitution of the free city of Cracow (1818) survived for only ten years. The prelates, lords, knights, and cities of the Bohemian estates counted for little. The Hungarian Diet, which met after a gap of thirteen years in 1825, represented the powerful Magyar aristocracy and gentry and had the power to vote taxes and recruits, but was described by Metternich as 'one of the most tiresome constitutional *divertissements* in the world'.[2]

In Germany there was a rash of constitution-giving after 1815, particularly in states that had fallen under Napoleonic influence. Baden and Bavaria received constitutions in 1818, Württemberg and Hanover in 1819, Brunswick and Hesse-Darmstadt in 1820. The purpose was both to establish a *Rechtsstaat*, the rule of law, that would prevent monarchs wielding arbitrary power, and to undermine noble privilege, by replacing the representation of orders by that of propertied individuals. This was achieved in south German states, where liberals and bureaucrats gained the upper hand. In Prussia, however, not only did Frederick William III refuse to grant a constitution, but the reforming minister Hardenberg was frustrated by aristocratic reaction in his attempts to strengthen bureaucratic centralism. In 1823 the nobles achieved the resurrection of the provincial estates, in which the owners of *Rittergüter* or noble estates, burghers, and the rural class were represented, and which controlled local government by the election of *Landräte* from among the owners of noble estates.

This situation may have suited the eastern provinces of Prussia, but did not suit the Rhineland, now annexed to Prussia, which had been thoroughly Frenchified and retained the Napoleonic Code. Rhineland liberals campaigned vigorously for *Staatsbürgertum* or equal citizenship against the system of estates, for vigorous parliamentary government against the dead hand of Prussian bureaucracy, and for the *Rechtsstaat* or constitutional state

---

[1] Quoted by Donald E. Emerson, *Metternich and the Political Police* (The Hague, 1968), 110.
[2] Metternich to Gentz, 17 Aug. 1825. Quoted by George Barany, *Stephen Széchenyi and the Awakening of Hungarian Nationalism, 1791–1841* (Princeton, 1968), 123.

against arbitrary power. In other German states such as Hesse-Cassel and Saxony, constitutions were not granted till 1831, while liberals had to force modifications of the constitution of Brunswick in 1832, the Duke of Brunswick being overthrown in the process. The Danish liberal Uwe Jens Lornsen, a former member of the *Burschenschaft* of Jena, mounted a propaganda campaign at Kiel in November 1830 in favour of a Norwegian-style constitution. He was arrested and the system of four consultative estates on the Prussian model conceded by Frederick VI of Denmark in 1834 was much more to the taste of the conservative, German-speaking *Ritterschaft* of Holstein. In Switzerland, where cantonal sovereignty and the dominance of the urban patriciates was underscored by the Constitution of 1815, a liberal movement in 1830–2 did force more popular constitutions on the oligarchies of half the cantons, but the Federal Diet was too weak to force 'regeneration' on the conservative forest cantons, led by the city of Basle.

In southern Europe constitutions were abrogated by returning monarchs and the Church and nobility were restored to some of their former powers. But there were no concessions to representative government and revolutionary opposition built up in the royal armies which were subjected to purges, cut down in size, and paid little and irregularly by bankrupt regimes. Secret societies riddled the armed forces and provided links with civilians who had also lost out at the Restoration.

On 1 January 1820 there was a mutiny at Cadiz among Spanish troops who were about to be sent to fight revolution in South America. Junior officers launched a *pronunciamiento* and forced Ferdinand VII to proclaim the Constitution of 1812 which he had annulled six years before, form a ministry of 'men of 1812', and summon the Cortes. This fell under the influence of *exaltados*, the radicals of Madrid and the provincial capitals who dominated the political clubs, press, and masonic lodges. However, counter-revolutionary resistance built up in Aragon, Navarre, and Galicia. Portugal was under the grip of the British military while King John VI remained in Brazil where he had become Emperor. But in August 1820 a military coup was executed in Oporto, a national junta and provisional government were thrown up, and the Cortes summoned. This met at Lisbon in January 1821 and published a liberal Constitution, including a single-chamber Cortes, which was accepted in 1822 by John VI who now returned from Brazil. But the Portuguese nobles and clergy, deprived of the privileged position that they had occupied in the traditional Cortes, made clear their opposition and looked to the Queen and her younger son, Miguel, to give a sign.

Even before the Portuguese rising, in July 1820, the Muratist army officers of the Kingdom of Naples, linked with discontented civilians through the secret society of the Carbonari, mutinied against the Bourbon King Ferdinand, in the hope that they could press the Spanish Constitution on him. The movement was echoed in Sardinia-Piedmont, where Victor Emmanuel I of

Savoy had returned in 1814 to restore the Church and aristocracy to their former glory. In March 1821 army officers, supported by a minority of nobles who belonged to another secret society, the Federati, forced the king to abdicate and found his cousin Charles Albert willing to accept the Spanish Constitution. These risings threatened the position of the Austrians in Italy. They ruled the Duchies of Parma and Modena indirectly, the first through Marie-Louise, the former wife of Napoleon, and Lombardy and Venetia directly from Vienna. These two provinces were permitted only consultative assemblies to remind the Emperor of the 'needs, desires and prayers of the nation', and the privileges of the Italian nobilities received scant recognition. Moderate liberal opposition focused on the *Conciliatore* journal of the Lombard noble Count Confalonieri and the young dramatist Silvio Pellico. But Metternich was taking no risks after the troubles in Naples and Confalonieri and Pellico were among a dozen patriots to be arrested, tried in secret in 1821, sentenced to death, reprieved, and sent to do long prison sentences in the grim Spielberg fortress in Moravia. The Papal States underwent a restoration that was positively medieval. Sales of Church lands were annulled. The Sanfedists were made into the irregular troops of the Papacy and all justice was dispensed in Church courts. Civil administration was given back to cardinals and bishops and conducted in Latin. Press censorship was extreme and there was no lay representative government to speak of. This was of course anathema to nobles, officials, and academics who had served in the Napoleonic Kingdom of Italy but it was not until February 1831 that they were able to take advantage of the absence of the cardinal-administrators in Rome to elect a new Pope, to launch a rising in Bologna, co-ordinated with other coups in Parma and Modena, and to establish a provisional government.

Counter-Revolution and Conquest

Whereas the peace settlement of 1814–15 had been dominated by the rhetoric of the balance of power, and hostility to France expressed a loathing both of expansionism and of revolution, once revolutions broke out in other parts of Europe hostility to revolution became explicit in the dialogue between the great powers. Metternich was adamant that the Quadruple Alliance and Holy Alliance, made flesh by the periodic meetings of the powers, should be used to authorize military intervention to put down revolution in any state and protect legitimate rulers. He obtained support for his policy of intervention from Russia and Prussia at the Congress of the powers at Troppau in Galicia in October 1820. At a second Congress at Laibach (Ljubljana) in March 1821 the Tsar, Frederick William of Prussia, and Ferdinand of Naples authorized Metternich to send in Austrian troops to crush the rebellions in Naples and Piedmont. Castlereagh on the other hand was adamant in his state paper of 5 May 1820 that the Quadruple Alliance had been made to free the Continent from the 'military domination of France' and not for the 'superintendance of the internal affairs of other states'.[3] Britain, though happy to treat Portugal as its own back yard, was keen to prevent the principle of intervention being used as a cover to extend Austrian hegemony, and boycotted the Congresses. Other powers soon saw the danger. Metternich's scheme at the Congress of Verona in November 1822 to set up a central investigating commission in Italy to co-ordinate the police surveillance of secret societies in the various states was resisted as an unwonted increase in Austrian domination not only by Tuscany and the Papacy but also by France and Russia. The tension between Austria and France in Italy almost reached the stage of war in January 1832, when Metternich sent troops to Bologna to suppress the rising and the French landed a force at Ancona.

Over Spain, Metternich was worried by Russian promises to send troops to crush the revolution, and at the Congress of Verona supported intervention by France as a way out of the dilemma. The 'Hundred Thousand Sons of St Louis' crossed the Alps in January 1823 to restore Ferdinand VII to absolute rule. George Canning, Castelreagh's successor after 1822 as Foreign Secretary, was opposed to French troops intervening again in Spain, but continued the policy of Britain protecting its interests in Portugal. On the death of John VI in 1826 a struggle for the succession broke out between his sons, Dom Pedro, Emperor of Brazil since 1822, and Dom Miguel. Dom Miguel, supported by Austria, had himself crowned King of Portugal in 1828. But Britain maintained the claim of Dom Pedro, sent the fleet to support the landing he made from the Azores in July 1832, and installed Dom Pedro's daughter Maria as queen, when Dom Pedro decided to remain in Brazil. Dom Miguel fled to Spain, where the death of Ferdinand VII in 1833 caused a similar succession crisis. The throne was claimed by his reactionary brother, Don Carlos, but the succession of Ferdinand's infant daughter, Isabella, was upheld by her mother, Maria Cristina, who acted as regent, and by the Spanish establishment. This represented the triumph of constitutionalism in Spain as well as Portugal, and was safeguarded after 1834 by the Quadruple Alliance of Britain, France, Spain and Portugal.

Despite the Holy Alliance there was also a danger of a confrontation between Austria and Russia in the Balkans, and the problem flared up with a rising of the Greeks against their Ottoman overlords in March 1821. In 1814 the Greek merchant colony at Odessa had founded a Philiki Etairia or Friendly Society, in secret, for 'the liberation of the fatherland from the terrible yoke of Turkish oppression'.[4] It was not quite certain where the fatherland was, since the Greek diaspora extended to Macedonia, Thrace,

---

[3] Quoted by R. W. Seton-Watson, *Britain in Europe, 1789–1914* (Cambridge, 1937), 74.
[4] Quoted by Richard Clogg (ed.), *The Struggle for Greek Independence* (London, 1973), 95.

Bulgaria, the Danubian Principalities, Asia Minor, the Levant, and trading cities from Marseilles to Odessa. Yet the Etairia aimed to trigger off a Balkan-wide rising against the Turks. The presidency of the society was refused by Capodistrias but accepted in 1820 by Alexander Ypsilantis, himself a Russian general and the son of the Hospodar of Wallachia who had entered Russian service. Ypsilantis established links with Ali Pasha, who had extended his hegemony from Epirus to Thessaly and western Macedonia and had many Greek landowners, captains of armed bands, and outlaws of the Peloponnese within his orbit. Ypsilantis made an alliance with Miloš Obrenović, the ruler of the Serbs since 1817 and, failing support from the Hospodar of Moldavia and the Romanian boyars, with the Romanian peasant leader Tudor Vladimirescu. This made it possible for Ypsilantis to cross the Prut from Bessarabia in March 1821 with a small army of some 700 Greek students. The Peloponnese rose in revolt at the same time, but then the movement fell apart. Obrenović made a deal with the Turks in pursuit of his goal of a hereditary principality. Vladimirescu could not be relied on and was executed by the Etairia in May 1821. Ali Pasha was captured by the Turks and executed in February 1822.

As the Turks gained the upper hand and multiplied instances of harsh repression, Capodistrias urged the Tsar to intervene on behalf of the Christians of the Ottoman Empire, whom he had a right and responsibility to protect under the Treaty of Kutchuk Kainardji (1774). Whereas Tsar Alexander was reluctant to go to war, his successor, Nicholas I, was more aggressive. Canning took the view that the best way to avoid a Russo-Turkish war was for Britain to combine with Russia to force the Porte to concede that Greece must be set up as an autonomous if tributary state. This was agreed by Britain, Russia, and France under the Treaty of London (July 1827). The Russians had Capodistrias installed as president of the new Greek republic, while the British took charge of the Greek army and navy. The Turks, however, rejected this mediation and were still determined to crush the Greek rebellion. In the event, the British and French fleets destroyed the Turkish navy at Navarino and Russian armies surged into the Balkans and forced the Porte to concede self-government for the Danubian Principalities and Serbia under the Treaty of Adrianople in September 1829. Capodistrias, seen as a Russian client, was assassinated in 1831, and Britain, France, and Russia agreed to offer the crown of Greece to Otto, son of Ludwig of Bavaria. British fears that Russia would acquire complete domination at Constantinople nevertheless seemed to be realized in 1833 when the Sultan pledged himself to close the Straits to all foreign warships. The Black Sea was now a Russia lake, and Russian merchant ships had easy access to the Mediterranean. In a statement of 11 July 1833 Palmerston laid the basis of a policy by declaring that 'the integrity and independence of the Ottoman Empire are necessary to the maintenance of the tranquillity, the liberty and the balance of power in Europe'.[5] It was a sentiment with which Metternich wholeheart-edly agreed.

The Russian autocracy was prepared to play with revolution in the Balkans, but not at home. The principles of 1789 had been kept out of Russia but the young army officers who crossed Europe in 1814, reached Paris, and occu-pied northern France in 1816–18 were enrolled into masonic lodges and there exchanged ideas with French and Belgian liberals. Returned to St Peters-burg, they transformed the lodges into secret societies and plotted to bring constitutional rule to an autocratic, caste-ridden, and militaristic state. On 14 December 1825 a group of army officers refused to swear loyalty to the new Tsar Nicholas I and tried to launch a rising. It was crushed; five Decembrist ringleaders were hanged, 121 were sentenced to hard labour or exile, and 300 others evacuated to remote garrisons.

The Congress Kingdom of Poland, which the Tsar ruled as king, had a con-stitution drawn up by Prince Czartoryski and a Sejm or parliament, of bish-ops, nobles, and townsmen. But the façade of constitutionalism could not disguise the iron grip of the Russian military and bureaucracy, and liberal opposition in the Sejm was supported by student fraternities at Warsaw and Vilna and secret societies such as the Patriotic Society among young officers of the Polish army and members of the cadet school at Warsaw. Through Kiev links were established with future Decembrists, but the Polish insurrec-tion did not break out till November 1830, when the Tsar ordered a general mobilization to deal with the revolutionary threat from France. The Sejm declared the rising national and moderates around Czartoryski tried to extract concessions from the Tsar. But Nicholas would have none of it and when the Sejm deposed him in January 1831 Russian troops invaded the Congress Kingdom. Leadership now passed to the radicals of the Patriotic Society. After six months of war the rising was suppressed, the Polish army, Sejm, and universities were abolished, and the kingdom was placed under the military rule of Field Marshal Paskevich. The containment of Poland was something on which Russia, Prussia, and Austria could all agree, and their agreement was sanctioned in 1833 by the Treaty of Münchengrätz, described by Palmerston as 'the Holy Alliance of the East'.

National Awakenings

Central and Eastern Europe were dominated by multinational empires—Russia, Austria, and, to some extent, Prussia. Coherence was maintained by personal loyalty to the monarch, state service in the army, Church, or civil bureaucracy, and respect for the privileges of provinces and estates. In all empires, however, there was an élite which was loyal to the monarch because

---

[5] Quoted by Donald Southgate, *'The Most English Minister ...': The Policies and Politics of Palmerston* (London, 1966), 65.

it monopolized the top positions in the court or state service, a peasant population which was loyal to the monarch because its main enemy was the serfowner, and between them a sub-élite or intelligentsia separated from the
mass by education and ambition, and from the élite by its exclusion from
office. In many countries, this sub-élite resorted to revolution, but revolution
had to contend with government repression and the indifference of the
masses to the sub-élite's thirst for office. As it happened, the language and
culture of the élite tended to be different from that of the people. The intelligentsia, composed of lower clergy, teachers, students, and lesser officials,
though conversant with both, often made the decision to formalize and promote the language and culture of the people, which, along with its religion
and memories of past struggles, were deemed to define it as a nation. The
idea of the nation had the advantage of bridging the gap between different
social strata and acquiring a mass base for the agenda of the sub-élite. It also
brought together members of the same nation divided until now between different states. Once the nation was defined, claims could be made for independence and self-government on its behalf, opening up an alternative route
to office. The struggle to achieve statehood for a given nation was the driving
force behind nineteenth-century nationalism.

The suppression of the Polish revolt in 1831 snapped the link between the
Russian autocracy and the Polish gentry. There was now no middle way
between loyalty and conspiracy. Five thousand Poles went into exile in
France, and not only radicals but also moderates such as Czartoryski. Czartoryski looked to convert the French and British governments to intervene militarily for the Polish cause. The radicals founded a Democratic Society in 1832
and conspired to resurrect Poland by means of national insurrection. They
preached that the Polish serfs should be emancipated so that they could lend
support against the regimes that had partitioned Poland.

Polish nationalism was confronted by two difficulties. First, the Poles were
divided between Russia, Austria, and Prussia, and would have to force concession from each of those empires in order to redeem Poland. Second, there
was a wide gulf between the Polish gentry and Polish and other peasants,
whose serf-owners they were. Adam Mickiewicz, the Polish poet, who was
elected professor of Slavic literature at the Collège de France in 1840, tried to
give Poles hope and unity by teaching that they were a crucified nation, the
Christ of peoples, who were on a pilgrimage to the Holy Land, and had a
divine mission to redeem other oppressed nations. On the ground, however,
things looked rather different. When the radicals planned an insurrection in
1846, they had to divide their forces between Prussian Posnania and Austrian
Galicia. Moreover, in Galicia the serfs turned on the Polish gentry who were
trying to raise revolt and massacred two thousand of them before Austrian
troops completed the suppression. Emancipation, the serfs calculated, if it
came at all, would come from Vienna.

The Italian nobility and middle class, living under Austrian rule in Lombardy-Venetia, suffered the domination of Austrian officialdom. The consultative assemblies were a fig-leaf, the provinces being ruled direct from the Italian Chancellery in Vienna. The Austrian law code was introduced into the law courts and was enforced by Austrian magistrates. The highest civil and military posts were reserved for Austrians and the careers of soldiers who had served in the Napoleonic Army of Italy were blighted. The Venetian tradition lived on in the Austrian Navy, which was largely staffed by Italian officers and in which the language of command was Italian. However, Lombard nobles often did better to enter the service of Charles Albert of Piedmont.

Giuseppe Mazzini, the son of a Genoese doctor, could never contemplate such a course of action. He joined the Carbonari in Genoa, was arrested in 1830 and went into exile in Marseilles. The failure of the risings in Parma, Modena, and Bologna convinced him that the era of coups by secret societies was over. 'The people', oppressed by foreign bayonets, must be involved in the struggle for liberation, and to this effect he founded 'Young Italy' in 1831. Without unity, he argued, there was no strength. The fragmentation of Italy into duchies and principalities also perpetuated the rule of monarchies and aristocracies, whereas a unitary, democratic republic would express the sovereign will of the nation.

Mazzini appealed to Charles Albert to lead the movement for Italian independence, but the king again ordered his arrest. He therefore organized a coup by officers of the Piedmontese army in 1833, a mutiny in the Piedmontese navy, based in Genoa, in 1834, which involved Garibaldi, and then, reflecting that all oppressed nationalities must work together to overthrow the old empires, founded 'Young Europe' and launched an invasion of Savoy by Italian, Swiss, German, and Polish patriots. None of these failed coups were especially popular, being confined to middle-class intellectuals and military men. Moreover, seeing the people as 'the aggregate of all classes', he was reluctant to make hard promises of land redistribution that would bring the masses onto his side. After he sought refuge in London in 1837, rival solutions to be rid of the Austrians without destroying the princely and aristocratic structure of Italy were put forward. Vincenzo Gioberti, formerly chaplain at the Court of Piedmont and exiled to Brussels in 1830 for his part in Young Italy, argued in 1843 in favour of an Italian Confederation under the presidency of the Pope with Charles Albert as his right arm. Cesare Balbo, whose father had played various roles in Napoleonic Italy and who himself had taken part in the rising of 1821, replied in 1844 that the goal must be a revival of the Napoleonic Kingdom of Italy, including Piedmont, Liguria, Lombardy, and the Papal Legations.

The Kingdom of Hungary was another difficult problem for the Habsburg Monarchy. The élite was the Hungarian aristocracy, which attended Court in Vienna, ran the Hungarian Chancellery there and, together with the Catholic

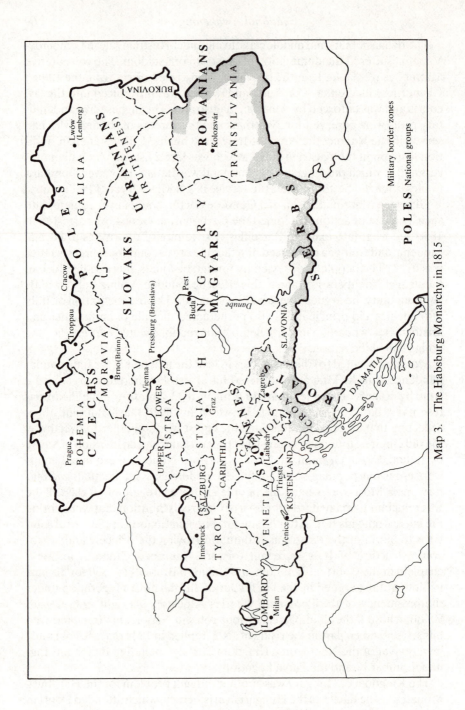

Map 3. The Habsburg Monarchy in 1815

Military border zones

POLES National groups

POLES
BOHEMIA
CZECHS
MORAVIA
Prague
Brno (Brünn)
Troppau
Cracow
GALICIA
Lwów (Lemberg)
UKRAINIANS (RUTHENES)
BUKOVINA
SLOVAKS
Pressburg (Bratislava)
Vienna
LOWER AUSTRIA
UPPER AUSTRIA
SALZBURG
Innsbruck
TYROL
CARINTHIA
STYRIA
Graz
CARNIOLA
SLOVENES
Laibach
Trieste
KÜSTENLAND
Venice
VENETIA
LOMBARDY
Milan
HUNGARY
MAGYARS
Buda
Pest
Danube
ROMANIANS
TRANSYLVANIA
Kolozsvár
SERBS
SLAVONIA
Zagreb
CROATS
DALMATIA

prelates, occupied the Upper Table of the Diet. They were fairly well Germanized and supported Metternich's plans to develop centralized bureaucracy. The sub-élite was the lesser nobility or gentry, who dominated the 52 county assemblies, which they regarded as so many republics, and the Lower Table of the Diet, but were entirely excluded from the spoils of high office. One of the aristocrats, Count István Széchenyi, in fact broke ranks to join the gentry, and campaigned to revive Magyar language and culture in order to preface demands for political autonomy. Magyar had declined to the status of language of the people in the eighteenth century, and the language of the Diet (despite Joseph II's attempts at Germanization) was Latin. In the Diet of 1825 Széchenyi spoke in Magyar to demand the introduction of Magyar as the official language, and helped to found the Hungarian Academy of Sciences, to develop Magyar as a literary language. The gentry, led by Lajos Kossuth, rallied to the cause, and Magyar was established as the official language of the Diet in 1845.

Less troublesome as yet for the Habsburg authorities were the Czechs of Bohemia and Moravia. The Bohemian nobility was German-speaking, imposed on the province from the seventeenth century, and loyal to the dynasty. The Czechs were a people of peasants, artisans, and traders but, like the Slovaks, were generating a priesthood and lay intelligentsia. A rigorous Czech grammar was published in 1791. Then in the 1830s a movement animated by František Palacký set up the Matice Česká (Czech Mother) to promote Czech publications, support a Czech dictionary and write Czech history in terms of its Hussite past and conflict with the Germans. To define the Czech culturally as a nation was the first step. But in 1844 a group of law and medical students with connexions among the working class of Prague formed a secret 'Repeal' organization which was named out of sympathy with O'Connell's Repeal Association, founded in 1840 to repeal the Act of Union imposed by Great Britain.

The self-definition of a nation was by no means an easy process. Hungarian nationalists dithered between the traditional view of the Hungarian nation, a political nation confined to the nobility alone, and a more modern view of nation which looked to give political rights to the urban middle classes and even emancipate the serfs. The Magyar revival threatened to divide the Hungarian nation between aristocrats and gentry, but was also intended to prevent the development of lesser nationalities in areas ruled by the Hungarian nobility, such as Slovaks, Croats, Serbs, or Romanians. Slovak intellectuals, who tended to have been trained at German-speaking universities, debated whether to define a Czech–Slovak nation on the basis of the language of the Hussite Bible, or a separate Slovak nation, on the basis of a spoken Slovak dialect.

While the promotion of a spoken language to the status of a literary (and printable) language was a key component of national identity, the previous existence of a separate state strengthened claims for national autonomy or even independence. The Slovaks could prove nothing here, nor could the Slovenes, who were sliced up between the Austrian provinces of Carniola, Carinthia, and Styria. As fervent Catholics they were happy with government from Vienna, where their leader was in fact Court librarian. The Croats had more history on their side, or rather two histories. On the one hand there was the Triune Kingdom of Croatia, Slavonia, and Dalmatia, on the other the Illyrian Provinces of Napoleon, which had included in addition the Slovene territories and the Military Border with the Ottoman Empire. A Kingdom of Illyria was reconstituted in 1816, without the strategically sensitive Military Border and Dalmatia, but this was disbanded in 1817 after protests from the Hungarians. So, while the Catholic nobility who controlled the Sabor or parliament demanded the return of the Triune Kingdom, a new generation of intellectuals launched the 'Illyrian' movement in favour of the Triune Kingdom enlarged by the Slovene provinces and the Military Border. Illyrianism was anathema to Metternich, who suspected that it was encouraged by Russia, and insisted that the Military Border was to remain intact at all costs.

In some cases a national group extended beyond the frontiers of the Habsburg Monarchy. The more independence the group outside had as a state, the greater the attraction it exercised over its compatriots within the Monarchy. This was known as irredentism. Before 1848 neither Serbia nor the Danubian Principalities had acquired full independence from the Ottoman Empire, and the Serbs living in Slavonia together with the Romanians living in Transylvania were more sophisticated than the Serbs or Romanians living outside the Monarchy. The centrifugal pull was at that stage not very strong. On the other hand the Romanians in Transylvania had to suffer the increasing chauvinism of the Magyars. They had no representation in the Transylvanian Diet which was monopolized by the Magyar nobility, German-speaking burghers and the *Szekelys*, who were free men by virtue of their Border Guard service. In 1842 the Magyars bullied their allies into accepting Magyar as the sole language of the Diet, administration, courts, schools, and Orthodox and Uniate Churches. This was refused by the Habsburg authorities in Vienna. Nevertheless Romanian opposition flared up, firstly among the Uniate clergy and secondly among the Romanian students who were studying in Paris and attended the Collège de France to learn about nationalism at the feet of Adam Mickiewicz and Jules Michelet.

The Prussian monarchy had less difficulty with nationalism than Austria or Russia. The attempted Polish rising in the Grand Duchy of Posen in February 1846 was scotched and 254 people were arrested. Eight leaders including Ludwik Mieroslawski, who was organising the insurrection for the Polish Democratic Society, were condemned to death in 1847. They were not executed and were to be released at the outbreak of revolution in Berlin in March 1848. Less dangerous but more intractable was the emergence of

Danish nationalism in the Duchies of Schleswig and Holstein. These were joined to the Danish Monarchy by a personal union, but Holstein was a member of the German Confederation. The northern part of Schleswig spoke a Danish dialect and after 1836 the Danish press, headed by Orla Lehmann, demanded the use of Danish in the administration, courts, schools, and churches of northern Schleswig. In 1842 the demand was raised for the inclusion of Schleswig into the Danish Monarchy. Christian VIII, who became King of Denmark in 1839, placated the nationalists in 1846 by ordering the Danicization of northern Schleswig. This was opposed by the German nobles of the Holstein estates, ably supported by the German academics of the University of Kiel. Such a challenge to German *Kultur* and administration sharpened German nationalism and began to transform it from a cosmopolitan into an exclusive kind.

Liberalism and Radicalism: Western Europe

Political regimes in Europe after 1830 were arbitrary, bureaucratic, and aristocratic in the east, and constitutional, representative, and oligarchical in the west. In the east liberal movements had a good deal of ground to make up. They demanded a wider civil society or freedom under the law, including a free press, freedom of association, trial in public and by jury, and representative institutions with legislative powers, and equality before the law, including the taxation of nobles and representation of property not privilege. In western Europe the main concern of liberals was to widen the franchise in order to broaden support for a campaign to displace the established oligarchy from office. They believed that only those who were independent by means of property ownership and education should vote, but that the popularization of property and education would bring ever greater numbers into the political nation.

All opposition in eastern Europe was in some sense radical, because the concept of a loyal opposition did not exist. In western Europe differences opened up between liberals and radicals. Radicals were democrats who preached the sovereignty of the people and agitated for universal suffrage. Their leaders tended to be intellectuals, the surplus product of the universities who had not found employment in the bureaucracy and professions and had taken to journalism and literary hack work. They did not try to efface the gulf between rich and poor, between educated and illiterate, but played on it. Many of them were becoming acutely aware of problems of unemployment, overwork and the loss of independence of artisans who were forced to become wage-labourers. At its fringe, the radical movement was socialist. Lastly, the radicals were not convinced that parliamentary debate, press articles, and political trials could achieve everything they wanted. They saw national guardsmen, the military, and the police behind even the constitutional, parliamentary regimes and were prepared to oppose force by force.

Great Britain was a prime example of the constitutional, representative, oligarchical system. The aristocratic Whigs had passed the Reform Bill in 1832 to hitch the middle classes to the constitution, but increasingly they faced criticism for standing in the way of democracy from Radicals. These included middle-class Benthamite or Philosophical Radicals, and working-class radicals of the nascent trade union movement. Fortunately for the Whigs, these two sorts of Radical did not always agree. Trade-unionists, supported by Anglican Tories, demanded a ten-hour working day, but the Benthamites opposed interference in the free market, and the factory act of 1834 legislated only on child labour. Benthamites pushed through the reform of the Poor Laws, to reduce dependence on parish relief and free the labour market, but Tories and working-class radicals campaigned against this in the industrial north, gripped by heavy unemployment.

The combined opposition of Tories and workers induced William IV to dish the Whigs in 1834, and ask Peel to form a Conservative government. The Whigs returned to office after the elections of 1835, and reformed municipal government. But by 1837 it was clear that the Whig leader Lord John Russell ('Finality Jack') was set against further parliamentary reform and would combine with the Tories in order to prevent it. Middle-class radicals now joined forces with the organized working class. The London Working Men's Association was formed by William Lovett in 1836, while in 1837 the Irish lawyer Feargus O'Connor founded the *Northern Star* in Leeds to co-ordinate radical associations in the industrial north. Seeking a political solution to social injustice, they drew up a Charter demanding universal suffrage, more MPs for large towns, the payment of MPs, the secret ballot and annual parliaments. It was endorsed by 1.3 million signatures and presented to Parliament in July 1839, but rejected.

The Chartist movement now began to break up. While the London radicals continued to defend legal action, others preached 'physical force', manifested by risings in Newport in 1839 and Bradford in 1840, which provoked the arrest of the leadership. Moderate Chartists became caught up with a middle-class movement that wanted parliamentary reform as a means to the repeal of the Corn Laws and the disestablishment of the Anglican Church. By 1842 they had left behind the mill-hands, stockingers, hand-loom weavers and miners of the provinces who had no interest in free trade and in Lancashire were more likely to be Catholic than Nonconformist. These launched a strike movement that brought out 500,000 workers from Scotland to Cornwall, but only confirmed their isolation from the middle classes.

The July Revolution in France displaced the ultra-royalist supporters of Charles X and benefited an oligarchy of the rich, educated, and well-born. It was anticlerical in tone but also a golden age for the Protestant bankers, merchants, and industrialists of Paris and the south. For some of the oligarchs the task of the revolution was finished with the ejection of Charles X. For others, the 'party of movement' as opposed to the 'party of order', Louis-Philippe had been chosen king in spite of his being a Bourbon and the programme of reform was by no means complete. The 'party of movement' enjoyed power under the banker Laffitte for three brief months in 1830–1 and prepared legislation to abolish the hereditary peerage, double the electoral body of the Chamber of Deputies to 200,000, enfranchise two million voters to elect muncipal councils, and permit National Guardsmen to elect their own officers. Out of power in March 1832 the 'party of movement' made common cause with the radicals who were angry that a republic had not been declared in 1830 and behaved like Jacobins of 1793. The radicals founded a Society of Friends of the People on 30 July 1830 and mobilized the crowds who turned out for the funeral of one of Napoleon's marshals, Lamarque, on 5 June 1832 to ignite the insurrection that Victor Hugo was to paint so dramatically in *Les Misérables* (1862).

A state of siege was declared in Paris and seven rebels were executed. The 'party of movement' pulled in its horns and abandoned the radicals. Alexis de Tocqueville warned in *Democracy in America* (1835) that in democratic regimes the tyranny of governments was replaced by the tyranny of the majority. In turn radical leaders like Auguste Blanqui formed societies which were ever more secret. The Society of Rights of Man triggered off risings in Paris and among the silk-workers of Lyons in April 1834. It made an attempt on the life of Louis-Philippe in July 1835 which provoked a batch of repressive laws. Republican feeling among junior officers and NCOs in garrisons along the eastern frontier was exploited by Louis-Napoleon Bonaparte, nephew of the former Emperor, who attempted to raise a mutiny at Strasbourg in October 1836. Blanqui's Society of Seasons attempted an armed coup in Paris in May 1839, and Blanqui was imprisoned for eight years.

By 1840 the Orleanist regime had recovered poise and solidity, and the radicals abandoned the weapon of insurrection. The working classes were setting up mutual aid societies to guard against sickness and here and there producers' associations to end the wage-slavery that made the capitalist his profits. Intellectuals who had been Carbonarist conspirators in the 1820s, then flirted with the doctrine of Henri, Comte de Saint-Simon that society should be reorganized according to 'capacities' and run by scientists who discovered, industrialists who acted, and artists and poets who felt. Many left the Saint-Simonian movement around 1830 when it changed into an ersatz religion and became critics of industrial society. Pierre-Joseph-Benjamin Buchez tried to reconcile democracy, Catholicism, and socialism after 1831 and after 1840 edited *L'Atelier* journal to support producers' associations. Pierre Leroux, who edited the *Globe*, believed that republicanism, religion, and socialism were all inherent in the revolutionary doctrine of fraternity. Flora Tristan sought to link socialism and feminism in her project of 1843 for a universal union to support employment, workers' education, and women's rights. In 1839 Louis Blanc argued that labour should be organised in social workshops which would receive an initial loan from the state and share proceeds equally among the workers. Pierre Joseph Proudhon, who was not an intellectual at all but the son of a cooper who became a printer at Besançon, argued that the state should be destroyed, and God too, and in *What is Property?* (1840) that all property that commanded rent, profit, or interest should be abolished. Exploitation should be replaced by the mutualism of free producers helping each other and aided (somehow) by free credit. It was the absence of credit that made these plans to bypass capital only dreams.

The Orleanist monarchy had to weather a challenge from the Right as well as from the Left. The legitimist supporters of Charles X mounted an unsuccessful counter-revolution in the west of France in 1832. Portugal and Spain had similar succession problems, for the claim of Maria II of Portugal, who succeeded her father in 1834, was challenged by Dom Miguel and that of Isabella of Spain was challenged by her uncle, Don Carlos. In both countries constitutional charters on the French model, including an upper house of peers, were promulgated, and the lower house of the Cortes was in each case dominated by moderates who represented land, wealth, and office. But the radicals, excluded from power, conspired to restore the Spanish Constitution of 1812 and the Portuguese Constitution of 1822, with their single-chamber assemblies that would break the power of the oligarchs. In 1835 the Spanish radicals, called Progressives, exploited the crisis caused by the Carlist war in the north and rising bread prices to organize provincial juntas in southern towns and force a ministry of their choice into power in Madrid. It was headed by a Jewish financier, Mendizábal, who began an orgiastic sale of Church lands and entailed lands to pay for the war and to satisfy his supporters. This was not good enough for the sergeants returning from the northern front who mutinied in August 1836, and forced the Queen Regent to summon a Constituent Cortes. In September 1836 there was a similar revolution in Portugal, undertaken by the National Guard. But in each case the radicals had to compromise, and the Spanish Constitution of 1836 and the Portuguese Constitution of 1837 provided for a second, elected chamber. This paved the way, with a little help from the military, for the return to power of the moderates, who restored French-style constitutions in Portugal in 1842 and Spain in 1845.

Liberalism and Radicalism: Central and Eastern Europe

On 27 May 1832 a National Festival of the Germans brought liberal and radical notables from south-west Germany together at Hambach Castle in the Rhenish Palatinate. Moderate speeches demanding greater German unity and more liberal constitutions were interspersed with radical speeches attacking the aristocracy and advocating popular sovereignty. The Hambachfest antagonized the governments of the German Confederation, and a battery of laws was passed, clamping down on freedom of speech, assembly, and association. In the wake of the repression, some radicals decided to imitate the French model of revolutionary action. Georg Büchner, the son of a regimental surgeon in Napoleon's armies, joined a Society for the Rights of Man at Giessen University in 1834. After an abortive attempt to incite the peasantry to revolt he fled to Strasbourg, where he wrote *Danton's Death* and *Woyzeck* before he died in 1837.

In Prussia Frederick William IV, who became king in 1840, reacted against the constraints of bureaucratic absolutism and attacked it by recourse to personal rule, concessions to the Junker aristocracy and a *rapprochement* with the Catholic Church in his 'Christian State'. This broadened the base of opposition to his regime. The Rhineland middle class dropped its separatism and tried to liberalize Prussia. David Hansemann submitted a memorandum to the king in 1840 in which he argued that a new constitution and representative government would mobilize the energies of the nation, hitherto insulated by the bureaucracy, behind the king, while to enfranchise property and education was the best way of cutting off revolutionary discontent. Civil servants and especially jurists became concerned both by liberal attacks on the bureaucracy and by the interference of the monarch in the independence of the judiciary. A group of academics specializing in German language, law, and history, led by the 'Göttingen Seven', dismissed for their views in 1837, met in conference in Frankfurt in 1846 and Lübeck in 1847 to examine legal paths towards constitutional monarchy, and founded the *Deutsche Zeitung* in 1847 to propagate their ideas.

While the liberal movement was gaining authority, the radicals were also seeking a voice. One of the editorial board of the *Rheinische Zeitung*, launched in Cologne in 1842, was Karl Marx, who had undertaken law studies at Bonn and Berlin and turned to journalism because his liberal views prevented him from obtaining a university appointment. At this period Marx was exposed to many influences which pulled him towards socialism. Like Moses Hess, who edited the *Rheinische Zeitung*, he had been brought up on Hegel, but was coming to see that Hegel's defence of what existed as successive embodiments of a World Spirit in its progress to perfection gave unwarranted justification to Prussian despotism, religion, and private property. Marx now believed despotism, religion, and private property enslaved man and dehumanized him. He came into contact with the writings of Wilhelm Weitling, a tailor of Magdeburg who had become caught up in Blanqui's Society of Seasons in Paris. Weitling believed that property was theft, and trade was the exchange of stolen goods. He was arrested in Zürich in 1843 and imprisoned for arguing that the true doctrine of Jesus Christ envisaged a communistic society of equality, harmony, and justice. That autumn Marx moved to Paris to escape the censor and in 1844 pushed his theory still further. Political revolution was not enough, he asserted, for it would 'leave the pillars of the house still standing'. Social revolution required 'a passive element, a material basis'. That basis must be a class that stood for the 'notorious crime of society', and 'the complete loss of humanity'. Through its redemption would come the 'complete redemption of humanity'.[7] That class was the proletariat and in June 1844 Marx saw the proletariat in revolt in Silesia.

In Russia, even more than in Germany, the shift from liberalism to radicalism and socialism was easily made. A French observer described the government of Nicholas I in 1839 as 'camp discipline substituted for the order of the city and the state of siege become the normal state of society'.[8] After the Decembrist revolt, in 1826, Nicholas transferred police matters from the Ministry of Internal Affairs to the Third Department of his own Chancellery, which was more closely under his control. This Department regarded itself as above the law, with unlimited authority to spy and interfere in the activities of the courts. The general who headed the Third Department also controlled the new paramilitary Corps of Gendarmes which was its executive arm and kept even provincial governors on their toes.

Both the army and the bureaucracy expanded under Nicholas I but the gulf between the service nobility and country gentry grew wider. In the army German officers enjoyed rapid promotion, discipline was harsh, senior officers insulted junior officers, and many gentry families preferred to send their sons to university rather than to cadet schools. The lower ranks of the bureaucracy, which was ill-paid and saw the prospect of ennoblement set further from its reach, became increasingly corrupt. But a law of 1831 restricted participation in the district assemblies of gentry that were set up by Catherine the Great in 1775 to only the wealthiest gentry, so that control of the bureaucracy, which was sporadic from above, became even more difficult from below.

Gentry who had served in the war against France and seen Europe retired to their estates. One of them, Peter Chaadaev, reflected that 'not one useful thought has germinated on the barren soil of our country, not one great truth has sprung up in our midst'. Alexis Khomiakov, who had fought in the Turkish War of 1827–9, rejected this view but looked back to a golden age before Peter the Great when the *sobornost* or brotherhood of the Russian people was expressed in the Orthodox Church, the Zemskii Sobor or Assembly of All the Land, and the peasant commune. Against this Slavophile nostalgia, Moscow circles of university-educated gentry and *raznochintsy* (men of no particular rank) like Vissarion Belinsky argued that the Orthodox Church was now the handmaiden of despotism and that only free institutions on the western model could liberate the human personality in Russia. Alexander Herzen, who met Belinsky in St Petersburg in 1840, believed that socialism,

---

[7] Karl Marx, 'Introduction to a Critique of Hegel's Philosophy of Right', in David McLellan (ed.), *Karl Marx, Early Texts* (Oxford, 1971), 124–8.

[8] Astolphe de Custine, *La Russie en 1839* (Paris, 1843), i, 255.

conceived as a more thoroughgoing 1789, was required for the regeneration of the individual and humanity. Mikhail Bakunin, the product of a cadet school who disgraced himself in the army and mixed with the Moscow intellectuals after 1835, left for Germany in 1840, met Weitling in Zürich in 1843 and Marx and Proudhon in Paris in 1844. As the Tsar deprived him of his noble rank and confiscated his property, so he became converted to anarchism.

In the Habsburg Monarchy liberal movements struggled to the surface, although they were often overpowered by nationalism or overtaken by radicalism. While Mazzini languished in exile there developed in Italy a current of equal strength which favoured greater representative government and a propertied franchise combined with moral education and material progress. It was particularly strong in Tuscany, among liberal nobles like Cosimo Ridolfi, and was not discouraged by the Grand Duke Leopold II. The same views were held in Piedmont by Massimo d'Azeglio who wrote in 1846 that 'if the Italian sovereigns do not wish their subjects to become violent liberals, they must themselves become moderate liberals'.[9] Similar attitudes were spread among the propertied and professional middle class of Lombardy by the Milanese professor and poet Carlo Cattaneo.

In Hungary, a Liberal party was formed first in the counties, then in the Diet, and was formally constituted in 1847. It demanded a ministry that would be responsible to the Diet, the right of the middle classes to sit in the Diet, and the emancipation of the serfs. They were opposed by a Conservative party, which supported royal absolutism and bureaucratic centralism. In Vienna itself, liberal ideas gained ground in the 1840s among the aristocrats of the Lower Austrian Diet, and among professional men, officials, and industrialists who formed societies like the Legal-Political Reading Club and Lower Austrian Manufacturers' Association. Unfortunately Metternich was convinced that liberalism would always be swamped by radicalism. He had nothing but contempt for the middle classes. And though he considered the minimal measure of enlarging the Staatsrat, which gave legislative advice and controlled the civil service, to include representatives from the provincial diets, he did nothing. This was not least because while he dominated the conference of ministers the greatest influence in the Staatsrat was his sworn rival, the Bohemian magnate Count Kolowrat. By such questions of personal politics were the fate of empires settled.

---

[9] Massimo d'Azeglio, *The Present Movement in Italy* (London, 1847), 16.

4

THE REVOLUTIONS OF 1848

The United Front

The Revolutions of 1848 ignited the countries of Europe in a way that would not be repeated until 1989. Violence broke out because legal and parliamentary movements for change were frustrated. The only countries where revolution was avoided were those where adequate concessions were made in time, such as Great Britain, Belgium, or the Netherlands, or, where opposition was negligible, such as Russia. Nobilities and middle classes demanded constitutional and representative instead of arbitrary and bureaucratic government. Artisans, industrial wage-workers, and peasants revolted against developing capitalistic practices that were reducing them to greater poverty. Emergent nations, such as the Poles, Danes, Germans, Italians, Czechs, Slovaks, Magyars, Croats, and Romanians demanded autonomy within or independence from the multinational empires that dominated them. The combination of grievances made an explosive cocktail, but in the long run divisions between the revolutionaries enabled governments to regain control.

In Great Britain, middle-class Radicals like Richard Cobden abandoned working-class Chartists to convert Whigs to a campaign to repeal the Corn Laws, for the benefit of the City and northern industrial interests. The repeal was actually undertaken in 1846 by the Conservative prime minister Robert Peel, a decision that was opposed by the protectionist squirearchy and split his party. The Whigs, known increasingly as the Whig–Liberals, returned to power, and committed themselves to free trade, responsible administration, and gradual reform. Unimpressed, The Chartists continued their campaign, and 50,000–100,000 joined a rally on Kennington Common on 10 April 1848 in support of another petition. Isolated from the rest of the political nation, they were confronted by up to 250,000 special constables, together with regular troops, under the command of the Duke of Wellington, and dispersed without trouble.

In Belgium, the Catholics and Liberals who had come to power in 1830 soon fell out amongst themselves. The Catholics monopolized power, founded a Catholic university at Louvain and gave the Church complete control of primary schooling in 1842. The Liberals who met in congress at Brussels in 1846 based their programme on anticlericalism. Prudent electoral reform and improvements for the working classes were included as a sop to the radicals of the Alliance démocratique. Elected to office under the journalist Charles Rogier, the Liberals forgot about electoral reform until a republic was proclaimed in France on 25 February 1848. Then Rogier, supported by King Leopold, decided that popular demonstrations would be met not by armed force but by the hasty enactment of a lower franchise (28 February) which left the radicals isolated in impotent rage. In the Netherlands, the autocratic William II decided on the same course of action. Opposition to the States-General, which was still based on the system of orders, built up among middle-class Liberals headed by Johan Thorbecke. On 25 March 1848 the Liberals were whisked into office by William II in order to revise the constitution and cut off radical agitators from their support.

Switzerland was still controlled by cantonal oligarchies who would cede very little of their sovereignty to the Federal Diet or Federal Directory. Some cantons had adopted a more liberal franchise for grand council elections in 1830; others had not. Radicals wanted to abolish the cantonal sovereignty which served only to shore up the local oligarchies and to move towards a democratic, unitary republic like the Helvetic Republic imposed by the French in 1798. They took power in the canton of Aargau and dissolved monasteries there, at which the Catholic cantons of Lucerne, Uri, Schwyz, Unterwalden, Zug, Fribourg, and Valais mobilized in a Sonderbund or Separatist League in order to defend religion and cantonal sovereignty. Liberals and radicals could at least agree on anticlericalism and the need to preserve the Confederation and they raised a citizen army through the Diet to defeat the Sonderbund in November 1847. A new Federal Constitution which gave some satisfaction to the radicals was adopted by plebiscite in September 1848.

The last Italian ruler who might be expected to take a reforming initiative in fact acted first. The Bishop of Imola, who became Pius IX in June 1846, decided to end the medievalism of the Papal States that threatened to provoke an uprising in the Romagna at any moment. Between July 1846 and July 1847 he released about 2,000 political prisoners, relaxed press censorship and removed it from the exclusive preserve of the Church, set up a Council of Ministers which included laymen as well as cardinals, and invited provincial delegates to a consultative assembly. These reforms were coupled with plans to improve popular education and develop prosperity through railways and an Italian customs union. A civic guard was permitted to arm in Rome and Bologna to control food riots and, so far as liberal notables were concerned, to act as a check on the papal irregulars.

Charles Albert of Piedmont and Leopold of Tuscany responded by granting a freer press. But in Vienna Metternich was furious. He decided to teach Pius IX a lesson and scotch reform by sending Austrian troops in July 1847 to reinforce the garrison of Ferrara in the Romagna. A storm of protest went up in the Italian states, and both Charles Albert and Leopold of Tuscany responded by making more concessions to liberal opinion. Moreover, agitation now spread to the Austrian provinces of Lombardy and Venetia. In the opera houses of Milan and Venice patriotic allusions in Verdi's operas were applauded and fights broke out between young bloods and Austrian officers. In Venice Daniele Manin, a lawyer of Jewish extraction, orchestrated a 'legal struggle' for self-government through scientific congresses, agricultural societies, and the Central Congregation (or powerless parliament) of Venetia. On 8 January 1848 he was thrown into prison.

The revolutionary breakthrough in Italy came in Sicily on 13 January 1848 where a popular rising of artisans in Palermo was aided and abetted by patriots of 1820. The movement was rapidly taken over, not least to control it, by merchants, professional men, and liberal aristocrats, some of whom had served under Lord William Bentinck, and demanded the restoration of the Constitution of 1812. In Naples there was little unrest, partly because of the concentration of military force there, partly because the *lazzaroni* or rabble were fanatical defenders (as in 1799) of the Bourbon monarchy against Jacobinism. But patriots triggered off risings in the provinces of Salerno and Calabria and on 17 January eminent citizens paraded in Naples to demand concessions of the king. Ferdinand II saw no alternative but to form a liberal ministry, authorize a national guard, and issue a constitution on 29 January which was modelled on the French Constitution of 1830. The Sicilians insisted on a separate parliament which was granted on 6 March. Then they deposed Ferdinand and set up a regency.

By then the pattern of politics in Europe had been completely changed by the revolution which broke out in Paris on 22–4 February 1848. The property franchise entitled a minority of 250,000 Frenchmen to elect deputies from an oligarchy of 56,000, and two-fifths of the ministerial majority that triumphed in the elections of August 1846 were government officials. The parliamentary opposition, composed mainly of professional men, introduced motions to lower the property franchise and disqualify 'placemen' from sitting as deputies. When these were rejected, they looked for extra-parliamentary support. Public meetings were banned, so 'banquets' were held up and down the country after July 1847 which were distinguished by their size and the political nature of the after-dinner speeches. The solid barristers of the dynastic opposition played into the hands of the moderate republicans of the *National* newspaper and the radicals of the *Réforme*, and at a banquet held in Lille on 7 November 1847 Ledru-Rollin advanced the demand for universal suffrage.

The government of Guizot tried to ban a banquet due to be held in an eastern district of Paris on 22 February 1848 and the opposition spilled into violence. Workers and students threw up barricades and the National Guard, which was composed of a middling and petty bourgeoisie rather than the rich and infiltrated by secret societies which organized the election of officers, refused to fire on them. This brought about a head-on collision of the crowd and the regular troops, who opened fire. The Guizot ministry fell and

Louis-Philippe, unable to form another ministry, was obliged to abdicate in favour of his young grandson, the Comte de Paris, and flee. The educated and propertied classes nevertheless gained control of the movement, and the provisional government set up at the Hôtel de Ville included representatives of all tendencies: the dynastic opposition, moderate republicans of the *National*, and radical republicans of the *Réforme* like Ledru-Rollin. There were also two socialists, Louis Blanc and a metalworker, Albert. The poet Lamartine, who was situated in the middle of the government, noted that it miraculously suspended the misunderstanding that existed between the different classes. And yet the alliance was precarious. The building workers of Paris, led by the Jacobin intellectual, François Raspail, a veteran of the secret societies of the 1830s, were not prepared to see the revolution confiscated by a narrow oligarchy, as in 1830; and on 25 February they marched on the Hôtel de Ville and forced the government to proclaim the Republic. In addition they demanded the implementation of the right to work and a Ministry of Labour to eliminate exploitation and unemployment. No ministry was founded but a commission of workers' delegates was set up under Louis Blanc and Albert in the Luxembourg palace which was now vacated by the peers of the realm and this legislated on shorter hours, a minimum wage, the protection of some trades against competition, and the relief of unemployment in national workshops. Unfortunately, as Marx observed, 'while the Luxembourg was looking for the philosopher's stone the Hôtel de Ville minted the current coins'.[1] In the spring of 1848 the radical press, political clubs, and the National Guard bubbled with activity in Paris and provincial cities as elections under universal manhood suffrage to the Constituent Assembly approached. Women's clubs and the *Voix des Femmes* newspaper demanded the extension of votes to women also. But for the radical leaders two months was not enough time to complete the education of a people who too often remained loyal to its traditional leaders. Moderate republican deputies did far better than radicals in the elections. Only thirty-four working class deputies were returned to the Assembly. Blanc and Albert resigned in disgust from the Luxembourg commission. The exploited woollen workers of Rouen, the overtaxed winegrowers of Languedoc, and the Alpine farmers who were being excluded from forest land, resorted to solving their problems by violence.

Unrest among peasants and workers was as much an effect as a cause of the political revolutions of 1848. The revolutions were not simply the fruit of demographic, agrarian, and urban tensions. 1846–7 was a year of hunger and hardship and in Prussia Frederick William IV summoned delegates from the provincial Landtage to a United Landtag in Berlin in February 1847. But in April 1847 he dismissed the United Landtag without granting a constitution,

---

[1] Karl Marx, *The Class Struggle in France, 1848–1850* (New York, 1924), 46.

and the deputies made no attempt to exploit the food riots in Berlin that month—nicknamed the 'potato revolution'—to force a crisis. Baden radicals who met at Offenburg the following September to demand the election of an all-German parliament were crying in the wilderness.

The revolution in France transformed German politics. A mass demonstration at Mannheim on 27 February and a march on Karlsruhe, the capital of Baden, forced the Baden government to concede a free press, trial by jury, and a civic guard on 29 February, and the Grand Duke to appoint liberal ministers on 2 March. On that day disturbances began in the Black Forest and swept across southern Germany. Forests were invaded, seigneurial archives destroyed, and castles set alight. In Baden the radicals gathered the peasants in mass meetings of three or four thousand but a radical who addressed peasants in Berg was rebuked, 'What does freedom of the press mean for us? Freedom to eat is what we want.'[2] The Grand Duchy of Hesse-Darmstadt and the Kingdoms of Württemberg and Bavaria, along with Baden, which retained the imprint of Napoleon's Confederation of the Rhine, conceded a free press, jury trials, wider representation, and, for the peasants, the abolition of seigneurial dues. There was one upset in Bavaria, where Ludwig I abdicated in favour of his son. But the radicals were arrested or driven underground and ministerial office was given to the liberals.

In the Rhineland the artisans of Cologne, under the leadership of the intellectuals of the Communist League, which had links with Marx and Engels, demonstrated on 3 March. A programme was advanced to establish a series of republics on the Lower, Middle, and Upper Rhine from the Rhineland to Baden-Württemberg. The cutlers of Solingen destroyed foundries that made cheap, cast-iron implements, the Rhine bargemen attacked the steamships that were stealing their trade, and Rhineland peasants surged into the forests to cut wood. Terrified, the liberal deputies of the Rhenish Landtag under Camphausen, who owned a steamship company, pressed Frederick William IV for reform so that revolution would be checked by 'the intimate fusion of the monarchical principle and popular liberties'.[3] In Berlin intellectuals, students, tradesmen, and artisans gathered after 6 March at noisy meetings in the Tiergarten and on their way back to the city on 13 March, clashed with troops. The city councils of Berlin and Cologne were received by the king and requested concessions. On 18 March a constitution, a free press, and a new assembly were promised. A large crowd of burghers gathered in the castle square that afternoon to applaud the king but could not persuade him to withdraw his regular troops which were, after all, the basis of the Prussian military monarchy. Stupidly, indeed, the troops were instructed to clear the square, and in reply barricades were thrown up by incensed

---

[2] Quoted by Rudolph Stadelmann, *Social and Political History of the German 1848 Revolution* (Athens, Ohio, 1975), 93.

[3] Quoted by Jacques Droz, *Les Révolutions allemandes de 1848* (Paris, 1957), 214.

journeymen—cabinet-makers, joiners, tailors, cobblers, and locksmiths. Many were killed before the king agreed to withdraw the troops to Potsdam and to replace them by a *Bürgerwehr*, or citizens' militia. This was the bourgeoisie in arms and served as much to keep public order as to restrain the military monarchy. On 25 March a liberal ministry was appointed, headed by Camphausen, with Hansemann as Minister of Finance. Whereas in France the liberal middle class took control of the popular movement in order to carry through a revolution, albeit for its own benefit, in Prussia it rallied to the support of the monarchy in order to prevent a revolution. The German middle classes desired the rule of law and consultation of the nation by the king, but they also wanted a political stability that could be guaranteed only by the Crown, bureaucracy, and, in the last resort, by the army. They had neither the nerve nor the will to alter radically the distribution of power in the Prussian state.

The revolution in Vienna on 13–15 March 1848, as well as the revolution in Paris, helps to explain why Frederick William IV stooped to make concessions. The Lower Austrian Estates which met on 13 March were besieged by students and workers, from inside and outside the city walls, to urge them to press for reforms. Crowds clashed with troops, and the mayor called out the *Bürgerwehr*, which had long been mainly ceremonial, to keep order. The military was withdrawn from the inner city and the students, *Bürgerwehr* and members of the estates, with the threat of popular violence, put pressure on the Court to dismiss Metternich, who had advocated military repression. On 14 March Metternich resigned and was replaced by his arch-rival, Count Kolowrat. A fully-fledged Civic Guard of 30,000, together with a separate student wing of 7,000, the Academic Legion, was authorized. On 15 March a constitution was promised.

The repercussions of the revolution in Vienna were felt all round the Monarchy, but as in Vienna it was the educated and propertied classes who remained in control. In Prague radical students, intellectuals, and artisans of the 'Repeal' organization organized a large meeting on 11 March to petition the Emperor for political and social reform, but the movement was taken over and moderated not only by liberals such as Palacký but the conservative property-owners and merchants blatantly opposed to their demands. On 8 April the Emperor merely promised a Bohemian Diet elected by the propertied classes, instead of the old Diet in which only prelates, lords, knights, and the free cities were represented. In Hungary radical agitation was led by the poet Sándor Petöfi, who addressed vast crowds and used the threat of 40,000 serfs marching on Budapest to force the city council to endorse their demands and to set up a Committee of Public Safety. But the liberal gentry based on the Diet at Pressburg sent Kossuth by steamboat to Vienna to gain from the Emperor on 17 March most of the concessions that the radicals demanded: a Hungarian ministry under a prime minister appointed by the Emperor, responsible to the Hungarian Diet, which would acquire the authority to legislate, and a separate national army. The Hungarian Diet then extended the franchise from nobles, *honoratiores*, and the burghers of free cities to property-owners in general, except Jews. Even so, the Magyar nobility was the real victor. Nobles both titled and untitled monopolized the Hungarian ministry, the officer corps, and the new assembly elected in June 1848. Only serfs who occupied land were emancipated and even those had to pay compensation to the landowners for dues and services abolished.

More dramatic still were the revolutions which spread to Lombardy and Venetia. Events in France and Naples knocked away the ability of other Italian princes to resist change. Leopold of Tuscany issued a constitution on 17 February. Charles Albert published another, called the *Statuto*, for Piedmont on 5 March. Pius IX granted a constitution with a two-chambered legislature on 14 March. In Milan the working classes manned the barricades against the Austrians for five days between 18 and 23 March. Radicals such as Carlo Cattaneo joined the rising on the second day but distrusted the lower classes of Milan as much as they feared alienating the upper classes. They did not proclaim a republic but looked for support to the Milanese patriciate who set up a provisional government and appealed for support to Charles Albert of Piedmont. The invasion of Lombardy by Charles Albert provoked Italian troops serving in the Austrian army to desert, and the Piedmontese entered Milan. In Venice, similarly, the rising of 17–18 March was the work of artisans and fishermen, but taken over by the educated middle class led by Manin. The civic guard which they formed was both to defend against 'anarchy' and to bully the Austrian troops, but they were powerless until the arsenal-workers attacked the garrison on 27 March. Then they proclaimed the resurrection of the Republic of Saint Mark and set up a provisional government of nobles, lawyers, and merchants. Everywhere in Europe, popular movements were at the root of revolution, but everywhere, under the guise of a united front, it was the propertied classes which benefited.

Division and Defeat

The initial success of the 1848 revolutions was explained by the unity of the revolutionaries. It soon dissolved. The propertied classes consolidated their position but left the masses, except in France, disfranchised. Radicals were eager to attract a popular base by championing universal suffrage and social reform, and were prepared to use force to press their claims, but this set them at odds with the liberals, who believed that the revolution had done its work. Unfortunately, the radicals themselves belonged to the educated and even propertied élite, and had little time for the pressing concerns of the mass of workers and peasants: land, employment, and lower taxes. Class interests divided them from each other, and when class war broke out the tide began to swing away from revolution.

Liberals, who feared for their property and security, forgot their programmes of responsible ministries and a free press and rallied to the old ruling class, which had lost its nerve in the spring but reorganized in the summer of 1848 around the principle of order. The achievements of the liberal-democratic revolutions were dismantled. On the other hand there was no aristocratic reaction, no return to state based on the system of orders. The revolution was put down by the military and it was the military and bureaucratic authorities that were strengthened. Finally, although popular sovereignty and popular suffrage were discarded, there was a sense in which authoritarian regimes relied on the acquiescence of the mass of the population, which was gratified by material benefits if not by a political voice.

Revolution flared up first in the Kingdom of Naples and was extinguished there first. The constitution granted by King Ferdinand on 29 January 1848 was in the interest only of the enlightened, possessing class. It excluded illiterates from the vote, which disfranchised ninety per cent of the population. The Neapolitan liberals made the revolution for themselves. When the agricultural masses, who were interested only in land, began to invade the larger estates they were driven off again by force to disabuse them of the idea that 'freedom was a banquet at which everyone was to sit and have his fill.'[4] The gulf between the liberals and the masses was exploited by Ferdinand when the parliament met on 13 May and tried to change the constitution. Two days later he launched a coup to close it down. Barricades were thrown up by about three hundred radical bourgeois, artisans, and a section of the National Guard, but the *lazzaroni* were faithful to the king, waved white banners and images of the Madonna and cried, '*Viva il Re!*' and 'Down with the Constitution!'. Sanfedism was still alive. Radical resistance in Calabria was soon put down and Sicily, which attempted to offer a crown to the Duke of Genoa, a younger son of Charles Albert of Piedmont, was invaded by the Bourbon army at the end of August.

The war against the Austrians started by Charles Albert on 25 March, and his defeat at Custozza four months later, gave the advantage in central Italy to the radicals. In Tuscany the ministry of the liberal aristocrat Cosimo Ridolfi, which represented the propertied élite of Florence and had no intention of joining in the war against Austria, was challenged by the radicals who found popular support among the building workers and dockers of the port of Livorno. Popular violence undermined liberal rule and on 27 October the Grand Duke had to ask the journalist and radical leader Giuseppe Montanelli to form a government.

In the Papal States, the Constitution of 14 March which provided for a nominated senate and a council of deputies elected on a narrow franchise (excluding Jews) satisfied the moderates but was challenged by a strong

---

[4] Quoted by A. W. Salomone, 'The Liberal experiment and the Italian Revolution of 1848: a re-evaluation', *Journal of Central European Affairs*, 9, no. 3 (1949), 285.

democratic movement. Ironically, Pius IX's amnesty of 1846 had permitted the return or release of former Carbonari and, thanks to his reforms, a radical press, political clubs, and a civic guard packed with undesirable elements flourished. During the summer of 1848 Pius tried to reassert his authority and called Count Pellegrino Rossi, a conservative professor of law at Bologna University, to form a government. The radicals feared that he was planning a *coup d'état* and on 15 November assassinated him. An insurrection followed and the Pope fled to Gaeta in the Kingdom of Naples. It was a turning point for him. From now on Pius IX was to crusade against every idea that the nineteenth century spawned.

Rome was in the hands of the radicals. The Council of Deputies elected a junta which organized elections to a Constituent Assembly, in the first place for the Papal States, then perhaps, if the example set by Tuscany were followed, for the whole of Italy. The Constituent Assembly abolished the Pope's Temporal Power on 9 February 1849 and proclaimed the Roman Republic. Mazzini, elected deputy for Ferrara, was made a citizen of Rome and First Triumvir. The hated grist tax was abolished, unemployed building workers were detailed to repair monuments and clear slums, and the land owned by religious orders was divided into allotments for poor peasants. But Mazzini's Rome was fiercely anticlerical, and the battering received by the Church and the clergy did not endear the regime to the Catholic masses. It was far from 'God and the People' in action.

In France, tension between moderates and radicals had been acute since the elections to the Constituent Assembly on Easter Day 1848, and the executive directory of five or Pentarchy elected by the Assembly included only one radical, Ledru-Rollin. The strength of the radicals was in the press, the political clubs, and the National Guard. On 15 May, when the Assembly was debating aid to Poland, the Palais Bourbon where it sat was invaded by club militants and National Guardsmen led by Raspail and Blanqui. They demanded that monarchs and reactionary regimes throughout Europe be overthrown, declared the Assembly dissolved and set up a revolutionary government in the Hôtel de Ville. The Pentarchy was able to regain control and crush the democratic leadership, but the rift that now opened between liberals and democrats endangered the revolution. It stood no chance at all once a chasm opened between the republican notables and the mass of the Parisian labouring population. After 15 May the government became concerned about the volume of migration from the countryside to the town, which served only to increase unemployment. The national workshops were no solution, and were seen as nests of idleness and revolutionary discontent. On 21 June, therefore, the workshops were ordered to close and young men registered there were conscripted into the army or sent to clear land in the Sologne or Landes. An insurrection was provoked—the famous 'June Days'—centred on the populous eastern quarters of Paris. It was led not by

the democratic intellectuals of the clubs but by building workers, metal-
workers and cobblers. Tocqueville made no mistake: for him, the fighting
that ensued between the workers of Paris and the National Guard and regulars was 'a class struggle, a sort of servile war'.[5] The bourgeoisie panicked,
and General Cavaignac, who put down the rising for the government, was
made Chief of the Executive Power by the Assembly, in the place of the
Pentarchy. For Marx the Second French Republic was now 'the dictatorship
of the bourgeoisie by the sabre'.

By-elections held on 17 September 1848 introduced a new force into
French politics. Louis-Napoleon Bonaparte, whose own reputation was
that of the Strasbourg mutiny of 1836 and his book on the *Elimination of
Pauperism* (1844), and who carried the immense mystique of the former
Emperor, was elected in Paris, Corsica, and three other *départements*. The
constitution that was finally ratified on 4 November provided for the election
of a President of the Republic by universal suffrage. Cavaignac stood on
behalf of the middle-class, governmental republicans. Ledru-Rollin and Raspail were the candidates of the democratic clubs. Louis-Napoleon Bonaparte
entered the contest as his own man. In the elections of 10 December 1848
Louis-Napoleon polled 5.4 million votes, nearly 75 per cent of the total,
against 1.4 million for Cavaignac and 500,000 between Ledru-Rollin and
Raspail. Support for Louis-Napoleon came from the rural and urban masses
who had been ruthlessly excluded from political life since 1815 and felt
betrayed by all parliamentary notables, whether royalist or republican. They
saw Louis-Napoleon obscurely as a man who had the interests of the people
at heart.

Louis-Napoleon was also supported by royalists who had been seething in
impotence since February and imagined that they could use him as a bridge
to the restoration of the monarchy. They were soon joined by moderate
republicans who had supported Cavaignac and wanted no recurrence of
anarchy. This 'party of order' forced the new President to accept a ministry
dominated by the rather conservative dynastic opposition to the July Monarchy. Against the 'party of order' the students, journalists, small-town
lawyers, doctors, pharmacists, and tradesmen of the democratic movement
tried to regain their influence over the working class and peasantry with a
view to the elections to the Legislative Assembly. They defended universal
suffrage and social reform, the interests of the people against those of the
privileged. These socialist-democrats, nicknamed the 'Montagne' in memory
of the radicals of the Constituent Assembly in 1792–3, used the café, club,
and village festival to undermine the natural deference of the peasantry to
the *curé* and *châtelain*; the revolt of women was expressed by the candida-
tures of two Saint-Simonian feminists, Jeanne Deroin and Pauline Roland.

---

[5] Alexis de Tocqueville, *Recollections* (London, 1948), 160.

In the Legislative elections of 28 May 1849 the Montagnards made a gallant showing, in the countryside as well as in the towns, especially in the Centre and South of France. Then they scuppered themselves by attacking the government's expedition to destroy Mazzini's Rome, and took to the streets in a futile demonstration on 13 June. In the period of the 'Republic without republicans' which followed the royalists who controlled the Assembly handed education over to the Catholic Church, stiffened censorship, and on 31 May 1850 deprived three million electors of the vote.

In Germany the radical movement that might challenge the gains of the propertied and educated middle class was much more narrowly based than in France. An insurrection in favour of a republic was triggered off in Baden on 13 April and on 24 April the German Democratic Legion of *émigrés* in Paris crossed the border into Baden. These were put down by Hessian troops sent in under the auspices of the Federal Diet to help the Grand Duke. The elections to the new Prussian assembly were delayed until May and on 20 April radical students tried to organize a mass demonstration to obtain an election under universal suffrage. They failed, and only about thirty per cent of the deputies elected were radicals, half of them university-educated, especially young jurists, the rest from the artisan and peasant classes. Most significant was the refusal of the Berlin working classes to join in the demonstration of 20 April, which attracted only 1,500 militants. Stefan Born, a printer who had associated with Marx and Engels in Paris and Brussels and joined the Communist League, was better known for organizing the Berlin printers' strike and founding the Central Workers' Club in Berlin on 29 March. He ignored the manifesto for Germany issued by Marx and Engels on 1 April which closely followed the programme of the *Communist Manifesto* for, as he put it, the workers 'would have laughed in my face or pitied me if I had presented myself as a Communist'.[6]

The separation of the organized working class from the liberal and democratic movements in Germany, and divisions between master-craftsmen and journeymen, and between these groups and the mass of unskilled and unorganized labour, enabled the conservative élites in time to regain the initiative. In July 1848 master-craftsmen convened an All-German Artisan's Congress in Frankfurt in an attempt to defend the privileges of the guilds that had been restored in many states after 1830 but that the liberal, middle-class Frankfurt Assembly was again abolishing. Excluded by their masters, journeymen held a rival General German Workers' Congress of their own in Frankfurt, which attempted to build bridges among wage-workers of all corporations and between craft-, factory- and domestic workers, illustrating a new class-consciousness. This was continued in the General German-Workers' Brotherhood, set up in Berlin in August 1848 by Stefan Born.

---

[6] Quoted by Stadelmann, *Social and Political History of the German Revolution*, 163.

Meanwhile, many of the unemployed in Berlin had been put to work by the government building canals and railways, but riots broke out on 28 June when piece-rates were introduced and again after 12 October when the work force was cut. The *Bürgerwehr* fired on the rioters and the propertied middle class drew closer to the traditional ruling class to build a dyke against social revolution.

The conservative nobility, which had lost power in March, were particularly antagonized after the shipowner Camphausen was replaced as Chief Minister on 20 June by the railway-owner Hansemann. His measures to complete the emancipation of the serfs, to tax hitherto exempt noble estates and to replace the manorial system by elective local government east of the Elbe threatened to break the back of the feudal class. The Court camarilla, which retained the ear of Frederick William IV, acted as a government-in-waiting. Conservatives launched the *Kreuzzeitung* and founded the Society for the Protection of the Interests of Landowners to fight for the survival of the agrarian, feudal, Christian monarchy. A conservative ministry was formed under Count Brandenburg on 2 November 1848. Berlin was reoccupied by 13,000 regular troops on 10 November, a state of siege was declared, the *Bürgerwehr* was dissolved and the Assembly was exiled from the capital. The mercurial Frederick William IV would have been quite content at this stage to go back to the autocratic and aristocratic polity that he favoured so well. But there was still the chance that he might become the constitutional monarch of a united Germany and on 5 December his ministers insisted on promulgating a constitution from above by royal edict and calling new elections in January. On 27 April 1849, after the breakdown of talks about a united, constitutional Germany, the Prussian government dissolved the new assembly. Representative institutions were not destroyed but they were put firmly in their place. A revised constitution issued in January 1850 made ministers responsible only to the king, not to parliament, and exempted the army from having to take an oath to the constitution. The Prussian military monarchy was back in business. After all, the revolution had been defeated by the military. 'The Prussian state cannot be based on corporate institutions', explained the Minister of the Interior, Otto von Manteuffel, for the benefit of Junkers who dreamed of closet politics and representation by estates. 'It is essentially a bureaucratic and military system.'[7] Besides, the propertied middle class had to be compensated for rallying so decisively to the monarchy. While the upper house was reserved for peers, the lower house, under the Suffrage Law of 30 May 1849, was to be elected by a three-tier system of electoral colleges graduated according to the amount of property owned. In the localities of East Elbia, on the other hand, the Junkers retained their patrimonial jurisdiction and their administrative and police powers. Watching

[7] Quoted by John R. Gillis, *The Prussian Bureaucracy in Crisis, 1840–60* (Stanford, 1971), 132.

from afar, Marx judged the German middle class incapable of undertaking a democratic revolution. That task was now incumbent on the proletariat. But Prussian legislation of February 1849 which reinforced the guild system on behalf of the beleaguered artisans, and of April 1849 which completed the abolition of serfdom made the proletariat extremely isolated.

In the Habsburg Monarchy the Constitution promised on 15 March and eventually published on 25 April with a Suffrage Law on 9 May was in no sense acceptable to the radicals. It provided for a senate of archdukes, royal nominees, and landed magnates, and a lower chamber elected indirectly by property-owners. But the radicals with their press, political clubs, and the Academic Legion had the support of the Viennese working class and 10,000 of them demonstrated on 15 May 1848 to demand a single-chamber Constituent Assembly elected by universal suffrage. Without the army, the imperial government lost its nerve and conceded the radicals' demands. The feeble-minded and epileptic Emperor Ferdinand, fearing the worst, left for Innsbruck. The government tried to exploit the hostility of the aristocrats, Viennese bourgeoisie, and provinces to the radicals and on 25 May ordered the Civic Guard to dissolve the Academic Legion. This only conjured up barricades and a revolutionary government in Vienna which was in a position to hold the ministry to ransom.

Outside Vienna, however, the Austrian army began to make its weight felt. Charles Albert of Piedmont was defeated at Custozza on 25 July and the Austrians reoccupied Milan. Field Marshal Radetsky took over the civil and military government of Lombardy-Venetia, pardoning common Italian soldiers who had deserted while punishing their leaders. Venice held out on its lagoon, but Daniele Manin was forced to establish a dictatorship in order to consolidate resistance. General Windischgrätz occupied Prague on 20 May and during the street-fighting of 12–17 June the barricades were manned only by students and young journeymen, without support either from the propertied classes or from the peasantry outside.

The government was able to play on a combination of fear and greed to isolate the radicals in Vienna. In the Constituent Assembly which assembled in Vienna on 22 July radicals were clearly outnumbered by Polish nobles, Ruthenian peasants, Czech liberals, and Tyrolese clericals. Unemployed workers given jobs on public works projects who rioted on 23 August when their wages were cut were crushed by the Civic Guard, as were indebted artisans and tradesmen who demonstrated when the Vienna city council refused to support a peoples' bank. The passage of the law to emancipate the serfs in Austria on 7 September cut off the urban radicals from the countryside. The radicals of the Central Committee of Democratic Clubs and the Academic Legion made a last bid to regain control in October 1848. An insurrection was staged to prevent Austrian troops from leaving to fight the Hungarians, who went to war with the Austrian government in September. The Magyar gentry who formed a National Defence Committee of the National Assembly to organize victory had enough trouble with Petöfi's radicals in Budapest and offered no help to the radicals in Vienna, though the Hungarian armies reached the gates of Vienna on 10 October. This was short-sighted, for the defeat of the revolution in Vienna would free Austrian troops to fight them.

General Windischgrätz bombarded the city into submission and declared a state of siege there on 20 November. The Academic Legion was disbanded, rebels were shot, and the assembly was exiled to Moravia. Prince Felix von Schwarzenberg, brother-in-law of Windischgrätz, formed a powerful conservative ministry on 21 November, with the support of the aristocracy and the Viennese middle class. Emperor Ferdinand, who fled to Moravia on 6 October, abdicated on 2 December in favour of his eighteen-year old nephew, Francis Joseph, who had a dramatic sense of kingship and saw the Monarchy almost through to its dissolution in 1918. The constitution drafted by the Constituent Assembly in January was rejected, an alternative constitution was imposed by the government on 4 March 1849, and the assembly was dispersed. Plans to undermine the power of the aristocracy in the countryside by elective local government were scrapped and the Catholic Church was released from all Josephenist controls to become a basic pillar of the state.

The Springtime of Peoples?

In the course of 1848 Poles, Danes, Germans, Italians, Magyars, Czechs, Slovaks, Serbs, Croats, and Romanians were all in arms against sprawling multinational empires in pursuit of the right of self-government. But much exertion achieved little success. Existing political structures were both larger and smaller than national groups, which were sometimes fragmented by separatism, and sometimes distracted by multinationalism. National self-consciousness was often the property only of a certain stratum of society, and nations which had reached different levels of development vied with each other for supremacy within the old empires instead of joining forces against them. Lastly, the policies and priorities of the great powers dictated in the last instance the fortunes of the nationalities.

The proclamation of a republic in France on 25 February 1848 sent a tremor through the Courts and chancelleries of Europe. It was feared that France would resort to the revolutionary imperialism of 1792, overrun Belgium and seize the port of Antwerp, extend her frontier to the Rhine and her influence in Germany, throw the Austrians out of Italy, resurrect Poland, and make war on Russia. The great powers orchestrated by Palmerston agreed that they would have to act in concert to put pressure on France. They rejected Metternich's maxim that the allies should intervene wherever an established government was overthrown by revolution, but threatened to do so if France attacked any part of Europe.

The response of the French Foreign Minister, Lamartine, enshrined in the manifesto of 2 March 1848, was a masterpiece of rhetoric and realism. The French Republic, he declared, did not recognize the humiliating peace treaties of 1815 and would defend by force of arms the rights of oppressed nationalities against any aggressor, mentioning the Swiss and Italians by name, but not the Poles. On the other hand Lamartine was afraid of the coalition of reactionary powers that had twice invaded France to defeat Napoleon, and as a historian of the Girondin party knew that war would provoke a shift to the Left if things went badly, and in the Montagnard Terror that followed the heads of moderates like himself would fall. 'Reassure yourselves', he therefore told the powers, 'if in error you take the Republic of 1848 for the Republic of 1792! We are not a revolutionary anachronism, we are not going against the stream of civilization.'[8]

The fact that France did not move in the spring of 1848 was of decisive importance for the outcome of national revolutions elsewhere. Lamartine offered no help to the Polish *émigrés* who lobbied him in Paris, but saw them as a nuisance and encouraged them to leave the country. The Prussian government was under no pressure to mobilize on the Rhine and even toyed with the idea, after the revolution of 13–16 March in Berlin, of resurrecting an independent Poland as a bulwark against Russia. Mierosławski was released from a Berlin prison to take charge of the Polish National Committee which sprang up at Posen (Poznań) and this was recognized by Prussia as the provisional government of Poland on 24 March. It was only when Polish patriots began to drill in armed camps for an invasion of Russia that Prussia agreed with Britain and Russia that European peace must not be set at risk.

The liberals and radicals of South Germany, especially Baden, Württemburg, and Hesse-Darmstadt, decided that the time had come to reorganize the Confederation, whose Diet represented only the state governments and had been an instrument of Metternich until his fall. Many of the liberal leaders, such as Heinrich von Gagern of Hesse-Darmstadt, acquired new influence as ministers at the beginning of March. Together with representatives of German state assemblies they gathered in a 'Pre-Parliament' at Frankfurt on 31 March to arrange the election of a full parliament that would represent not the state governments but the German nation. The first question was to agree what Germany was, for the complex of states which belonged to the Confederation and the community of German-speakers were two different things. Schleswig and the Grand Duchy of Posen, for example, had German populations (mixed with Danes and Poles, respectively) but did not belong to the Confederation.

Conflict between populations who rubbed shoulders produced a chauvinistic and exclusive nationalism that was quite unlike the cosmopolitan nationalism of the *émigrés* who dreamed of destroying empires. The German

---

[8] Quoted by Lawrence C. Jennings, *France and Europe in 1848: A Study of French Foreign Affairs in Time of Crisis* (Oxford, 1973), 10–11.

minority in the Grand Duchy of Posen, which had been a part of Prussia only in 1793–1807 and since 1815, feared that the duchy was about to become part of a new Poland and pleaded to be incorporated into Prussia. Early in April the Prussian army was sent in to disband the Polish irregulars and the Prussian government took steps to partition the duchy and have twelve German deputies sent to the Frankfurt Assembly. 'Freedom for all', proclaimed one member of the Assembly when it voted to incorporate parts of the duchy on 27 July 1848, 'but the strength and welfare of the fatherland above all!'[9]

Danish nationalism presented a similar challenge to German interests. On 21 March 1848 Orla Lehmann and his national liberals took office in Copenhagen and immediately declared the incorporation of Schleswig into the Monarchy. The German nobles of the estates of Schleswig-Holstein replied by declaring Schleswig independent of Denmark and requesting its inclusion in the German Confederation, Holstein being a member already. The Pre-Parliament voted the inclusion of Schleswig and the Federal Diet authorized the invasion of Schleswig on 9 April by the Prussian army. On 2 May the Prussians advanced into Jutland. This invasion alerted Europe for the first time to the dangers of German nationalism. Palmerston was not opposed to a united liberal Germany which might counterbalance France and Russia, and Russian ministers were not opposed to a united conservative Germany which would serve as a barrier against French republicanism. But territorial changes could not be entertained. Both powers together with France were bound to guarantee Danish interests in Schleswig under a treaty of 1720. Russia feared the eruption of Prussian power into the Baltic while Britain feared that Prussia would enlarge the Zollverein and drive Denmark for safety into the arms of Russia, which would then control the Sound as it threatened to control the Straits. Prussia was therefore forced to agree to an armistice at Malmö on 26 August, and the duchies were placed under a common Prussian–Danish administration. This caused havoc among the nationalistic deputies of the Frankfurt Assembly, especially those on the left. They narrowly failed to have the armistice rejected and then, on 18 September, headed riots in the city during which two deputies were lynched and a state of siege was declared. For German liberals freedom required unity and unity required power. It is no coincidence that the first keels of the German navy were laid in 1848.

The German Assembly in Frankfurt which opened on 18 May was dominated by a university-educated middle class, usually trained in the law, and over half were employed by the state as administrative civil servants, jurists, academics, teachers, and clergy. The caustic Engels described them as 'an assembly of old women … more frightened of the least popular movement than of all the reactionary plots of all the German governments put

---

[9] Quoted by Frank Eyck, *The Frankfurt Parliament of 1848–9* (London, 1968), 278.

together.'[10] Their task was to frame a constitution for the new Germany, but while the South Germans from Baden, Württemberg, Hesse-Darmstadt, and the Rhenish Palatinate wanted the national parliament and a central executive power to supersede the parliaments and governments of the thirty-seven states, deputies from the larger kingdoms of Bavaria, Hanover, Saxony, and Prussia defended states rights. Archduke John, who had led the Austrian campaign against the French in 1809 and was a bitter critic of Metternich, was elected *Reichsverweser* or Imperial Administrator. But the Assembly relied on the military might of Prussia to execute its policies and it is not surprising that the state governments rejected his decree of 16 July 1848 which required their armies to swear loyalty to him and their war ministers to obey him in a national emergency.

It became clear that the new Reich would have to be headed by a hereditary monarch who would be either the Austrian emperor or the Prussian king. On 19 October the Constitutional Committee of the Assembly recommended a *Grossdeutschland* that included the German-speaking parts of the Habsburg Monarchy. But it also laid down that an Austrian hereditary emperor of the Reich would be allowed only a personal union with his non-German territories. This came just as the Austrian Monarchy had subdued nationalist forces which were tearing it apart and had elaborated the constitution of 4 March 1849, which finally established the Monarchy, including Hungary and Lombardy-Venetia, as a centralized 'Reich of 70 millions', subsequently to be associated with a revived German Confederation directed by Austria and Prussia. The proposals of the Frankfurt liberals were ill-conceived and ill-timed, and duly rejected by Vienna. There was no alternative now to offering the crown of a *Kleindeutschland*, excluding the whole of the Habsburg Monarchy, to Frederick William IV. The constitution proposed for the Reich included a Staatenhaus representing members of state governments and state parliaments, a Volkshaus elected by universal male suffrage, and an hereditary emperor with a suspensive but not an absolute veto. Both the constitution and the offer of an imperial crown by a popularly elected assembly to a king by the grace of God were totally unacceptable to Frederick William. On 3 April 1849 he rejected the crown as a 'diadem moulded out of the dirt and dregs of revolution, disloyalty and treason',[11] dissolved the Frankfurt Assembly, and appealed to the German princes to set the German Confederation on a conservative footing. Radicals in Saxony, Baden, Hesse-Darmstadt, the Rhenish Palatinate, and Württemberg launched armed insurrections to defend the Frankfurt constitution (Bakunin and Wagner among the activists in Dresden) and the Grand Duke of Baden and the King of Saxony had to flee their capitals. On 26 May the rulers of Saxony, Hanover,

---

[10] Friedrich Engels, *Germany, Revolution and Counter-Revolution* (London, 1967), 51.
[11] Quoted by Helmut Böhme, *The Foundation of the German Empire* (Oxford, 1971), 66.

Prussia, Baden, and Württemberg formed a military alliance and the rebellions were crushed. The democrats of Saxony and South Germany would have time to reflect on invasion by Prussia and the execution of their leaders.

The movement for national unification was as unsuccessful in Italy as in Germany. One reason for this was the failure of France to move in 1848. Charles Albert of Piedmont went his own way by declaring war on Austria on 25 March. He did not in fact want the assistance of France, given its history of treachery since Campo Formio in 1797 and annexation of Piedmont in 1802. Palmerston recognized the implacable hatred of Lombards and Venetians for Austria but did not want the price of their liberation to be French expansion beyond the Alps. For him, the establishment of an independent neutral state in northern Italy would, as in Belgium and Greece, both satisfy national aspirations and offset the imperialist ambitions of the powers. The defeat of Charles Albert at Custozza on 25 July and the reoccupation of Milan by the Austrians put paid to such schemes. Charles Albert concluded a truce with the Austrians on 9 August, not least because he feared French intervention. He need not have worried. Intervention in France was the policy of the radicals who had invaded the French National Assembly on 15 May to demand aid for Poland. The bourgeois republicans who took control in Paris after the June Days rejected intervention which would only encourage the radical opposition.

French intervention—or its absence—mattered because the Italians did not rally to the flag of Charles Albert to free Italy of the Austrians. The Milan patriciate and Lombard aristocracy agreed to 'fusion' with Piedmont in a Kingdom of Upper Italy and organized a plebiscite to support their strategy on 8 June because that was the only guarantee against social revolution. The nobility of Venetia also accepted fusion but Manin had declared a republic in Venice precisely in order to define the autonomy of the city-state. It was not until the Austrians were battering at the gates, on 4 July, that the Venetian Assembly agreed to fusion, and the truce agreed by Charles Albert brought Piedmontese rule in Venice to an end after five days, to the delight of Manin. The liberal aristocrats of Tuscany cold-shouldered the efforts of Piedmont. Sicily was fighting a separatist war and offered a crown to one of Charles Albert's sons according to the principle, 'better Turin than Naples'. General Pepe, 'Calabrian Liberal and *beau sabreur* of the school of Murat',[12] who had joined the Carbonari and led the Neapolitan rising of 1820, led volunteers north to fight the Austrians. But the Pope's speech of 29 April, which did not oppose the right of individuals to fight Austria but refused to declare war himself, doomed any idea of a popular war of liberation. As significant as the Italians in the war against Austria was the Polish legion led by the poet Adam Mickiewicz which still proclaimed 'freedom is indivisible'.

[12] G. M. Trevelyan, *Manin and the Venetian Revolution of 1848* (London, 1923), 214.

Differences between regimes sharpened separatism. Gioberti summoned a congress of representatives from the Kingdom of Upper Italy, Tuscany, the Papal States, Naples, and Sicily to Turin in October 1848 to discuss a federation of Italian states, but he met with no success. The monarchists were divided from republicans like Manin. On the other hand Manin's republicanism was that of the ancient Venetian city-state, not the Mazzinian variety which preached republicanism as a pre-condition of national unity, and he took care to destroy the influence of the Mazzinian Italian Club in Venice early in October. The creation of a democratic, unitary republic was a possibility in 1848–9. The Tuscan radical Montanelli explained in Livorno on 8 October why the war with Austria had failed. 'There was no unity of direction, therefore there was no national government. We fought as Piedmontese, as Tuscans, as Neapolitans, as Romans, and not as Italians.'[13] When he came to power three weeks later he urged the convocation of an Italian Constituent Assembly, and victories of democrats at the polls in Piedmont, Rome, and Venice in January 1849 gave massive impetus to this scheme. Its price was the sacrifice of monarchy. The Pope had fled, and Leopold of Tuscany fled on 30 January. On the other hand Charles Albert was the only force who could challenge the Austrians, and his victory would strengthen the monarchical principle. He launched a new war on Austria in March 1849 and was defeated again, at Novara. The republicans were now confronted by the Austrians, who occupied Tuscany on 11 May and restored the Grand Duke, and by the French, who intervened to check the advance of the Austrians but on the same side. Despite gallant resistance by Garibaldi, the French entered Rome on 3 July and restored the ultimate obstacle to Italian unification, Pope Pius IX.

The Habsburg Monarchy was strained by the demands of different nationalities for autonomy. But many nationalities believed that their demands could be met within the framework of the Monarchy, and even that the Monarchy guaranteed that autonomy. Bohemia, with its mixed German and Czech population, was a part of the German Confederation and was invited to send deputies to Frankfurt. The Germans were eager to participate but Palacký replied on 11 April that he was not a German but a 'Czech of Slavic descent'. The future of the Czechs was not as a separate state but enjoying autonomy and protection from German persecution within the Habsburg Monarchy. 'If the Austrian state had not already existed for so long', he continued, 'it would have been in the interests of Europe, indeed of humanity itself, to endeavour to create it as soon as possible.'[14] A Slav Congress was held in Prague in June 1848, but did not unduly threaten the Monarchy. Viennese radicals feared Slav ambitions to create a vast Slavic empire, under the auspices of Russia, from the Arctic to the Bosphorus. Polish leaders reiter-

---

[13] Quoted by Giorgio Candeloro, *Storia dell' Italia moderna*, iii (Milan, 1960), 303.
[14] Quoted by Stanley Z. Pech, *The Czech Revolution of 1848* (Chapel Hill, 1969), 82.

ated the view that the Habsburg Monarchy should be destroyed and the Polish state reconstituted within its boundaries of 1772. But the Ruthenians of Galicia had no wish to be ruled over by Poles and drew close to the Czechs in defence of Austro-Slavism. So diverse were the languages of Czechs, Slovaks, Poles, Ruthenes, Croats, and Slovenes, that the plenary sessions had to be conducted in German.

The binding force of 'Austro-Slavism' was hatred of the Magyars. Having acquired autonomy from Vienna in March 1848, the Magyars in April constructed a unitary Hungarian Union that included Croatia-Slavonia, Transylvania, and Slovakia. Nationalities in these areas all requested from Vienna the same autonomy that the Magyars had won, but the Magyars considered that they were the only 'nation' with political rights in the Hungarian Union. Slovak leaders who demanded the use of Slovak in county assemblies and schools and on 10 May a federative reorganization of Hungary had to flee to Prague to avoid arrest by the Magyar authorities. Serbs meeting on the Military Border on 13 May demanded an autonomous Serbian province called Vojvodina and looked for support to the Croats. In Croatia the radical demands of the 'Illyrians' were contained by the Croatian nobility led by Josip Jelačić, who on 23 March 1848 was appointed 'Ban' or Governor of Croatia and general in command of the armies of both Civil Croatia and the Military Border. But the request of the Croatian Sabor or parliament to the Emperor on 5 June, demanding the reconstitution of the ancient Triune Kingdom of Croatia, Slavonia, and Dalmatia, together with the Military Border and the Slovene provinces, with a ministry responsible to the Sabor, was turned down. The Emperor Ferdinand confirmed the incorporation of Croatia within the Hungarian Union and dismissed Jelačić. The confirmation of the Hungarian Union was a blow also to the Transylvanians, who met 40,000-strong at Blaj on 15–17 May under the leadership of students, teachers, and Uniate priests to demand a separate national parliament. Yet they refused to join up with the Romanian rebels in the Danubian Principalities who wanted to reunite the Romanians on both sides of the Carpathians in a 'Daco-Roman' empire. For their pains, they were punished by a ruthless campaign of Magyarization.

Austria went to war with the Magyars in September 1848 in defence of the unity of the Habsburg Monarchy. The Magyar armies were joined by 20,000 Poles and placed under the command of the Polish general Bem, for Polish nationalists needed to destroy the Austrian Empire as well as the Russian in order to achieve their independence. The Austrian government, on the other hand, was able to play off the nationalities hostile to the pretensions of the Magyars against them. Jelačić was reinstated and invited to lead an army of regulars, *Grenzer*, and militiamen against the Magyars. The Romanian National Committee levied a national guard of 10,000 men. In the Austrian parliament on 19 September the Czechs refused aid to the Magyars on the grounds that they were oppressors of the Slavs. The Magyars found no sympathy from the great powers either. Palmerston urged that the Austrian position in northern Italy was untenable, but refused to give assistance to the Magyar revolt of 1848–9 because the integrity of the Habsburg Monarchy, which stood firm between French and Russian imperialism, could not be sacrificed. There was virtually no dissident movement in Russia in 1848, apart from a radical circle around the junior Foreign Ministry official, Mikhail Petrashevsky, including the writer Dostoevsky, which was rounded up in 1849. But Nicholas I was concerned that Polish fighting in Austria might spill into Russian Poland, and he was quick to respond on 17 June 1849 to a request for Russian support from Francis Joseph. Field Marshal Paskevich, who had put down the Polish rising in 1831, was put in charge of 190,000 Russian troops, and defeated 162,000 on the Hungarian side in August 1849. Finally, in October, Russian and Ottoman forces jointly suppressed the Romanian revolution in the Danubian Principalities.

Nationalism as a revolutionary movement thus failed in 1848–9. Nationalism would triumph later, but it would not be revolutionary. A breach between Austria and Russia, the defeat of Russia, and the re-emergence of French military power would be conditions of its success. The twin problems of multi-nationalism and separatism would be solved by the emergence of single states, Piedmont and Prussia, to defeat the Habsburg Empire and assert hegemony over the fragmented states which made up the Italian and German nations. And while the liberal-nationalist élites were still active, their campaigns would be cut off by governments in defence of the monarchical principle. Revolution would be averted by means of a simple strategem: national unification.

5

HIERARCHIES OF CULTURE

Language and Education

The historian of culture is like a solitary figure on the sea-shore. Here and there rises solid rock, the massive and imposing memorials of a Goethe or a Beethoven, but around them lie sheets of pebbles and sandbanks, formless and shifting, representing obscure artefacts, tales without authors, indeed all the values of society that received symbolic expression. Where should he start? With the brilliant or the mundane? With the conscious or the unconscious? With the culture of the social élite or the culture of the masses? In any country at any period there is no single culture but rather different layers of culture, superimposed one upon another, corresponding in a very general way with the different social strata of the population. There are hierarchies of culture, whether we look at the language in which people express their thoughts, the education they receive, or the forms of distraction in which they take part.

The idea that in the early nineteenth century language was what defined the population of one country from that of another must be modified. Some languages were cosmopolitan, the lingua franca of the European governing classes as a whole. Latin was the language of the Roman Catholic Church, of the universities of Europe, and also served as an official language in countries where a multitude of tongues were spoken. It had remained the official language in Poland down to the Partition of 1795 and was the language of the Hungarian Diet at Pressburg, where both Magyars and Croats sat, until the 1840s. The language spoken in European Courts and in aristocratic circles, from Paris to St Petersburg, the language, in a word, of polite society, was French. The presence of French *émigrés* in Russia in the 1790s and the presence of Russian officers in Paris in 1814 only reinforced the connexion. Tsar Alexander I addressed the Polish Sejm in French. It was the language of chivalry. French was spoken to ladies at balls and written in love letters. Tolstoy affirmed that love could be expressed only in French and would evaporate if Russian were used. Descartes wrote in Latin but Voltaire wrote in French. Clear and elegant, French was the language of the Enlightenment in Europe. It was the language of diplomacy. The last major peace treaty drawn up in Latin was the Treaty of Vienna which ended the War of the Polish Succession in 1738. The Congress of Vienna used French for all its proceedings and the reservation of Article 120 of the Final Act that this did not mean that a precedent had been set was purely formal and of little significance. French remained the accepted code of ambassadors and statesmen in the nineteenth century, so that even when they were at war they preserved a common system of values.

In a Europe dominated by empires it was necessary to learn the language of the dominant nationality in order to get on. So there were Frenchified Germans and Russians, Germanized Czechs and Magyars, Magyarized Slovaks and Croats, Polonized Lithuanian and Ukrainian gentry, and Ottomanized Bulgarians. From the end of the eighteenth century there was a good deal of opposition to this process of assimilation from intellectuals who argued that it should be possible to succeed and retain one's national identity, and that the defining ingredient of national identity was the language of the *Volk* or people. This argument began to bite when a dominant nationality imposed its own language as the official language of the administration, courts, churches, and schools on subordinate nationalities. Intellectuals replied by forging a national consensus and consciousness based on a common language, which could then be used to demand political autonomy for the national group. Speaking of the Austrian offensive against the French in 1809 the poet Heine wrote that 'August Wilhelm Schlegel conspired against Racine with the same purpose as that with which Minister Stein conspired against Napoleon'.[1] The Magyar aristocrat Count István Széchenyi, who kept his private diary in French, German, and English, but not Hungarian, spoke Hungarian at the Diet of 1825, rather than Latin (and certainly not German) to demand the introduction of Hungarian as the language of administration. The Polish gentry and intelligentsia developed Polish after the Partitions in order to resist attempts to impose German or Russian on them, and to create unity between lords and peasants, Catholics and Jews. Some Russian intellectuals, too, were having doubts about the French language. The conservative Karamzin, who visited the west in 1790 and discovered Englishmen who knew French nevertheless speaking English, asked, 'Is that not disgraceful for us? Why should we be ashamed of our mother tongue and turn ourselves into monkeys or parrots?'[2]

Yet the development of a modern literary language was not always easy. Between the fluid, everyday vernacular and the model for a written language, which might be an archaic, complex liturgical language, there was little resemblance. In the case of Russia, the written language was Church Slavonic, in which Church texts had been enshrined since the Byzantine period. In 1783 the Russian Academy decided to base a new literary language on the vernacular rather than on Church Slavonic, hoping to give it the subtlety and brilliance of French, and brought out a grammar between 1789 and 1794 and a dictionary in 1802. Less formally, Adamantios Korais, the son of a Greek

---

[1] Quoted by John B. Halsted (ed.), *Romanticism* (New York, 1969), 70.
[2] Quoted by Hans Rogger, *National Consciousness in Eighteenth-Century Russia* (Harvard, 1960), 108.

merchant of Smyrna who failed in commerce in Amsterdam and moved to Paris in 1788, elaborated a modern Greek literary language that was based on the spoken tongue, infused with words from Ancient Greek, and not on the language of the Greek Orthodox Church. Working in Pressburg in the 1840s the Slovak L'udovít Štúr abandoned his predecessors' attempts to develop a Slavic literary language derived from *bibličtina*, the language of the Hussite Bible, and adopted a narrower Slovak language based on the dialect of central Slovakia.

Dialect was a characteristic of all spoken languages, and was often a barrier between the educated and uneducated in a given country. There were three dialects in Slovakia. The Italian literary language was derived from Tuscan, and was spoken in Tuscany and by educated Romans. Otherwise Italy was a jigsaw of dialects, with Milanese incomprehensible to the speakers of Calabrian, and vice versa. The Swabian spoken in South Germany was quite different from North German, and in 1856, Thomas Mann tells us, the Bremen merchant Thomas Buddenbrook could speak the dialect of 'the ship-captains, the heads in the warehouse offices, the drivers and the yard hands', but his partner could not.[3] Even for the miners' children of the pit villages of County Durham it was said in 1861 that the language of their schoolbooks was as foreign to their dialect as medieval Latin.

The education of the social élite and that of the social mass had nothing in common for most of the nineteenth century. Governments were interested in the first to train the ruling class, and for a long time left the second to market forces. The first included secondary school and university education, the second elementary education only. The first was defined by the teaching of Latin, and even Greek, the second by the teaching of the language of the dominant nationality—and of religion.

At the end of the eighteenth century the education of the élite reflected the society of orders: colleges run by religious orders to train both the clerical and civil bureaucracy; cadet schools, knights' academies, and public schools to train the military aristocracy in Latin and French, mathematics, engineering, and geography, and the gallant studies of riding, fencing, and dancing. During the French Revolution the Directory sought to integrate the advances of the Enlightenment with the secondary school system through a network of Central Schools which taught mathematics, sciences, law, history, and drawing, as well as ancient languages, grammar, and rhetoric. In 1802 Napoleon replaced the Central Schools by *lycées*, run on military lines, to train the civil and military bureaucracy of the new French Empire. Here classics ousted everything else except mathematics, required for *grandes écoles* like the École Polytechnique, which trained soldiers and military and civil engineers. The defeat of Prussia by France in 1806 brought home the need for a highly trained

³ Thomas Mann, *Buddenbrooks* (1902, trans. 1924, Harmondsworth, 1982), 206.

bureaucracy composed of nobles and non-nobles that would be distinguished as a moral and intellectual aristocracy rather than an aristocracy of
birth. In 1812 the *Gymnasien* which taught Greek and Latin were raised
above all other schools, and the *Abitur* or leaving certificate which qualified
for university admission was made more rigorous. The genius behind the
reforms was Wilhelm von Humboldt, who had served in Rome after 1801 as
envoy to the Holy See but was more interested in classical Antiquity. He was
fascinated by the way the Ancients seemed to have harmonized the spiritual
and sensual sides of life, a balance he believed to have been upset by Christianity with its emphasis on poverty, humility, and sin. Appointed Head of
Education in the Prussian Ministry of the Interior, he developed the study of
classics not as stylistic or syntactical exercises but historically and philosoph-
ically, for the values that they disclosed. For Humboldt, classics offered a
general culture, distinct from the useful arts on the one hand, and aristocratic
play and dilettantism on the other, to ennoble the soul and develop a well-
rounded personality. In Russia, which had a much greater need to train its
bureaucracy, Alexander I founded a number of *lycées* while Nicholas I
adopted the *Gymnasium* system for the sons of gentry and civil officials after
1828. On the other hand, the tradition of a military education for sons of
nobles remained strong, and the number of cadet schools in Russia rose from
five to twenty-three during the reign of Nicholas I. There was no such system
of public secondary education in England, for the public schools were privately endowed. They were criticized as educational rotten boroughs, but
reform came from within, largely due to the influence of Thomas Arnold, the
headmaster of Rugby School (1828–42). Classical humanism, combined with
the muscular Christianity of the playing fields, became the model not only of
the public schools but also of the endowed grammar schools, even in industrial towns such as Leeds. The proprietary schools like Cheltenham (1841),
funded by subscription and run by the shareholders, offered Latin but not
Greek, and a more modern education which was useful for aspirants to the
military academies.

Just as the ambitious assimilated the language of the dominant nationality,
so they pressed to learn Latin which was the avenue to university, public
office, and the liberal professions. Ruling oligarchies became concerned
by the numbers who were using education to escape their social condition,
were overcrowding the professions or, failing to obtain the posts they coveted, were becoming discontented *littérateurs* and journalists. Attempts were
made to restrict access to secondary education by making the classical course
more demanding, as in France in 1840, or by raising fees and shutting out
all but the sons of nobles, officials, and rich merchants, as the Russian government did in 1845. In addition (and less clumsily), an 'intermediate' system
of schooling was designed for the children of small manufacturers and
tradesmen, low-grade officials, clerks, artisans, and rich peasants, for whom

elementary instruction was too little and who yet should be channelled away from the élite schools. This was the task of the burgher schools of Germany which were refashioned as *Realschulen* in 1832 and the higher primary schools set up in France in 1833. England had no such special provision but a thousand Dotheboys Halls performed the same function.

The European states had very little interest in primary education at the beginning of the nineteenth century. The schooling of the masses was abandoned to the law of supply and demand, supplied where it was demanded by underemployed artisans, demobilized NCOs, unfrocked priests, and penniless widows and spinsters. In Catholic countries teaching congregations of nuns and lay brothers resumed their work after the disturbances of the revolutionary wars. Gradually, governments did seek to intervene in elementary education, usually in conjunction with the established churches, more in the interest of social order than in order to promote literacy. In Prussia elementary education for the masses was compulsory from the early eighteenth century and the *Schulgeld* was levied on all parents after 1763. The framework of a system of supervision was established after 1817 under a joint Ministry of Education and Religious Affairs, and the Churches, both Protestant and Catholic, were closely involved as inspectors at all levels of their respective hierarchies. In France the compulsion ordained in 1833 by the Protestant Education Minister Guizot was not on individuals but on every commune to set up and fund one elementary school. Until 1830 the Catholic clergy were very much involved in the hierarchy of inspection, much less so after the anti-clerical Revolution of 1830. In Belgium, where the Revolution of 1830 was carried out by liberals and Catholics together, the influence of the Church in the structure of supervision and inspection was much greater. In the British Isles, Ireland was treated as a colony and a national system of primary education was organized in 1831, funded largely by the British Parliament and controlled by a Board of Commissioners in London. A radical move in 1833 to extend a similar system to England and Wales was rejected by Parliament as infringement of the liberty of parents to educate their children or not, and of religious toleration. Elementary education was left to the Church of England, which set up a National Society for Promoting the Education of the Poor in the Principles of the Established Church in 1811, and to the Nonconformists, who set up the rival British and Foreign School Society in 1812. Both movements were funded by voluntary subscription, although small grants-in-aid were made to voluntary schools after 1833. In Russia, finally, the education of serfs was left to the discretion of serf-owners under decrees of 1804 and 1828, and consequently very little was done until the Orthodox Church became more involved in rural schools after 1839.

The existence of state churches, their involvement in the provision of public education and the central part of religious instruction in popular education clearly raised problems for religious minorities. In Dutch schools after

1806 and in Irish schools, all pupils received a general moral education and Catholic and Protestant children received denominational instruction separately. In France and Germany, the parish school adopted the confession of the majority religion. As yet, pressure to exclude religious instruction from the classroom on grounds of toleration was weak, because after the revolutionary period there was generally seen to be no morality and no social order without religion. Frederick William III of Prussia told his officials in 1799 that he wanted children to be 'educated to become reasonable men, good Christians and decent citizens of the state'.[4] Guizot informed his primary schoolteachers in 1833 that they were 'one of the guarantees of order and social stability'.

The message given to primary schoolteachers was somewhat ambiguous. They were described as humble apostles of civilization, sent to redeem the masses from barbarism and pacify society. But most of them were from peasant or artisan backgrounds. The minority of them who were trained in normal schools or teachers' seminaries were not supposed to become 'intellectuals', which would give them airs about their station, and Swiss seminaries required two hours' vegetable gardening a day to preserve their rustic innocence. The teachers were supposed to stand out from the rest of the village as upright and sober envoys. But they were not salaried by the state and minimally, if at all, by the commune or parish. They had to collect the *Schulgeld* or school pence from the parents themselves, and eke out a meagre living by serving as secretary to the mayor or sexton to the priest. Schoolteachers in search of greater independence and status were both involved in the revolutions of 1848 and punished for their involvement.

Even if the schools functioned—and the towns were far better provided for than the countryside—attendance at them was very irregular. Cost was one obstacle, although larger towns took the burden of some pauper children on the rates and English 'ragged schools' and German *Armenschulen* made the education of the very poor their business. But free education made little difference where the children were required to contribute to the family economy. In the countryside children worked in the fields from haymaking to the harvest, and in southern Europe the wine, chestnut, and olive harvests came late. Children were employed in domestic industries, mines, and factories, and Factory Acts in Britain in 1833, Prussia in 1839, or France in 1841 could not overcome the eagerness of employers to hire child labour and the eagerness of parents to sell it.

A map of school attendance in Europe in 1839 coupled with a map of adult literacy in 1850 reveals three broad areas. In Switzerland, Germany, the Netherlands, Scandinavia, and Scotland, school attenders numbered one in ten, or fewer, of the population and illiteracy was under 30 per cent. In England and Wales, Ireland, Belgium, France, Austria, and northern Italy, school

---

[4] Quoted by Rudolf Schenda, *Volk ohne Buch* (Frankfurt, 1970), 45.

attenders numbered one in between 10 and 20 of the population and illiteracy was between 30 and 50 per cent. Far behind was a vast arc of southern and eastern Europe where only one in over fifty of the population attended school and illiteracy ranged from 75 per cent in Spain and central Italy to 85 per cent in southern Italy, 80 per cent in Poland and between 90 and 95 per cent in Russia, where only one person in 367 attended school in 1839. Illiteracy and semi-literacy determined many of the leisure activities of Europe.

Patterns of Leisure

Books were very expensive in the early nineteenth century but the reading public was expanding beyond the cultivated nobilities and university-educated bourgeoisie to include the educated middle classes. Book production rose in France from 3,357 titles in 1815 to 8,198 titles in 1827; in Germany it rose from 5,000 titles in 1827 to 7,617 titles in 1831 and 13,664 titles in 1843, and titles in German (as opposed to French) passed the 10,000 mark for the first time in 1841. The cultivated élite subscribed to plush reading rooms, which were like gentlemen's clubs, with smoking room and billiard room attached, and to circulating libraries, in order to vary their choice. But the middle classes demanded cheaper and more accessible reading matter. In England Dickens' *Pickwick Papers* was brought out in shilling monthly numbers in 1836 and had a readership of 40,000, three or four times that of Walter Scott's novels during the Regency. Book clubs made possible the exchange and second-hand purchase of books, and less select libraries and reading rooms were often attached to booksellers, stationers, tobacconists, and coffee-shops.

Coffee-shops and cafés were frequented for the daily newspapers that they kept. In 1820 Lille had three reading rooms and ninety-five cafés which took at least one paper. For newspapers were expensive, not least because of stamp tax, and had to be subscribed to, for copies were not sold on the streets. *La Presse*, launched in Paris by Emile de Girardin in 1836, was considered a cheap newspaper because the annual subscription was forty francs instead of eighty. His tactic was to reduce the political content and to publish novels from day to day as serials. Within months, the newspaper was selling 20,000 copies. The most popular novelist with readers was Eugène Sue, whose *Mysteries of Paris* was serialized in the otherwise staid *Journal des Débats* in 1842–3, and *Wandering Jew* in the Leipzig *Allgemeine Zeitung* in 1844. The Revolution of 1848 had a massive effect on newspaper reading, especially in France and Germany. In that year the number of inhabitants per newspaper was 40 in Great Britain, 44 in Germany, and 48 in France. Daily newspapers sold 65,000 copies in Berlin, 24,000 copies in Stuttgart, and 21,000 copies each in Augsburg, Hamburg, and Breslau. But a newspaper would be read by 4 people in Berlin and by 5 families or 20–25 people in North Germany, so that a quarter of the German population read local and political newspapers in 1848.

The reading public included the literate or semi-literate lower classes, and what they read was of concern to the authorities. The clandestine unstamped press of the English radical movement, including the *Poor Man's Guardian*, which passed from hand to hand in the public houses, had a circulation of 77,000 copies a week in 1833 and an audience of much more. Attempts were made to counter its influence by the propagation of 'wholesome' magazines. 1832 saw the appearance of Chambers' *Edinburgh Journal*, which had a circulation of 50,000, mostly in Scotland, and Charles Knight's *Penny Magazine*, sold under the auspices of the Society for the Diffusion of Useful Knowledge. A German society of the same name started a *Pfennig-Magazin* in 1833 and soon boosted its circulation to 100,000. German artisans were clearly more interested in honest self-improvement than English workers as the *Penny Magazine* had to close down in 1846, and a parliamentary inquiry of 1851 reported that sales of Chambers' *Journal* were 'almost exclusively confined to the middle classes ... chiefly among small shopkeepers, not among those dependent on weekly wages; not certainly among any portion of the working classes earning less than 16*s*. a week'.[5]

Much more popular among the English working classes were publishers like Edward Lloyd who sold 50,000 copies a week of his plagiarized *Posthumous Notes of the Pickwick Club* and brought out a *Penny Sunday Times* in 1840 (instead of sevenpence for the real thing) which consisted entirely of fiction and fabricated police-reports. Another publisher, G. W. M. Reynolds, leapt on to the Eugène Sue bandwaggon by issuing weekly numbers of *Mysteries of London* and in 1846 launched *Reynold's Magazine*, priced at one penny, which had a circulation of 150,000 copies in ten years.

These cheap books, newspapers, and periodicals gradually replaced the popular literature printed since the Reformation at Epinal and Tours, Hamburg, Reutlingen in Württemburg, Geneva, and Bassano in Venetia and carried across Europe by dynasties of pedlars. It was the only link that rural populations had with the printed word. Even if they could not read, they regarded print with superstitious awe as if it were a magic code. The pedlars responded by selling anything that could entrance the popular imagination: pious and devotional works, engravings of saints, alphabets for children, almanacks which reckoned the movement of planets and ventured prophesies, sensational *canards*, ballads of great robbers, the semi-pornographic memoirs of marchionesses and manservants, treatises on magic, and models for love letters, together with ribbons and buttons, rosaries, chains, and bracelets. For the mass of the population they were not only salesmen but bringers of news, street-entertainers, quacks, and sorcerers. For the authorities, who tried valiantly to control them, they were corrupters of morals and political agitators. Many of them indeed flitted from Switzerland to Alsace and the Rhineland and back, spreading democratic ideas. Everything they

---

[5] Quoted by G. A. Cranfield, *The Press and Society* (London, 1978), 147.

carried was plagiarized, filtered by penniless clerics and hack writers like F. G. Ducray-Duminil, who specialized in Gothic horror, but then most of it originated in a common fund of myths, legends and fairy-tales that was the patrimony of whole populations. The long-distance dynasties of pedlars, seasonal migrants from mountainous areas such as the Alps or Pyrenees, were rarely to be seen in Britain after 1830 or France after 1850, although they continued longer in Spain. They were replaced either by commercial travellers representing a single firm, with catalogues and samples, or by local, casual pedlars, who were scarcely distinguishable from vagrants.

Europe was crossed not only by lone pedlars but by troupes of players. Popular theatre celebrated the Christian tradition in nativity plays, passion plays, and paradise plays, from Catholic southern Europe to the Alps and the Rhineland. In Greece, southern Italy, and the French Basque country, where the story of Robert the Devil was popular in the eighteenth and early nineteenth centuries, the epic of the Crusades was re-enacted, pitting Christian knights against the Moorish infidel. Seasonal plays expressed the conflict between the New Year and the Old, between justice and injustice, between feasting and fasting, as in mid-Lent, when Carnival turned the world upside down.

The official and fashionable theatre of the eighteenth century was rather different from this, but during the French Revolution, in 1791, the theatre was freed from restrictions, leading to a glut of popular and highly political plays. National festivals, designed and choreographed by Jacques-Louis David, 'pageant-master of the Republic' were one attempt to control these, but it was Napoleon, with his distrust of 'mountebank stages', who tackled the problem effectively. A decree in 1806 ordered all theatre into the bright light of day and authorized only a hierarchy of professional theatres. At the bottom were the Théâtre de la Gaieté for pantomimes and harlequinades, the Porte-Saint-Martin Theatre for melodramas, and the Théâtre des Variétés for 'little plays of the bawdy, vulgar or rustic genres'. At the top were the Comédie Française for tragedy and comedy, and the Odéon for comedy, while opera was divided between the Opéra and the Opéra-Comique.

Censorship of the press made the theatre a powerful instrument of political or national opposition, but for that purpose the established theatre had to be modified. The Court theatres of Germany were patronized by the princes, and played French drama and Italian opera for the pleasure of a small ruling class. In 1767 the urban patriciate of Hamburg founded its own national theatre to perform serious and elevating pieces in German. The German influence was relayed to the Court theatre of Weimar, which was set up in 1791 and dominated by Goethe and Schiller. To the brilliance of Mozart's *Magic Flute* was added the passion and idealism of Schiller's own plays: *Wallenstein* (1800), *Mary Stuart* (1801), *The Maid of Orleans* (1803), and *William Tell* (1804). The theatre in Madrid also performed Schiller and, freed from

French occupation in 1808 and again in 1813, unleashed a riot of drama about 2 May 1808 and the Roman hero Brutus. Discontent with the reactionary Cortes after the restoration of Ferdinand VII was expressed loudly in the theatre. 'They act Jacobin plays almost every night', wrote the British ambassador Henry Wellesley to his brother in January 1814, 'and sing coplas against the Serviles which were more applauded than I ever recollect them to have been in Madrid.'[6] In England, the radical movement organized plays in saloons that expressed opposition to the government. These contravened the laws on theatre licensing and in September 1839 police raided the Royal Union Saloon in Shoreditch, where eight or nine hundred workers were watching a play, and made seventy arrests.

The 'singing saloons' of London and North-West England, like the *Star* which opened in Bolton in 1840, were early versions of the music hall. Against their 'wet' approach to music was the 'dry' earnestness of the Nonconformist amateur choirs, such as the Huddersfield Choral Society of 1836, which made use of the cheap sheet music being published by Alfred Novello and appealed strongly to the lower-middle class. Amateur choirs and music festivals called 'Olympias' sprang up in Germany in the 1830s, while the Paris Orphéon was founded in 1836. More popular with the courting couples of Paris were the promenade concerts promoted in a marquee on the Champs Elysées between 1837 and 1840 by Philippe Musard. These were copied from the promenade concerts and waltz nights of Johann Strauss, who was performing three times a night in Vienna by 1830 and then toured Europe. Strauss succeeded by glamorizing a strong Germanic tradition. Nearly all German towns had suburban pleasure gardens surrounding large houses with ballrooms upstairs, refreshment rooms downstairs, table and chairs outside, where all classes of people could afford to listen to the orchestra. 'Can an Englishman imagine', asked one observer, 'the inhabitants of the filthy cellars, alleys and courts of our towns, or the peasants of our villages, sitting in Kensington or any other gardens, mixed up with the gentry of our metropolis and the officers of our army? The idea seems to us preposterous.'[7] But after 1839 promenade concerts were brought to England by Louis Jullien, the son of a military bandmaster and failed student of the Paris Conservatoire. He composed countless marches, waltzes, and quadrilles and played in the Surrey Gardens, London and in the provinces to ecstatic audiences of young clerks, shop-assistants, and their girls who went to 'promenades always, never to a good concert, only rarely to the gallery at the opera'.[8]

The musical life of polite European society was a different world altogether.

---

[6] Quoted by F. D. Klingender, *Goya in the Democratic Tradition* (London, 1948), 139.

[7] Joseph Kay, *The Social Condition and the Education of the People in England and Europe* (London, 1850), i, 240.

[8] *Musical World*, 3 Dec. 1840. Quoted by William Weber, *Music and the Middle-Class: The Social Structure of Concert Life in London, Paris and Vienna* (New York, 1975), 109.

In Vienna the elegant ladies who presided over aristocratic salons organized recitals and benefit concerts at which virtuosi such as Paganini and Liszt would play. The university-educated official and professional class in Vienna waited until 1846 before setting up a Society of the Friends of Music to organize public concerts. This step was taken much earlier in London, where the Philharmonic Society was founded by an élite of the aristocracy, gentry, City, and professions in 1813. Opera did not take off in England in this period, partly because it was frowned on as immoral by stiff-necked Protestants, partly because no finance was forthcoming from the state, as in France, or from municipalities, as in Italy. At the King's Theatre in the Haymarket a Rossini opera was cancelled at short notice in August 1820 because further credit was refused by the banker Chambers.

The operas of Gioachino Rossini, with their rhythmic *élan* and endless stream of melodies, took Venice, Milan, and Naples by storm in the years after 1812. At the Theatre of the Italians in Paris the *Italian Girl in Algiers* was performed in 1817, the *Barber of Seville* in 1819 and Rossini became the director of the theatre in 1824. He had an important influence on Daniel Auber and his librettist Eugène Scribe who dominated the Opéra-Comique after 1830. But the rich bourgeoisie of the July Monarchy wanted sheer spectacle and pressed into the Opéra where the director, Louis Véron, provided them with the French grand opera of Giacomo Meyerbeer. A German by birth, Meyerbeer went to Venice in 1815 at the suggestion of Salieri, mastered the Italian style of Rossini, and went on to Paris in 1826. There he joined forces with Scribe and triumphed with *Robert the Devil*, sung in French, in 1831, and the *Huguenots* in 1836. This was opera on the grand scale: historical drama, sumptuous costumes, complex stage machinery, a huge cast, dazzling solo parts, and ballet in the entr'acte. The bourgeoisie certainly had its money's worth. Hector Berlioz's *Benvenuto Cellini*, which the composer later said contained a 'variety of ideas, an energy and exuberance and brilliance of colour such as I may perhaps never find again',[9] was not to its taste and closed after three nights in 1838.

'The Opéra has become reconciled with the enemies of music', wrote Heine in 1837, and 'the brilliant aristocracy, the élite distinguished by its rank, culture, birth, fashion and idleness, has fled to the Italian Opera.'[10] In 1835 it was Bellini who charmed the Theatre of the Italians with the *Puritans* and *Norma*, and in 1843 Donizetti electrified it with *Don Pasquale*. Paris had become the centre of the operatic world and non-French composers were often induced to go down the blind alley of French opera in order to succeed there. But Giuseppe Verdi had a triumph in Milan with *Nabucco* in 1842 and another in Venice with *Ernani* in 1844. Meanwhile composers in Germany were trying to break the monopoly of Italian taste. At the Court Opera of

---

[9] Hector Berlioz, *Memoirs* (London, 1969), 245.
[10] Quoted by Ernest Newman, *The Life of Richard Wagner*, i, *1813–48* (London, 1933), 257.

Dresden a Conductor of Italian opera was joined in 1817 by a conductor of the 'German department', Carl Maria von Weber. Weber created German opera at a stroke with *Der Freischutz* in 1821, hunting scenes, magic bullets, and all, but died five years later. Richard Wagner, who was captivated by *Freischutz* as a child, nevertheless felt the need to succeed in Paris. He stayed there from 1839 to 1842 without any luck, but triumphed with *Rienzi* at Dresden in 1842, and was appointed royal conductor there for life in 1843. Unfortunately or otherwise, his involvement in the Dresden rising of May 1849 put paid to that.

The seditious implications of reading and theatre were far more explicit in sport and games. G. M. Trevelyan observed that 'if the French *noblesse* had been capable of playing cricket with their peasants, their châteaux would never have been burnt.'[11] The hunting rights of the nobility which denied the peasants the right to kill the game that pestered their farms did not endear the nobles to them either. One result of the Revolution was to give peasants the right to kill game on their own land and, where landowners did not reserve shooting-rights, to open game-shooting to anyone prepared to pay a small sum for a licence. This was exceptional in Europe, where game reserves and game laws confined shooting for sport to a narrow upper class and punished poaching severely. Fox-hunting, which was built up in England between 1795 and 1815 and had some success in France and Spain, was the preserve above all of aristocratic gentry and tenant-farmers and reinforced the hegemony of the landed classes.

Blood sports were not the exception but the rule at the turn of the century. Aristocrats and plebeians shared in them together, gambling against each other. Hare-coursing, cock-fighting, dog-fighting, bull-baiting, bull-running, and prize-fighting were variations on the same theme. But the propertied classes, laced by a middle-class seriousness, became concerned that popular gatherings for blood-letting, drinking, and gambling could easily escalate into riot. The British Cruelty to Animals Act in 1835 enabled the authorities to suppress the annual bull-running at Stamford in 1838 and 1839, but did not include 'wildlife' (rabbits, deer, foxes) and thus preserved the pleasures of the gentry. Bull-running flourished unabated at small-town festivals in the south of France, although it was not until the 1870s that the full scale *corrida* was introduced from Spain. Dog-fights in Paris, notably at the barrier between Belleville and La Villette, were closed down in 1845 as the city was rebuilt, but cock-fighting remained as popular as ever in the north of France. The enclosure of common land and waste eroded cross-country football which was played between parishes in France and England. The traditional Shrovetide football of Derby, which invariably gave rise to violence, was banned by the town council in 1846, and special constables and dragoons were sent in to enforce the ban.

[11] Quoted by J. L. Carr, *Dictionary of Extraordinary Cricketers* (London, 1983).

The energies expended on violent sports were deliberately channelled into spectator sports, especially horse-racing. The English Jockey Club, founded at Newmarket in 1750, for the purpose of race-horse breeding, established the rules and rituals, the general public were kept in enclosures away from polite society, and off-track betting was severely controlled. Anglomania in France under the July Monarchy inspired the formation of a French Jockey Club in 1834 and the beginnings of horse-racing in the Bois de Boulogne and at Chantilly. The German tradition of organized sport was quite different. The Wars of Liberation stimulated the formation of gymnastic societies and the Swiss and Tyroleans, whose defence was based on the rifle-militia, had a passion for shooting matches. Everywhere however the trend was the same: towards the control of a turbulent society.

Religious Revival

There was a period of marked religious revival in the early nineteenth century, in reaction to the Enlightenment's belief in reason and to the French Revolution's attack on the churches and Christian religion. This revival took place more outside the confines of the established churches than within them. The religious revival nevertheless was balanced by two factors. First, though secular states recognized that religion was a useful instrument of social order, they were no longer prepared to accept churches as independent hierarchies that limited state power, and therefore imposed control over appointments of clergy and education as far as they could. Second, the idea of a state religion, whereby one particular religion was granted a monopoly of public worship in return for its support for the state—the traditional alliance of throne and altar—was attacked by anticlericals who opposed any political involvement of churches, and by minority religions which demanded the right to practice their own religion without fear of discrimination or persecution.

Joseph de Maistre, a Piedmontese noble who had been forced to flee to Switzerland before the French Revolutionary armies, asserted in 1797 that the Revolution was above all satanic and anti-religious. But he also argued that the Revolution had come as a divine punishment for the sins of humanity, which had deserted the true faith under the influence of the Enlightenment. In order to recover God's protection, the afflicted would either have to return to a life or prayer, or take up the sword of counter-revolution.

To re-establish the Catholic Church without playing into the hands of counter-revolution was the riddle that confronted those who wanted to bring the French Revolution to an end. The achievement of Napoleon was to restore the Catholic Church in France under the Concordat of 1802 with Pope Pius VII, but to impose a whole range of controls under the Organic Articles. He did not restore to the Church the lands confiscated by the revolutionaries, but compensated the clergy by paying their stipends from the coffers of the state, which served to make them even more dependent on the state. Moreover, the Catholic Church was now not the state religion but the religion of the majority of French people. The minority Protestant Church was fully tolerated and given its own organizational structure of elected consistories in 1802. In 1807 a Sanhedrin of rabbis and Jewish laymen, modelled on what was supposed to be the ancient supreme council of Palestinian Jewry, was summoned to Paris and a consistorial system was devised for the Jewish minority.

The conquest of Europe by Napoleon's armies did little for the Catholic Church. Monastic property was systematically confiscated. The Papal States were annexed in 1809 and in 1812 the Pope was kidnapped and lodged in the château of Fontainebleau. Jews were given civil rights in Baden and Westphalia in 1808, and in Hamburg in 1811, while the ghettoes were broken open in Rome in 1810 and in Frankfurt in 1811. In Spain, the religious orders were deeply involved in the War of Liberation. The Spanish clergy claimed that Napoleon's invasion was a punishment inflicted by God for the country's sins, that the struggle against Napoleon was a crusade, and that only a return to religion would drive out the invading armies.

The restoration of monarchies in 1814–15 heralded a wave of persecution by vengeful Catholics. Ghettoes were reconstituted in the Papal States and Sardinia-Piedmont. Protestants were slaughtered in the White Terror which swept southern France after Waterloo. Monarchies which had strictly supervised the Church before the Revolution now gratefully conceded it privileges. The Inquisition was brought back to Spain in 1814. The Jesuit order, suppressed in 1773, was formally reconstituted and returned to Sardinia, Spain, Piedmont, and even Austria, where otherwise the state-controls established by Joseph II remained intact. Religious congregations took over schools at all levels under the authority of bishops. In France a law against sacrilege, in 1825, punished the profanation of the sacred host, although the death penalty (after the offending hand had been cut off) was dropped.

Shattered by a quarter of a century of persecution, the Catholic Church was keen to rebuild its structures and authority. In 1814 France had only 36,000 priests, half of the number in 1789, and many parishes lay deserted. Ordinations, which varied between 350 and 500 a year under the Empire, were pushed up to 2,357 in 1830. Missions were preached in towns the length and breadth of France, and stone crosses were erected as symbols of Christ's suffering and powers of redemption. A crowd of 25,000 people attended at Cherbourg, and 40,000 at Avignon. A key role was played by women, whether in religious congregations or not. Women had kept the flame of religion alive in the communities during the 1790s, when the clergy were forced into hiding or exile. Now they flocked into new congregations, devoted to education, nursing, and poor relief. There were 12,300 nuns in France in 1808, 15,000 in 1815, 30,000 in 1830, and 66,000 in 1850. Alongside these operated 'third orders' of widows and spinsters who did not live in religious communities but acted as a spiritual leaven on the community at large, teaching catechism to children and visiting the sick. Lastly there emerged charitable associations of bourgeois women, providing soup for the poor, nurseries for infants, and support for the victims of prostitution. Male orders, though less numerous, were also active.

The renewed alliance of throne and altar and the increasingly high profile of the Catholic Church was opposed by liberals, for whom the revolutions of 1830 had an anticlerical dimension. A service held in the Paris church of Saint-Germain l'Auxerrois in 1831 in honour of the family of the deposed Charles X provoked riots in which both the church and the archbishop's palace were ransacked. Rumours that the regular clergy allied to Carlists were poisoning the wells in Madrid led to riots in 1834 in which 14 Jesuits and 14 Franciscans were killed. Though the authorities in no way approved of this violence, the July Monarchy reduced the influence of the Church in education and removed bishops from the Chamber of Peers, while the Jewish financier Mendizábal, who took office in Spain in 1835, dissolved monasteries and convents and sold off their land.

Though Catholics were in general allied to traditional monarchies and aristocracies, there was nevertheless a movement among some Catholic intellectuals to end the identification of the Catholic Church with despotism and aristocratic privilege, and to make clear that Catholicism could survive and even flourish under the rule of law, a free press, and parliamentary elections. Félicité de Lamennais, who founded a religious order in Brittany in 1828 to serve as the shock troops of Papal intransigence, turned to liberalism after the 1830 Revolution and broadcast his ideas among young clergy and Catholic laity in the *Avenir* newspaper. He had some support among Belgian Catholics and close links with the Polish rebels of 1831. The Papacy, which condemned the Polish insurrection, also condemned the views of Lamennais in the encyclical *Mirari vos* of 15 August 1832. A convergence was nevertheless established between Catholicism, liberalism, and nationalism that exercised many a government in countries that were not predominantly Catholic. The Belgian revolution of 1830 was largely in opposition to the anti-Catholic and anticlerical policies pursued by King William I of the United Netherlands. Irish Catholics were oppressed by a similar Act of Union, exclusion from office including the Bar, and by an Anglican state-church to which they had to pay tithes. Daniel O'Connell managed to squeeze Catholic emancipation from the Parliament at Westminster in 1829 by using the Catholic clergy to mobilize the tenantry. The Prussian government, which annexed the Rhineland in 1815, had to deal with a population that was liberal, Catholic, and for some time pro-French. It appointed loyal servants of the state to the bishoprics of Cologne and Trier and established a new university at Bonn, with a Protestant theological faculty. Catholic opposition in the Rhineland was led by Joseph Görres, who published *Der Katholik* at Mainz, but in 1825 he moved his journal and his circle of intellectuals to the Catholic Kingdom of Bavaria. The Catholics had their revenge in 1834, when the new Archbishop of Cologne, Clemens von Droste-Vischering, emptied the Protestant theological faculty of Bonn of its students. Fearing a separatist breach, the authorities in Berlin arrested the archbishop in 1837. Increasingly German Catholics looked 'beyond the mountains' to Rome for support. King Frederick William IV, who was crowned in 1840, defused the situation. He recognized that the intense conservatism of the Rhenish clergy and nobility could be mobilized against Rhenish liberalism and the new union of throne and altar was symbolized by his presence at the ceremony in 1842 to begin the completion of the magnificent Gothic cathedral of Cologne.

Protestant churches in Europe did not suffer the same degree of persecution, but were still subject to attempts by the state to increase its authority over them. In Prussia, on the three hundredth anniversary of the Reformation in 1817, the Reformed (Calvinist) and Lutheran Churches were fused as a single Evangelical Church, the better to be an instrument of state, an example that was soon followed in Hesse-Darmstadt, Baden, and Württemberg. The establishment of Anglican Church in Ireland was reduced in 1833, while in England an Ecclesiastical Commission was appointed by the government to reorganize Anglican endowments, sees, and bishoprics. This state interference in the Anglican Church was denounced as 'national apostasy' by High Churchmen in England. From their opposition grew the Oxford Movement, disillusion with the Anglican state-church and the conversion to Roman Catholicism of clerics like John Henry Newman (1843) and Henry Edward Manning (1850).

Protestantism witnessed a similar revival of faith to Catholicism, inspired by the same sense of guilt about the revolution and the same craving for redemption. It took place outside the establishment, which had fallen under the control of the state and was identified with the ruling class. Anglican parsons hunted, shot, and sat on the bench of magistrates, while German Protestant clergy were a highly educated ecclesiastical officer corps. The Protestantism of the educated classes and theological faculties in Europe was liberal. It held that man was perfectible. God was revealed by the life and teaching of Christ and the gospels could be freely interpreted by every Christian according to his own reason. Men had the free will to choose between good and evil and would be saved as much by the observance of duty and virtue as by faith. The teaching of the Protestant Revival or Awakening was quite different. It proclaimed that man was utterly sinful and that an unbridgeable gulf separated him from Almighty God. Redemption could be gained only by penitence and faith in the fact that Jesus Christ died on the Cross to save sinners. What was required of sinners was not intellectual effort but a child-like simplicity that would allow God's grace to flow into the empty vessel of the soul and work their conversion. It was then the task of the con-verted to go amongst other sinners, wherever they might be found, and cru-sade to save souls.

The roots of the Revival can be traced back to German Pietism and the Moravian Brethren of Saxony in the early eighteenth century. The move-ment came to England as Methodism after 1730, a movement that carried the gospel to industrial towns, mining communities, and sea-ports, which lay beyond the country-based and paternalistic influence of the Anglican Church. It then returned to the Continent with English and Scottish mission-aries, backed up by the propaganda of the British and Foreign Bible Society which was founded in 1804. In Geneva, the Calvinist national Church was lib-eral, controlled by an oligarchy of magistrates, and found no enthusiastic response among ordinary citizens. But the reformers set up an independent Church in 1817 and (with British help) a Continental Society which sent mis-sionaries all over France. The Revival in France, encouraged from Switzer-land and by English Methodists landing in Normandy, soon found a leader in Pastor Frédéric Monod, who organized his own propaganda machine in 1822. He was confronted by the liberals who dominated the consistories but asserted in 1840 that 'we will act with the consistories everywhere we can, without them if necessary and against them if they force us'.[12] Adolphe Monod, brother of Frédéric, appointed pastor at Lyons in 1827, broke with the liberal consistory in 1827 by adopting the orthodox cause, was dismissed in 1832 and organized the orthodox campaign from the Protestant faculty of theology at Montauban in south-west France. By 1849 the orthodox Protes-tants had triumphed in Geneva although in France, liberal Protestants still held the whip hand.

In Germany liberal Protestantism was the rule in the theological faculties, especially at Halle and Heidelberg, and among university-educated officials. The Awakening, which spread from Baden and Württemberg along the Rhine to the cities and ports of North Germany, rejected the Enlightenment and the Revolution as the work of the Devil. It emphasized sin, regeneration, and grace, and had a mystical, millenarian content. Preachers exalted the vic-tory of the Germans at Leipzig as the prelude to the battle against Antichrist and ascribed an apocalyptic role to Tsar Alexander I. Outside the territorial Churches, the movement was not altogether welcome to the authorities. But Ernst Wilhelm Hengstenberg, professor of theology at Berlin after 1826 and founder of the *Evangelische Kirchen-Zeitung*, who had contacts in aristo-cratic and official circles in Berlin, strove to purge the Awakening of mystical accretions, channel it into strict Lutheran orthodoxy and use it to reinforce the territorial Churches, Protestant Junkers, and Prussian monarchy. Fred-erick William IV was happy after 1840 to take Protestant orthodoxy together with Catholicism to build a Christian state that could fend off all revolution.

[12] Quoted by Samuel Mours, *Un Siècle d' Evangélisation en France, 1815–1914* (Paris, 1963), i, 55.

Just as Catholicism served to underpin nationalism in parts of the British, Dutch, and Prussian states, so Christianity underpinned nationalism in the Ottoman Empire. The Ottoman Empire was far from being a monolithic Islamic state. On the contrary it divided its subjects into different religious groups or *millets*, and gave to each autonomy in matters of worship, education, and justice, under the ministry of foreign affairs, so long as they paid taxes to the state. Thus there was an Orthodox Christian *millet* under the Patriarch of Constantinople, and the Ottomans recognized an Armenian Catholic *millet* in 1830, a Latin (Roman Catholic) *millet* in 1840, a Greek Catholic or Uniate *millet* in 1847, and a Protestant *millet* in 1850. Clearly there were advantages in converting to Islam—membership of the Ottoman élite for feudal lords, exemption from the poll tax for peasants—but there was no attempt at forcible conversion. If Christianity did become allied to Balkan nationalism, it was as much because of conflicts within the Orthodox Christian *millet* as because of conflicts with the Ottoman government. In 1766–7 the Patriarch of Constantinople abolished subordinate patriarchs in Serbia and Bulgaria, which had been crucial for the definition of Serb and Bulgarian identities. Patriarch Gregory V condemned the Greek rising of 1821. He was hanged all the same by the Ottomans on Easter Day, 1821, but the Greeks were careful to set up their own church, independent of Constantinople. Then they established state control over their Church by appointing a government procurator to supervise a Holy Synod which was chaired by the Archbishop of Athens.

The Greeks were imitating the example of Russia, which permitted no clash of loyalties between Church and state. The patriarchate of Moscow was abolished by Peter the Great in 1721 and replaced by a Holy Synod of bishops which was controlled by a lay official, the chief procurator. State control was coupled with the relentless persecution of religious minorities, especially under Nicholas I. The doctrine of Autocracy, Orthodoxy, and Nationality, devised in 1833, took the opposite line from that of the Ottomans and asserted that Orthodoxy alone supported the autocracy and defined Russian national identity. The Jews who were absorbed into Russia by the Partitions of Poland were forced by legislation culminating in 1835 to live in A Pale of Settlement along the western border of the Empire, not least to protect the Moscow merchants from competition. In 1827 Jews were constrained to twenty-five years of military service, without any compensating civil rights and in 1844 their right to tax themselves through the community (*kahal*) structure was abolished and replaced by a system of Jewish functionaries charged with collecting taxes. The Uniates of the Ukraine, who acknowledged the supremacy of Rome, were dragged back to Orthodoxy in a campaign of 1827–39. The insurrection of the Catholic Poles in 1831 was condemned by an encyclical of Pope Gregory XVI, who clearly esteemed the legitimate power of princes before religion. After the revolt was put down convents were closed and episcopal sees filled by reliable clients of the Tsar or, in the case of the See of Warsaw, kept vacant for all but eight years between 1827 and 1883.

The Birth of the Disciplined Society

Three factors in the early nineteenth century changed the relationship of the state and its subjects or citizens in matters of crime and punishment. These were state-building or the growth of bureaucratic centralism, the development of capitalist practices, and urbanization.

The thrust of bureaucratic centralism was to break down feudal structures that had set limits to the power of the state and to assert the monopoly of the legitimate use of force. In Naples and Sicily, where feudalism was abolished in the Napoleonic period, the state came into direct contact with the citizen for the first time, imposing its requirements of taxes and conscripts. Those who refused conscription were outlawed as bandits, and could be legally killed with impunity; but they tended to group in armed bands known as brigands, often under the protection of former feudal lords, who were keen to resist the centralizing state. Armed bands, undermining the state's monopoly of legitimate violence, clearly had to be wiped out.

The development of capitalist practices had the effect of separating peasants from traditional collective rights to woodland and waste, and workers from the ownership of the tools and materials of their trade, in the name of absolute property rights of the landowner or capitalist. The force of the law was brought to bear on any infringements of these absolute property rights, deemed 'inviolable and sacred' by the French National Assembly in 1789, punishing thefts of wood, poaching, arson, embezzlement, machine-breaking, and strikes. Crime rates (both reported and tried) rose dramatically in the early part of the century in Britain, France, and Germany, but there were fewer crimes of blood and more crimes against property.

Some law-breaking was habitually settled within the community, whether in the countryside or in the popular districts of towns, and was not brought to court or even reported. But as the countryside disgorged its population surplus into the growing cities, to seek employment (or remain unemployed), and as that surplus moved from shanty towns and working-class suburbs into the cellars and attics of bourgeois apartment buildings, so middle-class fears of a 'proletariat' which threatened its security and possessions became sharper. In the period 1825–30 French juries acquitted 50 per cent of those accused of crimes against persons, and were particularly indulgent in the south, where heated tempers and vendettas were part of the pattern of life. But they acquitted only 31 per cent of those accused of crimes against property, and were notoriously severe in the more prosperous and urbanized north. Crime against property was seen to be a form of social protest, and at the thin end of the revolutionary wedge.

Against such threats to social and political order the propertied classes had several lines of defence. The most recent were the civilian police who served as a uniformed presence in large towns and shifted the emphasis from the repression to the prevention of crime. The best examples—the Paris *sergents de ville* and the London metropolitan police—were both organized in 1829, and both came under the direction of central government. In England and Wales borough and county police forces were set up under the control of local magistrates in 1835 and 1839 respectively. In Germany, the police forces of Württemberg, Bavaria, and Saxony (with the exception of those of Munich and Dresden) were supervised by local municipalities; in Prussia, however, the municipal reform of 1808 left the control of police in the hands of the central government.

A second line of defence, based on the French model of 1791, was the *gendarmerie*. This was essentially a branch of the army, although placed under ministries of the interior, recruited from ex-soldiers and ordered with military discipline. Moving on both horse and foot, it was detailed to keep order above all in the countryside. Robert Peel set up such forces in Ireland in 1814, when he was Secretary of State for Ireland, but they were regarded as too 'French' and authoritarian for the mainland. Prussia adopted the system in 1812, Piedmont (the *Carabinieri*) in 1814, Russia in 1826, Naples in 1837, Spain (the *Guardia Civil*) in 1844. However, the coverage they provided was often patchy. France had 30,000 *gendarmes* in 1814 but, for financial reasons, the force was cut in Prussia from 9,000 men to little over 1,300 in 1820. In 1848 Berlin had only 120 *gendarmes* and 40 city police for a population of 400,000.

A third line of defence was the bourgeois militia or citizen guard. This force originated in the French Revolution as the armed instrument of property-owners to protect themselves against both popular violence and authoritarian measures. But such forces were held in profound suspicion by reactionary governments, not without reason on occasion, when liberal and even radical ideas infiltrated their ranks. The National Guard of Paris was disbanded by Charles X in 1827, and had to be hurriedly reconstituted during the July revolution. An armed citizenry was anathema to the Prussian government, and was confined to towns where no military garrison existed. The British militia was disbanded in 1814, but special constables mobilized in huge numbers in 1848 dealt effectively with the Chartists in London.

The regular military was the fourth and last line of defence against popular disorder. As a means of keeping civil order, it was essentially counterproductive, serving only to inflame the crowds. In Britain, regulars and the part-time yeomanry, though placed at the disposal of local magistrates, disgraced themselves by firing on the crowds at Peterloo in 1819 and at Queen Caroline's funeral in 1821. In France, military forces used for police purposes were answerable to civilian prefects, but the direct clash of regulars and crowds in 1830 and 1848 twice brought down the monarchy. In Prussia, garrisons fulfilled the functions that police forces served in Britain and France, and after 1819 local military commanders were empowered to use them without reference to civilian authorities in time of crisis. But the clash of the 12,000-strong military and the crowds in Berlin on 18 March 1848 deprived the monarchy of the initiative for eight months.

In times of trouble arrests rose and punishments became more severe. That did not necessarily mean more executions. Indeed, greater emphasis was placed on imprisonment in Prussia after 1797. Capital statutes which had risen in Great Britain from 50 in 1688 to over 200 in 1820 began to be repealed by Parliament in the 1820s and 1830s. The French Penal Code of 1810 shifted the weight of punishment from execution to incarceration and Napoleon established a network of central prisons throughout France. The terror of the death-sentence, a manifestation of arbitrary power made more arbitrary by unequal use of the pardon, gave way to punishments which were less violent but more certain in that a graduated scale applied fixed penalties to categorized crimes. This offered surer protection to property-owners and was supposed to make the potential criminal weigh risks against advantages before he acted.

Prison isolated criminals from society, but reformers felt that the dark gaols into which convicts were thrown served no useful purpose. In 1816 the Quaker Elizabeth Fry went into the women's wing of Newgate Prison, which was a den of idleness, fighting, and swearing. She had the women's earrings removed, their hair cropped, clothed them in plain smocks, and set them to sew and pray. Humiliation before God was a pre-condition of moral reformation. The Peterloo riots discredited Elizabeth Fry's Evangelical method as naïve. Magistrates and prison governors panicked and installed a regime of terror in English prisons. Between 1818 and 1824 treadmills were installed in prisons in twenty-six counties. In Prussia, prisons had once played an important economic role, working up raw materials for local manufacturers. Now outside labour did the job more cheaply and efficiently, and prison work tailed off. In 1818, the authorities in Düsseldorf became concerned that inactive prisoners of both sexes had started an orgy of self-abuse. For moral rather than economic reasons, marble-polishing was imposed under military discipline.

What kind of prisons should be built became a major concern of governments. In 1831 Alexis de Tocqueville was sent by the French government to visit the model prisons of the United States. An official British mission followed in 1834. Auburn and Sing Sing prisons in New York State practised the silent system, with prisoners picking oakum and crushing bones together in the same workshop. At Walnut Street Prison in Philadelphia the prisoners were confined permanently to separate cells, and did their work alone. All the visitors favoured the system of solitary confinement. It was less like a factory. The criminal subculture was completely destroyed and the prisoner was thrown back on his own conscience to feel guilt, repent, and reform. It became the model for a new generation of prisons, beginning with Petite Roquette (1836) and Pentonville (1842). Prisoners were required to wear leather hoods when they exercised, so that they could not recognize their fellows, and were penned up in little boxes facing the chaplain when they attended chapel. Prison chaplains favoured the system because it made the inmates open to religious conversion and moral reform. Utilitarians welcomed the new prisons as realizations of Jeremy Bentham's dream of the panopticon, in which all the prisoners were constantly visible from a central tower and, naked before inspections which served as a mirror of their own souls, were obliged by moral pressure rather than physical terror to behave. Practical problems nevertheless confronted reformers. As convictions increased, so did overcrowding, which undermined the ideal of solitary confinement. In many Prussian prisons, the prison population doubled between 1836 and 1840 alone. To build a satisfactory number of prisons was a financial impossibility for governments. In 1854, following the political unrest of 1848–52, the Second Empire revived the practice of transporting convicts to do forced labour in French Guiana.

'Poverty, misery, are the parents of crime', said William Cobbett in 1816.[13] A more far-reaching solution to the threat of crime was therefore the relief of poverty. But the European population was growing far more rapidly than sources of employment to maintain it. The private charity of manorial lords and churches was dealt a heavy blow during the Revolutionary years, and rural parishes which had some means of relieving their poor were losing much of their surplus population to urban parishes which could not. In the mid-1830s the proportion of the population receiving poor relief was 4 per cent in Geneva, 12 per cent in Paris and a staggering 45 per cent in Venice.

Simply to dole out more relief was no solution to the problem, and the bourgeois approach to reform was influenced as much by economy as the need for public order. A distinction had to be drawn between the deserving poor, who could not help themselves, such as foundlings, orphans, the aged, sick, crippled, and maimed, and the undeserving poor who preferred living on charity to honest labour. The French Constituent Assembly set up a commission on mendicancy and in 1796 legislation provided for hospices for the sick and required every commune to organize a *bureau de bienfaisance* for outdoor relief. The idle, on the other hand, were dealt with harshly to drive them back to the labour market. A decree of Napoleon in 1808 sent vagabonds to prison and beggars to *dépôts de mendicité* where they were subjected to forced labour.

The French established *dépôts* in Rhineland towns such as Trier which remained after 1815. Begging was prohibited in Germany and beggars were

---

[13] Quoted by Michael Ignatieff, *A Just Measure of Pain: The Penitentiary in the Industrial Revolution, 1750–1850* (London, 1978), 109.

shut up in prison or applied to forced labour in workhouses. Workhouses in Germany were open to free labour that was temporarily unemployed, and was set to spin linen and other tasks. Hamburg made contracts with local industrialists after 1788 to give the unemployed work in their homes. They were paid below the market wage in order to encourage them to find work elsewhere. After the emancipation of the serfs and with the annexation of the Rhineland there was a shift of population from east to west in Prussia. They went in search of work, but work was not always to be had. Neither beggars nor sick, they were nevertheless unable to fend for themselves. Urban communities resented having to shoulder the burden of rural communities and a Prussian Poor Law of 1842 required communities to provide relief only if the pauper had been accepted by the community and contributed to its expenses or been resident there for three years.

In England the agricultural counties of the south felt the burden of the poor more than the industrial north, where employment was expanding. The allowance system adopted in the south in 1795 whereby the unemployed were put to work on farms and their wages made up to subsistence level from the parish rates served only to tie up a surplus labour force where it was not wanted and became increasingly expensive after the Napoleonic Wars. Paupers, including the able-bodied, were also in receipt of outdoor relief from workhouses, which were meant primarily for abandoned children, the aged, and sick. A new Poor Law in 1834 did not resort to the French practice of forced labour but abolished outdoor relief for the able-bodied poor. They were given the choice either of entering a workhouse—and a string of new ones was built across the country—or of returning to the labour market in search of employment. Pauperism was to be reduced, public money saved, and the labour market stocked by making the alternative to honest labour unpalatable. Unfortunately, what reformers in England, France, and Germany refused to recognize was the phenomenon of involuntary unemployment: that people might be thrown out of work against their will by seasonal, cyclical, or structural changes. The New Poor Law was applied in the North of England just as a cyclical depression struck. Unemployed millhands and weavers were faced with the choice of the workhouse or starvation, and rioted. For the European middle classes unemployment was voluntary, nothing but idleness and work-shyness, a moral failing like any other.

'As soon as a good administration of the Poor Laws shall have rendered further improvement possible', concluded the English Poor Law Report of 1834, 'the most important duty of the Legislature is to take measures to promote the religious and moral education of the labouring classes.'[14] The previous year, arguing the case for a national system of elementary education, the radical Roebuck said that poor laws and prisons dealt only with the

[14] Quoted by S. F. Finer, *The Life and Times of Sir Edwin Chadwick* (London, 1952), 151.

evil, and that the evil itself was ignorance. The received view was
erty was the result of vice—of drunkenness, gambling, debauchery,
idence, and prostitution (which was badly paid). The middle classes
ssed fear and loathing of a race of degenerate and brutish men and
en who gratified their appetites instead of improving themselves. It was
d that they had no knowledge of good and evil, were 'without religion', and
ere consequently a menace to society. The Frenchman H. A. Frégier, who
coined the expression 'the dangerous classes' in 1840, observed that 'when
vice … allies itself with poverty in the same individual, it is a proper object of
fear to society, it is dangerous.'[15]

If the dangerous classes were to be won back to religion and morality some
framework to grasp them had to be found. Schools were one solution, but
schools had to be devised for children who had to work during the week,
including Saturdays, and for adolescents who had received only a minimum
of education. The corrupt reading material of the proletariat (for such as
could read) had to be fought by more improving literature. Lastly, the
deserving poor, including foundlings, orphans, the neglected infants of working mothers, adolescent girls on the streets, the sick, and the aged had to be
brought within the pale of religious life.

Followers of Jeremy Bentham were interested less in forming submissive
Christians than enlightened and industrious economic men. George Birk-
beck, who gave courses in applied science in Glasgow, was taken up by Henry
Brougham and the Benthamites after he moved to London and in 1823 the
London Mechanics' Institute was opened. By 1850 there were 610 Mechan-
ics' Institutes in England, with a membership of 102,000, although skilled
workers, clerks, and even young professional men far outnumbered the
unskilled working class. In France Baron Charles Dupin, a graduate of the
École Polytechnique who lectured at the Conservatoire Royal des Arts et
Métiers and was impressed by the commercial and naval supremacy of Great
Britain, persuaded the Minister of the Interior in 1825 to urge municipalities
to found courses in geometry and applied mechanics for the working classes.
The Society for the Diffusion of Useful Knowledge, founded by Henry
Brougham in 1827, aimed to teach workers the value of science in order to
make industry more productive and society more industrious and harmo-
nious. Not to be outdone, German Benthamites responded by founding the
Society for the Diffusion of Useful Knowledge in the Field of Natural Sciences, Technical Science, and Political Economy.

English Evangelicals began to tackle the problem in the 1780s and 1790s
with the promotion of the Sunday School movement, which was particularly
vigorous in the industrial Midlands and North of England. Hannah More,

[15] Quoted by Robert Tombs, 'Crime and the Security of the State: the "Dangerous Classes"
and Insurrection in Nineteenth-Century Paris', in V. A. C. Gatrell (ed.), *Crime and the Law*
(London, 1980), 217.

known to Cobbett as 'the old bishop in petticoats', and the Religious Tract Society, founded in 1799, distributed Bibles and other works of religion, no less than 314,000 copies of them in 1804 alone. In 1812 the British and Foreign School Society was set up to spread the system of mutual education which had been developed by the Quaker Joseph Lancaster. In these schools, small groups were placed under the supervision of older children who acted as monitors, multiplying the eyes and ears of the school teacher. A scale of rewards and punishments and emulation among sub-groups ensured the maximum industry and achievement. The mutual system was imported into France and supported by Napoleon's Minister of Public Instruction, Lazare Carnot, during the Hundred Days between the return from Elba and Waterloo. Largely for this reason it was opposed by the Catholic clergy and Restoration establishment, which denounced its pedagogy as mechanical and irreligious. But it enjoyed the support of ideologues, political economists, Protestant missionaries, and a minority of reforming prefects, all of whom argued that it provided a religious education, and it played an important role down to the Guizot law.

The Catholic Church responded quickly in France by resurrecting teaching congregations like the Frères des Écoles Chrétiennes, which had been abolished at the Restoration, and which royalist municipalities were happy to fund. Jean-Marie de la Mennais, brother of Félicité, and vicar-general of Saint-Brieuc in Brittany, set up a teaching congregation with special responsibility for rural schools in 1821. A Société Catholique des Bons Livres was founded in Paris in 1825 to counter revolutionary propaganda and to propagate 'those salutary doctrines that are the foundation of virtue and the guarantee of the stability of all social institutions'. Clerico-royalist nobles collaborated closely with the Catholic clergy in the foundation of the Société de Saint Vincent de Paul in 1833. Under the auspices of this society *patronages* were set up to provide innocent recreation and religious instruction for apprentices and young workers, to keep them away from drinking, gambling, blood-sports, and the theatre. Adolescent girls were set to work making lace and repeating the catechism in *ouvroirs*, under the eye of nuns, to safeguard them from falling into prostitution. Whereas the servants, seamstresses, and silk workers of Lyons either stopped work when they married or sent their children out to wet-nurses at considerable expense, the working wives of Milan had the free facility of the Catholic foundling hospital, which was far from being a dumping ground for unwanted babies, since most were collected again after a year or two.

Catholics had no monopoly of moral rescue. Protestants, and particularly the German Lutherans of the Awakening, were also struggling to save souls. Every village in the Grand Duchy of Saxe-Weimar, reported one French observer in 1831, had its nursery. The war had left tens of thousands of children orphaned or abandoned. The Royal Orphan House of Potsdam alone had a thousand boys in the 1830s, all sons of soldiers and destined to be soldiers themselves. Johann Heinrich Wichern, who had studied theology at Göttingen and Berlin but disliked the liberal, rarified world of the universities, threw himself into the work of organizing Sunday Schools, orphanages, and *Rettungshäuser* for abandoned children. Particularly successful was the *Rauhe Haus* or Rough House for homeless children that he set up in 1833 and ran like a large family instead of as a barracks. Amelie Sieveking, the daughter of a town syndic of Hamburg, who worked heroically in the city's hospitals during the cholera epidemic of 1831–2, sought to continue the mission through the Women's Society for the Care of the Poor and the Sick that she founded in 1832. The Prison Society of Rhineland-Westphalia, organized in 1827, trained women as 'deaconesses' to serve in prisons and hospitals, notably that of Kaiserwerth, where Florence Nightingale trained. The absence of religious orders in a Protestant country was no obstacle to what Wichern called the 'Inner Mission'.

The Romantic Revolt

Not all revolts against the established order ended in street-fighting. For some intellectuals, alienated from the real world, the main form of protest was aesthetic. This did not necessarily empty it of political content: art was, to some extent, the continuation of politics by other means. The manifestation of this protest was the Romantic movement, which revolutionized literature, painting, and music in the first thirty or forty years of the nineteenth century.

It is extremely difficult to pin down and analyse this movement, and it would be wrong to give too much unity to a phenomenon which threw up three distinct generations of artists and influenced educated Europeans from Madrid to Moscow. The first generation was that born around the year 1770, which had its roots in Germany and an elder statesman in Goethe. The second was born about 1790, and was attracted to the sunlit Mediterranean. The third generation was born around 1800, with a slightly smaller wave born about 1810, and was essentially French or based in Paris.

In the German states of the 1790s, young educated men were either excluded from careers in the public service by the monopolization of important offices by the nobility or abandoned them because of opposition to the military and autocratic regimes. The French Revolution appeared to them as a new religion of freedom, equality, and liberty and stirred up hopes of fashioning a better world in the light of reason. But the vision of a new world soon darkened, as constitution-making gave way to mob rule, regicide, terror, atheism, and then military dictatorship. Disillusionment set in; it seemed that mankind was as yet unfit for destiny.

Seeking consolation, a handful of German writers gathered at Jena around Friedrich Schiller. The circle included the brothers Schlegel, August Wilhelm and Friedrich, and Schelling, who became professor of philosophy at

Jena University in 1798. That year, which saw the first issue of the circle's review, the *Athenaeum*, may serve as the base-line of the German Romantic movement. These Romantics were ill at ease in the society in which they found themselves but were not activists who would take up weapons for a cause. Feeling themselves incomplete and pulled in opposite directions by the mundane and the sublime, by the rational and irrational in their hearts, they reached out to what was infinite and eternal in the world beyond the disappointments of everyday life, in a search for spiritual happiness. Schelling found satisfaction in a pantheistic interpretation of the world. For him, nature was not chaotic and senseless, but directed towards a higher goal. It was moved by a spiritual force, which strove to organize it into higher and higher forms, from stones to plants to animals, until it reached perfection in the mind of man. By exploring his own consciousness, therefore, man might come to understand the workings of this spiritual force in nature. Here the artist came into his own. For art was the means of expressing this spiritual dimension of the world, its timelessness and infinity, clothing it in sensuous form, whether in poetry, painting, or music. The artist was he who could reconcile the spiritual with the real by fixing it in the beautiful and end, for himself and those who shared in this creation, the inner discord in man.

The artist needed inspiration, and found it first and foremost in nature. To contemplate sheer mountain faces, the starlit heavens, storm-tossed seas, caves, and tall pine forests was to contemplate the divine in nature. The Creation was God's handwriting. The ancient world, whose ideals were essentially human and sensual, could not satisfy a craving for the world beyond, which presupposed Christianity. The Romantics therefore studied the Middle Ages, the Christian civilization *par excellence*, with its Gothic cathedrals, chivalrous knights, and popular faith. In the Courts of Europe, music, drama, and painting were all determined by classical models. These the romantics rejected as transplanted from other societies, and sacrificing truth to elegance. Instead, they turned to popular songs and stories, as told by bards and troubadours, which were not the work of individuals but, it seemed, the manifestation of the collective soul of the people, the *Volk*, and expressed its inner life. Fairy tales, with their caverns and forests, monsters and witches, seemed to betray primitive and unconscious fears and the fluidity of the division between fact and fantasy. Jakob Grimm, who collected them at Heidelberg in the years after 1805, believed that they were shorthand versions of the great myths and legends which were fundamentally the same all over Europe, and that they had been planted by God in the consciousness of the peasantry.

The Romantic poet was considered to be a seer or prophet who could lift the veil on the visible world and reveal the invisible. He was inspired, and his inspiration was interpreted as a divine visitation or as the surge of the unconscious over the conscious mind as he drifted into the realm of dreams, trances, and visions. This meant that in his search for a new language to express himself he was obliged to break existing artistic conventions which required an elegance and polish that stifled all feelings. Genius was diametrically opposed to rules. In addition, the Romantic poet communicated directly with his public, rejecting politeness and form, and baring his soul with all its pain and ecstasy. However, there were contradictions in the Romantic position. For all his inspiration, the artist still had to work at his art, and find people to buy it. Yet, because the common mass of humanity was so far beneath him, he had nothing but contempt for it. When Madame de Staël visited Goethe in 1803 she found him portly and satisfied with success, and not at all like the melancholy hero of his novel. 'Goethe really spoils the ideal of Werther for me', she wrote.[16]

Madame de Staël, who knew the Schlegels well, publicized German Romanticism in France in her study *On Germany* (1810), published in France as *De l'Allemagne* (1813). A parallel Romanticism had already taken some root as a result of the work of François-René de Chateaubriand, who returned from exile in England in 1800, after Bonaparte made conditions easier for royalist nobles. Yet as he wrote to Madame de Staël a year later, 'I have withdrawn a second time from the world, now that I can stay on French soil … I have returned to the desert, and am seriously thinking of dying there.'[17] In 1802 he published the *Génie du Christianisme*, which was a rehabilitation of the Catholic religion, not as a political force (although its political significance was appreciated by Bonaparte) but as poetry. Chateaubriand meditated on the Gothic cathedral, with its vaults and spires stretching towards heaven, and saw it as a petrified forest, which would eventually be reclaimed by nature as overgrown ruins.

Chateaubriand, who did not discover even the South of France until after his book appeared, was a representative of North European Romanticism. So also were the Romantics of the British Isles who were born around 1770— Sir Walter Scott, Samuel Taylor Coleridge, and William Wordsworth. Scott made his mark as a collector of ballads, which he published in 1802 as *The Minstrelsy of the Scottish Border*, and used the form of the romance in his own poetry, such as the *Lay of the Last Minstrel* (1805). However, he subsequently criticized many of the defects of the romance—supernatural interventions, a stereotyped cast of tyrannical counts and innocent maidens—and launched into the novel, which was set in the 'ordinary train of events' and allowed him to study the complexity of 'human passions and human characters'. Scott was not, like Chateaubriand, a very religious man, but he was fascinated by turning points in history, at which traditional communities and

---

[16] Quoted by W. H. Bruford, *Culture and Society in Classical Weimar, 1775–1806* (Cambridge, 1962), 393.

[17] Chateaubriand to Madame de Staël, 24 Aug. 1801, in *Correspondance générale, 1789–1807* (Paris, 1977), 144.

hierarchies were replaced by more materialistic, less honourable societies. His first concern, beginning with his novel *Waverley* in 1814, was the destruction of the clan system in Scotland after the suppression of the 1745 Jacobite rebellion. Only later did he take on medieval subjects, such as the clash between Saxon and Norman in *Ivanhoe* (1819) and the waning of feudalism and the spirit of chivalry in *Quentin Durward* (1823). These were not necessarily his best works, but they were certainly his most popular, both in England and on the continent. Paris was swept by a craze for Scott in 1822–7 and Scott was present at Rossini's opera *Ivanhoe* there in 1826.

The attitude of Wordsworth and Coleridge to historical change was ambivalent. At first they welcomed the French Revolution as a blow for hope and liberty. Later (in Coleridge's case after France's invasion of Switzerland in 1798) they turned against it and retreated to the Lake District. Coleridge, who saw himself as a philosopher as well as a poet, read German and travelled in Germany, was impressed by Schelling's pantheism. But his sense of wonder before nature was not unshakeable, and he wrote that when he observed nature, its message to him of the world beyond was less important than the meaning that his own feelings imposed on it. Wordsworth said in the *Prelude* (written 1798–1805) that the limits of ordinary experience could be transcended only in 'spots of time' and that Mont Blanc had appeared to him as 'a soulless image on the eye/ Which had usurped upon a living thought'. The Alps did not always generate sentiments of the divine. Wordsworth's dictum in the preface (1800) to the *Lyrical Ballads* published by Coleridge and himself that 'poetry is the spontaneous overflow of powerful feelings' points to the boundless inspiration of genius. But he went on to say that poetry resulted only from long and deep thought, and in 1810 warned that 'if words were not ... an incarnation of the thought but only a clothing for it, then surely will they prove an ill gift'.[18]

In order to express thoughts and feelings, some language was needed, but the medium of that language could distort or obscure the purity and immediacy of those feelings. Turner, who visited the Lake District in 1798 and was influenced by poetry which tried to express the moods of nature (though not by that of Wordsworth and Coleridge) took landscape painting as his medium. Yet instead of being trapped by the form of natural objects, he used light and colour to suggest the effects of sun, or rain, or storm. 'They are pictures of the elements of air, earth and water', wrote the essayist Hazlitt in 1816. 'The artist delights to go back to the first chaos of the world ... when the waters separated from the dry land and light from darkness .... All is without forms and void.'[19]

With plastic art, the medium was difficult to transcend. At the other end of

[18] Quoted by Jonathan Wordsworth, *William Wordsworth: The Borders of Vision* (Oxford, 1982), 210–11.
[19] Quoted by Jack Lindsay, *J. M. W. Turner, His Life and Work* (London, 1966), 109.

the spectrum was music, especially in the way it was revolutionized by Beethoven. 'It is the only genuinely Romantic art', insisted the writer and composer E. T. A. Hoffmann in 1813, 'for its subject is the eternal ... Music unfolds before men a new kingdom, a world that has nothing in common with the world of sensuous reality around us, and in which we leave behind all *precise* emotions in order to surrender ourselves to an ineffable yearning. Beethoven's music opens the flood gates of fear, of terror, of horror, of pain, and arouses that longing for the eternal which is the essence of Romanticism. He is thus a pure Romantic composer.'[20] To Wagner, Beethoven's deafness (which set in soon after 1800) seemed an advantage. 'Undisturbed by the bustle of life', he wrote, Beethoven 'only heard the harmonies of his soul'.[21] His *Eroica* symphony, completed in 1804, recast the symphony as a psychological journey of struggle and triumph. But Beethoven's struggle was not over. After its first performance in Vienna in 1805 the *Freymuthige* correspondant noted that 'The public and Herr Beethoven, who conducted, were not satisfied with each other this evening; the public thought the symphony too heavy, too long, and himself too discourteous, because he did not nod his head in recognition of the applause which came from a portion of the audience. On the contrary, Beethoven found that the applause was not strong enough.'[22] Moreover, Hoffmann's comment was written at the high point of Beethoven's career in the Vienna of the Congress. Between 1817 and the Ninth Symphony in 1824 he wrote virtually nothing.

When Rossini, composer of *The Barber of Seville*, visited Beethoven in 1822, he was told to stick to *opera buffa*, which suited the language and temperament of Italians. The difference between the two, nevertheless, was not just one of nationality. Rossini was twenty-two years younger than Beethoven, and belonged to a generation which had not experienced the French Revolution as trauma, but instead felt stifled by the rallying of conservative forces in Europe against France, the country of liberty. Young men in 1810 had an enthusiasm for life and liberty which was denied to them by their elders. They rejected established religion and the Middle Ages as reactionary, and sought a spiritual home in the Mediterranean. The French writer Stendhal, who settled in Milan for several years after 1814, said in 1824 that Rossini's music appealed especially to Italian lovers, for 'love in Italy is far more dynamic, more impatient, more violent, less dependent on dreams and imagination ... it takes the whole being by storm, and its invasion is the work of an instant; it is a frenzy'.[23] But Rossini's operas were also successful in France and provoked a *musicomanía* in Spain; they echoed the cult of a new sexuality.

It may seem strange to evoke Ingres as painting's response to this develop-

[20]   Quoted in Siegbert Prawer (ed.), *The Romantic Period in Germany* (London, 1970), 285.
[21]   Richard Wagner, *Beethoven*, trans. A. R. Parsons (New York, 1873), 78.
[22]   Quoted by Elliott Forbes, *Thayer's Life of Beethoven* (Princeton, 1964), i, 376.
[23]   Stendhal, *Life of Rossini* (London, 1970), 37.

ment. Yet Ingres, a native of Languedoc in southern France, reacted against the grand heroic style of his master, David, adopting a more graceful, intimate flavour inspired by Raphael and the Italian primitives. He went to Italy in 1806 after winning the Prix de Rome, worked for Murat while he was King of Naples, and stayed on in Rome and Florence for ten years after the collapse of French rule in Italy (1814). Between 1812 and 1826 he painted nothing that was inspired by the ancient world, but took his themes from the Middle Ages and Renaissance. His *Grande Odalisque*, with her soft, curving body and dream-like face, bewildered critics at the Salon of 1819. It was not until 1827 that Ingres took up the defence of the classical, academic tradition against the rising generation. Even then, the poet and art critic Baudelaire noted that 'for me, one of the things which distinguishes the talent of M. Ingres is his love of woman. His libertinism is serious and full of conviction.'[24]

In Great Britain, at war with Revolutionary France, radical Romanticism was all but stifled. The main exception was William Blake, an artisan engraver and Dissenter who was closely linked in the early 1790s with radicals such as Tom Paine and William Godwin. The reaction against the Revolution in France meant that his poem, *The French Revolution* (1791), was never published, and he was driven into a private world of his own, full of Biblical references and visions of the Last Judgment. He saw the war waged by Great Britain on France as a war waged against Liberty and Humanity, and a war which served only to increase exploitation at home, whether of conscript soldiers, transported slaves, starving children, chimney-sweeps, or of workers in the 'smokey dungeons' of mills and factories. Even thought was oppressed by 'mind-forg'd manacles'.

The call of liberty was taken up by a new generation of writers, over thirty years younger than Blake, led by Shelley and Byron. Neither could breathe easily in England, when reaction seemed institutionalized in Church and state. Shelley devoted his time at Oxford to electrical experiments, and was expelled in 1811 for publishing a pamphlet on the *Necessity of Atheism*. He then cultivated the radical atheist William Godwin, published *Queen Mab* (1813), which attacked Christianity, the monarchy, and marriage in the name of free love and eloped with Godwin's daughter Mary to Switzerland. In 1809–11 Byron had travelled to Greece and Turkey with a friend, mingled with the crowds in the streets and *souks*, picked up local dialects and venereal disease, and returned to write the self-dramatizing *Childe Harold's Pilgrimage* (1813). After the scandalous breakup of Byron's marriage and Mary Shelley's triumph with *Frankenstein* (1818), in which a creative dream turns out to be a nightmare, Byron and the Shelleys left for Italy.

The Middle Ages worshipped as a golden age by the previous generation of Romantics was rejected by Shelley and Byron as feudal and priest-ridden,

[24] Charles Baudelaire, 'Le Musée classique du bazar Bonne-Nouvelle', (1846), in *Œuvres complètes* (Paris, 1966), 872.

built on a Christianity which had divided man's soul between this world and the next. The voyage to Italy represented not a homage to classical canons of taste, nor a cult of Rome, which they found despotic, but a discovery of paganism, which placed man in the centre of the world, of Greek art, which harmonized man and nature, and of Italian women, for whom sex meant pleasure not guilt. Shelley was inspired by Aeschylus' drama, *Prometheus Bound*, and wrote *Prometheus Unbound* (1819), the story of the struggle of the fire-bringer and liberator of mankind against Jupiter, the author of darkness and oppression in the universe. Byron found his true voice with *Don Juan*, the first two cantos of which were also published in 1819. Conjured up by Dante, but even more by his rakish life in Venice, it provoked frenzied adulation in England, and an enormous fan-mail, especially from women, but also outright condemnation as wicked and pornographic. Byron defended it as 'quietly facetious', but also 'the most moral of poems', intended to expose English cant—'cant political, cant poetical, cant religious, cant moral'. One correspondant, 'John Bull' (who turned out to be Sir Walter Scott's son-in-law), said that it was 'written strongly, lasciviously, fiercely, laughingly; everybody sees in a moment that nobody could have written it but a man of the first order both in genius and dissipation—a real master of all his tools—a profligate, pernicious, irresistible, charming Devil'.[25]

Worshipped as 'stars', denounced as villains, expected to turn out only what their public wanted, and to behave in their lives as they did in their fantasies, Romantic poets like Byron and Shelley found their existence increasingly difficult. Both were enthusiastic about the liberal revolutions of 1820–1, and Byron had contacts with Carbonari who tried to launch a rising in the Romagna. Shelley drowned in a shipwreck in the Gulf of Spezia in 1822. Byron sailed for Greece in 1823 in order to help organize the Greek struggle for independence against the Turks, but he fell ill and died the following spring. Both were burnt out by their passion for life and liberty.

The third Romantic generation, the *enfants du siècle* born around 1800, were poignantly described by Alfred de Musset. 'Conceived between two battles, brought up in colleges to the roll of drums … They had dreamed for fifteen years of the snows of Moscow and the sun of the Pyramids.' Then Napoleon's Empire collapsed, and reaction set in. 'When the children spoke of glory, they were told, "Become priests"; when they spoke of ambition, "Become priests"; of hope, love, force and life, "Become priests".'[26] The Catholic Church held few charms for educated youth, but royalism was often another matter. For Victor Hugo, the Empire was represented by his father, who had fought under Joseph Bonaparte in Italy and Spain, and was inconsiderate and unfaithful to his wife. He took the side of his mother whose royalist background in the west of France he subsequently mythologized. In July

[25] Quoted by Leslie A. Marchand, *Byron: A Biography* (London, 1957), 750, 766, 900, 911.
[26] Alfred de Musset, *Confessions d' un enfant du siècle* (Paris, 1865) 6.

1815, Victor Hugo wrote 'Vive le roi!' in his Latin grammar and a year later proclaimed, 'I want to be Chateaubriand or nothing'.[27]

Unlike the generation of 1790, this generation searched for a spiritual dimension to life; unlike that of 1770, it saw art and politics as inseparably linked. Victor Hugo's concern for the greatness of France, which seemed irrelevant to the restored monarchy, and his sense that some of the essential gains of the Revolution had been saved by the Empire, led him back to a reverence for Napoleon by 1827. His (unperformable) play *Cromwell*, published that year, was a meditation on Napoleon, the preface of which served as an artistic manifesto. In it, he criticized the unity of place and time imposed by the classical theatre, which confined all the action to a banal peristyle and expelled all drama to the wings. He attacked the stilted rhetoric required of actors and the eternal cult of beauty. Inspired by Shakespeare, he noted that 'the ugly exists alongside the beautiful, the deformed close to the gracious, the grotesque on the reverse of the sublime, evil with good, shadow with light'. In 1829 he clashed with the government censor, who banned his new play *Marion de Lorme* on the grounds that it insulted Charles X through the person of Louis XIII. Victor Hugo replied with *Hernani*, where the action was transported to Spain, and the epithets 'coward', 'madman', and 'bad king' were addressed to the young Charles V. For fear of provoking a press storm, the censor let it through. At the first performance, on 25 February 1830, scuffles broke out between the partisans of the romantics, with their beards, long hair, and extravagant clothes, and the defenders of classicism. The critical reception was lukewarm, but popular acclamation was intense, and *Hernani* played right through the July Revolution until November.

July 28: Liberty leading the people is perhaps the most striking painting of the 1830 Revolution in Paris. Its author, Eugène Delacroix, had already caused something of a sensation at the Salon of 1827. He was criticized for not knowing the difference between a sketch and a painting, but as Baudelaire later remarked, 'Delacroix starts from this principle, that a painting must above all reproduce the inward thought of the artist … movement, colour and atmosphere … of necessity require a rather vague contour, light and floating lines, and bold brush strokes.'[28] Delacroix painted not heroism or sensuality but physical and mental anguish. The Greek struggle for independence inspired his *Massacre of Chios* (1821–4), Shakespeare and Dante appealed to him as portrayers of human suffering, and Byron's poem evoking the Assyrian King Sardanapalus, waiting for death, became his canvas of 1827–8. Because the painting of Delacroix did not have a fine finish, it was assumed that he worked like a madman possessed. Yet the contradiction for the Romantic artist was that the initial inspiration could not be sustained for the time needed to complete the painting. 'The result of my days is always the

---

[27] Quoted by Hubert Juin, *Victor Hugo*, i, *1802–1843* (Paris, 1980), 245, 264.
[28] Baudelaire, 'Salon de 1846', in *Œuvres complètes*, 891–2.

same,' Delacroix confided to his diary in 1824, 'an infinite desire which is never realized ... If only I could savour at leisure the impressions which I alone feel ... the innocent pleasures that every experience induces in a vivid imagination are not destroyed by the passage of years; every moment that passes distorts or dissolves them.'[29]

In 1838 Delacroix began a study of his friend, the musician Chopin, improvising at the piano, his face tormented by inspiration, with George Sand, his lover, beside him, her arms folded, deep in thought. The picture should have been executed rapidly, to capture the moment; instead, work was interrupted, and it remained unfinished. Chopin, a Pole who never returned to his native country after its invasion by Russia in 1831, racked by sickness, fearful of death, suave, and modest in society but expressing his inner feelings in passionate piano melodies, was almost a caricature of the Romantic composer. 'His creation was spontaneous, miraculous', wrote George Sand after his death at the age of thirty-nine, but to pin the dancing tune on to a score-sheet was 'the most heart-rending labour I have ever witnessed ... He shuts himself in his room for whole days, crying, pacing, breaking his pens, repeating and changing the same bar a hundred times, writing it and rubbing it out as many times ... He spent six weeks on a page only to return to what he had scribbled at the first attempt.'[30] Chopin played very little in public, partly because of his frail constitution, partly because he feared that he would not be understood. Instead, he gave salon recitals before a few intimate friends. Franz Liszt, who played much of Chopin's work in public and had women overcome with emotion, took the contrary view that 'the poet, torn from his solitary inspiration, can only find it in the interest—more than attentive, vivid and animated—of his audience ... He must *feel* that he moves, that he agitates those who hear him, that his emotions find in them the responsive sympathies of the same intuitions, that he draws them on with him in his flight towards the infinite.'[31] With Lizst, the magnesium sincerity of the Romantic soul was exploited as show business.

[29]   Eugène Delacroix, *Journal, 1822–1863* (Paris, 1980), 71–2.
[30]   George Sand, 'Histoire de ma vie', in *Œuvres autobiographiques* (Paris, 1971), ii, 446.
[31]   Franz Liszt, *Life of Chopin* (4th edn., London, 1872), 85.

PART II

Europe 1850–1880

6

MID-CENTURY PROSPERITY

Urbanization

The period between 1850 and 1873 in Europe was one of prosperity, marked off from the 'hungry forties' on the one hand and from the 'Great Depression' on the other. Doubts have been cast on the magnitude and continuity of the boom. Nevertheless, the population of Europe multiplied, foreign and domestic markets expanded, there was heavy investment in railways and urban development, prices remained high between the inflationary spurts of 1853–5 and 1870–2, real wages remained steady, and large profits were to be made where costs could be cut by mechanization and improved transport.

These developments did not occur everywhere at the same pace. From the demographic and economic point of view, the countries of northern and western Europe remained more advanced than those of the south and east, although the position of France was ambiguous. Between 1851 and 1881 its population scarcely increased at all. Germany, on the other hand, not only overtook France in terms of the number of its inhabitants, but also achieved a rate of population growth which was very close behind that of England. Within the British Isles, the population of Scotland rose more slowly than it had done earlier in the century, while that of Ireland, as a result of the famine, went into a steep decline. In Scandinavia, the rate of population increase was slightly faster than before 1850, but it could not match the growth of the Russian populations. Bringing up the rear were Austria-Hungary and the Mediterranean countries, where the population increase was altogether more sluggish.

Whereas the main cause of population increase in the first half of the century was the declining death-rate, the main cause in this period was a rising birth-rate. It was in the 1870s that the birth-rate, in western Europe at least, reached its peak for the nineteenth century. This was because industrialization in north-west Europe increased possibilities of employment and encouraged young migrants to the towns to marry earlier than they might have done in the countryside, where land was scarce. If women and children as well as adult males could find work in the mines and the factories, the incentive to raise large families was even greater. On the other hand harsh conditions of life and labour also pushed up the death-rate among the poor.

TABLE 4. *The population of European countries, 1851–1881 (m.)*

	1851	1881	Average annual rate of growth (%)
France	35.783	37.406	0.1
England and Wales	17.928	25.974	1.3
Scotland	2.889	3.736	0.9
Ireland	6.552	5.175	−0.8
Germany	33.413[a]	45.234[b]	1.1
Belgium	4.530[c]	5.520[b]	0.8
Netherlands	3.309[d]	4.013[e]	0.9
Denmark	1.415	1.969	1.1
Norway	1.490[f]	1.819[g]	1.0
Sweden	3.471	4.169[h]	0.9
Spain	15.455[i]	16.622[j]	0.7
Portugal	3.844[k]	4.551[l]	0.7
Italy	24.351[a]	28.460	0.6
Switzerland	2.393	2.846	0.6
Austria	17.535	22.144[b]	0.8
Hungary	13.192	15.739[b]	0.6
Russia	68.500	97.700[b]	1.2

[a] 1852. [b] 1880. [c] 1856. [d] 1859. [e] 1879. [f] 1855. [g] 1875. [h] 1870.
[i] 1857. [j] 1877. [k] 1854. [l] 1878.

Source: B. R. Mitchell, *European Historical Statistics 1750–1970* (1975).

In backward southern and eastern Europe the high birth-rate was almost cancelled out by a high death-rate. A cholera epidemic in Hungary in the early 1870s claimed over 300,000 victims, and drove the death-rate up to 44 per thousand. Large towns with their overcrowding and lack of sanitation, rather than industrial towns as such, were the real killers. In 1880, the average life expectancy at birth of a German male in rural Hanover was 43.1 years; his compatriot in the iron and steel town of Düsseldorf could expect to live 36.7 years, but for a Berliner the average span was only 29.9 years. By this time, the death rate in the far more salubrious and less urbanized Scandinavian countries had fallen well beneath 20 per cent.

Until the mid-nineteenth century, low agricultural productivity and frequent runs of bad harvests had set firm limits to population growth. But now transportation was improving, so that areas of food shortage could be relieved from areas of surplus, and agriculture flourished in this period in response to rising food prices. Until now also, the very size of the rural market and the emphasis in industry on consumer goods, particularly textiles, had meant that agricultural failure radically reduced demand for cloth and threw spinners and weavers out of work. The fortunes of agriculture dictated the fortunes of industry. After 1850, investment in capital goods, such as coal and iron, increased at the expense of consumer goods, and industrial production as a whole accounted for an ever greater share of total output. The industrial sector therefore gained a certain autonomy from agriculture, and economic fluctuations would henceforth be determined less by the state of the harvest than by the boom and slump of business. This, known as the trade cycle, was determined above all by patterns of investment.

TABLE 5. *Birth- and death-rates in Europe 1841–1880 (per thousand pop.)*

	birth-rate		death-rate	
	1841–5	1876–80	1846–50	1876–80
France	28.1	25.3	23.9	22.4
England and Wales	32.4	35.4	23.4	20.8
Germany	36.6	39.4	27.4	26.1
Belgium	32.5	32.1	25.1	21.8
Netherlands	34.4	36.4	28.4	22.9
Denmark	30.1	32.0	21.2	19.4
Norway	30.4	31.6	18.8	16.6
Sweden	31.3	30.3	21.0	18.3
Spain		35.8		30.4
Italy		36.9		29.4
Austria	39.6	38.7	36.5	30.5
Hungary		44.1		36.9
Romania		35.7		31.3
Serbia		38.6		35.6
Russia		49.5		35.7

The age of capital was characterized by periods of speculation, when the owners of capital expected high yields from investment in new sectors, such as the railways, so long as the cost of labour and raw materials was low. But as investment in these sectors reached saturation point, the prospects for profit-making began to darken, and the accumulation of capital drove up the price of labour and raw materials, now in short supply. Confidence wavered, panic set in, capitalists rushed to sell their shares before the market declined, enterprises went bankrupt and banks that invested in them were dragged down in their wake. And so things would remain, until brighter prospects and confidence returned. In this period, the years 1851–7 were years of boom, but these were followed by a sharp depression in 1857–8. Recovery came with the 1860s, despite the 'cotton famine' which resulted from the American Civil War of 1861–5, until another recession in 1866–8. The unification of Germany was followed by a period of feverish speculation, the so-called *Gründerzeit*, but there was a crash on the Vienna stock exchange in 1873, and recovery in the later 1870s was only a prelude to the Great Depression which lasted till the end of the century.

Industrialization transformed the demography of western Europe. It offered a solution to the problems of rural congestion, pauperism, and starvation that had afflicted so many countries before 1848. In Germany, after

1850, populations migrated away from agricultural regions like Baden-Württemberg and the north-east towards the expanding industrial areas of Saxony and Rhineland-Westphalia, where mining and metallurgy, rather than textiles, now provided the sectors of growth. In the coal belt that stretched from the Ruhr through southern Belgium to northern France, the population of the new mining towns grew in proportion to the tonnage of coal mined, but even faster where the metallurgical industry was present, and fastest where the industrial complex involved engineering and chemical works as well.

It is nevertheless clear that while the absolute numbers of industrial workers increased the industrial work-force did not necessarily become a larger proportion of the active population as a whole, except in those countries coming recently to industrialization, such as Austria, Hungary, the Netherlands, or Denmark. Between 1850 and 1880, the proportion of the workforce engaged in industry fractionally diminished in 'mature' industrial economies, such as those of Britain, Belgium, and France. In the first volume of *Capital* (1867), Marx observed that the accumulation of capital would require an increase in the size of the proletariat, but that as the demand for industrial labour outstripped its supply and wages began to rise, so entrepreneurs would be encouraged to replace men by machines. Mechanization created a pool of unemployed labour or an 'industrial reserve army' which would be available for employment (without putting wages up) in periods of boom, or as new sectors of investment, such as the railways, opened up. The increase in the proportion of the active population engaged in transport is clearly reflected in the figures for Great Britain, Belgium, the Netherlands, France, and Denmark. But what Marx failed to recognize was that the growth of the secondary sector (industry) entailed the expansion of the tertiary sector, including, apart from the retail trade, services such as teaching and administration. Already in 1880, a sixth of the work-force was employed in these tasks in France, a fifth in the Netherlands and Great Britain.

Industrialization in the mid-nineteenth century usually meant urbanization. This had not always been the case, for the first industrial revolution had taken place in the countryside. The rural industries were destroyed by mechanized, steam-powered factory production based in the towns, but those towns now offered employment for rural populations who were no longer able to supplement their meagre farm income with the product of cottage industry. The pattern of urbanization in Europe was now determined above all by the railways. In England, towns like Crewe and New Swindon were conjured out of nothing by the railway companies; in France the town of Alençon refused to accept the main line from Paris to Brest and stagnated while Le Mans, which accepted it, became a major industrial centre. Textile industries which had been dispersed became concentrated in towns like Roubaix in northern France or München-Gladbach on the left bank of the Rhine, which mushroomed within a few decades. But the industrial centre of

TABLE 6. *Structure of the active population in Europe, c.1880 (%)*

	Agriculture, forestry, fishing	Manufacturing, mining, building	Trade, banking, transport	Services, armed forces	Activity not adequately described
Great Britain 1881	13.3	48.5	9.7	21.1	7.4
Belgium 1880	39.5	36.3	10.0	14.2	—
Germany 1882	46.7	35.4	7.3	9.2	1.3
Netherlands 1889	32.9	30.2	16.1	19.3	1.5
France 1886	47.0	25.7	10.2	17.1	—
Italy 1881	51.4	25.4	3.6	9.3	10.5
Denmark 1880	50.4	23.8	8.2	7.7	9.9
Sweden 1880	58.5	9.5	4.0	9.3	18.7
Austria 1880	55.6	20.6	3.9	11.9	8.0
Ireland 1881	41.6	18.7	6.7	20.2	12.9
Hungary 1880	64.0	11.6	2.6	8.4	13.4
Spain 1877	70.5	12.6	4.8	12.1	—

Source: P. Bairoch, *La Population active et sa structure* (Brussels, 1968).

gravity in the Rhineland was shifting away from the older textile centres of Krefeld, Elberfeld, and Barmen towards the mining and metallurgical towns of the Ruhr, Duisberg, Essen, Bochum, and Dortmund, which were created by and for the railway. Railway connections were now essential for ports, the most successful of which developed shipbuilding and iron industries. The population of Rotterdam was 78,000 in 1840, 116,200 in 1869. On the Baltic coast, Stettin was linked to Berlin from 1843 and expanded far more rapidly than Danzig or Königsberg. In Britain, the railway network tended to link existing industrial centres rather than found new ones. Elsewhere in Europe, railways built to link Courts and capitals stimulated the growth of engineering and chemical industries in their suburbs, and changed them from parasitic to productive cities. This was clearly the case of Paris, Berlin, Munich, Karlsruhe, and Milan. Moreover, the annexation of unruly industrial suburbs by many cities for policing purposes in the 1850s dramatically increased their size overnight.

Large towns grew much faster than the population as a whole, especially in countries where industrialization was vigorous. This was the case even in France, where the total population increased only slowly in the middle years of the century. In England and Wales towns of over 20,000 inhabitants grew by 2.3 per cent in 1851–91 as against 3.1 per cent in 1811–51. In the industrial parts of Germany, on the other hand, the pace of urbanization was quickening. In both Prussia and Saxony, the average rate of growth of towns of over 200,000 inhabitants had been 2.2 per cent in 1815–49, but this increased dramatically in 1849–90 to 4.2 per cent in Prussia and 4.3 per cent in Saxony. Berlin, which had 400,000 inhabitants in 1850, had 1.9 million in 1890.

The connection between industrialization and urbanization was not one-way. Growing towns stimulated industry other than manufacturing industry,

TABLE 7. *Urbanization in Western Europe, 1836–1890*

	annual average increase of total population	annual average increase of population of towns over 20,000 inhabitants
France 1836–86	0.3	1.8
England and Wales 1851–91	1.2	2.3
Bavaria 1852–90	0.6	3.0
Prussia 1849–90	1.5	4.2
Saxony 1849–90	1.5	4.3

Source: A. F. Weber, *The Growth of Cities in the Nineteenth Century* (1899; Cornell, 1963).

especially the building trade. Whether in London, Paris, Berlin, or Vienna, the years 1863–5 and 1876–7 were the peaks of a building boom, of which the beautification of city centres was only one aspect. The erection of new public buildings, the demands of the railway companies for arteries linking termini, the lessons of 1848 which suggested that wide boulevards might ease the movement of troops, and the need to clear slums that were dens of cholera, typhus, crime, and discontent, together prompted redevelopment in most major European cities. But splendid façades and broad vistas could not mask some of the more tragic results of the rebuilding. Vienna was able to build the Ringstrasse on the open land between the walled inner city and the suburbs, but elsewhere rebuilding drove the poor into ever more crowded courts, garrets, and cellars in the working-class islands that remained in the inner cities, and the scourge of cholera was replaced in the large towns by the scourge of tuberculosis.

The growing towns nevertheless had complex and varied needs, so that not all migrants who arrived finished up at the bottom of the pile. Apart from the building trade, all aspects of commerce and the luxury trades flourished, affording employment for the Spaniards of Marseilles, the Belgians of Paris, the Czechs of Vienna. Some of the most rapidly growing towns in the mid-nineteenth century were the very antithesis of industrial centres: these were the seaside resorts, fashionable spas, and tourist attractions, such as Rome. In Rome, though, change was also explained by the unification of Italy. In 1848 two-thirds of the city's buildings belonged to ecclesiastical bodies, and the Church bred its own officials, pilgrims, and beggars. After 1860 Rome developed as a centre of litigation, education, and the press, while 1870 brought the new Italian government and thousands of civil officials and military men in its wake. Finally, it should be emphasized that the urbanization of Europe was a very uneven affair. In 1870, the proportion of the population living in towns of over 10,000 inhabitants was 57 per cent in England, 42 per cent in Scotland, and 26 per cent in Belgium. It was 21 per cent in France and

20 per cent in Germany, but also 31 per cent in the Netherlands, 24 per cent in Spain and 20 per cent in Italy. At the other end of the spectrum, the figure was less than 10 per cent in Hungary, Poland, Norway, Sweden, Finland, and Russia, while in the Balkans urbanization was quite insignificant.

Equally, it became apparent that agricultural and industrial prosperity could not indefinitely support the growing European population. Particularly vulnerable in this respect were regions where industry had not established itself, and where the problem of rural overpopulation had not been tackled. In Scandinavia, Danish agriculture had undergone something of a revolution, but in Norway and Sweden the subdivision of holdings was ludicrous. In the Baltic provinces of Germany, Mecklenburg, and Pomerania, emancipated serfs had been kept on to work the estates, paid partly in money and partly in kind. But the growth of world markets now threatened these areas with cheap Russian and American grain, and the surplus rural population was forced to move on or starve. Whereas rapid industrialization seemed initially to have solved the problem of the rural poor, an achievement that was reflected in the sharp decline of emigration from Europe in 1856–65, emigration shot up again in 1866–75. The outflow from Great Britain, including Ireland, still led the field in terms of absolute numbers. In Germany the source of emigration moved from the south-west to the north-east. But it is the dramatic increase in the sailings from Sweden and above all Norway, bound for North America, that catch the eye. The Statue of Liberty in New York harbour, completed in 1886, proclaimed a welcome for Europe's tired and poor, and 'huddled masses yearning to breathe free'. By then the ships which sailed for America were packed with emigrants of a quite different sort.

TABLE 8. *Rate of emigration per 100,000 inhabitants, 1851–1880*

	Europe	Great Britain	Germany	Norway	Sweden
1851–5	175	840	407	281	105
1856–60	86	430	288	204	40
1861–5	93	480	132	286	76
1866–70	144	560	286	864	464
1871–5	129	600	191	510	227
1876–80	94	420	104	432	301

Source: Walter F. Willcox, *International Migrations*, Vol. II (New York, 1931).

A World Market

By 1880 it would be fair to say that the international economy had become integrated, that a single world market had been created. This was partly the result of technological progress, as the routes of ocean steamers and railway tracks criss-crossed the globe, and partly the effect of lowering of tariff barriers between countries and the inauguration of an era of free trade.

International commerce multiplied in volume, stimulating the growth of both agricultural and industrial sectors of the economy. There were, however, always economic interests which resented exposure to the cold winds of competition, and at the end of the 1870s campaigns to restore protection intensified and found support with some governments.

In 1850 there were about 14,500 miles of railway track in Europe. Thirty years later there were 101,700 miles, and by then North America, too, had more than 100,000 miles built. At sea, the long haul was dominated in the 1850s by the graceful clipper that could sail from Liverpool to Melbourne in eighty-three days, or from Canton to New York in eighty-four. But steamships were improving as the screw-propeller replaced the paddle-wheel and iron replaced wood and they all but displaced the sailing ships on the major lines by 1880. The Suez canal, opened in 1869, shortened the route east for steamships, although sailing ships still went by the Cape. Submarine telegraph cables, such as that which spanned the North Atlantic (at the second attempt) in 1866, were laid by steamships. The encirclement of the world by telegraph by the early 1870s represented yet another revolution in communications.

These improvements brought down the cost of freight (of special importance for the transport of bulky goods such as coal and grain), increased competition to supply markets between different parts of Europe and indeed different parts of the world, and increased the volume of world trade. As markets expanded, the movement to lower or abolish protective tariffs and restrictive tolls, and to inaugurate the reign of free trade gained momentum. In 1857 the Danube and the Sound between Denmark and Sweden were declared freeways for the ships of all nations, and the Rhine followed suit in 1868. Somewhat more contentious were free trade treaties. In the next decade or so, several European countries followed the example of one signed by England and France in 1860.

The division for and against free trade was not so much between countries as between interests within those countries. In Great Britain the battle for free trade had been won in 1846, and the landowners looked to secure the domestic market by more efficient farming while the manufacturers required world outlets for their cheap, mass-produced textiles and metal goods. On the Continent the railway builders tended to favour free trade, both because it was the way to increase rail traffic and because in countries like France and Italy, and for some time in Germany, the native iron industry had not the capacity to produce enough pig-iron for the rails, which had to be imported. Bankers supported free trade in order to promote railway-building, one of their main interests in this period, and to open accounts with governments, which stood to lose from the reduction of customs revenue. It is significant that Émile Péreire, director of Compagnie du Midi and of the Crédit Mobilier, was one of the main advocates of the Anglo-French treaty. Free trade could only be in the interests of international traders, whether the wine-exporters of Bordeaux, the silk-importers of Lyons, or the patricians of the Hanseatic towns of Bremen, Hamburg, and Lübeck who founded the Congress of German Economists in 1857 to publicize their views. Lastly, as urban markets grew and agricultural prices remained buoyant, free trade was supported by the agrarian interests of most European countries, whether France or Italy, Hungary, Denmark, or Prussia. The East Elbian landowners, with their traditional outlets in industrial Britain, carried particular weight in the movement for free trade.

The opponents of free trade were by and large those interests that feared British competition in textiles, coke and coal, iron, steel, and machinery. Unless protective tariffs were maintained, they argued, the struggles of European industry to catch up with the British lead would be frustrated, and Britain would remain for ever the 'workshop of the world'. So the textile interests of northern France, South Germany and Saxony, Lombardy, and Catalonia, together with the coal and iron interests of northern and central France, Rhineland-Westphalia, and Silesia, threw themselves into the crusade against the treaties. In Germany, the battle between free trade and protection was a battle between Prussia and Austria for supremacy over the remaining states. In 1849 and again in 1852 Austria tried to reinforce her domination of the German Confederation by creating an economic *Mitteleuropa*, a customs union with high protective tariffs which would attract the industrialists of Saxony, Silesia, and southern Germany away from the Prussian-managed Zollverein, which offered them inadequate protection. The Austrian offensive did not succeed. The central and southern German states were dependent on the Zollverein and its Baltic and North Sea ports for their outlets, and Prussia threatened to break up the Zollverein if they drew too close to Austria. Moreover, political influence in northern Germany was wielded not by the industrialists but by the bankers, traders, and above all landowners, who were committed to free trade. Prussia acquired economic mastery in Germany as a result of her free trade policies before she completed it with political mastery, and Austria, after her defeat by Prussia in 1866, dutifully followed it, concluding free trade treaties with France, Belgium, the Netherlands, Switzerland, Germany, Spain, and Portugal, Norway, and Sweden.

It would be difficult to assess the relative contributions of improved communications and free trade in the expansion of the world market. Free trade was as much a response to the expansion as a contributor to it. Between 1850 and 1880 the value of European exports increased from $1,200 millions to $4,050 millions. Measurement by volume, to take price changes into account, reveals that the annual average rate of growth of European exports rose from 3.8 per cent in the 1850s to 5.2 per cent in the 1860s, the free trade era, falling to 3.1 per cent in the 1870s. A look at the relative performance of the different countries is also instructive. Great Britain remained at the head of the league, though its share of European exports fell from 29.8 per cent in 1860 to 26 per cent in 1880, and the growth rate of its exports in the 1860s was only 3.8 per cent. The growth rate of France's exports in the 1860s was 5.7 per cent, but its share of the total export market fell from 19.2 per cent to 16.3 per cent. The outstanding achievement was that of Germany. In the 1860s the growth rate of its exports was 6.7 per cent, and though its share of the European export market dropped fractionally from 18.4 per cent to 18.2 per cent, it had overtaken France as an exporting economy by 1880.

One way of examining the performance of the various European economies is to take the example of heavy industry, and specifically the challenge of the railways. For the railways in this period acted as a leading sector, stimulating the growth of the iron industry. In turn, the iron industry consumed coal, and the transportation of coal was one of the principal sources of freight charges for the railway companies. Lastly, the demand for locomotives was one of the main factors behind the development of the engineering industry. The manufacture of steel was made possible by two new inventions, the Bessemer converter of 1856 and the Siemens–Martin open-hearth furnace of 1864. These were dependent on Spanish and Swedish ores with a low phosphorus content, and in 1870 only 15 per cent of finished iron in Germany and 10 per cent in Britain was being turned into steel (the phosphorus problem was not solved until the Thomas–Gilchrist process of 1879). The expansion of the steel industry in the 1870s was largely directed towards the railways.

Britain's furnaces provided iron and steel not only for her domestic markets but also for export: between 1845–9 and 1866–70 the tonnage of iron and steel exported rose from 1.3 millions to 318 millions. Yet again the most dramatic performance was that of Germany. In the 1840s she was importing rails and rolling-stock from Britain and Belgium, because of the inadequacy of her own iron industry. But after 1850 capital and capacity were mobilized, and Germany used the challenge of the railways to consolidate a heavy industrial base. In the 1870s, the railways took about half of the output of the iron industry and one-tenth of that of the coal industry of the Ruhr. In turn, the iron industry consumed about one-third of the Ruhr's coal production, and the coal industry supplied about one-quarter of the railways' freight business. In France between 1840 and 1880 up to 70 per cent of French iron production went to supply the demands of the railways. But despite the switch from charcoal- to coke-fired furnaces at Fourchambault, Montluçon, Le Creusot, and Vierzon, France's productive capacity had not become adequate to her needs before the intervention of the trade treaty of 1860. The result of this was an increase in all imports including British and Belgian iron and a decline in the growth of all production, taking the years 1860–80 against 1840–60. The French iron industry, together with the Italian, came to excel in engineering rather than in the manufacture of pig- and cast-iron.

Nevertheless, the most conspicuous failure to respond to the railway age was that of Spain. Its General Railway Law of June 1855, to some extent imposed by foreign banking and railway interests, abolished import duties on rails and rolling-stock for a period of ten years. This meant that in the railway building boom of 1856–66 the nascent Spanish iron industry of the Basque province of Vizcaya remained stagnant while the country was flooded by foreign iron goods, mainly British and Belgian. The coal of the Asturias might well have been used to fire the excellent Basque iron ore, which with its low phosphorous content was first-rate for the manufacture of steel. But the difficulties of transporting coal from the Asturias to Vizcaya, the free trade treaty of 1869 which undercut the Asturias with cheap, seaborne British coal, and the greed of south Wales steel manufacturers for high-grade Spanish ore, meant that the axis between Gijón, the Asturian port, and Cardiff, exporting coal and importing iron-ore, became more important than the axis between Gijón and Bilbao. As a result, Spain remained a semi-colonial economy, plundered for its raw materials and confined to a state of backwardness.

There was therefore a clear distinction between countries which exported iron goods and capital to build railways abroad, and countries which constructed their railway systems with the help of foreign investment. In one case, the railways acted as a leading sector for the economy, in the other it did not. But there were other forms of export that could also act as a stimulus for national economies. That the Bordeaux Chamber of Commerce should be one of the most vigorous supporters of free trade was not surprising: between 1859 and 1868 the export of French wines to Britain more than quadrupled. In some economies, it was the export of agricultural produce that made possible the accumulation of capital for industrial investment. Denmark was one instance, as its farm products found growing outlets in industrial Britain, especially after 1860. Hungary was another, exporting vast amounts of cereal to Austria in the same period, so that the milling industry of Budapest developed as its prime manufacturing centre. In Russia, the black-earth provinces of the south were developed in response to the grain trade with western Europe. Odessa became a frontier 'boom town', its population rising from 32,000 in 1827 to 200,000 in 1875. It was not until the period 1875–80 that American grain exports began to displace Russian cereals in Britain, France, and Germany.

The appearance of large amounts of Russian and American grain on European markets from the mid-1870s had a disastrous effect on grain prices. Agrarian interests which for so long had been the champions of free trade now began to look to the restoration of protective tariffs to preserve domestic markets for their own crop. In Germany, to take one example, the iron and steel interest of Rhineland-Westphalia had formed a pressure group in November 1873 to demand protection, and were joined three months later by the iron masters of Upper Silesia. The cotton-spinners of South Germany, who were suffering competition from the cotton manufacturers of Alsace, which had been annexed by Germany in 1871, joined the alliance to form the Central Union of German Industrialists for the Promotion and Protection of National Labour in February 1876. The turning point came two weeks later, when the agrarians set up an Association of Tax and Economic Reformers, which was dominated by large Prussian landowners and dedicated to the restoration of the Corn Laws. The collaboration of industrial and agrarian interests, the 'marriage of iron and rye' as it was nicknamed, could not be ignored by Bismarck. Two other factors reinforced the drift back to protection. First, governments were in need of revenue after the wars of unification. France, which had suffered defeat in 1870–1 and was still required to pay an indemnity to Germany, was in particularly difficult straits, and Adolphe Thiers, when he was President of the French Republic in 1871–3, was prepared to listen to the massed voices of the protectionists who had been thrust aside in so cavalier a fashion by Napoleon III. Once the reparation payments to Germany ended, Bismarck found himself in financial difficulty, and the military preparations that surrounded the Balkan crisis and Russo-Turkish War in the years 1875–8 increased the weight on national exchequers. The case for slapping on tariffs to raise government revenues was therefore a strong one. Second, the liberal, free-trading interests that had held power in countries such as Germany and Austria since the mid-1860s fell from grace as the Depression began to bite and faith in the market economy gave way to disillusion. The shift to economic protection after 1878 was also a shift to political conservatism.

Agriculture: Profit and Loss

The middle years of the century were a period of rising prices and agricultural prosperity. The expansion of international trade and a growing and increasingly urbanized population pushed up a demand that was now becoming effective through the railway. More and more, agriculture became commercialized, part of the market economy, and specialized in the production of cash crops. And yet, despite this prosperity, the salient features of the European countryside remained inequality and poverty, the difference between a small number of rich landowners and substantial farmers and the mass of 'dwarf' proprietors and landless labourers. It was in the 1860s that serfdom was ended: the task begun in Austria and Hungary after 1848 was embarked upon in Russia, Poland, and Romania. Yet the emancipation of the serfs had to be reconciled with the interests of the ruling class of landlords and the security of the state, so that the countryside of eastern Europe, far from becoming a Garden of Eden, remained a dark valley of land-hunger, debt, secular routine, overcrowding, and misery.

  The growth of towns was made possible by increasing agricultural productivity. In turn, growing urban demand brought a healthy rise in agricultural prices. One exception to this general rule was England, where grain prices had been declining as the result of international competition, ever since the end of the Napoleonic Wars. The repeal of the Corn Laws in 1846 did not mark a decisive change in the long-term decline. But a glance at the fluctuation of grain prices in some countries of Europe does show a general trend upwards between 1840 and 1880 (except in England).

TABLE 9. *Agricultural prices in Europe, 1841–1880*

	Wheat			Rye		
	England	France	Italy	Netherlands	Germany	Austria
1841–50	132.1	111.5	107.0	81.5	72.4	63.5
1851–60	135.3	123.5	123.0	98.0	84.4	80.0
1861–70	126.4	125.8	115.8	90.2	85.4	76.4
1871–80	126.5	133.0	—	91.1	95.9	101.7

Prices are measured in grams of silver per hundred kilos.

Source: William Abel, *Agricultural Fluctuations in Europe* (London, 1980), appendix.

Figures for one or two cereal crops cannot suggest the complete picture for all agricultural products, not least because commercialization was taking agriculture away from obsessive cereal farming towards specialization in other commodities which could fetch high prices on the market. This specialization tended to define more boldly the regional character of European agriculture. Relatively backward economies in southern climates took on the appearance of granaries. Spain's subsistence crises were not altogether overcome, but a market for her wheat was opened up during the Crimean War and in all but seven years between 1849 and 1881 exports of cereal from Spain exceeded imports. Southern Italy including Sicily took on the role of a major grain producer after the unification of the country. And of course the fertile black-earth provinces of southern Russia responded to the repeal of the British Corn Laws by stepping up the production and export of grain, balancing the extra cost of transport by the exploitation of unpaid serf labour.

The Mediterranean countries were meanwhile discovering how to mass-produce wine. Until the middle of the nineteenth century the Mediterranean economy was a polyculture, combining cereal farming on the plains, vines scattered among the olive, fruit, and mulberry trees (which, in Lombardy and the Cévennes at least, provided leaves for the greedy silkworms), and chestnut groves and sheep-pasture in the hills. In France, urban demand and, after the treaty of 1860, foreign demand, provided the incentive to specialize, and increasingly the Midi went over to wine. Prices were buoyant, harvests were good, and the years 1855–80 were recognized as the 'golden age' of the vine. Tragedy was nevertheless to strike. The phylloxera epidemic created havoc by 1880, so that the average yield of 24.5 hectolitres per hectare in 1870–5 fell to 15.2 in 1885–90. This was disastrous for France, which embarked on a long programme of replanting with sturdy American vines, but excellent for the wine-growers of Spain and Italy, whose produce now flooded the French market. Piedmont and Tuscany switched from polyculture to the intensive planting of vineyards in the 1870s and 1880s, and even the wheat-growing south started to go over to growing cheap wines.

In Great Britain, where cereal prices were in a slow decline, the incentive for farmers was to switch to rearing cattle for the meat market. In northern Europe the consumption of meat rose with urbanization, and twice as much beef was eaten in France in 1882 as in 1840. Whereas earlier in the century cattle were turned on to common land or onto the stubble to graze, now artificial meadows were laid down and scientific stock-breeding—the perfection of Durham, Ayrshire, and other strains—caught on. Denmark founded a whole economy on cattle- and pig-farming. As yet, the emphasis was on meat rather than on dairy products, but that development would come towards the end of the century. Lastly, northern Europe was going over to 'industrial' crops—rape for oil, hops for beer, sugar-beet not only for sugar but for alcohol, and potatoes which could generate alcohol as well. No longer were roots farmed only as one phase of crop-rotation, for Chilean nitrates and phosphates were used to break free of conventional rotation. Beet fields encroached upon the bleak landscapes of eastern England, northern France, and central Germany; the produce was taken by rail to sugar-mills and distilleries, the first manifestation perhaps of the 'agricultural industry'.

As in industry, of course, the benefits of commercial farming were not spread evenly among the agricultural community. In Prussia, the Junkers were comforted by the doubling of farm rents between 1849 and 1869 and by a three- or four-fold rise in the value of large agricultural estates between the 1820s and 1870. On the other hand, the switch to specialized crops and the erection of mills, breweries, and distilleries on their estates rendered superfluous the mass of farm-servants and cottagers, who were mainly ex-serfs provided with small plots so long as they performed unpaid labour on the landlord's estate. Rising demand, land-values, and the seasonal nature of the work encouraged landlords to evict cottagers, many of whom were forced to move to industrial areas in search of work, and to turn to cheap, migrant labour from the eastern provinces, often female, and usually Polish. In Austria and Hungary landlords tried to follow the Prussian example of *Gutsherrschaft*, the direct commercial exploitation of their estates, once their serfs had been emancipated. This involved mortgaging those estates heavily to the government and using the capital for development and the hire of wage-labour. In Hungary, the population grew by 45 per cent between 1850 and 1900, but in the same period the number of agricultural wage-workers increased by 73 per cent.

Not all landlords by any means were interested in producing directly for the market. The leisured existence of the *rentier*, enjoying the social prestige and political influence that went with landownership, was often more congenial. In Spain, a general law of disentailment in 1855 brought vast quantities of municipal land, state and Church lands on to the market, while in Italy unification released much of the property of the Church and old nobilities, especially in the south. This was bought up in both cases by new men, bourgeois landowners, professional men, officials, merchants, and financiers, who were interested only in extracting the maximum rent, often through farmers-general who leased the land from them and sublet it at extortionate rates to the peasantry. On the large estates of Andalusia and Estremadura, vast tracts of uncultivated land coexisted with miserable populations of landless labourers, who launched a peasant revolt in 1861, taking possession of the town of Loja. Later the toilers of southern Spain would provide eager audiences for anarchist millenarians, who promised the great day of the *reparto*, when land would be restored to the people.

In England, the tendency had been towards the consolidation of large estates, but these were leased out to substantial tenant-farmers who provided their own capital and labour and, despite stiff competition for farms which pushed the rents up, enjoyed security of tenure. In Ireland the situation was quite different. Large properties were even larger, so that while in England and Wales 60 per cent of the land was owned by 4,000 people, who possessed an average of 4,500 acres around 1850, in Ireland an average of 10,000 acres was owned by 1,000 people, which accounted for 50 per cent of the land. On the other hand, farms were often tiny, having been divided almost infinitely before the famine. After the famine, as the population declined and rents fell into arrears, some landlords tried to consolidate these farms, in order to lease them to larger tenants. Unfortunately, these evictions of tenants violated the custom of Irish tenant-right, according to which the tenant had security of tenure and could buy and sell an occupancy as though it were his own property. This custom was not recognized by the landlords, who were themselves mainly Protestant, English, or Anglo-Irish, and absentees, and after 1867 the Irish Republican Brotherhood or Fenians organized a campaign of terrorism against the alien aristocracy. Gladstone introduced a bill to Parliament in 1870 which would provide compensation for evicted tenants and therefore recognized Irish tenant-right implicitly. But this bill was sabotaged not by the Tories but by the Whig magnates of the upper house, many of whom were Irish landlords. This gave a major impulse to the consolidation of the movement in favour of Irish Home Rule.

Mounting peasant unrest at the other end of Europe, indeed the fear of another revolt like that of Pugachev in 1774, was one pressing reason for the emancipation of the serfs in Russia under the law of 19 February 1861. Rumours that volunteers for the Crimean War would be freed on demobilization resulted in an increase in the number of disturbances that required military intervention from 86 in 1858, to 90 in 1859, and 108 in 1860. Russian peasants dreamed of the end of personal bondage, and of the dues paid, or labour-services performed for their lords in return for the allotments they held. Many anticipated the abolition of all taxes, conscription, and government, that is, anarchy. There could therefore be no question of a landless emancipation of the serfs, as in the Baltic provinces earlier in the century, without provoking a civil war. On the other hand, the Tsarist regime could not afford to alienate the landowning-official class on which its rule depended. It tried to steer a middle course, granting peasants their existing allotments, but also fixing statutory maximum and minimum allotments in each area, according to the fertility of the soil. There was of course a danger that the serfowners might confiscate land from the peasants, forcing all their holdings down to the minimum. As it happened, the minimum allotment for a peasant household should have been between five and eight hectares per soul, but almost three-quarters of the peasantry received allotments of less than four hectares per soul. It was only in Russian Poland, where the gentry again compromised themselves by insurrection in 1863, that emancipation was used to favour the peasants against their masters.

The peasant now had the property of his allotment, but the landlord had to be compensated for the loss of the dues or labour-services that he had received when the peasant was a serf. There were two schools of thought on this among the Russian gentry, the different attitudes explained to a large extent by the agricultural geography of Russia. In northern Russia, as a general rule, the land was poor and overcrowded, and the non-resident landlords had long commuted labour-services into dues paid in kind or money (*obrok*). Since they did not farm the land directly, these landlords were happy that the serfs should be granted generous allotments, on condition that the compensation for their lost dues would similarly be large. The attitude of the landlords of the black-earth and steppe provinces of the south was rather different. They did farm their estates directly, growing wheat for the expanding export market, and could not afford to lose their cohorts of unpaid *barshchina* labour. For them, the redemption of forced labour-services had no attractions, neither did they want to cede any of their valuable land to the peasantry.

The law of February 1861 attempted to satisfy both schools. The state would compensate the landlord for his lost dues or services to the tune of four-fifths of the capital value of the allotments he was ceding. On the face of it, the landlord would receive a large capital sum with which to develop his estate, but his mortgage debt to state banks was deducted from the compensation, and much of the rest had a tendency to evaporate at the gambling table. In their turn, the peasants were to pay a fifth of the capital value of their allotments direct to the landlord, and the rest to the state over a period of forty-nine years. But two provisions of the law were calculated to appease the landlord-entrepreneurs of the southern provinces, and perhaps explain the recurrence of peasant disturbances. For there were 844 outbreaks in 1862 and 509 in 1863. Peasants who decided on redemption were bound from February 1863 to 'temporary obligation', that is, they were obliged to provide their old dues and services until they had redeemed the value of their allotments. Those who wished to be free of all obligations at once (and the *barshchina* labour of the south was particularly onerous) could opt to receive so-called 'beggarly allotments', which were only a quarter the size of the maximum allotment in the given locality, but carried no obligations. Half a million peasants, or 5–6 per cent of the total, in fact took this way out, and whereas the peasantry lost on average 4.1 per cent of its old allotments to the former serf owner, it lost 23.3 per cent of its allotments in the sixteen black-earth and steppe provinces. Because of the inadequacy of these pocket-sized holdings for the maintenance of a peasant household, the peasants were driven back on to the estate of the large landowner in search of paid labour.

One common view is that the emancipation of the serfs released a mass of free workers who would constitute the shock-troops of Russia's industrial revolution. This view is mistaken. First, the peasant had acquired property in his old allotment and would not readily abandon it. Second, there was as yet no large-scale industrial sector which could provide employment for the rural surplus. Some *obrok* serfs had traditionally undertaken artisan crafts in the local town, and this they would continue to do. Other peasants with inadequate holdings remained on the land but hired themselves out as labourers to richer peasants or ex-serfowners. Third, the government expressed a horror of the 'cancer of the proletariat', whatever spectre it imagined by that term, and did not promote industrialization until the 1890s. Only 6 per cent of the rural population migrated between 1870 and 1896. Fourth, now that the abolition of serfownership had deprived the government of an excellent tool for coercing the peasantry into paying taxes and providing recruits, the government pressed the *obshchina* or peasant commune into providing the same services, including paying the taxes of any member who moved away. Not until their redemption payments had been completed would peasants be allowed to separate from the commune, and even then a two-thirds majority vote of the commune was necessary to approve it. Fifth, the retention of the commune, with its periodic re-allocation of strips according to the needs of the households that composed it, placed limits on agricultural productivity and made difficult the support of a large non-agricultural population. On the other hand it did mean that absolutely landless peasants were much rarer in Russia than in other eastern European countries.

Emancipation in fact did little in the short run to change the structure of Russian society. Its main achievement was to dash hopes and sharpen frustrations. Change was equally minimal in Romania, the former Danubian Principalities which were united under the auspices of Napoleon III in 1859.

The agrarian law of 1864 ended forced labour services and gave peasants the property of their allotments. But large landowners, the boyar aristocracy, retained 60 per cent of the land while 30 per cent of the peasants' plots were under two hectares in size. They could survive only by labouring on the large estates and the lords, who had not the capital to pay them wages, allocated them parcels of land on a share-cropping basis. Thus the landlords retained their old labour services without the traditional obligations of a seigneur, while the peasants continued to do their corvée with very little to show in the way of landownership. It was only in Bulgaria, which came into existence under the protection of Russia following the defeat of Turkey in 1878 that anything like a system of peasant proprietorship was created. For there the defeated Turkish feudatories could be expropriated for the benefit of the Bulgarian peasantry, whereas elsewhere the interest of the landed governing class had always to be respected.

The Accumulation of Capital

In a series of enormous booms between 1851 and 1873 the capitalist economy went into overdrive. It could call on armies of rural out-workers and rivet them to the large-scale, mechanized system of production that had destroyed their independence. What remained of the guild system was swept away in the name of free enterprise and repressive legislation choked the beginnings of the trade-union movement. Further legislation authorized businesses to raise capital wherever they could find it and at the same time offered protection to the private investor. Most important perhaps, there was a revolution in banking, which no longer restricted its lending to a charmed circle of kings and rich merchants, and became aware of the huge profits to be reaped in the promotion of railways and heavy industry.

This 'second' industrial revolution, based on railways, mining, and metallurgy, was distinguished from the 'first' industrial revolution, based on textiles, by a hunger for capital, a demand for massive, long-term fixed investment that made the textile revolution look like promotion on a shoe-string. Yet at the same time credit was becoming available. As a result of the 'gold rush' to California in 1849 and of similar discoveries in Australia it has been said that between 1850 and 1870 'more gold was brought into the markets of the commercial world than the mines of New Spain combined had furnished since the days of Cortez and Pizarro'.[1] The amount of gold coinage issued annually in Britain, France and the USA increased nearly six-fold in the early 1850s, and the amount of paper money securely backed by gold also multiplied. This made possible the adoption of the gold standard by most countries, and the formation of monetary unions, such as the Austro-German union of 1857–66, the Latin Monetary Union of 1865, joined by Austria in 1867, and the Scandinavian Monetary Union of 1875. These created

[1] L. H. Jenks, *The Migration of British Capital to 1875* (London, 1963), 161.

virtually fixed rates of exchange and greatly facilitated international trade and investment.

To cope with this sudden change the banking world was obliged to revise its ideas drastically. The view at one time put forward was that the 'old bank' was in this period entirely surpassed by the so-called 'new bank'. That is to say that the private banks of well-established Protestant or Jewish families like the Rothschilds, merchant banks which accumulated most of their capital from trade and either lent short-term commercial credit to known clients or raised funds for indebted governments, were overtaken by a completely different sort of bank, the most famous of which was the Crédit Mobilier of the brothers Péreire. These banks, constituted as joint-stock companies, were able to raise large amounts of capital from middle-class investors who sought high profits and were prepared to risk it in the financing of industrial enterprises. In fact, the distinction between 'old' and 'new' banks was not so clear-cut, and the old banks were quite capable of adjusting to new circumstances. For example, James de Rothschild had provided backing for the Péreires in the promotion of early French railways after 1835, while the Cologne banker, Abraham Oppenheim, was the financial power behind the Rhenish railway in the same period. The launching of the Crédit Mobilier would not have been possible had not the private bank of Fould and Fould-Oppenheim provided a large part of the initial share-capital, and Oppenheim was again a major backer of Gustav Mevissen's Bank für Handel und Industrie authorized at Darmstadt, much to the fury of the bankers of Frankfurt, in 1853. There was indeed a famous struggle between the Péreires and the Rothschilds, symbolizing the rivalry between old and new. But this would not have happened if their spheres of interest had sharply contrasted. On the contrary, the Péreires' Crédit Mobilier was as interested in negotiating government loans as Napoleon III was anxious to break the stranglehold of the Rothschilds on the treasury. And when the Péreires seduced the Austrian government in 1854 into hiving off the Austrian state railways to them for completion, the Rothschilds replied the following year with their own joint-stock bank, the Creditanstalt für Handel und Gewerbe, which secured the right to build a railway to Lombardy and Venetia. Moreover it was the Rothschilds who came best out of the crisis of 1857, and fended off the Péreires' challenge for the Vienna–Trieste line, the famous Südbahn, and for the Paris–Lyons–Marseilles and Lyons–Geneva lines. The 'old bank' had put together a formidable empire.

The initial boom of 1851–7 demonstrated that capital could be raised easily in the Paris and London markets, but only with great difficulty elsewhere, especially in southern and eastern Europe. This was either because capital-formation was minimal, or because investments inclined towards government bonds or land, a conservatism that was encouraged by native banking institutions. One danger was therefore that development would take place with foreign capital—French, British, or Belgian—and that joint-stock companies set up would be entirely in the hands of foreign directors. Prussia managed to escape this fate of financial colonization because, although native capital was scarce, the Prussian government (unlike the Austrian) refused to release its control of the railways in the 1860s and required a majority of German citizens on boards of directors. At the same time supreme efforts were made by banks like the Darmstädter to break the grip of foreign capitalists in the exploitation of the coal industry of the Ruhr. Elsewhere development was the achievement of foreign capital. The Genoa–Turin line and Mont Cenis tunnel were built for Piedmont by French capital. Spain was colonized after 1856 by the Péreires and Rothschilds who competed to build railways, and by French and British companies like Rio Tinto which were eager to plunder Spanish lead and copper. In 1856, after the end of the Crimean War, an international consortium, including Barings of London, Hope of Amsterdam, Mendelssohn of Berlin, Fould and Fould-Oppenheim, and the Péreires undertook to begin railway-building in Russia.

Whether the bank was 'old' or 'new', its main concern in the 1850s was the promotion of railways. Since the interest on shares was usually guaranteed by governments and the rate of return was high, no other investment was so popular. Manufacturing industry remained largely self-financing, and the isolation of industry was reinforced by the crash in 1857. Banks became more cautious. The Creditanstalt in Vienna went back to negotiating government bonds, and even German banks such as the Darmstädter and the Diskontogesellschaft, organized by David Hansemann and the Berlin banker, Gerson Bleichröder, in 1856, found a new role lending money to the Prussian government for its army reforms. Confidence returned with the 1860s and the German banks now effectively displaced foreign capitalists in Rhineland-Westphalia. Legislation in Britain in 1855 and 1862 and in France in 1863 and 1867 finally established the principle of limited liability, enabling joint-stock banks and businesses to raise the maximum capital while affording security for their investors. 'New' banks such as the General Credit and Financial Company were set up in London to assist industry, public works, and international trade, while in France the Crédit Lyonnais was set up in 1863 by Henri Germain, founder and administrator of the metallurgical company of Châtillon-Commentry, in order to modernize the iron industry. Yet even in the 1860s, the courtship between banking and industry was prone to upsets. The Crédit Lyonnais lost heavily by investing in a dye-works that failed and, now that the railway mania was over, turned (along with most French banks) to financing the rebuilding of Paris. Much later Henri Germain was to tell his shareholders that 'even the best conceived, most wisely administered industrial enterprises involve risks that we consider incompatible with the security indispensable in the employment of funds of a deposit bank'.[2] Real estate

---

[2] Quoted by Jean Bouvier, *Le Crédit Lyonnais de 1883 à 1932* (Paris, 1961), 369, note.

was an even safer investment than railways, as the cases of Spain and Russia were to demonstrate. For railways required traffic and traffic required industry and commerce. In the 1840s George Stephenson reported after a visit to Spain to survey prospects for railway building, 'I have been a month in the country, but have not seen during the whole of that time enough people of the right sort to fill a single train'.[3] No wonder that after a decade of speculation Spanish railway-shares lost their value, and their collapse in 1864 brought down the whole banking system which in Spain was pinned on the railways. In Russia, too, the railway shares floated on the Paris market lost value and the government, after several years of topping interest payments up to the guaranteed level, bought out the shareholders in 1867. Where the foreign capitalists could make no profit, the choice was between backwardness and state intervention.

It was not until the boom of 1867–73 that the marriage between banking and industry was properly consummated. A law of June 1870 in united Germany abolished the need for joint-stock companies to request authorization, and new banks such as the Deutsche Bank, promoted by the industrialist Georg von Siemens in 1870, and the Dresdner Bank of 1872, became involved in selling the industrial shares of the Rhineland and Saxony on the Berlin money-markets and the financing of industrial exports to all parts of the world. Unfortunately, many of the companies issuing shares during the boom existed only on paper, and a crisis of confidence and a rush to sell provoked a run on the Vienna market in May 1873. Those banks that survived, often by absorbing smaller ones, returned to the familiar task of selling government stock, whether that of France, which was obliged to pay an indemnity to Germany after its defeat in 1870, of the Spanish monarchy restored in 1875, of the Russian government, or of new borrowers such as Turkey and Egypt, where the Oriental railway and the Suez Canal seemed to promise an era of prosperity. Unfortunately, lending to governments could be every bit as risky as investing in industry. Revolt in the Balkans provoked panic among Turkish bondholders and the government at Constantinople went bankrupt in October 1875. A few weeks later the Egyptian government, in difficulty, tried to sell off its shares in the Suez Canal, and it was Disraeli's lightning move to buy them that committed Britain to a new phase of official rather than unofficial imperialism.

The dependence of industry on larger and larger amounts of capital clearly had some effect on the structure of entrepreneurship. Shareholders pressed for more involvement in the management of business and this was provided for under the legislation on joint-stock companies: the annual general meeting of shareholders could verify the firm's accounts and, when there were vacancies on the board, nominate directors. The industrialists themselves

---

[3] E. C. Blount, *Memoirs* (London, 1902), 245, quoted by Rondo Cameron, 'Crédit Mobilier and the economic development of Europe', *Journal of Political Economy*, 61, no. 6 (1953), 470.

were torn two ways. For while a joint-stock organization would permit them to raise large amounts of capital, a loss of independence to shareholders or banks was much to be regretted. In Prussia, joint-stock companies were rare until the law of 1870, but even when legislation permitted, industrialists did not rush to incorporate themselves. In France, 307 joint-stock companies were authorized between 1848 and 1867, but only 338 new ones were set up in the first five years after the law of 1867. In Britain, as late as 1885, only 5 or 10 per cent of the most important business organizations were joint-stock companies. Railways, shipping, the iron and steel industries, and utilities alone were predominantly organized on a joint-stock basis, because their capital demands were so high.

One way out of the dilemma was the *commandite* company or private company. This constitution permitted partners to draw on outside capital, but retained full liability for debts and full direction in the hands of the original partners or family firm. It was the usual formula practised by German banks, was adopted by the French iron-master, Schneider, at Le Creusot, and was popular in Great Britain. In both joint-stock and private companies there was the beginning of a separation of ownership and management. Whereas the early entrepreneurs had been both owners and managers, there might now be a distinction between the shareholders and board of directors on the one hand, and the directors of individual plants on the other. These posts were increasingly filled by a new class of managers, trained in France to a large extent at such *grandes écoles* as Centrale, Ponts et Chaussées, Polytechnique, and the École des Mines, but recruited in Britain from similar industries or increasingly, as in the case of railway managers, from within the industry itself. There was a risk that directorships would become hereditary fiefs within the founding family and that managers would never acquire influence in the firm, but the evidence for Britain after 1870 and for France after 1880 is that increasingly top managers were promoted to boards of directors.

Nevertheless, even in 1880 the vast majority of businesses in Europe were still based on the simple partnership or family firm, never approaching the banks or stock-markets but relying on self-financing. Owners were the same as managers, and the founder remained an all-powerful patriarchal figure. This might be the case even in rapidly growing businesses like that of Werner Siemens, established in Berlin in 1847 to manufacture cables and telegraph systems. Branches were opened in London and New York in the early 1850s, but these were run by his brothers, and managers were likewise recruited within the family. For Siemens, 'strange' managers who messed up his plans would have been as abhorrent as 'strange' shareholders who tried to influence them.

Finally, the terms on which labour was available were favourable to the capitalist in this period. Between the abolition of the guilds and the effective organization of trade unions industrialists were able to hire and fire workers more or less in accordance with market forces. An attempt had been made in 1849 to protect artisans by reintroducing the guild system in Prussia, but entrepreneurs were able to call upon urban craftsmen who had been undercut by large-scale production, on journeymen who were unable to gain satisfaction from their masters, on peasant-weavers or nailmakers who could not survive on their plots of land once their trade had become mechanized in neighbouring factories, and on the rural surplus obliged to migrate to industrial regions in search of work. The German Association of Handicraftsmen put up a last-ditch stand, meeting at Weimar in 1862, at Frankfurt in 1863, and at Cologne in 1864, in a bid to enforce monopolies of their crafts, but they were beset by divisions and the Prussian government was under the influence of the *laissez-faire* school. In 1869 *Gewerbefreiheit* or free enterprise was proclaimed throughout the North German Confederation, and relations between employer and employee were clarified as those of free contact.

What made possible the displacement of the skilled artisan by the semi-skilled worker was mechanization, and mechanization was necessary to step up productivity for wider markets. Mechanization in turn meant more capital investment, and capital-intensive industries required the presence of workers all the year round. Thus the coal and iron region of Saint-étienne saw migrant workers settling permanently, lone male workers joined by their families, and the development after 1860 of a working-class culture based on the café.

What the working-classes required to fight for a shorter working day, to fight against mechanization, to control the supply of labour when the market was rising, in order to gain higher wages, to resist wage-cuts and lay-offs in periods of depression was organization. But effective organization was what they lacked. The ancient associations of tramping artisans, called *compagnonnages* in France, which provided funds for sickness, festivities on patronal days, and even, in the case of the carpenters of Paris in 1845, could organize a successful strike, were falling into disuse. Friendly societies or mutual aid societies spread rapidly among the working-classes of Britain, and Belgium, France, Italy, and Germany, but their task was essentially to insure against sickness, which brought unemployment, against the cost of a funeral, and often to provide some form of education. Many of these workers' organizations were actually sponsored by the liberal middle classes, who looked to impose bourgeois values of hard work, education, and thrift in the interests of class harmony. From the mid-1860s, however, workers's organizations increasingly broke away from bourgeois patronage, articulating specific class interests. While liberal governments serving the interests of the bourgeoisie were keen at this point to invoke legislation against strikes and picketing, authoritarian governments took the view that to allow the working classes to form trade unions in defence of better wages and conditions would drive a wedge between them and radical, republican, or socialist agitators who were seeking their support. Restrictions on trade unions and strikes were therefore relaxed in Saxony in 1861, Prussia in 1863, and the North German Confederation in 1869. In France the Second Empire permitted combinations for strikes in 1864 (although the right to work was protected against picketing) and accorded *de facto* recognition to trade unions in 1868. In Britain, where trade unions had been legal since 1824, it was the Liberal government of Gladstone that outlawed picketing in 1867 and Disraeli's Tory government that removed picketing from the accusation of criminal conspiracy in 1875. Even so, where trade unions did form, they represented only a fraction of the industrial working class: élite groups of metalworkers, shipbuilders, boiler-makers, miners, building workers, printers, shoemakers, and spinners. Only 2 or 3 per cent of the German labour force was unionized by 1875, and that included self-employed masters who organized alongside journeymen and skilled factory workers. Moreover, they could operate successfully only when the demand for labour exceeded its supply; once depression set in during the mid-1870s not even the skilled workers were in a position to fight back.

Bourgeois Dynasties

By the middle decades of the nineteenth century the days of the self-made man were numbered. The commercial and industrial bourgeoisie consolidated its position, becoming less open to new blood from below, and more secure against the risk of fall-out from its own ranks. There was one exception to this rule. The Jews of Central Europe, who had hitherto been characterized either as Court bankers or poor artisans and pedlars, experienced a phenomenal *embourgeoisement*, moving into commerce, credit and (when legal restrictions were removed) the professions. Thus in the united Germany of 1871, 80 per cent of the Jewish population could be described as bourgeois.

The key to the success of the commercial and industrial bourgeoisie was the family firm. Whereas the nobility could bring new skills and resources into the family only by inheritance or marriage, this was achieved in the bourgeoisie by means of the partnership. Of course, the partnership was often cemented by marriage, as sisters married their brothers' partners, or sisters' husbands were brought into the partnership after marriage. Exceptionally, successful businessmen married their daughters into the aristocracy, as did Schneider of Le Creusot and the Rouen cotton magnate Pouyer-Quertier did. But as a general rule the family served the firm, and in turn the firm served the family. Industrialists came to look on the business as a patrimony, an estate on which to found and perpetuate their dynasty. 'From my early life', wrote Werner Siemens in 1881, 'I was enthusiastic about founding a world-wide business à la Fugger, which would give power and reputation not only to me but also to my descendants, and which would provide the means to raise my brothers and sisters and other near relatives to higher standards of life.'[4]

Whereas in the early part of the industrial revolution, women had often been involved in the firm, keeping accounts or supervising workers, in the mid-nineteenth century a division of labour was established, with the patriarchal businessman running the firm, and his wife running the household. It was a mark of a successful business and model family that the husband concerned himself with production, the wife with reproduction, education, and consumption. The bourgeois family no longer lived next to the factory, but in a tall bourgeois residence, with lavish, draped interiors, surrounded by a large garden or park. The bourgeois lady supervised the servants, educated the children, kept her hands busy with embroidery and needlework, wrote letters, visited and received lady friends in the afternoons, and organized receptions. She also attended church, sent her daughters to convent schools, and undertook charitable work, for the church legitimated the patriarchal family and provided the means for her to work in the wider community, counter-balancing the ravages of capitalism.

In order to succeed economically, the bourgeoisie had to create an environment in which capital could be accumulated, safe from the social threats posed by urbanization, industrialization, and radicalism. The tactics of aristocratic-run governments, which fostered the divisive rule of party, and which responded to popular outbursts by means of repression, lacked coherence and foresight as far as the bourgeoisie was concerned. They were also aware that cut-throat competition, though in the nature of capitalism, had to be balanced by the integration of the bourgeoisie as a class, to strengthen their hand in dealing both with governments and the urban masses. Given the breakdown of corporations and guilds, and the divisiveness of politics and religion, the vehicle of this integration was the voluntary association in which talk of politics and religion was banned. These took various forms, from literary and scientific societies, which proclaimed the virtues of useful as well as disinterested knowledge, to leisure associations, whether gentlemen's clubs on the English model or gymnastic, shooting, and music societies on the German model, and societies to improve the lot of the working classes through savings schemes, education, and temperance.

Some powerful employers provided such services through the firm, practising an 'industrial feudalism' to re-create a community of happy workers and reflecting the paternalism that agrarian landlords were said once to have shown to their peasants. Thus entrepreneurs such as Titus Salt at Bradford and Alfred Krupp at Essen provided canteens, and bath-houses, terraced cottages, evening classes, and chapels, allotments, and even holidays for their workers. Voluntary associations run by middle-class men concentrated on

---

[4] Quoted by Jürgen Kocka, 'Family and bureaucracy in German industrial management, 1850–1914', *Business History Review*, 45, no. 2 (1971), 138.

civilizing the male working class, while those run by their wives cared for single mothers, working mothers, and children. Though the grip of the middle classes on central government was still limited, they were increasingly active in municipal government. Limited municipal self-government was practised in Prussia after 1808 and copied by Russia in 1870, and the adoption of tax-weighted franchises in the towns and cities clearly favoured the bourgeoisie. Control of municipal government enabled the middle classes greatly to improve the urban environment in the middle years of the century by the provision of clean water supplies, sewerage, street cleaning, street lighting, and green spaces.

Attempts to integrate the middle class were, of course, only partially successful. The middle classes might be defined as all those in between the idle rich and the dependent poor, those who were independent economically by dint of property or education. By 'bourgeoisie' the French tended to mean an upper middle class of industrialists, merchants, bankers, professional men, and higher civil servants, separate from the *petite bourgeoisie* of artisans, shopkeepers, schoolteachers, lower civil servants, and white-collar workers. In Britain there was still a strong contrast between the City and northern industrialists. The financial and commercial bourgeoisie was generally richer than the industrialists, providing 16 of the 147 millionaires in Britain between 1858 and 1879, while the industrialists provided 13, and the landowners 117. Moreover the bankers and merchants were closer to the aristcracy in life-style. In Germany the *Bildungsbürgertum* or university-educated bureaucratic and professional middle class still looked down on the *Wirtschaftsbürgertum* or commercial and industrial bourgeoisie, although the latter, having closed the gap of wealth, were steadily closing that of status as well.

The rising status of the commercial and industrial bourgeoisie may be explained by a number of factors. One was the powerful economic spurt of the period 1851–73 and the cult of economic growth. In France a rival ideology to that of the classical-trained, leisured élite was provided by Saint-Simonism, preached by such gurus as Michel Chevalier, professor of political economy at the Collège de France between 1840 and 1879. According to this thinking, producers were more virtuous than the idle, society should be organized according to 'capacity' not birth, and co-operation in the industrial process would ensure social harmony. The *ingénieur*, understood in the wider sense of the technocrat, was honoured: in 1880 a dictionary of professions described him as 'the king of the epoch'. A second was the development of scientific and technical education to confer coveted academic qualifications on the captains of industry. Here, Great Britain fell some way behind. Physics and chemistry laboratories were set up at Oxford and Cambridge in the 1870s, and the experimental sciences became an integral part of the new universities of Manchester, Birmingham, and Leeds. But university science was never properly divorced from liberal education, engineering was not taught outside the universities in a distinct hierarchy of technical schools, and the British engineer remained a man who had risen from the ranks and gained experience 'on the job'. The pattern was entirely different in countries such as France, Germany, Switzerland, and even Russia. Faced with the problem of catching up in the industrial race, their governments sponsored scientific and technical education, which had direct relevance for industry. The University of Giessen turned out chemists who revolutionized the German chemical industry in the mid-1860s. The French *grandes écoles* provided the model for technical schools training engineers outside the universities, such as the Technische Hochschulen of Zürich (1855) and Berlin (1879), or the Technological Institute of St Petersburg (1862). Finally, the process of professionalization, by which professions established their own standards and conditions of entry, spread from the old liberal professions to the newer managerial professions. An Association of German Attorneys and a General German Teachers' Association were set up in 1848. Both were abolished after the Revolution and did not reappear until 1871. But an Association of German Engineers was authorized in 1856, made up of entrepreneurs and technical directors as well as of engineers, which campaigned among other things to achieve full parity of Technische Hochschulen with the established universities.

Despite the high status of the educated class in Germany, it always remained on a lower rung than the nobility. And the powerful position that the nobility occupied in the bureaucracy and army would have to be broken in many countries before the middle class could proclaim its triumph. The nobilities of the Italian states (except Piedmont) were broken by the process of unification, and the new state was run by a bourgeois political class of lawyers, civil servants, and landowners. In France, the destruction of two monarchies also served to weaken the grip of the nobility on office. The proportion of nobles among the French prefects declined from 53 per cent in 1852 to 36 per cent in 1870, and three-fifths of these were of the 'imperial' nobility of Napoleon I. In the French army, the proportion of sub-lieutenants belonging to the nobility fell from 27 per cent in 1825 to 5 per cent in 1840, not because of the 'internal exile' of the Legitimists after 1830 but because of the abolition of privileges of promotion accorded to the nobility. However, noble privilege was replaced by military and bureaucratic dynasticism. Of the entrants to the military school of Saint-Cyr in 1865, 50 per cent were sons of military men, 18 per cent sons of civil administrators.

England was a far less bureaucratic society, which tended to make it more aristocratic. The counties were supervised by the lord-lieutenants, who were invariably peers, and until the 1880s by the magistrates of the quarter sessions. As late as 1887, the gentry composed 81 per cent of the county magistracy, the clergy 6 per cent and peers or their heirs 7 per cent. The development of Poor

Law boards, sanitary boards, and school boards, together with the appointment of government inspectors, tended to favour the middle classes more, but appointment to central government departments by ministers and the purchase of army commissions tended to favour the aristocracy. It was the setbacks of the Crimean War, when foolhardy decisions were seen to be the fault of upper-class nincompoops, that provoked a movement for administrative reform. One of its leaders moved in the House of Commons in June 1855 'that this House is of the opinion that the manner in which merit and efficiency have been sacrificed in public appointments to party and family influence, and to a blind adherence to routine, has given rise to great misfortunes and threatens to bring discredit upon the national character and to involve the country in grave disasters'.[5] As a result, a government commission of enquiry was set up, but it was not until Gladstone came to power that recruitment to the civil service by open competition was established (1870) or that the purchase of army commissions was abolished (1871). Moreover, far from the floodgates being opened to social climbers, the examination system ensured that the civil service was dominated by a mandarinate educated at Oxford and Cambridge, while the paltry pay of army officers restricted the career in practice to those with private incomes.

But while England had nobles, it did not have a nobility; legally, the son of a duke or marquis could be only a commoner. In this respect it differed from Germany and Austria, where the nobility formed a caste. In those countries, moreover, unlike Russia or France, noble pedigree was of far more importance than official rank, so that a prime minister in Austria, if he were not of sufficient lineage, might be excluded from certain ceremonies of state. In the event, such a situation rarely arose, because of the near-monopoly of office of state and military commands held by the aristocracy. Between 1818 and 1871, 73 per cent of Prussian cabinet ministers were noble, as was 65 per cent of the officer corps in 1861, when William I became king. The noble ascendancy was less in other German states, such as Bavaria, but it was precisely this concentration of power in the hands of the nobility in Germany and Austria, the persistence of 'feudalism', the exclusion of the monied bourgeoisie and *Gebildeten* from political influence, that made tensions within the élite more acute than in England and France in the second half of the nineteenth century.

---

[5] Quoted by Southgate, *The Most English Minister* ... 364.

7

NATIONALISM AND UNIFICATION

Reaction: The 1850s

The tide was flowing strongly against revolution in the 1850s. The period between 1848 and 1855 has been described as 'the darkest hour in the night of Russian obscurantism in the nineteenth century'.[1] Constitutional and representative government had never existed in Russia; in the Habsburg Monarchy it came to an end. The Kingdom of Sardinia, which had challenged the imperialism of Austria in Italy, together with countries such as Great Britain, and Spain, Belgium, and the Netherlands, which had escaped relatively lightly from the violence of 1848, retained their constitutions and parliaments. Here were oligarchies which, by various combinations and coalitions in parliament, managed to navigate a difficult passage between revolution and reaction. It was only in France that there was a new political departure in this period, for the parliamentary notables were displaced by the President of the Republic who resorted to a *coup d'état* and established a regime that was both authoritarian and based on wide popular support.

In the Habsburg Monarchy the Constitution of 4 March 1849, which had been proclaimed by the government, not devised by an assembly, was never properly implemented before it was suspended on the last day of 1851. Martial law was in force in Vienna and Prague until September 1853, and in most other parts of the Monarchy until the marriage of the Emperor Francis Joseph in May 1854. The Minister of the Interior, Bach, eliminated all the forms of representative government, from communal assemblies up to Landtage, that had been envisaged by his predecessor in the spring of 1849. After 1851 the Reichsrat or Imperial Council was a purely advisory body of elder statesmen. The system of bureaucratic centralization was organized so that the great majority of officials in all parts of the Monarchy would be German-speaking. Lombardy-Venetia and Hungary, which had dared to rise in revolt against Vienna, were accorded no quarter but subjected from October 1849 to the rule of military governors. The Hungarian gentry were also punished ruthlessly, and deprived completely of the county assemblies and courts which had always been their arena. Radical elements around Mazzini and Kossuth, who had fled for his life into Ottoman territory only to be imprisoned by the Turks until 1851, formed secret societies and prepared for active resistance. But the insurrection staged by Mazzini in Milan on 6 February

---

[1] Isaiah Berlin, 'Russia and 1848', in *Russian Thinkers* (London, 1978), 3.

1853 was a fiasco, and the Austrian authorities now tracked down the Magyar conspirators to Transylvania and executed twenty-five leaders.

In Vienna the high aristocracy was back in the saddle. More significant still was the peace made between the imperial government and the Catholic Church. It was now understood that the Church could serve as the spiritual ally of the state in the struggle against revolution, and so by imperial rescripts of April 1850 and the Concordat of 1855, the anticlerical policies of Joseph II were reversed. Roman Catholicism was declared the state religion and at the same time the Church was given greater independence from the state. The Austrian example was imitated by many of the smaller German states. In Hesse-Darmstadt, the reactionary Chief Minister, Baron von Dalwigk, restored many of the privileges of the Roman Catholic Church in an agreement of 1856 with the influential Archbishop of Mainz, Wilhelm von Ketteler, and ensured that the Hessian nobility were entrenched in the upper house of the assembly. In Hanover, the nobility whose pre-eminence in the upper house and in the provincial estates had been undermined as the result of reforms in 1848, obtained their revenge in 1855 with the support of the blind, fanatical, and autocratic King George V, and of the Federal Diet at Frankfurt.

Although the King of Prussia had taken the leading role in suppressing the 1848 revolution in Germany, and was keen to reform the German Confederation in order to win more influence in it, the Austrian minister president Schwarzenberg was able to secure the support of the major German states at the Dresden conference of May 1851 for renewing the old-style Confederation under Austrian leadership. He also managed to secure a Prussian guarantee to back Austria if Lombardy-Venetia were invaded. Prussia, on the other hand, continued to dominate the Zollverein and keep Austria outside it. It also paved the way for a demonstration of power on both the German and European stages by strengthening the state. For the Chief Minister, Otto von Manteuffel, state-power, not aristocratic influence, was the strength of the Prussian monarchy, and if representative institutions were to be permitted to survive, they must be bent firmly to the will of the government. The patrimonial jurisdictions of the Junkers were finally abolished. Because many officials, especially young jurists, had sympathized with the revolution, the bureaucracy and judiciary were subjected to a political purge, and files on the conduct of public employees were reinstated. At the same time the bureaucracy was mobilized to supervise elections, and reliable officials were encouraged to put themselves forward as candidates. As a result the assembly of 1855 was nicknamed the 'Landratskammer', dominated as it was by those eyes and ears of the government in the locality, the district presidents.

Everywhere constitutional rule was under threat. Prussia, like Austria, was subjected to a period of martial law in 1849. After a Berlin jury acquitted a leading democrat in December 1849, administrative justice was extended.

The Berlin police chief became, in effect, the Prussian Minister of Police. A constitution was proclaimed by the government on 31 January 1850, but it was of an entirely authoritarian nature, ministers being responsible to the king alone. In Sardinia-Piedmont, the constitution remained intact, and that was the liberal Constitution of March 1848. But this was no thanks to the young king, Victor Emmanuel, whose father had abdicated after being defeated a second time by the Austrians. Autocratic by temperament, surrounded by the military men of the royal household, detesting the assembly which had fallen into the hands of a democratic '*canaille*', he wanted nothing better than a *coup d'état* against the constitution. However, Victor Emmanuel needed the support of liberal powers against Austria, and a prime minister like Camillo di Cavour needed parliament as a power-base to use against the king. Not for nothing was he an anglophile.

The parliamentary system constructed by Cavour, who became prime minister in 1852, was designed to exclude from power both the democrats and those clerical and aristocratic elements that looked to Austria and the Papacy to underpin their position. It was a *connubio* or marriage of his own centre-right with the centre-left of Urbano Rattazzi, which was held together by a policy of anticlericalism, including the dissolution of monasteries. There was a clerical reaction which made itself felt in the elections of 1857, but Cavour was cavalier with the parliamentary system when it suited him, and many of the right's seats were invalidated on the grounds that the pulpit and confessional had been used for electoral purposes. At the outbreak of war with Austria in April 1859 Cavour extracted from parliament authority for the king (and himself) to rule dictatorially for a year. The annexation of Savoy by France, foisted on parliament in the spring of 1860, got rid of the most clerical and conservative part of the country.

The stability of Cavour's parliamentary majority was secured by manipulating a tiny electorate. As Minister of Interior as well as Foreign Minister, Cavour could rely on provincial intendants to support government candidates by fair means and foul. The pattern in Spain was very similar. The moderate oligarchy of rich landowners, merchants, civil servants, and magistrates returned to power in 1844 and changed the constitution the following year. The franchise was restricted to substantial property-owners and the administration centralized so that provincial military governors could manage the elections. In the last resort the power of the oligarchy rested on the army of General Narváez, Duke of Valencia and Chief Minister between 1844 and 1851. In a society so divided between the propertied élite and the impoverished mass, constitutional opposition was very difficult. The Progressives were anxious to remain a respectable alternative. The Democrats who broke away from them in the 1840s flirted with republicanism, crusaded for federalism, and denounced conscription and the excise which weighed on the masses. But they were lawyers, academics, and *rentiers* who had very little support among the urban, let alone the agrarian poor, and relied on the ill-paid NCOs and junior officers in the army for political clout.

There was thus no 1848 revolution in Spain. That did not, however, remove the fear of revolution or prevent political use of it. The headstrong Queen Isabella and Court camarilla were eager to revert to absolute government, impressed by the example set in France by Louis-Napoleon. Narváez was therefore dismissed from office, a Concordat was concluded with the Catholic Church (1851) and the Cortes was dissolved in December 1852. Plans were elaborated to replace them by a small advisory assembly of appointed notables. The moderate oligarchy resisted these moves, and it was on their behalf that General Leopoldo O'Donnell mounted a coup against the Court in June 1854. He was sent into exile. Revolution was now the only means of stopping the Court. Insurrectionary juntas sprang up in Barcelona and other provincial centres. However it was not the Democrats who profited but rather the Progressives, who turned to their own general, Espartero. The popular movement was brought under control and elections to a Constituent Assembly held under the wider franchise of 1837, gave almost total control to the Progressives. But as in the 1830s the principles of these ambitious professional men, intellectuals, and landowners were only a cover for greed. They were concerned less with drawing up a constitution than with selling off the property of the secular clergy and the common land of the municipalities; they introduced foreign bankers and railway-builders to conjure prosperity out of arid soil. Opposition built up among the poor, Carlist counter-revolutionaries launched hostilities and the moderate oligarchs looked to O'Donnell to restore order. The Constituent Assembly was dissolved in September 1856 and the Moderates restored their own constitution of 1845. The parliamentary system that prevailed between 1858 and 1863, under the auspices of O'Donnell, was a coalition of Moderates and those Progressives who might be enticed by the spoils of office. The stability of this Liberal Union was ensured by the Ministry of the Interior, which provided patronage by means of which the caciques, or local big-wigs who had established powerful positions as a result of the land sales of the last twenty years, could build up a network of loyal dependants and ensure, at elections, the return of deputies who would support the government. It was a preview of the way in which Spain would be run after the Restoration of 1874.

Great Britain had neither the centralized administration nor, except in the dockyards, the volume of government patronage to influence elections in this way. But the landed gentry dominated the county magistracy and between the first and second Reform Acts, as Bagehot observed, the whole structure of British government rested on the deference of the lower orders to the ruling class of landowners—to whom might be added the large employers of labour in the industrial towns. Just as Piedmont and Spain were governed by parliamentary coalitions drawn from the landed oligarchy and avoiding the extremes of reaction and revolution, so also was Britain. The Repeal of the Corn Laws split the Conservatives into free trading Peelites (though Peel died in 1850) and die-hard protectionists under Lord Derby and Disraeli. The Whig–Liberals returned to office under Lord John Russell (1846–52), then formed a coalition with the Peelites, with the Peelite duo Lord Aberdeen as Prime Minister and Gladstone as Chancellor of the Exchequer (1852–5). In 1855 the Peelites resigned from the coalition, leaving the Whig–Liberals in power under Lord Palmerston. Reinforced by the elections of 1857, the Whig–Liberals renewed the coalition with the Peelites, and in 1859, drawing in a number of Radicals too, formed the Liberal party.

Belgium and the Netherlands had not been greatly threatened by democrats in 1848, for constitutional reforms had been brought in by the Doctrinaire Liberals. Likewise conservatism had nothing to bite on, for there was no royalism, feudalism, or clericalism in the Netherlands, and only Roman Catholicism in Belgium. So, when the Liberals were excluded from power in 1852 and 1853, they were replaced by moderate liberals, who were as opposed to Catholicism as to radicalism, and represented in the case of the Netherlands the old regent oligarchy of Amsterdam bankers and traders.

In France, the parliamentary oligarchy was not destined to have things its own way. The Legislative Assembly, elected in May 1849, was dominated by conservatives and royalists who were terrified by the resurgence of the socialist-democrats, the 'Montagne'. To stifle revolution they reduced the electorate, tightened censorship, and handed over the education system to the Catholic Church. Louis-Napoleon Bonaparte, elected President of the Republic by universal suffrage in December 1848, was threatened by a plot in the Assembly to secure the election as President in 1852 of the Orleanist Prince de Joinville, who would pave the way to royalist restoration. The only way to confound the conspiracy, in his eyes, was to change the constitution in order to secure the right to stand for a second term of office. In addition, he wanted to restore universal suffrage, the authentic voice of the people, to submerge political faction in a national consensus. Having failed to obtain the three-quarters majority in the Assembly required for constitutional revision, he turned to the army and mounted a *coup d'état* against the Assembly on the night of 1–2 December 1851. Royalist and republican leaders were arrested, but resistance to the coup was half-hearted because Napoleon immediately restored universal suffrage and was seen to have dealt a sharp blow to oligarchy. There was less popular opposition in Paris than in rural central and southern France. It was put down ruthlessly and insurgents were deported to Guiana or Algeria, but a plebiscite on the heads of the new constitution held on 18 December 1851 was ratified by 7.5 million 'yes' votes to 640,000 'no' votes and 1.5 million abstentions. The seizure of power was therefore legitimized by an *appel au peuple*, although the claims of the monarchy had still to be dispelled. The family property of the Orleanist dynasty was confiscated and in November 1852 another plebiscite conferred the title of Emperor on Napoleon, and made the title hereditary within his family.

The regime of Napoleon III was anti-parliamentary and authoritarian but above all Bonapartist. 'Since France has carried on for fifty years only by virtue of the administrative, military, judicial, religious and financial organization of the Consulate and Empire', asked Napoleon, 'why should she not also adopt the political institutions of that period?'[2] Those institutions included a head of state who was also head of government, his own prime minister, and responsible before the people alone. Ministers had no collective responsibility, which would present a 'daily obstacle to the individual initiative of the head of state', and were answerable to the Emperor, not to parliament, where they had no seats. Laws were drawn up by a Council of State of trained jurists, and voted by the lower house, the Legislative Body, but the Legislative Body could not present its own bills, or question ministers, or publish its debates. The Senate was not a Chamber of Peers, as the upper house of the July Monarchy had been. It was composed of marshals, admirals, cardinals, and government nominees, including famous scientists, who heard petitions, acted as guardians of the constitution, and might interpret it by means of the senatus-consultum.

The other side of the authoritarian regime was its popular basis in universal suffrage. This was called upon not only to ratify changes in the constitution, by the plebiscite, as under Napoleon I, but also at legislative elections, as in 1848–9. A favourable view is that the Second Empire undertook the political apprenticeship of the French masses; a more cynical view that Louis-Napoleon realized that the popular vote, which was above all rural, would not play into the hands of republican extremists. Both contain some of the truth. A large proportion of the French people was instinctively hostile to all notables, whether royalist or republican, as they had demonstrated in December 1848, and universal suffrage mobilized for the Empire the support of those beneath the political class. On the other hand there was no organized Bonapartist party, and the government could not rely on the natural governing class of France, which was Orleanist. It developed a system of official candidates, who were selected from 'men enjoying public esteem, concerned more with the interests of the country then with the strife of parties, sympathetic towards the suffering of the labouring classes'.[3] These were actively supported by prefects armed with government patronage, and police powers to suspend newspapers, and close the cafés and bars where the opposition held their meetings. The elections of March 1852 returned a very docile chamber, in which a quarter of the deputies were industrialists, non-political

---

[2] Quoted by Marcel Prélot, 'La Signification constitutionelle du Second Empire', *Revue française de science politique*, 3 (1953), 36.
[3] Quoted by Maurice Agulhon, *The Republican Experiment 1848–1852* (Cambridge, 1983), 177.

animals who were indebted to the government for the restoration of order and currently on the wave of an economic boom. Marx's portrait of a regime founded on bayonets and peasant ignorance is a caricature, but the opposition of the traditional élites to Napoleon III had to be answered by strengthening the executive.

The Crimean War

The Crimean War of 1854–6 may be seen as another episode of the perennial 'Eastern Question'. Russia again declared war on the Ottoman Empire and Great Britain again manœuvred to preserve the integrity of that Empire, as a buffer against Russian expansion. But there were also differences in the scenario. Great Britain was allied to France, and it was France that made the running for intervention, its aims as inscrutable as they were ambitious. The Balkan interests of the Habsburg Monarchy became clearer, and served to damage its relations with Russia in the long term. Lastly, the vulnerability of Tsarist Russia and its serf-armies was amply demonstrated, with important results both for its own internal development and for the resurgence of nationalist movements, once it had withdrawn from the European diplomatic scene.

Russia's place in the framework of European stability after 1850 was central. It had supported Austria in suppressing the Hungarian revolt in 1849. It supported Austria against Prussia's bid for leadership of the German Confederation in 1850–1, too, but at the same time had a common interest with Prussia in preventing the outbreak of revolution in Poland. It had co-operated with Turkey to crush the Romanian rising in the Danubian Principalities, where it had re-established a protectorate, although increasingly it considered that it should have a free hand in settling its differences with the Ottoman Empire.

Into this sedate gathering of European monarchs there now stepped an uninvited guest, Napoleon III. Tsar Nicholas was horrified by his appropriation of the imperial title, but Austria bullied Prussia and then Russia into recognizing Napoleon, so long as he agreed to observe the territorial status quo. Napoleon III had no such intentions. France had been driven back and hemmed in by the treaties of 1815, and Napoleon was the first head of state since then who was resolved to break out of that confinement and to redraw the map of Europe. As he looked around, however, he saw Great Britain standing over Belgium, Prussia standing over the Rhineland, Austria standing over Italy, and standing behind them all, Russia, the 'bastion of reaction'. France must go to the root of the problem, and challenge Russia. By challenging Russia at Constantinople, Napoleon would provoke confusion in the Ottoman Empire. That Empire could be used safely as a laboratory for testing the principle of nationalities, which directly challenged that of treaty rights, and the precedent could then be applied to other parts of Europe. In the first instance, however, France must play Russia at its own game, the protection of religious minorities. The ten million Christian subjects of the Sultan, ruled by the Greek Patriarch at Constantinople, came under the protection of the Tsar. But the Latin Christians, the Roman Catholics, had been recognized as a *millet* in 1840, and set under a Latin Patriarch in Jerusalem in 1847, for the first time since 1291. Napoleon seized the issue, and demanded of the Ottoman government that the keys to the Holy Places of Jerusalem be taken from the Orthodox clergy and given to the Latin clergy.

This dispute between France and Russia for influence at Constantinople, was won by France in November 1852. Nicholas was humiliated and incensed, and reverted to the view that only by the break-up of the Ottoman Empire could Russia gain control of Constantinople and the Straits. In the winter of 1852–3 Russia began to stir up trouble among the Balkan Christians—Montenegrins, Serbs, Bulgarians—and then demanded guarantees from the Porte that Balkan Christians would be protected, not put down. When the Turks refused these demands, Russian troops invaded the Danubian Principalities (July 1853).

Russian and Turkish troops clashed both on the Danube and in the Caucasus, and war seemed imminent. Austria, for whom any spark among Balkan Slavs threatened to light the powder-keg of Slav discontent within the Habsburg Monarchy, exerted pressure on Turkey, with the support of France, Britain, and Prussia, to make some concession to placate the Russians. But the Turks refused to give way. War broke out between Turkey and Russia, and on 30 November 1853 the Turkish fleet was destroyed off Sinope, on the southern coast of the Black Sea. What made the European situation different at this point was that both France and Britain were prepared to go to war to stop Russia. For France, the defeat of Russia was a necessary prelude to the re-assertion of French influence in Europe. In Britain, public opinion was hysterically anti-Russia, especially after Sinope. The government was divided between the doves under Lord Aberdeen and the hawks under Palmerston, at the Home Office, who urged the necessity of putting paid to Russian arrogance once and for all. He resigned on 15 December, placed himself at the head of bellicose public opinion, and was carried back to office as a leader of immense popularity. France had the men and Britain the ships, and paradoxically the only way Britain could be sure that Napoleonic ambitions would be kept within bounds was by entering an alliance with her. A combined fleet was sent to the Black Sea in January 1854, to clear it of Russian ships. War was declared in March, and an alliance of powers to check Russian expansion and open to all-comers was proclaimed on 10 April 1854.

Palmerston's private ambitions went a good deal further than merely standing up to Russia; in a memorandum which he drew up for Cabinet ministers on 19 March 1854 he spoke of her 'dismemberment'. Finland would be restored to Sweden, the Baltic provinces would go to Prussia, and Poland would become a sizeable kingdom. Austria would renounce her Italian possessions but gain the Danubian Principalities and possibly even Bessarabia in return, and the Ottoman Empire would regain the Crimea and Georgia. Most of the Aberdeen cabinet considered this a day-dream, and were preoccupied by the major problem of bringing Prussia and Austria into the western alliance. In Prussia there were some liberals who favoured an alliance with France and Great Britain and had the ear of the Minister-President, Otto von Manteuffel. But the aristocrats and high army officers of the *Kreuzzeitung* party regarded Russia as an ally against revolutionary movements, which they believed were generally stirred up by France; and they managed to convince Frederick William IV of their views. Prussia therefore maintained a position of armed neutrality.

The case of Austria was more complicated. Russia now posed a positive threat to her. The traditional vulnerability of Galicia was now compounded by the Russia occupation of the Danubian Principalities and, more dangerous still, by Russia's encouragement of Balkan nationalism against the Turks. The whole eastern part of the Monarchy was at risk. If Austria committed herself to the western powers, Russia would attack from the north and east and there would be precious little chance of support from sea-borne British and French troops. On the other hand if Austria allied with Russia to neutralize the threat to the Monarchy from the north, France might launch a war to 'liberate' the Italians and encourage the Hungarians and the Poles of Galicia to take up arms against Vienna. Within the Austrian government, the Foreign Minister, Buol, favoured supporting the liberal powers in the west, but the Interior Minister and the Chief of Military Staff refused to jeopardize the Holy Alliance with Russia upon which the stability of the Monarchy had traditionally depended. A compromise was reached, namely an alliance with Prussia, publicized on 20 April 1854. What this signified was difficult to say. For Buol, it strengthened Austria's northern flank and gave her the support to issue an ultimatum to Russia on 3 June 1854 to withdraw from the Principalities. For the Interior Minister and the Chief of Military Staff, as indeed for the Prussians, it was a means to bind Austria to the Holy Alliance and to prevent her declaring war on Russia.

As it happened, the gamble paid off. The Russians withdrew from the Principalities on 7 August, but on the understanding that in return Austria would steer clear of the western Powers. Buol, who had ambitions in the Balkans, did not listen. Together with the French Foreign Minister he elaborated 'Four Points' which summarized western policy and constituted a new ultimatum. These points included Russia's renunciation of its protectorate in the Principalities, a tightening up of the Straits Convention of 1841 which closed the Straits to warships in time of peace, the re-opening of the Danube whose delta had been controlled by Russia since 1829, and the end of Russia's claim since 1774 to be the special protector of the Christians of the Ottoman Empire. This time, however, Russia rejected the ultimatum (3 September 1854). The consequences of the rebuff would not immediately be apparent, but Austria now lost the Russian alliance that had enabled her to check for so long the fire of revolutionary nationalism within the Monarchy. Prussia on the other hand retained the support of Russia which was of the first importance to her in the pursuit of her German ambitions. On the other hand Austria, having joined the western powers to put pressure on Russia, saw no reason to fight once Russia had left the Principalities, which she then occupied (the Turks managed to recover only Bucharest). The Crimean expedition of September 1854 and the siege of Sevastopol was left to the British and French alone. Unfortunately, Napoleon III did not agree with Austria's occupation of the Principalities, for his plan was a united Romania under a single prince. This Austria could not contemplate, because it would sharpen the irredentism of Romanians living in Transylvania, and threaten the integrity of the Monarchy. The western powers had Austria as a diplomatic ally, but a tricky partner.

Great Britain and France were anxious to commit Austria more explicitly, and Buol was convinced that only an alliance with Britain and France could force Russia to make peace. In addition, he dreamed of an Austrian Empire which included not only Germany and northern Italy, Hungary and Galicia, but the Danubian Principalities, Serbia, Bosnia, and Herzegovina as well. For this purpose he concluded a treaty with Britain and France on 2 December 1854. The consequences for Austria in Germany were disastrous. Austria attempted, in the Federal German Diet, to drag the middle German states along with her. But Prussia's representative at the Diet, Bismarck, was able to persuade the middle German states of the treachery of Austria's anti-Russian policy, and of the illegitimacy of Austria's ambitions in the Balkans, and to assert Prussian hegemony over them. In Italy however, the Austro-French alliance gave Austria some respite. It killed hopes nourished by Italian patriots of a war of liberation fought by France against Austria and forced Piedmont to join the western alliance alongside Austria, to prevent the nationalist initiative passing to the revolutionaries.

The tide of events was nevertheless turning in favour of peace. Sevastopol fell to the allies in September 1855, after almost a year's siege. Public opinion in France was not as warlike as it was in Britain, and the constraints of great-power politics forced Napoleon III to realize that now he could do nothing for Romanian nationalism and nothing for Italian nationalism, let alone anything for Polish nationalism. Palmerston, a popular choice as Prime Minister in February 1855, was eager to go on fighting. The Russians broke through on the Caucasus front in November 1855 but Palmerston negotiated the opening of a front in the Baltic, brought Sweden into an alliance on 21 November 1855, and planned an attack on the Russia naval base of Kronstadt. However, most of the British Cabinet, together with the Queen and her Consort, were against continuing the war. Parliamentary criticism of British military and political leadership was mounting. More important was Palmerston's fear that France was on the verge of opening secret talks with the Russians, to reserve a friendship for the future; Britain could not fight on alone, and a separate peace must be prevented at all costs. In Russia, Nicholas I died on 2 March 1855 and Alexander II did not have the same commitment to the war, which was ruining both finances and foreign trade. Without the railway it took Russia three months to get troops from the Moscow area to the front, while Britain and France could ship them out in three weeks. The armies of conscripts were ill-equipped to fight, and recruitment was provoking unrest in the countryside. On the diplomatic front, there was the danger that Sweden and even Austria would enter the war. Tsar Alexander's uncle, Frederick William IV of Prussia, urged him to accept terms.

The terms of the Paris peace treaty concluded in April 1856 dealt a series of heavy blows to Russian power and Russian pride, though they were not unexpected. Her protectorate over the Danubian Principalities was replaced by the guarantee of the seven signatory powers, and she lost about a third of Bessarabia. The traditional neutralization of the Straits was extended to the Black Sea as a whole: there would be no warships there, and no arsenals. This was a triumph for Great Britain. The Danube was open to all navigation, under the supervision of a European commission. The powers guaranteed the independence and integrity of the Ottoman Empire, which was henceforth admitted to the Concert of Europe, but also claimed the right to intervene to protect the privileges of non-Muslims, now confirmed anew.

As a result of the war, the Russia whose armies had crossed Europe to Paris in 1814 was now a pale shadow of its former self. It would withdraw to contemplate internal reconstruction and could be discounted as the ever-present voice (and fist) of conservatism for the next generation. Austria was now isolated. It had repudiated and been rejected by Russia, and yet was distrusted by the western powers for failing to back up words with deeds. Prussia had improved its standing in Germany not only by its economic miracle but also by its diplomatic shrewdness. Napoleon appeared at the height of his powers at the Paris Conference, and yet his ambitions had been thwarted, whether in Italy, or on the Rhine, in Romania, or in Poland. Austria, in his view, had prevented the remodelling of Europe by refusing to fight alongside the allies; now it had everything to fear from French power. Cavour had come to Paris, hoping for some advantage, perhaps the addition of the Duchies of Parma and Modena to Piedmont, even a vice-regency for Victor Emmanuel in the Papal Legations. But Napoleon was as yet bound to respect the claims of Austria and could not afford to alienate the Papacy, for fear of turning the Catholic Church in France against him. Cavour came away from Paris empty-handed, but at least he had reached one definite conclusion: 'there is only one effective solution of the Italian question: cannon'.[4]

The Withdrawal of Russia

Between 1856 and 1875 the influence of defeated Russia counted for very little in Europe. One result of this was the flourishing of Polish, Finnish, and Romanian nationalism. Polish nationalism burst into another full-blooded insurrection in 1863, but Russia was able to bring it under control because the Crimean coalition against her could no longer be put together. Finland was a less dangerous problem, and concessions were made to prevent revolt spreading to that part of the borderlands. At the other extremity of the Empire, Russia's influence in the Danubian Principalities was terminated by their unification into the single state of Romania, the French strategy which Great Britain came to support. The formation of Romania acted as a powerful stimulus to Balkan nationalism, but in the 1860s Russia was ill-equipped to provide effective patronage for Bulgarians, Serbs, or Greeks, and Great Britain and Austria sided with Turkey to keep the peninsula from overheating.

Russia's defeat in 1856 forced the autocracy to think again about the system of bureaucracy and serfdom that prevailed from the time of Peter the Great. Russia was first and foremost a military machine, so that only the failure of that machine would induce the regime to re-examine its parts, and reform would always be approached from the military point of view. Dmitrii Miliutin, who was War Minister between 1861 and 1881, advanced a far-sighted critique of the military system of 1856. Since service in the serf-army was rewarded by emancipation at the end, service had to be long, conscription for twenty-five years. Under serfdom, agricultural productivity was low, and only two or three per cent of the total population could be kept under arms, which meant about 700,000 at the front line. There was no reserve to fill the gaps caused by casualties, with the exception of the militia, but that was more trouble than it was worth, for volunteers were not emancipated on discharge. Modern warfare required universal short-time conscription, followed by service in a reserve. Since under this reorganization all serfs would have passed through the army within a generation and earned their freedom, a modern army must mean the emancipation of the serfs. Emancipation came in 1861, universal military service in 1874. Six years' active service created a standing army of 800,000, nine years in the reserve (with the exemption of bread-winners) a force of 550,000.

As in Prussia after 1806, there was a case for mobilizing the support of the nation behind the Tsar, to establish some representative institutions which could channel opinion to an autocrat who, as things stood, remained insulated from the country by a bureaucratic caste. One or two gestures were

---

[4] Cavour to Cibrario, 9 April, 1856, quoted by Candeloro, *Storia dell' Italia moderna*, iv (Milan, 1964), 190.

made in this direction. The Russian gentry were consulted over emancipation, and invited to form committees in each province (November 1857). But because of the divergence of their views and the resistance of many gentry to emancipation, the whole matter was referred to the central government in 1858 and the Statute of 1861 was issued from above. Under a further Statute of 1 January 1864, *zemstvos* or local government assemblies were elected at the district and province level by the landed gentry, peasant communes, and townspeople formed into colleges. Permanent boards looked after business between sessions of the assemblies, and a new hierarchy of courts protected *zemstvo* officials from the arbitary commands of the bureaucracy. This was scarcely the introduction of a parliamentary system. There was no central, all-Russian assembly. The *zemstvos* had limited responsibility for roads and bridges, schools, hospitals, and the relief of famine, and could levy rates to discharge those functions. But they were not allowed to express political views, and were always contained by the Tsarist bureaucracy and police. Lastly, while the peasantry were fairly well represented at the district level, the landed gentry and officials had over four-fifths of the seats at provincial level and merchants and tradesmen felt particularly aggrieved. Their representation was low, and yet the *zemstvo* taxes deliberately penalized commercial wealth. Towns were given their own assemblies in 1870, but governors and police chiefs were always interfering, and drove independent-minded mayors to resign.

Under a reform of the law courts in 1864, jury trials were introduced, proceedings were now held in public, and the profession of barrister emerged. To deal with minor offences, JPs were elected by the district *zemstvos*. The intention was to promote a sense of law in educated society, but from this rural Russia remained sharply isolated. Peasant communities remained outside the new judicial system and vulnerable to the arbitrary intervention of officials. In the universities, where the regime had become more liberal after 1856, students, who were still overwhelmingly the sons of landowners and bureaucrats, suffered both anger and guilt over the terms of the emancipation. Protest was stifled by the stern Minister of Education appointed in June 1861, who banned student meetings, raised fees, and stepped up expulsions. But disturbances increased when the universities went back in the autumn of 1861, and a wave of university closures followed. Study groups now became secret societies, like the 'Land and Liberty' society at St Petersburg, but they had need of wider support. Later they would make contact with the peasants; for the moment the eyes of intellectuals were on the Poles.

The problem in Poland, or at least in the modest Kingdom of Poland which alone had any political significance, was that repression required an army of occupation and yet relaxation tended to conjure up all sorts of demons. In 1856 the viceroy, Field Marshal Paskevich, who had put down the Polish rising in 1831, died. The appointment of Prince Michael Gorchakov, cousin of the new Foreign Minister, indicated something of a thaw, although Alexander II, visiting Poland that year, warned, 'Pas de rêveries, Messieurs'.[5] Polish exiles who had been left in Siberia since 1831 were allowed to return, the Medical Academy if not the University of Warsaw was allowed to reopen, an archbishop was appointed to the vacant See of Warsaw, and an Agricultural Society of landowners set up to discuss the question of land reform. With 4,000 members and 77 branches over Poland–Lithuania, it might be seen as a substitute for the Polish Sejm.

These concessions were minimal, and served only to raise expectations. Secret groups of Polish students, who were more numerous in Russian universities than at home, together with young army officers, planned to mobilize the nation by emancipating both serfs and Jews, and to obtain autonomy for the Kingdom of Poland. On the day of one of the annual meetings of the Agricultural Society in Warsaw, 27 February 1861, the radicals planned a huge demonstration to urge their strategy on the land-owners. The crowd clashed with troops and five demonstrators were killed.

The danger of revolution and peasant war was now explicit. To contain it, an alliance was concluded between the Tsarist regime and the conservative upper class of Poland. It was symbolized by the appointment of Count Alexander Wielopolski, aristocrat and martinet, as the head of the civil administration. His policy was basically repressive: the dissolution of the Agricultural Society on 6 April 1861 and a massacre of 200 protesters in the streets two days later. On the other hand, he offered a few morsels: an advisory Council of State, the recruitment of more Poles into the administration and the founding of a 'Main School' to train them, the election of town and rural district councils, and the commutation of the labour services of serfs to the payment of dues.

But this puppet government of collaborating magnates could arouse only scorn and hatred. Opposition focused around the radicals, the 'reds', students, clerks, and army officers. They founded a Central National Committee which planned armed insurrection for Polish independence and the restoration of land to the peasants. Landowners, professional men, and the Catholic clergy opposed Wielopolski but disliked the strategy of insurrection: they constituted the 'whites', who tried to gain control of the opposition for moderate purposes.

As in 1831, it was the inept use of military mobilization that provoked rebellion. The conscription of 30,000 youths, from urban rather than rural areas, was announced; it was a clumsy attempt to destroy the 'reds'. But unlike 1831, the radicals were organized, with an underground network of 20,000 students, workers, petty *szlachta*, and priests. The Central National Committee unleashed a guerilla war, declared land restored to the tillers of

---

[5] Quoted by Davies, *God's Playground*, ii, 348.

the soil to arouse the peasantry, managed to spread revolution from Poland to Lithuania and White Russia, and held down a Russian army of 150,000 men.

Fortunately for the Russian authorities, the international situation was on their side. Prussia's loyalty during the Crimean War was now reinforced as General Alvensleben arrived in St Petersburg to negotiate the provision of Prussian troops. Napoleon III was eager to call a European congress, to deal once and for all with the Polish question, tearing up the treaties of 1815. But this was rejected not only by Russia but by Prussia and Austria, who had their own Poles to worry about, and by Britain, which was pricked by the old fear of Napoleonic ambitions. To ensure that revolution did not spread to Finland, and to undermine the ruling Swedish nobility Russia called a Finnish diet in September 1863 and conceded the equal status of Finnish beside Russian as an administrative language. But once insurrection had been stamped out in Poland, the Tsarist regime was merciless. 'The Russian order is personified in the mass of the rural population, in the common people, and in the Orthodox clergy,' wrote a leading Russian Panslav, Yuri Samarin, 'the Polish in the landed gentry and the Latin clergy.'[6] Thus the Polish serfs were emancipated in March 1864 in a way calculated to ruin the Polish *szlachta*. There was no question of *zemstvos* in the western borderlands. A campaign was mounted to convert the Uniates, who owed allegiance to Rome, back to the Orthodox Church. Not only was the Polish administration subjected to ministries in St Petersburg and filled with Russians, but Alexander II relinquished his duties as King of Poland and Poland was renamed simply Vistulaland.

Whereas Poland was wiped from the map, the Danubian Principalities finally came into their own as Romania. Russia had been obliged to give up its protectorate in 1856 to the supervision of the great powers and here, for once, Napoleon III was able to have his way. Romanian nationalism was running strong, and in 1857 the assemblies of Moldavia and Wallachia voted for the union of the Principalities under a foreign prince of international status, and autonomy under Ottoman suzerainty. Napoleon III declared himself in favour of these ambitions in January 1858; a united Romania would be an effective buffer against Russia and a victory for his nationalities principle. But Russia, Turkey, and Austria wanted to keep the Principalities divided and weak, and Britain was committed to the integrity of the Ottoman Empire. A conference of the powers in Paris therefore agreed on a convention (19 August 1858) whereby the Principalities of Moldavia and Wallachia would continue to have separate hospodars and assemblies, with the small exception of a joint legislative committee. This separation was cleverly foiled by the Romanians, for both assemblies agreed to elect the same hospodar,

⁶ Quoted by M. B. Petrovich, *The Emergence of Russian Panslavism* (New York, 1956), 195.

Alexander Cuza, a man of 1848. In 1861 Cuza undertook the administrative and legislative union of the Principalities, but rapidly made enemies among the ruling classes by emancipating the serfs, dissolving the monasteries of the Greek Patriarchate, and trying to increase his own authority at the expense of the assembly of boyars by use of the plebiscite. He was ousted by a palace revolution in February 1866, and the Romanians eventually secured their foreign prince. Another conference of the powers guided by Napoleon III, with Bismarck's support, settled on Charles-Louis of Hohen-zollern-Sigmaringen, who was allied to the Prussian ruling house but had a Beauharnais and a Murat for his grandmothers. Russia was infuriated but powerless, Austria was entangled in a war with Prussia, and the Turks planned to intervene until the British brought pressure to bear on them to refrain for the sake of peace. In October 1866 the Sultan recognized Prince Charles as the hereditary prince of Romania, under his suzerainty.

The influence of Russia had been eliminated north of the Danube, but there was always the possibility of increasing it in the Balkans. In St Petersburg the main concern of Gorchakov was to remain on friendly terms with the chancelleries and Courts of Europe. But Count Nicholas Ignatiev, who as director of the Asiatic department of the Ministry of Foreign Affairs had travelled to China, Japan, and Turkestan to push the boundaries of Russia's empire eastwards, could not be expected to keep a low profile when he became ambassador at Constantinople in 1864. He was one of the promoters of the Moscow Slavonic Benevolent Committee (1858) which financed the studies of Slav students, especially Bulgarians, in Russia. These Bulgarian intellectuals, who did most of their learning at the feet of Russian revolutionaries, returned to seek refuge in Romania, from where they launched unsuccessful military raids across the Danube in 1866 and 1868 into their Turkish-occupied homeland. More significant for the moment was Ignatiev's patronage of the campaign of the Bulgarian merchant colony at Constantinople to obtain a Bulgarian exarch. This was a head of the Orthodox Church in Bulgaria who would be independent of the Greek Patriarchate, which was both corrupt and hostile to national aspirations. A Bulgarian exarchate was granted in 1870, and was one step on the road to independence.

Serbia already had a ruling dynasty, or rather two rival ones, but was still bowed under Turkish suzerainty and the menace of Turkish garrison towns. Michael Obrenović, the son of Miloš, who became prince in 1860, was dedicated to the task of throwing the Turks out of Serbia. Whereas his father was a Serb peasant, Michael (having travelled in exile and married a Hungarian noblewoman) had the polished manners and military bearing of a Hungarian aristocrat. Serbia had no landed aristocracy, but he managed to increase his powers at the expense both of the bureaucratic caste, usually Serbs from within the Habsburg Monarchy, and of the French-educated intellectuals who dominated the triennial assembly and ran the liberal press. Having carved out absolute power for himself, he introduced a system of universal military service which by 1863 created an army of 90,000 from a population of only 1,138,000. It was a rough-and-ready peasant army, commanded by a handful of officers trained by a passing Czech soldier, but when clashes with Turkish forces in Belgrade in 1862 provoked the Turks to shell the town the Serbian government was able to mobilize a force of 15,000 and enlist the support of France and Russia to oblige the Turks to dismantle two garrisons. Michael Obrenović could not rely on any active Russian support at this stage and his strategy was to build a coalition of Balkan powers to eject the Turks from Europe. Conflicting claims to the same pieces of Balkan territory made the coalition very unstable. Nevertheless Serbia was able to reach agreement with Montenegro in 1866, with Croat and Bulgarian activists and the Greek government in 1867, and with the Romanian government in February 1868.

The most important link in that flimsy alliance was Greece, where the political situation had been transformed in 1862. This truncated kingdom, ruled by the Bavarian Prince Otto, without a constitution until one was forced on him in 1844, became increasingly unpopular with the commercial middle class, junior army officers, and the students, writers, journalists, lawyers, and politicians who frequented the cafés of Athens and subscribed to the 'Great Idea'—a Greek kingdom uniting all Greeks. Otto discredited himself not only by siding with Austria over the question of Italian unification, but, childless as he was, refusing to make provision, as the Constitution required, for an Orthodox heir. In 1862, while he was out of the country, he was ousted by a military coup. While the Greek parliament debated a constitution that would drastically curtail the influence of the monarchy, the great powers which had guaranteed Greece since 1832 settled on a candidate, the second son of Prince Christian, heir to the throne of Denmark, who became George I, king of the Greeks. George was essentially the British candidate, acceptable because he came in a package with the Ionian Islands, a British protectorate.

The intense desire of the Greeks in the Ionian Islands for *enosis*, or union with Greece, made the British only too happy to give up their protectorate. But *enosis* was also demanded by the Greeks of Crete, who rose in revolt against their Turkish overlords in August 1866. This rising was vigorously supported on the Greek mainland by a revolution committee which sent arms and volunteers, by the government, and by the Metropolitan Bishop of Athens. Prince Michael of Serbia now saw the chance of a general Balkan war against the Turks, and negotiated a treaty with them in the summer of 1867. King George of Greece, a prisoner of his warlike ministers, was obliged to sign. Each side pledged itself to be entirely rid of the Turks or, failing that, to gain Bosnia and Herzegovina for Serbia, and Epirus and Thessaly for Greece. In Constantinople, Ignatiev urged that Russia support the Balkan confederation to solve the Greek and Serbian problems at the same time. Napoleon III, never one to miss an opportunity, also put pressure on Russia to support Greek expansion.

For the moment, however, Russia was not strong enough and too many powers were interested in the status quo in the Balkans. Gorchakov himself, in St Petersburg, was reluctant to alienate Austria. Austria could suffer no trouble in Bosnia-Herzogovina that would encourage the Serbs within her own frontiers. Great Britain was still anxious to maintain the Ottoman Empire against Russia, and urged the Turks to withdraw their remaining garrisons in Serbia to weaken Serbia's commitment to Greece. Fortunately for conservative interests, Prince Michael was assassinated in June 1868, and Greece, which went to war alone with Turkey on behalf of Crete, was overwhelmed by Turkish sea-power. Balkan nationalism would now have to wait for the Russian Empire to reassert itself.

Unification: Italy

The failure of revolutionary movements to gain support, the separatism of the old city-states and the absence of foreign support had combined in 1848–9 to frustrate the liberation and unification of Italy. But within a decade the balance tipped towards the possibility of success. First, the revolutionary coups of Mazzinian conspirators were discredited. Mazzini organized a National Party in London in 1850, and staged a coup against the Austrians in Milan in 1853, but the middle-class conspirators were half-hearted, the popular support was betrayed, and Austrian troops quickly imposed order. Other revolutionaries concluded that only military strength would free Italy. 'To defeat cannons and soldiers, cannons and soldiers are needed', argued Giorgio Pallavicino, who had taken part in the Lombard rising of 1821 against the Austrians. 'Arms are needed, and not Mazzinian pratings. Piedmont has soldiers and cannons. Therefore I am Piedmontese. By ancient custom, inclination and duty, Piedmont these days is a monarchy. Therefore I am not a republican.'[7] If Italy were to be liberated, it would be by the military strength of Piedmont.

It followed that the federalist solution, looking to simultaneous risings in all the Italian states and the election of a constitutent assembly to organize the United States of Italy, must give way to the hegemony of Piedmont and the formation of a centralized Italian state. Carlo Cattaneo, the Milan revolutionary of 1848, still clung to federalism. But 15,000 Italian refugees had made their way to Piedmont, where alone in Italy constitutional government survived, and there, in 1857, the Italian National Society was founded. Committed to liberate and unify Italy under the auspices of Piedmont, it was headed by the Lombard, Pallavicino, the Venetian dictator, Daniele Manin,

---

[7] Quoted by Raymond Grew, *A Sterner Plan for Italian Unity* (Princeton, 1963), 10.

Giuseppe La Farina, the Sicilian leader of 1848, and Garibaldi. Above all, it had the confidence of the Piedmontese premier, Cavour.

The last question to be answered was whether, in a future war with Austria, Piedmont would obtain the support of France. The destruction of the French Republic by Louis-Napoleon came as a setback for those Italian patriots who looked to allied democratic movements in France, Germany, Poland, Hungary, and Romania to undermine the old empires. Napoleon had subsequently proclaimed his 'policy of nationalities' but his record was unconvincing and since 1855 an understanding with Tsarist Russia was central to his diplomacy. Felice Orsini, a Mazzinian who believed Napoleon to be the linchpin of the European system of reaction, tried to kill the Emperor by hurling a bomb at his carriage in Paris on 14 January 1858. He failed, but before he went to the scaffold he publicly urged the Emperor to intervene and liberate his country.

Napoleon III did intervene in Italy, a year later, but his aims could not be boiled down to the support of Italian nationalism. He was anxious to neutralize the Italian revolutionaries by seizing the initiative from them. French territorial and dynastic interests were well looked after. The outcome of Napoleon's meeting with Cavour at Plombières in the Vosges on 20 July 1858 and their secret treaty of 10 January 1859 was that Piedmont would be extended into a Kingdom of Upper Italy including Lombardy, Venetia, Parma, Modena and the Romagna, or Papal Legations. France would receive Nice and Savoy by way of compensation, and a Kingdom of Central Italy, grouping Tuscany, Umbria, and the Marches would be formed. The pact was sealed by the marriage of Napoleon's cousin, Prince Napoleon, and Princess Clotilde, the pious younger daughter of Victor Emmanuel, on 30 January. But Napoleon was acutely aware of the limits imposed by the international situation. The core of the Papal States could not be touched, neither could the Bourbons of Naples be challenged, without alienating Austria and Russia. At that moment Austria was uncomfortably isolated, and the Tsar offered Napoleon a benevolent neutrality. Prussia was ready to challenge Austria for hegemony within the German Confederation but Great Britain, under the Conservative cabinet of Lord Derby, was favourable to Austria and wary of Napoleon's ambitions. 'That Europe should be deluged with blood for the personal ambition of an Italian attorney and a tambour-major like Cavour and his master,' observed the Foreign Secretary, 'is intolerable.'[8] However, Great Britain was unlikely to intervene on the side of Austria.

Piedmont rejected Austria's ultimatum to disarm, and Austria invaded in April 1859. In the ensuing war, 70,000 Lombards and Venetians actually fought in the Austrian armies, while most of the fighting against Austria was undertaken not by Italian forces but by French. The battle of Magenta, the

---

[8] Quoted by R. W. Seton-Watson, *Britain in Europe*, 384.

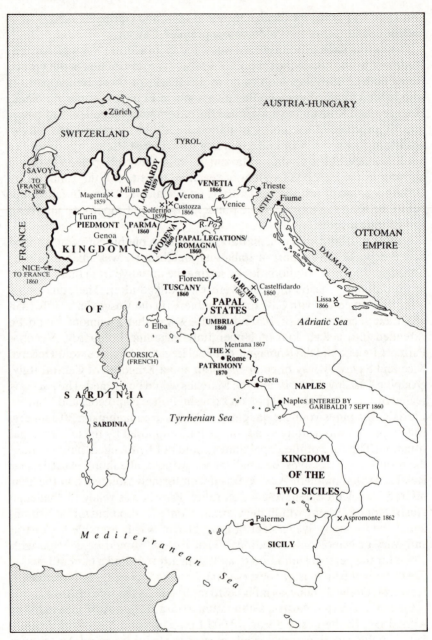

Map 4.　The Unification of Italy 1859–1870

entry into Milan, the battle of Solferino were triumphs of the French and of Napoleon III, not of the Piedmontese or of the Italian volunteers. The decision to call a truce with the Austrians was also French, and signed between Napoleon III and Francis Joseph at Villafranca on 11 July 1859. Napoleon had two reasons for calling the truce. First, there was the threat of Mazzinian revolution in central Italy, and the danger that Cavour might take advantage of the disorder to extend the boundaries of the new Italian state. In Florence, a popular movement led by Mazzinian democrats had forced the Grand Duke of Tuscany to abdicate in April. The liberal nobles and educated class had managed to form a provisional government, but their control was fragile and they appealed to Victor Emmanuel to assume the wartime dictatorship in Tuscany. This was something that Napoleon wanted to avoid and French troops under Prince Napoleon landed at Livorno to support the Tuscan provisional government. As Austrian troops withdrew from central Italy in June, so risings triggered by the National Society toppled the old dynasties in Parma and Modena, made way for provisional governments and governors appointed by Piedmont and supported by Piedmontese troops. In Umbria, the Marches, and most of the Papal Legations, the Papacy's Swiss troops managed to retain control. But in Bologna, the capital of the Legations, the vacuum left by the departing cardinal-legate and Austrians was filled by a provisional government of members of the National Society. This take-over was equally an embarrassment to Napoleon III, because the Catholic Church in France was one of the supports of his conservative order.

The second reason for Napoleon's negotiation of an armistice was his fear of a coalition of reactionary powers, similar to those that his uncle's ambitions had repeatedly provoked. Palmerston, the British Prime Minister, declared himself to be very anti-Austrian south of the Alps but pro-Austrian north of the Alps. Prussia offered to help Austria defend Lombardy-Venetia, in respect of the agreement of 1851, in return for the right to command the armies of the Confederation, which were mobilizing on the Rhine. Russia was prepared to give weight to Prussia in order to force a peace. It was therefore in Napoleon's interests to call a halt. Austria, as it happened, was reluctant to bow to Prussian demands, ever fearful of a Hungarian rising should the war go on, and was also inclined to end hostilities. The truce of Villafranca in July 1859 sacrificed Italian unification to French dynastic ambitions: Lombardy became part of Piedmont's Kingdom of Upper Italy, but Venetia was retained by the Austrians. In Central Italy, the *ancien régime* was to be restored: the Grand Duke of Tuscany and the Duke of Modena were to return to their duchies (nothing was said about the Duchess of Parma) and the Pope's Temporal Power was to be consolidated in the Legations.

The diplomatic settlement of the Italian question by France and Austria, without consulting the Italians, met with a storm of protest from Italian patriots which obliged Napoleon III to rethink his policy. Cavour resigned his premiership. The provisional governments in Tuscany, Parma, Modena and the Legations called assemblies on the franchise of 1848 which met in August and September 1859. These assemblies refused to accept the return of the old dynasties and, in the case of Legations, of the Pope's Temporal Power, and requested annexation by the constitutional Kingdom of Piedmont. Napoleon tried to shift responsibility for settling the question of Central Italy on to a European Congress, and this was provided for under the final Treaty of Zürich in November 1859. But on 22 December he published a pamphlet entitled *The Pope and the Congress* in which he argued that France would simply not accept the restoration by force and against the will of the people of the duchies to their old rulers or the Legations to the Pope.

This change of course by Napoleon III was decisive. At a stroke he alienated French Catholics, the Papacy, and Austria. Instead, he looked for support to Great Britain, where Palmerston's Foreign Secretary, Lord John Russell, was in favour of a strong Italy and the principle of self-determination, and negotiations for a free trade treaty were already under way. The understanding between France and Piedmont was renewed and Cavour returned to power in January 1860. Napoleon was now prepared to accept the annexation of the duchies and Legations by Piedmont, but this enlargement would have to bring compensation for France: the acquisition of Nice and Savoy. For his part, Cavour wanted to avoid negotiating with assemblies of notables in Central Italy which would haggle indefinitely over the terms of union. He therefore took a leaf out of Napoleon's book and organized plebiscites in Tuscany and the Legations on 11–12 March 1860. Though the Pope excommunicated those who took part in the plebiscite, pressure was brought to bear by the governors, who had almost dictatorial powers and, especially in Bologna, by the National Society. Victor Emmanuel took over the new territories by decree, and elections were held in Piedmont-Sardinia, Lombardy, the duchies, and Legations, this time on a restricted franchise, to a single parliament in Turin, which reconvened after a year's absence in April 1860. Its task was to ratify not only the annexation of the new territories, but the cession of Nice and Savoy, which had been decided by treaty on 24 March 1860 and endorsed, under the eyes of French troops, by plebiscite.

These rapidly executed deals were a snub to the conservative powers, Austria, Russia, and the Papacy, which promptly excommunicated Victor Emmanuel, but were based on the gamble that none would offer a serious challenge. The annexation of Nice and Savoy by France conjured up once again the spectre of Napoleonic imperialism, and Russell denounced Cavour as 'too French and too tricky',[9] but the mutual interests of Great Britain and France were strong enough to survive the jolt. Those who were dangerously antagonized by the surrender of Nice and Savoy were the Italian left, and

[9]   Quoted by Denis Mack Smith, *Victor Emmanuel, Cavour and the Risorgimento* (London, 1971), 164.

notably Garibaldi, a native of Nice. He sailed for Sicily with a thousand discontended intellectuals in April 1860, a move that may be interpreted as patriotic revenge for this diplomatization of the revolution. It was to have dramatic consequences. There is nothing to suggest that in the spring of 1860 Cavour envisaged uniting the whole peninsula of Italy. But once the *condottiere* Garibaldi had seized the initiative, landed in Sicily where the peasants had risen in revolt against their landlords, won them over by promises of land- and tax-reforms (rather cynically, as it turned out) and hurled them at the army of Francis II, the Bourbon King of Naples, Cavour was forced to act. Nationalism until now had been associated with revolution; national unification was an expedient to cut off revolution and control it.

The relationship between Cavour and Garibaldi was, to say the least, ambiguous. The popularity of the dashing, heroic Garibaldi was so immense that the frock-coated, bespectacled Cavour could not afford to challenge him. But the stability of the House of Savoy, its relations with the European powers, and his own influence depended on keeping Garibaldi on a tight leash. Thus, reflected Garibaldi, 'If the government stopped short of an absolute veto on the Thousand, it did not neglect to raise up an infinity of obstacles to our departure'.[10] As Garibaldi's men fought their way across Sicily from west to east, Cavour sent plenipotentiaries to prepare the way for annexation by plebiscite. But Garibaldi realized that annexation was an instrument 'to pull the fangs of the red revolutionaries'.[11] He therefore expelled the first plenipotentiary, and obliged the next to resign.

As Bourbon rule in Naples tottered, Francis II conceded a constitution (25 June 1860), brought in liberal ministers, and appealed to Napoleon III for support. Napoleon, wary of antagonizing the conservative powers further, proposed an Italian confederation that would include an enlarged Piedmont, the Papal States minus the Legations, and the Two Sicilies. But Britain refused to help by sending a squadron to the Messina Straits to stop Garibaldi crossing to the mainland, and Cavour refused to associate himself with the crumbling Bourbons against Garibaldi. Cavour nevertheless realized that 'once the Bourbons have fallen, the choice is between annexation and revolution.'[12] He was already planning, through his agents, a pre-emptive *coup d'état* in Naples to bring it under control before Garibaldi arrived there. A patriotic feather was needed urgently for the cap of Victor Emmanuel. If Garibaldi seized Naples, a humiliated Victor Emmanuel would have to launch a war to recover Venetia simply to 'save the monarchical principle'.[13] As it happened, Cavour's coup failed, the Bourbons gave way, and Garibaldi

---

[10] Ibid., p. 188.

[11] Denis Mack Smith, *Cavour and Garibaldi, 1860* (Cambridge, 1954), 186.

[12] Cavour to Nigra, chargé d'affaires in Paris, 4 July 1860, quoted by Lynn M. Case, *Edouard Thouvenel et la diplomatie du Second Empire* (Paris, 1976), 192.

[13] Cavour to Nigra, 1 Aug. 1860, quoted by Mack Smith, *Cavour and Garibaldi, 1860*, 132–3.

entered Naples on 7 September, greeted by the *lazzaroni* as a new Jesus Christ. Cavour now had to act to steal Garibaldi's revolutionary thunder. He also had to prevent Garibaldi from moving on to his next target, Rome. A repetition of 1849 would set every European power against Piedmont. Venetia was therefore forgotten. Napoleon's approval was gained for an advance by Piedmontese troops into the middle zone of the Papal States, Umbria, and the Marches (27 August 1860), and a secret agreement was concluded with Kossuth whereby a Hungarian rising would be generously supported in the event of an Austro-Italian war. Piedmontese troops crossed into the Papal States on 8 September and defeated a papal army reinforced by Catholic volunteers from all over Europe at Castelfidardo on 18 September. Garibaldi, whose forces began to lose ground against the Bourbons, was obliged to call on Piedmontese reinforcements. Cavour told the parliament at Turin on 2 October 1860 that the revolution was at an end, and was authorized to annex Sicily and Naples unconditionally after plebiscite by universal suffrage. Squeezed between Garibaldi's revolutionaries and peasant unrest on the one hand, and Bourbon reaction on the other, the notables of Sicily and Naples agreed to annexation for the sake of stability, and the plebiscite went through on 21 October.

Cavour had taken a desperate gamble. Lord John Russell, on behalf of the British government, congratulated him on carrying out unification without revolution, and on reinforcing constitutional monarchy. He spoke for a British public which welcomed the triumph of liberal, national, and anti-Roman forces. But Austria, Russia, and Prussia were incensed by what they saw as revolution and Napoleon III, the nightmare of a conservative coalition once more before him, backtracked speedily. The French ambassador in Turin was recalled and the French garrison that had protected the Pope in Rome since 1849 was pointedly reinforced. Fortunately for Napoleon, a meeting of Alexander II, William of Prussia, and the Emperor Francis Joseph at Warsaw in October 1860 was unable to agree on a concerted strategy against France. But for the first time Napoleon was faced by angry opposition in parliament when it met in March 1861, not only to his free trade policy but also to his violation of the Pope's Temporal Power. Cavour told the Italian parliament on 25 March 1861 that Rome would one day become the capital of Italy, although this would require guarantees for the Papacy— 'a free Church in a free State'—and agreement with France. Cavour's death on 6 June 1861 did not help to further negotiations, and Napoleon's Italian policy was now circumscribed by the conservative-clerical opposition in parliament and the menace of the conservative powers. He refused to withdraw French troops from Rome, which paralysed Cavour's successors and drove Garibaldi to launch a madcap expedition with the cry '*Roma o morte!*' to take the city by force. This was checked by Italian troops at Aspromonte (30 August 1864), but made negotiations no easier. Under a convention signed with France in September 1864 the Italian government was allowed to move the capital from Turin to Florence, but agreed not to invade the Papal States, while France made no clear commitment to withdraw from Rome.

The unification of Italy, or so far as it had got, was in many ways unsatisfactory. It had been made possible by a foreign power, but that foreign power was now defining its limits. The revolutionary movement of Garibaldi had exploited the masses rather than benefited them, and the masses were plebiscited only to ratify the transfer from old dynasties and nobilities to a new ruling élite. The Piedmontese were represented out of all proportion to their numbers in that new élite, because the regime that was imposed on unified Italy was one of extreme centralization, underpinning the hegemony of Piedmont.

The first stages of centralization went back to the war of 1859. Lombardy was integrated by decree, under the powers granted to the government by parliament, even before the Treaty of Zürich. There was no question of discussing the terms of fusion with a Lombard assembly vested with constituent powers; only confusion had resulted when this was tried in 1848. A law of 23 October 1859 imposed the Piedmontese system of provincial intendants and mayors, all appointed by Turin, while laws of 13 November 1859 imposed the Piedmontese system of justice and a comprehensive reorganization of all levels of education. All authority was concentrated in the Piedmontese Ministers of the Interior, Justice, and Education. The same system was extended by decree to Parma and Modena on 27 December 1859, three months before their inhabitants were consulted by plebiscite on annexation, in order to break down their 'municipalism'. Because of rising discontent, Tuscany was left provisionally with an autonomous government. But no constituent assembly was called: the legislative elections of March 1861 were to a single parliament at Turin, and the *Statuto* of 1848 was automatically extended to other parts of Italy. Carlo Cattaneo, elected Deputy for Milan, refused to take his place in the Chamber. Piedmont might have military superiority, he argued, but it was inferior in penal law to Tuscany, in civil law to Parma, and in municipal organization to Lombardy; the Piedmontese regime was if anything worse than the Austrian.

In May 1860 Cavour did promise the Chamber a more decentralized system, and a parliamentary commission was set up. Under the presidency of the Emilian, Marco Minghetti, it reported the following March, advising that the historic regions of Italy should have greater administrative autonomy. The report was ignored. In October 1861 a series of decrees dissolved the provisional governments in Tuscany and Sicily, where one of Garibaldi's lieutenants had been in charge since September 1860, and extended the system of intendants responsible to Turin to the whole peninsula; over half of these intendants in 1864 were of Piedmontese origin. For the French anarchist and federalist Proudhon, Italian unification entailed the creation of a 'prodigious bureaucracy' to keep twenty-six million subjects under control, but since the offices went to middle-class place-seekers, unification represented 'a form of bourgeois exploitation under the protection of bayonets'.[14]

Whether Italy could be controlled was in fact an open question. It was the ungovernability of the South, its population brutalized and corrupt to northern eyes, that convinced Turin that there was no alternative to administrative centralization on the French model. The secession of the southern states of America in the spring of 1861 did not reinforce the arguments of the federalists. Cavour's provisional governor of Naples reported in December 1860 on 'the impossibility of founding a government on anything other than force'.[15] Opposition was rife. The southern notables had supported the plebiscite on the understanding that some debate on a constitution and decentralization would follow. The destruction of the Bourbon regime provoked counter-revolution among dismissed officials, the army of 103,000 which was disbanded and 20,000 monks and lay brothers who were turned on to the streets when the Piedmontese law of 1855 on religious orders was extended to the South. Garibaldi's nominees and supporters were ousted by the new regime and did not hesitate to join forces with the Bourbon loyalists in a guerilla war. The imposition of conscription provoked a renewal of brigandage and in 1863 military law was imposed for two years as the state went to war on its new subjects. In Sicily, armed brigands became the clients of powerful landowners who replaced the authority of the state by a system of private justice; from 1865 this was known as the Mafia. In 1866 the Palermo garrison, weakened by the withdrawal of Piedmontese troops for the Austro-Prussian war, was attacked by Garibaldians as 40,000 Sicilians rose in revolt. Unification served only to exacerbate regional separatism and to sew the problem into the fabric of the young state.

Unification: Germany

The invasion of Italy by France in 1859 shaped both the timing and the nature of German unification. It revived fears of Napoleonic armies crossing the Rhine and provoked both the mobilization of 250,000 men in various German states under the authority of the Diet and an outburst of patriotic feeling across Germany. This was orchestrated by the German Nationalverein, founded in September 1859 by leading Hanoverian liberals such as Rudolf von Bennigsen, who wished to group German liberals (weak and isolated in their individual arbitrary and aristocratic states) behind a programme of constitutional reform and German unification. It was supported by hundreds of male-voice choirs, gymnastics and riflemen's societies that formed national confederations in 1861–2, and enthusiastically celebrated

[14] P. J. Proudhon, 'La Fédération et l'unité en Italie' (1862), in *Œuvres complètes*, xix (Paris, 1959), 99–101.
[15] Quoted by Candeloro, *Storia dell' Italia moderna*, v (Milan, 1968), 126.

the centenaries of the birth of Schiller in 1859 and of Fichte in 1862, and the half-centuries of the battles of Leipzig and Waterloo in 1863 and 1865.

After the painful experiences of 1848–9 German liberals realized that unification would take place not from the bottom up, by a German parliament, but from the top down, by the Prussian state. In 1858 the ailing Frederick William IV of Prussia retired in favour of the regency of his son, Prince William. A liberal–conservative or 'German Whig' ministry took office, inaugurating a 'new era' of parliamentary monarchy. Elections were no longer managed, and the liberals won a landslide in the Landtag elections of November 1858. Prussian leaders could agree with liberals that the achievement of German unification would require reigning in the states-rights of the thirty-three German governments outside Prussia, and a challenge to the leadership of the German Confederation by Austria, the defender of the confederal ideal. According to Otto von Bismarck, Prussia's representative at the Federal German Diet in March 1858, there was 'nothing more German than the development of Prussia's particular interests'.[16] When French armies invaded Italy in 1859, Prussia demanded of Austria the right to command the forces of the Confederation on the Rhine, but was refused. The moment for a confrontation between Prussia and Austria for leadership of Germany was fast approaching.

Initially, it was Austria that made the running. Her foreign minister between 1859 and 1864, Rechberg, had long been in correspondence with the exiled Metternich, and sought to ensure Austrian domination of Germany both by economic means and by the reorganization of the old Confederation. A plan was revived for an economic *Mitteleuropa*, protected by high tariff walls, which would win over the protectionist south German states and destroy Prussia's Zollverein. Austria also convened a summit of German rulers at Frankfurt in August 1863, and secured a majority for new confederal institutions of Byzantine complexity, including a five-man directorate of the Austrian emperor, king of Prussia and king of Bavaria, with two other rulers in rotation.

William I, king since 1861, received an invitation to attend the summit from Francis Joseph, but was pressed not to attend by his new minister-president, Bismarck. Bismarck's strategy to deal with Austria was threefold: to co-operate with her in defence of established dynasties and treaty rights, but independently of the German Confederation if possible; to revive the attractions of the Zollverein in the light of a free-trade treaty concluded with France in 1862; and to scupper Austria's plans to reorganize the Confederation by insisting upon the revolutionary solution of a directly elected German parliament.

The conservative alliance between Prussia and Austria was easily extended

---

[16] Quoted by Helmut Böhme, *Deutschlands Weg zur Grossmacht* (Cologne/Berlin, 1966), 84.

to Russia at the time of the Polish insurrection of January 1863; all three countries were troubled by Poles. In November 1863 a new provocation came from Denmark. On the grounds that most of the population of Schleswig was Danish, the Danish parliament ratified a constitution incorporating Schleswig (previously ruled only personally by the Danish king as its duke), and the new king, Christian IX, was proclaimed ruler of a kingdom that included Schleswig. Acting for the German Diet, Prussian and Austrian troops together invaded Schleswig in January 1864 and Jutland in March. Bismarck claimed that the Danish conflict was 'vital as an episode in the struggle of the monarchical principle against European revolution'.[17] Britain stood by treaty rights and therefore Prussia; France supported national self-determination, and therefore Denmark. In the absence of Anglo-French co-operation, Prussia and Austria were left free to overwhelm the Danish forces. In August the King of Denmark surrendered his rights in Schleswig to the Prussian king and Austrian emperor.

Bismarck's co-operation with Austria against revolutionary nationalism reassured the middle German states. Bismarck then set about negotiating the renewal of the Zollverein; the free-trade treaty with France now offered the prospect of wider markets in the west. It was a direct challenge to Austria's offer of a tariff union, and of course excluded Austria, but it was made under the cover of a conservative alliance with Austria. Saxony agreed to the Prussian proposals in May 1864, Thuringia, Brunswick, Baden, and Hesse-Cassel in June, and the traditionally pro-Austrian and protectionist southern states, Bavaria, Württemberg, Hesse-Darmstadt, and Nassau, which could nevertheless not survive without the markets and outlets controlled by North Germany, fell into line in September.

Having expelled Austria from Germany economically, Bismarck was ready to complete the task militarily. The *casus belli* was the settlement of the Schleswig-Holstein question. Austria and most of the middle states in the German Diet favoured bringing Schleswig into the Confederation alongside Holstein, and conferring them on the Duke of Augustenburg. This was opposed by Prussia. Ignoring the Diet, Bismarck made a treaty with Austria at Gastein (August 1865) whereby the duchies would be partitioned, Austria to administer Holstein and Prussia Schleswig. After this, however, Austria reverted to supporting the claim of Augustenburg, in an attempt to consolidate her influence within the German Confederation. Bismarck was by now bent on war. He concluded an alliance with Italy in April 1866 and entered into negotiations with Hungarian nationalists; in some situations, evidently, revolutionary nationalism was acceptable. He then bid for the support of German liberals, the men of the Nationalverein, by proposing on 10 June 1866 that the German Confederation be reorganized to exclude

---

[17] Bismarck to Werther, Prussian diplomat, 14 June 1864, cited by Böhme, *Deutschlands Weg*, 163.

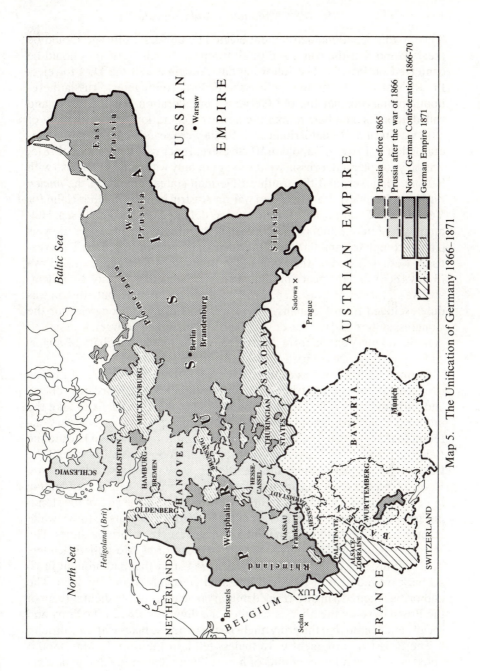

Map 5.   The Unification of Germany 1866–1871

Austria, that a national parliament elected by universal suffrage should be created, and that the command of all troops in North Germany should be conferred on Prussia. The following day Austria asked the Diet to reject Prussia's proposals and to mobilize the Federal contingents. Prussia thereupon announced that the old German Confederation was dissolved, and called upon its members to join the new Confederation. The settlement of 1815 was in ruins. Great Britain and Russia were scandalized by this unilateral action by Prussia. Napoleon III, an eternal enemy of the treaties of 1815, was only too pleased. Prussia went to war not only with Austria but also with Saxony, Hanover, and the southern German states supporting the *ancien régime* in Germany. Italy declared war on Austria in pursuit of her claim for Venetia, the Trentino, and Trieste but was defeated on land and at sea. Helmuth von Moltke, Chief of the Prussian General staff, put into operation his plan of complete annihilation of the enemy and limited war aims. The Austrians were defeated on the Main and in Bohemia at Königgrätz or Sadowa (3 July 1866), and the peace preliminaries were signed on 27 July. No indemnity was imposed on Austria and there was no occupation, but Austria was duly excluded from Germany. There was no European Congress, for the Congress system had broken down. Napoleon mediated between Prussia and Austria, taking Venetia from Austria to bestow on the humiliated Italians, and hoping for some compensation in the future for France.

German unification was characterized not only by the victory of Prussia over Austria, but by the triumph of authoritarian and military over liberal and parliamentary rule. German liberals had looked to Prussia to take the initiative in the process of unification, but Bismarck's solution was very different to that promised by the 'new era'. The confrontation went back to the Italian crisis of 1859. Prussia's mobilization of troops was a fiasco, and the Chief of the Military Cabinet and the Minister of War, General Albrecht von Roon, planned a reorganization of the army that was put before the Landtag in February 1860. Its main provisions were to increase the size of the standing army by raising military service in the line from two years to three, while incorporating the *Landwehr* or militia into the reserve or fortress duties. The liberals objected, and not only to the cost of the reforms. Most liberal leaders held commissions in the *Landwehr*, the citizen army that had brought Prussia back from defeat in 1806 and liberated Germany from Napoleon. The authorities wanted a highly-trained military machine, the obedient servant of the Prussian state; the liberals resented the divorce between the army and society and feared that the army might be used to raise taxes without consent.

The Prussian parliament nevertheless fell into the trap. In May 1860 it voted additional military credits of nine million taler on the understanding that the government was withdrawing its army bill and would strengthen only existing units; yet the new units were already being formed. The liberal opposition stiffened with the formation of the Progressive party, which was effectively an extension of the Nationalverein. Further military credits were now refused, and angry dissolutions and new elections ordered by the government in December 1861 and May 1862 only served to reinforce the opposition. In September 1862 Bismarck was called in to break the deadlock. It was at this moment that he made his famous reference to blood and iron. On 27 January 1863 he told the Prussian Lower House that if compromise should fail, conflict would follow, and 'conflicts became questions of power. He who has the power in his hands goes forward, because the life of the state cannot stand still even for one moment.'[18] Bismarck went on to purge the civil service of liberals, to muzzle the press, and to organize new elections in October 1863. The result was even worse than before, so at the beginning of 1864 the Landtag was simply disbanded.

The vital period of unification between 1862 and 1866 had thus been a period of non-parliamentary rule, one during which the 'conflict ministry' continued to rule without an approved budget. The government relied on the military–bureaucratic apparatus and the Junker landowning class which was Prussian, Protestant, subscribed to divine-right monarchy, and equated parliaments with revolution. The enemy was the liberal middle class; and Bismarck was prepared to enter into negotiations with one section of the organized working class. This was the General German Workers' Union which was founded at Leipzig in May 1863, and led by the lawyer, writer, and *galant*, Ferdinand Lassalle. Hostile to a bourgeoisie shored up by a property franchise and ruthlessly exploiting the workers, Lassalle demanded universal suffrage and producers' co-operatives, and looked to Bismarck's state to finance them. Another section of the organized working class, which opposed Prussian militarism and feudalism, and co-operated with radical elements among the middle class and petty bourgeoisie, as in Baden in 1848–9, threw up Peoples' Parties all over southern Germany in 1864. These came together in a German Peoples' Party at Darmstadt in September 1865.

Bismarck understood the contradictions of liberalism. The dramatic triumphs of his foreign policy enabled him to find a governmental majority in the Prussian parliament, to place the military and feudal monarchy on a popular basis in the new German Confederation and to rally the German bourgeoisie by the lure of wealth. In the election to the Prussian parliament, held on the same day as Sadowa, the liberals slumped from 247 to 148 seats, while the Conservatives improved from 35 seats to 136. The Conservatives in fact divided, for the Old Conservatives feared that Prussia would be swallowed up in a larger Germany while the Free Conservatives had no reservations. On the other side of the house King William's request in August 1866 for an indemnity bill to whitewash the government's period of rule without an authorized budget, in the light of its victories, split the Progressive party.

---

[18] Quoted by Böhme, *The Foundation of the German Empire*, 113–14.

Those who preferred power to law formed the National Liberal party, headed by the Hanoverian, Rudolf von Bennigsen, who was only too glad to be rid of the arbitrary and aristocratic government of George V. The National Liberals and Free Conservatives were to be the mainstays of Bismarck's rule.

After the victories of 1866 Prussia annexed not only Hanover but Schleswig-Holstein, Hesse-Cassel, and the part of Hesse-Darmstadt lying north of the Main. The rest of Hesse-Darmstadt, together with Saxony and Thuringia, were chained to Prussia rather than annexed by her. The constitution of this North German Confederation, approved by a constituent assembly in April 1867, had both authoritarian and popular elements. The Bundesrat, which represented the governments of the confederate states, not their parliaments, differed little from the Federal Diet of 1815. The hereditary president of the Confederation and commander of its troops was the King of Prussia, who embodied the principle of monarchical legitimacy. The new departure was the formation of a North German parliament, the Reichstag, elected by universal suffrage. In the Reichstag Bismarck rejected accusations of 'a deeply-laid plot against the freedom of the bourgeoisie, in association with the masses, to set up a Caesarian type of government'.[19] But Bismarck's policy cannot be described as wholeheartedly Bonapartist. It is true that he wanted to undermine the *Gebildeten*, the educated middle class of the Progressive party, which had so effectively exploited the three-tier suffrage and indirect elections to the Prussian Landtag, and he trusted in the instinctive conservatism of the German peasantry. But rather than employ political prefects to regiment them, as in France, he could rely on their deference to the German landowning class, a class much stronger than in France. And whereas French notables had little sympathy for the Napoleonic regime, Bismarck was able to ensure popular support for the perpetuation of that 'feudal' oligarchy on which the monarchy depended.

Another accusation levelled against the constitution was that it was 'nothing but the fig-leaf of absolutism'.[20] What Bismarck did was to enshrine the traditional division in Germany between civil society, the realm of private affairs, and affairs of state. Thus the military budget was taken out of the hands of parliament for a period of four years and fixed according to the size of the army, which in turn was to be one per cent of the population. There was no conception of the responsibility of ministers to parliament for their policies; only perhaps judicially, if they violated the constitution. When Bennigsen tried in 1867 to make Bismarck who, as Confederate Chancellor, was

[19] Bismarck on 28 March 1867, quoted by Lothar Gall, *Bismarck, the White Revolutionary* (1986) I, 322.
[20] Karl Liebknecht of the Saxon People's Party in the Reichstag, 17 October 1867, quoted by Roger Morgan, *The German Social Democrats and the First International* (Cambridge, 1965), 115–16.

merely the chairman of the Bundesrat, responsible for the acts of the President of the Confederation, the result was to make Bismarck the only minister of the German Confederation. His colleagues in the Prussian cabinet remained only Prussian ministers.

Finally Bismarck's triumphs rallied to him the German bourgeoisie for economic rather than political reasons. The cost of war opened up possibilities for bankers such as Gerson Bleichröder, who negotiated the sale of certain government-owned railways, and for the Diskontogesellschaft, whose directors interlocked with the leaders of the National Liberal party. The annexation of Schleswig-Holstein freed German exporters from overdependence on foreign middlemen, enabled them to trade their way out of the depression of 1866, and offered a new outlet for surplus capital: the Kiel Canal. The architect of Prussia's free-trade policy, Rudolf Delbrück, was appointed to preside over the Confederate Chancellor's office, and as a result the external tariff of the Zollverein was lowered, free enterprise established, and official authorization for joint-stock companies ended. Capital began to flow towards industry, much to the delight of the Rhenish and Silesian heavy industrialists, who were a bulwark of the Free Conservative party.

It is a commonplace that just as united Italy was an extension of Piedmont, so united Germany was only Prussia writ large. Austria was excluded from Germany (and Italy) in 1866, and the North German Confederation was Prussian, Protestant, and free-trading, for all to see. In Saxony socialists and radicals combined to form the Saxon People's Party to protest against annexation. Bismarck ruthlessly confiscated the wealth of blind King George V of Hanover because Hanoverian soldiers were organizing resistance in France; parliamentary opposition was continued by the Guelph party, led by Ludwig Windthorst, a Catholic and former Minister of Justice in Hanover. In the rump of Hesse-Darmstadt, too, the reactionary minister Dalwigk continued his struggles against Bismarck, looking to France for help.

The main problem, however, was the southern states of Germany. The peace treaty of Prague in August 1866 confined Prussian power to north of the river Main. Bismarck did not want to risk the southern states turning against him as they had in 1866. On the other hand clear attempts to integrate South Germany into the Confederation would antagonize not only Austria but also France, which wished to preserve its influence there and was embarking on serious military reform. His solution was to conclude secret military alliances with the southern states and then, turning again to the economic weapon, to float the idea of a Zollparlament, a common customs parliament elected by universal suffrage for the whole of the Zollverein, which included South Germany.

But South Germany was not to be swallowed easily. First, there were the governments—notably that of Bavaria, where Prince Chlodwig zu Hohenlohe-Schillingfürst became Minister-President in December 1866. He was anxious to keep the southern states together, and to negotiate from strength. A conference was called at Stuttgart in February 1867 to establish a common military organization for the southern states. Unfortunately, Bismarck had prevailed on Hesse-Darmstadt and Baden to accept military reforms on the Prussian model, pushed through with the help of Prussian generals, so that Hohenlohe's first plan collapsed. Hohenlohe was also concerned that a Zollparlament elected by universal suffrage would undermine the southern governments and lead straight to a unitary state. Instead, he proposed a 'wider Bund' of governments, an extension of the Bundesrat rather than of the Reichstag, and one that would maintain a close alliance with Austria. It was a last attempt to salvage the *grossdeutsch* solution against Prussian hegemony. But then the German public became outraged when Bismarck publicized a secret deal whereby Napoleon III was to purchase Luxembourg from the King of the Netherlands to compensate for Bismarck's gains. The wave of German patriotism undermined Hohenlohe's case, and the southern states were induced to accept the Zollparlament in June 1867.

By calling into existence the Zollparlament Bismarck in fact confronted himself with a new antagonist, popular opinion in the southern states. Meanwhile, in August 1867 Napoleon III and Francis Joseph of Austria met at Salzburg to consider Prussia's ambitions. Nothing concrete was achieved, for whereas France insisted on keeping Russia as an ally, Austria was already embroiled with Russia in the Balkans. But their meeting encouraged South Germans to assert their hostility to Prussia, and especially to the cost of military reforms that Prussia was demanding as the price of an alliance. In the elections to the Zollparlament, held in February and March 1868, the liberal nationalist parties in South Germany committed to integration with the north were swamped. The Catholic Patriot party in Bavaria, the democrats in Württemberg, and both Catholics and democrats in Baden routed the pro-Prussian parties, and repeated the performance in the Landtag elections. Military credits were everywhere refused. In February 1870 Hohenlohe lost a vote of confidence in the Bavarian parliament and was forced to resign. For the South German governments, the situation was intolerable. They would be obliged either to rely on liberal nationalist parties and thus become hostages to Prussia or to surrender to the Catholic and democratic opposition and to look to Austria and France for support. The danger that Ludwig II of Bavaria might throw in his lot with the Catholic opposition and Catholic powers had to be avoided at all costs by Bismarck.

It was events in a third Catholic power, Spain, that transformed the situation. Queen Isabella had been overthrown in September 1868 and the Progressive politicians were scouring Europe for a new monarch. An offer was made to Prince Leopold of Hohenzollern-Sigmaringen, of the Catholic branch of the Prussian ruling house, whose brother had accepted the Romanian throne in 1866. Bismarck seized the opportunity to eliminate the threat from the Wittelsbach dynasty of Bavaria. He coveted the imperial crown of Germany for William of Prussia, but this was claimed also by Ludwig of Bavaria. A Hohenzollern on the throne of Spain would increase the 'world-standing' of the Prussian dynasty and decide the issue. But there was the more acute danger that if a Hohenzollern declined the Spanish crown, and it were offered to a Wittelsbach, a south European Catholic coalition might come into being, with disastrous results for German unification. 'If Prince Adalbert's line or the ducal line accepts the offer', Bismarck told King William on 9 March 1870, 'Spain would have a ruling house which looked for support to France and Rome, maintaining contacts with anti-national elements in Germany and affording them a secure if remote rallying point.'[21]

Prince Leopold accepted the offer on 19 June, but before the Constituent Cortes in Spain could make the election the infuriated French threw themselves into the arena. Napoleon III had gained a massive majority in the plebiscite on the Liberal Empire in May 1870, and a dose of *gloire* would work wonders to ensure the popularity of the regime. The real issue at stake was which power was to be dominant in Europe, Prussia or France. Thus, when King William persuaded Prince Leopold to withdraw his candidature, the crisis was not defused. In pursuit of honour, rank, and greatness, the French government required the Prussian government to promise that the candidature would never be renewed. King William's refusal sent from Ems was doctored by Bismarck to imply that Prussia was breaking off diplomatic relations, and France declared war on 19 July. French 'aggression' solved the South German problem. Bismarck could now be sure that the southern German states would vote military credits and fight on Prussia's side. Despite the tremendous popularity of the war in France, the French armies were defeated at Sedan on 1 September, and Napoleon III surrendered to von Moltke. The German armies laid siege to Paris, and forced the new republican government to hand over Alsace and Lorraine and to pay a war indemnity of five billion francs. The southern German states now adhered to a united Germany, which was declared over the body of a prostrate France in the Hall of Mirrors of the Château of Versailles on 18 January 1871.

All the foundations of the German Constitution of 16 April 1871 had been established four years earlier. Sovereignty lay in the aggregate of German governments assembled in the Bundesrat, but the leading role of Prussia was indisputable. Of the 61 votes in the Bundesrat, Prussia had 17, Bavaria 6, Saxony and Württemberg 4 each, Baden and Hesse-Darmstadt 3 each, and all the others 1 each. The King of Prussia, formerly President of the Confederation, became Kaiser William I; Bismarck, his chief minister as Chancellor of the Confederation, became Imperial Chancellor, and was still the only responsible federal minister. The attributes of the Kaiser were ill defined, but

---

[21] Quoted by Georges Bonnin, *Bismarck and the Hohenzollern Candidature for the Spanish Throne* (London, 1957), 70–1.

it mattered little in practice. 'The Kaiser has no rights', explained William II on one occasion, 'and in any case it is of no importance. I have eighteen army corps and I can handle south Germans.'[22]

The Ausgleich

War was something that should have been avoided at all costs by the Habsburg Monarchy, a conglomerate of nationalities. Enemy powers might come to an understanding with revolutionary nationalists who would tear the Monarchy apart from the inside. Kossuth had been corresponding with Mazzini since 1850 and envisaged replacing the Habsburg Monarchy by a Danubian Confederation of Hungarians, Croats, Serbs, and Romanians. To confound the revolutionaries, Vienna avoided becoming involved in the Crimean War and, challenged by Napoleon III and Cavour, concluded an armistice at Villafranca as quickly as possible in July 1859. But France's patronage of subject nationalities made it clear that to cut the ground from beneath the feet of the revolutionaries the Austrian government would have to reach some compromise with conservative and moderate nationalists within the Monarchy, and restore some degree of self-government. Above all, the Magyar nobility, who had achieved autonomy in 1848 only to be defeated in battle and placed under military rule, had to be bought off for the long-term stability of the Monarchy. In 1848–9 the Austrian government had promoted 'Austro-Slavism' and used Slav peoples against the Magyars. Now it would make concessions to the Magyars, but at the expense of the Slavs— a discrimination likely to produce other and even more insidious forms of instability.

Reassured as it was at the time by the Prussian alliance, and thinking in wider terms of an economic *Mitteleuropa*, the Austrian government made an initial gesture towards the 'feudal' nobilities of the different parts of the monarchy, which had traditionally been close to the Court and ministries at Vienna. In March 1860 the Reichsrat or Imperial Council, a purely advisory body, was enlarged to include some fifty of them. What they demanded was the restoration of the historic rights of the Crownlands, which would provide forums for the old nobilities, and above all the return of the Hungarian, Croatian, and Transylvanian Diets. Under the 'October Diploma' of 1860, the government agreed to call the Diets.

These terms were agreeable to the Magyar aristocracy, but could not satisfy the revolutionaries or moderates among the lesser nobility. Déak, the leader of the moderates, wanted to go back to the 'April laws' of 1848: the Emperor to be King of Hungary in a personal sense only, with a Hungarian ministry responsible to the Hungarian Diet, and an Hungarian army. Another Austrian reform in February 1861 did nothing to satisfy the autonomists—it was

---

[22] Quoted by Jonathan Steinberg, *Tirpitz and the Birth of the German Battle Fleet* (London, 1968), p. 48.

more liberal, but also more centralist. The Reichsrat was transformed into a House of Lords, composed of archdukes, bishops, and landed aristocrats, and a House of Representatives was elected by the provincial diets of the Monarchy whose powers were reduced. The electoral system was devised to build in majorities for the German-speaking population in 'mixed' provinces like Bohemia and returned a chamber that was dominated by a German or Jewish upper bourgeoisie which was hostile to any form of separatism. For while federalism favoured the aristocracy, centralism favoured the middle classes.

So biased was the new system that no representatives from Hungary, Croatia, Transylvania, Slovenia, or Venetia turned up. Infuriated, the Austrian government dissolved the Hungarian Diet in August 1861, and reimposed military government on the country. However, there could be no question of going back to the repression of the 1850s. Revolutionary nationalism erupted in Poland, Romania, and Serbia;[23] on 13 March 1864 Kossuth's secret organization staged a massive demonstration in Pest to mark the anniversary of the 1848 Revolution. After the exclusion of Austria from Germany in an economic sense in October 1864 and the breakdown of the Austro-Prussian military alliance over the Schleswig-Holstein question, though, Austria no longer had the weight to enforce a purely German solution in the Habsburg Monarchy. Moreover the approach to compromise was not one-sided. Moderate nationalists, afraid of the rising tide of revolutionary nationalism, began to move towards the aristocratic position and to declare themselves in favour of talking to the Austrian government. 'Our goal is … to maintain the basic laws of the Hungarian constitution as far as possible', wrote Deák in April 1865, 'but we shall ever be prepared through the means provided by the law to bring our own demands into harmony with the demands of the complete security of the Empire.'[24]

Vienna agreed in September 1865 to call the Hungarian, Croat, and Transylvanian Diets. The elections to the Hungarian Diet, which opened in December 1865, were a landslide for the Deákists, who gained 180 seats. The conservatives, with whom they campaigned, acquired 21 seats, the left-centre of Tisza 94, and the extreme left only 20. This was a parliament dominated by the nobility, the aristocrats with 16 per cent of the seats, the lesser nobility with 62 per cent; the middle class and intellectuals had less than a fifth of the representation. The Transylvanian Diet, which was controlled by Magyars, asked to be incorporated into the Hungarian Diet, and they came, with only two Romanians, to reinforce the Deákists.

Negotiations between the Hungarian Diet and the Austrian government were interrupted by the Austro-Prussian War, but it made little difference to the outcome. The moderates were talking, and Bismarck's lightning victory gave the Magyar revolutionaries no chance to organize a strike. The *Ausgleich* or Compromise between the Austrians and Hungarian moderates was an agreement to prevent revolution. 'Dualism', said Kossuth at the end of 1866, 'is the alliance of the conservative, reactionary and any apparently liberal elements in Hungary with those of the Austrian Germans who despise liberty, for the oppression of the other nationalities and races.'[25] Above all it was an alliance against the Slavs. And because both Germans and Magyars feared the stimulation of Slav nationalism in the Balkans by Russia, so the agreement was by implication anti-Russian.

The *Ausgleich* was a complicated balance of royal prerogatives and national liberties. Francis Joseph was crowned King of Hungary on 8 June 1867, and had unlimited control over the imperial army, but the Hungarian parliament voted recruits. Ministers of Foreign Affairs and Defence were to be common to both parts of the Monarchy, as would be the financing of those two items, the budget to be hammered out by delegations from the two parliaments working together. But whereas the monarch in Austria could appoint a ministry in defiance of a hostile parliamentary majority, and had emergency powers to rule by decree, the Emperor as King of Hungary was ill-advised to ignore parliamentary majorities when appointing a ministry, and had no emergency powers. If the annual budget were not voted, a situation of *ex lex* came into being, and the counties and municipalities were free to refuse taxes. Moreover, since the joint budget for defence was financed largely from the joint customs duties of the Monarchy, which were to be renegotiated every ten years, the military strength of the Monarchy was mortgaged to the economic interests of the nobles in the Hungarian parliament. These had direct influence both over their own ministers in Budapest and over those in Vienna, where between 1871 and 1879 the joint Foreign Minister was the former Hungarian Minister-President, Count Andrássy.

The *Ausgleich* which was passed by the Reichsrat and became law in December 1867 created the 'Dual Monarchy' of Austria-Hungary. The other subject-peoples within the Monarchy did not do so well. Within the Austrian half were the Poles of Galicia, the Czechs of Bohemia, and the Slovenes of Styria, Carinthia, Carniola, and the Adriatic coastland. The Polish nobility were not anxious to repeat the tragedy of 1846, or to copy the insurrection of 1863 which had ended with the elimination of the Congress Kingdom of Poland. The Austrian government needed the support of the Poles in the Reichsrat to vote for the *Ausgleich*. Some compromise was therefore possible whereby, though the Galician Diet was not given legislative independence, Galicia acquired a Polish governor, and Polish became the official language throughout the education system, administration, and judiciary. As

---

[25] *Hungarian Political Trends between the Revolution and the Compromise, 1849–1867* (Budapest, 1977), 163.

a result four or five thousand German bureaucrats lost their jobs to Poles. These concessions were made at the expense of the largely peasant population of Ruthenes, who had saved the Austrian Monarchy by cutting down the Polish gentry when they rebelled in 1846. The Ruthenes now turned towards Russia for support, and became a focus for emerging Ukrainian nationalism.

The Czechs had likewise stood by the Monarchy in 1848 and were now also dealt a cruel blow. No longer simply the farmers and labourers of German landowners, or miners in the lignite mines of northern Bohemia, they had migrated to the towns as tailors, cobblers, and shopkeepers, and they were throwing up their own bourgeoisie of employers and intellectuals. But the German population was bent on retaining its supremacy. Andrássy argued in Vienna that any concession of 'Bohemian state-rights' would serve as the thin end of the wedge for the Slavs. The Bohemian Diet was therefore kept powerless with an artificial German majority, while German remained the official language in the secondary schools and universities, in the administration, and judiciary. Czechs were obliged to Germanize themselves if they wanted to get on, or to protest. 'We Slavs are peaceful people', wrote Palacký in 1865, 'but we warn you; do not sow the wind lest you reap the whirlwind.'[26] Czech deputies had walked out of the Reichsrat that was so heavily prejudiced in favour of the Germans in 1863, but would undoubtedly have voted against the *Ausgleich* in 1867. In April 1867 Palacký led a delegation of Slavs—mostly Czechs, with some Slovenes and Ruthenes—on a pilgrimage to Moscow for the Ethnographic Conference. Rejected by the Austria to which they had been faithful in 1848, they were now turning to a new patron: Russia. 'We Slavs were here before Austria', said Palacký in prophetic mood, 'and we shall be here after it.'[27]

The ascendancy of German liberals in Vienna was disastrous for other nationalities. However the conservative Minister-President Count Hohenwart, who took office in February 1871, was more favourable to federalism. He was prepared to make concessions to the Czechs in order to entice them back into the Reichsrat to reinforce his majority. But he reckoned without his opponents: the German deputies walked out of the Bohemian Diet, and German liberals boycotted the Reichsrat. Count Andrássy warned Francis Joseph against making concessions to Slavs. Hohenwart left office and the Czechs were unconsoled. In those parts of the Monarchy where the Germans' presence was important, the rights of other nationalities were severely restricted. A Slovene congress in Gorizia in October 1868 demanded a Slovene Diet and the use of Slovene in education and administration. But there was never any question of conceding a Diet, and German remained the official language in Styria, Carinthia, and Carniola. It was only on the Adriatic

---

[26] Quoted by Elizabeth Wiskemann, *Czechs and Germans* (2nd edn., 1967), 34. Wiskemann has 'storm' for 'whirlwind'.

[27] Quoted by C. A. Macartney, *The Habsburg Empire, 1790–1918* (London, 1968), 555.

coast, where the Italian minority which remained outside Italy was proving a nuisance, that any concessions were made to the Slovene languages.

The *Ausgleich* had destroyed two fundamental principles of the Habsburg Monarchy: that all the subject nationalities of the Emperor were equal and that their loyalty to him was its cement. Now the Hungarian part of the Monarchy had a new status, and the Magyar ruling class believed that only cultural assimilation, the Magyarization of other nationalities, could ensure their ascendancy in it. The tradition that the Hungarian 'nation' was the Magyars and the fact that *nemzet* meant both 'Hungarian' and 'Magyar' seemed to confer some legitimacy on Magyarization. The Nationality Law passed by the Hungarian Diet in 1868 made Magyar the official language of state, but authorized other national languages in the county and municipal assemblies, lower courts, churches, primary and secondary schools. It was never objectively enforced, the Slovaks in particular suffering the extremes of Magyarization. Their deputies to the Hungarian parliament were expelled in 1872. The three Slovak public secondary schools were closed in 1874 and the cultural association, Matica Slovenska, was disbanded a year later, on the grounds that they fostered Pan-Slavism. Coloman Tisza, who became Hungarian Minister-President in 1875, declared bluntly: 'there is no Slovak nation.' Under his rule, which was ostensibly that of the Liberal party, Magyarization became particularly ruthless, at all levels of the administration and judicial system, in the University of Pest, secondary schools, and eventually primary schools as well. It became impossible to enter the civil service or professions without relinquishing all traces of a non-Magyar background.

If there was a threat to Magyar supremacy, it was among the South Slavs. The Croat Sabor or Diet, meeting in 1865, had requested a union with the Monarchy that was purely personal (like that the Hungarians achieved two years later). But though they had supported the Monarchy against the Magyar rebels in 1848, the *Ausgleich* delivered them up to the Magyars lock, stock, and barrel. Andrássy, as Minister-President of Hungary, appointed a Ban of Croatia whom he could trust, to manage the elections and return a majority of pro-Magyar unionists. The Sabor then agreed to a law of 1868 that declared Hungary and the Triune Kingdom of 'Croatia-Slavonia-Dalmatia' to be 'one and the same state complex'. Under this settlement the Croats were cut off from Vienna by a Magyar barrier, which conducted foreign policy in the Balkans in the Magyar interest. Joint Hungarian–Croat questions were dealt with in Budapest, but there were only twenty-nine Croats in the Hungarian parliament, and the Croat minister who sat in the Hungarian cabinet was appointed by the Hungarian Minister-President. The Croats were granted autonomy in their internal affairs, and could use their own language in the administration, while the Ban was made responsible to the Sabor. But the Ban was also appointed by the Hungarian Minister-President, served as his agent, and was expected to keep Croat nationalists out of parliament. Lastly, Andrássy believed that the *Grenzer* units along the Military Border of Croatia-Slavonia might provide armed support for South Slav insurrection, whether Croat or Serb, and campaigned in Vienna after 1869 for their disbandment.

Fears about the South Slavs became acute in 1871, when the pro-Magyar Ban was obliged to resign and elections to the Sabor returned a vast majority for the Croat National Party, heirs of the Illyrians. Andrássy now managed to persuade the Austrian military that South Slav nationalism was more dangerous than Ottoman imperialism, and the Emperor agreed to order the demilitarization of the Military Border in June 1871. This provoked a mutiny among some of the *Grenzer* regiments: it was put down and martial law imposed. After mediation by the Catholic Archbishop of Zagreb, new elections in 1872 restored the official (mostly ecclesiastical) majority, and some compromise between Magyars and Croats was concluded.

The thorn in the side of the Magyars was in future to be not the Croats but the Serbs. Initially, they gave little sign of discontent; unlike other nationalities, they did not boycott the Hungarian parliament. Then, when an anti-Turkish revolt broke out among the Serbs of Bosnia and Herzegovina, in 1875, and the Serbian government in Belgrade teetered on the verge of intervention, a Serbian deputy set up a patriotic organization to send money and volunteers to assist the struggle against the Turks. At that time, it was Hungarian policy to support the Turkish Empire against Russia. It followed that Serbian nationalism, whether in the Ottoman or the Habsburg Empires, must be crushed. The Serbian agitators within the Monarchy were therefore rounded up. Andrássy began reluctantly to contemplate the occupation of Bosnia and Herzegovina in order to prevent trouble breaking out in future.

REVOLUTION CONTAINED

Constitutional Change

In the 1850s, a certain rigidity was observable in political life even in those liberal countries where representative government survived. The political nation was either so restricted in size that it did not challenge the ruling oligarchies, or else it was bullied or corrupted into docility by the government at election-time, or both. But from the early 1860s opposition groups which had been dormant since 1848–9 began to reassert themselves. The causes are not easy to pin down. Economic recovery in the early 1860s encouraged some workers to strike and organize in order to improve their wages. But the 'cotton famine' which resulted from the American Civil War provoked heavy unemployment locally, in Lancashire, northern France, and Catalonia, and the onset of another economic recession in 1866–8 was compounded by bad harvests in the same years. Yet the turmoil which overtook Europe in the 1860s was more than economic. Armies were on the march, battles were being fought and lost, and régimes became acutely conscious of their vulnerability. The unification of Italy and Germany undermined local nobilities, toppled petty princes from their thrones and obliged major ones to compromise with the principle of popular sovereignty. The success of Garibaldi and his Thousand had tremendous mythical power and seized the imagination of radical reformers in England, which he visited in 1864—and was encouraged to leave rather hastily when he became a political embarrassment to the government.

In England electoral reform was championed as a means whereby the middle class, reinforced by some of the working class, could attack aristocratic privilege and the established Church. The Reform Union, set up in April 1864, was organized by radical politicians, Lancashire merchants and manufacturers, and Nonconformist leaders. It took up the struggle against the defences of the aristocracy where the Anti-Corn Law League had left off. More significant was the Reform League, founded in February 1865 by the organized working-class élite, the unions of metalworkers, building-workers, and shoemakers who formed the London Trades Council, with the assistance of radical barristers and politicians. Radicals like Bright, who dominated one wing of the Liberal party, encouraged these organizations as valuable extra-parliamentary support and Gladstone himself, who lost his Oxford University seat in 1865, after coming out in favour of the disestablishment of the

Anglican church in Ireland, and was obliged to campaign in industrial south Lancashire, was won over to the cause of reform. In April 1866 Gladstone urged that the Liberals must 'be wise in time',[1] reform to avoid revolution, but he was also confident that the backing of the skilled, respectable portion of the working class, already acquiring property and becoming enfranchised as £10 rentpayer under the 1832 act, could only serve to strengthen the party and the constitution. But the gospel of this point of view, John Stuart Mill's *On Representative Government* (1861), made clear that the extension of the franchise must not be so great as to upset the balance of interests between the middle and working classes, and that if property became less important to qualify for the vote, education must become more so.

The death of Palmerston in October 1865, after the Liberal election victory in July, removed one obstacle to reform. The ageing Lord John Russell, who became Prime Minister, was happy to support the proposals of Gladstone, his Chancellor of the Exchequer. But the Liberal party was a broad coalition including not only radical intellectuals, Dissenting businessmen and Peelite administrators dedicated to some higher public interest, like Gladstone, but also Whig magnates in the Lords and their relations in the Commons, and a middle ground of Anglican landowners. When in March 1866 Gladstone introduced his bill to enfranchise house-owners and tenants paying a £7 rent in the boroughs, adding another 400,000 voters to an electorate of 1.1 million, Whiggish and dissident elements in the Liberal party rose in revolt, arguing that it would launch the workers as a class on property and government, allied with the Conservative opposition, and brought down the Russell ministry.

There was no question that Lord Derby, who formed a government in July 1866, could revert to the status quo. Hyde Park was invaded by rioters. Industrial disturbances increased with the onset of the slump. Irish Fenians stepped up their terrorist attacks. The Queen herself warned Derby and Disraeli that they must take up the issue of reform, and the fiasco of 6 May 1867, when the government had recourse to special constables and regular troops to confront a peaceful demonstration of the Reform League in Hyde Park, decided the issue. The Tory approach to reform was, however, entirely different from that of the Liberals. Once Disraeli had grasped the nettle, he was determined to pull it out by the roots. A carefully constructed system of checks and balances, as proposed by the Liberals, would serve no purpose. But a radical reform would break the ascendancy of Gladstone and Bright, terminate the reputation of being the 'stupid party' that had dogged the Tories since 1846 and cast them in the role of the 'national party'. Moreover, by going beneath the level of the skilled, organized working class, who were brought up on self-help, temperance, and Nonconformity, the Tories could tap what they saw to be the natural conservatism of the labouring masses.

---

[1] Quoted by Royden Harrison, *Before the Socialists* (London, 1965), 108.

They were moved by 'an impression—for it could be no more', as Lord Robert Cecil argued in 1869, 'that the ruder class of minds would be more sensitive to traditional emotions; and an indistinct application to English politics of Napoleon's supposed success in taming revolution by universal suffrage'.[2] More like Bismarck, they also trusted that the uneducated lower classes would defer to their employers and landlords in the exercise of their vote. 'Our social system', remarked *The Times*, 'is our real sheet-anchor, and that on which we may fearlessly ride.'[3]

In the short term, it seemed that they were wrong; the Reform Act of August 1867 did not play into the hands of the Tories. Their reform, which virtually established household suffrage in the boroughs, doubled the electorate to two million. Disraeli took over as prime minister in February 1868 and a general election was held in December. The Tories looked to break the Liberal hold on the boroughs, but achieved this only in Lancashire, where they played on Protestant fears of Catholics from Ireland. The Liberals, promising to disestablish the Anglican Church in Ireland, bid for the Irish Catholic vote and did well in the Celtic fringe, leaving only the English counties to the Tories. The Reform League supported the Liberals and a former Chartist, Ernest Jones, was a Liberal candidate in Manchester. Gladstone, and his first ministry of 1868–74, were the first beneficiaries of the Second Reform Act.

In countries more backward than Great Britain, the problem faced by the democratic opponents of the ruling oligarchy was that of mobilizing mass support. In Italy, where tax-paying and literacy tests confined the electorate to 529,000 or two per cent of the population, workers' societies for mutual aid and education had been developing since 1859, especially in Piedmont. At a congress of these societies at Florence in September 1861 Mazzini made a bid to win their support for his cause, but he was more concerned with the completion of national unification than with democratization, and many societies more interested in material and moral improvement than in politics refused to follow him. Dilemmas of strategy also beset the democrats. About fifty of them, mostly poor lawyers and hack literati, were active in the national parliament after 1861, but they were unable to impress their policies, including the demand for wider suffrage, on the parliamentary Left, which was part of the Cavourian *connubio*. Revolutionary activity seemed easier to some, especially at the time of the Polish insurrection, and Garibaldi led a spate of resignations of democrats from the Chamber to take part in wild attempts to conquer Rome or the Trentino by force. There is no doubt that Garibaldi had magnetic powers of leadership, but his cavalier disdain for legal forms and style of a popular dictator embarrassed those democrats who had decided

---

[2] Quoted by Paul Smith, *Disraelian Conservatism and Social Reform* (London, 1967), 95.
[3] Quoted by Gertrude Himmelfarb, 'The Politics of democracy: the English reform act of 1867', *Journal of British Studies*, 6 (1966), 132.

that the struggle for reform must take place within parliament. Lastly, though the democrats were marginal to the establishment, they were still educated and even propertied, and campaigned for narrow political and national goals. None of this promised them much influence over the poor and illiterate Italian people.

In Spain, a strategy to mobilize popular support was discovered in the later 1860s: federalism. Since 1858 a Liberal Union of Moderates and the majority of Progressives had maintained itself in power by the co-operation of government and caciques in the management of elections and the military support of the army and Civil Guard. In 1863, when Queen Isabella decided to be rid of her Chief Minister, General O'Donnell, the opposition, 'pure' Progressives and Democrats, tried to bully her into giving them office by means of a *retraimiento*, or refusal to take part in parliamentary politics. Since the Queen remained unmoved, the opposition had a choice between two alternatives. It could dig out support in the army, finding a *caudillo* of its own, like General Prim, or it could follow the advice of the Barcelona journalist and rising star of the Democrats, Pi y Margall, that they must look beyond a corrupt system controlled by politicians, generals, and landowners and harness the discontent of the landless peasantry by promising *reparto*, a massive redistribution of land. The impatient Prim launched a military coup early in 1866. It failed, the monarchy resorted to military dictatorship and the Democratic leaders were driven into exile. During his stay in Paris Pi discovered Proudhon, and above all his work on the *Federative Principle*, which he translated into Spanish. A vision of revolution and a federal republic was presented to him.

A second coup by Prim succeeded in September 1868. Queen Isabella was finally driven out, and a provisional government was set up, composed of Progressives and Liberal Unionists who rallied to the new regime. This was not just another *pronunciamiento*. Because of the Democrats, it was also a revolution. Revolutionary juntas were set up in Madrid and the provinces, especially in Andalusia, the Levant, and Catalonia. Military conscription and the excise were abolished. Convents were attacked and arms were distributed to Volunteers of Liberty, who would defend the revolution. The Democrats forced the government to decree universal suffrage, the freedom of the press, of association, and of religion, as the price of their support. But the Madrid authorities and the democratic movement very rapidly came into conflict. Prim was faced not only by revolution in the Spanish provinces but by revolt in the Spanish colony of Cuba; there could thus be no question of the abolition of taxes and conscription. The provisional government then contemplated summoning a constituent assembly and advertising in Europe for a new monarch. By October 1868, on the other hand, most of the Democrats had become rampant republicans. The provisional government retaliated by ordering the dissolution of the juntas and the demobilization of the

Volunteers of Liberty. In response the republicans denounced both the central government and the forthcoming election to the Constituent Cortes. There was an outbreak of local revolts, the republican intelligentsia found popular support in the new municipalities, clubs, Volunteers, and press. Pi y Margall's idea that insurgent towns should freely engage in agreements to set up a federal republic seemed to be taking shape. In the event it proved impossible to co-ordinate the various revolts. Prim's army restored order and the Progressives and Liberal Unionists who were elected to the Constituent Cortes in 1869 introduced a constitution which provided for religious toleration and both Chamber and Senate elected by universal suffrage. After the embarrassment of the Hohenzollern affair, the crown of Spain was accepted by Amadeo of Savoy, son of Victor Emmanuel of Italy; constitutional monarchy was to be given another chance.

It was of course in France that the republican pedigree was longest, but in the 1850s the republican opposition to the regime of Napoleon III was in a parlous state. Confronted head-on by repression, undermined by Napoleon's pre-emption of the principle of universal suffrage, and witnessing a steady increase in public prosperity, many republicans saw no alternative to parliamentary rather than revolutionary opposition. And so, while the unrepentant Blanqui vegetated in prison, a group of five Republican deputies elected in 1857, headed by Émile Ollivier, a former *commissaire* of the Republic in 1848, took the oath of loyalty to the Emperor which was required before they could take their seats in the Legislative Body. But there was a more prominent source of opposition to Napoleon's regime among the Orleanists, the natural governing élite of France, who dominated the administration, the law courts, the *conseils généraux* in the *départements* and the chambers of commerce, and from whom Napoleon, for lack of Bonapartists, was obliged to take several of his ministers. They challenged both the Emperor's Italian policy and his commercial policy, and in March 1860 took up clericalism and protectionism as two effective sticks with which to beat the government.

The Second Empire was not rigid. Napoleon himself realized that 'a constitution is the work of time'[4] and that rulers had to keep ahead of the ideas of their century if they were not to be overthrown. The issue was not popular suffrage, for that already existed, but liberalization: to decrease the role of the administration and to increase that of parliament. There must be progress from an authoritarian to a parliamentary Empire, without falling into anarchy on the one hand or ushering in restoration on the other. Decrees of November 1860 provided more muscle for parliament by permitting the publication of debates, the amendment of bills in committee and allowing ministers without portfolio to sit in the Chamber. In the elections of 1863, a Liberal Union of Orleanists, Legitimists, and Republicans made important

---

[4] Quoted by William H. C. Smith, *Napoléon III* (Paris, 1982), 201.

gains at the expense of official candidates. From 1865 Napoleon had his eyes on Ollivier as a future chief minister, but Ollivier as yet lacked a parliamentary following, and the balance of power was still held by the authoritarian ministers, led by Rouher.

The defeat of Austria by Prussia brought home to Napoleon the need to reconcile all classes, especially the educated middle classes, to the regime. Accordingly, the calling to account of ministers in the Chamber was authorized in 1867 and a liberal press law was passed in 1868. Both were quickly put to use by the opposition. The political press burst into life. The elections of May–June 1869, which were extremely agitated, resulted in significant gains by the Republicans. Ollivier now gathered 116 supporters for a vote of no confidence in Rouher's ministry, and to demand a new ministry drawn from and responsible to parliament. The authoritarian wing of Bonapartism collapsed; in January 1870 Ollivier was invited to form a ministry and preside over the drafting of a constitution for the Liberal Empire.

The new constitution was riddled with contradictions. The Emperor remained both head of state, responsible to the people alone, and President of the Council of Ministers. Ollivier was not prime minister but Minister of Justice and Keeper of the Seals. Ministers were deemed 'responsible', but it was not clear whether they were responsible to parliament or to the Emperor; in any case, Ollivier did not have a parliamentary majority and there was still no collective responsibility. Lastly, the Empire was 'parliamentary', but constitutional changes were still to be ratified by plebiscite, to maintain the personal authority of the Emperor. The plebiscite of 8 May 1870 was a triumph for him. Over 7.3 million people voted in favour of the constitution, only 1.5 million against. 'The Empire is stronger than ever', admitted the Republican leader, Gambetta.[5] And yet it was within a few weeks of being destroyed by Prussian armies. To a large extent its downfall was military. But the confusion that resulted from the reorganisation of the Empire in 1870 handicapped the government in the critical period of sparring with Bismarck and was fatal once war had broken out. The Second Empire almost solved the problem of reconciling monarchy and democracy—but not quite, and not in time.

Anarchism and Socialism

Universal suffrage might lead to social reform, but it might also serve only to reinforce support for the ruling class. Those who wanted to destroy social inequalities and exploitation found themselves facing three questions. Were they going to use revolutionary or legal means? Should a mass movement of peasants or workers remain entirely separate from the middle class, or should it collaborate with bourgeois radicals who shared some of the same goals? Lastly, should the aim be to seize political power in order to further

---

[5] Quoted by Jacques Gouault, *Comment La France est devenue républicaine* (Paris, 1954), 25.

social reform, or should political power itself be destroyed as exploitative and evil in itself?

Government repression after 1849 stimulated a new wave of secret societies in Europe, behind most of which seemed to be the irrepressible Mazzini. But as conservative regimes became entrenched, as pockets of resistance in France, Germany, and Italy were wiped out, and as prosperity began to return, radicals were obliged to take a long, cool look at their strategies. Karl Marx, who was reorganising the Communist League in London in 1850, criticized his rivals, for whom 'the motor of revolution is not the real situation, but will alone'.[6] For Marx now realized that revolutionaries could not trigger off coups wherever and whenever they fancied; a broad base of support would have to be built up in the working class by organization and education, through clubs, mutual aid societies, and trade unions, before any revolution would be effective. By the early 1860s a labour movement was emerging in England, France, Belgium, and parts of Germany like Saxony and the Rhineland, at least among an artisan élite of building-workers, metal-workers and shoemakers.

Marx's experience of the 1848 Revolution in Germany was that the middle class, however liberal, would throw in its lot with feudalism and the monarchy at the first whiff of revolution. It was therefore up to the organized working class alone to make the revolution permanent, to drive on from political to social revolution. Moreover his research for *Capital* convinced him more than ever that the wealth of the middle class was entirely derived from the cunning exploitation of wage-labour. 'Accumulation of wealth at one pole', he argued, 'is at the same time accumulation of misery, the torment of labour, slavery, ignorance, brutalization and moral degradation at the opposite pole.'[7] Marx was therefore happy to be on the platform at St Martin's Hall, Covent Garden, on 28 September 1864 when British and French labour leaders organized a meeting to launch the International Working Men's Association. The General Council which was elected to steer the movement was made up of twenty-seven Englishmen, three Frenchmen, two Italians, and two Germans, including Marx. Contacts had been made at a confident display of capitalism, the London Exhibition of 1862, and again through sympathy with the cause of the Polish rebels. But Marx was insistent that the *Address* adopted by the International set its sights on 'the abolition of all class rule' and declared that 'the emancipation of the working class must be achieved by the working classes themselves'.

It was essential to adopt some common strategy, but because the representatives came from countries where the balance of classes and questions of power-politics were entirely different, this was difficult to achieve. Initially,

      [6] Quoted by Jacques Droz, 'Les Origines de la social-démocratie allemande', in Droz, ed., *Histoire générale du Socialisme*, i (Paris, 1972), 773.
      [7] Marx, *Capital* (Harmondsworth, 1976), i, 779. This first volume of *Capital* was published in 1867.

Mazzinians had much influence on the General Council, but their concern with revolutionary conspiracy, class collaboration in the interests of national unification and the mystical force of the People was entirely foreign to working-class goals; they were eased out by 1865. The French representatives ran one of their leaders in a Paris by-election in March 1864, as a candidate of the working class who would have nothing to do with bourgeois republicanism. He gained few votes, but in an attempt to wean the workers away from republicanism to support the Empire, the imperial government passed a law authorizing coalitions for strike action and in 1868 gave *de facto* recognition to trade unions. The London trades which organized the International were also instrumental in founding the Reform League in 1865, and Marx told Engels that 'The Reform League is our doing.'[8] But it was not helpful that the working class should become distracted by parliamentary reform and swept into a struggle on behalf of Gladstonian Liberalism. Engels despaired in the elections of 1868 that 'everywhere the proletariat is the rag, tag and bobtail of the official parties'.[9] In Germany two labour movements had emerged, but the interests of neither coincided with those of the International. The General German Workers' Union, set up in May 1863 and headed by Ferdinand Lassalle, renounced co-operation with the middle class but looked instead to Bismarck and his feudal allies to provide universal suffrage and financial aid for their producers' co-operatives. The League of German Workers' Clubs, founded in June 1863, opposed Prussian militarism and feudalism, but because of that became caught up in the democratic, *grossdeutsch* policies of the Peoples' Parties. Wilhelm Liebknecht, who headed the League with August Bebel, a wood-turner from Leipzig, started 'from the viewpoint that the fall of Prussia equals the victory of the German revolution'. Marx called Liebknecht an 'ass', but 'the only reliable contact we have in Germany'.[10] The resolution of the German question in 1866, however, opened the way to class politics. The liberal bourgeoisie largely defected to the Bismarckian camp, while universal suffrage and the right to form trade unions were conceded in the North German Confederation. The League joined the International in September 1868 and reformed in 1869 as the Social Democratic Workers' Party.

Marx's plan for the International also faced direct opposition. The major formative influence on French socialist thought was that of Pierre-Joseph Proudhon, who died in 1865. 'We want neither the government of man by man nor the exploitation of man by man', Proudhon had written in 1848.[11] Labour alone was productive and yet because of rent and profit society was

[8] Quoted by David McLellan, *Karl Marx* (London, 1973), 368.
[9] Engels to Marx, 18 Nov. 1868, quoted by Harrison, *Before the Socialists*, 183.
[10] Quoted by Morgan, *The German Social Democrats*, 110, 120.
[11] Quoted by Daniel Guérin, 'Proudhon et l'autogestion ouvrière', in *L'Actualité de Proudhon*, Colloque des 24–5 novembre 1965 (Brussels, 1967), 68.

divided into two classes, 'one which works and does not own, the other which owns and does not work, which therefore consumes without producing'.[12] The unearned wealth of the financial and industrial barons was legitimized and secured by the apparatus of the state, the centralized administration, the police, the courts, the army, the Church, and that wealth served in turn to underpin the state. Instead, argued Proudhon, everyone must be owner of the fruits of his labour, and workers could achieve this by grouping in associations, the product of which would be shared out equally among them. Those associations, autonomous but freely federating together, would ensure both independence and harmony in society. There would be no government of some men by others in this anarchist Utopia. Proudhon criticized all forms of state socialism, nationalization, and public ownership, whether proposed by Louis Blanc or by Marx, on the grounds that they were as tyrannical as capitalism. He also advised the working class to separate itself from all political action, including participation in elections. The danger was that it would either vote for representatives who would betray its interest, or recognize a system that was loaded against it by the old parties. The working class should abstain, develop its own consciousness in isolation, and evolve its own tactics, which should be non-political.

Mutualism and federalism responded to the traditions of the French working class but were anathema to Marx. They contradicted his view that the working class must engage in political action to seize state-power, and then in the period of the 'dictatorship of the proletariat' take all the capitalist enterprises into collective ownership. Marx and the Proudhonists came into conflict at congresses of the International at Geneva in 1866, at Lausanne in 1867, and in Brussels in 1868, when Marx was able to mobilize the Belgian delegates behind his resolutions. But a more formidable antagonist was already on the horizon. Mikhail Bakunin, who had spent the 1850s in a Russian prison, knew no other answer to authoritarian regimes than revolutionary conspiracy, and in 1866 founded a secret society in Naples. His statement that 'we have faith only in the revolution made by the people for their positive and complete emancipation'[13] would have been applauded by Marx, but whereas Marx looked for support to the organized industrial workers of western Europe, Bakunin wished to harness the latent anger of the slum-dwellers and landless peasants of southern Europe. And though he did not have the sophisticated philosophy of Proudhon, he too was an anarchist who believed that the state was 'the most flagrant, most cynical and most complete denial of humanity', and must be destroyed.[14] In 1868 Bakunin founded a front-

[12] Quoted by Daniel Guérin, *Ni Dieu ni maître, anthologie historique du mouvement anarchiste* (Lausanne, 1969), 76.

[13] Quoted by Richard Hostetter, *The Italian Socialist Movement*, i, *Origins, 1860–82* (Princeton, 1958), 103.

[14] Quoted by Gerald Brenan, *The Spanish Labyrinth* (Cambridge, 1978), 133.

organization for his secret society, the Alliance of Social Democracy, in Geneva. Militants gathered groups of adherents in Naples, in Madrid and Barcelona, where the Revolution of 1868 provided a favourable atmosphere, in Geneva, and the little towns of the Jura. The membership was composed not as yet of the very poor but of disgruntled students and school-teachers, and the usual artisan élite of printers, builders, and shoemakers. Bakunin's ambition was to smuggle the Alliance into the International and take it over. Marx and the General Council in London ruled in 1869 that not the Alliance, but only its individual sections, could join. Even then, the watchmakers and jewellers of Geneva, who dominated the sections of the International in French-speaking Switzerland, objected to the Geneva section of the Alliance joining their Federation, and in the summer of 1870 Bakunin set up his own Jura Federation of sections which adhered to his anarchist Alliance. Sections of the International which spread rapidly across southern France in 1870, and accounted for much of the 'no' vote to Napoleon's plebiscite in May 1870, tended to look to Bakunin at Geneva rather than to Marx in London.

The collapse of the Second Empire during the Franco-Prussian War in August–September 1870 was accompanied by a resurgence of social violence. Bakunin and his followers briefly seized the town hall of Lyons, from which they proclaimed the abolition of the state. But France had its own revolutionary tradition which competed with anarchist influences. Napoleon III surrendered to the Prussians after the defeat of Sedan and a Government of National Defence set up at Paris proclaimed on 4 September 1870: 'The Republic was victorious over the invasion of 1792. The Republic is declared.'[15] Unfortunately, the Government of National Defence was divided between those like Thiers who, fearing disorder, wanted to make a peace as soon as possible, and those around Gambetta who ordered a *levée en masse* of National Guardsmen to support the line army in the struggle against the Prussians. Paris was besieged by the Prussians but it was alive with revolutionary institutions: clubs, vigilance committees which supervised the twenty mayors of the city, the radical press, and National Guardsmen. Many revolutionaries, inspired by Blanqui, believed that only an insurrectionary Commune, modelled on that of August 1792, could carry on the struggle against Prussia and against the conservative classes, who preferred to make peace with Bismarck and to safeguard their property and privileges rather than risk a revolutionary war. Bismarck granted an armistice in January 1871 to permit elections to a National Assembly that would ratify the peace, and it was against this defeatist Assembly that the working-class districts of Paris revolted on 18 March 1871 and established a revolutionary municipal government, the Commune.

---

[15] Quoted by J. P. T. Bury, *Gambetta and the National Defence: A Republican Dictatorship in France* (London, 1936), 125.

There has been much debate as to whether the Paris Commune of 1871 was a proletarian revolution and a conspiracy of the First International. The myth originates in two sources, namely Marx's reflections on the subject, *The Civil War in France*, and the findings of a commission of the conservative National Assembly, which gave rise to a law of 1872 prohibiting membership of the International. Subsequent historians have tried to play down its revolutionary and working-class nature, but its exceptional nature must stand. 80,000 Parisians, including a large proportion of the bourgeoisie, fled Paris before the elections to the Commune on 26 March 1871. A third of its members were manual workers and a third (interlocking with the first) were members of the International, whether of its Paris sections or affiliated unions. Workshops which had been abandoned by their owners were handed over by the Commune to associations of workers, most successfully to tailors, mechanics, and to workers in the metal, jewellery, and typographical trades. The absolute autonomy of every commune in France to undertake social and economic reforms as it saw fit, independent of the state authorities, was proclaimed,[16] in an attempt to link up with ephemeral communes in Lyons, Marseilles, Le Creusot, Saint-Etienne and Narbonne. At the same time the unity of France was to be preserved by a free federation of communes. Unfortunately, the members of the Commune were divided on how to ensure its survival in the short term. Jacobins and Blanquists proposed a Committee of Public Safety to exercise a temporary dictatorship; Proudhonists and Internationalists opposed. While the Communards were quarrelling amongst themselves Thiers and Bismarck agreed on a peace treaty which signed away Alsace and Lorraine and promised an indemnity of five billion francs. The way in which Thiers then 'hounded on the prisoners of Sedan and Metz against Paris by special permission of Bismarck' was held up to scorn by Marx.[17]

In the 'Bloody Week' during which the French army regained control of Paris, 25,000 people were massacred. 40,000 people were arrested and tried, of whom 10,000 were convicted. Half of these were imprisoned in New Caledonia. There were 93 death sentences, although only 23 judicial executions were carried out. The repression was a tribute to the fear of the French ruling class and behind it, that of Germany. In turn it had a dramatic effect on the socialist movement in Europe. In the first place, political action was now seen by many leaders to be dangerous if revolutionary, pointless if parliamentary, and anarchist alternatives were favoured. The attempt by Marx to impose the centralized control of the London General Council on the International in the interests of political action served only to provoke a schism. Bakunin and his allies in the Jura Federation, Italy and Spain saw the danger that the

[16]   Charles Rihs, *La Commune de Paris* (2nd edn., Paris, 1973), 163–5.
[17]   Marx, 'The Civil War in France', in Marx and Engels, *Selected Works in One Volume* (London, 1968), 276.

authoritarian behaviour of the London Council might give rise not so much to a dictatorship of the proletariat as to a dictatorship over the proletariat. In 1872 they set up an 'anti-authoritarian' International in which the autonomy of the sections and federations was recognized.

Second, a debate was fought out between those who argued that the only answer to repression by the authorities was revolutionary violence and terrorism and those who argued that the Commune had failed because the Parisian masses were insufficiently organized or aware of their goals. For the latter, opposition had to be extended beyond the ranks of intellectuals and skilled workers to the mass of the working class or peasantry, but a long-term programme of organization and education would be required. The Russian revolutionary Lavrov, who had witnessed the failure of the Commune, urged intellectuals to 'go to the people' in the towns and villages, to undertake propaganda, and to organize them. But the campaign of the 'Land and Liberty' movement in 1876–7 in the countryside of southern Russia, in Odessa, and St Petersburg was frustrated by popular indifference, mass arrests, and trials, and in 1879 the movement divided into two, one group favouring more popular campaigns, the other resorting to bomb-throwing to destroy the Tsarist state. In Italy, the sections of the International, which were particularly thick in the Romagna, declared for Bakunin, and though Marx's comment that these sections were run by 'a gang of *déclassés* ... by lawyers without clients, by doctors without patients, or medical knowledge, by students expert at billiards, by commercial travellers and clerks, and especially by journalists of the minor press, of more or less dubious reputation'[18] was prejudiced, it was not too far from the truth. Anarchists tried to ignite popular insurrection in the Romagna in 1874, but the peasantry showed their distrust and scorn for these outside agitators. In 1876 the movement split between conspirators who now tried to provoke insurrection in the countryside around Naples and others in the north of Italy who favoured propaganda. Anarchism found a popular base only in southern Spain. There, the apostles of anarchism travelled to the *pueblos* which longed to recover autonomy from the central government, caciques, and Civil Guard, and the promise of a distribution of the land took on the mythical power of a kingdom of God on earth replacing the Catholic message of patience, awaiting salvation in the next world.

The third effect of the Commune was that the working class became politically isolated and the socialist movement virtually outlawed. The forces of reaction in Europe rallied against what they took to be the International and all its works. Socialist leaders became oppressed by a siege mentality. August Bebel, about to serve a two-year sentence with Liebknecht for refusing to vote war credits in 1870, told the Reichstag in May 1871 that 'the

---

[18] Quoted by C. Seton-Watson, *Italy from Liberalism to Fascism, 1870–1925* (London, 1967), 70–1.

struggle in Paris is only a minor outpost skirmish, that the great issue in Europe is still before us and that before a few years pass the battle-cry of the Paris proletariat, "war on the palaces, peace for the cottages, death to misery and laziness!" will be the battle-cry of the whole European proletariat.'[19] But because the first aim of the socialist movement in Germany must be to shake off the coils of the authoritarian state, to win the right to free speech, a free press, and free association in order to be able to campaign for social justice, uniquely working-class concerns had to be set aside while essential democratic liberties were won. Marx condemned the programme of the German Social Democratic party drawn up at Gotha in 1875 as 'the old democratic litany familiar to all'. The irony was that the socialists had no support from bourgeois democrats, democratic though their programme was.

Stabilization: Liberal

After 1871 the trend in European politics was everywhere conservative. In the three eastern empires of Germany, Austria-Hungary, and Russia power was retained by the traditional ruling groups and government was authoritarian rather than parliamentary. But in western Europe revolution was controlled without the rehabilitation of old dynasties, nobilities, and Churches. In this sense the Restoration in Spain was something of an exception but there, as in Italy, France, and Britain, stabilization was achieved not by reaction but by a liberal, parliamentary oligarchy.

The events of 1870–1 greatly undermined the reputation of the French Republicans. Their pursuit of victory against the Prussians, the dictatorial attitude of the Government of National Defence and their association with the revolutionary violence of the Commune did not endear them to the millions who wanted peace, liberty, and order. France remained a Republic *de facto*, but a Republic without republicans. The Catholic Church recovered some of its authority. It was argued that France, having sinned by removing its troops from Rome and abandoning the city to the Piedmontese, had been punished by defeat, and could be redeemed only by repentence. The basilica of Sacré-Coeur was erected by subscription on the Communard stronghold of Montmartre, education was handed over again to the Catholic Church, and new campaigns were mounted to bring to working classes into the fold of the religion. Adolphe Thiers, who had directed the suppression of the Commune, was elected President of the Republic by the conservative National Assembly.

It nevertheless soon became clear to the Right that Thiers was not strong enough to prevent the recovery of the Republican party, and a coalition of royalists and Bonapartists overthrew him in 1873 and replaced him by a military man, Marshal MacMahon. The Right imagined that they could use

[19] Quoted by Vernon Lidtke, *The Outlawed Party: Social Democracy in Germany, 1878–1890* (Princeton, 1966), 41–2.

MacMahon as a bridge to the restoration of the monarchy which alone, it was argued, could safeguard religion, the family, and private property against revolution. In the summer of 1873 France came within an ace of restoration. But no compromise could be worked out between the childless Legitimist pretender, Henri 'V', and the Orleanist pretender, or between the autocratic ideas of Henri 'V' and those of royalist parliamentarians. In 1874 the picture was dramatically changed by a resurgence of support for Bonapartist candidates in a series of by-elections. The Bonapartists exploited the confusion in the National Assembly and presented the Empire as affording all the advantages of the monarchy together with the possibility of recall by plebiscite. The Orleanist branch of the monarchists and moderate Republicans could at least agree on one thing: that they did not want the Empire back. Early in 1875 they joined forces to vote two laws which amounted to the constitution of the Third Republic. The Orleanists could not obtain the abrogation of universal suffrage but accepted an indirectly elected Senate as the next best thing. And the President of the Republic, elected not by the people but by the two houses for a period of seven years, could never be a demagogue like Louis-Napoleon Bonaparte.

A republican constitution had been voted, but the Republicans were still in a parliamentary minority. Their image as war-mongers, dictators, and revolutionaries had to be changed. Under the brilliant leadership of Gambetta, they dissociated themselves from the Commune by rejecting the pressure of the radicals in the party to amnesty the Communards. Rural support was built up by warning the peasantry that a restoration of the monarchy would bring tithes and forced labour-services in its wake. Gambetta did not associate the Republicans with a particular class or even accept the term 'class': instead he appealed to the 'new social strata' of shopkeepers, small employers, teachers, and clerks who were striving to improve their lot and acquire property by hard work, thrift, sobriety, and education. Finally he demonstrated to professional men and industrialists that they must join the Republicans in their fight against monarchism, clericalism, and feudalism.

As a result, the Republicans won a massive majority in the parliamentary elections of 1876. But Marshal MacMahon was still president and the principle of ministerial responsibility was not established; they were not invited to form a government. Then, on 16 May 1877, MacMahon overreached himself by dissolving parliament and using all the administrative apparatus of the Second Empire to try to break the republican majority. He failed. But his dictatorial approach allowed the Republicans to publicize themselves as the only exponents of 'wise, firm, peaceful and progressive policies'.[20] The emphasis on peace was significant, for one of the aims of the conservative and clerical adherents of MacMahon was to launch a crusade to restore the

---

[20] Quoted by J. P. T. Bury, *Gambetta and the Making of the Third Republic* (London, 1973), 407.

Temporal Power of the Pope, the Papal States that had been annexed by the Italian state in 1870. However, as Bismarck noted on a memorandum from his military attaché in Paris, 'clerical France is altogether incapable of maintaining durable peaceful relations with Germany'.[21] A Catholic crusade, which stirred up Catholics in Alsace-Lorraine, south Germany, and the Polish provinces would force Bismarck to take retaliatory action against France. There is little doubt that Bismarck's favour counted in the second electoral success of the republicans in 1877. Republicans were now offered cabinet posts and in 1879 a republican president replaced MacMahon. The prime ministers whom he appointed were moderate men, the policies they pursued included railway-building programmes and a shift to protectionism which satisfied capitalist interests, and all projects of revenge on Germany for the humiliation of 1870 were shelved.

In Italy, the revolutionary activities of republicans and anarchists provoked a move to the Right, but there was never the possibility, as there was in France, of a Right based upon a fallen dynasty, old nobility, or the Catholic Church. The House of Savoy reaped the prestige of having carried through national unification, and Francis II of Naples had no popular standing after his deposition. The nobilities of the Italian states—one must use the plural— were gelded politically by administrative centralization. Only the displaced aristocracy of the south, still pro-Bourbon, and able to make use of peasant hostility to taxation to fight a guerilla war of resistance, and the 'black' nobility of Rome who still attended the Papal Court did not yet rally to the new regime. Neither did the Church provide a focus for political opposition. Pius IX never forgave Piedmont, 'the subalpine usurper' and confiscator of his Temporal Power. And though the Law of Guarantees of 1871 gave him the privileges of an independent sovereign in Italy, Pius repeated his instructions to the Catholic faithful that they should neither stand nor vote in parliamentary elections. The Church wielded immense influence after 1870 as an educational, cultural, and charitable body but did not exert that influence through any political party.

There was indeed a 'Right' and a 'Left' in Italian politics in the 1870s, but the terms represented only facets of a single liberal oligarchy, whose policies differed in emphasis rather than in kind. The 'Right' which held power down to 1876 was the old Cavourian, governmental party, which placed official patronage in the hands of provincial intendants in order to win elections. Rome had opposed it, so it was firmly, if moderately, anticlerical, and applied the 1855 law on religious congregations in the Papal States. It looked after the interests of a landed, professional, and industrial élite, and saw the Italian masses either as a source of revenue, to be mulcted by the grist tax of 1869, or as potentially explosive, to be put down by military force when they revolted

[21] Quoted by Alan Mitchell, *The German Influence in France after 1870* (Chapel Hill, 1979), 161.

(which they often did over taxation). The Left, which attained office in March 1876, was a coalition that included the Piedmontese centre-left, non-Piedmontese republicans who had since rallied to the monarchy, and the notables of the agrarian south. Once in power, the Left used all the instruments of state to manage the elections of November 1876, and in Sicily could rely on the Mafia bosses, suitably placated, to organize the return of loyal deputies. They enlarged the electorate in 1882, but only to two million or 7 per cent of the population; they also undertook to improve elementary education to ensure a tolerable degree of civic virtue and political discipline. The anticlericalism of the Left had a sharper cutting edge than that of the Right, although its bill on compulsory civil marriage in 1879 was rejected by the Senate. The Left agreed to abolish the grist tax in 1880, but its main concern was to win favour with banking, railway, and industrial interests by the promotion of vast railway-building programmes and a shift towards protection, in order to displace the Right as the classical governmental party.

The impact of revolution was much greater in Spain than it was in Italy. Southern Spain was the only region where the anti-authoritarian International found mass support. The effect on the republican movement was divisive. For Pi y Margall the lesson of the Commune was that Republicans must forsake revolutionary folly and, like the French Republicans, try to build up support in the Cortes. 'Intransigent' Republicans, on the other hand, were inspired by the Commune and urged the boycott of parliamentary politics together with revolution to establish a federal republic. Meanwhile the ruling coalition of Progressives, former Democrats, and Liberal Unionists was breaking up. The Progressives divided between those who wanted to take a conservative course, in closer alliance with the Liberal Unionists, and those, who now called themselves the Radicals, who wanted to move to the left to harness republicanism for their own purposes. The Radicals gained office in June 1872, fixed the elections to give themselves a majority in the Cortes, and launched attacks on the Catholic Church and the army. King Amadeo, cut off from the possibility of a conservative ministry, abdicated in February 1873 and brought the Radicals and the monarchy down with him.

The Republicans now secured their Republic and Pi y Margall became its first president in April 1873. Elections to the Constituent Cortes were ordered to be free, to break the link between the government and the caciques. Largely because three-quarters of the electorate abstained, a majority was won by the federal republicans and the Cortes was filled with lawyers, journalists, and club orators. Unfortunately the base of the new republican regime was very narrow. The federal republicans in the provinces, the militants of the cafés, clubs, and Volunteers of Liberty, were impatient to organize power by revolution from below, and would not calmly await instructions from Madrid. A wave of municipal revolutions established revolutionary juntas in the cities of the south: Cartagena, Granada and Malaga, Valencia and Castellón,

Seville and Cadiz. This 'cantonalist movement' inspired the French anarchist Paul Brousse, one of the Internationalists who tried to seize the town-hall of Barcelona in the confusion, with the view that socialists might in future take power municipality by municipality. But it brought about the fall of Pi, and subsequent republican presidents had to resort to the army to crush the revolts and revert to a unitary republic. A second reason why the army became necessary was to fight the Carlists, who responded to the fall of the monarchy by establishing a state in northern Spain that was virtually independent. But reliance on the army to crush rebellions resulted, by turns, in a republican dictatorship, the dictatorship of Francesco Serrano (a general of the 1868 Revolution, a Spanish MacMahon), and eventually, because the royalist generals in the army gained the upper hand, in a Restoration of the monarchy (December 1874).

The grey eminence behind the Restoration was nevertheless a civilian politician, Antonio Cánovas del Castillo. A protégé of O'Donnell and one of the architects of the Liberal Union in the period 1854–66, he had persuaded Queen Isabella to abdicate for the sake of the monarchy in 1870 and sent her son, Alfonso, to Sandhurst to learn how to be a constitutional king. Alfonso XII arrived in Madrid in January 1875, but it was Cánovas who was in charge of affairs. Freedom of the press was suspended, municipal councils and provincial assemblies were dismissed, officials were purged. A Liberal Conservative party, in the image of the Liberal Union, was hammered together from former Moderates and conservative Progressives who were willing to rally to the monarchy, in order to serve the interests of the government. Links were re-established with the caciques, who received immense powers to assess taxes locally, sell forest land, control the courts, and appoint to municipal and provincial offices, in order to build up a network of clientage that would vote in government majorities at every election. In the elections to the Constituent Cortes in 1876, republican and radical candidates were not allowed to stand, and the Constitution of 1876 abrogated universal suffrage, established a senate that was half-appointed, half-elected, and made the Catholic religion once again the religion of state. But it was not a restoration *à la* Ferdinand VII: absolutism was consigned to history and real power was vested in the Prime Minister, Cánovas.

In Britain, the radical agitation of the Reform League had been successfully appropriated by the Liberal party for the elections of 1868. The danger of revolution came from Ireland, where small-holding and extremely insecure tenants were now engaged in an agrarian war with their English or Anglo-Irish landlords. Their discontent was exploited by Fenian terrorists who were funded and armed in part by Irish Americans. The Gladstone government of 1868–74 was a familiar alliance of Whigs, Peelites, Dissenters, and Radicals. It was entirely united behind the plan to disestablish that privileged irrelevancy, the Anglican Church in Ireland, but was much more divided on Irish land reform.[22] The Irish land bill was a compromise which did not concede the principle of tenant-right demanded by Irish land-reformers and was thus directly responsible for the movement which began to demand the abolition of the Union and Home Rule. Moreover, the government's refusal to pare down the Anglican Church in England, and indeed its proposal to subsidize church schools from the rates under the Education Act of 1870 provoked a storm of anticlerical indignation from Dissenters and Radicals, the formation of a National Education League to fight the bill and almost the breaking away of a separate Radical party. The abolition of aristocratic privilege and influence in the civil service and army had broader support among the Liberals, but Gladstone was obliged to have resort to the royal prerogative to overcome opposition to army reform in the House of Lords. On the other hand, very little was conceded to the organized working class which had supported the Liberals in 1868, for while peaceful collective bargaining was permitted, picketing was still illegal and strikes could be punished for breach of contract.

The view of many of the propertied classes was nevertheless that the Liberal party was a hostage to its radical wing and insufficient guarantee against the tide of revolution. This was a sentiment that might be put to good use by the Conservative party, which remained a party of the county élites leavened by Tory radicals like Disraeli who had unsuccessfully gambled on popular suffrage in 1867. There was an urgent need to find support in the towns, among the commercial, industrial, and professional middle classes, and yet this would mean a revision of the philosophy that Toryism represented an alliance of aristocrats and plebeians against capitalist exploitation. At Manchester in April 1872 Disraeli played on middle-class fears by arguing that the Liberals were out to destroy the Church, the Lords, and the monarchy itself. At the Crystal Palace two months later Disraeli committed himself to improving the 'condition of the people' but counted above all on his sense that the working classes were 'proud of belonging to an imperial country, and are resolved to maintain, if they can, their empire—that they believe on the whole that the greatness and the empire of England are to be attributed to the ancient institutions of the land'.[23]

Disraeli's advocacy of more energy abroad, greater peace at home and above all the maintenance of established institutions, proved a successful formula in the elections of 1874. 'People are frightened', a Liberal peer told Gladstone afterwards. 'The masters are afraid of their workmen, manufacturers afraid of strikes, churchmen afraid of Nonconformists, many afraid of what is going on in France and Spain, and in very unreasoning fear all have taken refuge in Conservatism.'[24] Conservative support spread from its

[22] See above, p. 151.
[23] Quoted by Robert Blake, *Disraeli* (London, 1967), 523.
[24] Quoted by Smith, *Disraelian Conservatism*, 192.

traditional base in the counties to the large towns, where the new party machine had been working since 1870 to mobilize it. Disraeli's cabinet of 1874 was overwhelmingly aristocratic, and the government sought a balance between middle- and working-class interests. Thus picketing and strikes were no longer punishable as criminal offences, in the hope that the orga-nized working class would turn away from socialism. Workers' housing was to be improved, but always according to what the rates would stand, while freeing up the drink trade satisfied brewers and beer-drinkers alike. Above all, the emphasis of the government was on a dazzling and triumphant foreign policy. The Suez Canal shares of the Khedive of Egypt were bought up. The Queen was made Empress of India and a firm stance taken against Russian ambitions in the Straits and Balkans. But Disraeli's imperialism led straight to unsuccessful wars in Afghanistan and South Africa and in 1880 the British electorate deserted him.

Stabilization: Authoritarian

For a little while after 1867 parliaments in both Germany and Austria were dominated by liberals, who pursued policies of free trade, anticlericalism and antimilitarism. By the end of the 1870s both countries had become more con-servative and more authoritarian. The Catholic Church stood up to persecu-tion and had to be reconciled. The prosperity of the mid-century came to an abrupt end, and propertied classes demanded both the repression of social discontent and the protection of national economies against foreign compe-tition. Lastly, Russian militarism again endangered the peace of the Balkans, and governments were obliged to make commitments that were anathema to liberals.

In the first elections to the Reichstag of United Germany, held in 1871, the liberal parties, combining the National Liberals, Progressives, and other lib-eral fractions, won over half the seats, leaving the rest divided between the conservative parties, the Centre Party, and Polish, Danish, and Alsatian deputies. A liberal majority imposed constitutional, parliamentary rule, free-dom for trade, capital, and enterprise which was justifed by the boom of 1868–73, and war against the Catholic Church. Liberals had their reasons for attacking Roman Catholicism: the Church had often reinforced arbitrary and aristocratic regimes in states now annexed to the Reich and had opposed Prussian hegemony in Germany; moreover, liberals genuinely believed in a 'civilizing mission' against ignorance and superstition, and they were anxious still to appear militant, even after they had capitulated to Bismarck. Bis-marck had his own reasons for waging war against the Catholic Church in Germany, a war that became known as the *Kulturkampf*. First, he was con-vinced that not only the annexed Catholic populations of south Germany and Alsace but above all the Polish Catholics of West Prussia, Upper Silesia, and Posen were opposed to a Prussian-dominated Reich. He wanted to replace the religious, corporative, and regional loyalties cultivated by the Catholic Church by the loyalty of the citizen to the state. Second, he wished to secure a parliamentary majority by preventing a *rapprochement* between the Centre and the Conservatives, and making sure of the support of anticlerical Liberals. To do this, he needed to single out the Catholics as being guilty of separatism and ultramontanism. Third, when the Catholic clergy and the papacy opposed his policies, Bismarck argued that Popes were now challenging Emperors as in the Middle Ages, and that the state must tighten its control over the Church. To this end a law of 1872 made school inspectors into state officials and resulted in the sacking of clergy, especially Polish clergy, from the inspectorate. A series of laws passed in May 1873 empowered the state to direct the training of priests and to dismiss recalcitrant clergy, one of whom was the Polish Archbishop of Posen. A law of 1874 required Catholic couples to have a civil marriage as well as a church ceremony. Clergy were no longer allowed into schools to give religious instruction after 1876, and inter-confessional schools were imposed on the Polish provinces, and promoted by liberal-controlled cities like Cologne.

Bismarck's *Kulturkampf* was a failure. The Catholic laity rallied behind their clergy particularly in Rhineland-Westphalia, where the Catholic Centre party was founded in December 1870 and the Mainz Association in 1872. Instead of celebrating Sedan day on 2 September, Catholics celebrated 16 June, anniversary of the election of Pius IX, throughout the *Kulturkampf*. In the Reichstag elections of 1874 over four-fifths of German Catholics voted for the Centre party, which now returned ninety-one deputies. Worse still, the Protestant Church and its most stalwart supporters, the Prussian aristocracy defended confessional schools and Bismarck could not afford to lose their favour. Anticlerical legislation was voted with the help of liberal deputies, but Bismarck's dependence on the Left for a majority began to grow tiresome.

Bismarck and his ministers were in any case anxious to strengthen the executive at the expense of the Reichstag. Consideration of military affairs by the all-German Reichstag seemed particularly inappropriate because the army was overwhelmingly composed of Prussian contingents. The outgoing Prussian War Minister, Roon, wanted to establish the principle of a peacetime army of 400,000 men, maintained by an automatic per capita grant, which the Reichstag would not be required in future to debate. His concerns were not only related to national defence. 'An efficient army', he argued, 'is the only conceivable protection against the red, as against the black, spectre.'[25] But it was precisely the black and red spectres, the Centre, the left-wing of the National Liberals, the Progressives, and the nine socialists

---

[25] Quoted by Gordon A. Craig, *The Politics of the Prussian Army, 1640–1945* (Oxford, 1955), 221.

now in the Reichstag, who voted against this *carte blanche* to militarism. It was the National Liberals who rallied to the government and proposed the compromise solution of a military budget voted for seven-year terms, the Septennat. What Bismarck really needed to obtain his majority was a good war scare.

The liberal parties, who still held over half the seats in the Reichstag after the elections of 1874, were not broken until the onset of the economic depression. As prices fell and credit grew scarcer after 1873, a movement in favour of protective tariffs gathered momentum, first among iron, steel, and cotton manufacturers, then among East Elbian landowners.[26] Many *Mittelstand* groups were also interested in more protected markets. At the same time depression brought industrial discontent, which was symbolized by the formation of the Social Democratic party in 1875. The owners of mining and metallurgical plants feared the intrusion of socialist militants from the artisan trades in which they had bred. Political economists who had urged the workers to solve their problems by self-help, thrift, and education, had no answer in the face of strikes and unemployment except to call for harsh measures. 'Class domination, or more accurately the class order', wrote the historian Treitschke, 'is as necessary a part of society as the contrast between rulers and ruled is a natural part of the state.'[27]

Disillusionment with the liberal parties made itself felt in the Reichstag elections of 1877. As they lost ground a rift opened up between the left wing of the National Liberals, which looked towards the Progressives, and their right wing, which was determined to remain a governmental party. But Bismarck's aim was now to break free of the liberals and to draw closer to the conservative parties, which had gained ground. Since their power-base was outside the Reichstag, in the Court, army, bureaucracy, and Protestant Church, he would be able to refound the Reich as a more authoritarian regime. He seized on the chance of an attempt by an anarchist on the life of William I on 11 May 1878 to introduce an 'exceptional law' which virtually outlawed the socialists, who were nevertheless held responsible. It was designed to rally the forces of order, but the opposition of the Centre party, the left of the National Liberals, the Progressives, and socialists to a discriminatory and arbitrary measure proved too strong. Another anarchist assassination attempt prompted Bismarck to dissolve the Reichstag and hold fresh elections expressly to break the back of the liberal parties. He told the new Reichstag that the socialists were 'an enemy army living in our midst',[28] and in October 1878 the National Liberals fell into line and exceptional law was passed.

---

[26] See above, pp. 147–8.
[27] Quoted by James J. Sheehan, *German Liberalism in the Nineteenth Century* (London, 1978), 154–5.
[28] Quoted by Hans Rosenberg, *Grosse Depression und Bismarckzeit* (Berlin, 1967), 207.

The Chancellor now turned to the tariff issue. The right wing of the National Liberals, the Free Conservatives (representing heavy industry) and the Old Conservatives (representing East Elbian landowners), would all support protection. So would the Centre party, with its ninety-three deputies. It had opposed the anti-socialist law but had much agrarian and peasant support which was suffering as farm prices declined. The tariff voted in July 1879 thus cemented together an alliance of Conservatives, right-wing National Liberals, and the Centre party which effectively freed Bismarck from dependence on liberalism. The urban working classes were left to cope with the high price of foodstuffs. The jurists, lawyers, and academics who had annoyed Bismarck for so long now lost their influence. Manufacturers at last received economic protection but were subordinated politically to the Junker class, who were propped up by Corn Laws and still held the most important posts in the army and bureaucracy. But the real beneficiary was the military-bureaucratic regime itself, which now enjoyed increased revenues from customs duties and could afford to take a more disdainful view of parliament.

Despite its reliance on traditional élites and its ruthless suppression of dissident movements, the parliament of Imperial Germany was still elected by universal suffrage. The Prussian parliament, though, was elected by a three-tier suffrage weighted in favour of property-owners. A similar system operated in Austria-Hungary. The Hungarian parliament was elected on a high property franchise. The Austrian Reichsrat was elected indirectly by voters grouped into four curias, respectively of great landlords, chambers of commerce, urban and rural tax-payers. The regime in Hungary, an oligarchy of Magyar landowners and bureaucrats controlling a tiny electorate by means of governmental pressure, was not unlike that of Spain. The left-centre of Tisza, which in 1866 had wanted much greater independence from Austria, including a separate Hungarian army, came round to accepting the broad provisions of the Compromise for the sake of power, and in 1875 the left-centre coalesced with the Déakists to form the Liberal party. Tisza became Minister of the Interior, and was appointed Minister-President by the Emperor in his capacity as King of Hungary in October 1875. A new electoral law passed in 1874 set out conditions for the franchise based on property, taxation, and professional qualifications and limited the electorate to a mere 5.9 per cent of the population. And that was not the end of the matter. Constituencies were redrawn to give maximum weight to Magyars and minimum influence to other nationalities such as Slovaks, Serbs, and Transylvanians. The county assemblies, traditionally the parliaments of the local gentry, were virtually replaced by administrative committees which included ten members of the assembly and ten officials. These were entirely in the hands of the government's representative in the country, the High Sheriff, who was in turn directly subordinate to the Minister of the Interior. The High Sheriff oversaw the management of elections, and all varieties of bullying were employed to stifle opposition, especially Slav opposition. Slav candidates were prevented from standing or speaking, Slav voters were kept away from the polls, and those who could not make their declaration at the open ballot in perfect Magyar were disqualified. A Scottish historian noted in 1908 that this system 'actually eclipses that of England in its most corrupt epoch before the Reform Bill'.[29]

A similar hostility to Slav influence was manifested by the German Liberals who held power in Austria after 1867, but they were less successful in retaining their hegemony than their Magyar colleagues. Like the National Liberals in Germany, they pursued policies of free trade and anticlericalism. The traditional protectionist framework of the Habsburg Monarchy was dismantled and free trade treaties were signed; foreign capital was attracted, and railways and heavy industries promoted in the boom of 1868–73. Under the Concordat of 1855, marriages had been under the jurisdiction of canon law and elementary schools under the supervision of the Catholic Church, but in 1868 marriage disputes were withdrawn from church courts and state inspection was initiated for elementary schools. Then, the promulgation of Papal infallibility by the Vatican Council in 1870 was used as a pretext by the Liberals to abrogate the Concordat itself. The electoral system ensured that the German-speaking population was over-represented at the expense of the Slavs, and this advantage was reinforced by administrative centralization and the management of elections, which kept the Liberals in power in 1873, despite the slump.

The policies of the German Liberals nevertheless failed to withstand the stresses of the Balkan Wars of 1875–8. Foreign policy was in the hands of Andrássy, who opposed both Russian aggression and Slav insurrection. He came round to the view that Serb nationalism could best be checked by the Austrian occupation of Bosnia-Herzegovina, which was authorized by the Congress of Berlin in 1878. The German Liberals disliked the inclusion of more Slavs within the Monarchy and opposed the military commitments consequent upon the occupation and an alliance with Germany against Russia in 1879. This opposition was unpalatable to Andrássy and Francis Joseph; Count Eduard von Taaffe (descended from an Irish Catholic family that had migrated after the defeat of James II in 1690) was asked to form a ministry and to secure a majority in the Reichsrat for Andrássy's military plans. Taaffe turned his attention to the German clericals, the Poles, the Slovenes, and the Czechs, who had boycotted the Reichsrat since 1873. All these improved their representation in the 1879 elections and the Liberals, who lost ground, were unable to stop the government's Defence Bill. But Taaffe had to pay a price for securing the support of the nationalities, especially the Czechs, whose self-confidence was manifested in the Slavonic

---

[29] R. W. Seton-Watson, *Racial Problems in Hungary* (London, 1908), 268.

dances and rhapsodies of Dvořák (1878) and the opening of the Prague national theatre in 1883. A series of Language Ordinances of April 1880 thus required the use of Czech as well as German in the 'outer service' or lower levels of the administration and courts, and provided for a Czech section in the University of Prague. The way was now open for the Czech middle class to complete its education and find employment as lawyers, judges, and officials.

The Liberal ministers who still remained in the government resigned in June 1880. The 'Iron Ring' of Taaffe, dominated by aristocratic and clerical Germans and Slavs, was complete. The Catholic Church regained its influence and a protective tariff which pleased both industrialists and agrarians was passed in January 1879. But this was a balance that did not endear itself to Germans who regretted being shut out of the Reich in 1866 and resented the concessions that the Habsburg Monarchy was now making to the Slavs. In 1882 a movement was launched which favoured cutting off Hungary completely, Germanizing the Slavs who remained in the Austrian part of the Monarchy, and drawing closer to Imperial Germany by reinforcing the military alliance of 1879, and by the resurrection of a customs union for *Mitteleuropa*. It was the beginning of a Pan-German movement in Austria.

The Resurgence of Russia

Russia, the 'gendarme of Europe', had been defeated in 1856. During the next decade its former beat swarmed with revolutionaries and politicians pursuing their own interests at its expense. Revolutionary nationalism flared up amongst Romanians, Italians, Danes, Poles, Germans, and Magyars. European statesmen seized the opportunity to exploit these nationalist movements, while bringing them under a tight rein, in order to further the purposes of state-power. For Russia, Polish nationalism was nothing but a threat to military security and the internal stability of the regime, and had to be crushed at all costs. But further afield, in the Balkans particularly, Russia could afford to discard the role of policeman, learn from the example of Piedmont, Prussia, and especially France, and use revolutionary nationalism in order to throw off the chains imposed on it by the Treaty of Paris.

There were in the 1870s two schools of thought as to how Russia should go about recovering her great-power status. The conventional view, represented by ministers at St Petersburg like Prince Gorchakov, was the orthodoxy of the chancelleries of Europe. European affairs should be managed by statesmen in conference rooms or, in the last resort, settled rapidly by armies which executed their instructions on the battlefield. Good relations between Russia and Prussia had been reinforced by Prussia's help in suppressing the Polish insurrection of 1863, and when Prussia went to war with France in 1870 Gorchakov was happy to guarantee the neutrality of Russia. The price was support from Bismarck for Russia's unilateral repudiation in October 1870 of the clauses of the Treaty of Paris which banned all naval forces from the

Black Sea. Great Britain was not willing to fight for the clauses, and though Austria-Hungary was deeply concerned by Russia's intentions, Bismarck had been magnanimous towards Austria after his victory in 1866 and was able to prevail on her to agree to the revision. Bismarck capitalized on this agreement by resurrecting the Holy Alliance as the League of the Three Emperors in October 1873. The one principle on which all three Courts could agree was hostility to the International and the defence of monarchy. The alliance would be safe so long as the Eastern Question were not raised.

The second school of thought was that which prevailed among generals who had extended Russian imperialism in the Caucasus or central Asia, former Slavophils who promoted Russian cultural influence through the Moscow Slav Benevolent Committee (1858), and diplomats like Ignatiev whose point of view had been shaped in the embassy at Constantinople and whose fondest ambition was that Constantinople should revert to Russian hands. Responsibility for all Slavs of the Orthodox faith had been the guiding philosophy of the Slavophils. But the Polish revolt had rudely emphasized the fact that many Slavs were Catholic. The ideology of the Pan-Slavs who succeeded them focused on the struggle between Latin, Germanic, and Slav races, and argued that the destruction not only of the Ottoman Empire but also of the Austrian Empire was a pre-condition of the triumph of Slavdom. 'The way to Constantinople', ran the formula, 'lies through Vienna.'[30] The Slav peoples of the Balkans must be liberated from Ottoman and Austrian oppression, and then gathered in a federation under the aegis of the Tsar.

The question of oppression and liberation in the Balkans came sharply to life in the summer of 1875, when the Slav peasants of Bosnia and Herzegovina, weighed down by taxes and forced labour-services and suffering the effects of a bad harvest, rose in revolt against their Muslim overlords. An initial attempt by Ottoman troops to put down the rebellion failed, although the insurgents would not be able to hold out indefinitely without assistance. There was the possibility of support from Montenegro and Serbia, themselves still obliged to recognize Ottoman suzerainty and pay tribute to Constantinople, but otherwise independent. The ruler of Serbia, Milan Obernović, a cousin of Prince Michael who was assassinated in 1868, was half-Romanian, French-educated, and not particularly dedicated to Serb nationalism. He was wary of offending the governments of Russia and, above all, Austria. But in 1869 he had granted the Serbs annual assemblies and the elections of August 1875 were won by liberals who were committed to intervention and foisted an interventionist ministry on him. The pressure was building up against Turkish oppression and in May 1876 Bulgarian revolutionaries, trained in a Russian seminary in Odessa, launched an insurrection of their own. It was premature and a disaster, resulting in the massacre by

---

[30] Quoted by B. H. Sumner, 'Russia and Pan-Slavism in the Eighteen-Seventies', *Transactions of the Royal Historical Society*, 18 (1935), 42.

Map 6. The Balkans in 1878

the Turks of between 12,000 and 30,000 Bulgarians. European opinion was horrified, and Milan was forced to act, if only to save his reputation and his dynasty. Montenegro and Serbia invaded Ottoman territory on 30 June 1876.

It remained to be seen what the great powers would make of this revolutionary nationalism. For Austria-Hungary and its Foreign Minister, Andrássy, the situation was dangerous. Serbia must not be allowed to annex Bosnia or Herzegovina. A large Slav state outside Austria's frontiers would exercise a magnetic influence on Slavs within the Monarchy, and if Russia decided to back Serbia, the results could be catastrophic. Andrássy believed that the integrity of the Ottoman Empire must be maintained, although the Porte should make reforms to lighten the burdens on its Christian subjects. In Russia, two foreign policies operated in tandem. For the Pan-Slavs, Ignatiev returned to Constantinople and tried to urge the Porte to enlarge Montenegro, the highland state to which Russia had always looked first for a satellite; the deposition of Sultan Abdul Aziz in May 1876 was a blow to his plans. Inside Russia, Slav Benevolent Committees sprang up everywhere to send money and volunteers to help the Balkan rebels. A Pan-Slav general was sent with the blessing of the Moscow Slav Committee, but without that of the government, to organize the Serb troops for war. But official foreign policy was still in the hands of Gorchakov, who feared the repercussions of Slav rebellion within the Russian Empire, and was determined to settle the Balkan problem around the negotiating table and within the framework of the Three Emperors' League. In December 1875 he and Andrássy agreed to require the Porte to make reforms on behalf of its Christian subjects. Once Serbia had declared war on Turkey, the situation was somewhat different. Meeting at Reichstadt in July 1876, they agreed that if Turkey won the war, she should be restrained from taking vengeful action, and that if she lost, Turkey would be expelled from Europe and her European dominions partitioned. Austria specified that no 'great Slav state' should emerge in the Balkans, although there was some ambiguity in the agreement as to whether Bosnia and Herzegovina should go to Serbia and Montenegro respectively, or be annexed by Austria.

The war against Turkey did not go well for the Serbs. The ill-trained Serb forces lost five thousand men killed in action. A good many of the Russian volunteers did not arrive at the front but dozed in the cafés of Bucharest and Belgrade on the way. The contribution of the Russian Pan-Slav general was negative. 'Instead of saving Serbia', Ivan Aksakov of the Moscow Slav Committee later wrote to him, 'we almost ruined her. The charm of the Russian name has been destroyed both in Serbia and throughout the Slav world, yet outside Russia there is no future for Slavdom.'[31] The same point might have been made about Napoleon III and Italy: no revolutionary nationalism could succeed without the patronage of a great power, but were not great powers

---

[31] Aksakov to Cherniaev, 4/16 Jan. 1877, quoted by David MacKenzie, *The Serbs and Russian Pan-Slavism, 1875–78* (Cornell, 1967), 146–7.

given to pursuing only their own interests? Russia's only official action, as the Turks came within range of Belgrade, was to issue an ultimatum (30 October 1876) requiring them to make an armistice with Serbs on pain of Russian intervention. The Porte agreed, but Russia was being drawn into the conflict. The armistice began to run out. The influence of Ignatiev increased in Russian policy and Russia stepped up its demands. The Porte must concede not only reforms for Bosnia and Herzegovina but the creation of a Bulgarian state, which would serve Russians' interests in the Balkans much better than Serbia. These demands were refused. The demands of the Pan-Slavs for war became louder and louder, but Gorchakov could not afford to antagonize Austria in the Balkans, for the sake of the Three Emperors' League. Under a secret military convention of 15 January 1877 and a political convention of 18 March 1877, Russia agreed to keep her troops out of the western half of the Balkans, to refrain from creating a 'large Slav State', and to allow Austria to occupy Bosnia and Herzegovina. On 24 April 1877, Russia declared war on Turkey.

The ostensible reason for Russia's declaration of war was the protection of Balkan Christians. But she did not ask for their military assistance, and in turn expected to give very little away. Serbia could not count on Russian support and her interests, though she did not know it, had been mortgaged by Russia to Austria. Serbia concluded a separate peace with Turkey in February 1877, just before the armistice expired. Russia had to make some agreement with Romania, whose territory stood between Russia and the Danube frontier of the Ottoman Empire, to ensure a passage for her troops. In return, under a treaty of April 1877, Russia guaranteed the integrity of Romania, but in 1856 Russia had been forced to concede part of Bessarabia, which had been won in 1812 from the Ottoman Empire, to what was then the Danubian Principalities, and had not in fact given up the claim. If Russia was serving any Balkan interests, it was the creation of a Bulgarian state from the Ottoman Empire, but that would also serve Russian purposes: influence in the Balkan peninsula, access to the Aegean, and a frontier within shouting distance of Constantinople. It was only when the Russian armies became bogged down at the Turkish fortress of Plevna, just south of the Danube, between July and December 1877, that requests had to be sent out to the Balkan states for help. Romania joined in the war in September 1877, Serbia just after the fall of Plevna, and even Greece in February 1878. But this did nothing, in the eyes of Russia, to improve their bids for territorial compensation.

There was no possibility in 1877–8 of a 'Crimean coalition' against Russia. Disraeli persuaded the British cabinet and Parliament to authorize the sending of a fleet to the Dardanelles, to protect Constantinople. But Disraeli's attempts to bring Austria into an alliance foundered because of Andrássy's secret deal with Gorchakov by which Austria would gain Bosnia and Herzegovina from a Russian success. As during the Crimean War,

Austria was looking both ways and none. Again she miscalculated, because the treaty terms that were imposed on the Porte at San Stefano in March 1877 were entirely the work of the Pan-Slav, Ignatiev, and went against all international agreements. Russia did create a 'large Slav State' in the Balkans, although at the eastern end—Bulgaria. In the western Balkans Montenegro, which had continued fighting the Turks, was tripled in size, but Serbia got next to nothing, Greece nothing, and Romania lost Bessarabia to Russia. This was a slap in the face for most of the Balkan countries and Romania, and quite unacceptable to the European powers. The Congress System which was intended to maintain a balance of power in Europe had broken down after 1856, but it might yet be wheeled out to put Russia in its place. For British security was threatened and Austria realized that it had been double-crossed. At the Congress of Berlin, which opened in June 1878, Andrássy and the British envoy, Lord Salisbury, strove to clip Russia's wings and recover some satisfaction.

Both Britain and Austria were now forced to admit that the Ottoman Empire was a spent force, and that a settlement must be made at its expense. 'Big Bulgaria' was split down the middle along the Balkan mountains. In the northern part, Bulgaria proper, a Russian governor-general assumed military and financial control and presided over the drawing up of a constitution, the calling of a national assembly to ratify it and the election of a foreign prince, Alexander of Battenberg. The status of the southern part, Eastern Roumelia, remained somewhat confused. Austria was allowed to occupy Bosnia and Herzegovina, although the former rebels showed their dissatisfaction by inflicting 5,000 casualties on Austrian troops. Britain was no longer certain that Constantinople could close the Straits to a Russian fleet, but its main concern now was Egypt and the Suez Canal, and it acquired Cyprus as a base from which to survey Russian ambitions.

Russia retained Bessarabia and secured Batum, on the Caucasian Black Sea coast, but it had suffered a setback, always a threat to the survival of the autocracy. The war had already encouraged popular disturbances at home. The recruitment of half a million reservists deprived the countryside of manpower and ex-conscripts returned to spread rumours of a forthcoming partition of the land. Between 1875 and 1878 peasant revolts broke out in the Kiev region and there were strikes in the textile mills of St Petersburg. Young revolutionaries of the Land and Liberty movement 'went to the people' and tried to organize and educate these Ukrainian peasants and the workers of Odessa and St Petersburg to provide mass support for their cause. The Tsarist government acted fast, rounded up hundreds of young revolutionaries and attempted to discredit them by means of a show trial of 193 prisoners between October 1877 and January 1878. But the discredit rebounded on to the government itself. Seventy-five of the prisoners died, committed suicide, or went mad before or during the trial, and the day after it ended the

Governor of St Petersburg, who was responsible for their incarceration, was shot and wounded by a young revolutionary, Vera Zasulich. To the great delight of the public, at her trial she was acquitted.

The immediate response of the regime was to tighten up repression: state crimes could now be tried by military district courts. Among the liberal gentry of some *zemstvos* a movement began to find a middle course between revolution and repression, in support of the granting of constitutional liberties and greater representative government. It had little support. Most *zemstvos* feared terrorism and supported the hard line of the government. The revolutionaries scorned the ability of liberals to obtain any reform from the autocracy and their refusal to contemplate land reform. 'The people will not give a damn for your landowners' constitution', rebuked one of the Populist leaders, Mikhailovsky.[32] They continued with their revolutionary tactics, and on 2 April 1879 an attempt was made on the life of the Tsar.

Again, the government stepped up repression, appointing governors-general with dictatorial powers in the major cities. A score of dissidents were hanged and hundreds sent into exile. Some of the Populists wanted to go on educating and organizing the masses, but a terrorist group named the People's Will split off from the Land and Liberty movement in June 1879 to reply to the regime in kind, by murder.

At this point, paradoxically, those in high circles who believed that the government would have to make some concessions began to carry weight. They gathered around General Loris-Melikov, who had excelled himself in the Caucasus in 1877–8, been appointed Governor-General of the Ukraine in 1879, and Minister of the Interior and effectively Prime Minister in 1880. He was anxious to relax censorship of the press and discipline in the universities, and to include representatives of *zemstvos* and city councils on a general commission where legislation on administration and finance would be drafted for consideration by the Council of State. It proposed a 'listening autocracy', to promote the confidence of educated and propertied society, but in no sense a parliamentary monarchy. 'I know that people are dreaming about parliaments, about a central zemstvo duma,' he reflected, 'but I am not one of them. This matter is one for our sons and grandsons, and we can only prepare the soil for them.'[33] His proposals were presented to Alexander II and the Council of State in January 1881. William I of Germany urged his nephew not to relax the power of the government one iota. The terrorists were not impressed either, and a bomb thrown on 1 March 1881 blew off the legs of the Emperor and killed him. His son, Alexander III, was dull, fearful, and putty in the hands of the reactionaries. Loris-Melikov had no alternative but to resign and the faint hopes of constitutional and representative government in Russia evaporated.

[32] Quoted by S. Galai, *The Liberation Movement in Russia, 1900–1905* (Cambridge, 1973), 13.
[33] Quoted by Peter A. Zaionchkovsky, *The Russian Autocracy in Crisis, 1878–82* (Gulf Breeze, Florida, 1979), 151.

9

MID-CENTURY CULTURE

Schools

The prosperity of the middle years of the nineteenth century fed a demand for both secondary and primary schooling. Governments intervened to legislate on the provision of schools, provide funds and appoint inspectors in the more backward countries of southern and eastern Europe, which now followed where France and Germany had led the way. The emphasis on classical studies in secondary education and on religion in primary education was gradually undermined. But even in 1880 schooling was severely constrained by traditional values, class interests, and a lack of money.

The expansion of secondary education reflected the ambition of the middle classes to find employment in the public service and professions or, in France and Germany at least, to gain admission to the élite scientific and technical schools. Where the provision of secondary schools by the state or municipalities was inadequate, private schools of varied quality sprang up to meet demand. In Catholic countries private schooling was dominated by the Church, which provided seminaries for training priests and institutions run by the religious congregations which tended to serve the interests of the wealthier classes. In France, the state retained its monopoly of secondary education, with the exception of seminaries, down to 1850, but the opponents of revolution who then achieved power established the principle of 'liberty of education' and opened the way to a resurgence of Catholic colleges and convents. Between 1854 and 1876 the population of state-run *lycées* and municipal colleges increased by 71 per cent, while that of ecclesiastical secondary schools rose by 120 per cent. The education of young ladies was monopolized by nuns, and an attempt to introduce state secondary education for girls in 1867 was defeated by the French bishops at the head of Catholic opinion. In Italy, girls were uniformly educated in convent schools while the lack of state schools for boys, especially in the south, was compensated for by the existence in 1865 of 260 seminaries educating over 13,000 pupils. Only a fraction of these were destined for the priesthood: seminaries provided a cheap, Catholic education for those destined to be lawyers, clerks, and ushers. It was not until 1872 that they were subjected to state inspection. In Spain, a law of 1857 required every province to set up a *lycée*, but these were unpopular with the Catholic bourgeoisie, while the schools of the congregations, flourishing since the Concordat of 1851, continued to expand.

TABLE 10. *Pupils at public secondary schools, 1866–1867*

	Number of pupils	population per pupil
Scotland	15,946	205
Prussia	74,162	249
France	65,832	570
Italy	24,492	1,058
England	15,880	1,300

In 1876, over half the secondary school population in France was in fact educated in *lycées* and municipal colleges; but the clearest example of effective state provision was in Germany, where secondary education was entirely dominated by state *Gymnasien* and *Realschulen* financed by the municipalities. It may be argued that Prussia did not have the problem of a Catholic majority religion to contend with except in the Rhineland; but neither did England, and there the public provision of secondary schooling was minimal. A system of endowments and ancient foundations ensured the prosperity of nine public schools charging large fees and of a number of grammar schools which were no longer for 'poor scholars'. The only clientele it provided for, as Matthew Arnold observed, was the English upper class and 'a small fragment broken off from the top of our middle classes'.[1] The rest of the middle class went to proprietary schools which were financed by subscription, or to indifferent private schools. Arnold, who was greatly impressed by the Prussian system of education, tried to have it introduced into England through the recommendations of the Schools Inquiry Commission of 1868. But its plans flew in the face of a privileged system of education that suited the aristocratic establishment and were rejected in favour of a limited reorganization of endowments to make the best grammar schools more like public schools.

In Scotland the situation was even worse. The foundations of Eton and Winchester alone produced more revenue than the endowments of all the Scottish burgh schools and universities put together. An Education Act of 1872 grouped the burgh schools and academies as higher-class public schools which were inspected by officials responsible to a Scottish Education Department. But Parliament refused to approve the public funding of secondary education, and endowments and their management were not improved until legislation of 1878 and 1886.

The standard of classical education in the Scottish burgh schools was high, while in the academies there was a 'modern' tradition, strong in mathematics, modern languages, and drawing, that went back to the eighteenth century and provided an excellent training for commerce. But the balance in the secondary schools of Europe was overwhelmingly in favour of classical culture. It was not until 1848 that the hegemony of classics came in for any criticism.

---

[1] Matthew Arnold, *A French Eton or Middle-Class Education and the State* (1864; 1892 edn.), 68.

The view was then expressed that a training in letters sharpened ambitions that could not be fulfilled and bred generations of dangerous malcontents. Only in Russia was it argued that a pure diet of Latin and Greek insulated students from revolutionary ideas. In addition, to catch up with the industrial lead held by Britain an education that was altogether more practical and scientific was required. Attempts were made to develop the 'modern' side of secondary education, especially foreign languages and natural sciences. In Prussia the *Realschulen* were reorganized in 1859 as a six-year modern course without Latin, extended in 1878 to nine years in new *Oberrealschulen*; the *Realgymnasien* of 1882 taught Latin and foreign languages but not Greek, which was confined to the *Gymnasien*. In Italy, where the classical tradition was weaker, the education law of 1859 divided secondary education into two parallel streams: on the classical side, *ginnasi* up to about the age of fourteen, followed by *licei*; on the modern side, technical schools and technical institutes. In France, a reform of 1865 provided a four-year non-classical course, based on modern languages and science, to run alongside the eight-year classical course, though these 'special' courses continued to be housed within the *lycées* and municipal colleges. In England, the commission of 1868 proposed a hierarchy of grammar schools on the Prussian model, the top one teaching Greek to 18, the second Latin to 16, and the third, for the lower middle class, a modern course to 14, but these proposals, like the others, were rejected. Scientific education in English schools was encouraged by a system of payment-by-results financed by the Department of Science and Arts, set up on the initiative of the Prince Consort in 1856.

These different plans for a modern syllabus which would reduce the pressure on the liberal professions and direct talent towards more productive occupations had only limited success. Industrial development was uneven in Europe, and broad outlets in commerce and industry were required before *Realschulen* and special education would succeed. The training provided on these courses, and in spite of the boast of the Italian 'technical institutes', was not professional at all but at best non-classical. Moreover, industrial entrepreneurs were still essentially self-recruiting; these schemes were not breeding-grounds for 'captains of industry'. The other side of the argument is still more important. The material success of the mid-nineteenth century should not disguise the fact that the predominant social values were non-materialistic. A classical, humanistic education was still accepted as the defining culture of the élite. The liberal arts were held in higher esteem than the useful arts and owners of new wealth were anxious to polish it by giving their sons a classical education. Moreover, only a classical education led to the *baccalauréat* and *Abitur* which opened the doors to the university and thus to the liberal professions. The tendency of all 'modern' schools and courses was to drift towards a more 'legitimate' classical emphasis.

From secondary education the state turned its attention increasingly to primary education, the schools of the people. There were three ways of directing the masses to school: compelling individuals, as in Prussia; compelling communes, as in France; or supplementing the gaps left in private provision, as in England. In Spain in 1857, and in Italy in 1859, education laws imposed on communes the obligation to provide elementary schools and on parents the obligation to send their children there for at least two or three years. However compulsion was not enough. Only richer peasants could afford to send their children to school, unless it were free. But schooling would be free only if the commune paid. The Italian law of 1859 required communes to provide free education 'in proportion to their means and according to the needs of the inhabitants'.[2] Unfortunately the means of the communes were in inverse proportion to the needs of the inhabitants, which kept school attendance very low. In 1864, meanwhile, Russia followed the English model. Peasant communities were permitted to set up schools and the *zemstvos* were to inspect them and permitted—but not required—to allocate funds to education. However, such was the resistance to local taxes that, despite the poverty of Russia, most schools were sponsored by the peasant communities themselves. In England, where elementary education was in the hands of Church organizations helped along by a government grant, a system of public schools paid for out of local rates immediately appeared a threat to religion. And yet the provision of Church schools was completely inadequate in the growing industrial towns where organized religion was weak. The English Education Act of 1870 was therefore a compromise, leaving private Church schools alone in areas where they were strong, building non-sectarian schools, financed by the rates and inspected by local boards of ratepayers, everywhere else.

The basic functions of elementary education were first, to train individuals to be citizens of nation-states, some of which were brand new, instead of being loyal to local communities, provinces, corporations, or churches; second, to forget their *patois*, dialect, or peasant language and learn the language of the dominant nationality; and third, to 'moralize' the people. The prevailing view in Europe was that there was no morality without the sanction of religion. This was especially so in the 1850s when conservatives feared that over-education in literate skills would encourage pride, ambition, and ultimately anarchy. But a decade later, as it became clear that the universal Catholic Church stood in the way of national unification and secular citizenship, so a movement began to exclude religious education from publicly-funded schools, many of which in Europe (as well as private schools) were run by teaching congregations of nuns and lay brothers. This would be replaced by a moral and civic training to ensure that all children, irrespective of their religion, would grow up to become dutiful citizens of the state. The movement started in Belgium, where an Education League was set up in

---

[2] Quoted by Dina Bertoni Jovine, *Storia della scuola populare in Italia* (Turin, 1954), 284.

1864 to campaign for the neutrality of public schools in matters of religion. A similar League was established in France in 1866 and branches appeared in Italy in 1870. Even in England, where the established Church was Anglican, Nonconformists and radicals organized a National Education League to ensure that under the 1870 Education Act the catechism would not be taught in rate-supported schools. Liberals and radicals who obtained power excluded the catechism from publicly-supported elementary schools in Italy in 1877, in Belgium in 1879, and in France in 1882.

The imposition of a dominant national language in the new nation-states was no easy task. Outside Rome and Tuscany only 160,000 people spoke Italian in unified Italy in 1862–3, that is 630,000 altogether or 2.5 per cent of the population. Even in the elementary schools of Piedmont the teaching language was dialect. In 1864 over 13 per cent of the population in Prussian schools were Polish, and rates of illiteracy were far higher in the Polish provinces. Germanization was not an insuperable task in Prussia, but in Hungary the government ordered Magyar to be taught in all elementary schools in 1879, in order to Magyarize Slovaks, Romanians, and Serbs. Yet 47 per cent of the Hungarian population knew no Magyar in 1880, and the figure still stood at 44 per cent ten years later.

One continuing problem was still how to get the mass of children into elementary schools. As a general rule, the prosperity of the middle years of the century encouraged school attendance. Between 1847 and 1877, the primary school population of France rose by 33.6 per cent. But the number of boys at school rose by only 10 per cent to 2.4 million while the number of girls rose by 71 per cent to 2.3 million. Five years before universal free education was proclaimed in France, 57 per cent of these pupils were being educated free. But levels of school attendance in Europe were not determined only by whether schooling was free, or indeed compulsory. In poor regions where there was little more than a subsistence economy, children were required to work in the fields, or mind the sheep, or raise silkworms. In sharply stratified societies the gulf between the impoverished mass and the wealthy élite made social mobility impossible, and so education was of no value. In southern Italy, for example, there were only two ways to improve one's lot: brigandage or emigration. Industrialization did not immediately create a demand for education, because the requirement of the textile industry was for masses of unskilled labour. But in the period of high industrialization, railways, engineering, and shipyards required skilled labour, and employment prospects increased in white-collar occupations for clerks, accountants, teachers, and postal workers. It was these developments that set a premium on literate skills and increased the demand for schooling. Governments propagated elementary education in order to inculcate loyalty to the state and even to improve national security. 'We in Germany', said the *Militär Wochenblatt* in 1875, 'consider education to be one of the principal ways of promoting the strength of the nation and above all military strength.'[3] The quip ran after 1870 that France had been defeated by the Prussian schoolteacher, and it is true that in 1872–3, illiteracy in the Germany army ran at only 5 per cent, while in the French army it was 23 per cent. But there was always a difference between the official view and public consumption. The point of view of the clientele was that education was worthwhile only if it improved their material situation. School attendance therefore remained low in the backward regions of Europe, and illiteracy rates were correspondingly intractable: 68 per cent in Hungary in 1869, 72 per cent in Italy in 1871 and in Spain in 1877.

Philistinism

Though there were many individual exceptions, the broad middle class which carried so much weight in mid-nineteenth century Europe was educated but not cultivated. It was greedy for knowledge rather than meaning and consumed culture as it consumed material goods rather than using it as a means to self-perfection. Opulence of form excused poverty of thought; conformity and respectability were more important than individuality. The commonplace or rule of thumb stifled originality. Aristotle's dictum, 'things useful and necessary for the sake of things noble' would not have been appreciated. What mattered was what was useful: coal, railways, free trade, political reform, education, religion. Their usefulness showed them to be good in themselves. Some contemporaries were critical of the mentality. Monsieur Joseph Prudhomme, the quintessential bourgeois, the creation of the caricaturist and playwright Henry Monnier, became a stage personnage in Paris in 1852 and published his 'memoirs' in 1857. Flaubert's *Dictionary of Received Ideas* was a mocking collection of reach-me-down prejudices masquerading as profundities. The term 'Philistine' was popularized by the German poet, Heinrich Heine, who died in Paris in 1856 and Matthew Arnold, who admired him deeply, attacked 'the bad civilization of the English middle class' in his *Culture and Anarchy* (1869).

The typical bourgeois of the middle years of the century was too busy making money to be bothered with politics. The fact that in countries like France and Germany political censorship was fairly stiff between 1850 and the later 1860s did not inhibit the explosion of the printed word, because the demand was not for political journalism. Newspapers were bought for information, share-prices, law-reports, theatre guides, society gossip, and the serialized novel. In response to this demand the production of newspapers became a large-scale industry like any other, commercialized, served by modern technology, and offering the possibility of large profits. In England, the abolition of the stamp duty in 1855 immediately brought down the cost of newspapers. Increasing use of advertising brought it down still further. And the existence

---

[3] Quoted by Rolf Engelsing, *Analphabetentum und Lektüre* (Stuttgart, 1973), 102.

of a large and standard market was an incentive to develop and install new machines in the 1860s and 1870s: mechanical type-setting; the rotary press that could print up to 40,000 copies an hour; a device to feed in a continuous web of paper instead of sheets; the folding machine. Telegraph agencies provided instant news and the railways ensured a prompt and far-flung circulation.

Before 1850 most newspapers had been of limited circulation and sub-scription in advance, for up to a year, was required of readers. It is no surprise that reading-rooms were so popular. But cheap newspapers brought a change of practice: copies could now be bought from day to day. In England in 1856 the price of the *Daily Telegraph* came down to one penny. By 1880 its circulation was 250,000 and its owners were making a profit of £120,000 a year. The output of weekly newspapers and magazines was more varied. A popular English Sunday, like *Lloyd's Weekly*, which had an important fol-lowing among artisans and tradespeople, was selling 350,000 copies in 1863. In London and Paris there were journals for merchants and financiers. *Le Figaro* was launched in 1854 as a weekly review of society gossip and scandal, 'to recount Paris to Paris'. It was not until 1866 that it became a daily and introduced a political content only on the relaxation of press restrictions in 1868. One of the most important markets to open up was that of women. *La Mode illustrée*, which introduced the latest fashions and informed anxious women of what was done and what not done in polite society, sold 58,000 copies in 1866. Wide circulation attracted the advertisers and in the bour-geois family it was the women who saw to the business of consumption. It was largely for them that a new form of commerce, the department store, was conceived. Au Bon Marché, Le Louvre, Le Bazar de l'Hôtel de Ville, Print-emps, and La Samaritaine all opened in Paris during the course of the Second Empire.

In Germany and Austria the press was much more provincial than in Britain and France, and the *Mittelstand* was slower to catch up with reading the daily press. Even in 1881 the circulation of successful papers like the *Köl-ner Zeitung*, the *Dresdner Nachrichten* and the *Neue Freie Presse* of Vienna, founded in 1865, was not above 35,000 copies. Far more popular was a weekly started in 1853 by a Leipzig bookseller, *Die Gartenlaube*, which brilliantly combined instruction and diversion, and had a circulation of 400,000 copies in 1874. The most impressive breakthrough in this period was nevertheless made by *Le Petit Journal*, a Parisian daily of tabloid size, launched in 1863, and selling for one sou (five centimes). It was not registered as political, which avoided punitive taxation, and contained everything from news to financial and legal reports, literary reviews, human interest stories, and the *feuilleton*, or serial. It was the newspaper of the little man, extending to the provinces as well as Paris and in 1880, when the circulation of sixty Paris dailies was just under two million copies, 583,000 of those were accounted for by the *Le Petit Journal*.

Books became more accessible in the same period, partly because the distinctions between book, periodical, and newspaper were breaking down. Serialized novels, often little more than thrillers using the trick of the cliff-hanger, boosted the sales of the newspapers, and the technique spread from Britain and France to Germany, with the serialization in 1849–51 of Karl Gutzkow's *Knight of the Spirit*. Books were published in parts, as periodicals, with the added attraction of illustrations, for later binding. It was a response to the demand for encyclopaedic knowledge, but in an easily-packaged form. John Cassell's penny parts of the *Popular Educator*, the *Illustrated Family Bible*, and the *Illustrated History of England* together sold up to thirty-five million copies a year. Pierre-Jules Hetzel, a publisher who fled to Brussels after Louis-Napoleon's *coup d'état* and brought out Victor Hugo's attacks on the regime, returned to Paris to launch the illustrated periodical, the *Magasin d'éducation et de récréation* (1864). It was accompanied by a book-series of the same name, which included the best-selling titles of Jules Verne, Alphonse Daudet, and Erckmann-Chatrian. In England George Routledge's shilling Railway Library was aimed at the new public of railway-travellers. It specialized in reprints and in American writers such as Fenimore Cooper, Irving, and Longfellow whose works were not protected under British copyright law. The 1850s saw the appearance of the station bookstall, virtual monopolies of which were held by W. H. Smith in Britain and by Hachette in France. Books were also made available through public libraries. The Act of 1850 which authorized rate-supported public libraries in England was disappointing. In France and Germany associations dedicated to popular education received public support for their endeavours. A comparison of the clientele of select libraries of the Franklin Society in France and of the Berlin *Volksbibliotheken* in the early 1870s reveals *a petit-bourgeois* or *Mittelstand* readership of tradesmen, artisans, clerks, petty officials, and teachers, as well as women and schoolchildren.

The combination of bourgeois taste and technological innovation had its effect also on the world of music. The Victorian drawing-room with its piano, played by the daughter of the house, is the very image of middle-class comfort and respectability. But the industrial achievement behind this image cannot be ignored. In 1851 the piano industry was dominated by English manufacturers, centred on London, who produced about 15,000 instruments a year, many for export. But piano-making was either bespoke and artisanal, to provide the individual client with a luxury article, or the 'trash' fabrications of garret-makers, marketed by unscrupulous dealers. The revolution in piano-making, the iron-framed, overstrung piano, was the work of Heinrich Steinway, who moved from Brunswick to New York in 1850, and whose models made an immense impact on the London Exhibition of 1862 and the Paris Exhibition of 1867. The standardized, cheap but high-quality piano had arrived. But while British and French markets continued in their artisanal ways, the initiative was seized by German manufacturers. By 1884 there were 424 piano factories in Germany, notably in Berlin, Hamburg, Stuttgart, Dresden, and Leipzig, which turned out 73,000 pianos a year, half of which were exported.

The public which converged by rail and steamer on London and Paris for the exhibitions, to admire the artefacts of modern technology and to see the sights, was also the public of the theatres and concert-halls. It was provincial as well as metropolitan, cosmopolitan as well as native. But even the regulars had changed. Louis Véron noted in 1860 that the public, 'profoundly altered by new habits and attitudes', was 'too busy, too preoccupied by material interests, too exhausted by the duties and emotions of the day to be excited by the creations of the mind when they leave their dinner-tables'.[4] After his long day at the counting-house or government office, the bourgeois felt entitled to legitimate amusement.

The middle class was not the public of the subscription concerts of the Philharmonic Society or Paris Conservatoire. But neither was it the public of the music halls which sprang from the singing saloons and café-concerts around 1860. Their tastes were met by the impresarios of popular classical orchestras, who provided seats at reasonable prices and undertook gradually to educate as well as to divert their audience. Charles Hallé, a Westphalian who moved to Paris and came to England in 1848, was put in charge of an orchestra for the Manchester Exhibition of 1857 and kept it intact for a series of concerts launched at his own risk the following year. In Paris, Jules-Étienne Pasdeloup, himself a product of the Conservatoire, went outside fashionable Paris to hire a circus in the Boulevard du Temple in order to start his popular Sunday concerts in 1861. The basic repertoire was Haydn, Mozart, Beethoven, Weber, and Mendelssohn, but Pasdeloup also introduced the music of French composers and Wagner. Berlioz dismissed the audiences of five thousand people as 'virtually uneducated, like that of the boulevard theatres',[5] but that is not surprising, for Pasdeloup had established himself in the same street.

The middle-class public had no interest in the grand opera of Meyerbeer, which still dominated Paris in the 1850s. Giuseppi Verdi, who had just produced *Rigoletto*, *La Traviata*, and *Il Trovatore* for Italian audiences, lived in Paris from 1853 to 1857 and felt himself obliged to write a grandiose, Meyerbeerian opera, *Les Vêpres siciliennes*. Even the Opéra Comique was becoming serious. But at the Théâtre Lyrique the impresario Léon Carvalho rejected the heavy, spectacular, and entirely artificial genre of Meyerbeer for opera that was more delicately crafted, lyrical, and populated by human beings. His great success was with Gounod's *Faust* in 1859, which was followed by Bizet's *Pêcheurs de Perles* in 1863. At the other end of the spec-

---

[4]   Louis Véron, *Les Théâtres de Paris depuis 1806 jusqu'en 1860* (Paris, 1860), 109.
[5]   Quoted by Elizabeth Bernard, 'Jules Pasdeloup et les concerts populaires', *Revue de musicologie*, 56, (1970), 151.

trum from Meyerbeer, and aimed directly at the audience of the Exhibitions, was the *opéra bouffe* of the German-Jewish composer, Jacques Offenbach. He was authorized to open his own theatre, Les Bouffes Parisiens, in the Champs-Elysées, where the Exhibition of 1855 was to be held, and in time for its opening. Most of the capital was advanced by Hyppolyte de Villemessant, proprietor of *Le Figaro*. The success of *Orphée aux Enfers* (1858), a naughty parody of schoolboy mythology, was followed by *La Vie Parisienne* of 1866, which congratulated Parisian society on its chic, wit, and elegance, and *La Grande Duchesse de Gérolstein*, produced for the Exhibition of 1867, with Offenbach's diva, Hortense Schneider, in the title role. Another star of the 1867 Exhibition was Johann Strauss the younger, the Viennese waltz-master promoted in Paris by Villemessant. Offenbach encouraged Strauss to take up operetta, and though he lacked a good librettist, Strauss put on operettas at the Theater an der Wien after 1871, while Wagner played nearby at the new Court opera-house of Vienna.

Wagner was not a composer who commanded popular appeal, and he himself was quick to condemn successful Jewish musicians and the philistinism of the public in general. His ambition to use myth to express eternal truths of evil and redemption, to resurrect old German poetry for his text, and to squeeze vain soloists into the seamless web of the music-drama, went against the conventions and taste of his day. The rising tide of nationalism did not help his cause either. His *Tannhäuser* was performed at the Paris Opéra in 1861 under the patronage of Princess Metternich, wife of the Austrian ambassador. But, as the tenor, who had been told by Wagner to clip his virtuoso performance, noted, 'it was literally hissed off, hooted off, and finally laughed off'.[6] Between 1857 and 1864 he made no progress on the *Ring* cycle, whereas the nationalistic *Meistersinger* of 1868 gained an easy popularity in Germany. On the other hand anti-German feeling in France obliged Pasdeloup to stop playing Wagner after 1870, while the defenders of Italian opera in Italy assembled to shout down *Tannhäuser* when it was performed at Bologna in 1872. Wagner's project for a new opera-house at Bayreuth, in northern Bavaria, was snubbed by German plutocrats who would not contribute to an opera-house that was not to be based in Berlin or Vienna. Bayreuth was completed only by virtue of a generous subsidy from King Ludwig of Bavaria, and it was King Ludwig who heard the first performance of the *Ring* there, in August 1876, alone.

More cosmopolitan was the world of the spa towns and fashionable resorts, where cures were only one attraction among many. British tourists switched from Italy to the French Riviera in the 1860s not least for the delights of the casino of Monte Carlo. There were 200,000 visitors a year to French spas in the 1860s, mainly French. But when French gambling houses

[6] Quoted by Ernest Newman, *The Life of Richard Wagner*, iii, *1859–1866* (London, 1945), 115.

were closed in 1836 the leading casino owner set up his trade at Baden-Baden, and introduced a pump-room, baths, racecourse and theatre, to which Berlioz and the Bouffes-Parisiens were invited. There were 60,000 visitors a year to Baden-Baden alone on the eve of 1870, from all over Europe, the aristocracy setting the tone. Aristocratic leisure was nevertheless associated with idleness, and although the middle class had time on its hands, it was God's time and could not be frittered away uselessly. The Protestant bourgeoisie devised the alternative of 'rational recreation', time set aside to regenerate the body and refresh the mind, according to the formula *mens sana in corpore sano*, in order to return to the duties of work with that much more efficiency. Gymnastics associations and shooting societies were revived and co-ordinated in Germany when the threat from France made itself felt in 1859; the Prussian government tried to replace acrobatic activities on horizontal and parallel bars by military drill. In England the same threat gave rise to the Volunteer Force, which supplemented the regular army and militia. While the latter were officered by the gentry and drawn from the lowest ranks of the population, the Volunteer Force was a middle-class organization, who were attracted by the prospect of rifle-training, military drill, camps, and pub-crawling. After their defeat at the hands of Prussia, even the French turned to gymnastics. 'Next to the schoolteacher', urged Gambetta in 1871, 'we must place the gymnast and the soldier.'[7]

Whereas the middle class in Germany dedicated itself either to militaristic sports or to educational activities, in England it refined a whole range of sports, such as athletics, rugby, and rowing, that had little to do with militarism or culture and which were quite different from the sports that had brought aristocrats and plebeians together around the prize-fight or cock-pit, and still brought them together (though in separate enclosures) to gamble at the race-track. In middle-class sport there was no blood or violence. Competition was artificial, and took place according to a code of rules and, even more, according to conventions of fair play. The philosophy was that of the amateur. The desire to win at any price, by whatever means, was frowned upon, and gambling was outlawed. Individual talent was recognized, but in the team-game the individual player had to demonstrate team-spirit and self-discipline, under the leadership of the captain. Middle-class sport was the world of the capitalist market, but abstracted and idealized, anarchy made order.

Religion and Science

In the decade after 1848 organized religion, and especially the Catholic Church, was rehabilitated as a principle of order and authority in a turbulent world. But its position was coming under attack from a number of new directions. The Papal States' Temporal Power was held by Catholics to be

---

[7] Léon Gambetta, speech of 26 June 1871, in *Discours* (Paris, 1881), ii, 23.

essential for the spiritual independence of the Pope and for his influence over the universal Church. But because he was a secular Italian prince he stood in the way of the national unification of Italy. Second, the scientific discoveries and the scientific mentality of the mid-nineteenth century challenged not only the Churches but also religion itself by questioning the revealed truths on which faith was grounded. Third, although the Churches retained and even extended their hold on the middle classes, they lost their influence over the working classes, for reasons both political and demographic, if indeed that influence had ever been as strong as was alleged.

After 1848 governments were anxious to harness the authority of the Church as a force for order that they relaxed many of the state controls that had been imposed in more liberal times. Education was handed back to the Church and religious congregations were allowed to multiply. In France recruitment to religious congregations reached a high point in 1855–9, and the number of nuns multiplied from 66,000 in 1850 to 135,000 in 1878. The Spanish clergy, which had been deprived of most of its land, was salaried by the state under the Concordat of 1851. Austria agreed a Concordat in 1855 and in many of the smaller German states the clergy obtained the same privileges. After 1860, however, relations between Church and state changed once again. As a universal monarchy, the Roman Catholic Church stood in the way of movements of national unification. As a community of the faithful, it hampered the new relationship being forged between individual citizens and the state. As a defender of religious uniformity, it opposed ideas of religious pluralism and free thought championed by liberals and free-thinkers.

Though Louis-Napoleon as president of the French Republic had sent French troops to restore Pius IX to Rome and keep him there, in 1859 as French Emperor he sent French troops into war for the benefit of Italian unification and published the opinion that the spiritual influence of the Pope would be greater if he surrendered his Temporal Power to the emerging Italian state. This lost him the support of Catholics in France, and Orleanist notables like Guizot and Thiers joined in the criticism. In reply Napoleon began to replace, one by one, the controls that the state had formerly imposed on the Church. All Catholics in Europe opposed the interference of the state in what were regarded as the internal concerns of the Church, but at that point the Catholic opposition divided. The so-called ultramontanes believed that the state should serve as the secular arm of the Church and enforce its monopoly of the truth against all rival ideologies. The liberal Catholics, on the other hand, who met in congress at Malines in Belgium in 1863, argued that the Church should not use the state as a crutch. It should end its association with reactionary regimes, which only discredited the Church and numbed the minds of the faithful, they said, and descend into the market-place of ideas, to win the argument according to the rules of fair competition.

The liberal Catholics were strong in France and Belgium, weaker in Italy and virtually non-existent in Spain. They were isolated between on the one hand anticlericals, who now had the support of the French and Italian states, and on the other the Papacy, which made its position quite clear. *The Syllabus of Errors* issued by Pope Pius IX on 8 December 1864 listed a series of propositions with which the Papacy could not agree. These included the views that Catholicism should no longer be treated as an exclusive state religion, that the civil power had authority over the Church, that wicked acts done in the name of nationalism might be justified, and 'the Roman Pontiff can and ought to reconcile and harmonize himself with progress, with liberalism and with modern civilization'. This was a direct challenge to the national state and Napoleon III replied by banning the publication of the *Syllabus* in France. It was also a body-blow to enlightened Catholics who believed that modern civilization and the Catholic Church were not mutually exclusive. But the ultramontanes were cock-a-hoop, and interpreted the Pope's pronouncements in the most intransigent light. In the opposition camp, the anticlericals were stirred into action. The Belgian Education League was formed in December 1864 to campaign for the abolition of religious instruction in publicly-financed schools, and French and Italian anticlericals soon followed the Belgian example.[8]

The unification of Germany, as much as the unification of Italy, was a disaster for the Catholic Church. South German Catholics had preferred a loosely organized Confederation under the protection of Austria that preserved the liberties of the Church. The defeat of Austria by Prussia in 1866 threatened a Germany dominated by Protestant Prussia which would be much more centralized and bend the Church to the will of the state. Though some German Catholic bishops were ultramontane, most, together with the influential laity, were liberals. They viewed with apprehension the preparations that were being made in Rome for the Vatican Council that would proclaim the infallibility of the Pope when he spoke *ex cathedra* on matters of faith and morals. In September 1869 they met at Fulda and came out decisively against the doctrine which, if sanctioned, would bring down upon their heads accusations of Jesuitism and blind obedience to a foreign power. But the declaration of infallibility was part of the Pope's scheme both to insulate the Church from all modern errors and to subordinate the Catholic episcopate without question to the Holy See. It was duly voted by the Vatican Council on 18 July 1870.

Later in the year 1870 a heavy defeat was suffered by the Papacy. France was defeated by Prussia, and was forced finally to withdraw its garrison from Rome, which was duly occupied by Italian troops. The Pope was shorn of all his Temporal Power, with the exception of his palaces, diplomats, and Swiss

---

[8] See above, pp. 239–40.

guards. The principle of the universal monarchy was defeated by that of the nation-state, and it was on the grounds of loyalty to a foreign potentate that Catholics could now be persecuted in Germany, Italy, and France. Even the Jews of Rome were released from their ghetto and announced to Victor Emmanuel that 'under the sceptre of your Majesty we will from now on, outside our synagogue, be aware only of the fact that we are Italian and Romans'.[9]

European Jews tended to gain from the process of national unification and the retreat of the Catholic Church. They had prepared the way for their own emancipation by a process of urbanization, education, and *embourgeoisement*. Increasingly they moved to the big cities, restrictions on the residence of Jews in Vienna, for example, being lifted in 1848. They colonized secondary schools and universities and learned the language of the dominant nationality, be it French, German, Magyar, or Russian. They moved from petty trading and artisanal occupations to wholesale commerce, banking, and the professions. Emancipation, or the acquisition of civil and political rights, followed. In Russia, Alexander II granted rights after 1859 to a minority of 'useful' Jews, including merchants, artisans, and the university-educated. Swiss Jews, who were confined to the canton of Aargau, were emancipated under pressure from France in 1864. Jews in Italy were emancipated as each state became annexed to Piedmont. In Germany the way was led by the liberals of southern Germany. Baden emancipated its Jews in 1862, Württemberg in 1864. The North German Confederation followed in 1869 and imposed emancipation on Catholic Bavaria in 1870. Jews were emancipated in Austria and Hungary after the *Ausgleich* in 1867. In Great Britain, legal emancipation was completed in 1871. Emancipated Jews completed their assimilation into the dominant nationality and took up liberal politics, in order to defend their civil and political rights. This did not mean that they lost their Jewish identity. Only a small minority of Jews converted to Christianity, about 6 or 7 per cent in Germany between 1800 and 1870. Few intermarried with non-Jewish families. Jews tended to remain in certain residential areas and retained a distinctive socio-economic profile. In Vienna, Jews accounted for 61 per cent of doctors in 1881, 58 per cent of barristers in 1888, and an increasing proportion of teachers and academics. In France and Germany the pressure was great to join the dominant nation or *Volk*, whereas in the Habsburg Monarchy, because of its ethnic diversity, it was relatively easy for Jews to be politically Austrian, culturally German and ethnically Jewish. In eastern Europe, where the Jews dominated economic life and yet remained unassimilated, emancipation was retarded and anti-Semitic passions ran high. In Romania, a pogrom broke out in Bucharest when the parliament met to debate emancipation in 1866, while the Greek merchants of Odessa initiated a pogrom against their Jewish rivals in 1871.

[9] Quoted by Simon Dubnov, *History of the Jews*, vol. v (New York/London, 1973), 371.

National unification in Italy and Germany marked a defeat for the Roman Catholic Church. In a wider sense all Churches, and even religion itself, were threatened by the progress of science. In the early nineteenth century science was widely considered to be a branch of philosophy. Into the scientific world-view was built the notion of a divine creation and purpose of the universe, and thus that the natural world was a creation of the spirit and the spirit a driving force in nature. Particularly influential was vitalism which held that life was what connected matter and spirit. The vital principle safeguarded the distinction between soul and matter and postulated a divine Providence which ordered human affairs. Philosophical science was thus broadly compatible with the teaching of the Churches, and combined to justify the existing social order.

This system was rudely challenged by young German physiologists who laid the foundations of an alternative view on the eve of the 1848 revolutions and pushed home their arguments after the revolutions had failed. Jakob Moleschott, a Dutch physiologist studying at Heidelberg who was greatly influenced by Feuerbach, published his *Doctrine of Food* in 1850 which contained the statement, 'no thought without phosphorus'. Feuerbach put it over more succinctly in his review, asserting that 'man is what he eats'. For these scientists, the biological and physical worlds were one. Mind was the same as matter, and governed by the same scientifically verifiable laws. The existence of an immaterial soul and the divine purpose of the universe was contested. After the publication in 1852 of his *Cycle of Life*, which advocated the cremation of human bodies for fertilizer, Moleschott lost his teaching post and was driven to Switzerland and Italy to find support for his research.

Less polemical but more influential in the long term was the school of experimental medicine which developed in Germany and France. Its concern was to raise the biological sciences to the same level of rigour and certainty as the physical sciences by asserting that the phenomena of life were essentially the same as those of physics. The vital principle was discarded as unscientific and an unwarranted intrusion of philosophy into science. Abstract speculation was abandoned and a laboratory revolution took place, according to which all knowledge not discovered and verified by experiment was worthless. Clearly, experimentation in medicine posed difficulties, but the new generation of hard-headed physiologists were keen to establish their credentials. The leader of the German school, Emil Du Bois-Reymond, who became a full professor of physiology at the Prussian Academy of Sciences in 1858, measured the electric current in frog's legs. In France, the outstanding figure was Claude Bernard, appointed professor of physiological medicine at the Collège de France in 1854. His *Introduction to the Study of Experimental Medicine*, published in 1865, was an apology for vivisection. 'Dead anatomy teaches nothing', he wrote. Organisms must be observed at work, and if experiments on humans were impossible, inconceivable, experiments on living animals must serve instead. 'To learn how men and animals live', he continued, 'we cannot avoid seeing great numbers of them die.'[10]

The scientific view that man was part of the natural world and could be explained in terms of it was also advanced by Charles Darwin. After serving as a naturalist on a surveying expedition in the Pacific in 1831–6, and discovering Malthus in 1838, he published the fruits of his studies, *The Origin of Species*, in 1859. Darwin described how all organic beings struggled within their environment for food and habitat. Because these beings multiplied at a far greater rate than the resources available, there was competition for life between species and between individuals of the same species. Some individuals underwent small variations, and if these variations were useful in the struggle with the environment and with other organisms, they left more descendants and such variations became more frequent in following generations. By a process of natural selection the better adapted individuals and species survived while the others died out. Man himself was not created as a separate species but evolved like every other organism by a process of evolution.

Darwin was an objective scientist, and did not actually use the word evolution in the first edition of his work. But his findings provided high-calibre ammunition for the opponents of religion. It could be used to disprove the doctrine of the Creation and the Providential nature of history, for it implied that the world had evolved from time immemorial according to its own internal laws. Man himself was not created by God in his own image but was descended from the apes. The Churches were thrown on to the defensive. At a meeting of the British Association in Oxford on 30 June 1860 Samuel Wilberforce, Bishop of Oxford, challenged his audience to trace their descent from apes on the side of their grandmothers as well as on that of their grandfathers. Thomas Huxley, the British scientist who humbled the bishop by sarcasm, went on to become an influential popularizer of Darwin's thought. Two years later a Berlin zoologist, Ernst Haeckel, started to carry the gospel all over Germany, while the medical department of the University of Florence spread the message in Italy. An American, John William Draper, whose *History of the Conflict between Religion and Science* was published in New York in 1874 and translated into eight European languages, argued that every scientific discovery must undermine faith in God and denounced the Roman Catholic Church for fighting truth with mumbo-jumbo.

Another aspect of that conflict was the scholarly criticism of the Bible, which was held by the Churches to be the Word of God revealed, as a historical document. Ernest Renan, a Breton Catholic who gave one lecture as professor of Hebrew at the Collège de France in 1862 before being suspended, contested the historical accuracy of the Bible in many instances. His *Life of Jesus*, published in 1863, was an attempt to portray Christ (the title he chose

[10]   Claude Bernard, *Introduction to the Study of Experimental Medicine* (New York, 1949), 99, 108.

is significant) not as the son of God but as a historical figure, who inspired by the example of his life and teaching alone.

In the *Syllabus of Errors*, the Pope roundly denounced the views that the Bible contained 'mythical inventions', that spirit was the same as matter, and that God's hand had no influence in the world. This stubbornness only sharpened the attacks of the apologists of science. Even so, it would be wrong to imagine that religion and science were entirely irreconcilable. One of the most famous scientists of the nineteenth century, Louis Pasteur, director of scientific studies and then professor of physiological chemistry at the École Normale Supérieure between 1857 and 1877, whose work on microorganisms led to cures for anthrax, rabies, pebrine which destroyed vines, and to the sterilization of milk, always remained a good Catholic. Experiment, he said, constantly revealed that the least manifestation of nature was other than men initially supposed. The 'thick veil of the beginning and end of all things' could not easily be torn. Moreover, Pasteur, who lost three small daughters from typhoid fever, confided that 'my philosophy is all of the heart and not of the mind. I surrender myself to that which is inspired by those naturally eternal feelings that one experiences at the bedside of a child whom one has loved and just seen breathe its last. At that supreme moment there is something at the bottom of the soul that tells us that the world may very well not be a simple cohesion of phenomena like a mechanical equilibrium which has emerged from the eternal chaos by the gradual play of material forces alone.'[11]

Equally, the Churches could not afford to ignore the progress of science. After the Paris Commune a movement started among the Catholic clergy and laity in France to obtain authorization to set up Catholic universities. This was partly to endow young clergy with a solid intellectual training and partly to break the monopoly of the official University which was impregnated by Gallicanism, rationalism, scientism, positivism—in a word, by all the poisons condemned by Pius IX in the *Syllabus of Errors*. The Moral Order regime permitted the formation of Catholic universities with limited autonomy in 1875. That of Lille, founded by the Catholic clergy and local industrialists, opened in 1877. Despite the rhetoric about a Catholic and Roman counter-university, it was impossible for such a university to function without assimilating some of the fruits of modern research, in however harmless a form.

The Paris Commune reprieved the Catholic Church. The erosion of Catholic beliefs by Protestantism, philosophy, science, atheism, and socialism were all held responsible for the carnage. The execution of the Archbishop of Paris by the Communards did far more for organized religion than the *Syllabus*. Renan became a staunch conservative overnight. 'My belief is that society without Christianity is the Commune', wrote Cardinal Manning

---

[11] Louis Pasteur, letter to Sainte-Beuve, 22 Nov. 1865 in *Correspondance*, ii, *1857–77* (Paris, 1951), pp. 213–14.

of Westminster to Gladstone, 'What hope can you give me?'[12] 'No order, no institution, no government is secure', concluded the Catholic Association of Venice in October 1871. 'The ruler trembles on his throne, the priest at his altar, the magistrate on his bench, the private citizen in his home. All about there menace the plots of the revolutionary, the stones of the mob, the dagger of the assassin, the torch of the incendiary. The individual, the family, property, justice, the social order, all are threatened.'[13]

The return to religion was in the first instance a popular movement. The 1860s and 1870s were a time of troubles upset by war, national unification, revolution, and epidemics affecting both humans, and in the case of phylloxera, crops. Given that the Catholic hierarchy was itself a victim of the troubles, popular communities were obliged to fall back on their own devices to explain catastrophe and do something about it. Apparitions of the Virgin Mary, usually to poor peasant girls, were common in this period, from that at La Salette near Grenoble in 1846, to that at Lourdes in 1858, to Pontmain in western France, Alsace, Cremona and Soriano in Calabria in 1870–1, to Marpingen in the Saarland in 1876 and Knock in Ireland in 1879. Local cults sprang up spontaneously and the surrounding populations, usually led by women, made pilgrimages to the sites. The message of the Virgin was invariably that disaster had struck as punishment for men's sins, and that only atonement and a return to the faith would restore the protection of God. Women were keen to promote the cult of the Virgin, both as a way of feminizing Catholicism and of legitimizing the virtues of womanhood and motherhood.

The attitude of the Catholic hierarchy was ambivalent. For most of the century it had looked askance at pilgrimages, which tended to mix prayers and devotion with feasting, drinking, and dancing. Now, however, the clergy saw a way of using popular religiosity to protect the beleaguered Church. In the course of the 1870s, therefore, pilgrimages were purged of their profane accretions but commercialized through the railway network and organized on a national and even international, rather than just a local, basis. Three million faithful visited shrines in France in 1873, when the first national pilgrimage to Lourdes was held, and pilgrims came to Lourdes from Belgium in 1873, Germany, Poland, and Italy in 1875, Spain and Ireland in 1876, and Switzerland and Portugal in 1877.

The Catholic laity were keen to seize on the upsurge of religiosity to convert the working classes, whose atheism was believed to have been responsible for the Paris Commune. Bishop Ketteler of Mainz led the way with the foundation of workers' associations in the Rhineland after 1870. His example was followed by two French officers, Albert de Mun and René de la Tour du

---

[12] Letter of 23 November 1871, quoted by Owen Chadwick, *The Secularization of the European Mind in the Nineteenth Century* (Cambridge, 1975), 125.
[13] Quoted in Atti del quarto Convegno di storia della Chiesa, *Chiesa, e religiostà in Italia dopo l'unità, 1861–78* (Milan, 1973), 219.

Pin, who were captured in the Franco-Prussian War and interned at Aachen in the Rhineland. They returned to France to set up workers' circles in the early 1870s. The Opera dei Congressi which took off in Italy in the same period were inspired by the same vision of a Christian social order.

In France, the right-wing National Assembly decreed in 1873 that a basilica of the Sacred Heart should be built on the hill of Montmartre, to atone for the crimes of the Commune. In Germany, on the other hand, the government was fearful that pilgrimages might be used to whip up resistance to the *Kulturkampf*. Troops occupied the village of Marpingen for a fortnight in 1876 and the organizers of the local cult were put on trial in 1879, but acquitted. Governments came to realize that whereas national unification had sharply undermined the power of the hierarchy, Roman Catholicism was now the recourse of many who wished to defend local values and loyalties and resist national integration.

Positivism

Just as scientific laws were being developed to explain the relationship of man to the natural world, so also the view was put forward in the mid-nineteenth century that society was something more than the individuals who composed it, and that the relationship of man and society could also be explained in terms of scientific laws. In a word, sociology was born. This challenged religious and ethical systems, for if the good of society came first then the good of the individual had to come second. It also questioned the notion that man could successfully reform society purely in the light of his religious or political beliefs. Clearly, if society was shaped by social laws, those social laws would have to be understood before reform could begin.

The ideas put forward by the French mathematician and philosopher Auguste Comte in his *Course of Positive Philosophy* (1830–42) had a convincing scientific aura and served as the credo of the 'Positivist' school. Comte's argument was that the current political and moral crisis was the result of 'intellectual anarchy'. Two rival ideologies were still fighting for supremacy. The theological view held that man was corrupted by original sin and must be controlled by a Catholic and feudal hierarchy. The metaphysical view believed in the perfectibility of man and that his natural rights of liberty and equality should be realized in political democracy. The clash of these two conceptions was responsible for the chaos that had disrupted Europe since the Revolution, and even since the Reformation. Comte now proposed an alternative, scientific, conception that would make possible the reorganization of society along scientific lines. For Comte, man must now examine human society as if it were part of the natural world, and having discovered the laws that explained the phenomena of the natural world discover the laws that governed the relationships between men in society. These could be subdivided into the laws of social statics, or sociology, which started from the premiss that political institutions, social structures, and ideas were all interdependent in a given society, and the laws of social dynamics, or the laws of history. Man's mistake until now had been to try to remake society according to some blueprint, whether in the image of Heaven or according to the Rights of Man. But just as a physician had to understand the laws governing the human body before he could diagnose a disease and prescribe a cure, so the political scientist must establish the laws governing human society before he could pinpoint its weaknesses and propose reforms.

Comte was not an original thinker. Most of his thought was derived from that of Saint-Simon, whose secretary he had been in the years 1817–22. Later Comte tried to minimize this influence, and played down what he called 'the morbid liaison of his early youth with a depraved juggler'.[14] His logical exposition and confident system-building attracted a reverent following at the time but at the end of the century Renan, Engels, and Durkheim all rediscovered the genius of Saint-Simon, and even that of Condorcet, which Comte had tried to appropriate as his own. One reason for Comte's success was that after the death of Saint-Simon in 1825 his disciples followed him as exponents of a new religion of love and then became technocrats and planners, leaving Comte as the only scientist in the world of poets, industrialists, and scientists that Saint-Simon envisaged. Subsequently, the contradictions in Saint-Simon's thought caught up with Comte as well. His marriage was unhappy and broke up in 1842. He then fell in love for the first time, but Clotilde de Vaux, the object of his attentions, died eighteen months later. Whereas Comte had until now preached the superiority of the mind over the heart, his *System of Positive Politics*, published in 1851–4, a monument to Clotilde de Vaux, proposed that society's conflicts could be resolved by love, by a Religion of Humanity. This religion would centre on the cult of the woman, in her roles as mother, wife, and daughter. Nine 'social sacraments' were instituted, from 'presentation' (or baptism) to 'incorporation' (or canonization) after death. Public festivals would be dedicated to the glorification of fundamental social relationships, such as marriage and filial piety, and to the stages of human evolution, from fetishism and polytheism to monotheism. With its Marian cult, its sacraments, and calendar it strongly resembled, as Thomas Huxley said, Catholicism without Christianity.

Because of this about-turn, Comte left two sets of disciples when he died in 1857. There were those who were inspired by the later Comte and dreamed of establishing a Religion of Humanity. And there were those, led by the dictionary-maker Émile Littré and including Jules Ferry, the architect of the education reforms of the Third Republic, who subscribed to the earlier Comte and the cult of Science. However, even the latter were as estranged as Comte himself from the practicalities of social engineering, for they believed that education was the key to social harmony. In a speech of 1870 Jules Ferry

---

[14] Quoted by Émile Durkheim, *Socialism and Saint-Simon* (London, 1959), 106.

regretted social inequality but emphasized that he was advocating no social levelling. The solution was to educate rich and poor on the benches of the same school, to teach them that all occupations were socially useful and had equal dignity, and to develop a spirit of fraternity that would prove stronger than class differences. Fraternity was also at the centre of the positivists' moral teaching. The Church's view that there could be no morality without religion was rejected. Religion was wormeaten, no longer had a hold on the mass of the people and was basically antisocial, orientated as it was towards the salvation of the individual in the next world. Yet metaphysical morality, which was concerned only to assert individual rights, was socially disruptive. 'We realize', said Ferry in 1875, 'that in society there are only duties, and as Auguste Comte said, "each man has only one right, which is to do his duty".'[15] A system of ethics based not on divine command but on the notion of duty, which was derived from mutual interdependence in society and reinforced by the spirit of fraternity, was the positivists' answer to social tension. And because Ferry's speech was given on the occasion of his induction—with Littré—into one of the Lodges of the Grand Orient, it also represented the general view of French freemasonry, the hidden system through which so many Republican politicians were promoted.

Despite the translation (and abridgement) of the *Course of Positive Philosophy* by Harriet Martineau, published in 1853, Britain was not a particularly fertile ground for positivist thought. John Stuart Mill, though influenced by Comte's view of social statics, was wary of social determinism and keen to preserve a sphere in which the individual enjoyed the freedom to make moral choices. Herbert Spencer, whose *Social Statics* appeared in 1850, was very much Britain's own Comte, although he denied that he was influenced by the Frenchman, and claimed that he was ignorant of the *Positive Philosophy* until George Eliot introduced him to it in 1852. Spencer argued that man was subject to social laws, the most important being that men adapted to new environmental conditions imposed by the increase of human populations. Eventually, he claimed that individuals would learn to adapt perfectly to new challenges. As animal communities allowed the sick and malformed to die out, for the vitality of the race, so also for Spencer human societies should be subjected for their own good to the 'severe discipline' of the 'struggle for life and death'. Consequently, he proposed that the state should not concern itself with education, religion, poor laws, or health reform, for this would only increase human misery in the long run. Spencer criticized Comte for failing to grasp the notion of evolution, in this case from simple to complex societies. He seized on Darwin's concept of natural selection and in his *Principles of Biology* (1866) invented that of the survival of the fittest. Criticized in Britain for an affront to religious and ethical notions of duty and compassion,

---

[15]	Quoted by Louis Legrand, *L'Influence du positivisme dans l'oeuvre scolaire de Jules Ferry* (Paris, 1961), 243.

he enjoyed some popularity in the United States, whence his ideas returned in the 1890s as social Darwinism.

Meanwhile, in France, scientific laws accounting for competition and evolution were applied to races by Count Arthur de Gobineau. Briefly secretary to Alexis de Tocqueville when the latter was French Foreign Minister in 1849, he then served in the French diplomatic service in Switzerland and Germany, and in 1855 published an *Essay on the Inequality of Human Races*, which he dedicated to the reactionary George V of Hanover. He argued that a hierarchy of races existed, with the white (Aryan) race at the top and yellow and black races at the bottom. Though races had a tendency to mix, the greatness and brilliance of any civilization depended on the ability to maintain its purity. Thus the Franks had been weakened by mixing with Gallo-Roman blood south of the Loire, at the time of Charlemagne, while the Anglo-Saxons were mixing with Red Indians, Blacks, and Hispanics in the United States, so that modern civilization now depended on the survival of the Aryan race of northern Europe. Tocqueville had no time either for his determinism or for his pessimism. 'You profoundly despise the human race', he chided Gobineau in 1857, 'you consider it not only fallen but unable to rise again.'[16]

While Gobineau centred his scientific explanations of social evolution on race, Marx focused his on class. From London he issued his *Critique of Political Economy* in 1859 and the first volume of *Capital* in 1866. Like Darwin, he argued that man struggled with the environment to gain his subsistence, whether farming, mining, or manufacturing. But for Marx production was a social activity, and society was shaped both by the division of labour and by the rivalry between those who owned the land or capital required for production, and those who did not, and were exploited by the possessing classes. The legal system, state apparatus, and ideologies served only to reinforce and legitimate the domination of the possessing classes. However, the system was not static. For as capitalists invested in new technology to increase the productivity of the workforce and hence their ability to exploit it, so they both precipitated crises of overproduction and created an army of unemployed workers who would eventually turn against the system. What appealed to workers' leaders about Marx's message was the scientific demonstration that capitalism was doomed and that socialist society would inevitably take its place.

It was the influence of German thought rather than French thought that was felt among Spanish intellectuals from the later 1850s. But it was metaphysical German thought, that of the idealists, and notably a minor German idealist named Karl Krause, which was introduced to Spain by Julian Sanz del Rio, the professor of philosophy at the new University of Madrid. This

[16] Alexis de Tocqueville, *Œuvres Complètes (19). Correspondance d'Alexis de Tocqueville et d'Arthur de Gobineau* (Paris, 1959), 280.

philosophy held that the world was an emanation of God at a particular moment, and that all knowledge was ultimately knowledge of God. The task of the individual was to achieve an inner harmony between his nature and his spirit, and then to resolve the antagonisms of marriage, class, sect, or nation within ever higher associations, until a final harmony was reached in God. The Krausists, an elect upon whose self-education depended the destiny of humanity, floated about the universities in black garments and with serious mien, and acquired a certain amount of public importance after the Revolution of 1868. This was, in Comte's terms, progress from theological to metaphysical thought, and unfortunately it offered no practical programmes of social reform.

Between the depression of the 1840s and the depression of the 1880s social reform in Europe was minimal. It owed little to the academic theories of the Positivists and their rivals and was constantly frustrated by the obstinacy of hostile interests. After 1847 there were few important measures of factory reform in England, and in France child and female labour in the factories was not effectively limited until 1874, when Catholic conservatives dominated French politics. In the harsh world where sickness tended to bring unemployment in its wake a working-class élite was able to organize itself into friendly societies or mutual aid societies, which received some patronage from Napoleon III under a law of 1852. In Prussia the *Gewerbeordnung* of 1845 provided for sickness, invalidity, and old-age funds in the craft industries and these were extended to factory workers in 1849. But this system which was geared to the small workshop fell apart under the pressure of rapid industrialization in the 1860s and 1870s, and employers blatantly ignored the obligations laid upon them. The mass of the population fell back on poor relief. German workers who suffered accidents tended to return to the countryside from which they had come and increase the burden on the rural poor funds. In Britain, the rate of parishes for poor relief was calculated according to the number of poor, not according to the wealth of the inhabitants, which overburdened the districts that could least afford to pay. Everywhere, poor relief failed in the face of mass unemployment. The alternative of public works was tried in the French national workshops of 1848, in the Rhineland under the Elberfeld system of 1853 which set the unemployed to work repairing roads, improving town-squares, and reclaiming land, and in Lancashire during the cotton famine of 1863. But these schemes were not widespread enough, and public funds were always lacking. There was a reluctance on the part of local communities to pay rates on the one hand, or to accept central government interference on the other. Sanitary laws passed in England in 1848 and in France in 1850 applied neither to Paris nor to the City of London, which insisted on their own provisions, and provincial resistance in England resulted in the scrapping of the General Board of Health in 1858. Slum-clearance was hindered in both countries by the need to compensate slum-landlords, and the rebuilding of London and Paris in fact concentrated the working populations into smaller and more unhealthy ghettoes. Working-class life was still a vicious circle of exploitation, overcrowding, disease, and unemployment.

Realism

The challenge of a rapidly changing world was taken up by a movement of writers and artists who called themselves Realists. They were inspired not by history, legend, or the Bible, but by the contemporary world which forced itself upon their senses. Revolution and democracy had given expression to numbers, and workers and peasants now aroused the same interest as lords and ladies. Even the small-town bourgeoisie, with its pretensions, peccadilloes, and *ennui* was deemed worthy of artistic treatment. But above all it was the business of modern life that caught the eye: the race-tracks and regattas, the bars and boulevards, the department stores and apartment blocks, the railway stations and quaysides.

In some cases the change of approach came about very suddenly. The French novelist, Gustave Flaubert, wrote in November 1850 from Constantinople to his mistress, outlining three projects that he was considering. 'One: *Une Nuit de Don Juan*, which I thought of in quarantine at Rhodes. Two: *Anubis*, the story of a woman who wants to be seduced by God. This is the most exalted of the three, but has atrocious difficulties. Three: my Flemish novel about the young girl who dies a virgin and mystic in the arms of her father and mother in a small provincial town, at the end of a garden full of cabbages and fruit-trees, beside a stream the size of the Robec.'[17] But scarcely six months later, back in Rouen, Flaubert had dropped all three subjects and was planning a study of modern provincial life that was to become *Madame Bovary*, the story not of a romantic heroine, but a doctor's wife.

Of course urban and industrial life repelled as many writers and artists as it fascinated. The Romantic view of a higher world beyond the constraints of grim reality still had its exponents. In England the Pre-Raphaelite Brotherhood which was formed in 1848 took refuge for inspiration first in the life of Christ, then in the story of Dante and Beatrice, and Arthurian legend. It was a search for an ideal both chivalric and romantic. A leading German painter, Anselm Feuerbach, fled from the Realist obsession of artists in Paris and stayed in Rome between 1856 and 1873, his work influenced by the poetry of Dante, by the Madonnas of Raphael, and the apotheoses of Titian. The rejection of modern life was explicit among German novelists. Even so-called Realists like Gottfried Keller were still primarily interested in ethical questions, not in social and political problems, and confined their works to family circles, rustic settings, and the historical past.

---

[17] Gustave Flaubert, *Correspondance*, ed. J. Bruneau (Paris, 1973), i, 708.

One reason for the choice of historical and mythological subjects was their symbolic importance. Through them it was possible to portray the spiritual qualities of man's nature, cleansed of the tarnish of everyday life, and to fix the eternal values of love and beauty in a world that was far removed from the present. These were not the concerns of the Realists. They had experienced the Revolution of 1848 as young men and their hopes had been dashed. Eternal values of liberty and equality had been trampled underfoot and religion was now part of the apparatus of repression. They had no illusions at all about the higher qualities of mankind, and they were committed to show triumphant bourgeois society exactly as it was, warts and all.

Realism was the opposite of Romanticism or Idealism in that it had no faith in anything beyond the real world. Some artists of the period, such as the Frenchman, Millet, tended to idealize the people, portraying the peasantry and stylizing their work as a series of ritual acts, performed since time immemorial, to the greater glory of God. But the perspective of the leading Realist painter, Gustave Courbet, was quite different. His *Stone-Breakers* represented the most brutalizing and monotonous form of human toil, work as drudgery. His vast canvas, *The Burial at Ornans*, was a secular treatment of a religious ceremony, suggestive of no hope, the faces of the mourners mean and grim. 'Is it the painter's fault', asked the writer, Champfleury, 'if material interests, small-town life, sordid egoism, provincial narrowness have clawed their faces, dimmed their eyes, wrinkled their foreheads, made their mouths stupid?'[18] In the Salon of 1853 Courbet exhibited his *Bathers*, two podgy nudes on a slippery riverbank who seemed to the Empress to be carrying more weight than the plough-horses in the adjoining picture. Certainly they conveyed nothing of the ideal of beauty. Although the imperial authorities needed Courbet for the Universal Exposition of 1855, they wanted to vet sketches of a work to be commissioned. This Courbet refused, and set up a separate one-man exhibition under the banner of Realism.

The Realists were entirely cut off from the infinite and eternal. Absolute principles of good and evil, of right and wrong, seemed a long way off; people muddled along as best they could. Love was prosaic and usually disappointing, not a participation in the divine. In Flaubert's *Madame Bovary*, which starts with the boredom imposed by marriage to a country doctor, Emma consumes a succession of lovers in her desire to realize the ideal of romantic love that she has read about in novels, but she remains hungry for affection. She is driven to suicide by the pressure of debt and dies kissing the crucifix, but unrepentant. *Sentimental Education* (1869) is almost a mirror-image of *Bovary*. Flaubert's anti-hero, Frédéric Moreau, meets his ideal of a woman within the first pages of the novel. But he is weak-willed and indecisive. He is reluctant to confront obstacles in his path or to make sacrifices for a higher goal. Thus he refrains from approaching her and fritters way his life in a string

[18] Quoted by F. W. J. Hemmings, *Culture and Society in France, 1848–1898* (London, 1971), 105.

of other affairs. In Gottfried Keller's *Village Romeo and Juliet* (1855), two families quarrel over a small piece of land and make marriage between the young lovers impossible. But for them there is no question that death will permit in eternity the union that cannot be made in this world. Rather, they snatch their pleasure in this, the only world that exists, and then drown themselves. In a much more incisive way, Dostoyevsky confronted the issue of injustice in a world where God has ceased to exist. An individual like the poor student Raskolnikov in *Crime and Punishment* (1866) is driven to take the redress of evil into his own hands, to recreate a system of values, even if this involves brutal murder.

The enclosed world of the Realists flew in the face of a bourgeois society that believed in the observance of certain artistic conventions in order to suggest an ideal of beauty and to protect order, religion and morality. The Realists' concern with ordinary people was disapproved for political reasons. 'They had dissolved the national workshops, they had defeated the proletariat in the streets of Paris ... they had purged universal suffrage', wrote the critic, Castagnary, in 1851, 'and here was that vile multitude, chased out of politics, reappearing in painting.'[19] Under the Second Empire in France the law of 1819 against the publication of works which constituted 'an outrage to public and religious morality' was enforced in courts which sat without juries. Baudelaire's *Les Fleurs du Mal* and Flaubert's *Madame Bovary* were the subject of obscenity trials in the same year, 1857. The main contention of Flaubert's prosecutor was that Emma's approach to God was as lascivious as her approach to earthly lovers, and that she showed no repentence for her adultery. 'Art without rules is no longer art,' he concluded, 'it is like a woman who takes off all her clothes.'[20]

Artistic convention was the apparatus of bourgeois hypocrisy. A distinction was drawn between the nude, an alabaster column that was destined never to see a strip of clothing, and was usually portrayed in some exotic or mythological setting, and the naked woman, who had clearly just undressed and erupted into everyday life. Among the most established of nineteenth-century French painters were Jean-Léon Gérôme, who visited Cairo and Constantinople on several occasions and placed his nudes in the acceptable settings of seraglios, slave-markets, and Turkish baths, and William-Adolphe Bouguereau, whose diaphanous nymphs bathe in the evening light in forest pools. 'The public', according to Théophile Thoré, writing about the Salon of 1861, 'accepts monsters with goats' feet who carry off completely naked fat women, but it does not want to see the garters of the girls of the Seine.'[21] Courbet broke the rules by painting real women in real bathing-places, while

[19] Quoted by Linda Nochlin, *Realism* (London, 1971), 47.
[20] Pleading of Imperial procurator, printed in Flaubert, *Madame Bovary* (Paris, 1896), 410.
[21] Quoted by Linda Nochlin, *Realism and Tradition in Art, 1848–1900* (Englewood Cliffs, 1966), 55.

Manet scandalized the public by taking the conventions and making a mockery of them. In his *Déjeuner sur l'Herbe* well-dressed young men have joined a naked woman in her forest idyll, while his *Olympia* (1865) is not a classical odalisque, but, in the classical pose, a young prostitute who confronts the viewer with a direct gaze. Rejected by the Universal Exposition of 1867, he set up a separate exhibition in a private pavilion, next to Courbet's.

Bourgeois morality did not give ground that easily, and the pressure to conform weighs heavily in much Realist literature. The will of the anti-hero is so weak, and the norms of society so strong, that in Keller's novel *Green Henry*, written in 1854 and revised in 1879, the young artist of no particular talent would be happy to succeed without any effort on his part. When this proves impossible, he is just as happy to become a responsible member of the community, a minor official, and honest burgher of his home-town of Zürich. The intractability of bourgeois values, reinforced by the authority of the Catholic Church, is the theme of much of the writing of the Spanish novelist, Pérez Galdós. In *Doña Perfecta* the Catholic mother lives up to her name until her nephew, a liberal and free-thinker, determines to marry her daughter. At this point Catholic fanaticism and the prejudices of the provincial community are unleashed and Doña Perfecta combines with her confessor to kill the young man and drive the daughter to madness.

The Realists not only abolished the ideal world that was supposed to exist beyond the real world and give it meaning, they also tried to adapt the methods of science to their observations of society. The perspective of the scientist was supposed to be cool, detached, and impartial. Flaubert, who strove after the same impartiality, was said to have dissected the emotions of Emma Bovary like a surgeon with his scalpel. The Goncourt brothers, Edmond and Jules, insisted that massive documentation was required before a novel could be written about particular aspects of social life. On painting, the main influence was that of photography, which progressed from the daguerreotype of 1839, a metallic plate that could not be reproduced, to the wet collodion process of the early 1850s, from which multiple negatives and a high degree of accuracy could be obtained. The appeal for Realist painters was that the camera was a machine that would reproduce, quite objectively, what was placed in front of the lens. There could be no question of any idealization. That, for the critics, was the main drawback. In Courbet's *Burial at Ornans*, 'which one might mistake for a faulty daguerreotype', said one, 'there is a natural coarseness which one always gets in taking nature as it is, and on reproducing it just as it is'.[22] But even artists who were not Realists in the sense of painting subjects from contemporary life, such as Gérôme, aspired to the accuracy of the photograph, and Baudelaire noted in 1859 that 'the ill-applied progress of photography has contributed much, as do indeed

[22] Quoted by Aaron Scharf, *Art and Photography* (London, 1968), 96.

all material advances, to the impoverishment of the French artistic genius already so rare.'[23]

Curious though it may seem, the photograph exercised a powerful influence over the Impressionist painters who tried to fix on canvas, in the open air, the fleeting impressions of modern life. The 'bird's-eye' photographs taken from high buildings or by the famous photographer Nadar from his balloon made popular the view on to the street from above, with its sense of detachment. As camera speeds became quicker, so the image was transformed. The early snapshots of Paris were exposed for so long that it appeared that the city had no traffic. Then moving objects were registered as blurred and wispy shapes which were imitated by Monet in his *Boulevard des Capucins* in 1873. But already the exposure of 1/50 second made it possible to freeze rapid movements in print and see them in a totally new way. Impressionists like Degas, who was a photographer in his own right, were anxious to catch the instant of action in their pictures, whether it was the awkward gait of a galloping horse, the bow of a dancer, or an acrobat hanging by her teeth at the Cirque Fernando. Lastly, composition itself was influenced by the snapshot which cut off some figures at the frames and included others distributed in a wholly random manner in streets and on beaches. In many Impressionist pictures the only thing that the disconnected elements have in common is to be within the same frame at the same time.

Realism was not only a scientific means of observation. It followed science in its search for laws that determined the behaviour of human beings in society, whether they were laws of heredity or laws of the environment. At this point it is possible to speak of Naturalism, a subsection of Realism, which was extremely pessimistic about the scope of free will and portrayed individuals in the grip of genetic and social forces beyond their control. The Goncourt brothers were particularly interested by medical conditions and in *Germinie Lacerteux* (1865) they traced in vivid detail the physical and mental degeneration of a girl sent up to Paris from the country and falling prey to all forms of exploitation. Emile Zola devoured Darwin's *Origin of Species* when it was translated into French in 1862. The central thesis of struggle for survival between individuals and species and the determining roles of environment and heredity was applied to his twenty-volume 'natural and social history of a family under the Second Empire', the *Rougon-Macquart*. Zola also learned from Claude Bernard that the task of the scientist was to verify hypotheses by observation and experiment. His novels were planned as experiments in which the influence of hereditary factors such as alcoholism, and different environments from the slums of Paris to the coalfields of northern France, could be tested. Where the scientist remained uncertain, Zola argued that the novelist could use his intuition and forge ahead of him. Such

[23] Ibid., 110.

intellectual arrogance may be ridiculed, but the dramatic effect of his theories is remarkable. 'Subjective' individuals are no longer the mainspring of the plot, as in the Romantic novel. Instead, characters are the victims of forces greater than themselves and are swept up in the tide of the epic.

Naturalism had a certain amount of popularity in other countries, although few writers went to the extremes of Zola's determinism. In Italy Giovanni Verga started a cycle of novels, *The Tide*, that would interpret passions and emotions in purely mechanical terms, but he never got beyond the third volume. Galdós' novel *The Disinherited* (1881) is the treatment of a girl with a family history of insanity who is obsessed by the mission to prove her noble lineage; when she is rejected by the noble caste she descends into hysteria and prostitution. Inherited flaws and the evils of a rigid social hierarchy are brought out but Galdós does not imply that free will has been sacrificed on the altar of behaviourism. And despite the popularity of Darwinian theory in some German circles, the legacy of German idealism inclined writers there to repudiate a theory that undermined the ethical dilemmas that confronted the individual as a free moral agent. In art, as in religion, the challenge of a deterministic science was firmly contained.

PART III

Europe 1880–1914

IO

THE STRUGGLE FOR ECONOMIC SUPREMACY

Mass Migration

At the end of the nineteenth century Europe's political centre of gravity shifted from west to east. The cause was partly demographic. The rate of population growth in Mediterranean countries, Scandinavia, and the British Isles was sluggish and in the case of Spain, Norway, Sweden, England, Wales, and Scotland, slower in 1880–1910 than it had been in 1850–80. The population of France remained almost static. On the other hand the Netherlands, Belgium, Germany, and Austria grew faster than in the period 1850–80, while in eastern Europe there was nothing less than a population explosion. Numbers in the Hungarian part of the Habsburg Monarchy grew more vigorously than in the Austrian part, but the biggest leaps were achieved by Romania, the Balkan countries of Bulgaria, Greece, and Serbia, and, most of all, Russia.

The key factor behind population growth was falling mortality. A debate about the explanation of this change swings between medical discoveries and environmental causes, including better nutrition. Medical improvements were decisive only in the case of smallpox, following the introduction of compulsory vaccination by Norway and Sweden in 1810, the south German states between 1806 and 1817, and Great Britain in 1854, but smallpox deaths accounted for only a tiny proportion of the totals in these countries. Urbanization and overcrowded living and working conditions increased the risk of infection from airborne diseases such as tuberculosis in the middle years of the century. A rising standard of living and national campaigns to warn tubercular patients of the dangers of infecting others reduced mortality from tuberculosis at the end of the nineteenth century, but while improvement was marked in England, Wales, and Germany, countries such as France and Italy lagged behind. Other infectious diseases were carried by water. Contaminated water-supplies and the ineffective disposal of sewage were responsible for deaths from diarrhoea, dysentery, typhoid fever, and cholera, but urban improvements at the end of the century went a long way to reducing fatalities. The last major cholera epidemics in Europe took place in England in 1866, Austria-Hungary in 1872–3, France in 1884, and Germany in 1892, when there were 8,605 deaths in Hamburg alone. Typhoid fever was also water-borne, and whereas the number of deaths per million population was reduced in 1887–91 to 196 in England and 250 in the Netherlands, there were still 880 in Italy.

TABLE 11. *Birth- and death-rates in Europe, 1876–1910*

	birth-rate (per thousand population)		death-rate		infant mortality (death under age one per thousand live births)	
	1876–80	1906–10	1876–80	1906–10	1876–80	1906–10
France	25.3	19.9	22.4	19.2	166	126
England and Wales	35.4	26.3	20.8	14.7	144	117
Scotland	34.7	27.6	20.6	16.1	118	112
Ireland	25.5	23.3	19.2	17.2	99	94
Germany	39.4	31.7	26.1	17.5	227	174
Belgium	32.1	24.6	21.8	15.6	197	142
Netherlands	36.4	29.6	22.9	14.3	155	114
Denmark	32.0	28.2	19.4	13.7	138	107
Norway	31.6	26.4	16.6	13.9	101	69
Sweden	30.3	25.4	18.3	14.4	126	78
Spain	35.8	33.3	30.4	24.1	192	159
Portugal		30.9		20.1		134[a]
Italy	36.9	32.7	29.4	21.2	195	152
Switzerland	31.2	26.0	23.1	16.0	188	115
Austria	38.7	33.7	30.5	22.4	249	202
Hungary	44.1	36.3	36.9	24.9		206
Romania	35.7	40.3	31.3	26.0	205	
Bulgaria		41.8		23.7		161
Serbia	38.6	39.3	35.6	24.5		154
Russia	49.5	45.8	36.7	29.5	275	247

[a] 1910 only.

One of the most significant demographic changes was the decline of infant mortality at the turn of the century. This may largely be attributed to more rigorous standards of food hygiene. In particular, the widespread pasteurization of milk reduced infant deaths from gastro-enteritis. Infant mortality was still considerable in Germany in 1906–10, at 174 per thousand live births, whereas the rate was under 130 in France, the British Isles, the Netherlands, Scandinavia and Switzerland. However, the overall death-rate in Germany fell dramatically at the end of the century, and in 1906–10 was lower than that of France. The geography of mortality remained more or less constant. The highest death-rates were recorded in Mediterranean and eastern Europe, where diseases carried by insects were particularly rife. Deaths from malaria, carried by mosquitoes, in 1887–91 were only 6 per million population in England and Wales and 40 per million in the Netherlands, but 581 per million in Italy, of which 83 per cent were in the south or the islands. Typhus fever, carried by lice, erupted anew in the atrocious conditions of the First World War. A typhus epidemic in Serbia killed 150,000 people in 1915, including 126 of the 400 Serbian doctors. Even so, the overall decline of mortality was fairly dramatic in Serbia, dropping from 35.6 per thousand in 1876–80 to 24.5 per thousand in 1906–10.

TABLE 12. *The population of European countries, 1881–1911 (m.)*

	1881	1911	Average annual rate of growth
France	37.406	39.192	0.1
England and Wales	25.974	36.070	1.1
Scotland	3.736	4.761	0.8
Ireland	5.175	4.390	–0.6
Germany	45.234[a]	64.926[b]	1.2
Belgium	5.520[a]	7.424[b]	1.0
Netherlands	4.013[c]	5.858[d]	1.3
Denmark	1.969[a]	2.757	1.1
Norway	1.819[e]	2.392[b]	0.8
Sweden	4.169[f]	5.522[b]	0.7
Spain	16.622[g]	19.927	0.6
Portugal	4.551[h]	5.958	0.8
Italy	28.460	34.671	0.7
Switzerland	2.846[a]	3.753[b]	0.9
Austria	22.144[a]	28.572[b]	0.9
Hungary	15.739[a]	20.886[b]	0.9
Romania	4.600	7.000	1.4
Bulgaria	2.800	4.338[b]	1.6
Greece	1.679[c]	2.632[i]	1.6
Serbia	1.700[a]	2.912[b]	1.8
Russia	97.700[a]	160.700[b]	1.6

[a] 1880. [b] 1910. [c] 1879. [d] 1909. [e] 1875. [f] 1870. [g] 1877. [h] 1878.
[i] 1907.

Source: B. R. Mitchell, *European Historical Statistics, 1750–1970* (1975).

In eastern and southern Europe, birth-rates remained high, and in Romania and Serbia even increased in the last decades of the century. This went against the general trend in most of Europe, where the birth-rate began to fall. In France it dropped below 20 per thousand, and Scandinavia, the Low Countries, Switzerland, and the British Isles followed suit. In Germany, which started from a very high birth-rate in 1876–80, the downturn came later and had made less impression by 1906–10. The birth-rate fell sooner in towns than in the countryside and sooner among the upper and middle classes than among the lower classes. In 1907 there were 188 legitimate births for every thousand military, bureaucratic, and professional families in Germany, but 308 for every thousand agricultural families, and 315 for every thousand families of miners. As a result families grew smaller. At the turn of the century, the average Prussian family had five children, whereas in England the average was four and in France it was less than three. Because the death-rate was falling at the same time the proportion of the elderly in the overall population increased. This was particularly noticeable in France where between 1872 and 1910 the proportion of the population over sixty rose from 11.6 to 12.8 per cent while the proportion of the population under fifteen fell from 27.1 per cent to 22.5 per cent. In Germany, which retained a high birth-rate, however, only 8.5 per cent of the population was over sixty in 1910, while 34.1 per cent was under fifteen. This had very clear military consequences.

Though marriage continued to be later in western than in eastern Europe, the postponement of marriage was no longer the major force behind the falling birth-rate. Birth-control was being practised within marriage. In part this was a response to declining infant mortality, for there was less need to insure against the death of children by having a large family. In turn smaller families, in which the children were better spaced, ran less risk of infant mortality. But the underlying reason for the declining birth-rate was economic. This was not simply a reaction to the depression of 1873–95, because the birth-rate continued to fall as prosperity returned after 1895. Birth-control was rather a response to increasing prosperity; it allowed families to maintain or even improve their standard of living. The Scandinavians, Swiss, and French were particularly quick to see this. In addition, birth-control facilitated social mobility. For whereas in the early industrial revolution the demand for labour made children an investment, now factory acts and the importance of education made them an expense. It was better to travel light. So 'Malthusianism' percolated down the social scale, and after 1900 influenced even the working classes of England, France, and Germany. This irritated socialist militants who argued that only an ever larger proletarian army could solve problems of poverty and oppression.

Economic diversification was a precondition of social mobility. The birth-rate therefore remained higher in backward southern and eastern Europe than in the more advanced north and west. By 1910 the agricultural base had fallen below ten per cent of the active population in Great Britain and had been shrinking rapidly since 1880 in Germany and Belgium. But in France it was still 41 per cent in 1910. In Austria-Hungary, Italy, and Ireland it was static, while in a Balkan country like Bulgaria over four-fifths of the active population were still employed on the land. In Germany and Belgium, followed by the late developer Sweden, the active population was moving decisively from agriculture to industry. However the German economist Werner Sombart noted that for every hundred jobs in basic industry, another hundred would be created in trade, services, and administration. It was the size of this tertiary sector that was particularly striking, not only in Germany but also in the Netherlands and Belgium, Great Britain and Ireland, the Scandinavian countries, and France.

To move up the social scale required moving to a town, and to a large town at that. In France urbanization slowed down in the period 1880–1910, although the urban population was still growing at 725,000 every five years as against 780,000 in 1840–80. The proportion of the population living in cities of over 100,000 inhabitants grew between 1871 and 1911 from 32.6 per cent to 43.8 per cent in England, and in Germany from 4.8 per cent to 21.3 per cent,

TABLE 13. *Structure of the active population in Europe, 1910 (%)*

	Agriculture, forestry, fishing	Manufacturing, mining, building	Trade, banking, transport	Services, armed forces	Activity not adequately described
Great Britain[a]	8.8	51.1	14.2	21.4	4.6
Belgium	23.2	45.5	14.0	16.3	—
Netherlands[b]	28.4	32.0	19.6	19.0	1.0
Germany[c]	36.8	40.9	10.5	11.1	0.6
France[a]	41.0	33.1	13.2	12.8	—
Italy[a]	55.4	26.9	8.9	8.5	0.5
Spain	56.3	13.8	3.9	10.5	15.5
Portugal	65.0	24.9	6.5	3.6	—
Norway	39.5	26.0	17.0	16.4	1.1
Denmark[a]	41.7	24.2	14.6	16.1	3.4
Sweden	46.2	25.7	10.6	13.2	4.4
Switzerland	26.8	46.7	14.6	11.4	0.5
Austria	56.9	24.2	8.9	8.3	1.7
Hungary	64.0	17.5	5.7	9.2	3.3
Ireland[a]	42.9	23.2	8.3	16.3	9.5
Bulgaria	81.9	8.0	4.4	5.0	0.7

[a] 1911. [b] 1909. [c] 1907.

although in the Rhine province over half the population lived in such cities. The driving force behind urbanization was still industry and the railways, especially in countries like Sweden where large inland industrial towns sprang up only at the end of the century. In Germany, the most rapidly growing town was the Westphalian mining town of Gelsenkirchen, while the steel town of Ekaterinoslav in the Ukraine multiplied twelvefold between 1863 and 1914, but single-industry towns could go as fast as they came. Sustained expansion was experienced in towns to which new industries were being added or which provided services for a surrounding region. Rotterdam or Kiel with their shipbuilding industries came into the first category, Amsterdam with its financial and commercial services into the second. Berlin and Manchester came into both.

Few migrants to the cities, especially at the end of the century, found the streets paved with gold. Geographical mobility did not necessarily entail social mobility. This was clear in Gelsenkirchen where in 1907 60 per cent of the work-force were miners and half of those were immigrants from rural north-east Germany. In Vienna in the 1890s native-born Viennese provided 30.2 per cent of the work-force, but 35.7 per cent of salaried employees and only 23.6 per cent of unskilled labourers. In Paris an Auvergnat colony was well established by the Second Empire in the coal- and wine-trade and branched out into the hotel and restaurant business. But the Bretons who flowed into Paris during the agricultural crisis of the end of the century remained 'peasants of Paris', vegetating at the bottom of the pile as railway workers and labourers in the suburbs.

The problem was that even in the cities the class system was becoming more stratified, and in general, the larger the city, the greater the degree of stratification. The bourgeoisie became less open to penetration from the lower middle classes, among whom mobility was now basically sideways, from the old artisan and shopkeeper sector to the new white-collar sector. The separation of classes was underlined by the formation of middle-class suburbs, linked to the town centre by trams, omnibuses, or railways. The working classes were left isolated both geographically and socially. In the Ruhr town of Bochum only 18 per cent of manual workers moved into non-manual posts between 1880 and 1901, while only 3 per cent of white-collar workers or lesser officials sank into the manual trades.

In western European countries the scale of industrialization made it possible for the growing population to be absorbed even if it were only in hard manual labour. Because of this, whereas migrants had been forced to go abroad in the middle years of the century they were now able to find employment at home. The flow of emigrants from Ireland continued at a high rate, especially during the boom in the United States in 1887–92, and as the British economy stagnated after 1900, Scots and Welsh also migrated overseas. In Scandinavia and Germany on the other hand, the expansion of industry resulted in a radical decline of emigration after 1880. The development of the Ruhr sucked in a labour force from the eastern provinces of Prussia which had a large Polish contingent, and by 1913 over 400,000 Poles were working in the Ruhr. This in turn created a vacuum in the east, and Polish labour had to be imported from Austrian and Russian Poland, to work on the Junker estates or in the mines of Upper Silesia. Despite the concern of the German government and German nationalists, Germany became a net importer of labour after 1894.

Labour flowed from backward regions to the industrial areas of Europe. Italians from Piedmont and Venetia worked on building projects in Switzerland or the south of France, where local hostility to strike-breakers culminated in a lynching of twenty Italians at Aigues-Mortes in August 1893. After 1908 the French steel cartel began to import Italian labour into the metallurgical plants of Lorraine, and 13,000 Italians were employed there by 1913. But in southern Italy, Spain, Hungary, and Romania, which were isolated from centres of industry and where large landed estates predominated, the surplus population had to look further afield. In the period 1876–90 Italians migrated to Argentina and Brazil but after 1898 they turned to the United States and were followed by a mass of emigrants from eastern Europe. Employment prospects increased as the United States' economy boomed after 1898 and fares cheapened as the American shipping companies began a price war with the shipping companies of Liverpool, Hamburg, and Bremen in the period 1903–8.

TABLE 14. *Emigration from Europe, 1876–1910 (average annual emigration to non-European countries per 100,000 population)*

	1876–80	1881–5	1886–90	1891–5	1896–1900	1901–5	1906–10
Europe	94	196	213	185	147	271	322
Ireland	650	1422	1322	988	759	743	662
Great Britain	102	174	162	119	88	127	172
Denmark	157	380	401	338	117	292	275
Norway	432	1105	819	597	312	903	746
Sweden	301	705	759	587	249	496	347
Germany	108	379	207	163	47	50	44
Belgium			86	50	23	57	69
Netherlands	32	136	111	76	25	45	58
France	8	14	49	14	13	12	12
Spain		280	437	434	446	391	758
Portugal	258	356	423	609	417	464	694
Italy	396	542	754	842	974	1706	1938
Austria	48	90	114	182	182	355	469
Hungary		92	156	134	205	437	616
Russia	6	13	42	47	32	63	67

Emigrants from eastern Europe were very often persecuted minorities who were seeking a new home altogether. Migrants from Austria were mostly Poles and Jews from Galicia. Migrants from Hungary were not Magyars but Slovaks, followed by Serbs, Croats, and Romanians. Emigrants from Russia were Poles, Jews, Lithuanians, and Finns from the borderlands. In the generation before the First World War about 3.5 million Poles emigrated to the United States from Russia, Austria, and Germany. Between 1901 and 1905 11.2 per cent of immigrants into the United States were Jews and between 1899 and 1913 Jews accounted for 41 per cent of emigrants from Russia into the USA. The Jewish community in Britain—65,000 in 1881—increased fourfold over the next thirty years. On the other hand Russian peasants proper, in search of land and liberty, turned not westwards but eastwards. In the period 1901–10 there were 1,481,000 emigrants from Russia to the United States, Canada, England, Argentina, Brazil, South Africa, and Australia. But there were 2,257,000 migrants into Asiatic Russia, beyond the Urals, of whom 1,345,000 went to Siberia. And that does not count the 98,000 prisoners or exiles who travelled to Siberia against their own will.

The Great Depression?

The period 1873–95 has been called the Great Depression. Prices, especially the price of agricultural products, fell as supply overtook demand. New sheep farms were developed in Australia and Argentina and wheatlands were opened up in North America which surpassed those of the black-earth and Volga regions of Russia. Farm machinery was introduced. Above all, as railways were built far inland and shipping was improved by steel hulls, more efficient engines and the opening of the Suez Canal in 1869, so transport costs were reduced. The 'freight factor' in the total delivered cost of Black Sea wheat to Liverpool fell from 17.9 per cent in 1864 to 8.8 per cent in 1886. It was not until American wheat production levelled off in the 1890s, boll weevil struck the cotton plantations after 1892, and drought wasted Australia in 1895–1903 that agricultural prices began to rise again.

The depression was characterized not only by falling prices but also by slumps in the business cycle. However the slumps did not take place simultaneously in all countries. The 1870s were a depressed decade for the United States and Germany, but Great Britain did not reach the bottom of the cycle till 1879 while in France a government-sponsored railway-building programme of 1878 staved off the depression until 1882. In the 1880s the United States and Germany recovered as iron and steel production refloated their economies, but France and Britain failed to increase investment and sank into depression. After 1892 the economy of the United States slumped, but the German economy remained buoyant and pulled most of the European economies with it in the boom of 1895–1900.

It has been suggested in recent years that the Great Depression is something of a myth and that structural developments behind the cycles were more important. Moreover, while the picture looked fairly gloomy from the British point of view, it was much less so for western European countries in general. This was because the industrial lead established by Great Britain in the middle years of the century was being eroded by other countries such as Germany which were industrializing rapidly and narrowing the gap. They substituted their own manufactured goods for manufactured goods that they had hitherto imported from Britain, went on to challenge British exports in European and world markets and eventually began to push into the British market itself. Between 1880 and 1913 the British share of world exports of manufactured goods fell from 41.4 per cent to 30.2 per cent while that of Germany rose from 19.3 per cent to 26.6 per cent.

Within manufacturing industry, too, some sectors were expanding. Trade in textiles might be contracting and that in chemicals and metals, particularly steel, might be stable, but exports of machinery and transportation equipment were growing fast. The expansion or stagnation of a country's economy depended very much on the sectors in which it participated. The economies of Spain, Italy, France, and even Great Britain, which were heavily committed to the textile trade, stagnated. However, industrialization on a wide scale created an enormous demand for coal and Britain was able to meet that need, especially in anthracite, to an extent that other coal-producing countries like Belgium or France were not. In 1866–70 coal accounted for under 3 per cent of the value of British exports, but by 1896–1900 it had risen to over 9 per cent. As an exporter of textiles, coal, and iron plate Britain seemed at the turn of the century to be stuck in the rut of the first industrial revolution. The experience of Germany was quite different, perhaps because she was a late-comer. Germany managed the switch from iron to steel in the 1870s and 1880s and undertook pioneering work in engineering, chemicals, and electrical equipment. By 1913 she was the world's largest exporter of machinery and exported 40 per cent of world chemicals and 38 per cent of world steel. The industrial heartland of Europe had moved from the north-west to the centre.

At the end of the century there was a polarization between the industrial core and backward southern and eastern Europe, which was relegated to the function of providing food and raw materials for the industrial areas. Some countries were able to use the export of primary produce to pay for machinery and move towards an industrial base. In 1880 Sweden was an exporter of timber and iron ore. But she developed wood-processing and smelting with the benefit of hydro-electric power and became a major exporter of paper, cellulose, and steel. Hungary remained heavily agricultural but built up a flour-milling industry at Budapest that was second only to that of Minneapolis. On the other hand the Balkan countries were trapped in backwardness. Romania was plundered for her oil, Greece exported raisins, tobacco, wine, and olive oil, and Serbia pigs, and prunes, jam, and plum-based spirits.

TABLE 15. *Exports by sector of European countries, 1913 (%)*

	Food and drink	Raws, semi-manufactured goods	Manufactured goods
Germany	10.4	26.3	63.3
France	12.2	27.0	60.8
United Kingdom	6.1	33.9	60.0
Belgium	10.0	49.1	38.7
Austria-Hungary	27.2	40.4	38.7
Italy	30.0	38.0	32.0
Spain	43.8	30.9	23.3
Portugal	68.0	20.4	11.6
Sweden	12.8	63.1	24.1
Norway	36.6	50.5	12.9
Denmark	83.7	11.0	5.3
Russia	56.1	38.8	5.1
Bulgaria	71.5	18.1	10.4
Romania	71.4	27.7	0.9
Serbia	74.1	24.0	1.9
Greece	61.3	38.0	0.7

Source: A. S. Milward and S. B. Saul, *The Development of the Economies of Continental Europe* (1977).

As cheap foodstuffs flooded European markets, pressing down farm prices, and as industrializing countries struggled to find outlets for their manufactured goods, so there was a shift away from free trade towards protective tariffs in order to reserve home markets for home production and maintain levels of price, profit, and employment. Only three countries adhered consistently to free trade principles, namely Denmark, the Netherlands, and Great Britain. Because London wished to remain the leading financial and commercial centre of the world, it was in its interest to lend abroad and import heavily in order to spread sterling as far as possible. A protectionist lobby did spring up in the 1870s, but it was provincial, organized by the Birmingham iron and Bradford woollen industries, and carried no weight with the cotton barons or City, while the agricultural counties were divided on the matter. It had no influence either with the Liberal party, which won the elections of 1880, or with the Conservative party, which took power in 1886 and was reinforced by Liberals who represented commercial and financial wealth, and disagreed with Gladstone's Irish policy. Britain was prepared almost to liquidate its agricultural base, to import food cheaply, to accept competition from American or German manufacturers, and to offset the trade deficit by drawing interest on foreign capital investments.

Everywhere else in Europe, on the other hand, the protectionist shutters went up. The Italian parliament agreed in 1887 to tariffs on textiles, iron and steel, wheat, and sugar, even though this resulted in a tariff war with France and was disastrous for the Italian engineering industry, which required the import of cheap iron and steel. Castilian wheat-growers and Catalan manufacturers obtained a Spanish protective tariff in 1891. An alliance was formed in France in 1888 between agricultural and industrial interests to campaign for protective tariffs. In the elections of 1889 they secured the return of three or four hundred deputies favourable to their cause and their spokesman, Jules Méline, back in office, gave them a protective tariff in 1892.

Germany led the field by imposing tariffs in 1879 and raised agricultural duties in 1885 and 1888. Protective tariffs were imposed by Austria in 1887, Sweden in 1888, the United States in 1890, and Russia in 1891, in order to ensure that railway-building benefited its own iron and steel industry. The growing danger was that native industries would become asphyxiated for want of outlets for the products. Austria, whose industrial base was in Bohemia, solved the problem by unloading manufactures on to the Hungarian part of the Monarchy and bullying surrounding states like Serbia and Romania into accepting its exports. The position of Germany was more difficult. Bismarck's successor as Chancellor, Caprivi, feared that Germany's protectionist policy would check her industrial expansion, perpetuate the dominance of the Junkers and constrain her foreign policy. He therefore inaugurated a policy of seeking trade treaties with Germany's central European allies, from Italy and Austria-Hungary to Romania and Russia. But the combined power of heavy industry and agriculture, which organized in 1893 under the banner of the Agrarian League, mobilized against this repeal of Germany's corn laws. The Reichstag endorsed the treaty with Russia in 1894, but Caprivi reckoned without the influence of the Junkers in the Court, army, administration, and provincial estates and was obliged to resign his post. Despite the organization of the chemical, electrical, engineering, and armaments industries in defence of the treaties, because they could not survive without export markets, the protectionists secured a return to protection under the tariffs of 1902. In Great Britain, a new campaign for protection was launched in 1903 by Joseph Chamberlain, the Unionist politician, now Colonial Secretary, as the only way to defend national industries, finance social reform, and maintain the integrity of the Empire. But he was unable to convert the Conservative party to his cause. Financial and commercial interests still required free trade, and the principle of cheap bread for the working man could not be violated without losing support to Liberals or Labour.

The process of industrialization in Europe created a tremendous demand for food and raw materials from less developed countries. The first consignments of frozen meat arrived in Europe from Argentina in 1877 and from Australia in 1880. By 1914 half the beef and mutton consumed in Great Britain was imported. Argentina and Australia also provided wool, Brazil supplied coffee, and Chile sent nitrates for the chemical industry. Tea-growing spread from China to India and Ceylon. Ceylon and Malaya cultivated rubber for the tyre market which boomed after 1905, while Malaya also mined tin for oil-drums and canning. Java exported sugar to the Netherlands. Cocoa was cultivated on the Gold Coast, iron ore was mined in Algeria, and copper came from the Congo. Oil was drilled in Austrian Galicia, in Romania after 1895, in the Baku region of Russia, and after the turn of the century in Persia.

Commerce was followed by capital. To articulate trade with distant parts of the world railways, mines, oil-wells, docks, tramways, telegraphs, gas, and electrical installations had to be built, shipping lines created, and banks established. It is also clear that the rate of return on overseas financial assets was higher than in most European countries in the period 1870–1913. The interest rate on Latin America railway shares floated in London reached 8.4 per cent, and the rate on Latin American banking shares rose to 11.3 per cent. Interest in foreign capital markets varied from country to country. Great Britain was able to make up the deficit on its commodity trade (which rose from an average of £62.2m. per year in 1871–5 to £174.5m. in 1901–5) by the return on capital investments overseas. In 1914 Britain invested 2.8 per cent of its national wealth abroad, and those earnings accounted for 10 per cent of its national income. France invested 15 per cent of its national wealth abroad for 6 per cent of its national income in 1914, Germany 7 per cent of its wealth for 3 per cent of its national income.

It has been argued that there was a close connexion between overseas capital investment and imperialism in that western European countries had to assert political and administrative control over far-flung territories in order to protect their investors. The evidence is unconvincing. French and German governments were responsive to the demands of investors, and were prepared, for example, to guarantee a certain rate of interest on foreign railway shares, for without those guarantees timid investors would not risk their capital. But the British government had faith that the world of banking, investment, and speculation would follow its own nose in financial affairs, and stepped in only if, as in Egypt or Persia, its strategic interests were at risk. Moreover, the correlation between areas of financial investment and formal colonies was not very close. It was much more attractive that existing governments should provide the necessary security than that European governments should have to take over administration, with all the costs and concerns that entailed. By 1914 Britain sent 37 per cent of its capital exports to the Dominions and 9 per cent to India, but 18 per cent of its capital exports went to Latin America and 21 per cent to the USA. The case of France was rather different. In 1914 only 9 per cent of its capital exports went to French colonies, whereas 16 per cent went to the Americas, 8 per cent each to Scandinavia and central Europe, 11 per cent to the Near East, and 28 per cent to the Balkans, Romania, and above all Russia. The most attractive loans on the French money-market after 1888 were those directed to the Russian government, railways, or other utilities, and in the boom periods 1895–1901 and 1906–14 to fund the mines, steelworks, textile mills, and banks of Russia's late industrial revolution. In the 1880s Germany, which had hitherto imported capital to fund her industrialization, began to export capital, but her meagre colonies in south-west Africa and among Pacific islands scarcely benefited. The Deutsche Bank, acting as a siphon for German export capital, was far more interested in the oil fields of Galicia and Romania, in the Berlin to Baghdad railway that the Sultan authorized in 1901, and in bailing out the North Pacific Railway in conjunction with the American millionaire J. P. Morgan when it fell on hard times in 1893.

The cycle was complete when foreign investments and the import of primary produce created markets abroad that would take the surplus manufactured goods of the industrialized countries of Europe. The advocates of commercial imperialism were those representatives of light, export-oriented industries such as textiles, chemicals, and electrical goods whose interests had been damaged by protective tariffs. In France they found a lobby in the Colonial Union, which was set up in 1893 in answer to the Méline tariff and had strong support in Lyons, Marseilles, and Bordeaux. In Germany the Trade Treaty Association was formed in 1900 in an attempt to win heavy industry away from the agrarians who were demanding a return to protection. In addition German banks, which were closely involved in industry, succeeded in tying to many of their loans concessions for electrical engineering companies to build tramways and power stations. Up until 1896–7 the value of European exports to the rest of the world grew at a rate of under 2 per cent a year. Then the growth rate shot up to over 5 per cent, especially in the years

1903–7 and 1909–13. Between 1900 and 1910, Great Britain's share in the European export market fell from 26.0 to 23.7 per cent and that of France fell from 16.3 to 13.4 per cent. That of Sweden rose from 1.4 to 1.8 per cent, that of Russia rose from 6.7 to 8.9 per cent, and that of Germany rose from 18.2 to 19.6 per cent. If the Great Depression had struck in the 1880s its effects were clearly gone by 1914, and the shift in the balance of power was plain in economic terms at least.

Agricultural crisis

At the end of the nineteenth century European agriculture went through a very difficult phase. Over-production and cheap transportation drove down farm prices, especially those of cereals. Between 1871–80 and 1891–1900 the price of wheat fell in France from 133.0 to 96.6 grams of silver per hundred kilograms and in England from 126.5 to 69.9. In the Netherlands the price of rye fell from 91.1 to 63.3 grams of silver. Falling prices reduced land-rents and land-values, and the labour-force abandoned many rural areas to migrate to the towns or overseas.

The reaction of the agricultural lobby in many countries, as we have seen, was to press for tariff barriers against cheap foodstuffs. But in north-west Europe the challenge was met by more intelligent means that either (as in France) accompanied protection or (as in Great Britain, the Netherlands, and Denmark) served as an alternative to it. These included the mechanization of agricultural methods, a shift away from cereal farming to new specializations, and the organization of farm co-operatives.

In areas where there was significant rural depopulation, such as Great Britain, France, and Germany, and the wages of agricultural labour rose as a result, there was a strong incentive to replace costly human labour by machines. The horse-drawn reaper-binder, which made its appearance in the late 1870s, could reduce the cost of harvesting by two-thirds or three-quarters. Another innovation was the threshing machine, which was to be found on 374,000 holdings in Germany in 1882 and 1,436,000 holdings in 1907, although only a third of those machines were driven by steam and the rest were horse-powered. But where farms were small and rural labour was plentiful, there was little incentive to mechanize. At the turn of the century there was one thresher to every 111 hectares in Germany, but one to 945 hectares in Hungary and one to 1,194 hectares in Romania. In Bulgaria in 1900 only 10 per cent of ploughs used were made of iron; the rest were made of wood.

Because cereal prices slumped more sharply than other farm prices, there was also an incentive to switch from arable farming to other products. Moreover, improved communications and a widening market made specialization in certain cash crops a viable proposition. Some backward countries like Serbia had always preferred livestock-raising to arable farming, and in 1900 Serbia had the greatest number of pigs per head of population in the world. The tendency in east European countries such as Serbia, Bulgaria, and Romania at the end of the century was in fact to move into the production of wheat, largely because Austria-Hungary banned cattle imports in 1882 in order to encourage domestic cattle-breeding. In Germany the ratio of arable to pasture increased between 1870 and 1900, for despite the influx of cheap grain from Russia the phenomenal growth of the population and economy made it necessary to grow more grain, not less. Spain also resorted to intensive wheat-farming on newly enclosed lands after 1870. But the pattern in Great Britain, France, the Low Countries, and Scandinavia was different. Diminishing returns for cereals encouraged farmers to move over to livestock, and above all to dairy farming. Germany stopped importing live pigs from Denmark in 1887, but Denmark found new markets for its bacon, eggs, butter, and cheese in urban Britain, where dairy farmers fell back on the production of liquid milk.

Cattle-farming required a more intensive cultivation of fodder crops such as maize, potatoes, turnips, and mangels. Sugar-beet farming took off in Bohemia, Germany, northern France, eastern England, and even in Spain after the loss of its sugar-plantations in Cuba and the Philippines in 1898. In the Mediterranean improvements in irrigation and marketing made possible the specialist farming of fruit, such as oranges in Valencia and peaches, apricots, and cherries in Provence. More important was the wine boom in Spain and Italy in the 1880s which took advantage of the phylloxera epidemic in France. Between 1877 and 1886 Spain had 60 per cent of the French market, Italy 12 per cent. Then France replanted its vineyards, erected tariffs against Italy in 1887 and Spain in 1892, and provoked catastrophe among the wine-growers of those countries. In Catalonia, where the length of tenancies was tied to the life of the vine, the problem was compounded by the appearance of phylloxera after 1890, which provoked a wave of rural unrest, strikes, and clashes with the Civil Guard and military in 1893. After 1900 the crisis rebounded on France where huge domestic wine crops were topped up by Algerian imports, competition from beet alcohol, and the fraudulent sugaring of poor wines to produce a massive glut. Wine prices collapsed and in Languedoc, which had gone over to wine monoculture, there was a massive peasant revolt in the summer of 1907.

As farm prices declined the large estates which could cut costs tended to fare better than the small farmers who were enslaved to rural creditors, suppliers, and wholesalers. The only way to improve their competitiveness was through the co-operative movement, which could reduce costs and by-pass middlemen. The so-called Raffeisen system of rural savings banks spread through Germany, Austria, Belgium, and northern France after 1880 and made it possible for farmers to raise cheap capital for improvements. Consumer co-operatives were set up to purchase tools, machines, and fertilizer at discount prices. At the same time pooled expertise could insure against fraud, for as the use of chemical fertilizers increased so did the number of unscrupulous tradesmen who were happy to sell worthless products to an ignorant peasantry. The processing and marketing aspect of the co-operative movement was most fully developed in Denmark. The first dairy co-operative for making butter and cheese was set up there in 1882, and 90 per cent of Danish farms were linked to such co-operatives by 1909. Similar co-operatives were set up for processing bacon and eggs, and co-operative export companies were set up after 1895 to break the ring of British importers.

Declining prices threatened the small producer more than the large producer, but the effects of the agricultural depression must also be analysed as they affected landowners, tenant-farmers, and labourers. In general declining farm prices reduced rents and brought down the price of agricultural land after 1880. Where landowners also owned urban properties, which increased in value as a result of urban development, as in Great Britain and Russia, they were to some extent cushioned from the decline. In Prussia, on the other hand, where landowners tended not to own urban properties, they were forced into farming the land themselves or ever greater dependence on the state. Meanwhile British and French landowners who invested capital overseas also did well, particularly in the boom years after 1905.

As rents declined, so farmers were placed in a better position to negotiate easier terms, more secure tenure, and compensation for improvements made. This was clearly the case in Britain and northern France where large tenant-farmers predominated. But where there was rural congestion, as in Ireland, landowners were better placed to impose harsh terms on their tenants. Irish farmers replied to declining prices and continuing oppression by forming the Irish Land League in 1879 in order to campaign against rackrenting and evictions by the use of the boycott, and aiming in the long run to make tenants owners of their farms. After 1880 it had a mouthpiece at Westminster in the Irish Home Rule party and, not least to preserve the Union, Gladstone in 1881 conceded a Land Act which improved the position of the Irish tenant-farmer and broke the Land League.

In southern Europe tenant-farmers were a good deal worse off. Spanish landlords were notorious absentees and entrusted their estates to managers who sublet them at extortionate rents. Except perhaps in Galicia, leases were short and insecure, and no compensation was made for improvements. The sub-tenants of Estramadura were shunted from plot to plot to grow crops while the owner concentrated on cattle-breeding. Throughout southern Spain, in fact, where latifundia predominated, there was little land available for leasing, even though vast tracts lay uncultivated, and the majority of peasants were dwarf proprietors or landless labourers, who worked in gangs under armed foremen on horseback. Industrialization was inadequate to draw off the surplus population and the regions from which peasants emigrated overseas were not the south but Galicia and the Levante. The labourers stayed to fight for higher wages and launched strikes in Andalusia between 1902 and 1906. But they were ill-organized, and defeated by the import of blackleg labour from Portugal and drought which struck in 1905. In the Po valley of Italy, the proportion of day-labourers was increased by schemes to drain the marshlands of the estuary after 1872. But after the initial reclamation work there was little employment and frustrated labourers went on strike in 1897, 1902, 1907, and 1913. They were better organized than their Spanish counterparts and more successful.

TABLE 16. *Land distribution in Eastern Europe, 1895–1907 (%)*

Size of holding (hectares)	East Prussia 1907		Hungary 1895		Romania 1897		Bulgaria 1897	
	farms	area	farms	area	farms	area	farms	area
0–5	67.1	6.5	53.6	5.8	77.2	25.9 ⎤	87.3	49.0
5–10	20.1[a]	17.6[a] ⎤			18.2	14.7 ⎦		
10–100	11.3[b]	38.8[b] ⎦	45.4	46.5	4.0	11.1	12.6	44.5
100–1000	1.5	37.1	0.8	15.4	0.6	48.3	0.1	6.5
over 1000			0.2	32.3				

[a] 5–20 hectares.   [b] 20–100 hectares.

Sources: I. F. D. Morrow, *The Peace Settlement in the German–Polish Borderlands* (1936); I. T. Berend and G. Ranki, *Economic developments in East-Central Europe* (1974).

In eastern Europe, where large estates were directly cultivated, the situation of the rural population was particularly difficult. Some qualifications should nevertheless be made. In Bulgaria, whose Turkish landlords had been expelled after the war of 1877–8, Turkish estates were taken over by the village communities and parcelled out, so that small peasant proprietorship became the rule. Large areas of southern and western Germany were dominated by small farms, and even in Prussia the large Junker estate was something of a myth. While there were some wealthy nobles in Silesia, nobles in the core Prussian provinces of Brandenburg and Pomerania were often poor, and estates turned over rapidly because few were entailed. In Hungary the disease of the latifundia was much more explicit. At the turn of the century 0.2 per cent of the holdings were over 1,000 hectares in size, but this accounted for 32.3 per cent of the land area. A third of Hungary was entailed estate. The 324 largest landed proprietors occupied 19.3 per cent of the land, averaging 16,600 hectares, while Prince Esterhazy owned 230,800 hectares. At the other end of the scale over half the holdings were less than 5 hectares, but these accounted for only 5.8 per cent of the land area. Nearly 40 per cent of the agricultural population were labourers, who were unemployed for two-thirds of the year and whose misery drove them to launch strikes in 1891 and 1897. The strikes were broken up by the import of Slovak and Transylvanian labour, and a new 'slave law' was imposed on Hungarian agricultural labourers in 1898.

In Romania and Russia the serfs, though emancipated in the 1860s, had been left with derisory plots and, in Russia, with ongoing redemption payments in respect of dues and services abolished. In some areas, like the Baltic, White Russia, the Ukraine, and Black Sea areas, direct farming was the rule and peasants were landless or near-landless. Elsewhere, in the central black-earth and Volga regions of Russia, and in Romania, landlords were prepared to lease their land for rent paid in money, kind, share-cropping or labour-services. The subletting of estates by managers, usually of Jewish extraction in Romania, and the attempt by landlords to recoup on losses made as cereal prices fell, both had the effect of screwing rents up. In Romania, popular banks spread after 1900 to assist village co-operatives to lease land collectively, bypassing the manager, but these were resisted by managers and large landowners alike. In Russia, a Peasant Land Bank founded in 1883 assisted communes or co-operatives of richer peasants to purchase land from impoverished nobles, and between 1877 and 1905 peasants increased their holdings of non-allotment land from 7.2 million to 26.2 million hectares, to add to 137.2 million hectares of allotments. But this only had the effect of forcing land prices up, from 55 roubles per hectare in 1896 to 125 roubles in 1904. The grievances of the peasants gave rise to a wave of insurrections in the Ukraine, Volga, and central black-earth regions of Russia in 1902–3 and 1905–7, and a massive revolt of the Romanian peasantry in 1907.

Squeezed between peasant revolt and reliance on the nobility to consolidate its position, the Russian autocracy fought its way towards a solution of the land question. Redemption payments were halved in 1906 and finally abolished in 1907. An attempt was made to dissolve the commune, which had guaranteed the payment of redemption dues and yet acted as an organ of peasant insurrection, and to build a peasantry of individual proprietors, on the French model, which would stabilize rural society. Under legislation of 1906 and 1910 about 4.3 million of the 12 million households in European Russia separated out from the commune system and its periodic redistribution of strips, as hereditary tenures, although down to 1914 only about 1.3 million households managed to consolidate a farm from the scattered strips that they owned. There was no question of a massive expropriation of noble estates, even with compensation, but the Peasant Land Bank was extremely active in the period 1906–16, and about 11 million hectares of land passed to the peasantry from the nobility, about a fifth of the nobles' landholdings. Small and landless peasants made half the purchases and acquired a quarter of the land transferred. It was an improvement, but the spectre of rural revolution in Russia had in no sense been exorcized.

New Technology

If the industrial revolution of the early years of the nineteenth century was that of cotton, followed by that of coal and iron in the middle years of the century, then the new industries in the period after 1880 were steel, engineering, and chemicals, and the new sources of power were petroleum and electricity. Shipbuilding (from the 1880s), armaments, railways, and machine-building stepped up the demand for steel. Vickers, the British steel-making firm, moved into the armaments business in 1888 and into shipbuilding in 1897. The manufacture of steel was transformed by the Thomas–Gilchrist process of 1879 which, by adding limestone to the blast furnace to draw off the phosphorus impurities in a slag, made possible the use of the phosphoric iron ores of Lorraine and the Ruhr as well as the low-phosphoric ores of Spain and Sweden. Steel production in Great Britain, France, Germany, and Belgium rose from 125,000 tons in 1861 to 32 million tons in 1913. However, Great Britain was slow to adopt the Thomas–Gilchrist process and to establish large, mechanized steel plants. She was overtaken in steel production by the United States in 1889 and by Germany in 1893.

The British engineering industry made its mark with steam-engines and locomotives and still built 39 per cent of world shipping in 1914. Engineering was revolutionized by the production of small-arms, bicycles, typewriters, sewing-machines and automobiles, and the manufacture of machine-tools such as lathes, milling and grinding machines, which turned metal into machinery. But these developments, together with the perfection of steel alloys with manganese, chromium, or tungsten, which allowed the perfection of hard, steel-cutting tools, took place in America and on the Continent rather than in Great Britain. Great Britain provided nearly 70 per cent of French machine-tool imports in 1865 but only 7 per cent in 1909, having been overtaken by Germany in 1873, Belgium in 1883, and the United States in 1897.

Great Britain lagged behind also in the chemical industry. The growth of the textile, soap, and paper industries increased demand for alkalis, but Great Britain stuck to the Leblanc method of making soda that was superseded in the 1870s by the Solvay process, which used the ammonia produced in gasworks, and was adopted by Germany and France. Germany had a virtual monopoly of the production of artificial dyestuffs, in which the record of the Badische Anilin und Soda Fabrik at Ludwigshafen was outstanding. Only Swiss producers at Basle could compete. German capital owned almost all the French dyestuffs industry in 1914, when Great Britain imported 80 per cent of its dyestuffs, mainly from Germany. The Aktien Gesellschaft für Anilin Fabrikation (AGFA), which had produced photographic film since 1897, turned out a million metres of cinematographic film from a factory in Saxony in 1908. The French did better in the manufacture of synthetic fibres, such as the 'silk of Chardonnay' or rayon that was made at Lyons after 1891. The production of fertilizer, notably of phosphates, the output of which doubled between 1900 and 1910, was more evenly distributed across northern France, Belgium, and Germany.

The age of coal and steam did not come to an end but other sources of energy were developed. An internal combustion engine fired by a combination of gas and air was developed by the German engineer N. A. Otto in 1876. Rudolph Diesel, a German living in Paris, perfected an oil-fired engine in 1897. In 1900 world production of oil was about 150 million barrels, half of it in Russia, but the following year the rich oilfield of Spindletop, Texas, was opened up, and oil-drilling spread to Mexico, South America, Sumatra, and Borneo. Oil became cheap enough to substitute for coal. The Hamburg-Amerika line went over to oil in 1902, followed by the other big shipping lines, and the British Navy started to use oil in 1903. For other forms of transport the breakthrough came with the light, high-speed, petroleum engine developed in 1886 by Gottlieb Daimler, an apprentice gunsmith who then went to work for a gas-engine manufacturer. The rapid progress of the motor car was now possible. The licence to manufacture Daimler engines in France was acquired by Emile Levassor, who won the Paris–Bordeaux–Paris race in 1895, a distance of 732 miles, at an average speed of 15 m.p.h. Races and feats dramatized the advent of the car. Races were run between Paris and Amsterdam in 1898, Paris and Vienna in 1902, Paris and Madrid in 1903, Paris and Peking in 1907–8. The first Grand Prix of the Automobile Club de France was held in 1906, and won by a Renault at an average speed of 65 m.p.h. Hardy motorists travelled from New York to San Francisco in 63 days in 1903 and from Adelaide to Darwin in 51 days in 1907–8. The commercial production and sale of motor cars lagged some way behind. The total world production of motor cars in 1900 was 9,000. Nearly half of these came from the USA, which overtook France in 1906 as the leading car producer and moved on from artisanal to mass-production. Henry Ford's cheap Model T in 1908 changed the face of motoring. By 1916 Ford's factories were turning out 735,000 motor cars a year.

A further revolution took place in air transport. Count Ferdinand von Zeppelin launched a rigid airship in 1900, although a fully successful model was not developed until 1908 and did not come into commercial use until 1911. Wilbur Wright made the first petrol-engine powered, fixed-wing flight at Kitty Hawk in North Carolina on 17 December 1903 and demonstrated his plane to the French in 1908. The *Daily Mail* offered a £500 prize for the first plane crossing of the Channel, which was won by Louis Blériot in July 1909. Flying remained the preserve of eccentric sportsmen until the First World War stimulated the development of the aircraft industry, and there were no regular passenger air services in Europe until 1919.

Along with petroleum, the most important new source of energy was electricity. Electricity could be generated from the gases released from blast furnaces and coking ovens, as it was in the Rhine Valley by the Rheinisch-Westfälische Elektrizitäts-A.G., founded in 1900. Steam jets were put to use in the steam turbine to generate electricity by the British engineer Charles

Parsons, who set up a works at Newcastle in 1889 and supplied two massive turbo-generators to Elberfeld in Germany in 1900. France and Italy, which lacked coal resources, generated hydro-electric power from the fast-flowing waters of the Alps.

Demand for electricity came from many sources. The incandescent filament lamp was produced almost simultaneously by the American Thomas Alva Edison and the Englishman Joseph Swan. In Great Britain an ocean-going vessel, the Savoy Theatre, and the House of Commons were all lit by electric lamps in 1881. Electrometallurgy developed after the introduction of the electric furnace for producing steel alloys by the Siemens family in 1878. The production of aluminium from bauxite in 1886 marked the beginning of the electrochemical industry. In factories conveyor-belts, cranes, and other machines and machine-tools could now be powered by electricity. The demonstration of an electric railway at Berlin by Siemens in 1879 opened the way to a transport revolution based on electric traction. By the late 1880s electric tramways, which ran on rails and picked up power from overhead cables, were becoming established in the major capitals of Europe. Trolley-buses, which ran on pneumatic wheels and required no rails, were particularly popular in Germany and Austria after 1901. Electric transport tunnelled underground as well as overground: the first 'tube' was built in London in 1887–90. Horse-drawn buses disappeared from the streets of London in 1911.

Finally, a revolution in communications was made possible by electricity. Submarine cables had been the great triumph of the middle years of the century. In 1876 Alexander Graham Bell patented the telephone in the United States, and the new system caught on rapidly. In 1902 there were 2,315,000 telephone subscribers in the USA. Europe followed suit, although with less enthusiasm. There were 210,000 subscribers in Great Britain in 1900, but only 30,000 in France. European achievements were greater in other areas. The Scottish physicist James Clerk Maxwell discovered in the 1860s that light was electromagnetic and travelled in waves that spread out at right angles to the direction of propagation. His theory, which was empirically demonstrated by the German scientist Heinrich Hertz in 1888, made possible the transmission of radio waves by means of a spark discharged in an electrical system, undertaken by the Italian Guglielmo Marconi in 1896. Marconi sent radio waves across the Channel in 1899 and across the Atlantic in 1901. The first applications of wireless telegraphy were naval. The British navy took it up in 1900, the German government founded Telefunken in 1903 to catch up, and the battle of Tsushima in 1905 was fought between the Japanese fleet with Marconi and the Russian fleet with (less good) Telefunken sets. Civilian radio broadcasting had to wait until after 1920.

Industry: Ownership

New technological developments created a hunger for capital that could be satisfied only by raising funds on the stock markets or entering into a closer alliance with investment banks. But many firms, especially in Great Britain and France, were reluctant to raise outside capital for fear of losing complete management control, and they continued stubbornly to finance themselves from the profits they generated. Almost 80 per cent of British firms were still private in 1914. Some, like Harland and Wolff, adopted limited liability but never issued shares to the public. In northern France the steel firm of Denain-Anzin financed 80 per cent of new investment in 1910–13 from profits. Even in Germany there were industrialists like Werner Siemens who failed to move beyond the manufacture of electrical equipment because he refused to cede any control to outside capitalists. He was therefore overtaken by Emil Rathenau who obtained a patent from Edison to build power stations in Germany and borrowed heavily from the Deutsche Bank to found the Allgemeine Elektricitäts-Gesellschaft (AEG) in 1887. It was not until Werner retired in 1890 and was succeeded by his son Wilhelm that the family firm increased its capital by becoming a joint-stock company and merging with rivals, and moved into power-current projects.

The reluctance of firms to raise outside capital was paralleled by the reluctance of banks and stock markets to invest in industry. Long-term investment in industries that were involved in cut-throat competition, particularly when markets were depressed, was much less attractive than short-term credit in industry or buying government bonds. Yet long-term investment in industry was crucial for the development of new technology and increased competitiveness. Banks that did finance industry evolved strategies to eliminate the anarchy of competition that served only to push down prices and therefore profits. Monopoly was their ideal, cartels and trusts were approximations to it. Cartels or agreements between firms were organized, some to keep up the market price, others to fix production quotas, while syndicates centralized the marketing of several firms. The most radical agreement was a merger of firms in the same industry in a trust, which could then reduce competition by closing down the least efficient businesses.

A fundamental distinction can be made here between British and German financial markets and industry. German banks were ready to finance industry long term and, to safeguard their assets, set up cartels for potash (1881), coke, and pig-iron. The Rhenish-Westphalian Coal Syndicate, founded in 1893, controlled 98 per cent of Germany's coal production by 1904. In that year a cartel, the Steel Works Association, was organized. Plate-glass, cement, paper, and many chemicals were also brought into cartels. Some of the industrial concerns became so large that banks had to form consortia in order to raise enough capital to satisfy them, and the influence of bankers on the board of directors of industrial firms was matched by the influence of industrial magnates with the banks. In Britain, on the other hand, while local banks had provided short-term credit to local industries before 1880, the bank amalgamation movement of the 1880s and 1890s subordinated local bank managers to general managers in London who were keen to reduce the banks' commitment to industry. As late as 1913, moreover, only 37 per cent of prices quoted on the Stock Exchange were of domestic, non-government stock; government bonds and overseas investment held far greater appeal. As a result, there was no leverage for a process of cartelization in Britain.

In other parts of Europe there was the same reluctance on the part of the banks to become involved in industry. In Sweden, the Enskilda Bank of Stockholm which was in trouble in 1879 as a result of over-commitment in the railway industry, drew in its horns and reverted to lending to the Swedish government. However after 1896 it helped to promote Sweden's industrial 'push' by financing the iron-ore, timber, and electrical industries. On the other hand Austrian banks, which had lost heavily in the crash of 1873, and Bohemian banks, which had promoted the local sugar industry that suffered a crisis in 1884, remained altogether more conservative. They tiptoed back to financing industry after 1898, but on the basis of current-account credit and bills of exchange rather than the purchase of share-capital. Where they did invest, as the Credit Anstalt and Böhmische Escomptebank did in the Skoda arms-works in 1898, they insisted that the company became a joint-stock company so that they could spread the capital risk more widely. The banks transformed Austrian industry into one of the most heavily cartelized in Europe. There were forty Austrian cartels in 1897 and over two hundred in 1912. Even then, the Austrian and Bohemian banks played safe: lending money to the government was still a major preoccupation, and in 1900 over half their assets were mortgage loans, mostly on the security of large estates.

In eastern Europe deficiencies in private enterprise and the conservatism of the banks had to be compensated by the intervention of the state. The state with its military priorities had always closely supervised the railways which were vital for the swift transportation of troops. As financial crisis struck in 1873, so the German states were obliged to replace withdrawn private capital by the nationalization of the railways. This precedent was followed by Austria in 1877, Hungary in 1880, Russia in 1881, Italy in 1885, and even Belgium in 1897. In 1901 the Austrian Prime Minister Koerber tried to stimulate industry by direct government investment in rail projects to link Prague and Trieste, and a canal plan to link the Danube and the Oder. The naval expansion of the turn of the century meant government orders for the shipbuilding, steel, and armaments industries, especially in Germany and Great Britain, but it was such orders that almost alone maintained the somewhat artificial heavy industrial sector in Italy.

In a country as backward as Russia, state intervention went much further. There was little alternative to the forced transfer of capital from one sector of the economy to another. The industrialization planned by Sergei Witte, who became Russian Finance Minister in 1892, and which revolved around the construction of the 4000-mile Trans-Siberian railway (1891–1904), was carried out on the backs of the peasantry. Direct taxes accounted for only 17 per cent of government revenue in 1903, but between 1870 and 1910 indirect taxes on paraffin, matches, tobacco, sugar, and vodka (which became a government monopoly in 1895) quadrupled. Such heavy taxation contributed to the famine of 1891, caused peasants to default on taxes and redemption payments, which resulted in the forced sale of their property or forced labour, and depressed rural demand at the expense of Russian industry itself.

It was possible for countries which generated little surplus from agriculture, let alone from trade or financial dealings, to import capital for industrialization from those that did. Italy turned to France for capital, but French capital was interested mainly in building and municipal public works and withdrew after the collapse of the Italian building trade in 1887. It was replaced by German capital, which formed the Banca Commerciale Italiana at Milan in 1894 and the Credito Italiano in 1895, to fund the steel industries at Terni (Umbria) and on Elba and the shipbuilding, engineering, chemical, and electrical industries that carried Italy's industrial spurt of 1896–1908. The Russian experience was somewhat in reverse, because German investments which increased in the 1880s were replaced after a diplomatic row between St Petersburg and Berlin in 1887–8 by French capital. Between 1892 and 1908, about 60 per cent of the capital formation in Russia was foreign investment, compared with a foreign capital contribution of 45 per cent in Hungary between 1873 and 1900, and 35 per cent in Austria in 1900. French and Belgian capital built up the coal and metallurgical industries of Poland and the Ukraine; German capital developed chemical and electrical industries in the Baltic; and British capital exploited the oil wells of Baku and the Caucasus. Foreign firms and investors were attracted by the high profits in Russia, but they had also little alternative to investing in Russia because the tariff of 1891 virtually shut out imports. On the other hand the Russians had to export oil in bulk and more grain than was good for the subsistence of the population in order to pay the interest on foreign capital investment.

There was always a danger that capital for development would turn into financial imperialism. In Romania over 95 per cent of the oil industry in 1914 was in the hands of foreigners who were exploiting it for their own ends. Borrowing by poor Balkan countries was often not so much for industry but to build up their armies and to nationalize the railways that foreign powers were pushing across their territory. A country that defaulted on the repayment of loans risked foreign intervention to protect the interests of bond-holders, which would be ensured by the earmarking of taxes. Loans were accompanied by demands for railway concessions and contracts for the supply of arms. Portugal was able to avoid foreign controls when it defaulted on repayments in 1892, because it was a 'European' country; the Ottoman Empire and Egypt which defaulted in 1876, were not. Serbia was deeply in debt after it nationalized the part of the Vienna to Constantinople railway that ran through it in 1889–92, and had to accept the control of a consortium of foreign powers in 1895. Similar controls were imposed on the finances of Bulgaria in 1902 and on Greece after it was defeated by Turkey in 1898.

Industry: Management

In order to compete with their rivals, it was necessary at the end of the nineteenth century for firms to make economies of scale, to grow either by going public or by undertaking mergers. In Great Britain the biggest joint-stock companies were the railways, but in manufacturing industry family firms still predominated. A method was found to increase capital funding without ceding control to backers, through the private company. 'I have always had as much power as director of this company as I had as a partner', reported Thomas Vickers in 1886, 'and the resources of the company are greater than the resources of the old partnership.'[1] Mergers took place in Britain, but less in the new industries that mattered than in consumer industries such as brewing, food-processing, and textiles which were faced by falling prices. These included the Distiller's Company (1877), J. and P. Coats in textiles (1890), Tate and Lyle (1900), Lever Brothers in soap (1906), and the Imperial Tobacco Company (1901). But even with the mergers, the influence of the founding families on the new boards of directors was preserved to the extent that the Imperial Tobacco Company was described as akin to the original thirteen States of America, and the promotion of expert salaried managers to such boards, though increasing, was not always what it might be.

In France the small family firm was still the commonest, even in new sectors, as exemplified at Lyons by the car manufacturer Marius Berliet and the photographic and cinematographic brothers Auguste and Antoine Lumière. On the other hand the metallurgical and engineering firms of Lorraine and the electrical companies of Paris, Lyons, and Grenoble required outside capital. In the former the owners, who included large landowners, maintained their grip on management, but in the electrical industry there was a much clearer demand for the expertise of scientific managers on boards of direction.

Germany was at the other end of the spectrum. The capital demands of the new industries virtually closed them to small firms. Of the hundred largest German firms in 1907 only four were in food or brewing; 23 were in mining, 31 in metallurgy, 13 in engineering, 17 in chemicals, and 4 in electricals. Size was achieved not only by horizontal mergers but also by the vertical integration of an industry with the exploitation of raw materials in order to ensure their supply at fixed cost and the manufacture of by-products such as tar, naphtha, benzine, and ammonia from coal-mining, in order to avoid waste. Even in these large firms the influence of the founding families continued.

---

[1] Quoted by P. L. Payne, *British Entrepreneurship in the Nineteenth Century* (London, 1974), 20.

But a law of 1884 separated supervisory boards from executive boards in joint-stock companies, so that while in 1905 German banks had 29 per cent of the seats on the supervisory boards that were elected by the shareholders to protect their interests, they did not sit on the executive boards, which made room for the influence of scientifically trained managers.

This was clearly important because the new technology of the turn of the century required close co-operation between science and industry to promote the success of industry in world markets. In this field Germany made use of her advantage. German technical high schools, which were given the right to award doctorates in 1899 and thus achieved equal status with the universities, turned out three or four thousand graduates a year in 1900, as against a thousand a year from the *grandes écoles* in France. In addition, large firms like the Badische Anilin und Soda Fabrik at Ludwigshafen trained chemists and scientific managers for their own purposes. Over 77 per cent of salaried managers in Germany in 1907 had received some form of higher education.

The scientific training of managers was almost as effective in France. Traditionally the greatest of the *grandes écoles*, the École Polytechnique, had trained candidates for the army, the administration, and state-run monopolies such as the mining industry. Practical work in the metallurgical, glass, and chemical industries was undertaken by graduates of the École Centrale. But in the 1890s, as the military career lost its attraction and industrial concerns increased in size and status, so a greater proportion of Polytechniciens went into private industry, rising to over a third in 1900, and were responsible for major electrification projects. Among the more empirical technical schools, a private École Supérieure d'Éléctricité was founded in Paris in 1894 and a school of electrochemistry and electrometallurgy was established at Grenoble. By 1911–13 some 74 per cent of managers in large electrical firms in France had the diploma of *ingénieur*.

In Russia, the Ministry of Finance set up a network of polytechnic institutes between 1898 and 1902, but in Great Britain there was no equivalent. A scientific training that was capable of practical application was developed not in Oxford and Cambridge but in London and the civic universities which sprang up at the end of the century, often funded by local industrialists, in Manchester, Birmingham, Bristol, Leeds, Sheffield, Newcastle, and Glasgow. But the numbers involved were very small. Only 1,500 chemists, graduate or non-graduate, were employed by British firms in 1902, as against 4,000 in Germany. The conditions attached to government grants after 1889, the demand for school teachers after the Education Act of 1902, and the ethos of a scientific culture to match humanistic culture resulted in science becoming more abstract and less practical in British universities. As a result, manufacturers became even less interested in science graduates than they were before, and preferred to promote clever mechanics rather than engineers, and laboratory analysts rather than research chemists. Philistinism knocked yet another nail into the coffin of British industry; what was good for the eighteenth century was not good enough for the twentieth.

Industry: Labour

By the turn of the century it was possible to speak of a working class in Europe. The labour force was becoming less rural and more urban in origin, and migrant workers were leavened by generations of 'born proletarians'. There was still a strong contrast between western and eastern Europe. In Moscow 90 per cent of factory workers in the period 1880–1900 were migrant peasants, female workers tended to return to their village to raise families, and village solidarities dictated what trade peasants would take up and where they would live. In southern Russia, where the new mining and metallurgical industries were springing up, the population was scarce and labour notoriously expensive before the influx of a permanent work-force into mushroom towns like Ekaterinoslav. In the Ruhr area of Germany, the influx of Polish labour from the eastern provinces of Prussia and Silesia brought down the proportion of second-generation miners there from 75 per cent in 1850 to 37 per cent in 1893. On the other hand in a Ruhr town like Bochum there was a clear distinction between the floating, migrant work-force in the mines, foundries, and chemical plants and the stable, more often native-born, skilled labour-force in woodworking or machine-building. In Leipzig the 'proletarian' origin of workers increased from 57 per cent of those born before 1845 to 90 per cent of those born between 1867 and 1878. Trends were similar in France. In Saint-Étienne the proportion of workers born in the town rose from 39 per cent of men and 44 per cent of women in 1850–1 to 42 per cent of men and 59 per cent of women in 1901–11.

After urbanization, the working class was forged by mechanization. It has been suggested that the United States mechanized its industry far sooner than did Great Britain, because the relatively high cost of labour made it urgent to replace that labour by machines. On the other hand it is clear that the wages of workers were higher in Britain than they were on the Continent. A French survey published in 1907 calculated the average hourly wage of a sample of skilled workers to be 2.36 francs in New York and 2.1 francs in Chicago, 1.0 francs in London and 0.91 francs in Birmingham. In Paris the average hourly wage was 0.87 francs, in Berlin 0.81 francs, in Leipzig 0.66 francs, in Amsterdam 0.52 francs, in Brussels 0.46 francs, and this fell to 0.41 francs in Milan, and 0.35 francs in Rome.

To extend the length of the working day was still a viable alternative to increasing productivity by mechanization, as a way of extracting a surplus from the work-force. In the coal industry mechanization did not progress very fast, for whereas 51 per cent of coal was cut by machine in the United States in 1913, the proportion was 10 per cent in Belgium, 8 per cent in Great

Britain, and only 2 per cent in Germany. The miners' strikes which shook Germany in 1889 and 1905 were in pursuit of a shorter working day. Some 32 per cent of strikes in Germany between 1899 and 1914 were against long hours of work, whereas the figure was only 15 per cent in France.

The mechanization of many branches of industry took place later in France than in Britain, and made possible the employment of more female labour in France at the end of the century at a time when it was contracting in Britain. Stiffer competition and falling prices gave employers an incentive to mechanize, and women could be paid half the wages of men while being considered a more docile work-force. Women formed 30 per cent of the working population in France in 1866, but nearly 38 per cent in 1906. In Lyons, the introduction of the power-loom into the silk industry destroyed the *canuts* or hand-loom weavers and brought the female proportion of weavers in 1903 to 95 per cent. As a result of mechanization women took over the boot and shoe industry, the tobacco industry, and the bicycle workshops. A delegate to the congress of the metal federation in 1892 feared that 'husbands will be forced to do the cooking while women and children go to work outside'.[2] This view was somewhat exaggerated, for in many expanding industries such as mining, metallurgy, engineering, shipbuilding, and glass-making, there were few opportunities for women, and they were forced back on sectors such as textiles, dressmaking, and domestic service. For this reason the proportion of women employed in Great Britain fell by 8 per cent between 1881 and 1911 and, in contrast to France, the working class became more characterized by the adult male.

The main way by which mechanization made the working class more homogeneous was to reduce the difference between skilled and unskilled labour and to create a demand for a mass of semi-skilled workers who could learn a specific job in one or two weeks in order to operate the new machines or machine-tools such as lathes. Mechanization enabled employers to displace highly trained, versatile skilled workers who commanded high wages. On the other hand the introduction of new machinery provoked angry strikes, not so much, in the Luddite tradition, against the machines themselves, for they were accepted, but over whether they would be manned by the old skilled or imported semi-skilled workers. In Great Britain the Amalgamated Society of Engineers was involved in a protracted struggle with employers in 1897–8 over the introdution of machine-tools. In France, where mechanization came later, the agony was often sharper, as in the strike of filemakers in the Saint-Étienne region in 1910–11. The new machines carried the day and the exclusiveness of skilled workers who had established an almost dynastic monopoly of some crafts was broken down. In Germany, evidence from Leipzig shows that at the end of the century the sons of workers in one trade were far more likely to find employment in another trade than

[2] Quoted by Madeleine Guilbert, *Les Fonctions des femmes dans l'industrie* (Paris/The Hague, 1966), 47.

earlier on. A study of Bielefeld shows that more unskilled workers rose to become skilled workers in 1890–1910 than in 1860–80, and that conversely more skilled workers dropped into the ranks of the unskilled. The working class in Europe tended to become homogeneously semi-skilled.

Mechanization and the large-scale organization that went with it threatened the position of the small, independent producer. Accustomed to work for the specific order of a client, artisans were overtaken by the mass demand for cheap, standardized goods. Market prices were falling but their costs in terms of raw materials, rent, and the wages of apprentices and journeymen remained high. They had not the capital to adopt new machinery and enlarge their scale of production. In Germany the depression years of 1873–95 were particularly hard on small masters. Moreover the appearance of department stores like those owned in twenty-six different German cities in 1906 by Leonard Tietz, who had started as a haberdasher at Stralsund on the Baltic coast, undermined small retailers, with the exception of butchers and bakers. Reich legislation of 1897 protected artisans from proletarianization by permitting trades to set up compulsory guilds and semi-public craft chambers to represent their interests. In Great Britain, the labour aristocracy made the transition to the factory floor more painlessly, taking on the task of foremen. In France, where large-scale enterprise was slow to develop, the boutique of the artisan or retailer proved very resilient. Even so, the combination of economic pressure and the growth of department stores drove a third of jewellery, tailoring, clothing, and shoe traders out of business in the Palais-Royal district of Paris between 1885 and 1900, and a national organization was set up in 1888 to defend the interests of small shopkeepers.

As the old lower middle class struggled for survival, so a new lower middle class blossomed. This was the class that was thrown up by the revolution in transport, trade, and communications and included railway employees, clerks in banking, insurance, and shipping firms, shop-assistants, elementary schoolteachers, and post-office, telegraph, and telephone workers. With the development of girls' education and the acquisition of typing and shorthand skills, women increasingly made their mark on this sector. The degree to which these white-collar workers were separated from manual workers varied from country to country. In Great Britain, they were on a par with many skilled workers and the main division was between these two categories and the unskilled. In Germany and Austria the 'collar line' was much firmer, for the *Angestellten* or white-collar workers earned more than manual workers and enjoyed greater job security. In addition, they were a separately defined legal category from the point of view of social insurance, took part in the prestige accorded to 'intellectual' professions, and were assimilated both to civil servants as *Privatbeamten* and to the status-group of the *Mittelstand*. In France, on the other hand, the bourgeois aspirations of the white-collar workers were in conflict with the proletarian nature of their earnings, which became particularly acute as prices began to rise again at the turn of the century. Some employees in the state sector, notably post-office workers and primary schoolteachers, came to realize that they had more in common with the working class than with the middle class, launched strikes, and demanded the right to join trade unions.

Organization in pursuit of better wages and conditions was the concrete means by which the European working class defined itself. The artisan élite had long been organized. So also increasingly were the big battalions of coal, cotton, shipbuilding, engineering, and the railways towards which the balance of power in the labour movement was shifting. More difficult was the organization of the unskilled workers; indeed, it was largely against this industrial reserve army used by employers to keep down wages and break strikes that trade unions were formed. They were a floating population that moved from gasworks in the winter to brickyards and dockyards in the summer, and it was easy to break their strikes by calling on other casual workers. The net had to be cast as wide as possible, to regiment as many general labourers as possible, if the employers were to be defeated.

In Great Britain, the economic recovery of 1888–90 and the consequent demand for labour encouraged unskilled workers to raise their demands. In 1889 the gasworkers, followed by the London dockers, went on strike, and a wave of 'new unions' pushed up the number of organized workers from 750,000 (or 12 per cent of the manual labour force) in 1888 to 1,576,000 in 1892. Then there was a downturn in the economy, the employers organized themselves, and the bubble of the new unionism was burst. Between 1901 and 1905 trade-union membership fell. In Germany, the breakthrough to mass unionism came with the Hamburg dock strike of 1896–7, but whereas the Amalgamated Society of Engineers was confined to skilled workers alone, the Deutscher Metallarbeiter Verband, founded in 1891, enrolled all levels of skill and included gold- and silversmiths, fitters, turners, machinists, patternmakers, steelworkers, and labourers in the foundries. The number of unionized workers, which was held down by government repression between 1878 and 1890, rose from 250,000 in 1891 to 1,690,000 (including 119,000 women) in 1906. France was further behind, and the virulence of her strikes was in inverse proportion to the development of trade unions. Textile-workers, miners, metal-workers, and railwaymen did not become strongly organized till the period 1894–1906, when the number of unionized workers rose from 419,000 to 836,000. Even in 1913, there were only 1,064,000 unionized workers in France, as against 3,023,000 in Great Britain, and 3,317,000 in Germany. In Russia, finally, trade unions were not legalized until 1906, but by 1907 there were 2,853,000 unionized workers, 9 per cent of the labour force, both factory and artisanal workers, and up to 55 per cent among printers.

To the problem of how many workers were organized was added the problem of how local unions might be articulated to the best effect. The most powerful structure was again in Germany, where most unions adhered after 1890 to *Zentral-Verbände* or centralized unions for direction, and these came under a General Commission of the German Trade Unions. In 1906 there were 66 such amalgamations, and in 1913 the figure had been reduced to 47, compared with 1,135 unions in Great Britain. In Britain, the campaign to form national federations for each category of unions met with some success. The miners' federation, established in 1883, organized a strike in 1890, weathered a lockout in 1893, and after 1912 pressed for a national minimum wage. In France, by contrast, the miners' leaders never managed to put together an effective national federation, and the national strike that was called in 1902 was boycotted by the miners of the north of France, who thought it inopportune. Regionalism was the great barrier to organization in France and Italy, but an organ was devised in the 1880s to confront the difficulty: the chamber of labour. Local unions, instead of federating nationally with unions in the same category, federated at the municipal level with unions in the same town, as labour exchanges, which also encouraged workers to join unions, organized workers' education, supported strikes, and even contested elections. In 1894 the French chambers of labour set up a national organization, but this remained quite separate from the national organization of category federations until 1902.

Plutocracy

At the other end of the social scale, investments in railway shares, public utilities, urban development, and foreign and colonial bonds paid handsome dividends as the agricultural depression bit, so that the biggest fortunes were being made not by owners of land but by monied men: financiers, promoters, and speculators. In a word, aristocracy was displaced by plutocracy. In Great Britain landowners accounted for 73 per cent of millionaires in 1858–79 while commercial and financial magnates provided only 14 per cent. But by 1900–14 the proportion of landowners among the country's millionaires had been whittled down to 27 per cent while that of commercial and financial fortunes had risen to 38 per cent. In Prussia in 1912, 64 individuals had fortunes of over £1 million (20 million marks). These included 12 old nobles (princes, dukes, and counts), 28 lesser nobles, all of whom were from financial families ennobled during the previous half century, and 13 of whom were Jews, and 24 industrial and commercial magnates, all of whom were bourgeois and Christian. The wealthiest person in Prussia in 1910 was Bertha Krupp, the granddaughter of Alfred Krupp, who carried on the business dynasty after her weak-willed father, Friedrich, was driven to suicide in 1902 by a homosexual scandal. In Hungary the Magyar landowners were rivalled by Jewish capitalists who in 1910 provided 66 per cent of the commercial entrepreneurs and 90 per cent of the bankers in Budapest. The Budapest Jews were important buyers and even more important lessees of large estates, but new men were no longer under pressure to make their wealth respectable by sinking it in land. In the combination of landed and monied wealth that defined the plutocracy, it was monied wealth that dazzled.

If a landowning nobility was to prosper, it was well advised to diversify out of land and reap some of the gain of financial, commercial, and industrial growth. In France nobles held a third of the directorships of railway companies and a quarter of those of large banking and steel firms at the turn of the century. In Prussia, on the other hand, only the Silesian nobility were involved in industry, and consequently rich; most Prussian nobles remained 'cabbage Junkers', surviving by service to the state and thanks to the protective tariffs extracted from the government. Another solution was marriage into new wealth. After 1890 the endogamy of Spanish aristocrats and Catalan bankers and industrialists came to an end as the sons of the former married the daughters of the latter. The French Count Albert de Mun married his two daughters into a champagne and a cognac family respectively. Most spectacular in this period, however, were the marriages of European nobles to the heiresses of American millionaires. In 1894 Winaretta Singer, daughter of a German-Jewish immigrant to the United States who had invented and made a fortune from the sewing machine, married Prince Edmond de Polignac, son of a minister of Charles X of France, and as the Princesse de Polignac presided over one of the most brilliant artistic and musical salons in Paris. The following year Consuelo Vanderbilt married the Duke of Marlborough, bringing with her a fortune of $10m. Altogether, between 1870 and 1914, 60 British peers married American women. Marriage of German nobles and Jewish heiresses was unheard of, but a number of Jewish financiers revived the role of Court Jew, offering lavish entertainment, becoming connoisseurs and patrons of the arts, funding charities, and paying the gambling debts of kings and princes. Albert Ballin, promoted director of the Hamburg-Amerika line of luxury liners in 1899, became a favourite of Kaiser William II, not least because of his interest in German sea-power, and regularly entertained him at the Lower Elbe regatta at Hamburg, which preceded Kiel week. On the other hand he was never fully accepted, because of his Jewish origins, either by the Hamburg patriciate or by the Prussian aristocracy. Baron Maurice von Hirsch, a Jewish banker and builder of the Vienna–Constantinople railway, who owned vast estates in Moravia and Hungary, was snubbed by the Austrian aristocracy, but became the private banker of the Prince of Wales. After his death in 1896 he was succeeded in this role by Ernest Cassell, another Jewish banker who promoted South American railways, Egyptian dams, loans to the Mexican government, arms manufacture, and the London Underground. Cassell was knighted by Queen Victoria and became a leading light in the cosmopolitan entourage of the Prince of Wales; in 1922 his granddaughter Edwina was to marry Lord Louis Mountbatten.

In some countries, the financial, commercial, and industrial bourgeoisie integrated successfully with the bureaucratic and professional bourgeoisie; elsewhere, there were still divisions. In Great Britain, relations were close between the aristocracy and the City of London, in which many younger sons of the aristocracy and gentry worked, but more distant with northern industrialists. In France, the business, landed, professional, and official classes were amalgamated into a homogenous group of notables. The banking, commercial, and landed rich who paid for the education of their sons at the Law Faculties shared the top posts in the Cour des Comptes and financial inspectorate with the administrative dynasties. In turn, French officials and soldiers often married into landed or business families, both to eke out their salary with a dowry and to build bridges between the political class of the Republic and often royalist economic élite. In Germany and Russia on the other hand, though the commercial and industrial bourgeoisie were as often as not university-educated, ran municipal government and were often rewarded with the prestigious title of commercial councillor, they continued to be cold-shouldered by the bureaucratic and professional *Bildungsbürgertum*.

The balance of power between bourgeoise and nobility also varied between western and southern Europe, where the bourgeoisie made successful break-throughs into positions of power, and central and eastern Europe, where the nobility was able to defended its bastions. In France, Italy, and Spain by the turn of the century, the middle classes had effectively displaced the nobility as politicians, in the bureaucracy, and in the officer corps. Some aristocratic preserves remained, such as the diplomatic corps, since international relations were undertaken by small and often interrelated group of aristocrats. The British army was also more popular with sons of peers at the end of the century than it had been earlier on. It is also clear that the triumph of the middle classes was not a triumph for businessmen. The typical politician in France and Italy was now a lawyer, since economic élites tended to confine themselves to local government. The bureaucracy, moreover, was recruited through highly selective schools and institutions of higher education, which imposed their own *esprit de corps*. For example, recruitment to the British civil service, which expanded greatly in the Home, Indian, and Colonial sections, became more meritocratic, but between 1899 and 1908 public schools provided 42 per cent of the intake, and Oxford and Cambridge Universities 82 per cent.

In Prussia, the judiciary was colonized by the middle class, but provincial administration and ministerial offices were still dominated by the nobility. As late as 1911 over 78 per cent of Prussian higher officials came from noble, landowning, and official backgrounds; only 9 per cent came from professional and academic families and only 13 per cent from business circles. Though nobles had virtually monopolized the officer corps in 1860, and accounted for only a third of officers in 1913, the slack was taken up not by sons of the business classes but by the sons of soldiers and bureaucrats, so that military–bureaucratic dynasties now provided the backbone of the corps. Moreover, William II called in 1890 for a 'nobility of temperament' to replace the 'nobility of birth', and this was sustained by the practice of duelling in defence of personal honour, which was the privilege of the nobility and was imitated by student fraternities throughout Germany.

Bureaucratic and military careers were marginally more open in the Austro-Hungarian Empire. The Austrian aristocracy deserted the officer corps after the defeat of 1866, so that only a quarter of career officers were noble in 1910–11, and 17 per cent of reserve officers were Jewish. (In Prussia there were no Jewish reserve officers between 1885 and 1914.) Between 1890 and 1910 the proportion of aristocrats and gentry in the central Hungarian bureaucracy fell from 59 to 49 per cent, while that of commoners rose from 23 to 42 per cent. Jews found it more difficult to achieve public office, but by contrast they surged into the liberal professions. In 1910 they provided 42 per cent of journalists, 45 per cent of barristers and 49 per cent of doctors in Hungary. In Russia, under Alexander III, Jews were excluded from public office and their access to the professions was tightly controlled. The proportion of noble army officers fell from 90 per cent on the eve of the Crimean war to 20 per cent in 1913, but the judiciary (unlike in Prussia) and provincial governorships were dominated by the nobility, and between 1894 and 1914 90 per cent of the State Council, which was transformed into the upper house of the Duma in 1906, were drawn from the hereditary nobility.

In many countries, though not in all, the composition of the nobility reflected the greater weight of the plutocracy in public life. In Germany William II gave 14 per cent of his honours to bankers and businessmen, as against 6 per cent by William I, and 36 per cent instead of 49 per cent to army and navy officers. The proportion of nobles created from landowners and civil servants or judges was 25 per cent and 13 per cent in each case. Ennoblement in Austria was even more conservative. In the period 1885–1913 under 9 per cent of honours went to businessmen, as against 14 per cent to the civil administration, and 44 per cent to the military. Hungary stood out by ennobling bankers, traders, and railway magnates in significant numbers, and in 1890 the first Jew was promoted, without conversion to Christianity, to the baronage. In Great Britain, similarly, there was a sea-change in the creation of peerages between 1886 and 1914. Whereas a quarter of new peers came from old landed families and a third from the professions and public service, a third came from the plutocratic rich, who did not feel the need to gentrify their wealth by sinking it in landed estates before they accepted peerages. Nathan Mayer Rothschild became the first Jewish peer in Britain in 1885, a privilege denied his father by Queen Victoria in 1869, while the ennoblement of brewers such as Michael Bass and Arthur Guinness in the 1880s invited the remark that the British peerage had been reduced to a 'beerage'.

11

PROBLEMS OF NATIONAL INTEGRATION

Whereas the process of national unification until 1870 had been concerned to give the armature of statehood to emergent nations, in the period after 1870 states were concerned fully to integrate the nations over which they presided. This meant first, imposing a certain idea of the nation and second, ensuring that the loyalty of subjects or citizens to the nation took priority over loyalties to other communities.

There were several competing models of nationhood. One was the recognition of a common ancestry or descent. This was difficult to prove, so it was often linked to the idea of a homeland that had been occupied since time immemorial, famed for its natural beauty or natural frontiers. The combination of ancestry and homeland was expressed in the ideology of blood and soil, *la terre et les morts*, *Blut und Boden*. A second was the existence of a common religion. This might seem an unlikely element of nationhood, given the universality of religions, but the Poles, for instance, oppressed by Protestant Prussia and Orthodox Russia, identified themselves closely with Roman Catholicism, while the Russians asserted their Orthodox Christianity against the Muslim Turks on their southern frontier. Claiming a common language, third, was the most usual definition of a nation, since a language was held to express the soul of the people. The last model of nationhood was defined by Ernest Renan in a Sorbonne lecture of 1882. 'To have common glories in the past, a common will in the present,' he said, 'to have accomplished great things together, to wish to do so again, that is the essential condition for being a nation.'[1]

Once the nation had been defined, the priority of loyalty to the nation above all other loyalties had to be imposed. States had to ensure that other loyalties, to different regions or language groups, to other religions, to social classes or genders, did not assert themselves at the expense of loyalty to the nation. This was the work of national integration. Yet conflicting loyalties there were, and those conflicting loyalties were often subscribed to passionately, even dangerously, as far as the existence of the nation-state was concerned. Socialism asserted that the nation served the interests of the ruling classes and that the working classes had no other homeland than the international working class. A Second International was founded in 1889 to group

---

[1] John Hutchinson and Anthony D. Smith, eds., *Nationalism* (Oxford, 1994), 17.

socialist parties in different countries, to fight for the interests of workers and against nationalism and militarism. Roman Catholicism, a universal religion defeated by the process of national unification in 1870, provided an alternative focus of loyalty for communities opposed to the identification of the state with another religion or with no religion at all. The creation of nation-states was a complex affair for multinational empires, and generally meant nothing more than the identification of the state with the dominant nationality. This was resisted by minorities which were beginning to define themselves as nations and to demand home rule or statehood on the basis of that nationhood. Finally, in these states men not only monopolized political life but also exercised social and economic privileges. This lack of liberty and equality was now effectively contested by women organized in the name of feminism.

This struggle of conflicting loyalties was one of the dominant issues in European life down to 1914. It was a period in which the stakes were raised by the states' drive for colonies and world power. They also devised strategies to manage society and promote national integration. But it would also be fair to say that each movement that contested the primacy of the nation also had its own contradictions and weaknesses, so that the threats posed by socialism, Roman Catholicism, national minorities, and feminism were not always as strong as they might have been.

Socialism: Northern Europe

In the period after 1880 mass socialist parties were formed in Europe, which subscribed to the teaching of Karl Marx. They argued that the state was the instrument of the bourgeoisie to give force and legitimacy to its economic domination, that the workers should organize separate socialist parties ultimately to take control of the state. The orthodox Marxist view was that the state had resorted to legal and military repression to destroy workers' movements, and would do so again, and that socialists must therefore counter repression by revolution, leading to the dictatorship of the proletariat and the expropriation of capitalism. They also held that since the socialist workers were involved in relentless class struggle, they should not make alliances with other parties which, even in opposition, were by definition part of the bourgeois system. There were, in addition, revisionist Marxists who argued that revolution was needless and dangerous in democratic societies where popular suffrage existed and that it was possible for socialists to come to power by legal, parliamentary means. Moreover, they pointed out that as the industrial working class was a minority in society, and that not all workers voted socialist, socialist parties would be well advised to make alliances with bourgeois parties with whom they had something in common, in the first instance to correct the worst aspects of capitalism and to improve gradually the lot of the working classes. Not all leaders of the organized working class, however, were Marxist. There were those who thought Marxist parties centralized and doctrinaire, and who feared that the dictatorship of the proletariat would be the dictatorship of Marxist parties over the proletariat, and no better than bourgeois dictatorship. These thinkers were anarchists. Often they acted as loners, but they also tried to convert the working classes to their cause. They argued that the working classes should organize independently of socialist parties, in occupational trade unions and local chambers of labour, and forsake the political process, which served only the politicians, in favour of using their industrial muscle through the general strike. This combination of anarchism and socialism, which flourished mainly in southern and eastern Europe, was called anarcho-syndicalism. The problem in Great Britain was for a party serving the working class to break the influence of the Liberal party over those workers who gained the vote when the franchise was again extended in 1884. The Fabian Society, founded that year by George Bernard Shaw and Sidney Webb, an official in the Colonial Office, was influenced by Marx's *Capital*. On the other hand it took the view, following the American Henry George, that property-owners should not be expropriated but simply have their assets taxed for the good of the community as a whole. George's main influence was on Liberals in London who called themselves Progressives in order to campaign for the new London County Council in 1888, and demanded a shift of the burden of rates from occupiers to urban landowners. The Fabians had little choice but to fall in with the Progressives.

Fabians took their name from the Roman General Fabius Cunctator who acted only after 'long taking of counsel' and was a master of delaying tactics. Theirs was a natural response to British conditions. Revolution was needless in a country which had first parliamentary and now municipal representative government. Conditions in Ireland were different, and the only prominent socialist to advocate revolution in England was an Ulster Protestant whose father had made his fortune in the West Indies, Henry Hyndman. Hyndman met Marx in 1880, founded the Democratic Federation in 1881 (it became the Social Democratic Federation in 1883), and took advantage of rising unemployment to hold a rally at Trafalgar Square on 8 February 1886 which became extremely violent. But the following year, like the Fabians, he urged the creation of a socialist municipal council in London, which would take over the gas, water, and transport services for the public good.

Both movements lacked the support of organized labour—the Fabians because they were intellectuals, the Hyndmanites because they scorned the trade unions for representing only a fraction of the total working population. And so the twain scarcely met. The London Trades Council, reinforced by dockers and gasworkers, aimed to run labour candidates for Parliament and the LCC after 1891, but had to rely on co-operation with the Progressives. Organized labour in Yorkshire and Lancashire, which wanted nothing to do with 'continental revolutionists' but only to elect working men to Parliament, founded the Independent Labour Party at Bradford in 1893. But its decision to campaign against the Liberals as well as against the Conservatives in the general election of 1895 met with no success. Moreover, the Trades Union Congress was dominated by coal, which tended to be Liberal, and cotton, which in Lancashire supported Conservatives because of their stand against the Catholic Irish. It was not until trade-union rights were threatened by a lock-out of engineers in 1897–8 and a clamp-down on the South Wales railwaymen who struck during the Boer War in 1900 that the TUC accepted the need for the separate representation of labour.

In Belgium, both Liberal and Catholic parties were united in defence of the Constitution of 1831 which disfranchised the masses by a narrow, propertied franchise. Liberal influence over the working class was much less than in England. The Belgian Workers' Party was set up in 1885 not by intellectuals but by skilled, unionized labour led by a typographer and a marble-worker. But anarchism remained very strong, especially in the French-speaking districts, and was responsible for a wave of strikes at Liège and among coalminers of Charleroi in March 1886. Despite its commitment to legal means the Belgian Workers' Party was forced to accept the tactic of the general strike, both to head off anarchist influence and to exercise pressure on the Constituent Assembly that was elected in 1892 but refused to concede universal suffrage. The big guns of a general strike launched in April 1893 induced the Assembly to change its mind.

The use of the general strike to obtain universal suffrage was debated elsewhere. The Swedish Social Democratic Party which emerged from the labour movement in 1889 under the leadership of August Palm, a young tailor expelled from Germany, proposed it in 1893. However, it was brought into line by its Liberal allies, who preferred to make their point by the election of 'alternative' people's parliaments under universal suffrage (although without success until 1909). In the same summer of 1893 extremists in the Austrian Social Democratic Party urged the use of the general strike to obtain suffrage reform after a demonstration of 50,000 people outside the parliament building in Vienna. But Viktor Adler, the Jewish doctor who led the party, managed to dissuade them.

The model for all European social democratic parties was the German Social Democratic Party (SPD), founded in 1875. Outlawed under the antisocialist law of 1878, it was forced into a position of revolutionary opposition to the authoritarian German state and to the feudal and bourgeois parties that underpinned it. On the other hand, elections to the Reichstag were by universal suffrage and after the lapse of the anti-socialist law in 1890, the SPD emerged as a mass party. Moreover, whereas in states such as Prussia and Saxony the suffrage was massively weighted in favour of property-owners, and the SPD on principle boycotted elections to the Prussian state parliament, in the south German states the suffrage was broader and possibilities of reform clearer. Georg von Vollmar, a soldier from an old Catholic noble family who became leader of the SPD in Bavaria, caused a sensation in 1894 when his party voted for the Bavarian state budget on the grounds that it included social reforms. In 1899 his party also made an electoral pact with the Centre party in order to obtain a more generous electoral law. Even more important was the debate over the so-called catastrophe theory. The Erfurt programme of the SPD had been drafted in 1891 by Karl Kautsky and Eduard Bernstein. Kautsky, who considered himself the heir to Engels, described the long-term goals. These were based on Marx's laws of capitalist development, notably those predicting the sucking of artisans and peasants into the proletariat, the growing industrial reserve army of the unemployed, and the declining rate of profit, and held that in time capitalism would inevitably self-destruct. Bernstein, who remained in London after the lapse of the anti-socialist law and was close to the Fabians, dealt with the short-term aims. However, in a series of articles published in the party newspaper, *Die Neue Zeit,* between 1896 and 1898, he started to question the catastrophe theory. He pointed out that the emergence of a new lower-middle class of managers, technicians and white-collar workers belied class polarization, that the organization of the working class in trade unions was helping to push up real wages, and that capitalists were learning to cope with falling rates of profit by throwing up tariffs and cartels and exporting surplus goods and capital abroad. The corollary of this analysis was that the SPD should not indulge in revolutionary politics, but commit itself to a strategy of reforming the worst abuses of capitalism.

Bernstein's opinions were broadcast just as the German and European economy in general started on an upswing. But they clashed with a doctrine that offered immense hope to a persecuted and struggling party. As Bebel had told Engels in 1885, 'Every night I go to sleep with the thought that the last hour of bourgeois society strikes soon.'[2] Kautsky argued that Islam had conquered the world until it ceased to believe in itself. Bernstein was dubbed a heretic and was effectively put on trial in his absence at the Stuttgart conference of the SPD in 1898 and the Hanover congress of 1899. Kautsky, Bebel, and the Polish socialist Rosa Luxemburg reaffirmed the catastrophe theory and the doctrine of revolution. Bernstein was accused of looking at events 'through English spectacles'; authoritarian, feudal Germany was quite different. It was asserted that if the SPD ever looked like achieving a majority in the Reichstag, it would be destroyed by a *coup d'état* rather than allowed to take political power. Bernstein's views were rejected, and the SPD went on to develop its own contradiction, that of a revolutionary class party, but one wedded to parliamentary politics and so bureaucratic that it trembled at the thought that it might ever have to resort to violence.

[2] Quoted by Vernon L. Lidtke, *The Outlawed Party: Social Democracy in Germany 1878–90* (Princeton, 1966), 233.

Socialism: Southern Europe

In France, the Paris Commune had been brutally suppressed in 1871. The labour movement remained in a state of shock until the national workers' congress of 1876, and militants suffered until in 1880 an amnesty was granted to those who had been involved in the Commune. On the other hand, unlike Germany, France was a democratic Republic in which, after 1877, governments reflected the majority in parliament.

The strategy of the French Workers' Party (POF), founded at the workers' congress of 1879 by Jules Guesde, a former anarchist who had learned his Marxism from German *émigrés* in Paris, bore the mark of this tension. Guesde adopted a revolutionary tactic because, as he told Marx, he needed to 'cut the cable that kept our workers in radical or bourgeois Jacobin waters'[3] and to emphasize the separation of classes. The principle of class struggle had to be embedded in the mind of the workers, and from this followed the principle of revolution. Every year after 1880 Guesde lead his party to the Père Lachaise cemetery in Paris, where the heroes of the Commune had made a last stand. Workers had to grasp the fact that the French bourgeoisie was always prepared to resort to repression, so they must reply with revolution. By 1880, however, the democratic Republic was in the hands of genuine republicans, and elections beckoned. There could be no excuse for the POF not putting up candidates. Guesde visited Marx in London to take advice on drawing up an election manifesto. Not surprisingly, it combined long-term goals, based on the catastrophe theory, and short-term electoral promises.

As a Marxist, Guesde was dedicated to the conquest of state-power, but he had to contend with the anarchist followers of Proudhon who wanted to replace the state by a federation of free communes and preferred to abolish wage-labour through workers' associations rather than the nationalization of large combines. They rejected the catastrophe theory, and they disliked being dictated to by an authoritarian socialist party. In 1881 many anarchists who had joined the Workers' Party when it was set up in Marseilles left. The following year the former anarchist Paul Brousse led away another breakaway group, christened the Possibilists, who wanted to take control of France commune by commune, establish a municipal socialism of gas, water, and transport services, and convert the working classes to socialism by the immediate, practical results they obtained. In 1887 nine Possibilists were elected to the municipal council of Paris. Soon, however, the Possibilists began to behave like bourgeois politicians, making pacts with bourgeois parties, and many of the rank-and-file of the movement, inspired by a former Communard, Jean Allemane, themselves broke away in 1890 to form a movement

---

[3] Quoted by Claude Willard, *Le Mouvement socialiste en France, 1893–1905. Les Guesdistes* (Paris, 1965), 18.

dedicated to the emancipation of the working class by direct action, and specifically by the general strike.

A struggle ensued between Guesde, Brousse, and Allemane for control of the labour movement, which was growing in strength after the legalization of trade unions in 1884. Guesde set up a National Federation of Trade Unions in 1886 in order to bend the labour movement to the purposes of the POF. Despite its revolutionary rhetoric, the POF enjoyed considerable electoral success, winning a string of town councils in 1892 and returning six deputies to parliament in 1893. These were joined by middle-class intellectuals converting to socialism from bourgeois radicalism, such as Jean Jaurès and Alexandre Millerand. Outside parliament, the POF adopted the device of May Day demonstrations in favour of an eight-hour day, as recommended by the Socialist International which met in Paris in 1889, to keep the trade unions active but under control. The Allemanists were resolutely opposed to the reduction of the labour movement to a mere transmission belt of socialist parties. They seized control of the Bourses du Travail, which were clusters of trade unions in the same town, from the Broussists between 1890 and 1892, and in 1894 took over the National Federation of Trade Unions from the Guesdists by securing a majority in favour of the general strike. The Federation was reorganized as the General Confederation of Labour (CGT) in 1895, and an appeal went out to anarchists to join the new movement. Anarchists had been involved in a series of individual terrorist attacks, culminating in the assassination of the President of the Republic, Sadi Carnot, in June 1894. But they were weakened by repressive government legislation and a show trial in August 1894, and had been driven out of the Marxist-dominated congress of the International at Zürich the previous year. French anarchists therefore joined the labour movement and, building on the tactic of the general strike, developed that explosive mixture of anarchism and trade unionism, anarcho-syndicalism.

In the Mediterranean countries the grip of Marxist orthodoxy was tenuous. Democratic Radicals, who opposed the governing 'Left', had a good deal of influence among the working class of Milan. When the franchise was extended in 1882, a Workers' Party was set up by Milanese printers to win back the workers. They looked for support to peasants in the Po valley and organized strikes there between 1882 and 1886, when the party was banned as criminal and its leaders arrested. Violent opposition to the dominant oligarchy was the popular tradition in Italy, and was urged once again by anarchist leaders who returned from South America in 1889. The Marxist movement was very small in Italy, based on Milan and headed after 1891 by a lawyer, Filippo Turati, who had met European Marxists in Brussels, and by his mistress, the Russian revolutionary *émigrée*, Anna Kuliscioff. They founded an Italian Socialist Party (PSI) in Genoa in 1892, defeated a takeover bid of the anarchists and forced Italian socialism down the path of parliamentary legalism. What happened in Milan and Genoa was one thing; what happened in the south was quite another. In 1893 the Sicilian peasants, faced by rising wheat prices and falling sales of wine, fruit, and sulphur since the tariff war began with France in 1887, erupted in revolt. Socialist intellectuals from Palermo and Catania tried to organize the peasants into workers' *fasci* (unions), and bring in the sulphur-miners and railwaymen. Antonia Labriola, the Neapolitan philosopher and the only Marxist thinker of stature in Italy, called the rising 'The first appearance of the proletarian or semi-proletarian mass on the Italian political scene'.[4] But Anna Kuliscioff was more realistic when she told Engels that 'the socialist party is scarcely born in Italy and it is not possible to talk of a socialist revolution in a country which is two-thirds medieval, where the peasants are in conditions analagous to France before 1789'.[5] Though in no way involved with the Sicilian *fasci*, the Socialist Party was dissolved by a wave of government repression (October 1894), and decided to join the Democratic Radical and Republican parties in a union of progressive forces to defend liberty. This paid off with the election of 12 socialist deputies in 1895, and 16 in 1897.

Even more divorced from the masses was the Spanish Socialist Workers' Party (PSOE), founded in 1879. It was a servile copy of the French Guesdist party, led by a puritanical Madrid printer, Pablo Iglesias. It was committed to class struggle in a country that had scarcely had a bourgeois revolution, and to political action in spite of the manipulation of elections by local landowners or caciques. The socialists only polled 20,000 votes in 1898, and had no deputy elected until 1910. The spontaneous revolutionism of the masses was, by contrast, fully exploited by the anarchists who in 1881 set up the Federation of Workers of the Spanish Region. Within a year it had nearly 20,000 members in 179 sections in western Andalusia alone. There was in fact a good deal of tension within the anarchist movement. In southern Spain the members were peasant communities, often hungry and unemployed, and prone to violence, whether the assassination of Civil Guards or informers by the Black Hand Gang, or a mass march on the town of Jerez by six thousand Andalusian peasants early in 1892. In Barcelona, on the other hand, the anarchists were skilled workers who were organized into trade unions and used the strike weapon to considerable effect. But the socialist party, as a Madrid party, made no headway in Barcelona, the largest industrial city in Spain. It acquired some support among the metallurgical workers of Bilbao and the miners of Asturias in the north, but the General Union of Workers (UGT), set up in 1888 to bring the organized working class over to Marxism, had to move its headquarters back from Barcelona to Madrid in 1899. The workers of Barcelona rarely bothered to vote. When they did, in

[4] Quoted by Leo Valiani and Adam Wandruszka, *Il movimento operaio e socialista in Italia e in Germania dal 1870 al 1920* (Bologna, 1978), 15.
[5] Quoted by Giorgio Candeloro, *Storia dell' Italia Moderna*, vi (Milan, 1970), 433.

the municipal election of 1901, they did so for a demagogue of the republican party, Alejandro Lerroux. Between their anarcho-syndicalist unions and their republican ballots there was little room for Marxism.

Socialism: Russia

The task of the Populists of the Land and Liberty group had been agitation among the peasant masses in order to bring about agrarian revolution and the destruction of the state. For them, the struggle for political power was irrelevant, if not evil. But the Tsarist police clamped down and Populist leaders like Plekhanov fled westwards to Geneva in 1880 where they came in contact with European conditions and the 'scientific socialism' of Marx. Plekhanov realized the importance of political liberty to organize a party and build up support by propaganda. He set up the Liberation of Labour group in 1883 which looked for its base not to the peasantry but to the industrial proletariat. Russia was backward, but Marx's laws of historical development predicted that capitalism would evolve in Russia and with it a revolutionary working class. 'We indeed know our way,' he affirmed, 'and are seated in that historical train which at full speed takes us to our goal.'[6]

There were other Populists who clung to the notion of a separate path for Russia. They argued that industrialization, undertaken on the backs of the peasantry, would destroy demand and therefore never take off. They pointed to the peasant commune as the cell of the new communist society. Surely Russia would be able to avoid belching smoke-stacks and the misery of a growing proletariat and leap over capitalism into the socialist Utopia? Vera Zasulich wrote to the aged Marx from Geneva in 1882 to obtain confirmation for this view, and Marx conceded that if Russia could be insulated from market forces it might be possible. But the Russian Marxists, who wanted to throw off backwardness and were mesmerized by European capitalism, democracy, and culture, were already looking for signs of class differentiation in Russia that would herald the arrival of capitalism.

Marxist intellectuals, fleeing repressive regimes, tended to congregate in Switzerland. In 1893 Rosa Luxemburg and her lover Leo Jogiches set up the Social Democratic party of the Kingdom of Poland and Lithuania in Zürich. This meant that they were entirely isolated from the working-class movements in their own countries, and prone to misjudge them. Yet there were strategic points in Russia and Russian Poland where the proletariat was concentrated and volatile, even if it was only a small proportion of the total population, and was very susceptible to agitation. In 1892 there was a strike in the Polish textile town of Lódz. In 1894 there was a wave of strikes among textile and clothing workers in the Jewish Pale, from Vilna, Bialystok, and Brest-Litovsk to Minsk and Vitebsk. These were stimulated by Jewish intellectuals

---

[6] Quoted by Arthur P. Mendel, *Dilemmas of Progress in Tsarist Russia* (Cambridge, Mass., 1961), 112.

Map 7.   The Borderlands of Russia

like Arkady Kremer and Julius Martov with the help of young Jews who were shut out of secondary education by the quota system imposed in 1887–8, and who knew Yiddish, and the ways of the ghetto. In 1895 Russian social democrats including Vladimir Ulyanov (Lenin) began to agitate among workers in St Petersburg, where they set up a Union of Struggle for the Emancipation of the Working Class. They were arrested in December and January 1896 but even without them, in May 1896, a massive strike of 30,000 textile workers broke out in the city.

These events were very important for the development of Marxist strategy. In *On Agitation*, written in 1894, Kremer argued that agitators must concentrate on concrete economic needs such as wages and hours. The workers would strike, come into conflict with the authorities, and realize that it was impossible to improve their lot under existing political conditions. At that point they would become converted to political action and social democracy. This was also the view of the clandestine *Workers' Thought* paper put out by the St Petersburg Union of Struggle, without Lenin, from the end of 1897. In 1899 *Workers' Thought* published an article by Bernstein which argued that 'every kopek increase in wages, every hour less in the working day, brings us nearer to the socialist future.'[7]

These ideas were extremely worrying for the Marxist exiles in Switzerland. Plekhanov was at that time taking Bernstein to task in the columns of *Die Neue Zeit* for undermining faith in the inevitable rise and collapse of capitalism, which offered the only hope for backward Russia. This heresy was now merging with the view that the Russian working class knew its own way, and had no need for guidance from intellectuals abroad. The nettle was grasped by Lenin, who was allowed to leave Siberia in 1900 and settled in Stuttgart, where he brought out the first number of *Iskra* (*The Spark*). Workers, left to themselves, he said, were capable only of a trade-union consciousness. 'The labour movement, separated from social democracy, inevitably becomes bourgeois.'[8] The intellectuals were back in business, for without a revolutionary theory there could be no revolutionary movement. That theory must be kept inviolate, like the Holy Grail, by an élite of professional revolutionaries who formed the party, and would be injected as necessary into the labour movement which remained separate from the party and over which the party exercised hegemony.

Much of the old conspiratorial tradition echoed in Lenin, and to some extent he was continuing the work of his brother, executed in 1887 as one of five members of the Peoples' Will group plotting to assassinate Alexander III. But after his own imprisonment Lenin realized the need to establish political democracy in Russia if socialist agitation were to be successful. The manifesto

    [7]   Quoted by Alan K. Wildman, *The Making of a Workers' Revolution* (Chicago, 1967), 141.
    [8]   Quoted by Richard Pipes, 'The Origins of Bolshevism: the intellectual evolution of young Lenin', in Pipes (ed.), *Revolutionary Russia* (Cambridge, Mass., 1968), 49.

of the Russian Social-Democratic Labour party (RSDLP), which was penned by his contemporary Peter Struve after the party was formed at Minsk in March 1898, noted that Russia had escaped the 'life-giving hurricane of the 1848 revolution' that had conferred freedom of speech, writing, organization and assembly on Europe. The Russian working class had to conquer these liberties as a pre-condition of the struggle 'for its final liberation, against private property, for socialism'.[9]

The struggle for political democracy ushered in the possibility of collaborating with other classes in Russia. Unfortunately, Struve's manifesto asserted that 'the farther east one goes in Europe, the weaker, meaner and more cowardly in the political sense becomes the bourgeoisie, and the greater the cultural and political tasks which fall to the lot of the proletariat.' The historical task of the proletariat was not only to carry out the socialist revolution but also, before that, to push the fearful bourgeoisie towards undertaking its own, democratic revolution. Struve, who saw working-class agitation decline in Russia after 1900 and, as an accomplished economist, was impressed by Bernstein's views on the improving condition of the working class and the attenuation of class struggle, began to move closer to opposition groups in the *zemstvos* and their administrative organs. In 1901 he launched a paper called *Liberation* around which all supporters of a constituent assembly in Russia might gather. Lenin was not impressed by Struve's analysis. For him, 'The coarse, haggling nature of the common liberal lay hidden beneath the dapper, cultured exterior of this latest "critic".'[10]

Roman Catholicism

Although 1870 was a setback for the universal Catholic Church, the political power of the Catholic Church was still a force to be reckoned with in Europe. It had lost from the unification of nations—and was a bad loser and did not make light of its opposition to many of the new regimes. Liberal states which challenged traditional élites and traditional beliefs were cold-shouldered by the Catholic Church, and the French Republic was anathema. In turn, liberal and radical parties redoubled their efforts to destroy the political influence of the Catholic Church. Radicals were more uncompromising than their liberal allies, who might be content with some form of accommodation with the Church and Catholic parties. This was particularly the case when the threat of socialism became manifest. Liberals then realized that they had a common interest with many Catholics: the defence of private property. Sometimes a consensus of ruling groups was achieved, and anticlerical strife abated. On other occasions Catholic hostility to the regime was too strong to be overcome.

In Belgium, Roman Catholic politicians came to power in the summer of 1870. The liberal opposition was divided on the question of suffrage reform

---

[9] Quoted by E. H. Carr, *The Bolshevik Revolution, 1917–1923* (London, 1950), i, 3.
[10] Quoted by Galai, *The Liberation Movement in Russia*, 103.

between Progressists, who wanted it, and Doctrinaires, who did not. They could, however, agree on an anticlerical programme for the elections of 1878, which they won, and abolished the use of the catechism in municipal schools the following year. Unfortunately the vexed question of electoral reform returned to split the liberals, and Catholics returned to power in the elections of 1884. When universal suffrage was demanded by the socialists after 1886, the reaction was rather different. Liberals and Catholics united in defence of the constitution.

Monarchy was not an issue in Belgium whereas in France a republic had been established and the republicans felt anxious about its survival. The experience of 1848 showed that to establish universal suffrage without educating the new electors in civic virtue only played into the hands of reaction, whether royalist or Bonapartist. For the republicans who took power in 1877–9, the political influence of the Catholic Church was pernicious. It seemed still to be encrusted with the privilege, feudalism, and intolerance of the *ancien régime*, and it had been the spiritual arm both of the authoritarian Empire and of the monarchy that had almost been restored in 1873. To reduce that influence the republicans expelled the Jesuits in 1880 and eliminated the teaching of catechism from municipal schools in 1882.

Among the republicans there was disagreement between moderates and radicals. The Opportunists or moderates declared before the general elections of 1885 that they had conquered the support of rural France, but were concerned that harsh anticlerical measures would alienate republicans who were also practising Catholics and drive them into the arms of the Right. The radicals, on the other hand, savoured the rhetoric of anticlericalism against Vaticanism, monasticism, and the *Syllabus of Errors*, and demanded the expulsion of teaching congregations from all publicly supported schools together with the separation of Church and state. Opposition to the Republic's anticlerical measures indeed strengthened the Right in the elections of 1885, and Opportunists were able to secure a majority, ironically, only with the support of the radicals. The radicals then demanded cabinet posts and forced through a law in 1886 expelling teaching congregations from all publicly supported schools.

The intensification of social conflict and the rise of socialism worried Catholics as much as it did Opportunist republicans. Pope Leo XIII urged French Catholics in 1892 to accept the Republic as the existing form of government and to devote themselves to the main task of re-Christianizing society. The Pope's quarrel with the Italian state which had usurped his position in Rome made it all the more necessary to reach a settlement with the French Government. This proposal of a *Ralliement* found favour with many Opportunist republicans, and there was some co-operation between Catholics and Opportunists in the elections of 1893. Unfortunately there were some Catholic clergy and laity, especially in traditional areas of counter-revolution such as the west

and the Midi, who refused to abandon their royalist principles. The accommodation of the élites therefore left much to be desired. Moreover, as the
Catholic Church made clear its support for the rich against social revolution,
so the working class became more virulent in its anticlericalism.

As a republic, France was unique among European great powers. In Spain,
the monarchy was restored in 1875 and the Catholic Church sought its
revenge. Cánovas del Castillo, the architect of the restoration and leader of
the Liberal-Conservative party, refused to give it everything it wanted. The
constitution ended total Catholic uniformity, tolerating the practice of other
religions in private at least. The bishops condemned this 'national apostasy'
and Carlism took up the defence of the true faith, even though Leo XIII
pressed Spanish Catholics in 1882 to accept the constitutional monarchy. On
the other hand, the Church assumed control of all levels of state education,
and the lectures of professors at the Central University of Madrid were cen-
sored, to stop French ideas seeping into Spain.

Such policies alienated the Liberals under Sagasta, who was able to use the
defence of free thought and state control of education as a bridge to the republican movement and a stick with which to beat the government. As a result,
Sagasta was invited to form a Liberal ministry which lasted from 1885 to 1890.
Many of the privileges of private Catholic schools were now removed. But, as
in France, the upsurge of revolutionary movements after 1890 made the liberals less fanatical about their anticlericalism. It was a question of the ruling oligarchy pulling together. Thus Sagasta's Liberal ministry of 1892–5 did not
question the compulsory teaching of religion in primary schools and even
agreed to the founding of chairs of religion and ethics in state secondary
schools.

In Italy, anticlericalism was built into a regime which had united the country in 1870 at the expense of the Papal States. The Papacy made it clear that
Catholics should neither vote nor stand in parliamentary elections. The Left
removed the catechism from the compulsory syllabus of municipal primary
schools in 1877, but it had to take into account the profound Catholicism of
the population and repeatedly made clear that the catechism had not actually
been abolished in schools. Even so, the Temporal Power of the Papacy was
always a stumbling-block in the path of *rapprochement*. When a 'government
of national unity' was formed under Francesco Crispi in 1887, negotiations
began with the Vatican. But Crispi was forced to listen to the radicals in his
coalition, who were resolutely anti-Austrian and anticlerical, and the talks
were called off. The growth of social unrest nevertheless altered the balance
of forces in Italy, as in France and Spain. Catholics were not prohibited from
voting in provincial and municipal elections, which were deemed 'administrative' rather than 'political'. In 1895 a pact was therefore concluded in
Milan between 'clerico-moderates' and liberals to defeat the democrats and
socialists in the municipal elections. It was an attempt to reconstitute the

political unity of the bourgeoisie against the forces of revolution but the Papacy's hostility to the Italian state made an Italian *Ralliement* unthinkable.

German unification had similarly been carried out at the expense of Roman Catholics, who had been denounced by Bismarck as separatist and ultramontane. His alliance with the liberals in the 1870s was based on the anticlerical policies of the *Kulturkampf*. But by 1878–9 the threat from socialism had driven him to obtain the anti-socialist law from the Reichstag and his protectionist policies had broken the marriage with liberalism. Bismarck became anxious to bring the Catholic Centre party into his governing coalition.

Unfortunately, the Centre party did not represent the German establishment but the 'losers' from unification: south Germany against Prussia, rural Germany against the *Industriestaat*, the Catholic middle class that was discriminated against in the universities, civil service, and professions, and the Polish miners of the Ruhr. In his bid to bring over the Centre party Bismarck opened negotiations in 1879 with the Vatican and in 1886 with the Catholic episcopate. But the Centre party wanted only the abolition of state controls over the Catholic Church, not greater political power for the Church in the state. It was not a tool of the Vatican and the Catholic bishops, and it did not agree to become part of the Bismarckian system, in alliance with the Protestant Conservative party, in return for an inadequate modification of the state controls imposed on the Church. In 1887 Bismarck abrogated the anticlerical May Laws of 1873, but the Centre party did not compromise itself by voting the seven-year military appropriations law. In 1893 the Silesian nobles who represented the right-wing of the party were keen to vote another army bill in order to become part of the German establishment. But they were defeated by the Rhinelanders and south Germans who saw the party as the vehicle of another Germany and wanted to maintain its freedom of manœuvre. The *Kulturkampf* was ended, but the coalition of élites in Germany was incomplete. Moreover, the presence of large Polish minorities in the eastern provinces of Prussia highlighted the way in which Roman Catholicism and unfulfilled nationalism could combine to menace the unity of nation-states.

National Minorities

One powerful obstacle to national integration was the existence of national minorities within states. For most European states were not nation-states in any clear sense, but multinational states dominated by one nationality in particular. While the English, French, Spanish, Germans, Austrians, Magyars, and Russians had achieved statehood and were keen to impose their national language and ideology on all subjects or citizens, intellectuals or sub-élites were emerging at the end of the nineteenth century among peoples who had long been mainly of peasant stock, to define their peoples as nations and make demands for them. They struggled with the dominant nationality over landownership and land-tenure, over churches and schools that they wanted in their own religion and their own language, over representation and office-holding. The government of the multinational state was caught on the horns of a dilemma. If it made no concessions, it risked insurrection by inferior nationalities. If it did make concessions, it risked confrontation with the dominant nationality and undermining national integration. Things were made more complicated still by the division of some national minorities, such as the Poles, between a number of states, which converted a national problem into an international one.

The Irish nationalist movement was a land-war against an alien landlord class, and a demand for a national parliament in Dublin instead of, or in addition to, the imperial Parliament at Westminster. After 1883 the Catholic clergy and hierarchy in Ireland were won over to the movement. But the concession of Home Rule and land reform proposed by Gladstone in 1886 outraged both the English aristocracy, many of whom were Irish landlords, and the loyalist Protestant majority in Ulster. The Conservative party was prepared to support them, in the name of the integrity of the Empire, and triumphed in the elections of 1886. The conversion of Gladstone to Home Rule, meanwhile, prompted Scottish Liberals to form a Scottish Home Rule Association in pursuit of 'Home Rule All Round'. Welsh nationalism was about neither land nor Home Rule but was founded on the Nonconformist campaign to disestablish the Anglican Church, which was maintained by the payment of tithes. The Welsh voted Liberal and depended on a Liberal government to deliver the goods. However the unreasonableness of their demands served to undermine the Liberal ministry of 1892–5.

In Spain nationalist movements in Catalonia and the Basque provinces were based on the economic weight of the periphery: textiles in the first, steel and shipbuilding in the second. In the 1870s their opposition to Castilian centralization was expressed as Carlism in the Basque country and as federalism in Catalonia. But these movements were defeated by the restoration, and in Catalonia the opposition looked for a broader base among landowners, industrialists, and peasants. Revolution was forsaken. The separate identity of Catalonia was defined in terms of its language, culture, and history, and a programme of 1892 demanded Home Rule: a Catalan parliament, Catalan as the official language, and the reservation of all official posts to Catalans. The Basques took up the cry, and a Basque Nationalist party was set up in 1895 to defend the *fueros*, language, and Catholic religion of the Basque race against the anticlerical politicians in Madrid.

Breton nationalism was also a device to defend the religion of a very Catholic province against anticlerical ministers in Paris. The Breton Regionalist Union that was founded in 1898 also wanted to restore the Breton language, which had traditionally cocooned the Breton faith but was now spoken only in the west of the peninsula. But Brittany was a poor province, dominated by priests and nobles, and any Breton who wanted to get on learned French and left. The pattern in Belgian Flanders was similar. The use of both French and Flemish in the courts, administration, and secondary education was conceded by the government between 1873 and 1883, but after the extension of the franchise in 1893 a popular Flemish nationalist movement took off. A key demand was for a Flemish university in Ghent, but the Flemish middle class learned French to further its ambitions, and gave no support to a proposal that could only trap it in a position of inferiority.

The question of Alsace-Lorraine was rather different. It had been annexed to Germany by force and placed under German military–bureaucratic rule. It was allowed fifteen seats in the Reichstag in 1874, all of which were won by opponents of the annexation. The education system was Germanized. Most of the population spoke German or a German dialect, but the Catholic clergy protested against the imposition of German in the schools in the 1870s as they had against the imposition of French by Napoleon III in the 1860s: it was a question of local autonomy. As a result Bismarck extended the *Kulturkampf* to Alsace-Lorraine. In 1887, when war with France seemed likely, political life was all but blacked out in the province.

The tension between Germany and Russia in 1887 made more precarious the position of minorities further east. The German nobility in the Baltic provinces of Courland, Livonia, and Estonia had traditionally been loyal servants of the Tsar. But now the government in St Petersburg undertook the Russification of education, administration, and justice in the provinces, and built Orthodox cathedrals to convert the population from Lutheranism. German nobles returned to Germany and fomented anti-Russian feeling in university and military circles. The undermining of the German nobility in turn stimulated the national consciousness of the largely peasant Latvians (in Livonia and Courland) and Estonians, who accepted Orthodoxy but not Russification. At the same time Bismarck tried to uproot the Polish minority in the eastern provinces of Prussia lest a Polish state that emerged from a Russo-German war tried to claim them. Poles of Russian or Austrian origin were forcibly expelled after 1883, German teachers were introduced into Polish schools and in 1886 a Prussian Colonization Commission was set up at Posen to buy out Polish landowners and parcel out their estates among German colonists. Chancellor Caprivi was obliged to make concessions to the Polish minority in order to get his army bill through the Reichstag, but this only provoked a backlash among German nationalists, who founded a German Society for the Eastern Marches in 1894. It had the support of Prussian ministers like Miquel who declared in 1897 that 'we must strengthen national sentiment by treating the Poles harshly'.[11]

Only Poles of the Austrian province of Galicia were allowed any autonomy. In the Russian government, it was debated in 1898–9 whether *zemstvos*

---

[11] Quoted by William W. Hagen, *Germans, Poles and Jews: The Nationality Conflict in the Polish East, 1772–1914* (Chicago, 1980), 176.

might be conceded in the 'western borderlands' of Poland–Lithuania. Sergei Witte scotched the idea, on the grounds that Polish landowners, rather than Lithuanian, White Russian, or Ukrainian peasants would dominate them. This did not hamper the development of Polish nationalism, far from it. On the one hand, the insurrectionary tradition of the Polish nobility in search of the historic pre-Partition frontiers was revived by Jozef Pilsudski, a young noble of Lithuanian descent who was exiled to Siberia for five years in 1887 and founded the Polish Socialist Party (PPS) in Paris in 1892. On the other the National Democratic Party of Roman Dmowski, a graduate of Moscow University, was founded in Austrian Galicia in 1897. Whereas Pilsudski saw Russia as the main obstacle to the resurrection of the Polish-Lithuanian Commonwealth, Dmowski wanted to build a Poland including the Polish provinces of Germany and saw Germany as the main enemy. Whereas Pilsudski's Poland was historical, Dmowski's was ethnic. He considered the Polish people the bedrock of nationality and saw the development of a national consciousness among Lithuanians, Ukrainians, and Jews as a threat to the consolidation of the Polish nation.

It was a point of some debate whether the Jews, who were scattered in a diaspora across Europe from Moscow to Paris, were a nation rather than a religious group. Moreover, their instinct until now had been to profess loyalty to the state in which they lived and to assimilate with the dominant nationality in order to gain emancipation. The pogroms in the southern Pale of Russia, in which Ukrainians were particularly active, convinced many Jews that assimilation was now impossible and that they had no choice but to migrate. Most headed for the European cities and ports, but a group of students at Kharkov began to organize a migration to Palestine. Leon Pinsker, a Jewish doctor educated in Germany, who spoke Russian, and had a practice in Odessa, argued that anti-Semitism was inescapable and that the Jews must become a people again, with one territory instead of the diaspora, and that in Palestine. Hibbat Zion was founded at his house in 1883 to promote settlement in Palestine, and obtained financial support from Baron Edmond James de Rothschild. The early Zionists had little support among the Jews of western Europe, who survived by assimilation, were embarrassed by the arrival of the orthodox, Yiddish-speaking Jews of eastern Europe, and believed that a Jewish state in Palestine would undermine their claim to civil rights in France, Germany, or Austria. The Universal Israelite Alliance which was based in Paris encouraged the eastern Jews to go to the United States of America and not to Palestine. Another option was represented by Joseph Bloch, a Galician-born rabbi who edited the *Österreichische Wochenschrift* in Vienna from 1884, was elected to the Austrian parliament, and in 1886 set up the Austrian Israelite Union. He argued that the Jews should stay and fight anti-Semitism, developing their ethnic Jewish consciousness, speaking German, Polish, or Czech, but professing loyalty to the Austrian state above all, as 'the only Austrians in Austria', as the guarantee of their rights. But Theodor Herzl, a cultivated Viennese and Parisian correspondent of the *Neue Freie Presse*, realized that anti-Semitism would be provoked not only by Jews standing out as a foreign body but also by their assimilating, competing, and becoming successful. In 1896 he published his *Jewish State* in favour of a Jewish Palestine. Having failed to win over the Kaiser, Lord Salisbury, or the Sultan to his scheme, he organized a Zionist congress in Basle to gain Jewish support for the Palestine plan. But the Jews who attended were educated, liberal, and middle-class, even if mostly from eastern Europe. The Yiddish-speaking, orthodox Jewish workers of Vilna and the northern Pale who went on strike, usually against Jewish employers, for better pay and conditions, wanted something more than a vision of the Promised Land. Encouraged by local Jewish intellectuals like Arkady Kremer, they founded the social-democratic Jewish Bund in 1897. It was Jewish, because they were isolated in the ghettoes and suffered as Jews as well as workers. But it was socialist too, affiliated to the Russian Social-Democratic Labour party that was organized at Minsk in 1898, and had little in common with middle-class Zionism.

The deterioration of relations between Austria and Russia in the Balkans heightened Austrian fears of Slav nationalism. In Bohemia the Old Czechs, of landowning and business stock, who supported Taaffe, were challenged by the Young Czechs—lawyers and journalists with the support of the commercial middle class and even the peasantry—who demanded Czech as the state language in Bohemia and helped to overthrow Taaffe in 1893. In 1897 Count Badeni, who needed Czech support to push the ten-yearly Austro-Hungarian tariff through the Reichsrat, agreed to make language concessions to the Czechs in Bohemia that would mean dismissal for hundreds of German officials unless they learned Czech. Georg von Schönerer, darling of the German nationalists, unleashed a campaign of such ferocity inside and outside the Reichsrat that Badeni was forced to resign. Schönerer was convinced that the multinational Habsburg Empire was doomed. The German nation must cut its losses and request inclusion into the German Reich, even if that meant converting to Protestantism. But when the Badeni decrees were withdrawn in 1899 the Czech leader Thomas Masaryk wrote: 'Palacký said that we were here before Austria, and that we shall be here after Austria has gone. But whereas for Palacký that was only a phrase, I want that to become a fact.'[12] Given the hostility of the Bohemian Germans, Masaryk based his Czech nationalism not (like Palacký) on Bohemian state-rights, but on the ethnic solidarity of the Czechs of Bohemia, Moravia, and Silesia.

The Austrian Monarchy found it difficult to abandon the German ruling class. Vienna supported the claims of Germans against Italians in Trentino

---

[12] Quoted by Bruce M. Garver, *The Young Czech Party, 1874–1901* (Yale, 1978), 264.

and Trieste, and even the claims of loyal Catholic Slovenes in Trieste and Istria against Italians, although that provoked a resurgence of Italian nationalism which threatened the Triple Alliance. The Magyars were more fully committed still to the suppression of any rival national claims in the Hungarian Union. Count Khuen-Hédervary, who was appointed Ban of Croatia in 1883, maintained his ascendancy by expelling dissident Croat deputies from the Sabor and abolishing juries in press trials. Fortunately the Croat opposition was at daggers drawn with the Serbs, and the Serbs within the Monarchy were kept on a leash until 1903 by good relations between Vienna and the Obrenović dynasty in Belgrade. A Romanian National party petitioned the Emperor in 1892 to restore autonomy to Transylvania, and it enjoyed much support in the Kingdom of Romania. For that reason the entire committee of the party was tried before Magyar judges for 'incitement against the Magyar nationality', and imprisoned. It remained to see how long peace would endure on the Danube and in the Balkans.

Feminism

The modern feminist movement can be dated to the end of the nineteenth century. It is not that, until then, women remained invisible in the home. Women were a mainstay of agriculture, the labour force of the consumer goods industries such as textiles, clothing, luxury goods, and foodstuffs, often in sweatshops or at home, so that they could continue work after marriage and childbearing, and they provided the armies of domestic labour. Prostitutes were often recruited from seamstresses and servants who had been impregnated by their employers and then dismissed. But women were rarely educated above the elementary level, were excluded from Latin-based secondary schooling and access to universities, and were therefore unable to qualify for the professions or bureaucracy. Women who had taken a prominent part in running family businesses at the beginning of the century were excluded after 1850, as the bourgeoisie affirmed its ideal of separate spheres: for men the marketplace and public life; for women the home, raising and educating the children, and supervising the servants.

At best, women found a semi-public role, exercising a 'spiritual motherhood' in society at large, seeking to alleviate the social evils inflicted by their capitalist menfolk. In Catholic countries, unmarried women went into religious congregations, devoted to education and nursing: there were 135,000 nuns in France in 1878. In Protestant England, there were 25,000 governesses at any one time. Married women of the middle classes, often under the patronage of upper-class ladies, busied themselves with charitable works, visiting hospitals, prisons, poor houses, and asylums, founding crèches and nurseries, visiting working-class mothers in their own homes. Public life was barred to them. Despite, or because of, Jeannine Deroin's *Politique des femmes* and Louise Otto's *Frauen-Zeitung* in 1848–9, women were banned from attending political meetings or joining political organizations after 1850 in France, Germany, and Austria. In addition, under the civil law, they were deprived of essential rights in order to enthrone the patriarchal family. The married woman was an eternal minor. Napoleon's Civil Code of 1804 summed up the position of married women thus: 'A husband owes protection to his wife, a wife owes obedience to her husband.' She lost control of her inherited wealth and earnings, and she had few legal rights over her children. Divorce was prohibited in most countries, adultery by women was heavily punished but scarcely sanctioned when committed by men, and abortion was criminalized in Britain in 1803, in France and Belgium in 1810, and in many other countries subsequently.

The organization of women to demand fuller rights developed slowly. The demand for suffrage was not made with any force until the turn of the century. Most middle-class women took the view that political rights had to be earned, not demanded as of right, by demonstrating their capacity as educated, employed, and propertied women, and that therefore the demand for civil rights to open up these areas should come first. Even these rights women tended to demand not for themselves, but so that they could fulfil their duties to society more effectively and make the world in which they lived more civilized.

The first public movement led by women was the campaign against the regulation of prostitution. From the First Empire in France, and from the 1840s in Russia and the 1860s in Britain, any woman suspected of being a prostitute was liable to arrest, registration with the authorities, and compulsory vaginal examination to check for venereal disease. Brothels were tolerated by the law, but had to be licensed by the state. Public order, decency, and hygiene were the overriding concerns. The Contagious Diseases Acts in Britain provoked a movement of revulsion led by Josephine Butler. In 1875 she founded the British, Continental and General Federation for the Abolition of the State Regulation of Vice. She argued that the regulation of prostitution sanctioned vice and criminalized women, while leaving men, who were just as responsible for spreading disease, scot free. The only way to stop prostitution and ensure sexual justice, she asserted, was for men to refrain from sex outside marriage. Her movement had the regulation system lifted in Britain in 1883, and was copied by Anita Augspurg of the Frauenwohl Association in Germany, but the French solution to the problem was to tighten up state regulation, and the question was not debated in Russia till 1910. Butler then moved on to trying to stamp out the 'white slave trade' of child prostitution, and organized an international conference on the subject in 1899. This was not attended by Italy or Spain, and a French bill on trafficking failed, but a Russian Society for the Protection of Women, founded in 1900 by the cream of St Peterburg society, had the age of brothel girls raised to 21 in 1909.

A second line of campaign centred on securing the rights of women to gain a good education, pursue professional careers, secure control of their earnings, and be able to divorce their husbands. Barbara Leigh Bodichon and her group of women at Langdon Place, London, launched the *English Woman's Journal* in 1858, campaigned for married women's property rights, which were secured by Act of Parliament in 1870, set up the National Society for Promoting the Education of Women (1859), and helped to found Girton College, Cambridge, in 1869. Louise Otto, now Louise Otto-Peters, founded a General German Women's Association at Leipzig in 1865 and published a journal, *Neue Bahnen*, in which she argued that since women could not base their claim to rights on military service, they must base it on education, employment, and service to the community. 'Through the education of the female sex and through the spread of women's employment', she wrote in 1872, 'we will prepare the foundation for the structure, of which women's suffrage will be the capstone.'[13] In France, restrictions on public associations under the Second Empire, then the priority given by liberal women to establishing the Republic, delayed the women's rights movement, but a journalist, Léon Richer, and a woman of independent means, Maria Deraismes, set up a Society for the Amelioration of the Condition of Women in 1875, which was relaunched as the League for Women's Rights in 1882. They campaigned for better women's education, the right of women freely to dispose of their income, and the right to divorce. A divorce law was passed in 1884, but a law on women's property had to wait until 1907. Meanwhile, the marginalization of the question of suffrage was illustrated by their row with the young Hubertine Auclert. Auclert was keen to have the vote discussed at an International Women's Rights Congress in 1878, which was sponsored by Richer and Deraismes, but Richer replied with the familiar anticlerical argument that women were under the thumb of nuns and priests and would only vote to overthrow the Republic. Auclert launched her own newspaper, *La Citoyenne*, dedicated to the cause of women's suffrage, before marrying and emigrating to Algeria.

In 1888 an International Council of Women was founded in Washington to co-ordinate moderate women's organizations world-wide. These included the League of German Womens' Associations (BDF), founded in 1894, and the National Council of French Women (CNFF), dominated by Protestant and Jewish ladies, established in 1901. These organizations were still in the first instance philanthropic, although increasingly they campaigned for civil rights. In Germany, civil law for the whole Reich was only slowly being unified, and when its draft proposals were released in 1896, it appeared that women's rights were to be circumscribed instead of enlarged. The BDF, prompted by activists like Auspurg, launched a protest movement and collected a petition of 25,000 signatures.

Some progress was made in these traditional areas. The university of

---

[13] Ann Taylor Allen, *Feminism and Motherhood in Germany, 1800–1914* (New Brunswick, 1991), 109.

Zürich was opened to women in 1865, and was especially popular with Russian women, who did not have access to Russian universities until 1905. The university of London was opened to women in 1878, Scottish universities followed *en masse* in 1889, Heidelberg was opened in 1901, and German universities as a whole followed in 1908. Gradually women entered first the medical, then the legal professions. Female suffrage, however, still eluded them. A female suffrage amendment to the British Reform Act in 1867 was voted down, leading John Stuart Mill, inspired by his wife Harriet Taylor, to leave Parliament and write *On the Subjection of Women* (1869). In some northern countries, women were allowed the vote in local elections— Scotland in 1881, Iceland in 1882, Denmark in 1883, Norway in 1901. In Britain, women were eligible for the school boards of 1870 and two women were elected to the London County Council in 1889. However, the franchise act of 1884 gave votes to farm labourers, not to women. Local suffrage and local eligibility were seen as an extension of women's role in the local community, but breaking into national suffrage was a different matter.

In 1902 an International Women's Suffrage Alliance broke away from the ICW to co-ordinate the struggle for women's suffrage. Movements affiliated to it included Millicent Garrett Fawcett's National Union of Women's Suffrage Societies (NUWSS), set up in 1897, Anita Augspurg's German Union for Women's Suffrage (1902), and the French Union for Women's Suffrage (1909) of Jeanne Schmal, who had just seen through the law on married womens' property. The strategy of these movements was to use legal methods, and to put pressure on established parties and governments. But male-dominated parties and parliaments were reluctant to concede votes for women—the exceptions being Finland in 1906, during its insurrection against Russia, and Norway in 1907, after it won its independence from Sweden. The question then arose as to whether women should resort to direct action. A demonstration organized by the NUWSS in Hyde Park on 21 June gathered a crowd of 500,000, but to no effect. A bill to give women the vote in local elections was introduced into the French parliament in 1906, but was promptly lost. Hubertine Auclert, returning to active campaigning, and a young psychiatric doctor, Madeleine Pelletier, who had been on the Hyde Park demonstration, overturned ballot boxes in a Paris town hall during the municipal elections of 1908. In 1908 women were finally allowed to participate in political life in Germany. The German Suffrage Union demonstrated in Berlin in 1910 for a propertied women's franchise, and the SPD, prompted by the Saxon socialist Clara Zetkin, organized a Proletarian Women's Day in 1911 in support of both women's suffrage and universal manhood suffrage in those states, like Prussia and Saxony, that did not have it. Meanwhile, the persistent wrecking of suffrage bills by the Liberal government drove Emmeline Pankhurst's Women's Social and Political Union in 1912 to attacks on golf courses, letter boxes, and 10 Downing Street.

Four problems faced the movements for women's rights. First, they remained essentially bourgeois movements which failed to build a mass base. The former actress and socialite, Marguerite Durand, who launched *La Fronde* in 1897 to promote women into the professions and unionize women workers, clashed with the print union, which refused to print her paper at night. The BDF excluded associations of women workers on the grounds that they were political, and the women attending French Feminist Congresses in 1900 and 1908 refused to give their maids the day off. The Zürich-educated Russian socialist Alexandre Kollontai walked out of the first All-Russian Women's Congress in 1908 and wrote that 'between the emancipated women of the intelligentsia and the toiling women with calloused hands, there was such an unbridgeable gulf, that there could be no question of any point of agreement between them'.[14]

Second, in order to secure those rights, womens' movements had to attach themselves to existing political parties, either liberal, or socialist, or conservative, and convert them to their cause. Liberal parties were the most obvious, because they were traditionally committed to the idea of a public sphere underpinned by civil rights, and believed in granting political rights to those who met certain property and educational qualifications. But they were very reluctant to deliver votes for women, mainly for the pragmatic reason that they might benefit the opposition. British suffragists and suffragettes discovered that renewed though it was, the Liberal party that returned to office in 1906 in no sense had votes for women on the agenda. Anna Milyukova of the All-Russian Union for Women's Equality, founded in 1905, clashed over the vote with her husband, Paul Milyukov, at the opening meeting of the Kadet party in October 1905, the latter fearing what Russian peasant women would do with their ballots. The French Radicals were an immovable obstacle to female suffrage, the Prime Minister, Georges Clemenceau, stating in 1907 that 'if the right to vote were given to women tomorrow, France would all of a sudden jump back into the Middle Ages'.[15]

Some feminists looked to socialist parties, which tended to oppose discriminatory legislation because they suffered from it themselves. But Marxists also took the view that feminist concerns with higher education and married women's property rights were essentially bourgeois concerns, that proletarian women had to be emancipated as proletarians before they were emancipated as women, and that feminist movements threatened to distract working-class women from the primacy of socialist goals. In a word, the class struggle came first. The crop-haired Madeleine Pelletier had to work hard to extract commitment to women's rights from the French Socialist Party (SFIO) in 1906, and then, attempting to build a bourgeois feminist-socialist

[14] Richard Stites, *The Women's Liberation Movement in Russia* (Princeton, 1978), 228.
[15] Steven C. Hause and Anne R. Kenney, *Women's Suffrage and Social Politics in the French Third Republic* (Princeton, 1984), 99.

front at the Stuttgart Congress of the Socialist International in 1907, was lambasted by Clara Zetkin, defending hard-line socialist values in a flowery hat. Lastly, while feminism and conservatism were in some sense mutually exclusive, conservatives also realized that to give women the vote might boost their own fortunes. The first Reichstag deputy to support female suffrage, in 1902, was Wilhelm von Kardorff of the Free Conservatives. However, the order that women propped up by voting conservative would not necessarily be that most ready to deliver the rights they craved.

This leads on to a third point, that the feminist model was not always the most attractive to women. The model of wife and mother was far more powerful, and endorsed in different ways by Churches, bourgeois morality, and socialist and trade-union thinking alike. Many socialists and trade unionists believed that women were better off in the home than undercutting men's wages at work. In Germany, women accounted for under 9 per cent of the socialist trade union membership in 1913, and when, in the same year, the Lyons printer Emma Couriau asked to join the printworkers' union, she was refused, and her husband expelled from the union too. French suffragists tended to think the antics of British suffragettes ridiculous, and were certainly not prepared to risk prison sentences. Campaigns in favour of sexual liberation through contraception and the right to abortion, led in France by the anarchist Paul Robin after 1896 and by Madeleine Pelletier after 1910, were also roundly condemned, both by conservatives like Jacques Bertillon of the National Alliance to Increase the French Population, who argued that it was the duty of women to breed to provide recruits for national armies, and by socialists who argued that it was the duty of women to breed to provide recruits for the armies of the proletarian revolution. Marie Stritt was forced to resign the presidency of the BDF in 1908 when she demanded the deletion of the article of the Civil Code that prohibited abortion. Women were as likely to be found in religious and patriotic movements as they were in feminist organizations. In 1912 the BDF was joined by the German-Evangelical Women's League, which was opposed to female suffrage and was affiliated to the League of Patriotic Women's Societies, founded in 1871. This included such movements as the Naval Association of German Women, an auxiliary of the Navy League, set up in 1905, and the Women's Association of the German Colonial Society, founded in 1908, which boasted 18,000 members by 1914.

Fourth, the progress of feminist movements contributed to a widespread crisis of masculine identity at the end of the nineteenth century. The bourgeois order had been based on a clear distinction of male and female roles and identities, which were now being thrown into confusion. Men started to denounce the 'mannishness' of women and became obsessed by images of castrating women, the theme of so much Symbolist art.[16] At the same time

---

[16] See below, pp. 381–2, 386.

men started to question the whole issue of schoolboy friendships and male comradeship and to worry about homosexuality, a term coined in the 1890s. Oscar Wilde, brought to trial in 1895 for gross indecency under the Criminal Law Amendment Act of 1885, failed to convince the jury by comparing his friendship with the young Lord Alfred Douglas to that between David and Jonathan. Strategies were sought to reassert traditional gender stereotypes in reassuring ways. The cult of the big-game hunter was extraordinarily seductive at the turn of the century. There was a revival of duelling, not only in Germany but also in France where duels ran at 200 a year between 1875 and 1900 and fencing academies were adorned by such mottos as 'Honour to Arms. Respect for Ladies'. Finally, militarism was developed as an antidote to feminism just as much as it was designed to fight socialism. In 1912 General August Keim founded not only the German Army League but also the German League to Combat Women's Emancipation, dedicated to returning women to the home.

THE RACE FOR EMPIRE

Colonialism

For Great Britain in 1880 Empire meant first and foremost 'Greater Britain', the colonies that had been settled mainly by British emigrants in Canada, South Africa, Australia, and New Zealand. Under the protectionist system, these colonies had provided reserved markets for British exports, and in return exports for those colonies to Great Britain were admitted at lower customs rates than those paid by other countries. However, the establishment of free trade by Great Britain opened her markets to the goods of all nations and in the third quarter of the nineteenth century commercial independence had to be conceded to these colonies, to raise tariffs for revenue and protection as they saw fit. At the same time the threat to Canada during the American Civil War and the cost of suppressing rebellions of Maori or South African tribesmen brought home to the government in London the need to devolve the task of colonial defence on to colonial forces; the only exception to this rule were the British troops left at the Cape, to defend the naval station. It followed from this that the colonies should be granted internal self-government under a governor appointed by the crown. New Zealand, New South Wales, South Australia, Tasmania, and Queensland became self-governing in the 1850s, while the Dominion of Canada was formed in 1867 as a federal union of Nova Scotia, New Brunswick, Ontario, and Quebec. In Canada, settlers of British and French origin could be reconciled. In South Africa, relations between the British colonists at the Cape and the Dutch colonists (Boers) who had trekked into the interior were much more strained. Great Britain had annexed Natal in 1844 but granted internal self-government to diamond-rich Cape Colony in 1872 in the hope that it would become the centre of a South African federation, which would include the Boer republics of Transvaal and the Orange Free State. The Boers required British military assistance to defeat the Zulus between 1877 and 1880, but after this the British tried to annex the Transvaal. The Transvaal Boers under their President, Paul Kruger, were prepared to defend their independence by force of arms, and achieved this by defeating the British at Majuba Hill in 1881.

In West Africa, British power was established at Sierra Leone, the Gold Coast, and Lagos (annexed 1861) in order to suppress the slave trade and promote legitimate commerce, notably that of palm oil. In East Africa, the British propped up the Sultan of Zanzibar and developed trade with India in the 1870s. No other colony could compare with India. After a mutiny by Indian troops in 1857 the administration of India passed from the East India Company to a Secretary of State in London, to whom the Governor-General and Viceroy were subordinate. A sub-continent of 250 million Indians with only a smattering of British colonists could not be considered for internal self-government. Native princes retained their autonomy under treaties with the British, but the opening of the Suez Canal in 1869 and the completion of a submarine cable to India in 1870 brought the Viceroy and his council under even tighter control by the Secretary of State and Queen Victoria became Empress of India in 1876. Unlike the white colonies, the government in India was not allowed the liberty to establish customs for protection or to raise revenue, and was rapped on the knuckles for trying to do this in 1875. Neither was defence a matter that could be devolved. Unreliable Indian units were disbanded after 1857 and replaced by British troops. In 1878 the Indian army was 200,000 strong, including 65,000 British and 135,000 Indian troops. Its importance became greater as Russian power expanded into Central Asia and as Great Britain took on commitments in the Near East and Far East. Lord Salisbury, later Disraeli's Secretary of State for India, described India in 1867 as 'an English barrack in the Oriental seas from which we may draw any number of troops without paying for them'.[1]

In 1880 France too had colonial possessions. Algeria, which it occupied in 1830, was the cornerstone of her Mediterranean and African ambitions. It was a military base comparable with India rather than a white settlement colony; indeed, France did not have much of a surplus population and the French were not keen to emigrate. Trade was an important feature of French colonialism. Ground-nut oil and palm oil were exported from Senegal, and Saigon was occupied after a war with China in 1858–60 as an entrepôt for the import of raw silk destined for Lyons. The Suez Canal was built between 1859 and 1869 largely by French enterprise, and French capital, and increased French economic interests in the Far East. However, Saigon was also a naval base and France was in pursuit of power in South-East Asia as well as profit. Cochin-China, the southern part of Indo-China, was brought under direct French rule in 1867, and protectorates were established over the local rulers of Cambodia in 1863 and Annam, the central part of Indo-China based on Hué, in 1874. There is a parallel here between Great Britain's direct rule in India and indirect rule in Burma.

Defeat in 1870 made the acquisition of empire even more important for France. Not only Alsace and Lorraine but also the title of Emperor passed from the ruler of France to the ruler of Germany. Disraeli's purchase of the shares of the Khedive of Egypt in the Suez Canal Company was a further blow to the French, who had not forgotton that Great Britain had displaced

[1] Quoted by B. R. Tomlinson, *The Political Economy of the Raj, 1914–47* (London, 1979), 179.

French power in Canada and India in the eighteenth century. France moved away from a system of free trade and made Senegal and Algeria into economic dependencies (reserved markets for French exports and given preferential duties on their exports to France in return) in 1877 and 1884. In 1879 the Governor of Senegal won over the French government to the idea of building a railway eastwards into the African interior to meet the river Niger. Both commercial and military ambitions would be satisfied. In particular, the thrust of British trading companies up the Niger would be checked. French interest in North Africa also increased. From Algeria influence could be extended eastwards into Tunisia. One difficulty was that there were only a thousand French colonists there, as against an Italian settlement of 25,000. But the Bey of Tunis was heavily indebted to French creditors, which served as a lever after 1878 for French companies to win concessions to build a railway across the Algerian border to Tunis, to sink mines and develop land, in preference to Italian speculators. The Italian clergy, especially the Capuchins, were another barrier to French influence in Tunisia. However, Charles-Martial Lavigerie, the French Bishop of Algiers since 1867, founded a missionary congregation of White Fathers who established a community in Carthage. In 1878 he sent twelve White Fathers into Equatorial Africa on apostolic safaris to establish four mission centres. Lavigerie informed the French government in 1880 that 'from the frontiers of Algeria to those of the British and Dutch colonies of the Cape of Good Hope, all the interior territory is henceforth placed, from the religious point of view, under a French authority'.[2]

The possession of colonies was a factor of world power and also increased the standing in Europe of the country that possessed them. In the 1880s, conversely, the structure of power in Europe also influenced the drive for more colonies. After the unification of Germany and the war between Russia and Turkey, Bismarck constructed a system of alliances which ensured German security in Europe and forced international conflicts to be played out in a wider sphere. A Dual Alliance between Germany and Austria was concluded in October 1879 which was to be of central importance down to 1914. But whereas Bismarck saw the alliance as a step towards a renewal of the *Dreikaiserbund*, including Russia, the Austro-Hungarian Foreign Minister, Andrássy, saw its purpose as to strengthen Austria in the Balkans against Russia. Unfortunately for Austria, the British general election of April 1880 returned the Liberals to power, and Gladstone supported Russia's patronage of oppressed Balkan Christians against Turkey. Austria was now isolated, and forced in June 1881 to accept a *Dreikaiserbund* between herself, Germany, and Russia which guaranteed for Russia the closure of the Straits to British warships and German and Austrian neutrality in the event of a war between Russia and Great Britain.

---

[2] Quoted by J. Dean O'Donnell, *Lavigerie in Tunisia* (Athens, Georgia, 1979), 44.

France still floated free of Bismarck's system, and no alliance was conceivable so long as Alsace-Lorraine was annexed to Germany as a *Reichsland*. Accommodation was possible only outside Europe, and Bismarck indicated at the Berlin Congress that he would not oppose France acquiring Tunisia, the claims of Italy notwithstanding. In May 1881 French troops established a protectorate in Tunisia and Lavigerie became a cardinal, Apostolic Administrator of Carthage and Tunis, with authority over the Italian clergy, and Primate of Africa. Gambetta announced that 'France is becoming a great power again'.[3] Radicals who opposed colonialism made possible by the good offices of Bismarck and for the benefit of plutocrats alone, formed a Ligue des Patriotes in 1882 to demand revenge against Germany. Italy, which regarded Tunisia as part of the old Roman empire, was extremely disconcerted by French aggression. King Umberto, himself the son and grandson of Austrian princesses, accepted a Triple Alliance with Germany and Austria (May 1882) as an insurance policy against France. This marked a defeat for the Italian 'irredentists', who were mostly anticlerical and republican, and demanded the recovery of Trieste and Trentino from Austria. They were gagged in the interests of diplomatic and political stability. Guglielmo Oberdan, an Austrian subject of Italian descent, who tried to assassinate Francis Joseph, was executed in December 1882 and became a martyr to their cause.

The next wave of expansion followed from an upset between France and Great Britain in Egypt. Both powers had financial and strategic interests there because of the Suez Canal. But in 1876 the government of the Khedive went bankrupt, and Britain and France agreed to bail him out only on condition that their representatives were given financial and political controls to protect the interests of bondholders. The Khedive conceded, but then became difficult and was forced by the French and British to abdicate in favour of a more pliable successor. An Egyptian nationalist movement gathered momentum among junior army officers and students and forced the new Khedive to appoint a nationalist ministry and to call a parliament. This immediately demanded control of the budget from the British and French. Britain and France decided on joint action against the nationalists, but in the French parliament the radical opposition refused the government credits for the expedition, and in September 1882 the British entered Cairo alone.

This was the start of a chain-reaction. France was humiliated and deeply jealous of British colonial supremacy. But the soldier and explorer de Brazza had just returned from Africa with a treaty signed on the banks of the Congo with one King Makoko, who ceded his territory to France. The French press demanded that the government ratify the treaties, and they were massively endorsed by parliament in November 1882. Another French officer was sent out to the Lower Niger to conclude similar treaties. These developments

---

[3] Quoted by Henri Brunschwig, *French Colonialism, 1871–1914: Myths and Realities* (London, 1966), 57.

gave cause for concern to other colonial speculators, notably King Leopold II of the Belgians who was himself collecting treaties from African chiefs in the Congo, with the help of the explorer Stanley and hoped to found a vast central African state. British trading interests in West Africa insisted on the maintenance of free trade in the Congo and Niger, and the British government stepped in and concluded a treaty with Portugal (February 1884) using the Portuguese as a cat's paw to safeguard its own interests in the Congo.

At this point Bismarck made a move. As the economic depression bit, so Bremen and Hamburg firms looked to export their goods further afield, to West Africa, East Africa, and the Pacific. A Bremen merchant, Lüderitz, built a trading station on the south-west African coast at Angra Pequeña in 1883 threatening Britain's Cape route to India, while in 1884 Karl Peters arrived in East Africa, challenging British trading and strategic interests in Zanzibar. In response, Bismarck declared South-West Africa a German protectorate, then sent a naval vessel to Togoland and the Cameroons, hemming in British interests on the Niger, and proclaimed them German protectorates also. Bismarck's thinking was threefold. First, he decided that it was time for Germany to enter the colonial race and establish a German *Mittelafrika*. Second, he was keen to boost the National Liberal party and bind it more closely to the government coalition. Johannes von Miquel, the leader of the National Liberals, was also vice-president of the Colonial League, founded in 1882 to press the government to take colonial action. 'All this colonial business is a sham,' he confessed in September 1884, 'but we need it for the elections.'[4] Third, he was keen to exploit the rupture between Great Britain and France in Egypt to win France over to his side and to bully Great Britain into making concessions to Germany. He therefore refused to recognize the Anglo-Portuguese treaty and summoned an international conference to Berlin to settle the African question once and for all.

The main purpose of the Berlin conference of 1884–5 was to impose free trade in the Congo. But it also gave countries a free hand to establish a sphere of influence in areas they effectively occupied, and resort to force if necessary to extract trading concessions from African rulers. The upshot was a rash of companies, chartered by their respective governments, which drove into the African interior in pursuit of commercial and strategic interests. Karl Peters founded a German East Africa Company in 1885 and signed treaties with local rulers in Tanganyika. William Mackinnon replied with the British Imperial East Africa Company (1888) to claim Zanzibar, Kenya, and Uganda. Cecil Rhodes established the British South Africa Company in 1889 to stake out British claims in Bechuanaland, which boxed the Germans into South-West Africa, and also in Rhodesia and Nyasaland.

Even with German help, France did not manage to release the British grip

---

[4] Quoted by H. Pogge von Strandman, 'Domestic origins of Germany's colonial expansion under Bismarck', *Past and Present*, 42 (1962), 146.

on Egypt, but she established a protectorate in Tunisia and then turned her attention to Indo-China, where the Emperor of Annam had died in 1883. The native mandarinate organized a rebellion against the French and were supported by Chinese regulars and irregulars. The rebellion was put down and in 1885 China ceded Tonkin, or North Vietnam, to France as a protectorate. In parliament the French premier, Jules Ferry, justified expansion in terms of a substitute for revenge against Germany and a means of reversing the economic depression by exporting goods up the Red River to '400 million consumers' in China. But neither the Right nor the radicals would have anything to do with his colonialism, which they denounced as wasteful, corrupt, and dangerous. Ferry's government fell over the Tonkin question in March 1885 and in the October elections both the radicals and the Right made important gains.

The colonial adventures of the 1880s were not generally popular with public opinion, especially on the political Left. They were variously considered wasteful of resources, provocative of dangerous colonial wars (for local tribes, kingdoms, and empires often fought back), an encouragement to militarism, beneficial only to capitalists, and a diversion from pressing national interests, either in Europe or in other global spheres. The French Ligue des Patriotes argued that France should be ever watchful on the Rhine; the Imperial Federation League was concerned not with India or Black Africa but with bringing the white settled colonies of Canada, Australia, New Zealand, and South Africa into an imperial federation under an imperial parliament. Not until the 1890s would public opinion see the struggle for colonies as a projection of and a decisive factor in the struggle for supremacy in Europe.

Chauvinism

The *Dreikaiserbund* of 1881 gave Russia a strong base from which she could complete her expansion into central Asia. Great Britain had fought the Afghan War of 1874–7 to reinforce the defences of India by annexing the Khyber Pass and establishing control over local Afghan chiefs, but in March 1885 Russian and Afghan troops clashed at Pendjeh, much to the discomfort of the Gladstone government. In addition, the *Dreikaiserbund* advanced Russian ambitions in the Balkans. Austria allowed Russia to look forward to the unification of Bulgaria and Eastern Roumelia, in return for the right to annex Bosnia and Herzegovina, which she had occupied.

But Austria too had ambitions in the Balkans. Serbia, which had been abandoned by Russia in 1878, was tied to Austria in 1881 by a commercial treaty and a secret political convention by which Prince Milan could make himself king when he liked (which he did in 1882) and have a free hand in Macedonia, provided that he ensured that Serbian nationalism was gagged and that no Russian forces were admitted into Serbia. The railway being built from Vienna to Constantinople was the vehicle of Austrian interests in the

Balkans, and both Serbia and Bulgaria were obliged to accept that it crossed their territory.

Russia looked on Bulgaria as its backyard in the Balkans and after troops were withdrawn in 1879 the military was keen to build a railway across Bulgaria to Constantinople. Two Russian generals were appointed to the government of Prince Alexander of Battenberg, as Ministers of War and the Interior. A power struggle developed and in 1883 Prince Alexander appealed to his parliament for support and dismissed the Russian-dominated ministry. Two years later a group of Bulgarian revolutionaries in Philippopolis, the capital of Eastern Roumelia, overthrew the Turkish governor and appealed to Prince Alexander to intervene. In order to retain popular support, the Prince marched to Philippopolis and took control of the movement. The Russians, who had favoured the unification of the two halves of Bulgaria in order to create a satellite state, now had second thoughts. Their traditional policy of 'liberating' Balkan Christians from Turkish rule in order to build a highway to Constantinople was futile if peoples like the Bulgarians demonstrated only ingratitude and unreliability. The situation was made worse by the impetuosity of Serbia. King Milan, greedy for compensation, declared war on Bulgaria in November 1885, but Alexander moved his forces across from the Turkish front, captured Nis and threatened Belgrade. Only a threat from Austria to intervene in support of Milan stopped the Bulgarian army in its tracks. The Russians were incensed; the influence that they had once wielded in Balkan affairs had now passed decisively to Austria. Tsar Alexander III began to think that the *Dreikaiserbund*, which was renewed for another three-year period in 1884, did more to hinder Russian ambitions than to further them. The Pan-Slav press was quite convinced of this. 'We would like Russia to be in free, though friendly relations with Germany', wrote Mikhail Katkov in his *Moscow News* on 30 July 1886, 'but we would like to see similar relations with other powers, and the same with France.'[5] The first problem was dealt with first. On 21 August 1886 a group of Russian officers kidnapped Prince Alexander of Battenberg and under pressure from the Tsar he abdicated.

Austria and the British government of Lord Salisbury, who had just returned to office, protested but took no firm action. Tension between Russia and Germany increased, and that tension was now exploited by radicals and chauvinists in France who had revolted against colonial adventures undertaken with the approval of Bismarck and thirsted for revenge on the Rhine. They now had a leader in General Georges Boulanger, who in January 1886 became Minister of War in a cabinet that was heavily spiced with Radicals. Boulanger had his eyes on the recovery of Strasbourg. He introduced a bill to reduce military service from five years to three but to

---

[5] Quoted by George F. Kennan, *The Decline of Bismarck's European Order* (Princeton, 1979), 180.

close the loopholes by which seminarists, students, and the rich could obtain exemption. He set about purging the officer corps of royalist and Bonapartist elements and took advantage of the law of June 1886 exiling the heads of France's ruling families to dismiss half a dozen royal dukes and counts from their posts in the army. Such gestures did little to endear the French Republic to the Tsar's Court, but the possibility of an alliance between France and Russia against Germany was explored unofficially by radical activists like Paul Déroulède, President of the Ligue des Patriotes, who visited Katkov in Moscow in July 1886, and by Boulanger through the French military attaché in St Petersburg.

Bismarck faced the danger of war on two fronts and in 1886 Germany had a standing force of 435,000 against a French force of 524,000. In January 1887 Bismarck decided, a year in advance, to ask the Reichstag to enlarge the German army under a new Septennat. The Reichstag agreed to the increases, but only for a three-year term, not for seven. Bismarck promptly dissolved the Reichstag, called elections, and whipped up fears of Boulangist aggression in the press and by calling up 75,000 reservists. It was the manufacture of a war scare in order strengthen the governmental coalition of Conservatives, Free Conservatives, and National Liberals. The anti-militarism of the left liberal and Social Democratic parties was publicized as anti-patriotism, and the wave of chauvinism that swept Germany knocked away their support.

Against the combined threat of France and Russia the Triple Alliance with Austria and Italy, though renewed in February 1887, was not enough for German security. But through the Triple Alliance it was possible to make overtures to Great Britain, which was antagonized by Russia in Afghanistan as well as in the Straits and harassed by France for staying put in Egypt. There was no question that Lord Salisbury would commit Britain to an alliance that would engage her forces if one of her allies were attacked. But Britain was as concerned about Russia as Austria was concerned about France and Italy. Under the Mediterranean agreement, which was an exchange of notes between the British and Italian governments in February 1887 and between the British and Austrian governments the following month, the status quo in the Mediterranean, Aegean, and Black Sea was upheld.

In the event Bismarck was let off the hook abroad as well as at home. In May 1887 the Radical-dominated cabinet of which Boulanger was War Minister was overthrown in the French parliament by moderate republicans with the support of royalist and Bonapartist deputies, in order to avoid war with Germany, and a republican ministry with the support of the Right was formed. The Radicals and the Ligue des Patriotes were incensed by this 'German ministry' and gathered in their thousands to cheer Boulanger at the Gare de Lyons when he was sent off to a command in central France. In June 1887 the *Dreikaiserbund* expired but Bismarck was able to negotiate a Reinsurance Treaty with Russia alone. Strictly speaking, this was incompatible with the Triple Alliance, for the one committed Germany to give Russia a free hand in the Straits while the other committed her to keep Russia out of the Straits. But Bismarck was safe so long as secrecy was maintained and Russia was pledged to remain neutral if Germany were attacked by France.

Unfortunately for Bismarck relations with Russia deteriorated further. The Bulgarian parliament elected a candidate unacceptable to Russia as their new prince: Ferdinand of Saxe-Coburg-Gotha, a grandson of Louis-Philippe who also enjoyed the full support of Francis Joseph and the Austrian government. In November 1887 Bismarck instructed the Reichsbank not to sell Russian bonds on the Berlin money-market and French financiers were quick to step into the breach. This was an important move towards a Franco-Russian alliance. Bismarck was grateful that Francesco Crispi, the premier of Italy, who was engaged in a tariff war with France, should be keen to sign a military convention with Germany in January 1888. Further moves were made to bring Lord Salisbury into an alliance, but Salisbury did not want to be dragged into a war against France and the connection went only as far as a renewal of the Mediterranean agreement, this time including Turkey, in December 1887. Moltke, the Chief of the German General Staff, was eager for a preventive war against Russia, but at least Bismarck managed to head off that proposal.

Imperialism

In 1886 Eugène Melchior de Vogüé introduced the French public to the works of Turgenev, Tolstoy, and Dostoyevski in his *Russian Novel*. Immediately it became a best-seller. But the new interest of the French in Russia was not only literary. After the Berlin money-market was closed to Russian bonds in 1887 the trade switched to Paris, and Russian bonds were a great success with French investors. In 1889 the sale to Russia of Lebel rifles, which used smokeless powder, was approved by the French government. At the same time relations between Germany and Russia deteriorated. After the dismissal of Bismarck in March 1890 the management of foreign affairs passed in effect to Friedrich von Holstein, director of the Foreign Office's political department. He was as hostile to Russia as Bismarck was respectful, and in June 1890 allowed the Reinsurance Treaty to lapse on the grounds that it gave support to Russia's ambitions in the Straits that was incompatible with the Triple Alliance. Russia was no longer bound in toils to Germany and was free to conclude an alliance with France. In July 1891 a French squadron was received at Kronstadt and Alexander III stood bare-headed to the *Marseillaise*. A secret military convention in August 1892 committed Russia to help France in a Franco-German war and France to help Russia in a Russo-German war, and a Russian squadron paid a return visit to Toulon in 1893. The convention was endorsed by the French and Russian governments in 1894, and a bridge dedicated to the memory of Alexander III was officially named during a visit of

Nicholas II to Paris in 1896. Until now, German strategy in the event of a war on two fronts had been to defeat Russia first. But the Chief of General Staff between 1894 and 1905, Count Schlieffen, argued that France would have to be put out of action by a lightning campaign of 40 days while Austria held the eastern front, and that only then would German troops be fully engaged against Russia.

As a counterweight to the Franco-Russian alliance a *rapprochement* with Great Britain would have been a natural option for Germany. But although William II was a grandson of Queen Victoria there was a growing feeling in Germany that the maintenance of German power in Europe now required her establishment as a world power. Without naval power, Germany risked both losing her colonial possessions and being strangled by an economic blockade. The British Naval Defence Act of 1889, which inaugurated a naval building programme, supported by the foundation of a Navy League in 1895, raised the stakes at sea. An attempt by Cecil Rhodes in 1896 to overthrow the Boer Republic of the Transvaal, which was growing rich on gold and drifting closer to Germany, not only provoked William II to send a telegram of support to its president, Paul Kruger, but decided the German government to assert the equality of Germany with other global powers, namely Great Britain, the United States, and Japan. In June 1897 the naval minister, Admiral Tirpitz, advised the Kaiser that 'for Germany the most dangerous naval enemy at the present time is England. It is also the enemy against which we most urgently require a certain measure of naval force as a political-power factor.'[6] He submitted a 408m. Reichsmark programme of naval expansion until 1905, not only to protect Germany's overseas trade and colonies but also in order to challenge Great Britain in the North Sea while her fleet was overstretched in the Mediterranean and Far East and force her to concede world superiority to Germany.

In the Near East British relations with Austria and the Ottoman Empire also grew cooler. Between 1895 and 1897 the Turks massacred Armenians, suppressed a Bulgarian-inspired rising in Macedonia, and defeated Greece, which went to the aid of Cretans who rose in revolt against Turkish rule. Lord Salisbury would have no public support in Britain for shoring up the Ottoman Empire and adopted a Canningite policy of combining with Russia and France to force sweet reasonableness on the Porte. In addition, he was less worried about a Russian presence at Constantinople so long as Britain was secure in Egypt and could obtain guarantees from Russia to secure British interests in India. Great Britain therefore failed to renew the Mediterranean agreement in January 1897 and Austria, deprived of British support, had no choice but to come to an understanding with Russia in May 1897 to put the Balkans on ice.

[6] Quoted by Steinberg, *Tirpitz and the Birth of the German Battle Fleet*, 126, 209.

The Balkans had peace for almost a decade, not least because Russia was pursuing ambitions in the Far East. China and Japan remained closed to western trade until the mid nineteenth century. Western military and naval power then forced China in 1842 and 1858 and Japan in 1854 and 1858 to make important trade concessions under treaty, but there the similarity between the fate of the two countries ended. In Japan the supreme warlord or Shogun who had capitulated to the western powers was overthrown and the Meiji Emperor restored to full authority in 1868. The hierarchy of feudal vassals on which the power of the Shogun rested was abolished and replaced by a centralized system of government and a modern army. Taxation of the peasantry and the export of raw silk provided capital to build railways and establish an industrial basis of military power. Within a generation Japan was transformed from a medieval to a modern state. China, on the other hand, failed to reform itself and became a prey to western imperialism. Russia acquired a base at Vladivostok in 1860. The tributary state of Tonkin was lost to the French in 1885 and that of Burma to the British to 1886. Military power remained in the hands of regional governors who were little more than independent warlords. Western powers provided funds for military and naval reforms but the Dowager Empress spent half the naval budget on the royal palace. The Manchu dynasty itself was supported by foreign loans.

In 1894 Japan went to war with China for the possession of Korea and inflicted a humiliating defeat on her. Under the Treaty of Shimonoseki in 1895 China was obliged to pay a massive indemnity to Japan, which greatly assisted her military and industrial programme. China was forced to appeal to the western powers for more loans, and those loans were granted only on condition that the Chinese government would grant concessions to build railways and sink mines. Russia was interested in building a short cut in the Trans-Siberian railway across Manchuria to her naval base of Vladivostok and founded a Russo-Chinese bank, financed largely by French capital, to build it. But Vladivostok was ice-bound for much of the year and Port Arthur, further south on the Yellow Sea coast of China, was an attractive proposition. In November 1897 Germany suddenly seized Kiaochow on the Yellow Sea as a coaling station to make possible the pursuit of *Weltpolitik* in the Far East. Russia acted fast and early in 1898 bullied the Chinese government into leasing Port Arthur to her as a naval base. Great Britain, not to be excluded, obtained Wei-hai-wei, on the opposite shore and the French secured Kwangchow. In fact the western powers decided that the imperial dynasty was so weak that it could no longer be relied upon to protect their interests and began to stake out their own spheres of influence in China.

The focus of British concerns was nevertheless not in China but in East Africa, which guaranteed the security of India. The British position in Egypt was shaky now that fanatical Mahdists had reconquered the Sudan and other powers pursued ambitions around the headwaters of the Nile. In 1885 the

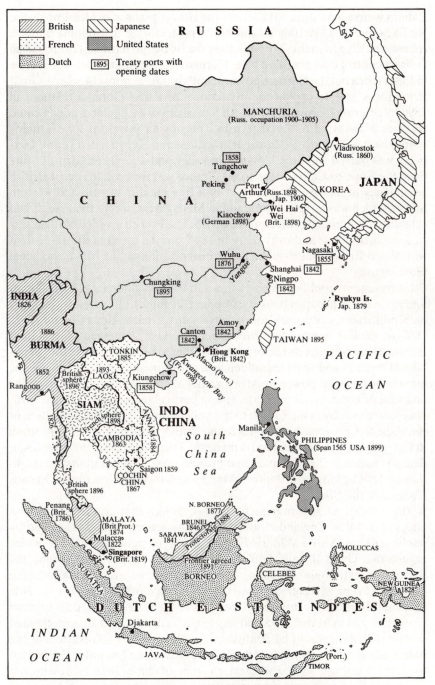

British ⧄

French ⬚

Dutch ⬚

Japanese ⧅

United States ▨

1895 Treaty ports with opening dates

R U S S I A

MANCHURIA
(Russ. occupation 1900–1905)

Vladivostok
(Russ. 1860)

1858
Tungchow

Peking
Port
Arthur (Russ.1898)
(Jap. 1905)

KOREA

JAPAN

C H I N A

Kiaochow
(German 1898)

Wei Hai
Wei
(Brit. 1898)

Nagasaki
1855

Wuhu
1876

Yangtse

Shanghai 1842
Ningpo
1842

Ryukyu Is.
Jap. 1879

INDIA
1826

Chungking
1895

Amoy
1842

Canton
1842

Hong Kong
(Brit. 1842)

TAIWAN 1895

P A C I F I C

O C E A N

1886

BURMA

1852

Rangoon

TONKIN
1885

British
sphere
1896

1893
LAOS

Kiungchow
1858

Macao (Port.)

Kwangchow Bay
Fr. 1898)

SIAM

French sphere
1898

ANNAM 1884

INDO
CHINA

CAMBODIA
1863

S o u t h

C h i n a

S e a

Manila

PHILIPPINES
(Span 1565 USA 1899)

Saigon 1859

COCHIN
CHINA
1867

British
sphere 1896

N. BORNEO
1877

BRUNEI
1846

SARAWAK
1841

Protectorate 1888

Penang
(Brit.
1786)

MALAYA
(Brit Prot.)
1874

Malacca
1822

Singapore
(Brit. 1819)

SUMATRA

Frontier agreed
1891

BORNEO

MOLUCCAS

CELEBES

NEW GUINEA
1828

D U T C H   E A S T   I N D I E S

I N D I A N

O C E A N

Djakarta

JAVA

(Port.)

TIMOR

Map 8.   Imperial Expansion in the Far East

Italians were encouraged to take over the British garrison of Massawa on the Red Sea and in 1889 Italy established a protectorate in Ethiopia under a treaty with King Menelik. Through Italy the British government exercised an indirect control over the Blue Nile. German trading companies were active in East Africa but the German government's interests were elsewhere. Great Britain was able to exploit the breakdown of Russo-German relations in 1890 by offering Germany the North Sea island of Heligoland, which could serve as a naval base, together with Tanganyika in return for Germany renouncing her claims to Zanzibar, Uganda, and Kenya. As a result, Germany was barred from the Upper Nile valley and a projected British route from the Cape to Cairo safeguarded. France was induced to accept British ascendancy in this area by the offer of a free hand in central and western Sudan, which was largely desert, and in Madagascar, where the French had established a nominal protectorate in 1885. The French invaded Madagascar to consolidate their authority there in 1896, but the result of the agreement with Great Britain was to make the British position on the Nile a good deal more secure.

Governments could not, however, act in total isolation from public opinion. In France, a group of bankers, shipping magnates, industrialists, military men, politicians, writers, and journalists set up a French Africa Committee in 1890 to protest against the government's abject agreement with Great Britain. It organized lectures, brought together a colonial group in the Chamber of Deputies and acquired influence in government circles. Its aim was the pursuit of imperial power in Africa rather than the promotion of specific financial or commercial interests, and in particular to extend French influence westwards from the Congo to the upper Nile, to prevent completion of the Cape to Cairo route and to force the British to reconsider their position in Egypt. The alliance with Russia made the French government more confident to challenge Great Britain and in June 1896 a French military expedition under Captain Jean-Baptiste Marchand left Marseilles for the French Congo and the Nile.

The Gladstone government of 1892–4, unlike that of Lord Salisbury, adopted a 'Little Englander' attitude, but its actions were constrained by public opinion. Alfred Milner's *England in Egypt*, published in 1892, which argued that Great Britain should not only retain Egypt but reconquer the Sudan, was extremely influential. Lord Rosebery, who replaced Gladstone as Liberal Prime Minister in March 1894, tightened Britain's grip on the Nile by establishing a protectorate in Uganda. For the Foreign Office Sir Edward Grey declared in March 1895 that any French advance into an area claimed by Great Britain would be considered by Her Majesty's Government 'an unfriendly act'. The triumph of the Conservatives and Liberal Unionists led by Lord Salisbury in the general election of June 1895 represented a groundswell of feeling in favour of imperial greatness. Queen Victoria's

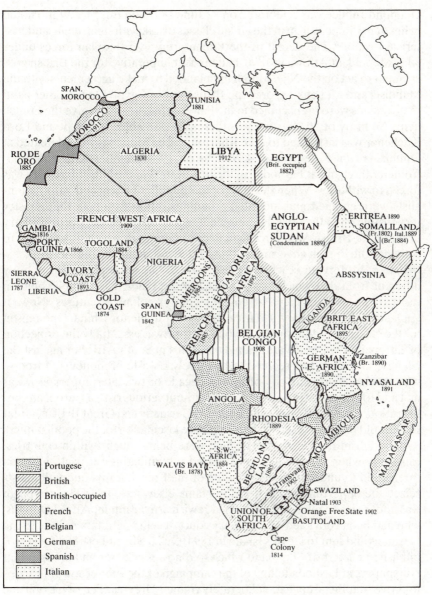

SPAN.
MOROCCO

TUNISIA
1881

MOROCCO
1911

RIO DE
ORO
1885

ALGERIA
1830

LIBYA
1912

EGYPT
(Brit. occupied
1882)

ERITREA 1890

SOMALILAND
(Fr.1802) Ital.1889
(Br. 1884)

FRENCH WEST AFRICA
1909

ANGLO-
EGYPTIAN
SUDAN
(Condominion 1889)

GAMBIA
1816
PORT.
GUINEA 1866

TOGOLAND
1884

NIGERIA

ABSSYSINIA

SIERRA
LEONE
1787
LIBERIA

IVORY
COAST
1893

GOLD
COAST
1874

SPAN.
GUINEA
1842

CAMEROONS
1885

FRENCH EQUATORIAL AFRICA
1895

UGANDA

BRIT. EAST
AFRICA
1895

BELGIAN
CONGO
1908

GERMAN
E. AFRICA
1890

Zanzibar
(Br. 1890)

NYASALAND
1891

ANGOLA

RHODESIA
1889

MOZAMBIQUE

MADAGASCAR

S.W.
AFRICA
1884

WALVIS BAY
(Br. 1878)

BECHUANA
LAND
1885

Transvaal
1902

SWAZILAND

Natal 1903

Orange Free State 1902

UNION OF
SOUTH
AFRICA

BASUTOLAND

Cape
Colony
1814

	Portugese
	British
	British-occupied
	French
	Belgian
	German
	Spanish
	Italian

Map 9. Imperial Expansion in Africa

Diamond Jubilee was celebrated on 22 June 1897 and Beatrice Webb noted in her diary 'imperialism in the air, all classes drunk with sightseeing and hysterical loyalty'.[7] The defeat of the Italian army by Ethiopian forces under King Menelik at Adowa in 1896, had made it imperative for the British government to act on the Nile. Marchand planned to make agreements with the Mahdists and Menelik to force the British out of Egypt. On the other hand the Russians were preoccupied in the Far East and unable to give the French help. An army of 20,000 men was therefore assembled in Egypt and Lord Kitchener was instructed to take Khartoum. The Mahdists were defeated at Omdurman on 2 September 1898 and on 19 September Kitchener confronted Marchand at Fashoda, on the headwaters of the Nile. Marchand was forced to withdraw. When the news of this humiliation reached Paris nationalists were enraged and mounted a demonstration to topple the ministry responsible on 25 October. Fearing a military coup in France, Lord Salisbury ordered the British Mediterranean fleet to Gibraltar, which was enough to convince the French government that Marchand should be recalled.

Imperialist fervour reached a peak in 1898. The atmosphere was entirely different from that which had prevailed in the 1880s. Then, public opinion resisted the entanglement of governments in colonial ventures. Now, it applauded the scramble for Africa and the scramble for China. One reason for the change was that rivalry beyond Europe was essentially the projection of European rivalries. Wars against the Zulus in South Africa or against the Chinese in Indo-China seemed to be merely a waste of money and troops, with no clear European pay-off. But a decade or two later imperialism was first and foremost a struggle for power, without serious risk of European conflagration, between Russia and Germany, Germany and Great Britain, Great Britain and France. As such, it held immense fascination for the popular mind.

Imperialism fuelled conflicts which were being fought within countries, especially when those countries suffered a humiliating set-back. Fashoda threatened to undermine the standing of the French army, but nationalists seized the opportunity to deflect the blame elsewhere. In 1898 a campaign was under way to reopen the case of a Jewish army captain, Alfred Dreyfus, who had been convicted by a military court of selling military secrets to the Germans and sent to Devil's Island in 1894. On 20 November 1898 *Le Figaro* published a letter of Marchand which told how Kitchener had brought him newspapers at Fashoda telling of the campaign of the supporters of Dreyfus to prove that the army had deliberately framed Dreyfus. Ten of his officers, learning of the infamy of their fellow countrymen, broke down in tears, and immediately gave ground to Kitchener. French nationalists blamed Fashoda not on the army but on the 'enemy within' which discredited the army and divided and weakened France for the benefit of foreign powers. These

[7] Beatrice Webb, *Diary* (London, 1983), ii, 118.

traitors, they claimed, were not true Frenchmen but members of an international conspiracy of Jews, Protestants, and Freemasons which aimed to subvert and destroy the Republic. Frustrated imperialist feeling turned inwards in 1898–9 as an orgy of anti-Semitic, anti-Protestant, and anti-British feeling.

There was a sense in which imperialism was a new religion. Moreover, the religious content of imperialism was very marked. In the 1880s it had been opposed in many quarters as conquest, plunder, profit, exploitation, and brutalization. Now imperialism was defended as sanctioned by high moral principle, as a vehicle of peace, Christianity, and civilization. The French spoke in terms of a civilizing mission and exempted missionary orders from legislation which banned other congregations in France. Abroad, missionaries laboured on behalf of French civilization in general; anticlericalism was not for export. For German imperialists, *Kultur* as well as capital was carried along German shipping routes and railway lines. The publication of Rudyard Kipling's poem, 'The white man's burden', early in 1899, salved the conscience of many a reluctant British imperialist. Kipling's message was that imperialism was a moral responsibility according to which advanced peoples should take it upon themselves to raise sullen, benighted peoples to a higher level of civilization.

Such justifications of imperialism were sometimes hypocritical and always one-eyed. In the French colonies, only a tiny minority of the indigenous populations were ever assimilated. To win French citizenship, a Senegalese or Vietnamese had to obey French (not local) law, and be adopted by a French family, marry a French national, obtain a French secondary education, or do French military service. All others remained 'subjects' without political rights, and were subject to forced labour for the benefit of French colonists. The propagation of the Christian gospel involved missionaries in the protection of their converts from rough local justice and consuls in the protection of missionaries. Riots against missionaries as agents of foreign and devilish powers became a commonplace in China after 1891, and in 1897 the German authorities used the pretext of the death of two missionaries at the hands of the Chinese to occupy Kiaochow, and to obtain the support of the Catholic Centre party to do so. Attacks on European populations in the name of imperialism also posed moral dilemmas. The pretext offered by the British in 1899 for going to war with the Boer Republic of the Transvaal was to protect the poor English or *Uitlander* population of the Transvaal which was denied the vote by the Boers. Nevertheless, war against settlers of Dutch origin was opposed in many British circles. W. T. Stead, an influential journalist who praised Kipling's view of Empire, denounced the Boer War as oppression at the service of the private fortune of Cecil Rhodes.

For the mass urban populations of western Europe, imperialism had very little to do with a civilizing mission. 'Give 'em hell!' was the basic sentiment behind popular jingoism in 1898. The superiority relished was less moral than technological, summed up in the words of Hilaire Belloc: 'whatever happens, we have got/The Maxim gun and they have not'. The art of Kipling was to combine high moral purpose with the cult of brute force and to write in the slang of the ordinary British soldier. Contemporaries dubbed him 'the Burns of the music-hall' and the 'Banjo-bard of Empire'. He caught a current mood, although he was not able to satisfy it. 'Wilder and wilder grows the popular taste for blood', ran the account of one critic. ' "More chops", goes up the cry more fiercely every hour, "more chops, bloody ones with gristle". No one writer can keep pace with the gruesome demand for blood-stained fiction, and so a vast school of battle-and-murder novelists arises.'[8]

Paradoxically, jingoism seized Europe precisely at the moment when the influence of Europe on the rest of the world was decisively challenged. The United States of America went to war with Spain on behalf of a revolt against Spanish rule in Cuba and destroyed the Spanish fleet off Manila in May and in Santiago Bay in July 1898. Cuba was ostensibly given independence although the USA reserved the right of intervention after it ended military occupation of the island in 1902. Moreover, it annexed the Philippines, which formerly belonged to Spain, at the end of 1898. The British Colonial Secretary, Joseph Chamberlain, argued in a speech at Birmingham on 13 May 1898 that Great Britain should abandon its splendid isolation and make alliances with the United States and Germany. Lord Salisbury did not approve of his initiative, and the struggle for naval supremacy stood in the way of a real understanding, but Britain was able to come to an agreement with Germany over southern Africa in August 1898 which ended German patronage of the Transvaal and gave Britain a free hand to deal with the Boers.

Co-operation between Great Britain, Germany, and the United States was possible also in China, where a popular rising against the imperialists who were partitioning the country, orchestrated by the Righteous and Harmonious Fists Society, received the name of 'Boxer rebellion'. In June 1900, supported by the Manchu dynasty, the Boxers laid siege to the foreign legations in Peking. British, French, German, Russian, American, and Japanese troops were all involved in the relief of Peking and the restoration of order. Russia took advantage of the situation to oblige the Chinese government to agree in November 1900 to a thinly-disguised Russian protectorate over Manchuria allowing her to complete a railway to Port Arthur by 1903. Great Britain was extremely worried by the emergence of Russian power in the Far East and persuaded Germany to sign an agreement to uphold the territorial integrity of China against Russian expansion. However, in March 1901 Chancellor Bülow declared to the Reichstag that the fate of Manchuria was a matter of absolute indifference to him. The seizure of Kiaochow had been a spin-off from Germany's *Flottenpolitik*, and that *Flottenpolitik* was directed against

---

[8] Richard Le Gallienne, *Rudyard Kipling: A Criticism* (London/New York, 1900), 157.

British navalism. Great Britain found itself confronted not only by German naval power but also the ambition of Russia to become a naval power in the Far East, with France in tow. The solution was an alliance concluded by Great Britain in 1902 with Japan. Japan was keen to uphold the integrity of China, given her protectorate in Korea, which was now threatened by Russian expansion down to Port Arthur. The alliance gave Britain joint naval superiority in the Far East against Russia and France and liberated British ships for use in home waters against Germany. For her part, Japan demanded of Russia that she confirm the integrity of China and recognize the Japanese domination of Korea. When Russia refused, in February 1904, Japan launched a torpedo attack on Port Arthur and the Russo-Japanese war began.

13

THE MANAGEMENT OF SOCIETY

The accepted task of government at the turn of the century was to reduce the strains in the system imposed by labour unrest, socialism, anarchism, feminism, religious conflict, and the demands of national minorities for autonomy. Their survival depended upon their ability to bring about national integration. Many instruments short of the suppression of all opposition were at their command and at the end of the nineteenth century these were brought out in array.

Because the first educational concern of governments was to train servants of the state, secondary and higher education were developed long before elementary education. Elementary schooling for the masses was a relatively late arrival, and its main purpose was not to universalize basic skills and facilitate social mobility but to reinforce nationality and the existing social order. Churches which undertook popular education on their own account in some sense rivalled government enterprise, but in another sense were valuable allies. The balance was often a delicate one. Likewise, Churches had their own programmes of social welfare to relieve poverty and insulate the masses against the appeal of revolutionary agitators. Governments might approve this concern and even undertook legislation to improve working conditions at the behest of Churches or religious interests. On the other hand they brought forward their own plans for social insurance that were beyond the financial and administrative capacity of churches. One popular reaction against poverty and exploitation was socialism; another was anti-Semitism. In some cases, as in Russia and Romania, governments used anti-Semitism to reinforce their authority. Elsewhere they stopped short of this, but established interests such as landowners, industrialists, and the Churches manipulated anti-Semitism to their own benefit. In particular Churches which were anxious that their influence on the masses was decreasing, saw anti-Semitism as an indirect means of promoting loyalty to Christian values.

Mass Education

Between 1880 and the First World War, the governments of north-eastern Europe completed the provision of state-funded primary schools, salaried teachers, compulsory and free mass education. In 1901 Germany spent 12 per cent of its budget on public education, England 10 per cent, France 8 per cent, but Spain only 1.5 per cent. School provision was very inferior in southern and eastern Europe. In the first decade of the twentieth century the school population, as a proportion of the total population, was 17 per cent in Germany and Great Britain, 14 per cent in France and Sweden, but only 4 per cent in Russia.

The main function of primary schooling was national integration, and the old empires discovered at the end of the nineteenth century that a single language was a far greater force for unity than loyalty to a ruler. Unfortunately, language was also what defined the nationalities that were struggling for autonomy within these empires, and the clash could be very violent. The imposition of Russian on elementary schools in Poland only created a clandestine school system in which Polish was taught by local clerks, priests, apothecaries, organists, the children of local gentry, and above all women. Konrad Prószyński's Polish primer, published in 1875, went through 42 editions and sold 750,000 copies by 1906. By 1901 a third of the country's population was encompassed by the clandestine school system and most peasants owed their literacy to it. The movement was encouraged by Polish nationalists and the factory strikes of January 1905 stimulated a school strike or boycott of official schools that lasted until 1911.

Many governments subscribed to the view that there was no morality without religion and were quite content to hand over the education of the people to the state Church. But as the government increased its funding of primary education so it assumed control of the elaboration of syllabuses, teacher training, inspection of schools, and examinations. This could result in conflict with the Church which had assumed responsibility for education until then. Conflict was particularly sharp where the government was liberal and insisted, not least for the stability of the regime, that the education provided by state schools must be not religious but secular.

In Russia the ministers of Alexander III responded to revolutionary violence by restoring the influence of the Orthodox clergy in education. The Holy Synod, itself a department of state, took over the direction of parish schools, run by priests, from the Ministry of Education, and multiplied them from 4,000 in 1884 to 32,000 in 1894. The *zemstvos* were antagonized into developing the network of secular schools, and the number of pupils in primary schools in Russia rose from one million in 1878 to six million in 1911. The Prussian state relieved the manorial lords of the eastern provinces of all responsibility for education in 1886 and in 1906 organized elementary schooling on a national basis, funded by a general tax instead of the traditional school tax on heads of families. But after the excesses of the *Kulturkampf* the National Liberals concluded that religion was an indispensable barrier to socialism, and therefore, rather than support the Progressives' demand for secular education, joined the Conservatives in defence of confessional schools. In England and Wales the Conservatives' Education Act of 1902 replaced the school boards by Local Education Authorities at county and county-borough level. But the Church of England continued to supervise religious instruction in the schools and its own voluntary schools were to be supported from the rates. Nonconformists were antagonized by public funding of the Church of England. Joseph Chamberlain managed to control his Birmingham constituents by promises of tariff reform but Wales rose in revolt behind Lloyd George and Nonconformity, allied to free trade, carried the Liberals to victory in 1906.

The existence of teaching congregations complicated matters in Catholic countries. In France the republicans made primary education free in 1881. In 1882 they made it compulsory for individuals (not just binding on communes), excluded the catechism from state primary schools and expelled the teaching congregations from them after 1886. A private sector sprang up, which received no funds from the state, but which taught catechism in school, employed teaching congregations, and was directed by the episcopate. Émile Combes, the small-town radical who headed the Left Bloc between 1902 and 1905, was determined to complete the work of the Enlightenment and had the teaching congregations expelled from private schools as well. He could prevail only so far against Catholic France, which set up private Catholic schools with lay teachers or 'secularized' nuns. In Catholic Italy, the educational influence of the Church was even more difficult to combat. The anticlerical Left did not abolish the catechism in state schools in 1877 but made it no longer compulsory. Giolitti, looking to the Right for support in 1908, introduced a bill requiring communes that were opposed to religious instruction to provide it if some heads of families so wished. The socialists led a ten-day attack on the bill in parliament and the press, but were defeated and abandoned Giolitti. What was difficult in Italy was impossible in Spain. In 1902 the Liberal Minister of Education, Count Romanones, established a national system of public primary education with salaried teachers and supervision by municipal and provincial boards. But the Catholics and Conservatives fought tooth and nail to preserve the Church's control of private education. As members of teaching congregations trickled over the border from France, Romanones tried to clamp down on congregations that were not authorized under the Concordat, but in 1904 there were 10,600 men and 40,000 women in religious congregations (as against 1,750 and 13,350 respectively in 1861). In 1913 Romanones tried to make religious instruction no longer compulsory in state schools, but again the Catholic organizations rose as one against him.

The exclusion of religious instruction from state schools did not mean the end of moral education. French republicans replaced religious obedience by a 'scientific' ethic of social solidarity. Because of the fact of the division of labour and the interdependence of all individuals in the social organism, the child must subordinate his interests to those of society. This morality that owed nothing to religion did not have the compelling simplicity of heaven and hell. Attempts were also made in the schools to combat the physical and moral degeneration that derived from life in large towns and cities. Alcoholism and tuberculosis were two major concerns, and the first was said to lead to the second by undermining the body. Another view was that industrialization and urbanization disrupted family life and that alcoholism, vagabondage, and prostitution were the consequences of the disruption of the family. The education of girls was less intellectual than that of boys. They did less arithmetic and no science other than domestic science. They learned to make and mend clothes, wash and iron linen, and cook. It was argued that the simple domestic comforts provided by the 'angel of the hearth' would keep her husband out of the café or public house and her children off the streets. The irony was that the majority of working-class women had to work, outside, for decent wages before they were married and at home, for very little, afterwards. Yet the middle-class woman who did not have to work was held up as a model. Indeed, the imposition of the bourgeois virtues of hard work, sobriety, thrift, and cleanliness on the idle, uncouth, and drinking populace was one of the major tasks of primary education. This was glaringly obvious to the anarchist thinkers of France and Spain. To convey an alternative proletarian morality Francesco Ferrer set up the first anarchist school in Barcelona in 1901 and there were forty-seven in the province by 1906.

What governments and Churches wanted children to learn in school and what their parents wanted them to learn was often very different. In a word, those in authority wanted to reinforce the existing social order while those who acquired an education did so to penetrate it. The diversification of the economic and social structure was a powerful incentive to obtain qualifications. The revolution in trade, transport, and communications, especially in northern and western Europe, at the end of the nineteenth century opened new horizons and offered new possibilities of employment beyond the village or small town for those with an elementary education. There were jobs to be had in the railway, train, and metro services, in the post office, in the offices of banking, shipping, and insurance firms, in teaching, nursing, and the police force. Opportunities for girls as well as boys were opening up: no longer did girls from poor families have to resign themselves to textile mills, dressmaking, and domestic service. School attendance and literacy rose, although in proportion to the opportunities and incentives to study. Despite the progress being made in Russia, only 48 per cent of all children aged 8–11 attended school in 1911. In 1912, the proportion of children between six and twelve years old enrolled at school in Italy ranged from 97 per cent in Piedmont and 86 per cent in Lombardy to 38 per cent in the Basilicata and 31 per cent in Calabria in the south. In 1900 the illiteracy rate was 47 per cent in Italy, although this concealed great differences between 11 per cent in Piedmont and 13 per cent in Lombardy on the one hand and, on the other, 65 per cent in the Basilicata and 70 per cent in Calabria. In the Austrian Empire the Italian population had an illiteracy rate of 16 per cent as against 3 per cent for the

Czechs, 6 per cent for the Germans, 40 per cent for the Poles, and 77 per cent for the Ukrainians or Ruthenes. The overall illiteracy rate in the Austrian part of the Monarchy was 26 per cent, while in the Hungarian part it was 41 per cent. The illiteracy rate was 79 per cent in the Kingdom of Serbia, 78 per cent in Romania, and 72 per cent in Bulgaria. Three years earlier it had been 69 per cent in the Polish provinces of Russia, 79 per cent in Russia as a whole. At the other end of Europe, illiteracy rates were eroded to 14 per cent in Great Britain and France in 1906–7.

Pressure for education built up not only at the elementary level, but higher up. Economic hardship as well as new opportunities played its part. As the depression of 1873–95 bit deep, so the families of peasant farmers, artisans, shopkeepers, clerks, lower officials, and elementary schoolteachers coveted a secondary and higher education for their children that would afford them a career with security and status. This demand for an education traditionally reserved for notables caused concern among established interests. The propertied, official, and professional élite became anxious about the challenge to its monopoly. It denounced the mania for public office, the overcrowding of the professions, the shortage of posts and university places that left stranded a half-educated intellectual proletariat, the danger of being educated out of one's class of origin, and the damage done to the economy by the flight from productive occupations. One weapon it had was that classical education still held the key to the universities, state bureaucracy, liberal professions, and Churches and a classical education required a good deal of capital, both financial and cultural. Half the problem could be dealt with simply. Though the secondary education of girls expanded greatly after 1880, governments were slow to permit girls to receive a classical education and allow them to take the *baccalauréat* or *Abitur*, which gave access to the universities. The other half of the problem was tackled by diverting boys away from *Gymnasien* and *Real-gymnasien*, or the classical side of *lycées* and colleges, towards secondary courses based on modern languages and sciences, or towards 'higher primary' schools which provided a practical training after the standard primary education. In Germany ambitious sons from poorer families were directed towards *Realschulen*, completed after 1878 by *Oberrealschulen*, which together delivered a nine-year modern course. In 1887 the Russian Education Minister Delianov advised that *gymnasia* and pro-*gymnasia* should be closed to 'the children of coachmen, servants, cooks, laundresses, petty tradesmen, and other such persons'.[1] This gave rise to the notorious 'circular on cooks' children', of 18 June 1887 and between 1884 and 1892 the proportion of children of urban estates in Russian *gymnasi* fell from 36 to 31 per cent while that of children of gentry and officials rose from 49 to 56 per cent. In French *lycées* and colleges non-classical 'special' education

---

[1] Quoted by Peter A. Zaionchkovsky, *The Russian Autocracy under Alexander III* (Gulf Breeze, Florida, 1976), 208.

was upgraded to 'modern' education in 1891. It offered a modern *baccalau-réat* instead of a special diploma, but that gave access only to *grandes écoles* and not to faculties of law and medicine. Much more popular were the higher primary schools developed after 1881 which offered a short, practical, and above all free education to the lower middle class that was interested in careers in business, white-collar occupations, teaching, and the lower ranks of the administration. Similarly successful were the higher grade schools in the industrial north of England. They were run by the school boards and very much part of the primary school system, but offered an excellent training in mathematics, science, technical drawing, and commercial techniques for the labour aristocracy. In England and France higher primary education replied to a powerful demand for rapid training and modest but remunerative occupations. By the turn of the century secondary schools there were desperate to regain a clientele which had abandoned them. One of the aims of the English Education Act of 1902 was to channel the higher primary school pupils back into the grammar schools.

While some students preferred the higher primary track, students embarking on secondary education wanted it to pay and resisted diversion towards modern courses which did not have access to universities. The gradual lengthening of modern courses was one response to this pressure. Another was to make technical high schools more attractive, although in Russia the polytechnical institutes, set up after 1898, and which offered economics as well as engineering, were far more popular than the technical high schools. Eventually, governments had to concede the principle of equal access to university of students from modern schools as well as from classical schools. This occurred in Germany in 1900 and France in 1902. At the same time the medical and legal professions had to drop their requirement of knowledge of Latin and even Greek. Universities began to open up, in terms of both social origin and gender. After 1900 *Mittelstand* groups arrived in German universities in greater numbers, and seeing the law and medical faculties blocked by the propertied and educated classes, ironically favoured the theological and philosophical faculties as a quick track to teaching and the Church. Women also gained entry to universities in greater numbers. The proportion of women in university populations in 1914 was 7 per cent in Germany, 10 per cent in France, 20 per cent in Great Britain, and (though they attended separate universities) a striking 30 per cent in Russia.

Social Welfare

Socialism, for many notables in Europe, was a disease which fed off the misery of the working classes. Improve the condition of those classes, and they would become immune to it. But rapid industrialization and urbanization had made the Churches' system of charity inadequate, and mutual aid societies were the creation only of skilled workers. Governments had to find a

middle way between *laissez faire* liberalism and collectivism in order to head
off the socialist threat. Repression was not enough.

The pace was set in Imperial Germany by Bismarck and the heavy industrialists who were anxious to keep socialism out of their factories. The system
of social insurance agreed by the Reichstag rested on three legs: compensation for industrial accidents to be the responsibility of employers alone
(1884); sickness benefits, which would also cover the first thirteen weeks of
an accident, to be funded one-third by employers and two-thirds by workers
(1883); and old-age and disability pensions, which would be funded equally
by employers and employees and include a state contribution (1889). The
package was meaner than it appeared. The scheme was largely financed out
of workers' contributions, or by workers through indirect taxes that fell predominantly on them. Benefits were earnings-related, so that better-paid
workers paid in more and received higher benefits. Finally, the scheme was
open only to industrial wage-workers, not to domestic servants, agricultural
labourers, or the self-employed. The SPD opposed the schemes as insufficient, although its right wing was attracted by echoes of Lassallean state
socialism. Left liberals feared that industrialists' costs would increase and
exports suffer. The aristocratic wing of the Centre party was ready to support
Bismarck, but the Rhineland Catholics opposed state intervention and state
contributions to buy the souls of Catholic workers.

Rhinelanders in the Centre party were far happier with the Factory Act
that was passed in 1891 after the fall of Bismarck, to protect female and child
labour. Indeed, they had been campaigning for such legislation since 1887.
The Centre also had its own schemes for preserving Catholic workers from
social democracy. Catholic workers' associations, which provided sickness
benefits, education, leisure activities, and religious instruction, had about
60,000 members by 1895. In the face of the great expansion of the centralized
trade union movement, the Centre party organized rival Christian trade
unions in 1893, which had a membership of 160,000 members by 1900 and did
much to block the expansion of social democracy in Rhineland-Westphalia.

The Catholic hierarchy opposed Christian trade unions because they
accepted the strike weapon and instead gave support to the 'Trier faction' of
Catholic aristocrats and clergy who wanted to resurrect the guild system.
Industrialization had gone too far in Germany to make this more than a pipe-
dream, but in Austria the struggling artisans found support among the lower
clergy who organized them after 1887 into Christian Social Associations.
More important, Austrian artisans had the ear of the Catholic, federalist
aristocracy which gathered around the *Vaterland* journal of Baron Karl
von Vogelsang, a Lutheran noble from Mecklenburg who had converted to
Catholicism and moved to Austria in 1865. This aristocracy, which passionately opposed the centralized, secular regime and 'Jewish' capitalism of the
Austrian liberals, that could only breed class conflict and socialism, aimed to

restore a Christian-corporative social order and actually carried sufficient weight in Taaffe's Iron Ring after 1879 to achieve something. The government extended the franchise to artisans in 1882 and needed to retain their support. As a result the Reichsrat passed a *Gewerbeordnung* in 1884. This protected craftsmen by requiring them to join associations in their trade, which were open only to those who passed a proficiency test. In addition, a Factory Act was passed severely restricting the employment of child and female labour, much to the consternation of liberal industrialists. Lastly, accident insurance (1887) and sickness benefits (1888) were established on the German model. The social-democratic leader, Viktor Adler, had to admit that he was impressed by the government's programme.

In Great Britain the influence of the industrialists was much greater and the dominant ideology sanctified individual liberty, freedom of contract, and private property. Even the trade-union movement, with its own mutual aid schemes, preached self-help. Fabian socialists and Radicals led by Joseph Chamberlain pressed for more government intervention to relieve poverty, exploitation, and unemployment, but the Liberal government of 1892–5 was far from Bismarckian. Gestures were made, with a bill to make employers responsible for industrial accidents and bills to limit working hours, firstly of railwaymen, then of miners, and finally of women and children in docks, dangerous trades, and domestic industry. But railway, mining, and manufacturing interests mobilized their spokesmen in the Liberal party and the House of Lords, and bills were emasculated and defeated. The Liberals went down in the elections of 1895 to the Conservative and Unionist parties, whose policies echoed something of Bismarck's. 'Social legislation', said Arthur Balfour, 'is not merely to be distinguished from socialist legislation, but it is its most direct opposite and its most effective antidote.'[2] They introduced a Workmen's Compensation Act in 1897 which finally made employers responsible for industrial accidents but refused to consider a pension scheme because of the cost. Meanwhile the trade unions and the poor-law reformer Charles Booth set up a National Committee for Promoting Old-Age Pensions to campaign for a system of universal pensions financed out of general taxation.

French republicans went scarcely further along the road of social reform than British liberals. An alliance of moderate republicans and royalists passed a law in 1893 limiting female labour to eleven hours a day and introduced a bill on accident insurance. But by the time it became law in 1898 the Senate had watered it down so that it was not compulsory for employers, and employees had to take them to court. In 1899 a government of moderate republicans and radicals took office and offered the Ministry of Commerce to the socialist Millerand. He introduced an Associations Bill to permit trade unions to own property, and another bill to provide for arbitration in

---

[2] Quoted by J. R. Hay, *The Origins of Liberal Welfare Reforms, 1906–14* (London, 1975), 35.

industrial disputes which was rejected both by employers and unions. His main achievement was a Factory Act of 1900 that reduced the working day to ten hours in workshops which employed women as well as men. No pensions bill was introduced until 1906.

In Catholic countries the Church stepped in alongside the state to advocate its own programme of social reform. Inspiration was provided by the encyclical *Rerum Novarum* of Pope Leo XIII, published in 1891, which declared private property to be sacred but condemned the brutal exploitation of man by man under naked capitalism. Workers must be encouraged to improve their lot, in order to render them less vulnerable to socialist demagogues, by joining in associations. These might be workers' circles or unions, composed of workers only or mixed with employers, but their purpose should be not strife but justice and harmony.

Rerum Novarum was clearly a response to the threat of socialism. But its message was ambiguous. It encouraged the social Catholic movements that existed already to win back workers, artisans, and peasants to the Church in order to strengthen a conservative, hierarchical social order. It sanctioned the work carried out in France by Count Albert de Mun in favour of workers' circles, mixed unions, factory legislation, and social insurance. It supported the charitable Opera dei Congressi in Italy and the rural credit bank and co-operatives propagated in Venetia and Lombardy after 1892 by Giuseppe Toniolo, a professor of political economy at Pisa University who was fighting to stop the penetration of socialism into the countryside. The archbishop of Valencia gave his full backing to the Catholic workers' circles founded by the Jesuit Antonio Vicent, and gathered in a National Council of Catholic Workers' Corporations in 1896. Cardinal Manning, who played a key role in negotiating a settlement of the London dock strike in 1889, welcomed the encyclical. But other Catholics, who were just as opposed to the liberal, capitalist system but more open to the modern world, claimed the sanction of *Rerum Novarum* for the work that they were undertaking. These Christian democrats were mainly young priests who rejected the political pretensions of the Catholic Church and accepted lay education. They also rejected the alliance of the Catholic Church with the rich and sought to spread the gospel among the poor. For this reason they accepted the principle of class conflict, the strike, and the right of workers to form separate unions, independent of their employers. In France their leader was the abbé Jules Lemire, who was elected to parliament from a Flemish constituency in 1893 and organized two congresses of Christian democrat priests, at Reims in 1896 and at Bourges in 1900. In Italy their leader was Romolo Murri, who had attended the lectures of Labriola while a seminarist in Rome, and began to found workers' groups in the Marches, Emilia-Romagna, Piedmont, and Liguria after 1900. Both movements came into conflict with social Catholics, the ecclesiastical hierarchy, and Vatican officials, and before he died in 1903 Leo XIII made it clear that they must fall into line.

Anti-Semitism

The assassination of Tsar Alexander II in March 1881 was attributed to Jews and unleashed a series of pogroms in the southern Pale and the Polish provinces of Russia that lasted for over a year. A mass exodus to cities further west of Jews, mostly orthodox and Yiddish-speaking, began. Between 1880 and 1900 the Jewish population of Warsaw rose from 99,000 to 219,000, that of Budapest from 70,000 to 168,000, that of Vienna from 73,000 to 147,000. A sharp increase in anti-Semitism after 1880 was partly a response to this influx of *Ostjuden*. Soon the Jews became scapegoats for changes in Europe for which they bore little responsibility. One problem was the rapid and uneven development of capitalism. In backward Russia and eastern Europe the vast majority of the population were peasants while the Jews, who were not allowed to own land, were peddlers, small traders, innkeepers, money lenders, small manufacturers, and sweated labourers. At a time of political crisis and agricultural depression, it was easy to single out Jewish middlemen as exploiters. Where capitalism was developing fast, as in Germany and Austria, the establishment of free trade and free enterprise occurred at about the same time as the emancipation of the Jews, so that large-scale enterprises employing cheap labour and large-scale outlets that undercut small businesses could be denounced as Jewish. Even in mature capitalist economies, where businesses were used to turning to the money-markets for credit, banking and stock-exchange crises which provoked bankruptcies and the centralization of capital were laid at the door of speculation by 'parasitic' Jewish financiers.

In central Europe the passage from arbitrary, authoritarian regimes in which what representation there was was based on estates and favoured the nobility, to constitutional, parliamentary regimes in which the franchise was based on wealth or education, was comparatively recent. Such regimes were promoted by the liberal middle classes, who were reinforced by emancipated Jews. Wealth and education combined in a political press that was often Jewish-owned and Jewish-run, and was used to influence public opinion and maintain liberal parties in power. This was anathema both to the traditional Right and to democratic and socialist movements which found it easy to dismiss liberalism as Jewish.

Modernism and Jewishness might also be thrown together. Conservatives who were concerned by anticlerical attacks on the Catholic Church blamed them on Jews, who were said to have invented freemasonry as a front organization for this work. The expansion of education was seen to favour Jewish ambitions, while the education of women and divorce laws were denounced as Jewish attacks on the traditional family. Modern art, modern literature, modern theatre, which seemed to have so little regard for conventional morality, were attacked as the work of Jewish publishers, producers, dealers, and critics.

The pogroms in Russia were endorsed both by certain revolutionary groups, who were happy to denounce the Jews as exploiters, and by the reactionary advisers of Alexander III, who saw the possibility of harnessing popular anger in defence of 'Autocracy, Orthodoxy, and Nationality'. Jews were expelled in tens of thousands from the countryside to urban ghettos and from Moscow and St Petersburg to the Pale. The sale of spirits, which had provided an income for many Jews in the villages, became a state monopoly. In the Pale, where Jews accounted for between 30 and 80 per cent of the population, they were allowed 10 per cent of the places in secondary schools and universities. Jews were excluded from public office and access to the professions was restricted, but they did more than their fair share of military service. Jews lost their voting rights in the towns but continued to pay taxes.

Romania passed very similar legislation and in addition prohibited Jews from peddling, which was often their last resort. In the Habsburg Monarchy, the Poles of Galicia, with the help of the Catholic clergy, founded a Polish People's Party to exclude Jews and Ruthenes from various sectors of economic life. The Jews of Prague included few migrants from the east and were well established in business and the professions. They were fully Germanized and underpinned the ascendancy of the Christian German middle class, but attracted the hostility of Czech artisans, tradesmen, and skilled workers. In Hungary the anti-Semites tried to make capital of what they described as the ritual murder of a fourteen-year-old Christian girl. But the strategy of the Liberal party which monopolized power down to 1905 was that the Jewish financial and professional middle class should be used as an ally on condition that it Magyarized itself. Although most Jews in Hungary remained orthodox and Yiddish or German-speaking, the Liberals refused to allow anti-Semitism to take a grip.

In Austria, and particularly in Vienna, the situation was rather different. Artisans, who were suffering competition from large-scale industry, were enfranchised in 1882. Georg von Schönerer, a Liberal who broke from his party because it failed to adopt a Pan-German nationalism, decided to tap popular anti-Semitism in 1884 by organizing a petition to nationalize the Northern Railway Company of Salomon Rothschild. In 1885 Schönerer was elected to the Reichsrat along with Karl Lueger, a self-made lawyer and Democrat who realized that the Democrats' hold on the lower middle class was weakening. He supported Schönerer's motion to restrict Jewish immigration from Russia, but avoided the excesses of the followers of Schönerer, who was imprisoned in 1888 for smashing up a Jewish newspaper office. Lueger wanted to make anti-Semitism respectable. He fell in with the Christian Social movement of the Catholic lower clergy, met Karl von Vogelsang and brought the Conservatives into a United Christian front in 1889, to exclude Jews from public, professional, and business life and to break Liberal-Jewish political power. The return of the Liberals to office in 1893 sharpened the conflict. Lueger was elected mayor of Vienna three times in 1895–6, but three times the government refused to confirm his election; he was not yet respectable. But in the Reichsrat elections of 1897, in which wage-workers voted for the first time and the Social Democrats won fourteen seats in Austria, Lueger's Christian Social party denied them a single seat in Vienna. Anti-Semitism demonstrated its use as the 'socialism of fools' that deflected class hatred on to the Jews in order to safeguard capitalism as a whole. Lueger was now recognized as *staatserhaltend*, or state-preserving, and his fourth election as mayor was confirmed by the Emperor.

In 1880 the Jewish population of Germany was 562,000, about half that of the Austrian part of the Habsburg Monarchy, and that of Berlin was 54,000. It was Germanized, and played a full part in Germany's economic expansion and in the National Liberal party. But many *Mittelstand* groups held the Jews responsible for the crash of 1873 and read in the *Gartenlaube* journal that 'the social question is the Jewish question'. When Bismarck broke with liberalism in 1878–9 the position of the German Jews became more precarious. Adolf Stöcker, the Court chaplain and a leading Conservative politician, was keen to win the Berlin workers away from social democracy, but realized after the Reichstag elections of 1879 that he had little chance. He turned his Christian Social party towards the *Mittelstand* and campaigned for the return of the guilds and against the Jews. In Hesse, where the peasants were suffering from falling prices, high taxes, indebtedness to Jewish moneylenders, and the danger of foreclosure, Otto Böckel, the librarian of the University of Marburg, formed an Anti-Semitic People's Party and inaugurated a new kind of populist, demagogic, nationalist politics. This threatened not only the National Liberals, who were seen to favour the Jews, but also the Conservative parties, which lacked his popular appeal. In an attempt to recover support, the Conservative party, persuaded by Stöcker among others, adopted an anti-Semitic platform at its 1892 conference. This, however, did not prevent the election of 18 anti-Semitic deputies in the 1893 Reichstag election, 10 at the expense of the Conservatives. In 1893 they therefore tried another tactic, sponsoring an Agrarian League to draw farmers west of the Elbe into a coalition with the Junkers to the east. The success of the Agrarian League, which had a budget larger than that of the SPD, was such that the Conservatives were able to drop anti-Semitism in 1896, leaving Stöcker to form a separate Christian Social party.

In France, the Jewish population fell from 89,000 in 1866 to 49,000 in 1872, after the loss of Alsace-Lorraine, and was only 71,000 in 1897. But that did not hinder the emergence of a virulent anti-Semitism, which had a left-wing pedigree going back to the July Monarchy, that relished attacks on Jewish financial feudalism, speculation, and the thirst for monopoly. The collapse of the Catholic Union Générale bank in 1882, which was attributed to Jewish manipulation of the money-market, came as a gift to the anti-Semites. Édouard Drumont's *La France juive*, which denounced the Jewish grip on economic,

political, and cultural life and painted a picture of an Arcadian, rural, Christian France without them, became a best seller when it appeared in 1886. His
journal, *La Libre Parole*, founded in 1892, exposed the corruption of deputies
and ministers by two Jewish intermediaries on behalf of the Panama Canal
Company and led the attack on Captain Dreyfus as a German spy in 1894.

The Catholic Church was quick to see the benefits of anti-Semitism. By
attacking the Jews as the people who had killed Christ and been sent to the
four corners of the earth to grovel in materialism they could harness the persecuting instinct to bring the masses back to the Catholic faith. All elements
which challenged the Catholic Church, from freemasons and Protestants to
supporters of divorce and state education for women could be labelled
'Judaizing Christians, worse than the Jews themselves'. The circulation of the
Catholic paper *La Croix* rose to 130,000 in 1889, after it adopted an anti-
Semitic position, and ran into several provincial editions. *La Croix du Nord*,
for example, had a strong following among factory workers. At a time of
social unrest, the capitalist class was vulnerable to criticism, but in anti-
Semitism it found a solution to its ills. 'In the end,' explained *La Croix* in
1894, 'the social question is the Jewish question.'[3] Be rid of the Jews, and
exploitation and misery would cease. Bernard Lazare, a Jew who had taken
to anarchism and was one of the first champions of the innocence of Dreyfus,
was quick to see the sleight of hand. Only a minority of Jews, he argued, were
rich; the rest, from Vilna to the lower east side of New York, lived in extreme
poverty. 'Anti-Semitism is a capitalist trick designed to safeguard the totality
of the banking, industrial and landowning class by a small and cleverly limited operation.'[4] 'The Christian bourgeoisie', echoed Theodore Herzl in
1898, 'seems quite disposed to throw us to the socialist wolves.'[5] In the elections of 1898, twenty-two anti-Semites were elected to the French parliament, along with fifty-seven socialists. But one of the socialist leaders, Jaurès,
favoured the campaign to retry and acquit Dreyfus, while Jules Guesde
declared that the guilt or innocence of a Jewish army captain was of no consequence to the labour movement.

Authoritarianism

The government of the French Third Republic was criticized, even at the
time, for being weak. Parliamentary deputies were considered by many too
powerful and corrupt. They received jobs, scholarships, and contracts from
ministers to nourish support in their constituencies for the next election, on
condition that they supported those ministers in the next vote of censure or
confidence, of which there were many. They received money from railway,

---

[3]   Quoted by Pierre Sorlin, *'La Croix' et les Juifs* (Paris, 1967), 109.
[4]   Bernard Lazare, *Contre l' Anti-Sémitisme* (Paris, 1896), 32.
[5]   Quoted by Stephen Wilson, *Ideology and Experience: Anti-Semitism in France at the time
of the Dreyfus Affair* (London/Toronto, 1982), 357.

canal, and industrial companies to pay for their election expenses or fund the newspapers that put across their viewpoint, in return for obtaining concessions and contracts from ministers for those companies. Deputies were therefore always looking to their constituents, and ministers to the deputies. Leadership seemed to be absent. In fact the regime was more stable than it seemed. The Constitution of 1875 provided for a parliamentary republic, in which an indirectly-elected Senate represented the moderation and continuity of rural and small-town France. The president of the republic was also indirectly elected, by the Chamber and Senate sitting as a National Assembly, so that he would not dispose of the authority that Louis-Napoleon was accused of misusing. The president nevertheless chose the prime minister, and President Grévy (1879–87) was biased against insufferable radicals like Gambetta, who was Prime Minister for only two months. Ministries rose and fell but the ministers were drawn from the same pool and enjoyed long periods in office. The main disadvantage seemed to be that the parliamentary oligarchy monopolized power and did not take sufficient pains to conceal the way in which the spoils system operated.

A sharp attack on the parliamentary republic was made by the radical partisans of General Boulanger when he was removed from office in 1887. The Ligue des Patriotes turned up *en masse* at the Gare de Lyon to wave him off to his new command in central France. The conservatives supported the Opportunist ministry until, at the end of the year, it fell when it was revealed that President Grévy's son-in-law was selling Legion of Honour ribbons. Both the radicals and the conservatives were now stranded. The radicals ran Boulanger in a series of by-elections in favour of the dissolution of parliament and a revision of the constitution which would make it more responsive to the popular will and have a stronger executive power. Behind the scenes both Bonapartists and Orleanists saw the opportunity to exploit the mass support that Boulanger's campaign generated and use him as a Trojan Horse for the restoration of their own claimants. Boulanger's campaign electrified the country in 1888 and reached a climax in January 1889 when he won a by-election in Paris. At that moment he might have marched on the Elysée Palace with his supporters and staged a *coup d'état*. But he panicked, fled to Brussels, and later committed suicide on the grave of his mistress.

The failure of Boulanger illustrated the resilience of the moderate Republic. Conservatives, discredited by their association with Boulanger, lost ground in the general election of 1889. Socialists who had been mesmerized by Boulanger's populism decided to have no more to do with bourgeois leadership. Strikes, May Day demonstrations, the formation of new federations of unions by railwaymen and textile workers, a federation of chambers of labour, socialist gains in the municipal elections of 1892, and the legislative elections of 1893, when their representation jumped from twelve to forty-eight seats, all marked a resurgence of class politics. Many conservatives realized that they must collaborate with moderate republicans to ensure the stability of the existing political order, and the protective tariff of 1892 and *Ralliement* were bridges over which they could march. Tough measures were taken by the republican government in an attempt to check the tide of revolution. The Paris chamber of labour was shut down by force in July 1893 for political activities and remained closed for three years. After a bomb was lobbed into the Chamber of Deputies in December 1893, so-called 'villainous laws' were passed which restricted civil liberties in order to break the anarchist movement, and a show-trial of thirty alleged anarchists was held in 1894, following the assassination of President Carnot. A radical ministry which gained office with socialist support in 1895 and tried to introduce graduated income and inheritance taxes was brought down by the Senate. The ministry of Jules Méline (1896–8), one of the longest in the Third Republic, was supported by Conservatives and represented the closest they came to exercising power within the Republic. For landowners, industrialists, financiers, the Catholic Church, and the military who witnessed the consummation of the Russian alliance in the state visit of Nicholas II to France in October 1896, it was an Indian summer.

The defeat of the French Right in the elections of May 1898 was a heavy blow. A republic which was tolerable while they could exercise the dominant influence in it became anathema once they were excluded from power. The campaign of left-wing intellectuals to reopen the case against the Jewish army captain, Dreyfus, was interpreted as a smear campaign against the army, which had tried and sentenced him. Fashoda, which conservatives argued was the result of the demoralization of the army, made it all the more necessary to silence the intellectuals before they took power in the Republic. The Ligue des Patriotes, which was banned after the Boulanger Affair, was resurrected at the end of 1898 and mobilized support on behalf of the conservatives. Its leader, Déroulède, tried to win over the military at the funeral of the President of the Republic, on 23 February 1899, to occupy the Elysée Palace, but without success. The decision of the Appeal Court to reopen the Dreyfus trial provoked a massive demonstration by nationalists in support of the army. Fortunately a government of 'republican defence' which included moderate republicans, radicals, and a socialist minister took office in June 1899 and blocked the threat from the Right. On the other hand the government could not afford to embarrass and anger the military to the extent that they would attempt a *coup d'état*. Dreyfus, retried by a military court at Rennes in August 1899, was found 'guilty with extenuating circumstances'. No proceedings were therefore brought against the high-ranking army officers so cordially detested by the intellectuals. The new President of the Republic duly pardoned Dreyfus, to appease his supporters, and the government tried to deflect their frustration by punishing Déroulède and launching a new attack on religious congregations.

In Italy, King Umberto feared that the French Republic was funding the republican opposition, and suffrage was kept limited, even after 1880. On the other hand unification had undermined the Italian nobilities and caused the Catholic Church to forsake politics, so that there was no basis for strong right-wing opposition to the liberal Italian state. Deputies accepted patronage from the government in order to build up local support as the price of being 'transformed' from one political allegiance to that of the government majority. This *trasformismo* which combined the forces of Left and Right was the outstanding achievement of Agostino Depretis, who was Prime Minister between 1876 and 1887. But it divided the insiders from those who received nothing from the spoils system: the socialists, the democrats, and the conservatives. Francesco Crispi, who saw himself as an Italian Bismarck and despaired that 'after 1878 there were no more political parties, only politicians'[6], attacked the system when he became prime minister in 1887. In impassioned speeches he appealed over the heads of the politicians directly to the electorate and reinforced the executive power. The political role of prefects was made explicit, and they were given much tighter control over provincial councils, while administrative justice was introduced to protect officials. In 1892–3 the ministry of Giolitti, which was based on the Left, demonstrated only that it was corrupt and powerless to put down disorder in Sicily. Crispi returned to power to organize the repression of socialists and anarchists, repeatedly prorogued parliament, governed by royal decree, dissolved town councils, banned opposition newspapers, outlawed socialists, and drafted 40,000 troops into Sicily, before using force and fraud to create a huge majority for his government in the elections of 1895.

The military defeat of Italy at Adowa in 1896 finished Crispi's political career. In 1898 bad harvests and the war between Spain and the United States drove up wheat prices to a level that provoked bread riots all over Italy. These were exploited by the socialists, who demanded that the agrarian–industrial élite cut tariffs and taxes. 80 people were killed and 450 injured when the military put down demonstrations in Milan in May 1898. States of siege were proclaimed in the provinces of Milan, Florence, Livorno, and Naples, and in June King Umberto asked General Pelloux to form a government and put paid to parliamentary rule. Early in 1899 Italy was humiliated in the scramble for China. Germany, Russia, Great Britain, and France had all acquired naval bases there, but Italy's request for one was rejected by the Peking government. Pelloux resigned, and then formed a new ministry that was based on the Centre and Right of the assembly. As discontent grew he introduced a Coercion bill to silence 'seditious' meetings, strikes, associations, and newspapers. When the extreme Left of radicals, republicans, and socialists held up the bill by obstruction, Pelloux prorogued the assembly and

---

[6] Quoted by Christopher Seton-Watson, *Italy from Liberalism to Fascism* (London, 1967), 93.

on 22 June 1899 the coercion measures were promulgated as a royal decree. His unconstitutional behaviour convinced the constitutional Left of Giolitti and Zanardelli that they must join the socialists to fight for democratic liberties. In the general elections of June 1900 the constitutional Left and socialists made heavy gains, King Umberto was killed by an anarchist soon afterwards, and General Pelloux, though he still held a majority, resigned in February 1901. Zanardelli was invited by the new king, Victor Emmanuel III, to form a ministry, and took Giolitti as his Interior Minister. The Socialist party had adopted a reformist strategy the previous autumn and joined the democratic block. In Italy at least authoritarian measures were checked.

In Spain elections were in the hands of powerful caciques who used government funds and force to return ministerial candidates. In the Cortes Cánovas perfected the *turno pacífico* or peaceful alternation in power of his own Liberal Conservative party and the Liberals of Sagasta, who thus won their own chance to manage the elections. This he saw as preferable to the military *pronunciamiento* as a way of sharing the spoils of office, and it was only frustrated republicans who were driven to foment a mutiny, in the garrison at Badajoz, in 1883. Cánovas handed over power to the Liberals in 1881–3 and again in 1885, when Alfonso XII died. He believed that the Liberals were in a better position to weather the regency of Alfonso's widow and prevent Carlist or republican revolts. Sagasta conceded universal male suffrage in 1890, but after that the social order was threatened by anarchist insurrections in Andalusia and bombings in Barcelona. 'The army', Cánovas was forced to admit when he resumed power in 1890, 'will remain for long, perhaps forever, the robust supporter of the social order, and an invincible dyke against the illegal attempts of the proletariat, which will accomplish nothing by violence but the useless shedding of its own blood.'[7] As it happened, anarchists responded to the mass torture, court martial, and execution of anarchists in the fortress-prison of Barcelona in 1896 by the assassination of Cánovas the following year.

Military defeat, as in France and Italy, provoked an internal crisis. Defeat at the hands of the United States, the triumph of the New World over the Old, of Protestantism and materialism over the secular arm of Roman Catholicism, was particularly galling. It caused an epidemic of introspection among Spanish intellectuals. The 'generation of 1898' around Joaquín Costa believed that Spain had been punished for its backwardness. It must bury The Cid, spend less on the army and more on roads, schools, and irrigation. But Catholic conservatives around Menéndez y Pelayo asserted that Spain had been punished for letting in Masonic liberalism, Jewish capitalism, and French anticlericalism. Spain was defined by her Catholicism and she must return to the tradition of the *Reconquista* and the Counter-Reformation, excluding all dissent and division in order to carry out God's will.

The cliques of politicians who had shared power amongst themselves so

---

[7] Quoted by Stanley G. Payne, *Politics and the Military in Modern Spain* (Stanford, 1967), 60.

cynically since the Restoration now came under attack. The frustrated military contemplated a *pronunciamiento*. Catalan industrialists and agrarians protested about having to pay taxes to such a corrupt regime. The Liberal government of Sagasta, which had presided over the defeat, was replaced in 1899 by a Conservative government under the relatively high-minded Francisco Silvela. He was not able to satisfy the Catalans, who organized a tax strike and in 1901 founded the Lliga Regionalista to fight for autonomy. In 1903 Silvela was replaced by Antonio Maura, who wanted to break caciquismo by an appeal to public opinion, but opinion that was articulated through corporative institutions and limited by authoritarian government. He lost the support of the Liberals, who joined with the republicans to oppose him. Neither could he count on the young king, Alfonso XIII, who relied on the military for advice, dreamed of personal rule, toppled Maura, and closed the Cortes in 1904 in order to install his favourite general as Minister for War.

In Great Britain the parliamentary system remained intact. But the threat of violence, less from socialists than from the land war and terrorist outrages mounted by the Irish nationalists, altered the pattern of politics. After the general election of November 1885 the Irish nationalists held the balance in the House of Commons. But in seeking to placate them by the introduction of a Home Rule Bill, Gladstone was seen to be giving way to revolution and was abandoned by both Whig aristocrats and the middle-class radicals around Joseph Chamberlain, who as Liberal Unionists allied with the Conservatives in defence of the Union of Great Britain and Ireland. The Liberals were again defeated at the polls in July 1886, and two decades of almost unbroken Conservative and Unionist rule began under the Marquess of Salisbury. This combined the aristocratic landed interest led by Salisbury and Balfour, the suburban middle classes empowered by the Redistribution Act of 1885 and given a powerful voice in Joseph Chamberlain, and the masses given more influence by the Franchise Act of 1884. 'I think a democratic government should be the strongest government from a military and imperial point of view in the world,' he told Balfour in 1886, 'for it has the people behind it.'[8] The Local Government Act of 1888 created the LCC of which the Liberals won control, but did not affect the ascendancy of the landowners in the counties. And while there was much criticism of the control of the army by civilian ministers and officials, Salisbury retained a distrust of military experts and professionals, and successive reforms in 1888 and 1895 stopped short of establishing a Chief of General Staff to advise the Secretary of State for War.

Mass support for imperialism carried the Conservative and Unionist parties back into power in 1895, with Joseph Chamberlain going to the Colonial

---

[8]   Quoted by Andrew Porter, *The Origins of the South African War: Joseph Chamberlain and the Diplomacy of Imperialism* (Manchester, 1980), 32.

Office. The Boer War, resorted to in October 1899 to bring the Transvaal firmly into a South African Federation under British paramountcy, was exploited by the Conservatives to win the elections of October 1900. The relief of Mafeking on 17 May 1900 after 217 days' siege gave rise to wild torchlit celebrations in England. The popular *Daily Mail*, founded by Alfred Harmsworth in 1896, trumpeted the message of Empire. The Liberal politician Asquith denounced Chamberlain's jingoistic appeals to the masses in the election campaign as 'the worst fit of vulgar political debauch since 1877–8'.[9] But the patriotic tide induced Asquith and other influential Liberals such as Grey and Haldane to support the war and the Empire, which divided them from the Liberal leader, Campbell-Bannerman. Lord Rosebery, who had succeeded Gladstone as Prime Minister in 1894–5, staked a claim to be the head of a future government of national unity by rejecting Home Rule for Ireland in 1902.

During the Boer War there was much criticism of party politics. Rosebery argued that it put forward not the best men but the most eligible and proposed a non-party cabinet which would include successful generals and admirals, expert administrators and imperial proconsuls like Lord Milner, the High Commissioner in South Africa. But Rosebery was not in office and when Salisbury retired in 1902 the middle-class, authoritarian, Liberal Unionist Joseph Chamberlain remained isolated from the Conservative leadership. The new Conservative Prime Minister was a stalwart of the British landed establishment, Arthur Balfour. Chamberlain was equally unsuccessful in forcing his policies of imperialism and social reform on the Conservative party. In 1903 he proposed a federation of the white, self-governing British colonies, which would be ringed by tariffs to keep out cheap foreign goods. The colonies would be allowed tariff concessions on their exports, if they made tariff concessions to British exports. The tariffs, he claimed, would reduce unemployment, raise wages, and pay for social reforms such as old-age pensions. Most of the Conservative cabinet objected that tariffs would raise food prices, hinder exports, and jeopardize the invisible earnings of the City of London. Chamberlain resigned from the cabinet in the autumn of 1903.

Party politics and parliamentary institutions were far weaker in Germany than Great Britain, and more vulnerable to authoritarian measures. Kaiser William II, who succeeded in 1888, took advice first and foremost from his military entourage, especially the Chief of the Military Cabinet and the Chief of the General Staff, who were beyond parliamentary scrutiny. He refused to bow to the experience of his Chancellor, Bismarck, rejected Bismarck's plan to make the anti-Socialist law permanent, and dismissed him in 1890. In military and naval matters the Kaiser exercised an absolute right of command that was not covered by the responsibility of the Chancellor, but William II

---

[9] Quoted by H. C. G. Matthew, *The Liberal Imperialists* (Oxford, 1973), 129.

was inclined to generalize from this to other areas of policy-making. This was unfortunate, because a Reichstag majority was necessary for military appropriations bills, and in 1890 Bismarck's ruling coalition broke up and lost ground heavily in the elections. The contradiction became plain when the new Chancellor, General von Caprivi, saw that he would have to reduce military service from three years to two and make concessions to the Catholic Centre party in order to get an army bill through the Reichstag. The Kaiser, on the other hand, would brook no compromise. In 1894 Count Botho zu Eulenburg, the Prussian Minister-President, encouraged by heavy industry and agrarian interests, proposed an anti-revolution bill. If this were rejected by the Reichstag a *coup d'état* to abolish universal suffrage would be justified. Rather than accept it Caprivi resigned, and was succeeded as Chancellor by Prince Hohenlohe, the former Minister-President of Bavaria, now aged 75. Hohenlohe was himself hard pressed to prevent the military bringing forward another anti-revolution bill in the winter of 1894–5. Tension increased between the Kaiser and his military headquarters on the one hand, and his ministers, including the Prussian Minister of War and Reich Secretary of the Navy, on the other. These were unable to obtain credits from the Reichstag for military and naval expansion without unacceptable concessions. In June 1897 William II completed the dismissal of most of his ministers and installed reliable confidants such as Bernhard von Bülow as Reich Foreign Secretary. 'Bülow will be my Bismarck', announced the Kaiser at the end of 1895, 'and just as he hammered Germany together externally with Grand Papa's help, so shall we two clean up the rubbish-heap of parliamentarism and the party system at home.'[10]

After the ministerial reshuffle of 1897, the East Elbian agrarians and heavy industry organized themselves and obtained direct access to the Prussian Foreign Minister, Miquel, over and above the Reichstag, in order to pave the way to the restoration of protective tariffs when Caprivi's treaties expired in 1902. Heavy industry in the Ruhr, together with the shipping interests of Hamburg and Bremen, stood to gain also from the government's programme of naval expansion, but this could not take place without recourse to the Reichstag for credits. Tirpitz introduced his first Naval bill there in December 1897, but the Kartell of Conservatives, Free Conservatives, and National Liberals did not command a majority and the Conservatives only voted for the fleet as a quid pro quo for tariff reform. Fortunately it was possible to win over the Centre party to support both the naval bill and the government coalition in the elections of June 1898. This was largely because the fleet was an imperial institution (unlike the very Prussian army) and had a much more middle-class officer corps than the army.

A coup against the Reichstag should it refuse naval credits, and a change in

---

[10] Quoted by J. C. G. Rohl, *Germany without Bismarck* (London, 1967), 158.

the electoral law, were out of the question in 1898. But tension with Great Britain could be used to mobilize public opinion by propaganda and extra-parliamentary organizations, to place the Reichstag deputies in the glare of publicity. It was made clear that any reluctance to vote credits would provoke a dissolution and an appeal to patriotic sentiment in the country. At the same time a successful *Welt-* and *Flottenpolitik* would increase the power and prestige of the military, the government, and the Kaiser himself, at the expense of the Reichstag. Propaganda was orchestrated by the Colonial League, the Pan-German League, founded in 1897, and the Navy League, set up in 1898 by the Reich Navy Office and heavy industry, and grouping 270,000 members by 1900. For some radical nationalists such as Friedrich Naumann and Max Weber, a German empire was necessary to alleviate the problem of over-population and hunger in Germany, and empire-building must be combined with social reform to improve the condition of the working class. But for Foreign Secretary Bülow a successful foreign policy was enough to 'reconcile, pacify, rally, unite', and was combined with the Kaiser's labour policy which proposed to sentence pickets who intimidated strike-breakers to three years' hard labour.

In Austria, the breakdown of the parliamentary system was explained as much by nationalism as by socialism. The triumph of the Young Czech opposition in the Reichsrat elections of 1891 gave rise to anti-dynastic riots and the proclamation of a state of siege in Prague. One solution offered by the government was to balance middle-class nationalists by loyal working-class voters. A fifth curia enfranchising non-taxpayers was created in 1897, but the following elections saw the rise not only of the Social Democrats and Christian Socialists but the Young Czechs as well. Minister-President Badeni made concessions to the Czechs which served only to provoke a backlash of German nationalism. After his resignation and the assassination of the Empress Elizabeth in 1898 Austria went over to a period of government by non-party ministries of civil servants and non-parliamentary rule under emergency legislation. In Hungary, parliamentary government survived, but the majority enjoyed by the Liberals was maintained by methods that were more and more authoritarian. Between 1885 and 1888 hereditary peers were replaced by pliant life peers in the upper house, the franchise in the lower house was restricted, and the county assemblies were packed with non-elected members and brought under the strict control of the *foispán* or lord lieutenant, who represented the central government.

After the assassination of Alexander II in Russia Count Dmitry Tolstoy, who was appointed Minister of the Interior by Alexander III, presided over the virtual annihilation of political life. Organizers of meetings and strikes were made liable to administrative exile, and the *Okhrana* or secret police was set up in 1883 to prevent them happening in the first place. The University Statute of 1884 imposed state controls on university administration, courses, examinations, and student discipline. Public trials and jurors became rarer and elective JPs were replaced in 1889 by appointed land captains who had total control of peasant affairs and were increasingly drawn less from the gentry than from the bureaucracy. Provincial governors and the reactionary press of Katkov campaigned for the abolition of the *zemstvos*, but though this did not happen a statute of 1890 reorganized *zemstvo* elections on the basis of estates, which increased the representation of nobles, and brought them under tighter control by governors. A movement began among some *zemstvo* nobles, supported by the doctors, veterinary surgeons, teachers, and agriculturalists employed by the *zemstvos*, in favour of the rule of law and a central Duma to articulate the opinion of the nation above the heads of the bureaucratic caste. But Nicholas II, who succeeded to the throne in 1895, warned against 'senseless dreams' of the participation of *zemstvo* representatives in the affairs of the internal administration. 'I shall maintain the principle of autocracy', he said, 'just as firmly and unflinchingly as did my unforgettable father.'[11] Only defeat at the hands of a foreign power could force the autocracy to change its mind. That defeat was to be administered in 1904, by Japan.

[11] Quoted by Galai, *The Liberation Movement in Russia*, 26.

CULTURE AT THE TURN OF THE CENTURY

Mass Culture

The broad public which had received an elementary education created a mass demand for cheap entertainment. It has been calculated that of 50 million Germans in Germany and Austria in 1886, 45 million could read and write. 20 million, especially in the countryside, were 'Sunday readers' of almanacks, the Prayer Book, and the Bible, 30 million read newspapers, 10 million read some popular literature, 2 million read the classics and 1 million followed literary developments. Novels were still expensive and libraries were patronized by the middle classes. More accessible to popular taste and means were the thrillers in pamphlet form, with garish illustrated covers, that sold for a penny or 25 pfennig. They were in the tradition of *colportage*, hawked by street pedlars who entered bars and workshops, or sold by tobacconists, newsagents, or at railway kiosks. The Mannheim publisher Julius Bagel brought out 967 stories in his *Kleine Volks-Erzahlungen* series between 1877 and 1906, rehashing the same adventures of pirates, smugglers, highwaymen, hangmen, explorers, settlers, and redskins. But imported American cowboy and detective stories transformed pulp fiction. Charles Perry Brown's Aldine Publishing Company introduced English readers to Buffalo Bill and Deadwood Dick at the turn of the century. In Germany the Dresden publisher Adolf Eichler launched Buffalo Bill in 1905 and the tough American detective Nick Carter in 1906. The most successful thriller series, written by Pierre Souvestre and published in Paris by Fayard, featured the masked bandit Fantomas. Between 1911 and 1914, thirty-two separate volumes sold about 600,000 copies each.

Conservative, religious, and cultivated circles were eloquent in their denunciations of the 'trash' and 'filth' that was corrupting the masses. The German Poets' Memorial Foundation was set up in 1901 to buy up wholesome literature for subsequent sale to public libraries. But a survey of 1902–3 showed that the municipal public library of Bremen was used almost entirely by *Mittelstand* groups, male and female; industrial workers accounted for only eight per cent of the readership. The socialist and trade-union organizations were equally concerned by the corruption of the masses and wanted to train informed, upright proletarians fit for the new society. Together they founded a Central Workers' Library in Bremen, but on the eve of war only a sixth of the books borrowed were socialist literature and two-thirds were fiction. Both bourgeois and proletarian moralists were fighting a losing battle against popular taste and the organized book trade. Cheap literature had to be fought on its own territory and on its own terms. In England George Newnes began *Tit-Bits*, a penny periodical of miscellaneous scraps and competitions, in 1880, and in 1896 introduced his Penny Library of Famous Books, a cheap edition of the classics. In 1879 the Religious Tract Society brought out the *Boy's Own Paper*, which was wholesome but not too anodyne and enrolled masterly story-tellers such as R. M. Ballantyne, G. A. Henty, Conan Doyle, and Talbot Baines Reed (who invented the 'Fifth Form at St Dominic's'). It was soon selling 250,000 copies. Alfred Harmsworth, a brilliant plagiarizer, followed *Tit-Bits* with *Answers* in 1888 and the *Boy's Own Paper* with *Comic Cuts* in 1890, which halved the price of a penny dreadful, and the *Halfpenny Marvel* which started the English detective Sexton Blake on his career. The rot had to be stopped early, but at the same time a new market had been discovered: that of the adolescent.

The reputation of Harmsworth was made by the *Daily Mail*, which he founded in 1896. Calculating that 'where one man will spend a shilling 5,000 will risk a halfpenny', he priced his newspaper at a halfpenny when other dailies were selling for a penny and *The Times* cost three pence. He rode the crest of jingoism and employed first-class reporters such as George W. Steevens, whose own *With Kitchener to Khartoum* (1898) went into thirteen editions in a few months. By 1900 the paper had a circulation of 1,250,000. In Paris the *Petit Parisien*, owned by a former notary's clerk, Jean Dupuy, was selling more copies than the *Petit Journal* in 1901 and reached the one-million mark in 1902. The German press remained more regional but the *Berliner Morgenpost*, launched by Leopold Ullstein in 1898, a year before his death, and selling at 10 pfennig rapidly achieved a circulation of 160,000.

These daily newspapers were the staple of the lower middle class and much of the working class. They did not represent the views of any party and indeed were scarcely 'political' at all. Comment and opinion gave way to the front-page sensation and news as education was replaced by news as entertainment. The international news agencies—Reuter, Havas, and Wolff—relayed news by telegraph and increasingly after 1887 by telephone. Financial news and racing news, including starting prices, were printed out in newspaper offices on tickers. Photographs were published in newspapers after 1880, first in separate supplements, then in the regular dailies. Competitions were held, with prizes to be won. Rising circulation attracted advertising which formed an important part of a newspaper's revenue. The *Petit Journal* drew 15 per cent of its income from advertising in 1884 and 24 per cent in 1909. This in turn kept the price of newspapers down and increased circulation.

While the press of mass circulation undermined popular literature hawked by pedlars, café-concerts and the music hall challenged the boulevard theatre and low drinking dives. In France the café-concert, which played hit tunes and entrance could be had for the price of a drink or an ice cream, expanded after regulations were relaxed in 1864; in 1889 there were as many café-concerts in Paris as theatres. In the same year the impresario Joseph Oller founded the Moulin Rouge, which was only the most famous of his string of theatres, while the Folies Bergère came under new management and was raised to European fame by Édouard Marchand. In Germany, Tingel-Tangels or tavern theatres providing rowdy entertainment and prostitutes for the lower classes were challenged by music halls such as the Apollo theatre, Düsseldorf, which opened in 1899. In Great Britain tighter building and licensing regulations drove out the gin palaces and saloon theatres and brought in specialized variety theatres in which drink was banned from the auditorium. Horace Edward Moss, the son of a diorama promoter, opened a music hall in Edinburgh in 1875 and another in Newcastle in 1884. After 1895 he built a chain of 'Empires' across Scotland and England, culminating with the Hippodrome which opened its doors in London in 1900. From the large towns variety theatres spread to the seaside resorts which in the 1890s thronged with holiday-makers ferried by cheap railway transport to enjoy pleasures that until then had been reserved for the middle class. At Blackpool Alderman William Broadhead built the South Pier in 1893 and the 518-foot Tower in 1894. Billiard halls and roller-coasters vied for attention with 'nigger' bands, complete with concertinas and banjos, and pierrot troupes imported from France.

The 'kinetograph', a device that would transform popular entertainment, was patented in the United States by Thomas Alva Edison in 1891. Emil Rathenau acquired the rights for Germany, but in November 1895 another German, Max Sklandonowsky, gave a public projection of moving pictures in the Berlin Wintergarten. More successful was the cinematograph of the Lumière brothers, which showed film at the Grand Café of the Boulevard des Capucines on 28 December 1895 and then toured England. There, Robert William Paul produced a cheaper version of Edison's kinetoscope and gave a public performance in March 1896. The demand for film grew, and early clips of weightlifters and performing animals were supplemented in 1896 by newsreel of the Epsom Derby and the coronation of Tsar Nicholas II. The Frenchman Charles Pathé, after earlier careers as a pork butcher, solicitors' clerk, and dealer in phonographs, went into the business of film-making and increased the capital of his business from one million francs in 1897 to thirty millions in 1913. By 1910 Max Linder, an actor who worked for Pathé, was the first screen star. A branch of the Pathé company in Italy, Cinès, inaugurated the era of the epic in 1912 with *Quo Vadis*, which was acclaimed in Paris and London. Early cinema performances were given in tents by travelling fairground showmen, and were then taken up by music-hall proprietors. In 1901, thirteen of the sixty large music halls in Great Britain regularly showed films and the following year they took off in the French café-concerts. Purpose-built cinemas appeared in Britain after 1909. In 1911 there were 3,000 cinemas in Great Britain, 1,500 in Germany, where young and working-class audiences watched 'junk films', the equivalent of pulp fiction, and 1,200 in Russia, where audiences reached seven million in 1912.

Not only bourgeois moralists but also anarchist, socialist, and trade-union activists became concerned that the working class was becoming demoralized by drink and semi-pornographic entertainment in the theatres and music halls. Romain Rolland, a French socialist intellectual, set out to create a simple, moral, class-conscious proletariat through a popular theatre which would arouse its nobler passions. His *14 July*, in which the hero is the Paris crowd, was staged in a commercial theatre in 1902. A first popular theatre was opened in the Paris suburb of Belleville in 1903, showing Rolland's drama *Danton*, but the auditorium was rarely more than a quarter full and the theatre closed in 1905. A second popular theatre opened in the Batignolles district in 1903 with Zola's *Thérèse Raquin*, but that too soon had to move and close. It was clear that the Parisian populace preferred the boulevard theatre, cabarets, and café-concerts.

The popular theatre, characterized by cheap, unreserved seats, a late start, and a repertoire to elevate the working classes, was a German creation. In opposition to the commercial theatre in Berlin which played Scribe and Dumas the Younger to easy-going bourgeois audiences, the theatre critic Otto Brahm founded the Freie Bühne in 1889 to perform Ibsen's *Ghosts*. This was still too expensive for the skilled workers who, restricted politically by the anti-socialist legislation, turned to the theatre to seek a response to their views. Bruno Wille, a freelance writer and lecturer, obliged them by establishing the Freie Volksbühne in 1890, which charged 50 pfennig a seat to see Ibsen's *Pillars of Society*. Two years later Wille founded the Neue Freie Volksbühne to perform plays of sharper social criticism. But there was always a struggle between the demands of proletarian consciousness and the demands of artistic and commercial success. The membership of the Neue Freie Volksbühne dropped to 200 in 1895 but rose after 1905 to 15,500 in the 1906–7 season, largely because it put on plays by Schiller and Shakespeare.

The working men's choral societies faced a similar dilemma. They sprang up during the period of the anti-socialist law as a 'cover' for socialist organization and to provide the battle-hymns for the class-conscious workers' army. But they were in competition with the middle-class, nationalistic clubs of the Deutscher Sängerbund and acquired artistic pretensions to increase their following. By 1912 the Deutscher Arbeiter Sängerbund had 192,000 members, 6,000 more than the Deutscher Sängerbund, included women, and performed Bach, Handel, and Beethoven. The director of the movement made clear in 1911 that it did not 'consider its sole purpose to be politically useful to the proletariat; its desire is rather to allow the proletariat to enjoy the finest fruits from the cornucopia of the goddess of music.'[1]

[1] Quoted by Dieter Dowe, 'The Workingmen's Choral movement in Germany before the First World War', *Journal of Contemporary History*, 13 (1978), 288.

The working classes of Europe were also making their influence felt on the world of sport. A book entitled *Sport in Europe*, published in 1901, was a guide to hunting and shooting from Spain to Russia for the European upper class.[2] Sport was also the turf, which was followed with equal interest by aristocrats and plebeians. Middle-class sports were of two traditions. The German tradition was gymnastics, a military and patriotic training organized by the Deutsche Turnerschaft. This had had 627,000 members in 1898. It was taken up by the Czech nationalists, whose movement was called Sokol (Falcon) and held its first congress in Prague in 1882. French gymnastics clubs sprang up in the wake of the defeat in 1870. They were concentrated in north-eastern France and were often founded by exiled Alsatians and Lorrainers who called them 'Le Souvenir' or 'La Revanche'. Membership was dominated by the petty bourgeoisie until the 1880s, when there was an influx of working-class youth who discovered the joys of evening exercise, travel to competitions, sociability, and (despite the organizers) acrobatics and drinking.

The English tradition was athletics. It was taken up by the *lycées* of Paris who formed the Racing Club of France in 1882 as racing on foot, with runners divided into stables, wearing jockey costumes and even carrying horse-whips. Hygienists encouraged the foundation of athletic clubs in schools to correct 'overtaxing' academic work and confinement in cramped boarding schools. One of them, Baron Pierre de Coubertin, was convinced that the strong, virile, physical and moral education of the British public schools was responsible for the prodigious expansion of the British Empire. In addition, he was troubled by quarrels between different sportsmen, whether gymnasts and rowers, marksmen and tennis-players, and within sports, as between German and Swedish gymnasts. Making money out of sport was on the increase but not to the taste of Coubertin. His aim was to 'unify and purify' sport under the auspices of the Olympic games of classical Greece. Almost single-handed he drew together a congress of delegates of as many sporting societies in the world as possible, interested the princes of Europe in his enterprise, and launched the first modern Olympic games at Athens in 1896. On that occasion, the Germans excelled at gymnastics, the Greeks at shooting and fencing, the Hungarians at swimming, the French at cycling, the Americans at athletics, and the English at lawn tennis. Further games were held in Paris in 1900, St Louis (USA) in 1904, London in 1908, and Stockholm in 1912.

Only sports that were practised by a number of countries qualified for the Olympic competition. Association football and rugby football, which both developed out of athletics, did not come into that category. In this case the prime mover was England. English firms introduced these games into Europe through its ports and commercial cities: Le Havre in 1872 followed by Bordeaux and Hamburg in 1881, Turin in 1887, Bilbao in 1898. The

---

[2] F. G. Aflalo (ed.), *Sport in Europe* (London, 1901).

French bourgeoisie preferred rugby to soccer, partly because of the popular image that the latter had in Britain. It flourished in the Paris region and south-west, nurtured by the wine trade and the English colonies of Pau and Biarritz. A French schoolmaster noted in 1891 that 'the Grand Prix at Longchamp attracts over fifty thousand, a football match hardly five hundred.'[3] It was not until 1900 that soccer became popular in France, catching on in the industrial towns of northern France, but the average gate rarely rose above a thousand.

This was quite different from the British experience. Association football began in the universities and public schools but soon teams were being formed by churches, chapels, Sunday schools, Board schools, public houses, factories, and railway works. West Ham Football Club was started in 1895 among the employees of the shipbuilding firm of Thames Ironworks in the aftermath of a strike by an employer who was anxious to promote industrial peace and prosperity. But the demands of success in the competition circuit led to the drafting in of professional players. Gates of 10,000 were common at English football matches from the 1880s, brought in by tram and railway, and were increasingly working class in composition. Football coupon betting spread in the 1890s and Manchester's *Athletic News*, a football weekly, was selling 180,000 copies by 1896. The FA Cup Final at Crystal Palace was seen by 66,000 in 1897 and 120,000 in 1913.

There were a million club football players in Great Britain in 1914, but only 200,000 in Germany. These were overwhelmingly made up of white-collar workers, students, and young professionals. The football team of the Ruhr town of Schalke, founded in 1904 and relying on miners' families for 60 per cent of its membership, was exceptional. The labour movement, rather than take up football and make it into a proletarian sport, condemned it as brutal. Instead it formed an Arbeiter Turnerbund in 1892 to rival the middle-class, chauvinistic Deutsche Turnerschaft and tried to win working-class members back from it. Its membership rose from 27,000 in 1898 to 187,000 in 1914, but it could not compete with the large, bright, well-equipped gymnasia of the Turnerschaft, and the more it competed, the more the workers' gymnastics movement abandoned the ideology of training for the class struggle for the Greek ideal of bodily training, in which the whole *Volk* should now participate.

The Arbeiter Turnerbund despised the cyclists of the Arbeiter Radfahrerverein, which had 130,000 members in 1910, on the grounds that they were exercising only their legs. Italian socialists rejected the middle-class values of the Italian Touring Club (1894) until the Red Cyclists were formed in 1913 to propagate anti-militarism.Cycling was above all the sporting mania of France. By 1910 the Touring Club of France had 125,000 members, but it had virtually no working-class membership. Cycling was popular as a spectator

---

[3] Quoted by Eugen Weber, 'Gymnastics and Sport in *fin de siècle* France', *American Historical Review*, 76, no. 1 (1971), 85.

sport in France, as football was in England. In 1895 the Paris municipal council built a cycle track in the working-class east of Paris to set off the posh racecourses of the west of Paris at Auteuil and Longchamp. Competitions such as the Six Days, culminating in a Saturday night sprint, offered huge profits to promoters and punters. Track racing was followed by road racing, which was admirably suited to small-town and rural France. Newspapers that were backed by cycle and car manufacturers to increase the sale of machines in turn sponsored road races to boost their circulation. In 1903 *L'Auto* launched the Tour de France with 20,000 francs in prize money and its circulation rose from 20,000 to 65,000 copies, and 320,000 copies by 1914. The wheel had come full circle, as business, sport, and the popular press all fed off each other.

Secularization?

At the end of the nineteenth century religious practice was under heavy assault from a number of quarters. Governments were intent on limiting the political influence of churches either by bringing them under tighter control or by cutting off funds. Urbanization and the Churches' endorsement of the existing social order alienated the mass of populations from organized religion. Intellectuals rejected the faith in the name of science. On the other hand, contrary developments could also be seen. Attacks by governments often served to galvanize communities around the defence of religion, which articulated communal interests and values. Not all urban or working-class populations abandoned religion, while on the other hand the threat of socialism stimulated at the same time social Catholicism, which looked to defend the existing social order, Christian Democracy, which endorsed the legitimate grievances of the masses, and integralism, which rejected liberalism and capitalism as well as socialism. Many intellectuals, unhappy with the claims of science, returned to the faith, and popular irreligion was countered by religious revivalism.

A Russian mystic, Vladimir Soloviev, regretted that the Russian Orthodox Church 'slumbered under the canopy of state tutelage'.[4] Konstantin Pobedonostsev, who was Overprocurator of the Holy Synod between 1880 and 1905, turned it into a tool of political reaction. Parish priests were an isolated caste of sons of priests. They were paid little by the state and acquired a reputation for charging extortionate fees and for drunkenness. The religion of the peasants was defined by the externals of candles, icons, and incomprehensible Church-Slavonic texts. The spiritual vacuum was filled by dissent. The puritanical Old Believers who waited on the imminent Apocalypse were joined after 1870 by the Stundists of the Ukraine who rejected sacraments for salvation by faith and adult baptism. Mystical sects of self-mutilators and flagellants united with the divine by means of incantations, dancing, and sexual

---

[4]   Quoted in Robert L. Nichols and T. G. Stavrou (eds.), *Russian Orthodoxy under the Old Regime* (Minneapolis, 1978), 30.

orgies. There were about 17.5 million Old Believers and sectarians in Russia at the census of 1897, or 15 per cent of the population. This does not include Poland where 233,000 Uniates, persecuted since 1875, returned fully to the Catholic Church when the government, under pressure from the *zemstvos*, increased toleration in 1904.

In Russian Poland Catholic bishoprics were either kept vacant or filled by political appointees of the Tsar. The lower clergy were sons of the Polish people and remained close to them, but, abandoned by their superiors, looked to other sources of authority. One of these was a nun, Feliksa Kozlowska, who claimed a divine mission to save the world from God's justice by slavery to the Virgin Mary. She gathered a community of priests together at Plock on the Vistula after 1893 and became its Little Mother. The priests who made pilgrimages to Plock were jeered as bleating rams led by a lecherous she-goat. A papal encyclical of 1905 ordered the congregation to disband and the following year Kozlowska was excommunicated. The Mariavites, as they were called, left the Roman Church, returned to the Polish people and replaced the Latin liturgy by Polish. They controlled 70 parishes and had 100,000 followers.

In the Roman Catholic Church liberals who had sought to compromise with secular authorities under the slogan 'a free Church in a free state' were undermined by attacks on the Church by those authorities, and other schools of Catholicism flourished. In Austria the episcopate was neo-Josephenist and anxious not to provoke the government. In 1894 it condemned the Christian Social activities of the lower clergy who were organizing the artisans of Vienna and peasants of Lower Austria. Rome however supported the Christian Socials because they preached a return to a Christian social order. The minority of Italian bishops who desired *rapprochement* with the Italian state were defeated by the question of the Temporal Power and by the ascendancy of the integralists, headed by Mgr Umberto Benigni, who was appointed Under-Secretary of the Congregation of Ecclesiastical Affairs in the Vatican in 1906. The integralists denounced capitalism, liberalism, and modernism in the same breath. So also did the Christian democrats. Unfortunately Christian democrats like Romolo Murri supported the demands of the working class and wanted to form a Catholic mass party. By 1907 he was outside the Church. The tension between the priest of the people and the reactionary hierarchy was brilliantly portrayed by Antonio Fogazzaro in his novel *Il Santo*, published in 1905, which immediately became a best-seller in several languages. Ironically Italian Catholics, though they did not form their own party, supported the governmental candidates of Giolitti in the election of 1913 against socialists and the extreme Left, now that Giolitti had defended religious instruction in state schools and declared his opposition to divorce.

In France the *Ralliement* between Church and Republic was scotched by the Dreyfus Affair and by the *rapprochement* between anticlerical France and the anticlerical Italian state in 1898–1904. The Radical Prime Minister, Combes, wanted to tighten state control over the Church under the Concordat but the socialist allies on whom he depended insisted that the Concordat be abrogated and that state payments to the Church and clergy be stopped. A law of December 1905 separated Church and state in France. Moderate bishops and Catholic mandarins of the Académie Française, nicknamed the 'green cardinals', fought for one last compromise: the acceptance of lay 'associations of worship' proposed by the government to manage Church property. But these were condemned by Pope Pius X in August 1906 as a violation of the ecclesiastical hierarchy (and a lesson to Spanish liberals that separation was not an option to be considered). The integralists and ultramontanes triumphed in France and Rome. In one sense they were close to popular Catholic opinion in France, for Catholics gathered in force early in 1906 to prevent officials, supported by gendarmes and troops, from making inventories of Church property. On the other hand the Christian democratic movement, especially the 'Sillon' of Marc Sangnier, which took seriously the problems of the working classes, was condemned by the Papacy in 1910 for wanting to rebuild the social order, defying the hierarchy, and indulging in politics. This of course did not prevent wealthy Catholics from rallying lock, stock, and barrel behind the presidency of Raymond Poincaré in 1913.

Protestant churches also developed strategies to deal with the threat of socialism. A Lutheran pastor from Alsace, Tommy Fallot, broke with his Marxist friends in 1888 and founded a Protestant Association for the Study of Social Questions. It proposed a middle way between socialism and capitalism based on the co-operative movement, but needed the support of the largely bourgeois French Protestant Churches. In Germany Adolf Stöcker helped to found the Protestant Social Congresses in 1890. These met annually to discuss labour protection, working-class housing, and the development of Protestant working-men's associations. There was no question of being soft on socialism, and during the miners' strike of 1905 the German Evangelical Church defended King, fatherland, and Christianity. In the Church of England a thin red line of Christian socialism was represented by the Guild of St Matthew, which was founded in East London in 1877 by Stuart Headlam, an Anglo-Catholic curate who was educated at Eton and Cambridge. Its first task, however, was to fight the atheism spread among the working classes by Charles Bradlaugh. When the London dockers went on strike in 1889 the Anglican Bishop of London, Temple, did nothing while Cardinal Manning of Westminster intervened to find a compromise.

Religion had nevertheless a role to play in the urban cauldron. The parish system of the established Church was less able than the sects to cope with the flood of immigrants. But the particular sect that individuals or families espoused frequently defined their class. In England, for example, Primitive Methodists were mainly working class, Congregationalists were a cut above

Baptists, while Unitarians and Quakers were predominantly the families of professional men and businessmen. Nonconformity was adopted by skilled working-class men as a badge of their respectability and by working-class women as a way of socializing outside the home. It was not to the taste, however, of the hunting classes or drinking classes.

Because Protestantism meant respectability and independence the task of those evangelical missionaries who campaigned to restore the urban masses to the faith was first to restore them to a decent life. William Booth, the founder of the Salvation Army in 1878, established food depots, night shelters, labour yards, and 'rescue homes' for women, but he made clear that 'it is primarily and mainly for the sake of saving the soul that I seek the salvation of the body'.[5] The Salvation Army began work in Paris in the 1880s but French Protestants saw themselves as superior to the Catholic masses and found the Army's revivalist hymn-singing, accompanied on the accordion, somewhat vulgar. The Catholic Christian Social movement in Austria and Lombardy-Venetia also believed that the lot of the poor must be improved by the foundation of mortgage banks, co-operatives and labour unions before they could be won for the Church. 'It is necessary that we organize them, that we give them bread', said a deputy at the Catholic Congress of Genoa in 1908. 'Then, once their faith is gained, we will get them to vote for religious instruction too.'[6]

There were exceptions to the phenomenon of urban irreligion. The antithesis of religious countryside/irreligious town is too simple. Immigrant communities such as the Italian and Irish Catholic populations in London retained their religion because they lived as colonies in foreign lands. At the same time there were vast rural areas, such as central France and southern Spain, where religious practice was at extremely low levels, lower even than in the towns that dotted them. Religious practice varied between regions which included both town and country. It was high in Belgian and French Flanders, including the conurbation of Lille–Roubaix–Tourcoing, in the French and Swiss Jura, in both Alsace and the highly urbanized Rhineland, in Savoy, the Valais, and northern Italy, and in northern Spain—not least in the industrialized Basque country. A high level of religious practice often underlined regionalism and even nationalism. Strong Catholicism reinforced Basque, Breton, and Alsatian regionalism, and Polish and Irish nationalism. After 1886 the disestablishment of the Anglican Church in Wales became an article of faith less of British Nonconformity than of Welsh nationalism.

One final (and desperate) way of whipping up religious feeling among populations who were losing touch with it was by the negative device of anti-Semitism. 'One power alone can oppose the invasion of the Jew', declared the Assumptionist Father Bailly in *La Croix* in 1889, 'and that is the Church.'[7]

---

[5] William Booth, *In Darkest England and the Way Out* (London, 1890), 45.
[6] Quoted by Richard A. Webster, *Christian Democracy in Italy* (London, 1961), 18.
[7] Quoted by Pierre Sorlin, *'La Croix' et les Juifs* (Paris, 1967), 94.

Hatred of the people who crucified Christ would extend the influence of Catholicism. In Protestant Germany, Adolf Stöcker remarked in 1879 that anti-Semitism was necessary for 'the strengthening of the Christian soil'. However, within a few years anti-Semitism in Germany had become not a religious hatred, opposing Jew to Christian, but a racial hatred, opposing Jew to Aryan. It rejected the Christianity that consoled the weak and sick and humanity at large for a Christianity that exalted man's appropriation of divinity by the Incarnation and above all the strength, health, will, and destiny of the German race. In 1892 Stöcker confessed that he saw 'a great danger in having the struggle against Judaism detached from Christian soil. ... Such an error is to treat the Jewish question as a racial question. This is not a Christian treatment.'[8]

Anti-Semitism adopted a spurious scientific rationale at the end of the century. The scientific mentality reigned supreme. But there was a movement at the same time among some intellectuals away from science and back to religion, if not back to the established Churches. In France Ferdinand Brunetière, editor of the liberal *Revue des Deux Mondes*, published an article in 1895 entitled 'Science and Religion'. In it he attacked the positivist cult of scientific inquiry and claim to formulate scientific laws that governed man's origin, behaviour and destiny. 'The unknowable', he said, 'surrounds us, envelops us, grips us.'[9] In addition the search for a morality independent of religion was doomed to fail. Man was not perfectible but burdened by Original Sin. Social inequalities could never be eliminated, only attenuated. A tough Catholic (not Protestant) morality was therefore for Brunetière the only force that could guarantee the social fabric.

Other thinkers found their way back to religion by aesthetic routes. The novelist Joris-Karl Huysmans rejected the materialism of the world and experimented with the aesthetic and sensual pleasures of the dilettante in his novel *À Rebours* (1884). In *Là-Bas* he played with satanism and black magic. But the hero of *En route*, written in 1892–3, made a pilgrimage to the Virgin of Suffering at La Salette, and the inspiration of Gothic cathedrals and the Catholic liturgy played a part in his becoming a Benedictine oblate in 1908. Charles Péguy, a left-wing intellectual and defender of Dreyfus's innocence, came to see that the childhood innocence, humility and trust of the peasant-saint Joan of Arc and the peasant-Virgin Mary was the way to God. Thérèse Martin, a Carmelite nun of Lisieux who died of consumption in 1897 at the age of twenty-four, reflected this ideal of a simple faith. The *Story of a Soul* which she left behind was published in 1898 and had sold 410,000 copies by the time she was canonized in 1925.

In Russia there were intellectuals who in the 1890s had placed their hopes in Marxism as the scientific solution to the problems of a backward country. Among them were Nikolai Berdyaev and Sergei Bulgakov who were close

[8] Quoted by Uriel Tal, *Christians and Jews in Germany* (Cornell, 1975), 258–9.
[9] Ferdinand Brunetière, *La Science et la Religion* (Paris, 1895), 20.

associates of Struve and followed him into the Union of Liberation in 1903. They associated with symbolist poets and toyed with mysticism before the failure of the 1905 Revolution drove them to look for eternal spiritual values in the Orthodox religion. Bulgakov argued that whereas the Gothic cathedral represented a yearning for God but never fulfilment, the Orthodox religion was the re-enactment of the mystery of the Incarnation among the faithful on earth. Attempts were made to draw the higher clergy of the Orthodox Church into discussion but Pobedonostsev would have none of it. For him, Orthodoxy was first and foremost the pillar of autocracy.

The Unconscious

The positivists' search for iron laws that determined human behaviour and eliminated all traces of free will reached something of a climax in the 1880s. Darwinian notions of reverse evolution invaded the field of criminology. In *Criminal Man*, published in 1876, Cesare Lombroso, a professor of legal medicine at the University of Turin, claimed to have discovered a race of 'born criminals', who were marked out by certain cranial and facial irregularities and who were cases of atavism, or throwbacks to a primitive stage of evolution. Madmen were little different: they were cretins in a moral sense. Society's defence against crime now became a very simple matter. Since these degenerates had no sense of moral responsibility and could not distinguish bad from worse, they must be eliminated by artificial social selection— transportation, perpetual imprisonment, or death.

The Darwinian credentials of this theory, and its appeal to a bourgeoisie terrified by crime, carried conviction at the first International Congress of Criminal Anthropology which was invited to Rome in 1885. Lombroso's work was translated into French in 1887 and a letter from Taine, the grand old man of positivism, printed in the second edition (1895), congratulated Lombroso for showing us 'libidinous, ferocious orang-outangs with human faces. … If they rape, steal or kill, it is infallibly because of their nature and their past. All the more reason to destroy them as soon as it is discovered that they are and will always remain orang-outangs.'[10] But by the second Congress of Criminal Anthropology, held in Paris in 1889, the French medical world had recovered itself. Lacassagne, professor of legal medicine at Lyons, and Gabriel Tarde, a statistician in the Ministry of Justice, attacked Lombroso for criminalizing certain physical features like large jaws and prominent ears and argued that crime was not a hereditary but a social phenomenon, the fruit of poverty, ignorance, alcoholism, and vice. The criminal still had a capacity for good and, isolated in a prison cell, could be reformed.

For Tarde, crime was committed because it was fashionable in a certain milieu and became crystallized as the habit of that milieu. Words, craft

[10] Taine to Lombroso, 12 April 1887, in C. Lombroso, *L'Homme criminel* (2nd edn., Paris, 1895), pp. ii–iii.

techniques, moral maxims, articles of law, and religious rites were copied from one individual by another, whether son from father, apprentice from master or peer from peer, so that all social norms were merely imitative. The free will of the individual was restored to pride of place. This individualistic view, however, was not accepted by Emile Durkheim, professor of sociology at the University of Bordeaux. In his *Rules of Sociological Method*, published in 1895, he asserted that social norms were 'things' which existed objectively, outside the individual, and exercised a coercive power over him. Any deviation from the norm was punished by society either informally or, in the case of a crime, formally. For Durkheim crime was not, as Tarde said, a disease but rather a revolt against despotic states of 'collective consciousness', like religion, without which no change would be possible. In modern industrial societies, Durkheim observed, collective beliefs tended to lose their grip and new forms of social solidarity emerged, based on the interdependence of individuals who specialized in very different forms of labour. But even then, individuals were always striving to improve their lot and were confronted more often by failure than by success.

The positivists had argued that morality based on religion was out of date in a scientific age and became less and less effective as religion lost its hold on the masses. Some of them tried to replace religion by a secular morality that owed much to the German philosopher Kant. Morality was to be universal. That is to say that each individual was to regard himself as, in a sense, legislating for the whole of mankind by his actions. He should do nothing which, if done by everybody, would tear apart the social fabric. Both religions and secular forms of morality laid heavy constraints on the individual, constraints that were intolerable for Friedrich Nietzsche, a young professor of classical philosophy at the University of Basle who resigned his chair for medical reasons in 1879. For the next ten years, before he collapsed from tertiary syphilis, he struggled to find a new morality for the individual that would restore him to his freedom and to his central place in the universe. God was dead, and that was as it should be, because Christianity impoverished man by subordinating the sensual to the spiritual, the mortal to the immortal, life to afterlife. Kantian morality was just as oppressive, because equality required the good of the individual to be subordinated to the good of all, and the conception of goodness which it promoted was, Nietzsche claimed, a disguised form of what was expedient for society. People conformed through fear and outsiders were stamped upon. And yet, argued Nietzsche, meaning had to be created in *this* world. What was true and had value for the individual was only what furthered *his* life. Fearless individuals who felt the will to power within them must refuse to compromise, overcome the weakness that led them to imagine that morality was something independent of their own wills, and strive to create new values for themselves. Their actions might be denounced by society as evil but only out of destruction could come creation; evil and good blurred into one another. The only rule constraining the individual was that what he willed now he was prepared to will again, indeed, to will its eternal return. 'Dear Professor,' he wrote in his last letter to his older colleague Jakob Burckhardt in 1889, 'in the end I would much have preferred being a Basle professor to being God. But I did not carry my private egoism so far that I should omit the creation of the world. You see, one has to make sacrifices, however and wherever one lives.'[11]

The exponents of the human will found another idol in Henri Bergson, an altogether more sedate Parisian professor of philosophy who gave public lectures at the Collège de France after 1900. Bergson reacted against the neo-Kantian view that it was not possible to know ultimate reality but only approximations to it which could be subsumed under scientific symbols and laws. In his work, which culminated in *Creative Evolution*, published in 1907, Bergson agreed that the human intellect could analyse only space and matter, that was 'ready made'. But there was also the inner life-force of things, a flux or process of becoming that was like an electric charge. It penetrated matter and organized it into higher and higher forms of evolution, culminating with the human intellect. Human beings were part of that current of energy, charged with matter, but only that matter was accessible to the intellect. Yet if the mind did violence to itself and substituted intuition for intellect, it could put itself in contact with the life-force, of which the human will was only a prolongation. By that the will was energized and endowed with creative power.

Bergson's ideas influenced a whole generation of thinkers, including Georges Sorel, an engineer who retired to a Paris suburb and religiously followed the Friday lectures. The extraordinary result of his studies was *Reflections on Violence* (1908). Sorel argued that 'myths', such as the Holy Grail, Reign of Saints, or Second Coming had immense and irrational powers to drive men to act. The myth of the general strike, as a complex of images of class war, had the power to provoke feelings of anger in the working class and to inspire actions that would transform the world. Because the myth was grasped intuitively by the workers there was no need for a Leninist élite schooled in the scientific theory of Marxism. But Sorel and Lenin agreed that revolutionary will must now supplant the unfolding laws of the contradictions of capitalist society which left the workers as impotent pawns of fate. Similarly, Sorel disliked Jaurès and his parliamentary compromises and justified proletarian violence which embodied the Bergsonian life-force and the Nietzschean will to power. However, like Jaurès, Sorel was interested in the triumph of moral values. For Jaurès that meant justice for the working class. For Sorel, as for Nietzsche, it meant the triumph of any values, so long as they were won by struggle. At about the time Sorel's book was published, the working-class strike movement in 1906–8 lost its momentum and Sorel

[11] Quoted by J. P. Stern, *The Mind of Nietzsche* (Oxford, 1980), 22.

looked to the right radicalism of the Action Française, which was not afraid of street violence, to continue the fight against decadence.

At the turn of the century there was a reaction against the positivist doctrine, so influential in the middle years of the century, that the behaviour of men in society could be explained by general laws. For many thinkers this had the effect of reducing individuals to leaves in a swirling current. German idealists distinguished between *Naturwissenschaft* or natural science, in which it was possible to derive general laws, and *Geisteswissenschaften*, or cultural sciences, where subject and object were of the same kind, namely human beings with thoughts, feelings and intentions. Because the subjective motives of individuals had to be taken into account in a discipline such as history, it was not possible to derive general laws that would make it possible to predict their future behaviour. This mode of thinking was revived by Wilhelm Dilthey, who became professor of history at Berlin in 1882. For him, the only way for the historian to explain the past was to re-experience in his own mind the thoughts, feelings and intentions of historical figures. The free will of individuals made their actions unpredictable, so that while it was possible to understand why a particular revolution happened it was not possible to discover a law governing why revolutions in general happened.

Max Weber, whose career progressed from law practice to academic law, and to ancient and medieval economic history before he was appointed professor of political economy at Freiburg in 1894, accepted the difficulties posed by the subjective intentions of individuals but thought that it was still possible to reconcile them with general laws of social behaviour. To be free was in fact to be rational, establishing certain goals, and working out the best means to achieve them. True, man was not an island but had to take account in his actions of other people, both his relations with them and the expectations they had of him. These relations and norms constrained his actions and made them more predictable. Weber however preferred 'the subjective understanding of behaviour', explanations based on the mind-sets of particular groups, rather than those based on external circumstances. Ironically, he believed that the more rational men became in pursuit or profit, order or salvation, the more effectively they built 'iron cages' of capitalism, bureaucracy and religion which limited their freedom.

Weber, like Bergson, stopped just short of postulating the existence of the unconscious. The revolt against the determination of human behaviour in the name of free will was obliged to. The essence of freedom was self-expression, and there was a sense in which the unconscious was a prey to dark forces over which the individual had no control. Freedom and submission to the unconscious might be considered to be mutually incompatible. There were scientists at the turn of the century who oriented their research to discovering the laws which governed the unconscious mind. In the long term it might become possible to understand and control mental phenomena. The

Paris neurologist Jean Charcot began his science of the mind with hysteria. He isolated it as a nervous disease and explained it physiologically as a disorder of the brain. He experimented with hypnosis as a cure, for hypnosis suspended the patient's faculty of concentration which could then be re-directed by suggestion to a particular object. Gustave Le Bon, who turned from medical studies to become a popular writer on science, was terrified by the scenes of the Paris Commune in 1871. He attended the lectures of Charcot in the late 1870s and was influenced by Lombroso. In his *Psychology of Crowds*, published in 1895, he argued that men who were conscious, rational beings in isolation descended several rungs of civilization when they became swept up in a crowd. They became slaves to impulse, began to hallucinate, and, in a hypnotic trance, became completely vulnerable to the suggestions of leaders who might be thrown up. For Le Bon revolution was a return to barbarism that could be equated with hysteria; the most terrible of revolutionaries, from the *tricoteuses* of 1793 to the *pétroleuses* of 1871, were invariably women.

The thought of Le Bon was that of a provincial bourgeois frightened by the 'age of the masses' and finding a cathartic explanation in physiological and anthropological determinism. Sigmund Freud, who studied with Charcot in Paris in 1885–6 and hung Brouillet's 'Clinical Lesson of Dr Charcot' in his Vienna study, was a good deal more sophisticated. Freud asserted that mental disorders were not physiological but psychological in origin. Essentially, they derived from the repression of sexual desires that was required by society. Middle-class men placed their wives on a pedestal of chastity and satisfied their lusts in illicit relationships with women of a lower class. Middle-class wives were supposed to be above sexual desire but were often no strangers to adultery. The personality of the individual was thus not a coherent whole but fragmented, torn between primitive desires and social expectations, racked by neurosis and guilt. Freud approached the unconscious, in which these battles were fought, not by means of hypnosis but using the technique of relaxed narration by the patient, until he no longer believed their traumatic stories of actual seduction by their parents. The death of his father in 1896 precipitated a period of self-examination and he hit on the dream as the 'royal road to knowledge of the unconscious activities of the mind'. Dreams were not representations of the future but regressions to the past, to childhood, which was far from being innocent. Dreams were the disguised fulfilment of suppressed wishes, especially the unpermissible longing of the child for the parent of the opposite sex and feelings of jealousy and hostility towards the other parent, which Freud christened the Oedipus complex in 1897. In *The Interpretation of Dreams*, published in 1900, Freud suspected that 'Friedrich Nietzsche was right when he said that in a dream "there persists a primordial part of humanity which we can no longer reach by a direct path" '.[12] In *Totem*

---

[12] Sigmund Freud, *The Interpretation of Dreams* (3rd edn., London, 1932), 506.

and Taboo (1913) he tried to uncover the primordial myth which lay at the root of the human psyche. Freud tapped the unconscious through the dream, asserted that most anxiety was sexual in origin and tried to elicit the laws that governed it. The revolt against positivism resurrected free will and restored meaning to life, but at the same time discovered that 'free will' was compressed by unconscious forces which could themselves be explained scientifically.

Symbolism

Whereas the Realists were enthusiastic about the modern world, the Symbolists felt alienated from everything it stood for: the mechanization of life, the march of democracy, the degeneration of the race. They had a sense of the decay of civilization and tried to flee it. Unlike the Romantics, however, they found no compensation in Nature, which seemed cruel, or in love, for they thought women voracious and dangerous. Instead, they sought refuge in an inner life, that of instinct or the unconscious, though their inner selves were often fragmented, tortured, or unstable. They searched for 'artificial paradises' in the world of drugs, dreams, or sexual experience. For that reason, Symbolism was closely associated with Decadence.

While the Realists had sought to represent reality, to subjectify the objective, Symbolists tried to fix the moods of the unconscious, to objectify the subjective. A new language had to be found to convey their message. They were keen to break down the barriers between art, literature, and music, exploring the colour of sounds and the music of words. Some Symbolists were proficient as painters as well as musicians, or poets as well as painters. They were a self-conscious avant-garde, meeting in cafés and cabarets, from Le Chat Noir, which opened in Paris in 1881, and Berlin's Schall und Rauch, which opened in 1901, to Moscow's Bat (1908). Here artists experimented with their art, away from the gaze of the masses, often parodying the grand opera or bourgeois theatre of the previous evening, developing night-club sized art forms, such as *chansons* in which the text mattered as much as the music, puppet shows, and Chinese shadows.

Symbolist painting was distinctly post-Impressionist, about moods clothed in elaborate forms, not about the play of light. Myths and legends, such as those of the Sphinx, Oedipus, and the Biblical story of John the Baptist, Salome, and Herod's wife, were the rage, and design was central, whether Japanese, Islamic, medieval, or primitive. It had its precursors in the Pre-Raphaelites and French hallucinatory painters such as Gustave Moreau, rediscovered after 1880 and described by Huysmans as 'a mystic shut up in the heart of Paris ... Plunged into ecstasy he sees the radiance of fairy-like visions, the sanguinary apotheoses of other ages.'[13] His *Oedipus and the Sphinx*, shown in the Paris Salon of 1864, expressed a deep fear of women.

---

[13] Quoted by John Rewald, *Post-Impressionism* (New York, 1962), 158.

These were overtaken by a new generation of artists. Vincent van Gogh came from Belgium to Paris, where he met Paul Gauguin in 1886. Early in 1888 he went to Provence, where he was intoxicated by the Mediterranean sunlight. He projected his own violent moods on to the canvas in red and green. After he was transferred to a lunatic asylum in 1889 he painted landscapes that were tortured heaps of colour edged in black, his anguish pent up in the swirling impasto. A year later he shot himself. Gauguin, who spent his child-hood in Peru and left a seminary to go to sea, was inspired by the primitive societies of Brittany and Tahiti which he imagined to be closer to the eternal truths of humanity. He raised the background and flattened the figures into a single plane, as in Japanese prints. He simplified the design into blocks of vivid colours, which were outlined in black like stained-glass windows, to concentrate the sensation.

The impact of post-Impressionist art on younger German artists provoked the so-called Secessions from mainstream art in Munich in 1893 and Vienna in 1897. In Munich Franz von Stuck exhibited a painting entitled *Sin* (1893), portrayed as a *femme fatale*, and revived the images of antiquity to challenge the powerful Bavarian Church. In Vienna Gustav Klimt scandalized the pro-fessors with his allegorical paintings on the ceiling of the main university auditorium (1900–7), rendering Philosophy by angst-ridden figures and Medicine by pregnant women, apes, and skulls. Refused a professorship him-self, he reverted to portraits of women in an exotic, Byzantine style. The new century saw a new wave of symbolist art in Paris. Henri Matisse, a Picard who abandoned a career in law for art, made his impact at the Autumn Salon in Paris in 1905. His emphasis was on the flat, smooth surface, the curving shapes of figures like paper cut-outs (which at the end of his life they became), and bright, purified colours vibrating together. Everything was brought to a state of equilibrium and ideal being. In Dresden a group of artists calling them-selves Die Brücke (the Bridge) formed around Ernst Kirchner, an architec-ture student at the Technische Hochschule. They followed developments in Paris but were also inspired by the Norwegian Edvard Munch, and by the German art of Grünewald, and Gothic woodcuts. Where Matisse seemed to be happy with line and colour in themselves the German Expressionists, especially after they moved to Berlin in 1911, were inspired by an inner vision which was twisted, distorted, even demonic.

The predicament of these artists was that they still painted objects, while objects interfered with the emotions that they were trying to suggest. In the end the object had to be destroyed. A start was made in Paris after 1908 by the Spanish painter Pablo Picasso and the Frenchman Georges Braque. They abolished perspective and combined in a single image objects seen from several different viewpoints. Between 1909 and 1911 they broke the objects up into fragments and concretized the spaces between so that the boundary between the object and its surroundings no longer existed. Another

Spaniard, Juan Gris, intellectualized what they were doing and imposed a linear grid on the patterns that were emerging. By 1912 the abstract composition came first, models were no longer used, and rectangles here and there might suggest an object, like a newspaper article or sheet of music, that could be painted in or pasted on. This technique came to be described as Cubism.

Paris intellectuals loved to sit in cafés, found schools, and issue manifestos. Picasso and Braque were Cubists but somewhat indifferent to the Cubist school that met at the Closerie des Lilas. This school used the poet Guillaume Apollinaire as its spokesman and made a sensation at the Salon des Indépendants in 1911. Its leader, Robert Delaunay, was the link between the Paris Cubists and the Blaue Reiter (Blue Rider) school which held its first exhibition in Munich in December 1911. This included the Russian Vassily Kandinsky who turned down a post in academic law to follow the avant-garde in Germany and Paul Klee, son of the German conductor of the Berne Philharmonic Orchestra. They felt that primitive peoples, children, and even animals had more insight into the inner life of the world than civilized men, and that colours were like musical tones, playing on the emotions of the soul.

The Italian Futurists, based in Milan, published a manifesto in *Le Figaro* in 1909 in praise of energy, speed, struggle, violence, and war. Unlike *fin de siècle* Symbolists, they were passionate about new technology, aeroplanes, and fast cars. In 1911 a group of them was brought to Paris by their promoter, Filippo Marinetti. They did not adopt the grid system of the Cubists but painted the lines of force of a street in movement or the rhythm of a violinist. They crammed things remembered, premonitions, and associations of ideas into their pictures under the banner of *simultaneità*. In Moscow Mikhail Larionov, the son of a military doctor who organized exhibitions of French and German painters, tried to paint not matter but the energy that it emitted, in rays or waves. He publicized what he called Rayonism in 1911 as the pictorial equivalent of music. There was a response even in England. Percy Wyndham Lewis founded the school of Vorticists and in July 1914 published a review unhappily entitled *Blast*.

There was a good deal of cross-fertilization among artists and writers in the cafés of Paris. In 1890 Gauguin was mixing with Symbolist poets at the Café Voltaire. As with Cubism, the masters of the genre were one thing, the movements another. Huysmans introduced the public to the masters through his novel *À Rebours* (1884), the hero of which read Verlaine, Mallarmé, Baudelaire, and Edgar Allen Poe. The previous year Paul Verlaine, who had spent time in English preparatory schools and Belgian prisons, and would spend more drying out in French hospitals, announced the *poètes maudits*, who included himself, Stéphane Mallarmé and Arthur Rimbaud. Rimbaud, with whom Verlaine had travelled in 1873 after his marriage broke up, was the adolescent poet of revolt. His plunge into the unconscious was traced by the titles of his poems—'The Drunken Boat', *A Season in Hell*, *Illuminations*. By the 'alchemy of the word', rhythms, images, and colour-coded vowel sounds, 'I noted the inexpressible,' he said, 'I fixed giddiness.'[14] Then inspiration left him. In 1886, when the *Illuminations* were finally published, he was trafficking skins, ivory, and guns in East Africa.

Mallarmé, a provincial schoolmaster reared on 'art for art's sake', had not a whit of romanticism or religious feeling about him. His quest for the ideal was haunted by the fear that behind the azure sky there was nothing. In *Hérodiade* (unfinished) and the *Afternoon of a Faun* (1876) he invented a hermetically sealed world in which beauty reflected itself. He sought to unveil the mystery of the universe in poetry. But words too often signified things and to signify was not to suggest. He wanted to 'paint not the thing but the effect it produced', to make the reader forget that he was using words. So he evoked impressions that shimmered, consumed themselves, and dissolved in light. Mallarmé wrote very little after 1876 and had nothing to do with the Symbolist manifesto that was published in 1886 by a group of poets led by Jean Moréas, and stated that 'symbolist poetry seeks to clothe the Idea in sensible form'. On the other hand his Tuesday soirées in the rue de Rome became the meeting place for all symbolist writers.

One of the visitors in 1891 was Oscar Wilde, who had made a reputation in London as a poet, playwright, and high priest of decadence. He was inspired by the ongoing *Hérodiade* to write *Salome* (1892), later made into an opera by Richard Strauss, and his French friends were much more upset that the English when he was sent to prison in 1895. Mallarmé had also been visited in 1889 by a young Rhinelander, Stefan George, who refused to follow his father into commerce or enter the civil service when he left the Gymnasium at Darmstadt, and began to translate Baudelaire's *Fleurs du mal* into German. In Vienna in 1891 George met Hugo von Hofmannsthal, who was still at school, and invited him to collaborate on the *Blätter für die Kunst*, a review that he launched in Berlin in 1892. George and Hofmannsthal abandoned the tormented ecstasies of Goethe imitators and developed a more lyrical German poetry, which suggested the changing moods of their inner life. But the legacy of German Romanticism was difficult to shake off, and George turned to distant worlds of pastoral Antiquity, the chivalric Middle Ages, and the Persian Orient to explore men driven by Fate and the Gods, and torn between love and duty to a higher ethic.

Drama as well as poetry lent itself to the exploration of an inner world in which men were constrained by Fate or by subconscious forces. In the plays of the Norwegian Henrik Ibsen characters destroyed themselves by sacrifice to a mission or duty that no longer had any sense, instead of surrendering themselves to love. Not until the *Master Builder* (1892) in which the builder is driven to climb as high as he has built in order to deserve the love of a

[14] Arthur Rimbaud, *Poésies complètes* (Paris, 1963), 120.

younger woman was there a sense in which the characters were gripped by forces over which they had no control. But Max Reinhardt, who moved from the cabaret Schall und Rauch to succeed Otto Brahm as director of the Deutsche Theater in Berlin in 1905, presented *Ghosts* (1881) as a drama of destiny rather than moral dilemma, in which the actors were dwarfed and suffocated by the jagged mountains of Edvard Munch's set (1906).

Maurice Maeterlinck, a Flemish law student who took to writing plays when he went to Paris in 1885, caused a sensation with *Pelléas et Mélisande*, which opened there in 1893. The conflicts and anxieties of the lovers, doomed to die, were conveyed by the remote, northern fairy-tale setting with its dark forests and subterranean passages beneath castles, and the repetition and unfinished sentences of the dialogue. Belgian, German, and Polish writers, much more than the French, used myths as a path into the recesses of the human soul. Russian symbolism was very close to mysticism and religion and somewhat obsessed by the archetype of the Eternal Feminine. Alexandr Blok, who came from a respectable legal and academic family in St Petersburg, began in this vein with his *Poems on the Beautiful Lady* (1905). But when his wife left him to become an actress he wrote the *Puppet Show* (1906) in which the Eternal Feminine represented Death to the frock-coated mystics but Columbine to Pierrot and Harlequin.

Dramatists were fascinated by puppets in the early years of the century. Puppets were human symbols manipulated by outside forces, but they were also papier mâché manipulated by men. They were mute and could only gesture; they wrote with their bodies. 'People are tired of listening to words', said Hugo von Hofmannsthal, ten years before he wrote *Prelude to a Puppet Show* (1906), 'for words have pushed themselves in front of things … This has awakened a desperate love for all those arts which are executed without speech: for music, for the dance, and all the skills of the acrobats and jugglers.'[15] In 1906 Hofmannsthal's *Oedipus and the Sphinx* was produced by Max Reinhardt at the Deutsche Theater in Berlin and Richard Strauss asked him to adapt it as the libretto for an opera. The result was *Elektra*, performed in Dresden in 1909, the first fruit of a collaboration between Hofmannsthal, Reinhardt, and Strauss, which continued with *Der Rosenkavalier* in 1911 and *Ariadne auf Naxos* in 1912.

Links between musicians and Symbolist writers were numerous. Claude Debussy, who survived a rigorous classical training at the Paris Conservatory and in Rome, was attracted by poets who merely hinted at things and allowed him to graft on his thoughts. He wrote songs for poems by Baudelaire and Verlaine. In 1894 his setting of Mallarmé's *Afternoon of a Faun* was performed. But what inspired him from its first production was Maeterlinck's *Pelléas et Mélisande*. He made as much use of silence as of sound to express emotion, and in the orchestration each instrument was given a delicate

---

[15] Quoted by Michael Hamburger, *Hofmannstahl: Three Essays* (Princeton, 1972), 67.

colour of its own to blend into the painting. Instead of the rhythm, phrasing, dynamic, articulation, and accent all being determined by the melody and harmony, as in the German and Italian tradition, Debussy made them all into variables that depended equally on the atmosphere of sound that he wanted. And the first performance in 1902 was a success, despite the threat of Maeterlinck to challenge him to a duel for failing to cast his mistress as Mélisande.

In his *Images* for piano of 1905–12, orchestrated in 1910–13, Debussy abandoned literary allusions and tried to create 'an effect of reality'. He also wrote the score for *Jeux*, a ballet performed by Diaghilev's company in Paris in 1912. Ballet had collapsed at the Paris Opera by 1880 and was considered unworthy of the serious composer, who must concern himself with opera. But in Russia the tradition was maintained by the choreographer Marius Petipa and the ballets of Glinka were followed by those of Tchaikovsky. The revolution in ballet was initiated by the Irish-American dancer Isadora Duncan who rejected elegance and brilliance for a simple, free style and used the dance to express the human soul. In 1904 she visited St Petersburg and impressed Sergei Diaghilev, a rich aesthete who edited *The World of Art* journal. Diaghilev formed a dance company, took Michel Fokine as his choreographer, Anna Pavlova and Nijinsky among his dancers, Alexandre Benois and Léon Bakst as his designers, Igor Stravinsky as his composer, and brought them to Paris in 1909. Stravinsky, the son of a leading bass at the Imperial Opera in St Petersburg, composed *The Firebird* for the company in 1910 and *Petrushka*, with Nijinsky playing the unhappy puppet who fails to win the love of the ballerina, in 1911. Stravinsky then turned to a pagan rite of a girl dancing herself to death before the elders in order to propitiate the god of spring. Bakst designed the production as a bas-relief with the figures in profile and Stravinsky based his music on rhythm to elicit from the dancers 'a series of rhythmic mass movements of the greatest simplicity which would have an instantaneous effect on the audience'.[16] Diaghilev wanted Nijinsky to undertake the choreography, but unfortunately Nijinsky understood nothing of music and was already half mad. The first performance of the *Rite of Spring* in May 1913 was ill-received, although the score was later described by Debussy as 'a beautiful nightmare'.[17]

In Vienna, musically one of the most conservative cities in Europe, another breakthrough was made by Arnold Schoenberg. The son of a shoe-shop owner, a bank employee for four years and then the choirmaster of a metal-workers' union, Schoenberg had to go to Berlin in 1901 to find a remunerative teaching post, with the help of Richard Strauss. He also painted, seeking 'only to pin down the subjective feeling' in the view of Kandinsky,[18] and had three works in the Blue Rider exhibition of 1911. His

[16] Igor Stravinsky, *Chronicle of My Life* (London, 1936), 83.
[17] Debussy to Stravinsky, 8 Nov. 1913 in Robert Craft (ed.), *Conversations with Igor Stravinsky* (London, 1959), 50.
[18] Quoted by Willi Reich, *Schoenberg: A Critical Biography* (London, 1971), 41.

Gurrelieder, finished in the same year, first performed in Vienna in 1913, was well received because it was richly orchestrated and based on a familiar Danish legend. But Schoenberg was abandoning the cumbersome harmonies and swollen melodies of the tonal tradition in order to create a new musical language of simplicity and versatility. He also set aside the clutter of literary allusion for a music that was more abstract and expressed the depths of the unconscious mind. *Pierrot Lunaire*, performed in Berlin in 1912, was scored for eight instruments and a voice for which relative pitches were notated to form a speech-melody. In *Die glückliche Hand* (*The Knack*), finished in 1913, the fears and anxieties of the main character were to be 'projected' as a spectral choir of six men and six women looking through keyholes, their faces illuminated by green or red light. Asked whether he would be interested in making a film of the piece, Schoenberg demanded 'the utmost unreality. The whole thing should have the effect not of a dream but of chords ... sounds for the eye.'[19] It was not performed until 1924.

The search for a new language of expression was the overriding concern of the French novelist, Marcel Proust. The son of a prosperous doctor of medicine and an artistic mother who was the daughter of a Jewish stock-broker, he was racked by illness and at the age of thirty-five retired to a cork-lined room to write. The three thousand pages of his *À la Recherche du Temps Perdu*, written (except for the last volume) before 1913, relate, on one level, the apprenticeship of Marcel in the aristocratic salons of the Faubourg Saint-Germain, in love with both men and women, and in politics. On another level the book traces the apprenticeship of the artist and his struggle, punctuated by periods of hope and depression, to find a voice, and some of the most important characters in the novel are artists whom he observes. Proust rejected the realism epitomized by the Goncourt brothers and by those who believed that 'reality' was a world of objects which could be painstakingly documented. For him, our senses registered impressions that are only signs or symbols of a meaningful world existing beyond them. This world is not comfortable, for the signs are difficult to interpret. His characters are unable to go beyond appearances really to know each other; they do not know whether they are loved or in love, and whether or not they are socially acceptable. Moreover, everything is in a state of flux: people age and become unrecognizable; love can never be durable; and what confers social status at one moment, may no longer do so the next. For Proust, the subjective world constructed by the individual has the virtue of illusion, whereas reality inevitably brings disappointment. Art, because it can preserve illusion, seems to provide a resting-place. At the end of Proust's novel, finished after the First World War, Marcel has cracked the code and is ready to write his own novel in the light of his new vision.

[19]   Schoenberg to Emil Hertzka, autumn 1913, in Schoenberg, *Letters* (London, 1964), 44.

15

THE BREAK-UP OF NINETEENTH-CENTURY EUROPE

1905: Revolution in Russia

The 1905 Revolution in Russia was a nationalist, liberal, socialist, and popular explosion, triggered by the defeat of Russia in the Russo-Japanese war. The Russian autocracy never reformed itself unless constrained by military defeat, which made repression impossible, but now it was forced down the path of concessions for the first time since the Crimean War. And yet, in the short term, the revolutionary movement failed. The opposition was too divided, fear of revolution caused the propertied classes to rally to the regime, and the government recovered its nerve.

The western and southern borderlands of the Russia empire were both its most industrialized regions and the thickest with national minorities. This mixture of labour and nationalist grievances was highly unstable, although movements of Finns, Latvians, Lithuanians, Poles, Jews, Georgians, and Armenians tended to divide between nationalist and socialist wings. In the western provinces Jews suffered both as Jews and as workers, and were split between middle-class Zionists, labour Zionists, the Bund, which was socialist but demanded cultural autonomy for Jews, and the Russian Social Democratic and Labour Party (RSDLP), from which it broke in 1903. The Bund was on even worse terms with Pilsudski's Polish Socialist party. The PPS tried to recruit Polish-speaking Jews and yet was tainted by anti-Semitism. It was interested only in founding a Polish democratic republic, not a Russian democratic federation. For his part, Pilsudski was at daggers drawn with the National Democratic party of Dmowski. Dmowski was no longer interested in socialism, and opposed to use of violence that would only invite repression. When the Japanese attacked Port Arthur in February 1904, Pilsudski went to Tokyo to plan a national insurrection in Poland and Dmowski went there to urge the Japanese not to give him any help. The socialist parties of Pilsudski and Rosa Luxemburg tried to whip up strikes that erupted in January 1905 into a full-scale rising; Dmowski set up a National Workers' Union to organize workers who opposed strike action and the two movements clashed violently. Dmowski was closer to the Finnish nationalists who were struggling against the tyranny of the Russian autocracy: the emasculation of their Diet in 1899, a Russification edict in 1900, the abolition of the separate Finnish army in 1901 and the assumption of dictatorial powers by the Russian governor-general Bobrikov in 1903. After the failure of petitioning and passive resistance movements, Bobrikov was assassinated in 1904, and in November 1905 Finland was in the grip of a general strike.

The liberal and democratic opposition to the autocracy formed a Union of Liberation in Switzerland in 1903. It was the organ of *zemstvo* gentry who wanted a constitution and of radical intellectuals led by the former Marxist, Struve. It did not speak for the 'Slavophile' members of the *zemstvos*, such as D. N. Shipov, who believed in a trust between Tsar and representatives of the Russian people, and held their own *zemstvo* congresses, but it built a bridge to professional associations of lawyers, medical personnel, engineers, and teachers, many of whom formed the *zemstvos'* expanding civil service, and to unions of white-collar and railway workers. These gathered in May 1905 in the Union of Unions, which was 100,000-strong by October that year.

No revolution would be possible in Russia, however, without a mass movement of peasants and workers. After 1902 there was an upsurge of peasant unrest in the black-earth belt of the Ukraine and along the Volga. Strike activity gathered momentum in southern Russia, where the enterprises were large-scale, often foreign-owned, and isolated from student activists in Kiev or Kharkov. There were general strikes at Rostov in November 1902 and at Odessa in July 1903, which began in the port and spread to the railway workers. Socialist parties needed to find a way of harnessing such peasant unrest for their revolutionary aims. In 1900 heirs of the Populists set up an Agrarian Socialist League in Paris. It had a terrorist wing, which assassinated the Interior Minister Plehve, in 1904. It made use of village schoolteachers and seminarists to draw peasants into the Socialist Revolutionary Peasant Union (SRs), set up in 1902, and also developed a base among industrial workers in Odessa, Kiev, Ekaterinoslav, and the Urals.

Lenin's RSDLP was struck by rural unrest, but took the view that socialist revolution would be made not by peasant proprietors, however land-hungry or indebted, but by the industrial proletariat, aided by a landless rural proletariat. As far as the industrial proletariat was concerned, moreover, it was divided over strategy. At its second congress in Brussels in 1903 Martov argued in favour of a mass party that overlapped broadly with the organized labour movement and was decentralized and sensitive to local conditions. Lenin conceded that the working classes were 'spontaneous' but not that they were 'conscious' in a class sense. This was the privilege of a small party that should control the labour movement by means of a seamless ideology and centralized organization, and guide it away from questions of hours and wages to the seizure of political power. Lenin's argument won a majority and the Bolsheviks separated from the Mensheviks behind Martov. But Plekhanov, who had supported Lenin, soon concluded that he was guilty of 'confusing the dictatorship of the proletariat with the dictatorship over the proletariat' and Trotsky attacked Lenin's methods as 'a dull caricature of the tragic intransigence of Jacobinism'.[1]

The government attempted to gain control of workers through unions organized in Moscow by the chief of secret police, Zubatov, and in St Petersburg by Father Gapon's Assembly of Russian Factory and Millworkers. But when 120,000 of Gapon's workers marched peacefully to the Winter Palace on 9 January 1905 to petition the Tsar troops opened fire on them, killing 170. Bloody Sunday destroyed the faith of the workers in the Tsar and drove them towards socialism. Protest strikes broke out all over Russia. They were particularly severe in the borderlands—from Tbilisi and Baku to Lódz, Bialystock, Vilna, and Riga—where national and class grievances were combined. As the Russian armies crumpled in defeat the railway workers paralysed the country by a strike on 8 October 1905 which soon became general. In St Petersburg the metallurgical, textile, and print workers found a new organization to cap the factory committees and trade unions: the soviet or parliament of 500 workers' delegates who represented a work force of 200,000. The soviet sprang up independently of social democracy. The Mensheviks, who were prepared to meet the workers on equal terms, acquired some influence there, as did Trotsky. But Lenin, who did not arrive in St Petersburg until 8 November, did not, and the Bolsheviks switched their attention to Moscow where they organized a futile armed insurrection on 10 December. Meanwhile the countryside was in a state of anarchy, with the peasants organizing strikes, invading forest and farmland, and burning manor houses. Peasant unions were set up, dominated by the SRs, and an All-Russian Peasant Union met in congress in November to demand the confiscation of state, Church, and gentry land.

Nicholas II favoured repression, but Bloody Sunday had failed, and now the army could not be relied upon to remain loyal. On 9 October 1905, as the strike movement spread, Witte urged the Tsar to make concessions, since 'it is not on the extremists that the existence and integrity of the state depend. As long as the government has support in the broad strata of society, a peaceful solution to the crisis is still possible.'[2] On Witte's advice, Nicholas II issued a manifesto on 17 October 1905 promising an Imperial Duma elected on a broad franchise to consent to laws and oversee the legality of government actions. Witte became Chairman of a Council of Ministers with collective responsibility that prevented the Tsar from playing off one minister against another. The Slavophile branch of the *zemstvo* movement, the so-called 'Octobrists', duly accepted these concessions and rallied to the throne. The other branch, and most of the radical intellectuals, based on the Union of Liberation, continued to demand a constituent assembly elected by universal,

---

[1] Quoted by Carr, *The Bolshevik Revolution*, 32–3.
[2] Quoted by Geoffrey A. Hosking, *The Russian Constitutional Experiment, 1907–14* (Cambridge, 1973), 5.

equal, direct, and secret suffrage, declared its support for the strike movement, and demanded agrarian and labour reform. It contested the elections
as the Constitutional Democrats or Kadets.

Russification measures were suspended in Finland and its Diet decided to
hold elections under universal suffrage. Dmowski's National Democratic
party took part in the Russian elections but the two Polish socialist parties did
not. Neither did the Russian Social Democrats or the SRs. Strikes and trade
unions were legalized, but an extension of the franchise in December 1905
still included only a minority of the working class. A constitution was issued
from above on 23 April 1906, four days before the opening of the Duma.
Under it, no law would be valid without the consent of the Duma, but legislation was initiated by the Tsar, who retained 'supreme autocratic power', and
he had the right to issue emergency legislation when the Duma was in recess.
The Russian state was declared to be 'one and indivisible' and the Poles were
refused a separate parliament. Witte, who was opposed by the Court, military
leadership, conservative bureaucrats, the Church, and emerging parties of
the Right, was kept on until he had secured a huge international loan to
bail out the government, then dropped before the Duma met. The Duma,
dominated by Kadets, Polish nationalists, and a non-socialist Labour group,
passed a vote of no confidence in the cabinet, and demanded a government
responsible to itself. It was promptly dissolved on 9 July 1906. In the second
Duma, which met on 20 February 1907, the Social Democrats, Social Revolutionaries, and Labour group were heavily represented, as were the national
minorities. Dmowski proposed a plan for national autonomy and Stolypin,
the Chairman of the Council, ordered a dissolution. Stolypin, whose military
courts had executed a thousand revolutionaries, now changed the electoral
law unilaterally by what amounted to a *coup d'état* on 3 June 1907, to clear the
way for the return of the Octobrists and the Right. The third Duma, which
met in November 1907, was propertied, Great Russian, pliable, and pro-
longed until 1912.

1905: Tremors in the West

The outbreak of revolution in a country as backward as Russia, with a small
and barely organized proletariat, came as something of a surprise to Russian
Social Democrats. Lenin argued in 1905 that the passage to a socialist revolution in Russia would succeed only if the European proletariat threw off the
yoke of bourgeois rule and came to the help of the Russian working class.

The message that the October strikes in Russia had forced the Tsar to grant
a constitution spread rapidly to Austria. Street demonstrations in support of
universal suffrage reached a climax in the first week of November 1905. Barricades were thrown up in Prague and clashes with troops left scores of dead.
The Austrian government promised a reform bill but this only provoked the
social democrats to screw up the tension by calling a one-day general strike

on 28 November. The trade unions were reluctant to join in, but a million workers attended protest rallies in Vienna, Prague, Graz, Laibach, Trieste, Lvov, and Cracow. Electoral reform was opposed in the Reichstag by the Poles, Pan-Germans, and German Liberals, but the Social Democrats turned to the Christian Socials, Young Czechs, Ruthenes, and Slovenes for support and threatened more general strikes until the Emperor sanctioned the law in January 1907.

In Germany the Social Democrats exploited universal suffrage in Reichstag elections to return 81 deputies in 1903. They were able to join with Centre and left-liberal parties to democratize the franchise in south Germany between 1904 and 1905, but in Prussia and Saxony the franchise was so unfair that the SPD failed to win any seats in the 1903 state elections, while in Hamburg a more restrictive franchise was planned to reverse the socialist gains of 1904. A 'suffrage storm' erupted in Saxony, Hamburg, and other parts of Germany in January 1906 as demonstrating crowds came on to the streets. Rosa Luxemburg, who left Germany to throw herself into the revolutionary movement in Poland in December 1905, published a pamphlet entitled *Mass Strike, Party and Trade Unions* in 1906, in which she argued that the Russian and Polish revolutions were mass strikes launched spontaneously by the class-conscious proletariat. Far from having to educate the proletariat, the party must ensure that it never fell behind its fervour. Neither must the trade unions paralyse the movement by bureaucratic organization. But the trade unions feared anarchist infiltration and Bebel wanted to stick to parliamentary action. At the SPD congress at Mannheim in September 1906 the trade-union movement achieved parity with the party in party decisions and the mass strike was outlawed. 'The revisionism which we have killed in the party,' noted the *Leipziger Volkszeitung*, 'rises again in greater strength in the trade unions.'[3]

In Great Britain a judicial decision in 1901 that trade unions could be held responsible for damages inflicted during a strike confirmed the wisdom of the decision of the Trades Union Congress to engage in political action through the Labour Representation Committee, formed in 1900 to return Labour candidates to Parliament. But the LRC was not committed to class war or the socialization of the means of production. The Social Democratic Federation, which failed to obtain this commitment, left the LRC in 1901 and the Labour leader Ramsay MacDonald proclaimed 'The complete failure of the Marxian movement' in England.[4] In 1903 the LRC entered into a pact with the Liberal party to ensure as far as possible that they fought against the Conservative party and not against each other in the next elections. Labour obtained 29 seats in the elections of January 1906, which were a Liberal landslide. Labour was certainly tamed, if not in the pocket of the Liberals.

---

[3] Quoted by Carl E. Schorske, *German Social Democracy, 1905–1917* (Harvard, 1955), 52.

[4] Quoted by Ralph Miliband, *Parliamentary Socialism: A Study in the Politics of Labour* (2nd edn., London, 1973), 21.

The French experience at the turn of the century was of class collaboration against political reaction on the British model rather than class separation on the German. At the founding congress of the Parti Socialiste Français in December 1899 Jaurès defended the acceptance of ministerial office by the socialist Millerand on the grounds that the Republic was in danger from counter-revolutionary forces and that a collectivist society could be promoted gradually from within a bourgeois government. Jules Guesde disagreed. Social reforms were slow in coming and after the shooting of three strikers by troops at Chalon-sur-Saône in June 1900, he announced that 'the war on the working class has never been so implacable as under the Waldeck–Rousseau–Millerand government.'[5] The Guesdists and Blanquists broke away to found a rival Parti Socialiste de France.

The elections of 1902 marked a shift to the Left and in the Left Bloc of the Radical premier Émile Combes a considerable influence was exercised by Jaurès. But Combes was obsessed by the elimination of religious congregations from private as well as public schools, and avoided issues of nationalization and progressive income tax that would have split his majority in two. Anticlericalism, observed Guesde, was 'merely a manœuvre of the capitalist class to divert the workers from their struggle against economic slavery'.[6] At the Amsterdam congress of the Socialist International in 1904, Guesde was able to call upon August Bebel to denounce the collaboration of French socialists with the class enemy. In his own defence, Jaurès argued that they were only making use of democratic liberties won on the barricades and taunted the SPD that they would never have the chance of holding office because their parliament was 'only half a parliament' in 'predominantly a feudal, police-controlled country'.[7] Jaurès was defeated, the Left Bloc fell and in April 1905 Jaurès and Guesde joined to form a single socialist party, the French Section of the Workers' International (SFIO).

It soon became clear, however, that despite the rhetoric of class struggle the SFIO was wedded to parliamentary politics. The labour movement, converted to anarcho-syndicalism, turned away from socialist politicians and looked to direct action. The General Confederation of Labour (CGT) called for a massive general strike on 1 May 1906. Over 200,000 workers took action, turning a deaf ear to the Guesdists who were anxious to maintain the hegemony of the party over the labour movement and urged the workers not to strike but to vote socialist in the elections of 6 May. The Amiens Congress of the CGT in October 1906 asserted the independence of the labour movement from any political party, and on 30 July 1908 the CGT called another general strike.

    [5] Quoted by Williard, *Le Mouvement Socialiste*, 446.
    [6] Quoted by René Rémond, *L'Anticléricalisme en France de 1815 à nos jours* (Paris, 1976), 219.
    [7] Quoted by Julius Braunthal, *History of the International, 1864–1914* (London, 1966), 280.

The pattern in Italy was similar. The parliamentary socialists led by Turati supported the Zanardelli–Giolitti government of 1901 in order to defend democracy and argued that the 'advanced' bourgeoisie could be pressed by socialists towards collectivist reforms. Unfortunately the majority in parliament was still held by the Centre and Right, which rejected tax reforms, and Giolitti as Minister of the Interior took a hard line against strikes by public employees, and sent in the army to take control of the railways in February 1902. The parliamentary socialists came under pressure from the Marxists to abandon the government, which they did in 1903, and Turati, offered ministerial office by Giolitti, now premier, turned it down.

The balance was now shifting from political to direct action. The organized labour movement spread from the chambers of labour of Milan, Turin, and Genoa to the landworkers of Emilia, who set up a national federation at Bologna in 1901. Southerners in the socialist party such as Arturo Labriola argued that collectivization would never be achieved by parliament but only by strike action. He carried the Bologna Congress of April 1904 and that September northern and central Italy were in the grip of a general strike. This provoked a division between the party leadership, now radical, and the moderate parliamentary party of Turati. This joined forces with moderate trade unionists who organized a General Confederation of Labour (CGL) at Milan in 1906 to try to check wildcat strikes.

In Spain there was a revival of anarchism after the defeat of 1898. Francisco Ferrer, who had been in exile in Paris since 1886, returned to Barcelona in 1901 to launch the anarchist school movement to free the individual from debauchery and religion. Anarchism penetrated the trade unions of Barcelona and a strike of tramway operators and metal-workers developed into a general strike in February 1902. The strike failed and the anarchists turned to assassination attempts against Alfonso XIII. The army, increasingly attacked by anarchists and Catalan nationalists, obtained the right in 1906 to try anti-militarists and separatists in military courts. This only served to exacerbate anti-militarism, and when, in July 1909, the Maura government mobilized troops to fight in Morocco, opposition was led by Catalan nationalists, anarchists, with socialists and Lerroux's Radicals obliged to join the protest for fear of losing support. In the 'Tragic Week' that followed troops were sent into Barcelona, martial law was imposed, and cases of 'armed rebellion' went before military courts. The Radical politicians managed to wriggle out; Francisco Ferrer was executed on 13 October 1909. In response to this repression, the socialists accepted that a bourgeois revolution would have to come first, joined the republicans, and secured the election of Iglesias to the Cortes in 1910. On the other hand a National Confederation of Labour (CNT) was set up in Barcelona (1909), dedicated to secure the rights of workers and women by means of the general strike, and destined to become the most powerful instrument of anarcho-syndicalism in Europe.

1905: Germany's Bid for Power

The German Social Democrats improved their position in the Reichstag election of 1903 because of their opposition to the protectionist tariff of 1902. The Conservative parties, for whom it had been passed, lost ground, and the National Liberals did not have enough weight to give the government a majority. To survive, it was dependent on the goodwill of the Catholic Centre party. This was uncomfortable for Chancellor Bülow and anathema to the nationalists of the Pan-German League and the Navy League who still saw the Centre party as separatist, ultramontane, and opposed to military credits. The nationalists were also frustrated at the lack of success of *Weltpolitik* and made no secret of their frustration to Bülow.

Germany's expansionism was in fact tightening the circle of hostile powers around her. In April 1904 the Franco-Russian alliance was extended by an agreement constituting the *Entente Cordiale* between France and Great Britain. Britain was concerned lest France, as Russia's ally, enter the war against Japan in the Far East, which would oblige Britain, as the ally of Japan, to go to war with France. But as Balfour told King Edward VII in December 1903, it was 'impossible to contemplate anything at once so horrible and absurd as a general war brought on by Russia's impracticable attitude in Manchuria'.[8] The alternative was to enter an agreement with France. However, the underlying reason for the *Entente* was to lay to rest a generation of colonial disputes which had brought France and Britain to the brink of war in 1898. France finally recognized Britain's paramountcy in Egypt and in return Britain recognized hers in Morocco. This in fact went against an international agreement signed at Madrid in 1880 which guaranteed an open door to trade in Morocco.

Bülow, under pressure from the nationalists, attempted to break the imaginary ring. On 31 March 1905 William II landed at Tangier on the Moroccan coast to assert the open door and endorsed the suzerainty of the Sultan. It was a direct challenge to France. Russia was immobilized by war and revolution and was unable to help her ally. It was thought in Germany that Great Britain was opposed to French power in Morocco and would welcome Germany's move. Germany insisted that France's claims be examined by an international conference that could not fail to increase Germany's prestige.

Unfortunately Bülow miscalculated. The French Foreign Minister, Delcassé, stood by France's claims and would hear nothing of an international conference. However, he was compelled to resign by his more squeamish colleagues in June 1905. In April 1905 Admiral Sir John Fisher, the First Sea Lord, told the Conservative government that the British and the French fleets were one and could seize the Kiel Canal in a fortnight. The newly-formed

---

[8] Quoted by Ian Nish, *The Anglo-Japanese Alliance, 1894–1907* (Westport, Conn., 1966), 286–7.

British General Staff was in touch with the French General Staff and for the first time since the Napoleonic Wars the British contemplated military action on the continent of Europe. In January 1906 a Liberal government took office with Sir Edward Grey as Foreign Secretary. It was more suspicious of Germany than its Conservative predecessor and stood resolutely by the Anglo-French *Entente*. Russia too was prepared to stand by its alliance with France and after its defeat by Japan needed French loans more than ever. The defensive treaty signed by William II and Nicholas II on the Tsar's yacht at Björkö in the Gulf of Finland on 24 July 1905, unbeknown to their foreign ministers and incompatible with their respective treaty obligations, was simply one of the more outrageous manifestations of personal diplomacy. Germany was not even able to rely on the Triple Alliance, for Italy was drawing steadily closer to France. A Franco-Italian treaty in 1896 secured Italy's position in Tunisia; another in 1898 ended the tariff war. In June 1902, two days after the Triple Alliance was renewed, a third treaty with France gave Italy a free hand in Tripoli so long as she remained neutral in the event of a Franco-German war. At the international conference which opened at Algeciras in January 1906 Germany was left isolated. Italy abstained in the vote and William II spoke of war against his 'useless' ally. The Dual Alliance with Austria-Hungary was all that Bülow had to fall back upon.

The crisis could nevertheless be put to some use. Although Schlieffen presented his famous plan in December 1905, William II never really contemplated war against France. 'Because of our socialists', he told Bülow, 'we cannot take a single man out of the country without extreme danger to the life and possessions of our citizens.... Let us first shoot down the socialists, behead them and render them harmless, and then let us have a war against the outside world, not before and not *à tempo*.'[9] For all the Kaiser's verbal violence, a *coup d'état* against the socialists was out of the question. But Bülow used criticisms of German colonial administration in South-West Africa by the socialists, the Centre party and the Progressives to fight the Reichstag elections of January 1907 as a plebiscite on the government's foreign policy. He counted on a wave of patriotic opinion to reinforce the authority of the government and to undermine those parties that did not subscribe whole-heartedly to *Weltpolitik*. The Progressives decided to go with the current and join the government majority. The Centre party just about held its own. In the socialist camp, Bebel was right to predict that should war break out a chauvinist 'fever... will grip the masses',[10] for the SPD slumped from 81 to 43 seats. In the Reichstag debates that spring, Bebel argued that the Social Democrats were good patriots and opposed military budgets only because the financial burden fell on the classes least able to pay. At the Stuttgart congress of the Socialist International in August 1907

---

[9] Quoted by Fritz Fischer, *The War of Illusions* (London, 1975), 57.
[10] Quoted by Schorske, *German Social Democracy*, 73.

French, Belgian, Polish, and Russian delegates were eager to sanction the general strike as the ultimate weapon of the working class against war. But Bebel would have none of it. The party had decided once against the general strike to retain political control over the labour movement. Now it decided against the general strike in the event of the outbreak of a war, which would leave it isolated from the mass of patriotic Germans. The government had discovered the Achilles' heel of German socialism.

Slav Nationalism Contained

As Great Britain became less interested in shoring up the Islamic despotism of Sultan Abdul-Hamid against Russian ambitions, so a new presence made itself felt at Constantinople: that of Germany. A German military mission had gone to Turkey as early as 1883 to reorganize the Ottoman army after its defeat by Russia and arms sales were stepped up. In exchange for loans to the bankrupt Ottoman government German banks won concessions to extend the Berlin to Constantinople railway into Asia Minor and between 1899 and 1903 a contract was negotiated between the Deutsche Bank and Constantinople to extend the railway across Mesopotamia to Baghdad. The German government put its weight behind a scheme that would open up new markets and tap cotton, coal, and oil by an overland route. German influence would be built up in the Near East to an extent that would never be possible in the Far East. The Pan-German press was captivated by the idea and Paul Rohrbach, a Baltic German who had moved to Berlin as Russification intensified, struck a vein of popular interest with his book, *Baghdad Railway*, published in 1902.

German ambitions infallibly aroused the suspicions of both Russia and Great Britain. Britain was opposed to a route eastwards that would outflank its own sea-passage through the Suez Canal and Red Sea. Baghdad was a good 200 miles from the Persian Gulf but after 1899 German shipping began to establish branches in the Gulf and Lord Curzon, the Viceroy of India, tied the Sheikh of Kuwait by an agreement not to make possible the extension of the Baghdad railway to the Gulf by ceding any of his territory. The threat to India was not the least of British concerns. Russia, which posed that threat, was also worried by German plans. In 1900 the Porte agreed not to grant concessions in northern Anatolia or Armenia to any power other than Russia, in order to protect Russia's border along the Caucasus. Now Russia and Great Britain found a rare opportunity for agreement. Persia at least must be free of German influence, and the Anglo-Russian *Entente* of 31 August 1907 divided Persia up into a Russian sphere of interest including Tehran, a British sphere of interest bordering Afghanistan and the Gulf of Oman, and a neutral zone along the Persian Gulf. A Triple Entente between Great Britain, Russia, and France was consolidated against German expansionism.

At the same time the Habsburg Monarchy was being shaken by the claims

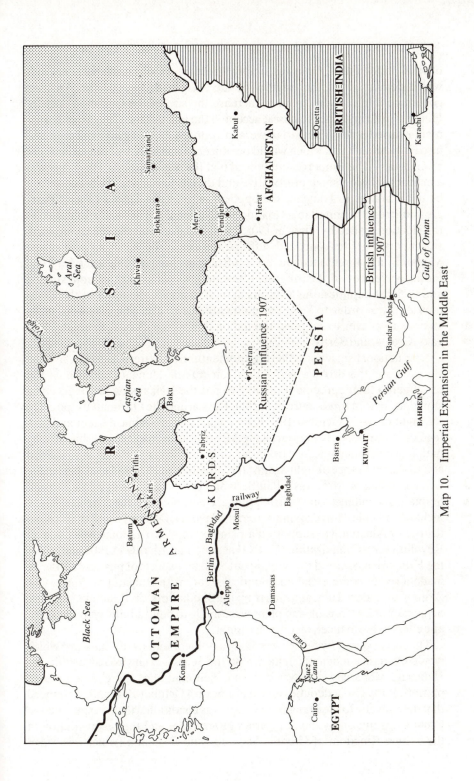

Map 10. Imperial Expansion in the Middle East

of rival nationalities. One was simply a recurrence of Hungarian demands which demonstrated the fragility of the *Ausgleich*. In 1902 the Austrian government introduced a bill to increase the size of the Common Austro-Hungarian Army. The Reichsrat accepted the bill, but the Hungarian parliament refused unless Hungarian were introduced as a language of command into Hungarian units, which would be officered uniquely by Hungarians, not by Germans. The Emperor announced that the organization of the army was a matter for his personal prerogative and that its unitary character could not be undermined. In Hungary the opposition to István Tisza's Liberal Party grew in strength, united in a Coalition of National Parties and triumphed in the elections called by Tisza in 1905. The Emperor retained the trump card. In January 1907 he conceded suffrage reform in the Austrian part of the Monarchy and threatened universal suffrage in Hungary unless the National Parties gave ground. Fearing the eruption into parliament of non-Magyar and socialist deputies, the Magyars agreed to accept the unity of the Common Army in order to keep out political reform. The Magyars were more anxious than ever to suppress the national movements of Romanians, Slovaks, Croats, and Serbs.

Slav nationalism was gathering momentum in eastern Europe and the Balkans, and this drove a wedge between Austria-Hungary and Russia and endangered their agreement of 1897 to put the Balkans on ice. It received stimulation from three sources: Serbia, Russia, and the Ottoman Empire. On the night of 10–11 October 1903 King Alexander of Serbia, a client and protégé of Austria like his father, King Milan, was murdered with his wife by nationalist Serbian officers. His successor, Peter Karageordjević, who trained as a soldier in France, fought against the Prussians in 1870 and took part in the Bosnian rising of 1875, was a Pan-Serb and pro-Russian who wanted to end Serbia's dependence on Austria-Hungary and unite all the 'Serbian lands' including Bosnia-Herzegovina, Croatia, Slavonia, Dalmatia, and the Kosovo district of Albania. He supported a rising by the International Macedonian Revolutionary Organization (IMRO) against Turkish rule in 1903 and, when the Hungarians insisted on keeping out Serbian exports of pigs and cattle, he made a secret commercial and political treaty with Bulgaria in April 1904. Arms were ordered not, as usual, from the Skoda works in Bohemia, but from Schneider of Le Creusot, and plans were made to build a railway to the Adriatic coast to be financed by French capital.

The threat posed by Serbia was that of a 'Piedmont of the Balkans' which would exercise a magnetic influence on the Serbs—even Croats—within the Habsburg Monarchy as, it was believed, Piedmont once exercised on Italian patriots. Forty Croat deputies met at Fiume on 4 October 1905 and announced that their loyalty to the Hungarian Union was conditional upon respect for the Croat Constitution by the Hungarian government and the reconstitution of the Triune Kingdom of Croatia, Slavonia, and Dalmatia (which was ruled from Vienna) as an equal partner of Austria and Hungary within the Monarchy. On 26 October a meeting of twenty-six Serb deputies at Zara adhered to the resolution. Though Croats were Catholic and Serbs Orthodox, their linguistic and ethnic unity was proclaimed: Croats and Serbs formed 'one nation'. These events have been seen as the emergence of Yugoslav or South Slav nationalism, inspired by Serbia or Russia. There was certainly opposition to German and Magyar domination, and the case was clearly made for replacing the Dualism of 1867 by a Trialism that could solve the South Slav problem within the Habsburg Monarchy instead of without it. It remained to see whether the Austro-Hungarian leadership would take up the challenge.

The Russian revolution of 1905 gave encouragement to Slav nationalism in the Habsburg Monarchy but it also stimulated class politics. In the Reichsrat elections of May 1907 the national vote was challenged by the class vote. The Social Democrats obtained 23 per cent of the vote overall, and 40 per cent in Vienna and Bohemia. The Young Czechs and Old Czechs won 20 seats instead of 53 in 1901. But together with the Poles, Ukrainians, Serbs, Croats, and Slovenes the Slavs could, for the first time, form a majority in the Reichsrat if they joined forces. This was one root of the Neo-Slav movement which preached the brotherhood of all Slav peoples, announced by the Young Czech leader, Krámar. The other root was the success of the national minorities of the Russian Empire, especially in the second Duma of February–June 1907. In May 1908 Krámar visited St Petersburg, met the Polish leader Dmowski and the Prime Minister, Stolypin, and defined his goal of replacing the oppression of one Slav people by another, as in Poland, by a fraternal union in which the linguistic and religious individuality of each people would be respected. Slavs in the Russian and Austrian empires would combine against the Pan-German nationalism suffered by Poles in Prussia and Czechs in Bohemia.

A Neo-Slav congress was held in Prague in July 1908. Attended by Czech, Pole, Ukrainian, Croat, Serb, Slovene, and Russian delegates, it discussed the establishment of a Slav bank to end enslavement to German capital and the organization of a Slav exhibition. Its success was limited. Dmowski shook hands with the leader of the Russian delegates but the anti-national reaction in Russia had already begun. Slovaks did not appear in order not to provoke Magyar chauvinists. Many Serbs felt that the South Slav question could not be settled without destroying the Monarchy. The existence of the Monarchy was not questioned by the congress, but relations between Austria-Hungary and Russia were deteriorating and the Russophile element in Slav nationalism, however covert, could not be ignored by Vienna.

For that reason Baron von Aehrenthal, who became Austria's Foreign Minister in 1906, initiated a forward policy in the Balkans and Near East. In January 1908 he announced plans to extend Austrian influence across Macedonia to the Aegean by building a railway through the Sanjak of Novi

Bazar, bypassing Serbia and cutting it off from the Adriatic, to join the Turk-ish line that pushed up from Salonika. This antagonized Great Britain and Russia, and in May 1908 Edward VII and Nicholas II met at Reval in Estonia to urge reforms in Macedonia on the Porte. In particular, a governor should be appointed there only with the consent of the powers. This intrusion was rejected by Austria-Hungary and Germany. But all foreign intrusions in Macedonia were rejected by the junior officers of the Ottoman Third Army Corps, which was stationed in Salonika. Exasperated by the despotism of Abdul-Hamid, its surrender to foreign influence and the crumbling of the Ottoman Empire at the edges, it mutinied on 25 July 1908 and threatened to march on Constantinople unless the Sultan changed his advisers and pro-claimed a constitution.

The immediate effect of the Young Turk revolt was to undermine the Ottoman Empire still further. In the first week of October 1908 King Ferdi-nand of Bulgaria declared his independence of Ottoman suzerainty, the Cre-tans proclaimed *enosis* or union with Greece, and Austria announced that it had annexed Bosnia-Herzegovina, a direct affront to Serbian nationalism. The Austrian Chief of Staff, Conrad von Hötzendorf, urged war against Ser-bia, but was restrained by Aerenthal and Francis Joseph. The first reaction of the German government was anger that it had not been consulted in advance by Austria and embarrassment because of the long period spent building up influence at Constantinople. But Germany had to stand by Austria 'as a solid bloc', in Bülow's words, because Germany had no other ally. Germany now had ambitions of her own in the Balkans and Far East which brought her into direct conflict with Russia, and made her leaders more willing to support Austria in the Balkans than Bismarck had ever been. In January 1909 the German Chief of Staff, Moltke, assured Conrad that if Austria had to invade Serbia and Russia mobilized, Germany would mobilize against Russia (whatever the priorities of the Schlieffen Plan). Aehrenthal warned Serbia on 19 March 1909 that she must accept the annexation and guarantee a 'cor-rect and peaceful policy' if she did not want war. Three days later Bülow demanded that the Russian government accept the annexation, if it did not want war.

On this occasion the bullying tactics paid off. Despite Austria's violation of the 1897 agreement with Russia and the provisions of the Treaty of Berlin, Russia was too weak after her defeat by Japan to contemplate war on behalf of the Serbs and too fearful of revolution to place great-power prestige above the security of the dynasty. Neither did the Triple Entente do its job. France was governed by Radicals who were not enamoured of Russia and would cer-tainly not risk war with Germany to support Russia in the Balkans. In the British government the Russophiles were in a minority and in February 1909 Edward VII undertook a state visit to Berlin. Five years later, in almost identical circumstances, things turned out quite differently.

The Attack on Privilege

In the first decade of the twentieth century the major European governments were confronted by two massive items of expenditure: the cost of rearmament, which now included navies as well as armies, and the price of defusing social tension by welfare policies. Existing tax systems were not geared to take account of these wider obligations, and the ruling classes ensured that the existing burden was passed on to the poor in the form of consumption taxes or the high cost of living imposed by protective tariffs. The question was whether the resistance of the traditional élites to new taxes, especially direct taxes, could be broken in order to pay for navies and social reform, or whether the only solution to class conflict was war.

Great Britain responded to the threat of German sea-power not only by making alliances with Japan and France but also by developing a bigger, faster, all-big-gun battleship, the first of which, the *Dreadnought*, was launched in 1906. Germany might now have settled for a fleet that could protect its commerce and colonies, but Tirpitz dreamed of a navy that would provide 'world-political freedom', and though various gestures were made in 1907 to check the arms race, notably at the Hague Peace Conference, the German Naval Law of 1908 provided for the building of four capital ships a year. William II, who repudiated every suggestion of disarmament, told the *Daily Telegraph* in October 1908 that while he was not personally hostile to Great Britain, most of his subjects were.

The cost of the German navy rose from an average of £10.5m. between 1900 and 1905 to £21m. in 1909, on top of an army budget of £40m. But in Imperial Germany only the individual states were empowered to raise direct taxes, and that privilege was stoutly defended by the Conservatives and the Centre party, which had to look to its Bavarian vote. The federal government had to rely on indirect taxes on the consumption of sugar, brandy, and beer, stamp duty, the receipts of the post and railways, and tariffs. Bülow's nationalist Bloc of 1907 included Progressives and some National Liberals who wanted to combine *Weltpolitik* with tax and suffrage reform, and in the spring of 1909 Bülow decided to shift some of the burden of taxation onto the property-owners by introducing a Reich inheritance tax. This was a challenge to the privileges of the Junkers and the states-rights that underpinned them. On 24 June 1909 a majority of Conservatives, Centre party and right-wing National Liberals threw the bill out of the Reichstag. Bülow resigned and was replaced as Chancellor by Theobald von Bethmann Hollweg, who built his Reichstag majority around a 'Blue-Black' Bloc of Conservatives and Centre party, together with Polish Conservatives and Alsatians to whom he offered greater autonomy.

The German middle classes had one last chance to head a popular movement in order to end the domination of the Reich by a reactionary caste of

Junkers and heavy industrialists. In Baden and Württemberg the example was set of National Liberals co-operating with Progressives and Social Democrats in a 'Grand Bloc' against Catholics and Conservatives. The SPD was open to reformist arguments at its Nuremberg party congress in 1908 and among the National Liberals the young Saxon leader Gustav Stresemann was concerned that socialist gains in the Prussian Landtag in March 1908 would condemn the National Liberals to remain a party of professors and businessmen and, because of the Centre party, Protestant ones at that. In April 1909 he helped to found the Hanse Union which drew together the interests of light as well as heavy industry, banking, commerce, crafts, and white-collar organizations behind a policy of free trade, suffrage reform, and direct imperial taxation. Unfortunately the interests in the Union were too divergent. The Central Union of German Industrialists, which represented heavy industry, retained its commitment to protective tariffs and cartels and its hostility to organized labour. The National Liberals were deeply divided between Right and Left, and the Right feared that Prussia would be handed over to the SPD if universal suffrage were conceded there. The deep fear of socialism of the German middle classes drove them into the arms of the reactionary nobility that still dominated the Prussian Landtag, bureaucracy, army, and court. In turn class strife became sharper and the problem of integrating the working class into the Reich more and more difficult.

In Great Britain Joseph Chamberlain's campaign for tariff reform ended by breaking up the Conservative party, as he had helped to break the Liberal party over Ireland, while by defending the almost religious doctrine of free trade, the Liberals won a landslide victory in the elections of January 1906. But the Liberals had moved beyond the era of Gladstone. They left 30 constituencies open in the elections to the Labour Representation Committee, which returned 29 Labour MPs. Liberal thinkers justified the use of taxation to redistribute wealth for the good of the community as a whole. The Boer War had brought home the need for social reform and Haldane and Grey were among the 'Coefficients' gathered by Sidney and Beatrice Webb in 1902, who believed that education, preventive medicine, and a national minimum wage were the prerequisites of a strong empire. In April 1908 the dying Liberal leader Campbell-Bannerman resigned and a new set of 'radicals' were promoted by the new Prime Minister, Asquith. Winston Churchill became President of the Board of Trade and Lloyd George, who became Chancellor of the Exchequer, introduced a bill for a state-financed old-age pension scheme and that summer visited Germany to study the Bismarckian system of social insurance.

The election of 1906 was won on the traditional policy of retrenchment, but in the winter of 1908–9 the Admiralty became concerned about Germany's new battleship-building programme. In March 1909 it insisted on not four but eight battleships in 1909–10. The cabinet was divided and Asquith tried to find a compromise of four now and, if necessary, another four later. The Conservative press trumpeted, 'we want eight and we won't wait', and in July 1910, when news came in that Austria was building three or four dreadnoughts, the government decided on eight, without prejudice to the 1910–11 programme.

Free-trade finance was clearly inadequate to pay for dreadnoughts and pensions, and Lloyd George decided to shift the weight from indirect to direct taxes and to tap the resources of the rich. His 'People's Budget' of 29 April 1909 increased the rate of income tax, with concessions on earned incomes up to £3,000, imposed supertax on incomes over £5,000, raised death duties, and taxed undeveloped land (except agricultural land), and the unearned increment of land values. The People's Budget was unacceptable to the landowners, the City, the tariff reformers, the Middle Class Defence Organization, and to the peers who threw it out on 30 November 1909 and provoked a general election.

The election of January 1910 reduced the Liberal lead over the Conservatives to three seats. Labour was contained with 40 seats but the reform of the House of Lords seemed unavoidable. This was not only because of the budget but also because the Irish Nationalists, with 82 seats, held the balance as they had in 1885 and required the reform of the House of Lords to get Home Rule through. The Liberal leadership was anxious to avoid constitutional conflict and one possibility was the formation of an English 'Blue–Black' Bloc. In a memorandum of August 1910 Lloyd George proposed a coalition with the Conservatives in which the Liberals would concede tariff reform and conscription if the Conservatives agreed to National Insurance and Home Rule. But tariff reform was as unpalatable to Asquith as Home Rule was to Balfour and the plans for coalition fell through.

At this point the British experience diverged from the German. The Liberals introduced a bill to restrict the financial powers of the House of Lords and held another general election in December 1910. The result was stalemate between Liberals and Conservatives, but the Liberals gathered their Labour and Irish Nationalist allies to push against privilege. The new king, George V, agreed to create enough Liberal peers to pass the Parliament bill through the House of Lords, should the Conservative peers continue their obstinacy. The threat worked. The House of Lords accepted reform and Balfour resigned as leader of the opposition. Lloyd George then introduced his National Insurance Bill of 1911 to provide, on top of old-age pensions, contributory but flat-rate sickness, accident, and (as yet unknown in Germany) unemployment insurance. In Great Britain the landed élite accepted the responsibility of paying taxes, and in 1914 death duties paid for the army, income tax paid for the navy, and customs and excise more than paid for education, pensions, and national insurance.

Between 1906 and 1909 France was in the hands of the Radical cabinet of

Georges Clemenceau. Anti-militarism had been satisfied by the reduction of military service to two years in 1904, anticlericalism by the Separation of Church and State in 1905. The Radicals held private property to be sacred and Clemenceau took a hard line against anarcho-syndicalism and strikes, but they attacked monopolies on behalf of the small man and in 1906 introduced a pensions bill and nationalized the Western Railway, if only to save it from bankruptcy.

Clemenceau's Finance Minister, Joseph Caillaux, inherited a tax system that relied on tariffs, heavy consumption taxes on necessities such as sugar, and for direct taxation levied a fixed percentage on income from land, houses, businesses, and stocks and shares, in a way designed to keep the state off the back of the bourgeoisie. It was totally unsuitable for the new demands of military expenditure and social reform. Caillaux decided to introduce a British-style graduated income tax on unearned income from rent and interest, profits, and earned income, with supertax on incomes over 5,000 francs. In March 1909 the income-tax bill was passed by the Chamber of Deputies, with the support of the socialists. But it was buried under formalities and amendments by a commission of the Senate. Clemenceau was not anxious to press the matter. France did not have a plutocracy on the same scale as England, and the supertax threshold included rural notables such as country doctors who were the backbone of local Radical committees. Clemenceau's ministry was made unpopular by Caillaux's income-tax bill; the socialists under Jaurès were more bitter towards him than ever as he tried to move his majority towards the moderate republicans. The resources for social reform and military expenditure were therefore not available. Clemenceau fell in July 1909 after criticism by Delcassé of his naval programme of building light cruisers instead of battleships. The pensions bill, requiring contributions from employees as well as from employers and the state, was passed in 1910, although the trade unions argued that they were exploited enough already, while the Senate was careful to minimize the contribution of the state.

The Disintegration of the Ottoman Empire

In a bid to mobilize the energies of the Ottoman Empire and save it from destruction the Young Turks had risen in revolt and obtained a constitution and a parliament that met in December 1908. Turks, Arabs, Greeks, Armenians, Slavs, and Jews were represented. These concessions were opposed by the Islamic conservatives and elements of the military, who launched a counter-revolution in April 1909. But the Young Turks retained their hold on Macedonia, marched on Constantinople, deposed Sultan Abdul-Hamid, and inaugurated a period of military rule under a Committee of Union and Progress. They were humiliated by the loss of Bulgaria and Bosnia-Herzegovina, feared the growth of national feeling among Macedonians, Albanians, Armenians, and Arabs and had to replace loyalty to the Sultan-Caliph by a new principle of unity.

They therefore began the Turkification of the Empire. In August 1909 the closure of all political organizations based on nationality was ordered, according to the formula 'no distinction of race or creed'. National opposition only intensified as a result. The Albanians, for example, rather than accept the imposition of the Turkish alphabet on their schools, new taxes, and compulsory military service, rose in revolt in 1910 and 1911 and demanded a separate Albanian parliament, army, and administration.

As the Ottoman Empire fell to pieces, so the European powers gathered round like vultures. The Algeciras conference in 1906 had re-established the rights of France, Germany, and Spain in Morocco. Spain feared that France would absorb its interests there and in July 1909 Maura ordered a call-up of reservists for an expedition—the only result was revolution in Barcelona. In France, there was a shift of influence from the old school of republicans who were prepared to come to terms with Germany and recognized that German constitutional concessions to Alsace-Lorraine in 1910–11 now bound the provinces firmly to the Reich, and the ambitious young men of the Foreign Office who came under the influence of the Colonial party. They used the pretext of riots in Fez to convince a weak foreign minister that troops must be sent. In May 1911 the French occupied Fez and established a *de facto* protectorate in Morocco.

It was up to Germany to defend her interests if she dared. Foreign affairs were in the hands of the irascible Alfred von Kiderlin-Wächter, who was closely associated with the Pan-German leader, Heinrich Class. The ambition of Class was to establish a German *Mittelafrika* from the Cameroons to Tanganyika that would require the French and Belgians to make concessions in the Congo. At the same time a strong German response in Morocco ran the chance of driving Great Britain away from France and splitting the *Entente*. Kiderlin and Bethmann Hollweg won over the Kaiser and on 1 July 1911 the German gunboat *Panther* appeared in the South Moroccan port of Agadir. In compensation for the French seizure of Morocco, the Germans demanded the surrender of the entire French Congo.

The *Entente* gave Great Britain certain responsibilities towards France, but the Liberal premier Asquith was under pressure from 'radicals' to insist that France give ground and avoided confrontation. The hawks argued that only a united front by Britain and France would check Germany's pretensions and in a speech at the Mansion House on 21 July 1911 Lloyd George, presumed to be a 'radical', announced Britain's full support for France. This was a shock to the Germans. However, the British government was not prepared to send ships and troops if the Germans landed in Morocco and Joseph Caillaux, who became the French Prime Minister in June 1911, was told by the French Chief of General Staff, Joffre, that France did not have a seventy per cent chance of winning a war with Germany. Caillaux therefore decided to negotiate a compromise, using his banking connections in

Berlin, and a treaty of 4 November 1911 secured France's protectorate in Morocco in return for the cession of part, but not all, of the French Congo to Germany.

In Germany there was an outcry from nationalists, National Liberals, Conservatives, and the military at this capitulation. But in France the nationalist backlash was much sharper. In the Chamber of Deputies the Right denounced the sacrifice of France's African empire by Caillaux, although a majority ratified the treaty. A commission of the Senate which included Clemenceau and Raymond Poincaré, a scrupulously honest and patriotic Lorrainer, revealed Caillaux's secret negotiations behind the back of his own foreign minister, and forced him to resign. He was replaced in January 1912 by a ministry headed by Poincaré.

Italy, which had been humiliated by Austria's annexation of Bosnia-Herzegovina, now feared that France might seek to recover its prestige by occupying the only patch of Ottoman North Africa that remained free of foreign domination: Libya. In December 1910 a Nationalist Association was formed in Florence under the presidency of Enrico Corradini, a journalist and man of letters, to press for an African adventure. Giolitti, who returned as premier in March 1911, was in danger of alienating the employers' organization, Confidustria, because his 'new deal' for the workers promised pensions and universal suffrage. A successful foreign policy bringing financial and commercial advantages could serve to buy them off. Great Britain and France opposed Italy's ambitions in the eastern Mediterranean. Austria and Germany could not be relied on for support. So Giolitti went it alone, issuing an ultimatum to the Turks to surrender Tripoli on 28 September 1911, and declaring war on them the next day.

'What if, after we attack Turkey', asked Giolitti, 'the Balkans move? And what if a Balkan war provokes a clash between the two groups of powers and a European war? Is it wise that we saddle ourselves with the responsibility of setting fire to the powder?'[11] Italy's declaration of war certainly undermined Ottoman defences and encouraged Russian activities in the Balkans. Russian military strength was still being rebuilt after the defeat of 1905, and after the Bosnian crisis in 1908 Russian foreign policy was devoted to supporting a league of Balkan states which, on behalf of Russia, could act as a barrier against Austrian ambitions. Success came with the secret treaty between Serbia and Bulgaria signed on 13 March 1912, which was extended to Greece in May, and to Montenegro in September 1912. For the Balkan League, however, the main enemy was the Ottoman Empire, the main aim, to divide up Macedonia, and the fiery little state of Montenegro began the war by attacking Ottoman forces on 8 October 1912.

A tussle developed between the general staffs and civilian ministries in

---

[11]   Quoted by R. J. B. Bosworth, *Italy, the Least of the Great Powers* (Cambridge, 1979), 145.

Map 11.   The Balkans in 1914

Austria, Russia, and Germany. The Austrian General Staff was eager to intervene against Serbia, whatever the Russian reaction, but the Austrian Foreign Minister, Count Berchtold, refused to take the risk. The Russian General Staff and Minister of War planned a mobilization on 22 November 1912, to back Serbia's claim to an Adriatic port, but the Foreign Minister, Sazonov, and the Chairman of the Council of Ministers, Kokovtsev, persuaded the Tsar to have the mobilization cancelled. On 8 December, in a German war council meeting with the Kaiser but without Chancellor Bethmann Hollweg or Foreign Minister Kiderlin, the German Chief of General Staff, Moltke, and that the German attitude to a European war should be 'the sooner, the better'.

Whether Austria-Hungary was able or willing to deal with the Serb and Croat question within the Monarchy was a crucial issue. Neo-Slavism had been shattered by the annexation of Bosnia-Herzegovina. In the Reichstag the Czechs, Serbs, Croats, Slovenes, and Austro-Ukrainians combined in a Slavic Union in 1909 to attack the government on national issues. The parliamentary system broke down and the Austrian Minister-President Count von Stürgkh ruled by decree between 1911 and 1914. But the Austrian government made absolutely no attempt, as the heir to the throne, Archduke Franz Ferdinand urged, to reconcile the South Slavs who lived within the Monarchy. Dualism was held to be sacrosanct. Trialism was not considered, for fear of antagonizing the Magyars and placing the Common Army in jeopardy once again. Leaders of the Slavic Union were put on trial and the government made clumsy efforts to have them convicted as paid agents of Serbia. Conrad, the Austrian Chief of General Staff, was dismissed in November 1912 for suggesting that Austria should attack Italy and reoccupy Lombardy and Venetia, but the army was allowed to maintain its political weight by establishing military rule in Bosnia. Khuen-Héderváry, now the Minister-President of Hungary, realized that the government could not win elections in Croatia and suspended the Croatian constitution in March 1912. The Ban of Croatia was now an absolute ruler and attempts on his life multiplied.

Outside the Monarchy the Austrian government did everything possible to prevent the emergence of Serbia as a 'Piedmont of the Balkans'. The first priority was to dissuade Serbia from seeking an outlet on the Adriatic coast. An Albanian assembly declared independence of the Ottoman Empire as a sovereign state and was recognized by the great powers. But the Serbs and Montenegrins had designs on Albanian territory and laid siege to Scutari until the Austrians threatened to drive them out by force. The Turks signed a peace treaty in London in May 1913 which marked the end of Turkey-in-Europe. Austria was happy with the 'big Bulgaria' that resulted, which absorbed most of Macedonia, and obtained Salonika as a port on the Aegean. Serbia was not so happy, especially since Austria had cut if off from the Adriatic by the creation of Albania. The enemies of Bulgaria—Serbia,

Greece, Romania, and even Turkey—started a war against her in June 1913. Bulgaria appealed to Austria to intervene and Austria threatened Serbia with war unless she made peace with Bulgaria. But what emerged from the Treaty of Bucharest in August 1913 was a 'big Serbia' that shared Macedonia with Greece and increased its population from 2.9 to 4.4 millions. For all her efforts, Austria was now confronted by a 'Piedmont of the Balkans', and an angry one at that.

The Bitter Pill of Militarism

The Morocco crisis and the Balkan Wars increased the sense of international insecurity and intensified the pressure on states to rearm. Rearmament was opposed by the Left and anti-militarism boosted its success at the polls. States and international socialism confronted each other. Yet means were found to defuse the situation, both by tax reform and by nationalist propaganda to which the masses were always susceptible.

During the Morocco crisis, in the autumn of 1911, Admiral Tirpitz reversed an earlier decision to reduce the tempo of battleship-building to two a year in 1912–17 and asked the Kaiser for a navy bill to maintain the tempo of four a year. His bargaining position was not strong. *Flottenpolitik* had failed to win Germany a place in the sun, and the Conservatives could not be persuaded to help pay for what they called the 'detestable navy'. On the other hand the Conservatives were in favour of expanding the army to exploit Germany's large and youthful population and to restore the prestige of the military in the best Prussian tradition. In January 1912 an Army League was set up to campaign for a large army bill.

Unfortunately the Conservatives enjoyed less and less electoral support. In the Reichstag elections of January 1912 the Conservatives slumped from 60 to 43 seats and the Free Conservatives from 24 to 14 seats, while the Social Democratic party obtained 35 per cent of the popular vote and 110 seats. In the aftermath of the socialist victory a massive coal strike broke out in the Ruhr. The National Liberals set themselves against any consideration of a popular base and their right wing expelled moderates like Gustav Stresemann from the party executive. Class lines were drawn more firmly than ever and the SPD stuck to its principle, 'To this system, no man and no penny' by opposing the army and navy budgets in 1912.

The deadlock had to be broken. During the first Balkan War the government decided to expand the standing army to 750,000 in 1913–14, and to 820,000 by October 1914. The cost of the army was to rise from £40.8m. in 1910 to £88.4m. in 1914. Bethmann Hollweg decided that the propertied classes must share the burden and in April 1913 proposed to cover military expenditure by death duties and a tax on the annual increment of property values. The SPD were prepared to vote a military budget which lightened the weight of taxes on the working class and, by taxing the propertied classes, might make them less militaristic. They were also subjected to a barrage of anti-Russian propaganda by the press, Defence League, and Pan-German League. On 7 April 1913 the Chancellor warned the Reichstag of the possibility of a 'European conflagration which will line up Slavs against Teutons'.[12]

The budget for the army bill was opposed by the Conservatives, Free Conservatives, anti-Semites, and 20 deputies of the Centre party, but they were left in a minority of 63 against 280 of the Centre, National Liberals, Progressives, and SPD on 30 June 1913. The imperial government seemed to have found a way to bring the socialists into line. But for the Conservatives, the problem was made only more explicit. The Reichstag, elected by universal suffrage, seemed to be swimming with revolutionaries. In August 1913 the Agrarian League, the Central Union of German Industrialists, and the German Mittelstand Association met at Leipzig to form the Cartel of Productive Estates. Its task was to put pressure on the government outside the Reichstag to remove the menace of trade unions, strikes, and socialism. In October 1913 the industrialists put forward a plan to impose an Imperial Upper House on top of the Reichstag, with representation for the professions and productive estates. The Agrarian League was closer to the Pan-German League whose leader, Heinrich Class, published a book in 1912 entitled *If I were Kaiser*, in which he advocated a victorious war and a coup against the Reichstag to abolish universal suffrage.

Humiliation over Morocco stimulated the 'awakening of national feeling' in France. Just as the populations of Alsace and Lorraine were becoming reconciled to the German Reich, so nationalist writers like Maurice Barrès romanticized the idea of their stolid resistance. They were Catholics in a Protestant Reich and Catholicism, which for so long had been dismissed by republicans as anti-national, was now integrated as essential to French nationalism. Joan of Arc, born in Lorraine, beatified in 1909, became a national heroine. Count Albert de Mun, leader of the Catholic Right, threw his weight behind the moderate republican Raymond Poincaré who was elected President of the Republic by the National Assembly in January 1913. The candidate of a strong executive and a tough foreign policy, he disproved Charles Maurras's assertion that republicanism and nationalism were contradictions in terms and that only restored monarchy could restore France's *grandeur*. Poincaré, for the poet Charles Péguy, was a sort of royalty within the Republic, carried to the presidency by a 'movement of national energy'.[13]

The first task of Poincaré was to enlarge the French army to about 700,000 men in order to provide a match for the growing German army. This would be done by extending military service, which had been reduced to two years by the Radicals in 1904, to three years, as in 1889. The Three Year Law passed the Chamber of Deputies on 19 July 1913 by 358 votes to 204, and was

---

[12]   Quoted by Fischer, *The War of Illusions*, 187.
[13]   Charles Péguy, *L'Argent Suite* (Paris, 1913), 74.

to be paid for largely by borrowing. But the CGT and the socialist party were violently opposed to the law and while Radicals such as Clemenceau supported it, the hard-core 'Radical and Radical-socialists' who gathered their forces at Pau in October 1913 and elected Caillaux as their leader, did not. It was not that the opposition was anti-patriotic or even narrowly anti-militaristic. It believed that better military training and the use of heavy artillery were valid alternatives to building up numbers alone. In addition, it argued that military expenditure must be met from direct taxes and it disliked the way in which the government was reneging on anticlerical legislation. The Radical-socialists and socialists agreed on a common programme of opposition to the Three Year Law, tax reform, and the defence of lay education for the elections of April 1914. The formula was powerful. The socialists returned with 101 seats and the government coalition of Radicals, moderate republicans, and the Right was soundly beaten.

France was faced with the same problem as Germany, but two years later, Poincaré, unlike Bethmann Hollweg, was obliged to defer to the parliamentary majority. Yet he was anxious to prevent Caillaux, whom he cordially detested, from becoming prime minister. Fortunately for Poincaré, Caillaux's wife was on trial for shooting the editor of *Le Figaro* which had been mounting a smear campaign against her husband and Poincaré was able to nominate the independent socialist, René Viviani. Behind the scenes, a way out of the impasse was discovered. Viviani agreed not to tamper with the Three Year Law. In return, the Senate finally voted Caillaux's Income Tax Bill on 2 July 1914.

The issue of military service did not matter to the same extent in Great Britain. A National Service League was founded after the Boer War in 1902, boosted by the presidency of Lord Roberts from 1905, to press for the introduction of compulsory military service. In 1906 the Liberal Secretary for War, Haldane, radically altered the organization of the armed forces. A British Expeditionary Force of 158,000 men was planned, together with an auxiliary of Special Reserves. The Volunteers were replaced by a Territorial Army which would fight at home, not abroad, although individual territorials might volunteer for overseas service. Haldane's reform was, if anything, a guarantee against conscription. It did not please the National Service League which had 100,000 members in 1912, but Haldane founded the Voluntary Service League in 1913 to attack its arguments and among the Conservatives only the 'Die-Hards' were prepared to adopt a policy that was an electoral liability.

Large armies were still suspected as a threat to democracy, and the navy was much more popular as the key to Britain's strength and security. Class tension was evident in the national coal strike of 1912 and the formation of a triple alliance of miners, railwaymen, and transport workers in 1914. Doctrines of direct action were in the air, but the triple alliance was geared not so much to a general strike as to preventing the escalation of conflicts in the three closely interlocking sectors which could damage the livelihood of their members. In any case, the railwaymen were much less militant than the miners. The parliamentary Labour party opposed the mass strike and argued convincingly that in Great Britain the evils of capitalism would be eliminated only by the achievement of political power through the ballot box. The Labour party was itself contained electorally, and learned the hard way in January 1910 that it was fruitless to run against Liberals as well as Conservatives. Finally, the Labour press was far from being unpatriotic. Robert Blatchford's influential *Clarion*, which was fiercely opposed to the 'Liberal capitalist party', was forever warning workers of the dangers of German militarism.

War against Revolution

In the approach to the outbreak of the First World War, four factors were crucial. First, the ambitions and strategies of the great powers. Second, the system of alliances, the danger of which was less to drag allies into the abyss as to make them concerned lest their opposite numbers renege on their commitments at the last moment. Third, the balance of power in the decision-making process between military men and civilian politicians. Last, the pressure of both nationalist and socialist, antimilitarist opinion, and the opportunity offered by the war to achieve the ultimate in national integration.

After the second Morocco crisis the division of Europe into the Triple Alliance and the Triple Entente became a little more fluid. Germany had failed to unseat Great Britain as the leading sea-power, as Britain refused to surrender her naval superiority and Tirpitz was denied the naval bill he wanted. At this point a *rapprochement* between Britain and Germany seemed possible. Germany reverted to her drive to become the dominant continental land-power, and sought to increase her influence in the Ottoman Empire and Near East, along the line of the Berlin to Baghdad railway. This brought her into direct confrontation with Russia, a confrontation that was no longer mediated by Austria-Hungary. Turkey, defeated by the Balkan alliance in the first half of 1913, invited the Germans to send another military mission to Constantinople. Its head, Lieutenant-General Otto Liman von Sanders, would not only inspect troops and direct manœuvres, like the mission of 1883, but be seconded to the Turkish General Staff and Ministry of War. In addition Liman von Sanders asked for command of the Turkish First Army Corps which garrisoned the Constantinople area and for German control of the Straits. Fearing that Germany would build up Turkish military and naval power and threaten her in the Black Sea, Russia protested vehemently in November 1913, three weeks before the mission left for Constantinople, and prevailed upon France and Britain to sign the protest note.

Relations between Great Britain and Russia were in fact very poor after

1912, because of the shadow cast by Russia over Persia and India. In Persia Russia was trying to extend its influence from the northern (Russian) zone to the neutral zone, but the Anglo-Persian Oil Company, set up in 1901, claimed the right to drill for oil throughout Persia. This was a vital British interest for the navy was switching from coal to oil-firing, and in February 1914 Churchill persuaded the Cabinet to buy a controlling interest in the company. The following month, Great Britain signed an agreement with Germany whereby Germany recognized the exclusive rights of the Anglo-Persian Oil Company in central and southern Persia and southern Mesopotamia, while on 15 June 1914 Britain agreed that the Germans could extend the Baghdad railway to Basra, just north of the Gulf. On 25 June Grey noted that 'we are on good terms with Germany and we wish to avoid a revival of friction with her.'[14]

Germany was nevertheless fearful of being encircled. Since Russia's defeat in 1905 the Franco-Russian alliance had not given cause for concern. But now Russia was recovering its military strength, drawing on huge manpower resources, and in *Germany and the Next War* (1912) General Friedrich von Bernhardt argued that Germany must beat back the Slavic tide in order to preserve German and European civilization. In March 1914 the Russian Duma voted massive credits for a three-year military programme. This was aimed to increase the standing army to almost two million men by 1917. A strategic railway network was being built to facilitate mobilization. Naval expansion came late but rapidly. The naval budget leapt from £9.4m. in 1910 to £23.6m. in 1914, which was greater than that of Germany, and the new Baltic fleet under construction threatened Germany's northern coastline. The Russians were anxious for a naval convention with Britain whereby the British fleet would occupy the German fleet in the North Sea while the Russians landed in Pomerania. Under pressure from the French, Britain agreed to secret naval talks with the Russians in May 1914. These were exposed by the Berlin press early in June and undermined the confidence that had been building up between Britain and Germany. The solution urged by the German Chief of Staff, Moltke, on Conrad, who was now reinstated as Austrian Chief of Staff, when they met at Karlsbad in May 1914, was for a pre-emptive strike against Russia and France before their rearmament programmes were complete. 'To wait any longer means a diminishing of our chances; as far as manpower is concerned, one cannot enter into competition with Russia.'[15]

The reassertion by the military authorities of their supremacy over the civil authorities goes a long way to explaining the outbreak of war in 1914. In Germany the issue was as much domestic as foreign. The militarization of the administration in Alsace and the insults aimed at the citizens of Zabern by a

[14] Quoted by Zara S. Steiner, *Britain and the Origins of the First World War* (London, 1977), 123.
[15] Quoted by V. R. Berghahn, *Germany and the Approach of War in 1914* (London, 1973), 171.

German officer provoked a Reichstag majority of Social Democrats, Progressives, Centre, and National Liberals to pass a vote of no confidence in the government of Bethmann Hollweg in December 1913. Squeezed between the military and the parliamentarians Bethmann opted to support the military. It was made clear once and for all that Germany was not a constitutional state with responsible government. Advocates of a *Staatsstreich* began to bay louder. A *Staatsstreich* could not be entertained, but the opposition could be broken by war.

On 28 June 1914 the Austrian Archduke Franz Ferdinand and his wife were assassinated in the Bosnian capital of Sarajevo by Bosnian students. They opposed the Trialism that he advocated and demanded the integration of Bosnia-Herzegovina into the Kingdom of Serbia. The Serbian government was not responsible for the killings; the Serb Prime Minister had warned the Habsburg authorities on 5 June of possible trouble during the Archduke's visit. None the less, the bombs and guns were provided by Colonel Dragutin Dimitrijević, who was head of the Intelligence Bureau of the Serb General Staff and also head of the secret society of 'Union or Death', known as the 'Black Hand'. Over his activities the Serb government had virtually no control. In Vienna, Conrad had wanted to settle the South Slav question once and for all by military means since 1908. Foreign Minister Berchtold, who was a dove in 1912, was now prepared to go along with the military. Count Tisza, who became Minister-President of Hungary once again in June 1913 was stubbornly against war, but was brought into line by the promise that no more Serbs would be included in the Monarchy. The aged Emperor Francis Joseph wavered, but when William II failed to attend the funeral of Franz Ferdinand and his wife in Vienna, Berchtold sent the head of his private office, Count Hoyos, who happened to be a friend of Bethmann Hollweg's nephew, to Berlin to secure a promise of unconditional German support for Austrian military action. It was hoped that this support would either cause Russia to back off, in which case the war would be localized in the Balkans, or enable Austria and Germany to deal with Russia between them. The 'blank cheque' was signed by Germany on 5 July 1914. On 23 July the Serbian government received an ultimatum from Vienna to eliminate Pan-Serb propaganda and bring the perpetrators of the assassination to trial. The Serb government agreed, except to the demand for Habsburg participation in an inquiry. However, the ultimatum was designed to be rejected. Austria declared war on Serbia on 28 July, and immediately Conrad moved most Austrian forces to the Serbian front, in spite of plans made with Moltke for the Austrians to be ready to engage the Russians in Galicia.

Austria has to bear some responsibility for the outbreak of the war, because of her aggression against Serbia and extraction of the promise of German support. The Italian government, which had not been consulted by Austria on the declaration of war, took the opportunity to bow out of its

Triple Alliance commitments. In any case, she had to deal with the break-through of the Italian Socialist party in the first parliamentary elections held under universal suffrage in 1913, and a 'Red Week' of nationwide strikes called by the PSI and CGL after several antimilitarist demonstrators were shot by police at Ancona in June 1914. Germany, on the other hand, seized her historic moment. For her, the war against Serbia was only a sideshow. The urgent task for Moltke was a pre-emptive strike against Russia, and this, according to the Schlieffen Plan, required a lightning war against France to put her out of action. German armies would have to move through Belgium, and take the key fortress of Liège, but since 1913 they had a howitzer that could convert it to rubble. William II returned from the Kiel regatta to Berlin after the Sarajevo assassination and met the military and Bethmann on four successive days. Bethmann was persuaded of the need for war, wheat and bullion were bought up on the world markets, and troops were refused leave. The authorities were, of course, worried about the strength of socialist oppo-sition to war. The majority of the SPD had voted against launching a mass strike in the event of war in 1906, 1907, and most recently at the Jena congress in September 1913. On 25 July the SPD leadership nevertheless proclaimed that 'the class-conscious proletariat of Germany, in the name of humanity and civilization, raises a flaming protest against the criminal activity of the warmongers'[16] and called for mass demonstrations against war. Two days later 60,000 marchers were on the streets of Berlin. But the socialist objection to the war collapsed. The SPD and trade-union leaders feared that on the outbreak of war a state of siege would be declared, which would play into the hands of the extreme Left, and the military would smash their organization and finances. On 28 July SPD leaders met Bethmann Hollweg and disavowed any intention to strike in return for the continuing legality of the labour movement. In addition, Bebel's prediction of anti-Russian chauvinism came true. Hugo Haase, a leading German socialist, told the French socialists at a last desperate meeting of the International Socialist Bureau in Brussels on 29 July that 'what the Prussian boot means to you, the Russian knout means to us'.[17] Just as France had been cast in the role of the aggressor in 1870 to seduce the south German states into a united Reich, now Russia was cast as the aggressor to ensure the loyalty of the German working classes.

The attitude of Russia was that, although she was not ready for war, she desperately needed to avoid another humiliation as in 1905, or a loss of face such as she had suffered in 1908. Not to respond to the plight of Serbia would be to go the same way as Turkey or China. Chairmen of the Council of Min-isters who had taken the view that war meant revolution, such as Stolypin and Kokovtsev, were gone, the first assassinated in 1911, the second dismissed in January 1914, and the clamour for war was led by the Minister of Agriculture,

[16] Quoted by Schorske, *German Social Democracy*, 286.
[17] Quoted by Georges Haupt, *Socialism and the Great War* (Oxford, 1972), 208.

Krivoshein. True, internal unrest had been growing since the shooting of 172 miners at the Lena goldfields in Siberia in April 1912, and St Petersburg was in the grip of a general strike between 4 and 15 July 1914. The government, however, felt that war would enable it to step up repression. Meanwhile, such public opinion as existed, whether in the press or in the Octobrist-dominated Duma, was keen for Russia to help her Slavic brothers and to flex her great-power muscles. Russia ordered a partial mobilization on 24 July, then, under pressure from the General Staff, a general mobilization on 29 July, after Serbia was invaded. A hesitant Tsar withdrew the mobilization order under pressure from Germany on 30 July, but was told by Foreign Minister Sazonov, another dove in 1912, that if he gave in to Germany and heaped shame on the Russian people, they would never forgive him. The general mobilization was ordered again on 31 July and Germany declared war on Russia on 1 August.

The French government was literally all at sea during the July crisis. President Poincaré, Prime Minister Viviani, and the head of the Quai d'Orsay left France by ship on a state visit to Russia on 16 July and returned on 29 July. It may be argued that their business in St Petersburg was to reassure themselves about the solidity of the Franco-Russian alliance, given the danger of a German attack under what was understood of the Schlieffen Plan. The French ambassador in St Petersburg, Maurice Paléologue, has also been accused of encouraging the Russians to take a hard line against Germany. On the other hand the French cabinet, meeting on 30 July, was aware only of Russia's partial mobilization order, and Poincaré urged St Petersburg by telegram not to provoke Germany. The French public was more interested in the trial of Madame Caillaux, who had shot the editor of *Le Figaro* to defend her husband's reputation and her own, than in Serbia. The French government also had its socialists to worry about. In theory the SFIO and CGT were committed to resist war, in the last instance by a general strike. But Léon Jouhaux, the leader of the CGT, met Karl Legien, the secretary of the German trade-union organization in a Brussels café on 27 July and became convinced that a united proletarian front was impossible. The CGT was also worried about government repression and when, on 31 July, it renounced the use of the general strike the Ministry of the Interior withdrew its list of persons to be arrested at the outbreak of war, the notorious *Carnet B*. Jaurès, the socialist leader, was shot dead by a right-wing fanatic on 31 July, but paradoxically this helped to draw together socialists and the nation. Poincaré's letters of sympathy were published in the socialist paper, *L'Humanité*, and Jaurès, though an antimilitarist, was also a patriot who believed that the task of the armies of the Republic was not only to defend French soil but to propagate the principles of 1789. 'If Jaurès were still here', Jouhaux said at his grave on 4 August, the day the German socialists in the Reichstag voted war credits, 'he would tell you, comrades, that above the national cause, in the harsh struggle that is beginning, you will be defending the cause of the International, and that of civilization, of which France is the cradle.'[18]

The German ambassador to Paris pressed the French on 31 July to remain neutral in the event of a Russo-German war, but the Chief of Staff, Joffre, threatened to resign unless France mobilized, and the government decided to mobilize on 1 August. German forces invaded Luxemburg on 2 August and demanded a free passage through neutral Belgium to invade France. This was refused by King Albert and Belgium was promptly invaded. Germany then claimed, fantastically, that French planes had bombed Nuremberg, and declared war on France on 3 August.

Great Britain was reluctant to become involved in the war, despite its commitments under the Triple Entente. On 26 July, hearing of the Austrian ultimatum to Serbia, the British Foreign Secretary, Sir Edward Grey, urged Bethmann Hollweg to restrain the German militarists and join a Four-Power conference of Great Britain, Germany, France, and Russia on the Serbian question. It has been said that if, instead of trying to rekindle the spluttering flame of nineteenth-century Congress diplomacy, Grey had warned Bethmann bluntly on 26 July that Britain would intervene on the side of France and Russia, he might have deterred Germany from pushing Austria into a war with Serbia. Bethmann rejected the proposal of a conference on 27 July but gambled on British neutrality, telling the British ambassador in Berlin on 29 July that Germany would not annex any French territory if Britain remained neutral.

The British government had problems of its own to deal with, namely strikes, suffragettes, and a revolt by Ulster Unionists against another Home Rule bill. A majority of the cabinet was against war on 29 July, and again on 31 July. George V appealed to the Tsar early on 1 August to delay Russian mobilization, but too late. German violation of the neutrality of Belgium, which since 1839 had been under the protection of the great powers, was for Britain the formal *casus belli*. More influential was the fear that a Franco-German war would open the way to German naval activity in the Channel, and to French ports facing England falling into German hands, if not to the fall of France altogether. Turkey, which feared destruction at the hands of Russia, entered the Triple Alliance on 2 August. German military and economic domination of the Ottoman Empire could only threaten the security of Britain in the Persian Gulf and India. On 3 August Great Britain issued an ultimatum to Germany. It was August Bank Holiday, and crowds massed outside Buckingham Palace, shouting 'We want war!' There was little trouble from the Labour party. Ramsay MacDonald had opposed war but resigned and was replaced by Arthur Henderson. The Conservatives, who had denounced the Liberal government as a 'revolutionary committee' when

[18] Quoted by Jean-Jacques Fiechter, *Le Socialisme français de l'affaire Dreyfus à la grande guerre* (Paris, 1965), 209.

it introduced a new Home Rule bill in 1912, fell into line, as did the Irish Nationalists, who had criticized the Home Rule bill for not going far enough. Germany had its *Burgfrieden*, France its *Union Sacreé*, Great Britain its party unity. The spectre of socialism had been exorcized, but at the expense of a European war. The moment to begin a revolution, it turned out, was not at the beginning of a war.

BIBLIOGRAPHY

General

General Surveys

The relevant volumes of the *New Cambridge Modern History*, namely, vol. ix, *1793–1830* (1965), vol. x, *1830–70* (1960), vol. xi, *1870–98* (1962), and vol. xii, *1898–1945* (1960 and 1968), are unwieldy and now rather dated; volume ix has weathered the passage of time best. By contrast the *Cambridge Economic History of Europe*, vol. vi (1965) and vii (1978), are well integrated and reflect recent research. In the *Fontana History of Europe*, George Rudé, *Revolutionary Europe, 1783–1815* (1967) and Norman Stone, *Europe Transformed, 1878–1919* (1983), are better than Jacques Droz, *Europe between Revolutions, 1815–1848* (1967), which takes the Rhine as its centre of gravity, and J. A. S. Grenville, *Europe Reshaped, 1848–78* (1967), which confines itself to political and diplomatic history. The *Fontana Economic History of Europe*, edited by Carlo Cipolla, on the other hand, is a first-rate work of international collaboration. Vol. iii and iv, in two parts (1973), cover the nineteenth century. The *Longman General History of Europe* is crisp and accessible, the relevant volumes being Franklin Ford, *Europe 1780–1830* (1970), H. Hearder, *Europe in the Nineteenth Century, 1830–1880* (1966, 2nd edn., 1988), and John Roberts, *Europe 1880–1945* (rev. edn., 1986). Eric Hobsbawm's *Age of Revolution, 1789–1848* (1962), *Age of Capital* (1975), and *The Age of Empire, 1875–1914* (1987) contain stimulating ideas. James Joll, *Europe since 1870: An International History* (1973), is a good introduction to the later period.

International history is still dominated by A. J. P. Taylor, *The Struggle for Mastery in Europe, 1848–1918* (1954), which is witty and provocative but in the time-honoured tradition of diplomatic history. It is now complemented by Paul Schroeder's immense survey, *The Transformation of European Politics, 1763–1848* (1994). For the first part of the century, Derek McKay and Hamish Scott, *The Rise of the Great Powers, 1648–1815* (1983), Geoffrey Best, *War and Society in Revolutionary Europe, 1770–1870* (1982), and Alan Sked (ed.), *Europe's Balance of Power, 1815–48* (1979) are scholarly and up-to-date surveys. F. R. Bridge and R. Bullen, *The Great Powers and the European States System* (1980) and Alan Palmer, *The Chancelleries of Europe* (1983) are succinct guides to the whole period while F. H. Hinsley, *Power and the Pursuit of Peace* (1967) is perceptive on international relations. M. S. Anderson, *The Eastern Question, 1774–1923* (1966) is the clearest introduction to a thorny problem. R. W. Seton-Watson, *Britain and Europe, 1789–1914* (1937) has now largely been replaced by Muriel E. Chamberlain, *'Pax Britannica'? British Foreign Policy, 1789–1914* (1988). Recent literature on the question of nationalism includes Ernest Gellner, *Nations and Nationalism* (1983), Eric Hobsbawm, *Nations and Nationalism since 1780* (1991), Benedict Anderson, *Imagined Communities: Reflections on the Origin and Spread of Nationalism* (1983), Anthony D. Smith, *Theories of Nationalism* (1971), John Breuilly, *Nationalism and the State* (2nd edn., 1982), and Mikulás Teich and Roy Porter, *The National Question in Europe in Historical Context* (1993).

A simple introduction to demographic history is E. A. Wrigley, *Population and History* (1960). Marcel Reinhard and André Armengaud, *Histoire générale de la population mondiale* (1961; 3rd edn., 1968) is standard. D. V. Glass and D. E. C. Eversley, *Population in History* (1965) and W. R. Lee (ed.), *European Demography and Economic Growth* (1979) contain useful essays. On urban history, Adna Ferrin Weber, *The Growth of Cities in the Nineteenth Century* (1899, republished 1963) is the best starting point and may be supplemented by Paul Bairoch, *Cities and Economic Development* (1988), part III. On migrations Walter Willcox, *International Migrations*, vol. ii (1969), a good statistical source, may be supplemented by Dudley Baines' concise *Emigration from Europe, 1815–1930* (1991), P. C. Emmer and M. Mörner (eds.), *European Expansion and Migration* (1992), and Klaus J. Badie, *Population, Labour and Migration in 19th and 20th Century Germany* (1987). Sidney Pollard's readable *European Economic Integration, 1815–1970* (1974) should be supplemented by A. G. Kenwood and A. L. Loughheed, *The Growth of the International Economy, 1820–1960* (1971) and Simon P. Ville, *Transport and the Development of the European Economy, 1750–1918* (1990). The best summary of agricultural developments is William Abel, *Agricultural Fluctuations in Europe* (1980). David Landes, *The Unbound Prometheus: Technological Change and Industrial Development in Western Europe from 1750 to the Present* (1969) is a classic. Good general surveys of the industrialization of Europe include Jordan Goodman and Katrina Honeyman, *Gainful Pursuits: The Making of Industrial Europe, 1600–1914* (1988), Sidney Pollard, *Peaceful Conquest: The Industrialization of Europe, 1760–1970* (1981), Derek Aldcroft and Simon P. Ville, *The European Economy, 1750–1914* (1994), and Tom Kemp, *Industrialization in Nineteenth-Century Europe* (1969) which has short chapters on the major countries. *L'Industrialisation en Europe au XIXe siècle*, the proceedings of an international colloquium of the Centre National de la Recherche Scientifique (1972), is an admirable collection of surveys. P. K. O'Brien and C. Keyser provide a good example of the new economic history in *Economic Growth in Britain and France, 1780–1914* (1978) while Richard Sylla and Gianni Toniolo, *Patterns of European Industrialization: The Nineteenth Century* (1991), offers a critical reassessment. On eastern Europe, Alexander Gerschenkron, *Economic Backwardness in Historical Perspective* (1962) is a collection of once-controversial essays; Doreen Warriner, *Contrasts in Emerging Societies* (1962) quotes accounts of contemporaries and a major scholarly contribution has been made by I. T. Berend and G. Ranki, *Economic Developments in East-Central Europe in the Nineteenth and Twentieth Centuries* (1974). Louise Tilly and Joan Scott, *Women, Work and Family* (1978, 2nd edn., 1987), explore the changing contribution of women to industrialization. On social history, the different strata of society are dealt with admirably by Dominic Lieven, *The Aristocracy in Europe, 1815–1914* (1992), Jürgen Kocka and Allan Mitchell (eds.), *Bourgeois Society in Nineteenth-Century Europe* (1993), and Ira Katznelson and Aristide R. Zolberg (eds.), *Working-Class Formation: Nineteenth-Century Patterns in Western Europe and the United States* (1986).

Cultural questions may be approached through Carlo Cipolla's brief *Literacy and Development in the West* (1969). *Education and Society in Modern Europe* (1979) by Fritz Ringer is a masterly survey, but limited to Great Britain, France, and Germany, and to secondary and higher education. On Great Britain, Anne Digby and Peter Searby, *Children, School and Society in Nineteenth-Century England* (1981) is a good recent collection of texts and commentaries and John Roach, *History of Secondary*

Education in England, 1800–1870 (1987) is a much-needed survey. Robert Anderson, *Education and Opportunity in Victorian Scotland* (1983) is first-class. The standard survey of Antoine Prost, *Histoire de l'enseignement en France, 1800–1967* (1968) may now be supplemented by Françoise Mayeur, *De la Révolution à l'école républicaine* (1981) and Françoise Furet and Jacques Ozouf, *Reading and Writing: Literacy in France from Calvin to Jules Ferry* (1983). Friedrich Paulsen, *German Education Past and Present* (1908) and R. H. Samuel and R. Hinton Thomas, *Education and Society in Modern Germany* (1949) have to a large extent been supplanted by Ringer (above), but Nicholas Hans, *History of Russian Educational Policy 1701–1917* (1931) is still serviceable. Hans-Eberhard Mueller, *Bureaucracy, Education and Monopoly: Civil Service Reforms in Prussia and England* (1984), is a useful comparative survey. Willem Frijoff, *L'Offre de l'école: Eléments pour une étude comparée des politiques éducatives au XIXe siècle* (1983), contains articles in English and French (with summaries in the other language) about many European countries.

Press history is well covered for France in Claude Bellanger *et al.*, *Histoire générale de la presse française*, vol. ii, *1815–71* (1959) and vol. iii, *1871–1940* (1972). For England there is G. A. Cranfield, *The Press and Society* (1978). Contributions to popular culture include Richard Altick, *The English Common Reader: A Social History of the Mass Reading Public, 1800–1900* (1957; 1967) David Vincent, *Literacy and Popular Culture. England, 1750–1914* (1984), Peter Burke, *Language, Self and Society: A Social History of Language* (1991), on France, James Smith Allen, *In the Public Eye: A History of Reading in Modern France, 1800–1940* (1991) and Martyn Lyons, *Le Triomphe du livre: Une Histoire sociologique de la lecture dans la France du XIXe siècle* (1987) and, on Germany, Rudolf Schenda, *Volk ohne Buch* (1970) and Rolf Engelsing, *Analphabetentum und Lektüre: Studien zur Sozialgeschichte der populären Lesestoffe* (1973). Religious sociology is now well developed. Useful introductions are Alan Gilbert, *Religion and Society in Industrial England: Church, Chapel and Social Change, 1740–1914* (1976), Fernand Boulard and J. Rémy, *Pratique religieuse urbaine et régions culturelles* (1968), and Bernard Plongeron, *La Religion populaire: Approches historiques* (1976). A new comprehensive, but rather conventional, history of Roman Catholicism, edited by H. Jedin and J. Dolan, has been translated from the German as the *History of the Church*. Vol. vii, viii, and ix (1981) cover the nineteenth century. The third volume of Emile Léonard's masterly *Histoire générale du Protestantisme* (1964), covering the nineteenth and twentieth centuries has not, unlike the first two, been translated. S. M. Dubnov, *History of the Jews*, vol. iv (1973) and v (1971) are indispensable. Owen Chadwick, *The Secularization of the European Mind in the Nineteenth Century* (1975) traces mainly intellectual developments.

The *New Grove Dictionary of Music and Musicians* (1980) is the indispensable starting-point for the history of music. Donald Grout, *A Short History of Opera* (1965) and Cyril Ehrlich, *The Piano: A History* (1976) cover two important aspects of musical life. E. D. Mackerness, *A Social History of English Music* (1964) relates music to popular culture. On the theatre there is F. W. J. Hemmings, *The Theatre Industry in Nineteenth-Century France* (1993) and *Theatre and the State in France, 1760–1905* (1994). The social history of leisure is now coming into its own with Peter Bailey, *Leisure and Class in Victorian England* (1978), James Walvin, *Leisure and Society, 1830–1950* (1978), Richard Holt, *Sport and Society in Modern France* (1981) and Holt, *Sport and the British: A Modern History* (1989).

National Histories

On Great Britain, Asa Briggs, *The Age of Improvement, 1783–1867* (1959) is still very worthwhile and Harold Perkin, *The Origins of Modern English Society* (1969) is bold and stimulating. The numerous series are being published, of which the best are probably the *Short Oxford History of the Modern World*, including Norman McCord, *British History, 1815–1906* (1991) and T. O. Lloyd, *Empire, Welfare State, Europe: English History, 1906–1992* (4th edn., 1993), the *Paladin History of England*, including Richard Shannon, *The Crisis of Imperialism, 1865–1915* (1976), and the *New History of England*, including Norman Gash, *Autocracy and People: Britain 1815–1865* (1979) and E. J. Feuchtwanger, *Democracy and Empire: Britain, 1865–1914* (1985). On the Celtic fringe there is Gareth Elwyn Jones, *Modern Wales* (1984), William Ferguson, *Scotland 1689 to the Present* (1968), J. C. Beckett, *The Making of Modern Ireland, 1603–1922* (1966; 2nd edn., 1981), Roy Foster, *Modern Ireland 1600–1972* (1988) and Theo Hoppen, *Ireland since 1800* (1989).

On Belgium and the Netherlands there is now a survey of quality in E. H. Kossmann, *The Low Countries, 1780–1940* (1978), although Henri Pirenne, *Histoire de la Belgique*, vol. vi (1926) and vol. vii (1948) remains stimulating. Alfred Cobban's *A History of Modern France*, vol. ii, *1799–1871* (1963) and vol. iii, *1871–1962* (1965) is now rather dated. Theodore Zeldin's *France 1848–1948*, vol. i (1973), vol. ii (1977) is a cornucopia of information, with clever insights but entirely idiosyncratic; the beginner would do best to start with the paperback volume, *Politics and Anger* (1974). *France 1815–1914: The Bourgeois Century* by Roger Magraw (1983) surveys contending interpretations but has its own strong bias. Good recent studies now include François Furet, *Revolutionary France, 1770–1880* (1992), Peter McPhee, *A Social History of France, 1780–1880* (1992), Maurice Agulhon, *The French Republic, 1879–1992* (1993), Christophe Charle, *A Social History of France in the Nineteenth Century* (1994), and Annie Moulin, *Peasantry and Society in France since 1789* (1991). Robert Gildea, *The Past in French History* (1994) examines collective memory and political culture. François Caron, *An Economic History of Modern France* (1979) is clear and concise. The relevant volumes of F. Braudel and E. Labrousse, *Histoire économique et sociale de la France*, vol. iii (1976) and vol. iv (1979), contain important contributions by a range of historians, as does the new social history edited by Yves Lequin, *Histoire des Français, XIXe–XXe siècles* (3 vol., 1984).

Italian history is now well served by introductions. Stuart Woolf, *A History of Italy, 1700–1860: The Social Constraints of Political Change* (1979) and Derek Beales, *The Risorgimento and the Unification of Italy* (1971) offer interpretations of the same period from two different perspectives. Christopher Seton-Watson, *Italy from Liberalism to Facism, 1870–1925* (1967) is rather densely written but a valuable work of reference. Recent studies by Harry Hearder, *Italy in the Age of the Risorgimento* (1983) and Martin Clark, *Modern Italy 1871–1982* (1982) are good companion volumes. Giuliano Procacci's *History of the Italian People* (1970) and Gianni Toniolo, *An Economic History of Liberal Italy, 1850–1918* (1990), are clear and succinct. Much fuller and very useful is Giorgio Candeloro, *Storia dell' Italia moderna*, vol. i (1956), ii (1958), iii (1960), iv (1964), v (1968), vi (1970), and vii (1974). The best introduction to Spain remains Gerald Brenan's colourful and evocative *Spanish Labyrith* (1943; 2nd edn., 1950). Raymond Carr, *Spain 1808–1939* (1966; 2nd edn.,

1982) is a detailed but very readable account. The last chapter of Jaime Vicens Vives, *An Economic History of Spain* (1969) covers the nineteenth century. Very useful also are Joseph Harrison, *An Economic History of Modern Spain* (1978), Nicholas Sánchez-Albornoz, *The Economic Modernization of Spain, 1830–1930* (1987), and Adrian Shubert, *A Social History of Modern Spain* (1990). E. E. Malefakis, *Agrarian Reform and Peasant Revolution in Spain* (1970) is compulsory reading on the land question.

On Germany, James J. Sheehan, *German History, 1770–1866* (1989) and Gordon Craig, *Germany 1866–1945* (1978) are now the standard texts. Helmut Böhme, *An Introduction to the Social and Economic History of Germany* (1978) throws into relief basic structures and trends. On the later period, H.-U. Wehler, *The German Empire, 1871–1918* (1985) is a welcome translation of a good survey. Michael Hughes, *Nationalism and Society. Germany, 1800–1945* (1988) is serviceable, but David Blackbourn and Geoff Eley's controversial *Peculiarities of German History: Bourgeois Society and Politics in Nineteenth Century Germany* (1984) show how far German historiography has come. For recent views on the German economy see W. R. Lee (ed.), *German Industry and German Industrialization: Essays in German Economic and Business History in the Nineteenth and Twentieth Centuries* (1991). On Prussia, H. W. Koch, *A History of Prussia* (1978) and E. J. Feuchtwanger, *Prussia, Myth and Reality* (1970) are useful. A simple introduction to the maze of the Habsburg Monarchy is Hugh Seton-Watson, *The 'Sick Heart' of Modern Europe: The Problem of the Danubian Lands* (1975). C. A. Macartney, *The Habsburg Empire, 1790–1918* (1968) is a monument of scholarship but exhaustive and to be read in short bouts. Alan Sked, *The Decline and Fall of the Habsburg Empire* (1987), John W. Mason, *The Dissolution of the Austro-Hungarian Empire* (1985), Peter Sugar (ed.), *A History of Hungary* (1990), chs. 11–15, Jörg Hoensch, *A History of Modern Hungary, 1867–1986* (1988), John Komlos (ed.), *Economic Development in the Habsburg Monarchy in the Nineteenth Century* (1983), Andrew C. Janos, *The Politics of Backwardness in Hungary, 1825–1945* (1982) are extremely useful recent studies. A. J. P. Taylor, *The Habsburg Monarchy, 1815–1918* (1942), has pace. There are valuable ideas and insights in older works such as Elizabeth Wiskemann, *Czechs and Germans* (1938; 2nd edn., 1967), Oskar Jaszi, *The Dissolution of the Habsburg Monarchy* (1929), Henry Wickham Steed, *The Habsburg Monarchy* (1913), and R. W. Seton-Watson, *Racial Problems in Hungary* (1908).

Robert Okey, *Eastern Europe, 1740–1985* (2nd edn., 1986) covers the Balkans and Poland as well as the Habsburg Monarchy. On Balkan countries, Charles and Barbara Jelavich, *The Establishment of the Balkan National States, 1804–1920* (1977), is a good introduction. Barbara Jelavich, *History of the Balkans* (2 vols., 1983), is very full. John Campbell and Philip Sherrard, *Modern Greece* (1968), Richard Clogg, *A Short History of Modern Greece* (2nd edn., 1986), Douglas Dakin, *The Unification of Greece, 1770–1923* (1972), Richard Crampton, *A Short History of Modern Bulgaria* (1987) and Michael Petrovich, *A History of Modern Serbia* (2 vols., 1976) are valuable surveys. Piotr S. Wandycz, *The Lands of Partitioned Poland, 1759–1918* (1974) takes a chronological route whereas Norman Davies, *God's Playground: A History of Poland*, vol. ii (1981) is more thematic, and brilliant. Good introductions to Russian history include Robert Auty and Dimitry Obolensky, *Introduction to Russian History* (1976), J. N. Westwood, *Endurance and Endeavour: Russian History 1812–1992*

(1973; 4th edn., 1993) and Hugh Seton-Watson, *The Russian Empire, 1801–1917* (1967), which is bulky and detailed but very readable. Barbara Jelavich, *Russia's Balkan Entanglements, 1806–1914* (1991) gives continuity to a recurrent problem. On the economy, Olga Crisp, *Studies in the Russian Economy before 1914* (1976) may be read with Peter Gattrell, *The Tsarist Economy, 1850–1917* (1986). More of a rag-bag, but with some interesting contributions, is C. E. Black, *The Transformation of Russian Society: Aspects of Social Change since 1861* (1967).

Two parts of Europe which seem often to be left out of general surveys are Scandinavia and Switzerland. B. J. Hovde, *The Scandinavian Countries, 1720–1865*, vol. i (1943) covers the earlier period decently. W. Glyn Jones, *Denmark* (1970) is useful but Franklin D. Scott, *Sweden: The Nation's History* (1977), is somewhat disappointing. Much better are T. K. Derry, *A History of Modern Norway, 1814–1972* (1973), J. Paasivirta, *Finland and Europe: International Crises in the Period of Autonomy, 1808–1914* (ed. and abr. by D. G. Kirby, 1981) and Fred Singleton, *A Short History of Finland* (1989). The standard history of Switzerland is E. Bonjour, *A Short History of Switzerland* (1952). To this may be added Jonathan Steinberg's interrogative *Why Switzerland?* (1976).

Chapter 1

Malthus's *Essay on the Principle of Population* (1803 edn., Everyman 1973) is an essential starting-point. The demographic and economic studies listed above are full of relevant material. Other interesting perspectives on population and subsistence include K. H. Connell, *The Population of Ireland 1750–1845* (1950), John Post, *The Last Great Subsistence Crisis in the Western World* (1977), on the famine of 1817, Frederick Marquardt, '*Pauperismus* in Germany during the *Vormärz*', *Central European History*, 2 (1969), Vera Bácskai, *Towns and Urban Society in Early Nineteenth-Century Hungary* (1989), Johan Söderberg *et al.*, *A Stagnating Metropolis: The Economy and Demography of Stockholm, 1750–1850* (1991), and John Merriman, *The Margins of City Life: Explorations on the French Urban Frontier, 1815–1851* (1991). François Crouzet, 'War, blockade and economic change in Europe 1792–1815', *Journal of Economic History*, 24 (1964), reprinted in *Britain Ascendant: Comparative Studies in Franco-British Economic History* (1990), is an excellent introduction to the problem of markets in the Napoleonic period, to which may be added Geoffrey Ellis, *Napoleon's Continental Blockade: The Case of Alsace* (1981). The impact of military factors on economic growth is studied by Gautram Sen, *The Military Origins of Industrialization and International Trade Rivalry* (1984) and Immanuel Wallerstein, *The Modern World System III: The Second Era of Great Expansion of the Capitalist World Economy, 1730–1840* (1989), while Rick Szostak, *The Role of Transportation in the Industrial Revolution: A Comparison of England and France* (1991) is good on the late eighteenth century. For a later period, W. O. Henderson, *The Zollverein* (1968) and Bernard Semmell, *The Rise of Free Trade Imperialism* (1970) are useful. On agriculture there is material in B. H. Slicher van Bath, *The Agrarian History of Western Europe, 500–1850* (1963), while Jerome Blum, *The End of the Old Order in Rural Europe* (1978) is a packed synthesis which centres on central and eastern Europe. Michel Confino, *Systèmes agraires et progrès agricole. L'assolement triennal en Russie au XVIIIe et XIXe siècles* (1969) is a sensitive appreciation of the benefits of communal agriculture. François Crouzet has edited important collections of essays, notably *Essays in European Economic History, 1789–1914* (1969) and *Capital Formation in the Industrial Revolution* (1972). His lectures on *The First Industrialists: The Problem of Origins* (1985) concentrates on British entrepreneurs. Leland Jenks, *The Migration of British Capital to 1875* (1927; rep. 1971) may be supplemented, for a wider European view, by Rondo Cameron, *Banking and Economic Development* (1972). Kent Roberts Greenfield, *Economics and Liberalism in the Risorgimento* (1965) is perceptive on the Italian case. Mack Walker, *German Home Towns: Community, State and General Estate 1648–1871* (1971) includes an interesting picture of the guild system in its latter stages, while Rudolf Stadelmann, *Social and Political History of the German 1848 Revolution* (1975) has useful background chapters. W. L. Blackwell, *The Beginnings of Russian Industrialization, 1800–60* (1968) is comprehensive. Much good recent writing has focused on the Low Countries, in particular, Joel Mokyr, *Industrialization in the Low Countries, 1795–1850* (1976), Richard T. Griffiths, *Industrial Retardation in the Netherlands, 1830–50* (1979) and Pierre Lebrun, *Essai sur la révolution industrielle en Belgique* (1979). Peter Mathias's admirable *The First Industrial Nation* (1969) on Great Britain is now in a second edition (1983).

The study of élites has made big strides in the last twenty years. David Spring, *European Landed Elites in the Nineteenth Century* (1977) contains essays of varying quality. F. M. L. Thompson, *English Landed Society in the Nineteenth Century* (1963) remains worthwhile, although controversy has been stirred up by Lawrence and Jeanne Stone, *An Open Elite? England 1540–1880* (1984) and there is now G. E. Mingay, *Land and Society in England, 1750–1980* (1994). There is excellent work on the British middle classes by Harold Perkin, *The Origins of Modern English Society* (1969), Leonore Davidoff and Catherine Hall, *Family Fortunes: Men and Women of the English Middle Class, 1780–1850* (1987), R. J. Morris, 'Voluntary societies and British urban élites, 1780–1850: an analysis', *Historical Journal*, 26 (1983), and Morris, *Class, Sect and Party: The Making of the British Middle Class. Leeds, 1820–1850* (1990). Michael McCahill, 'Peerage creations and the changing structure of the British nobility, 1750–1830', *English History Review*, 96 (1981), makes an important contribution. A good introduction to work by German historians is Hartmut Kaelble, 'Social stratification in Germany in the nineteenth and twentieth centuries', *Journal of Social History*, 10 (1976); Wolfgang Köllmann, *Sozialgeschichte der Stadt Barmen im 19. Jahrhundert* (1960) was one of the pioneering studies. To these may be added Hans Rosenberg, *Bureaucracy, Aristocracy and Autocracy: The Prussian Experience 1660–1815* (1958), Charles McClelland, *The German Experience of Professionalization* (1991) and the first-rate collection edited by David Blackbourn and R. J. Evans, *The German Bourgeoisie* (1991). John Gillis, *The Prussian Bureaucracy in Crisis 1840–1860* (1971), relates social to political tensions. David Sorkin, *The Transformation of German Jewry, 1780–1840* (1987) is a study of *embourgeoisement*. Walter McKenzie Pinter has done scholarly work on the Russian bureaucracy in 'The Russian higher civil service on the eve of the Great Reforms', *Journal of Social History* 8 (1975), and (with D. K. Rowney) *Russian Officialdom, the Bureaucratization of Russian Society from the Seventeenth to the Twentieth Centuries* (1980). Lenore O'Boyle broke new ground with 'The image of journalists in France, Germany and England, 1815–48', *Comparative Studies in Society and History*, 10 (1967–8) and 'The problem of an excess of education men in western Europe, 1800–50', *Journal of Modern*

History, 42 (1970). Two massive contributions by French historians are Adeline Daumard, *La Bourgeoisie Parisienne de 1815 à 1848* (1963) and André-Jean Tudesq, *Les Grands notables en France, 1840–49* (1964). More accessible is the collection of readings by Guy Chaussinand-Nogaret, *Une histoire des élites, 1700–1848* (1975).

Chapter 2

Good introductions to Napoleonic France are provided by Martyn Lyons, *Napoleon Bonaparte and the Legacy of the French Revolution* (1994), Geoffrey Ellis, *The Napoleonic Empire* (1991), D. G. Wright, *Napoleon and Europe* (1984), and Louis Bergeron, *France under Napoleon* (1981). Essential reading is the scholarship of Jean Tulard, including *Napoleon: The Myth of the Saviour* (1977; trans. 1984), *Le Grand Empire 1804–1815* (1982), which surveys Napoleonic Europe, and the work of Guy Chaussinand-Nogaret on Napoleonic notables, *Les Masses de granit. Cent mille notables du Premier Empire* (1979). Clive Church, *Revolution and Red Tape: The French Ministerial Bureaucracy 1770–1850* (1981), Edward Whitcomb, 'Napoleon's prefects', *American Historical Review* 79 (1974), and Tulard, 'Les composants d'une fortune: le cas de la noblesse d'Empire', *Revue historique*, 253 (1975), add to the study of the élite; Irene Collins, *Napoleon and his Parliaments* (1979) is a little pedestrian. Much of the *Revue d'histoire moderne et contemporaine* 17 (1970) is given over to important articles on 'France a l'époque napoléonienne'. Education is treated in *Annales historiques de la Révolution française*, 53 (1981), and the final chapter of R. R. Palmer, *The Improvement of Humanity* (1985). There are different perspectives on opposition to the regime in Claude Langlois, 'Le plebiscite de l'an VIII' and Jean Vidalenc, 'L'opposition sous le Consulat et l'Empire', respectively in *Annales historiques de la Révolution française* 44 (1972) and 40 (1968), Jean Vidalenc, *Les Emigrés français, 1799–1825* (1963), and Richard Cobb, *The Police and the People: French Popular Protest, 1789–1820* (1970).

On the Napoleonic order in Europe, the indispensable introduction is now Stuart Woolf, *Napoleon's Integration of Europe* (1991). To this may be added Ellis (1991) and Wright (1984), cited above. On military developments there are Geoffrey Best, *War and Society in Revolutionary Europe, 1770–1870* (1982), Jeremy Black, *European Warfare, 1660–1815* (1994) and Robert M. Epstein, *Napoleon's Last Victory and the Emergence of Modern War* (1994), a study of the campaign of 1809. There is much of interest in Otto Dann and John Dinwiddy (eds.), *Nationalism in the Age of the French Revolution* (1988), the Colloque de Bruxelles, *Occupants et occupés, 1792–1815* (1969) and the Société des études robespierristes, *Patriotisme et nationalisme en Europe a l'époque de la Révolution française et de Napoléon* (1973). Penetrating articles on Napoleonic Italy include P. Villani, 'Le Royaume de Naples pendant la domination française, 1806–15', *Annales historiques de la Révolution française* 44 (1972), those collected in the same review, 49 (1977), under the title 'L'Italie jacobine et napoléonienne' and a pair by Michael Broers, 'Napoleonic Piedmont, 1801–1814', *Historical Journal* 33 (1990), and 'Patriotism in Piedmont, 1794–1821: Revolution as Vendetta?', *Historical Journal* 34 (1990). Other Studies include Adrian Lyttelton, 'The National Question in Italy', in M. Teich and R. Porter, *The National Question in Europe in Historical Context* (1993), Franco Della Peruta, 'War and Society in Napoleonic Italy', in John A. Davis and Paul Ginsborg (eds.), *Society and Politics in the Age of the Risorgimento* (1991), E. E. Y. Hales, *Revolution and Papacy 1769–1846*

(1960), Angelo Varni, *Bologna napoleonica* (1973), and Reuben Rath, *The Fall of the Napoleonic Kingdom of Italy, 1814* (1941). Simon Schama, *Patriots and Liberators* (1977) is the definitive study of the Batavian Republic and Kingdom of Holland. T. C. W. Blanning, *The French Revolution in Germany: Occupation and Resistance in the Rhineland, 1792–1802* (1983) and Jeffrey Diefendorf, *Business and Politics in the Rhineland, 1789–1834* (1980) are first-class contributions. Solid older works on the Confederation, like Michel Dunan, *Napoléon et l'Allemagne. Le Système continental et les débuts de Bavière, 1806–10* (1942) and Charles Schmidt, *Le Grand Duché de Berg, 1806–13* (1905) have been supplemented by William O. Shanahan, 'A neglected source of German nationalism: the confederation of the Rhine, 1806–1813', in Michael Palumbo and William O. Shanahan (eds.), *Nationalism: Essays in Honour of Louis L. Snyder* (1981), and by recent German scholarship, notably Helmut Berding, *Napoleonische Herrschafts- und Gesellschaftspolitik im Königreich Westfalen, 1807–13* (1973) and Berding (ed.), *Deutschland zwischen Revolution und Restauration* (1981). On Spain there is Charles J. Esdaile, *The Spanish Army and the Peninsular War* (1988), which is broader than its title suggests, the sturdy narrative by Gabriel H. Lovett, *Napoleon and the Birth of Modern Spain* (2 vols., 1965), and Raymond Carr, *Spain, 1808–1939* cited above. The brief reign of Paul I of Russia is explored by Hugh Ragsdale (ed.), *Paul I: A Reassessment of his Life and Reign* (1979). Eugène Tarlé, *Napoleon's Invasion of Russia, 1812* (1942; 1970) is still serviceable, Marc Raeff, *Michael Speransky: Statesman of Imperial Russia, 1772–1839* (1975) and Alan Palmer, *Alexander I, Tsar of War and Peace* (1974) are valuable biographies but there is now also Janet M. Hartley's admirably concise *Alexander I* (1994). For the Congress Kingdom, see W. H. Zawadski, 'Russia and the Reopening of the Polish Question, 1801–1814', *International History Review* 7 (1985). On Scandinavia, H. Arnold Barton, *Scandinavia in the Revolutionary Era, 1760–1815* (1986) is first rate, while F. D. Scott, *Bernadotte and the Fall of Napoleon* (1935) is a good narrative. The Prussian predicament after Jena is dealt with by Marion Gray, *Prussia in Transition: Society and Politics under the Stein Reform Ministry of 1808* (1986), W. M. Simon, *The Failure of the Prussian Reform Movement, 1807–19* (1955) and R. C. Raack, *The Fall of Stein* (1965). Robert Berdahl, *The Politics of the Prussian Nobility* (1988) is a powerful work about ideas and institutions covering the late eighteenth and early nineteenth centuries. The resurgence of Austria is covered in terms of propaganda by W. C. Langsam, *The Napoleonic Wars and German Nationalism in Austria* (1930; repr. 1970) and in terms of military organization by Gunther Rothenberg, *Napoleon's Great Adversaries: Archduke Charles and the Austrian Armies* (1982). Metternich's mentor is discussed by P. R. Sweet, *Friedrich von Gentz, Defender of the Old Order* (1941) while Enno E. Kraehe, *Metternich's German Policy*, vol. i, *The Contest with Napoleon, 1799–1814* (1963) explains much about the emergence of the German Confederation. On German nationalism in general, Hagen Schulze offers *Nation-Building in Central Europe* (1987) and *The Course of German Nationalism: From Frederick the Great to Bismarck* (1991). British reactions to Napoleon are dealt with superbly by Linda Colley, *Britons: Forging the Nation, 1707–1837* (1992), by A. D. Harvey, *Collision of Empires: Britain in Three World Wars, 1793–1945* (1992), and in essays by Colley, Cottrell, Cunningham, Dreser, and Surel in Raphael Samuel (ed.), *Patriotism: The Making and Unmaking of British National Identity* (3 vols., 1989). Less well-charted territories are explored by Domokos Kosáry, *Napoléon et la*

Hongrie (1979), C. M. Woodhouse, *Capodistria: The Founder of Greek Independence* (1973), Notis Botzaris, *Visions balkaniques dans la préparation de la révolution grecque, 1789–1821* (1963), Georges Castellan, *La Vie quotidienne en Serbie au seuil de l'indépendance, 1815–39* (1967), William W. Haddad and William Ochsenwald (eds.), *Nationalism in a Non-national State: The Dissolution of the Ottoman Empire* (1977), and Stanford Shaw, *Between Old and New: The Ottoman Empire under Sultan Selim III, 1789–1807* (1971).

Chapter 3

On international questions, Paul Schroeder, *The Transformation of European Politics, 1763–1848* (1994), has now displaced C. K. Webster, *The Congress of Vienna, 1814–15* (1919) and Harold Nicolson, *The Congress of Vienna, 1814–15* (1948), but Alan Sked (ed.), *Europe's Balance of Power, 1815–48* (1979), may be more accessible in the first instance. On France, G. de Bertier de Sauvigny, *La Restauration* (1955) is admirable; he also wrote the corresponding chapter in the *New Cambridge Modern History*. Gwynn Lewis, *The Second Vendée* (1978) and Brian Fitzpatrick, *Catholic Royalism in the Department of the Gard, 1814–1852* (1983) study the violence of restoration politics in one part of the Midi. Other work on the Restoration includes William Fortescue, *Revolution and Counter-Revolution in France, 1815–1852* (1988), Philip Mansel, *Louis XVIII* (1988), and Stephen Holmes, *Benjamin Constant, the Making of Modern Liberalism* (1984). On the revolution of 1830 there are provincial as well as Parisian perspectives in Pamela Pilbeam, *The 1830 Revolution in France* (1991), David Pinkney, *The French Revolution of 1830* (1972) and John Merriman (ed.), *The 1830 Revolution in France* (1975). Douglas Porch, *Army and Revolution: France 1815–48* (1979), examines the continuity of republican sentiment in the army. H. A. C. Collingham, *The July Monarchy: A Political History, 1830–1848* (1988), is comprehensive. Good recent writing on republican and socialist politics after 1830 includes Maurice Agulhon, *The Republic in the Village* (1982), Robert J. Bezucha, *The Lyon Uprising of 1834* (1974), Edward Berenson, *Populist Religion and Left-Wing Politics in France, 1830–1852* (1984), a collection of writings by Paul E. Corcoran, *Before Marx: Socialism and Communism in France, 1830–1848* (1983) and Máire Cross and Tim Gray, *The Feminism of Flora Tristan* (1992).

The continuity of revolutionary politics in the military is treated in Eric Christiansen, *The Origins of Military Power in Spain 1800–54* (1967) and George T. Romani, *The Neapolitan Revolution of 1820–1* (1958). The importance of *émigré* politics is examined in Lloyd S. Kramer, *Threshold of a New World: Intellectuals and the Exile Experience in Paris, 1830–1848* (1988). The formation of Belgium is admirably covered by J. S. Fishman, *Diplomacy and Revolution: The London Conference of 1830 and the Belgian Revolt* (1988). J. M. Roberts, 'Italy, 1793–1830' in the *New Cambridge Modern History*, vol. ix (1965) is a valuable introduction to the Italian question. Alan J. Reinerman has analysed Metternich's policy in Italy in a series of articles in *Journal of Modern History*, 42 (1970) and 46 (1974), *Historical Journal*, 14 (1971), and *Central European History*, 10 (1977), and in *Austria and the Papacy in the Age of Metternich*, (2 vols., 1979, 1989). Different aspects of Metternich's Italy are covered by Laurence Sondhaus, *The Habsburg Empire and the Sea: Austrian Naval Policy, 1797–1866* (1989) and his *In the Service of the Emperor: Italians in the Austrian Armed Forces, 1814–1918* (1990), Adrian Lyttelton, 'The Middle Classes in Liberal Italy' in

John A. Davis and Paul Ginsborg (eds.), *Society and Politics in the Age of the Risorg-imento* (1991), and Denis Mack Smith, *Mazzini* (1994). Metternich's policies in both Italy and Germany are covered in Arthur G. Haas, *Metternich, Reorganization and Nationality, 1813–18* (1963) and Donald E. Emerson, *Metternich and the Political Police* (1968). A very useful *vol d'oiseau* is Clive Church, *Europe in 1830: Revolution and Political Change* (1983). The key book on Germany is now James J. Sheehan, *German History, 1770–1866* (1989). To this may be added Hagen Schulze, *The Course of German Nationalism*, and cited above, Robert Berdahl, *The Politics of the Prussian Nobility*, cited above, Alf Lüdtke, *Police and State in Prussia, 1815–1850* (1989). On German liberalism there is John L. Snell, *The Democratic Movement in Germany 1789–1914* (1976), John Gillis, *The Prussian Bureaucracy in Crisis*, Loyd E. Lee, *The Politics of Harmony: Civil Service, Liberalism and Social Reform in Baden, 1800–1850* (1980), Jacques Droz, *Le Libéralisme rhénan, 1815–1848* (1940), Jonathan Sperber, 'Echoes of the French Revolution in the Rhineland, 1830–1849', *Central European History* 22 (1989), and R. Hinton Thomas, *Liberalism, Nationalism and the German Intellectuals, 1822–1847* (1951). W. Carr, *Schleswig-Holstein 1815–1848: A Study of National Conflict* (1963) cuts through the tangles of a tricky subject. On left-wing politics Carl Wittke, *The Utopian Communist: A Biography of Wilhelm Weitling* (1950) has flavour while David McLellan, *Karl Marx: Early Texts* (1971) and his mas-terly biography of *Karl Marx: His Life and Thought* (1973) are essential reading.

On Great Britain, Michael Brock's scholarly *Great Reform Act* (1973) should be supplemented for the assumptions behind it by D. C. Moore, *The Politics of Deference* (1976). There is now a plethora of works on Whig–Liberal politics, but T. A. Jenkins, *The Liberal Ascendancy, 1830–1886* (1994) is conveniently concise, to be matched by Paul Adelman, *Peel and the Conservative Party, 1830–1850* (1989). Good biographies of front-rank politicians and statesmen include C. J. Bartlett, *Castlereagh* (1966), Oliver MacDonagh, *O'Connell: The Life of Daniel O'Connell, 1775–1847* (1991), Norman Gash, *Lord Liverpool* (1984), *Mr Secretary Peel* (1961) and *Sir Robert Peel* (1972), and Muriel Chamberlain, *Lord Palmerston* (1987). Introductions to popular radicalism include J. R. Dinwiddy, *From Luddism to the First Reform Bill* (1986) and D. G. Wright, *Popular Radicalism: The Working-Class Experience, 1780–1880* (1988), but the serious student should tackle E. P. Thompson's brilliant *Making of the English Working Class* (1963; 1980). John Foster, *Class Struggle and the industrial revolution* (1974) has encountered criticism from Gareth Stedman Jones, *The Languages of Class: Studies in English Working-Class History, 1832–1982* (1983), which also reassesses Chartism. Joseph Hamburger, *Intellectuals in Politics: John Stuart Mill and the Philosophic Radicals* (1965) examines the dilemma of a middle-class radical.

There are two good short biographies of Metternich by Alan Palmer (1972) and Andrew Milne (1975). Administrative politics in Vienna are admirably treated by Egon Radvany, *Metternich's Projects for Reform in Austria* (1971). The nationalities problem in the Habsburg Monarchy has been the subject of much recent scholarly research. Miroslav Hroch, *Social Preconditions of National Revival in Europe* (1985) is an indispensable starting-point. Contributions include George Barany, *Stephen Széchenyi and the Awakening of Hungarian Nationalism, 1791–1841* (1968), Istvan Déak, *The Lawful Revolution: Louis Kossuth and the Hungarians, 1848–9* (1979), R. J. W. Evans, 'The Habsburgs and the Hungarian Problem, 1790–1848', *Transac-tions of the Royal Historical Society* (5th ser., 39, 1989), Iván Zoltán Dénes, 'The

432   *Bibliography*

Value Systems of Liberals and Conservatives in Hungary, 1830–1848', *Historical Journal* 36 (1993), Joseph Zacek, *Palacký: The Historian as Scholar and Nationalist* (1970), Peter Brock, *The Slovak National Awakening* (1976), Jan Kosik, *The Ukrainian Nationalist Movement in Galicia, 1815–1849* (1986), Keith Hitchens, *The Rumanian National Movement in Transylvania, 1780–1849* (1969), and Gunther Rothenberg, *The Military Border in Croatia, 1740–1881* (1966). Alan Sked, *The Survival of the Habsburg Empire* (1979) concentrates on Lombardy-Venetia. On the Greek revolt, Douglas Dakin, *The Greek Struggle for Independence, 1821–33* (1973) and Richard Clogg (ed.), *The Struggle for Greek Independence* (1973) set high standards; J. A. Petropulos, *Politics and Statecraft in the Kingdom of Greece 1834–1849* (1968) continues the story in great detail. The essence of John S. Koliopoulos, *Brigands with a Cause: Brigandage and Irredentism in Modern Greece, 1821–1912* (1987) may be found in his article in *East European Quarterly* 19 (1989).

The brief history of the Congress Kingdom of Poland is well covered by Frank W. Thackeray, *Antecedents of Revolution: Alexander I and the Polish Kingdom, 1815–1825* (1980), R. F. Leslie, *Polish Politics and the Revolution of November 1830* (1956), and M. Kukiel, *Czartoryski and European Unity, 1770–1861* (1955). To Marc Raeff, *The Decembrist Movement* (1966) may be added an interesting collection of essays edited by Alexandre Burmeyster, *Le 14 Décembre 1825. Origine et héritage du mouvement des décembristes* (1980). The regime of Nicholas I is covered by David Saunders, *Russia in the Age of Reaction and Reform, 1801–1881* (1992), W. Bruce Lincoln, *Nicholas I* (1978), John Shelton Curtiss, *The Russian Army under Nicholas I, 1825–55* (1965), Sidney Monas, *The Third Section: Police and Society in Russia under Nicholas I* (1961), P. S. Squire, *The Third Department* (1968), and S. Frederick Starr, *Decentralization and Self-Government in Russia 1830–70* (1972). Studies of Russian power now include Edward C. Thadden, *Russia's Western Borderlands, 1710–1870* (1984), which deals with Poland, Finland, and the Baltic, and John C. K. Daly, *Russia's Seapower and the Eastern Question, 1827–1841* (1991). Nicholas Riasanovsky, *A Parting of Ways: Government and the Educated Public in Russia, 1801–55* (1976) analyses the origin of the intelligentsia. Martin Malia's essay, 'What is the intelligentsia?' in Richard Pipes (ed.), *The Russian Intelligentsia* (1961) is fundamental, as is his brilliant *Alexander Herzen: The Birth of Russian Socialism* (1961). Isaiah Berlin's essay on Vissarion Belinsky is conveniently republished in his *Russian Thinkers* (1979).

Chapter 4

Accessible introductions to the 1848 Revolutions include Peter N. Stearns, *The Revolution of 1848* (1974), Roger Price, *The Revolutions of 1848* (1989) and Jonathan Sperber, *The European Revolutions, 1848–1851* (1994). Lewis Namier, *1848: The Revolution of the Intellectuals* (1946, repr. 1971), is a classic. William Langer, 'The pattern of urban revolution in 1848' in E. M. Acomb and M. C. Brown, *French Society and Culture since the Old Régime* (1966) provides a useful model. On the Low Countries there are Brison D. Gooch, *Belgium and the February Revolution* (1963) and Siep Sturman, '1848: Revolutionary Reform in the Netherlands', *European History Quarterly* 21 (1991). On Switzerland Joachim Remak, *A Very Civil War: The Swiss Sonderbund War of 1847* (1993) is excellent. The best introduction to France is Maurice Agulhon, *The Republican Experiment, 1848–1852* (1983). Roger Price's *The*

Second French Republic: A Social History (1972) is both scholarly and readable while his (edited) *Revolution and Reaction: 1848 and the Second French Republic* (1975) is a useful collection of essays. Peter Amann, *Revolution and Mass Democracy: The Paris Club Movement in 1848* (1975) and Rémi Gossez, *Les Ouvriers de Paris*, vol. i, *L'Organisation, 1848–51* (1967) concentrate on Parisian politics; John Merriman, *The Agony of the Republic: The Repression of the Left in Revolutionary France, 1848–51* (1978) is strong on regional perspectives. Clare Goldberg Moses, *French Feminism in the Nineteenth Century* (1984) has a chapter on 1848. Karl Marx, *The Class Struggle in France, 1848–50* and *The Eighteenth Brumaire of Louis Bonaparte*, in various editions, are good history as well as polemic and theory. A. J. Tudesq, *L'Election présidentielle de Louis-Napoléon Bonaparte, 10 décembre 1848* (1965) is an excellent monograph.

Lawrence C. Jennings, *France and Europe in 1848: A Study of French Foreign Affairs in Time of Crisis* (1973), goes a long way to accounting for the failure of the revolutions of 1848, especially in Italy. On Italy, Frank Coppa, *The Italian Wars of Independence* (1992), has material on 1848. E. E. Y. Hales, *Pio Nono* (1954) and Harold Acton, *The Last Bourbons of Naples, 1825–61* (1961) remain central, but G. M. Trevelyan, *Manin and the Venetian Revolution of 1848* (1923) now has to be supplemented by Paul Ginsborg, *Daniele Manin and the Venetian Revolution of 1848–9* (1979). Other useful works include H. Hearder, 'The making of the Roman Republic, 1848–9' in *History*, 60 (1975), Denis Mack Smith, *Mazzini* (1994), Lawrence Sondhaus, 'Prince Felix zu Schwarzenberg and Italy', *Austrian History Yearbook* 22 (1991), and Alan Sked, *The Survival of the Habsburg Monarchy: Radetsky, the Imperial Army and the Class War, 1848* (1979).

For other parts of the Habsburg monarchy R. J. Rath, *The Viennese Revolution of 1848* (1957) is very thorough. Stanley Pech has covered *The Czech Revolution of 1848* (1969). Istvan Déak, *The Lawful Revolution* on Kossuth has already been cited. Jurai Krnjević, 'The Croats in 1848' in *The Slavonic and East European Review*, 28 (1948) and G. Georgescu-Buzău, *The 1848 Revolution in the Rumanian Lands* (1965) are useful accounts of lesser-known arenas. A welcome recent study is Lawrence D. Orton, *The Prague Slav Congress of 1848* (1978). The best introduction to Germany in 1848 is Rudolf Stadelmann, *Social and Political History of the German 1848 Revolution* (1975). Jonathan Sperber, *Rhineland Radicals: The Democratic Movement and the Revolution of 1848–1849* (1991) is an important regional study while William Carr, *The Origins of the Wars of German Unification* (1991), illuminates the great-power dimension. Friedrich Engels, *Germany, Revolution and Counter-Revolution* in Leonard Krieger (ed.), *The German Revolutions* (1967) blames fairly and squarely the German middle class. Very useful are L. O' Boyle, 'The Democratic Left in Germany, 1848', *Journal of Modern History*, 33 (1961) and Frank Eyck, *The Frankfurt Parliament of 1848–9* (1968). The issue of nationalism is treated by C. E. Black, 'Poznań and Europe in 1848', *Journal of Central European Affairs*, 8 (1948), Eric Hahn, 'German parliamentary and national aims, 1848–9', *Central European History*, 13 (1980), and W. E. Mosse, *The European Powers and the German Question* (1958). Theodore Hamerow, *Restoration, Revolution, Reaction* (1958) is now rather dated but his article 'The German Artisan Movement of 1848–9', *Journal of Central European Affairs*, 21 (1961) together with the chapter by J. Kocka in Ira Katznelson, *Working-Class Formation* (1986), cited above, may give focus to P. H. Noyes' important but rather turgid

Organization and Revolution: Working-Class Associations in the German Revolution of 1848–9 (1966). On South Germany, Charles Dahlinger, *The German Revolution of 1848–9* (1903) is still very useful. On political reaction there is David E. Barclay, 'The Court camarilla and the politics of monarchical restoration in Prussia', in Larry E. Jones and James Retallack (eds.), *Between Reform, Reaction and Resistance: Studies in the History of German Conservatism from 1789 to 1945* (1993). Studies of the Russian dimension include Judith E. Zimmerman, *Mid-Passage: Alexander Herzen and European Revolution, 1847–1852* (1989), Joanna Seddon, *The Petrashevsky: A Study of the Russian Revolutionaries of 1848* (1985), and Ian W. Roberts, *Nicholas I and the Russian Intervention in Hungary* (1991).

Chapter 5

On education, apart from the general works cited above, there is useful information in T. W. Bamford, 'Public schools and social class, 1801–50', *British Journal of Sociology*, 12 (1961), R. D. Anderson, *Universities and Elites in Britain since 1800* (1992), E. G. West, *Education and the Industrial Revolution* (1975), Michael Sanderson, 'Literacy and social mobility in the industrial revolution', *Past and Present*, 56 (1972), Anthony Lavopa, *Prussian Schoolteachers. Profession and Office, 1763–1848* (1980), W. H. Bruford, *The German Tradition of Self-Cultivation* (1975), which is good on Humboldt, and Hermann Boon, *Enseignement primaire et alphabétisation dans l'agglomération bruxelloise, 1830–79* (1969). There are approaches to popular literature in C. P. Magill, 'The German author and his public in the mid-nineteenth century', *Modern Languages Review*, 43 (1948), Rudolf Hackmann, *Die Anfänge des Romans in der Zeitung* (1938), and Louis James, *Fiction for the Working Man, 1830–50* (1963; 1974). The frontiers of literacy and illiteracy emerge from Lawrence Fontaine, *History of Pedlars in Europe* (1995), Achille Bertarelli, *L'imagerie populaire italienne* (1929), William Harvey, *Scottish Chapbook Literature* (1903), and Yvonne Castellan, *La Culture serbe au seuil de l'indépendance, 1800–40* (1967). On the theatre, Leopold Schmidt, *Le Théâtre populaire européen* (1965) ranges widely. Very useful also are Maurice Albert, *Les Théâtres des boulevards, 1789–1848* (1902), Louis Véron, *Les Théâtres de Paris depuis 1806 jusqu' à 1860* (1860), F. D. Klingender, *Goya in the Democratic Tradition* (1948), on Madrid, W. H. Bruford, *Theatre, Drama and Audience in Goethe's Germany* (1950), Lawrence Senelick (ed.), *National Theatre in Northern and Eastern Europe, 1746–1900* (1991), a collection of documents, and Kenneth Richards and Peter Thompson, *Essays on Nineteenth-Century British Theatre* (1971). William Weber, *Music and the Middle-Class: The Social Structure of Concert Life in London, Paris and Vienna* (1975) is provocative but rather schematic and ignores opera. This may be remedied by Roger Parker, *The Oxford Illustrated History of Opera* (1994) and for France at least, by Jane L. Fulcher, *The Nation's Image: French Grand Opera as Politics and Politicized Art* (1987). It should be supplemented by Alice M. Harison, *Musical Life in Biedermeier Vienna* (1985). Ernest Newman's *Life of Richard Wagner* is standard; the first volume (1933) covers the years 1813–48. The history of sport is still in its infancy. Alongside Holt, cited above, there is Joseph Antoine Roy, *Histoire du Jockey-Club de Paris* (1958), Timothy Mitchell, *Blood Sport: A Social History of Spanish Bullfighting* (1991), Raymond Carr, *English Fox-Hunting: A History* (1976), Robert W. Malcolmson, *Popular Recreation in English Society, 1700–1850* (1973) and scholarly essays in Brian Harrison, *Peaceable Kingdom: Stability and Change in Modern Britain* (1982).

The key text on changing models of crime and punishment is Michel Foucault, *Discipline and Punish. The Birth of the Prison* (1975; trans. 1977). Other theoretical works include Anthony Giddens, *The Nation-State and Violence* (1985), esp. ch. 7, and Charles Tilly, *Coercion, Capital and European States,* AD *990–1990* (1990). Problems of state control are examined by John A. Davis, *Conflict and Control: Law and order in Nineteenth-Century Italy* (1988), Giovanna Fiume, 'Bandits, violence and the organization of power in Sicily in the early nineteenth century', in John A. Davis and Paul Ginsborg, *Society and Politics in the Age of the Risorgimento* (1991), and Alf Lüdtke, 'The role of state violence in the period of transition to industrial capitalism: the example of Prussia from 1815 to 1848', *Social History* 4 (1979). The industry on crime and criminality has thrown up useful works by J. J. Tobias, *Nineteenth-Century Crime: Prevention and Punishment* (1972), Howard Zehr, *Crime and the Development of Modern Society* (1976), Dirk Blasius, *Bürgerlich Gesellschaft und Kriminalität. Zur Sozialgeschichte Preussens im Vormärz* (1976), V. A. C. Gattrell (ed.), *Crime and the Law* (1980) and Martin S. Wiener, *Reconstructing the Criminal: Culture, Law and Policy in England, 1830–1914* (1990). Policing is studied in Clive Emsley, *Policing and its Context, 1750–1870* (1983), Stanley H. Palmer, *Police and Protest in England and Ireland, 1780–1850* (1988), and Hsi-Huey Liang, *The Rise of the Modern Police and the Modern State System from Metternich to the Second World War* (1992), which concentrates on international policing. Prison systems have been studied by U. R. Q. Henriques, 'The rise and decline of the separate system of prison discipline', *Past and Present*, 54 (1972), Michelle Perrot, 'Délinquance et système pénitentiaire en France au XIXe siècle', *Annales*, 30 (1975), and Michael Ignatieff, *A Just Measure of Pain: The Penitentiary in the Industrial Revolution, 1750–1850* (1978). The best introduction to poverty and poor relief is Stuart Woolf, *The Poor in Western Europe in the Eighteenth and Nineteenth Centuries* (1986). Moral and religious education is discussed by Richard Johnson, 'Educational policy and social control in early Victorian England', *Past and Present*, 49 (1970), Thomas Laqueur, *Religion and Respectability: Sunday Schools and Working-Class Culture, 1780–1850* (1976) and Brian Harrison, cited above. The 'social' side of religion can be studied through K. S. Inglis, 'Patterns of religious worship in 1851', *Journal of Ecclesiastical History*, 2 (1960), which uses census material, Thomas Bebbington, *Evangelicalism in Modern Britain* (1989), chs. 1–4, Ralph Gibson, *A Social History of French Catholicism, 1789–1914* (1989), Hazel Mills, 'Negotiating the divide: women, philanthrophy and the "public sphere" in nineteenth-century France', in Frank Tallett and Nicholas Atkin (eds.), *Religion, Society and Politics in France since 1789* (1789), William J. Callahan, *Church, Politics and Society in Spain, 1750–1874* (1984), William O. Shanahan, *German Protestants and the Social Question* (1954), Robert Bigler, *The Politics of German Protestantism: The Rise of the Protestant Church Elite in Prussia, 1815–1848* (1972), John E. Groh, *Nineteenth-Century German Protestantism* (1982), Jonathan Sperber, *Popular Catholicism in Nineteenth-Century Germany* (1984) and Gregory Freeze, *The Parish Clergy in Nineteenth-Century Russia* (1983).

On Romanticism there is much good writing. John B. Halsted (ed.), *Romanticism* (1969), Lilian Furst, *Romanticism* (2nd edn., 1976), and Hugh Honour's lavishly illustrated *Romanticism* (1979) make good introductions. Rupert Christiansen, *Romantic*

Affinities (1988) examines key themes while Maurice Cranston, *The Romantic Movement* (1994), goes country by country. M. H. Abrams, *The Mirror and the Lamp: Romantic Theory and the Critical Tradition* (1953) examines the Romantic genius. German Romanticism is treated by Roger Cardinal, *German Romantics in Context* (1975), Oskar Walzel, *German Romanticism* (1932), and Siegbert Prawer, *The Romantic Period in Germany* (1970). The standard biography of Beethoven is Elliott Forbes, *Thayer's Life of Beethoven* (2 vols., 1964). Marilyn Butler, *Romantics, Rebels and Reactionaries* (1981), is an admirable study of English Romanticism while Edgar Allison Peers, *A Short History of the Romantic Movement in Spain* (1949) is still useful. Andrew Cunningham and Nicholas Jardine (eds.), *Romanticism and the Sciences* (1990) offers a different perspective. On specific writers there is David Erdman, *Blake, Prophet against Empire* (3rd edn., 1977), Jonathan Wordsworth, *William Wordsworth: The Borders of Vision* (1982), Richard Holmes, *Shelley, The Pursuit* (1974), Paul Graham Trueblood, *Byron's Political and Cultural Influence in Nineteenth-Century Europe* (1981) and Philip W. Martin, *Byron, a Poet before his Public* (1982). Hubert Juin, *Victor Hugo*, vol. i, *1802–1843* (1980), vol. ii, *1844–1870* (1984) and Alain Decaux, *Victor Hugo* (1984) are works proportionate in size to the greatness of the man. Eugène Delacroix, *Journal, 1822–1863* (1980) and Franz Liszt, *Life of Chopin* (1872) are very evocative.

Chapter 6

Among studies of urbanization and industrial revolution, E. A. Wrigley, *Industrial Growth and Population Change* (1961) examines northern France and north-east Germany, and Germany is covered by J. J. Lee in Philip Abrams and E. A. Wrigley, *Towns in Societies* (1978) and Klaus Bade, *Population, Labour and Migration in Nineteenth and Twentieth Century Germany* (1987). On France and Belgium there are articles by Georges Dupeux, 'La croissance urbaine en France au XIXe siècle', *Revue d'histoire économique et sociale*, 52 (1974) and Allan H. Kittel, 'Industrial innovation and population displacement in Belgium, 1830–1880', *Journal of Social History*, 1 (1967). There are good essays on Great Britain, the Netherlands, Germany, and Italy in H. Schmal (ed.), *Patterns of European Urbanisation since 1800* (1981). Philip Waller surveys the English urban scene in *Town, City and Nation: England 1850–1914* (1983). Mack Walker, *Germany and the Emigration, 1816–1885* (1964) is very readable, but a veritable mine of interesting contributions is the Commission internationale d'histoire des mouvements sociaux et des structures sociales, *Les Migrations internationales de la fin du XVIIIe siècle à nos jours* (1980).

The question of widening markets is examined by Paul Bairoch, 'European foreign trade in the nineteenth century', *Journal of European Economic History*, 2 (1973), James Foreman Peck, *A History of the World Economy: International Economic Relations since 1850* (2nd edn., 1995), Patrick O'Brien, *The New Economic History of the Railways* (1977), which goes further than merely quoting lengths of track, and the critical assessment by Roy Church of *The Great Victorian Boom, 1850–1873* (1975). Daniel Headrick, *The Tentacles of Progress: Technological Transfer in the Age of Imperialism, 1850–1940* (1988), deals with shipping and the telegraph. Free trade versus protection is examined by Ivo N. Lambi, *Free Trade and Protection in Germany, 1868–79* (1963) and Michael S. Smith, *Tariff Reform in France, 1860–1900* (1980).

The land question in Ireland is tackled by Barbara Solow, *The Land Question and the Irish Economy* (1971), which plays down the extent of exploitation and E. D. Steele, *Irish Land and British Politics: Tenant-Right and Nationality 1865–70* (1970), which plays it up. There is a wealth of good material on the emancipation of the Russian serfs, from Terence Emmons's essay in W. C. Vucinich (ed.), *The Peasant in Nineteenth-Century Russia* (1968), which looks at peasant mentalities, and Terence Emmons, *Russian Landed Gentry and the Peasant Emancipation of 1861* (1968) to Alexander Gerschenkron, 'Agrarian policies and industrialization, 1861–1914' in *Continuity in History and Other Essays* (1968), David Field, *The End of Serfdom: Nobility and Bureaucracy in Russia, 1855–61* (1976) and David Moon, *Russian Peasants and Tsarist Legislation on the Eve of Reform* (1992). The scholarship of P. A. Zaionchkovsky's *The Abolition of Serfdom* (1978) is unduly constrained by a feudalism-to-capitalism framework, and is not his best work.

On mid-century industrialization, there is much in *L'industrialisation en Europe an XIXe siècle* and the *Cambridge Economic History*, vol. vii, already cited. W. O. Henderson, *The Rise of German Industrial Power, 1834–1914* (1975) and Martin Kitchen, *The Political Economy of Germany, 1815–1914* (1978) are two efficient studies of the main emergent economy. David Landes, 'The old bank and the new' in Crouzet (ed.), *Essays in European Economic History* (1969) is central. Following his *France and the Economic Development of Europe, 1800–1914* (1961) Rondo Cameron has edited *Banking and Economic Development* (1972) which includes essays on Italy, Spain, Austria, and Russia. Jean Bouvier, *Le Crédit Lyonnais de 1863 à 1882* (1961) and Richard Tilly, *Financial Institutions and Industrialization in the Rhineland, 1815–70* (1966) are important contributions to banking history. Entrepreneurship is discussed by Peter L. Payne's succinct *British Entrepreneurship in the Nineteenth Century* (1974) and in the collection edited by Maurice Lévy-Leboyer, *Le Patronat de la seconde industrialisation* (1979). There is a useful survey of labour legislation in Great Britain, France, and the USA in G. V. Rimlinger, 'Labour and government: a comparative historical perspective', *Journal of Economic History*, 37 (1977). Labour history moves between the formation of working classes, such as Michael Neufeld, *The Skilled Metalworkers of Nuremberg: Craft and Class in the Industrial Revolution* (1989), and Michael P. Hanagan, *Nascent Proletarians: Class Formation in Post-Revolutionary France* (1989), and their organization, which features more prominently in Bernard H. Moss, *The Origins of the French Labour Movement: The Socialism of Skilled Workers* (1976), Robert Gray, *The Aristocracy of Labour in Nineteenth-Century Britain, 1850–1900* (1981), and E. H. Hunt, *British Labour History* (1981). Roger Magraw offers a synthesis on France in *The Age of Artisan Revolution, 1815–1871* (1992), while Ira Katznelson and A. Zolberg, *Working-Class Formation*, cited above, compares labour in France and Germany.

The relationship between monied and landed wealth is analysed by W. D. Rubinstein, 'Wealth, élites and the class structure of modern Britain', *Past and Present*, 76 (1977), adducing statistical evidence, and more impressionistically by Martin J. Wiener, *English Culture and the Decline of the Industrial Spirit, 1850–1980* (1981). A more traditional trading community is portrayed by Thomas C. Owen, *Capitalism and Politics in Russia: A Social History of the Moscow Merchants, 1855–1905* (1981) and by Alfred J. Rieber, *Merchants and Entrepreneurs in Imperial Russia* (1982). Important studies of the bourgeoisie include Jürgen Kocka and Allan Mitchell (eds.),

Bourgeois Society in Nineteenth-Century Europe (1993), Pamela Pilbeam, *The Middle Classes in Europe, 1789–1914* (1990), Bonnie G. Smith, *Ladies of the Leisure Class: The Bourgeoises of Northern France in the Nineteenth Century* (1981), Jean-Pierre Chaline, *Les Bourgeois de Rouen: Une Élite urbaine au XIXe siècle* (1982), Adeline Daumard, *Les Bourgeois et la bourgeoisie en France depuis 1815* (1991) and David Blackbourn and R. J. Evans (eds.), *The German Bourgeoisie* (1991). Jürgen Kocka examines the Siemens family in 'Family and bureaucracy in German industrial management, 1850–1914: Siemens in comparative perspective', *Business History Review*, 45 (1971) and the training of managers in 'Capitalism and bureaucracy in German industrialization before 1914', *Economic History Review*, 34 (1981). This is covered for France by F. Perroux and P. M. Schuhl, 'Saint-Simonisme et pari pour l'industrie, XIXe—XXe siècles', *Économies et sociétés*, 4 (1970), and for Great Britain by Michael Sanderson, *The Universities and British Industry, 1850–1970* (1972). A good comparative study is P. W. Musgrave, *Technical Change, the Labour Force and Education: A Study of the British and German Iron and Steel Industries 1860–1964* (1967). On service and nobility, useful studies include William Serman, *Les Origines des officiers français, 1848–1870* (1979), Albert V. Tucker, 'Army and Society in England, 1870–1900: A reassessment of the Cardwell reforms', *Journal of British Studies*, 2 (1963), and Walter L. Arnstein, 'The survival of the Victorian aristocracy' in F. C. Jaher (ed.), *The Rich, the Well-Born and the Powerful* (1973). Two illuminating contemporary studies are T. H. S. Escott, *England, its People, Polity and Pursuits*, vol. ii (1879) and D. Mackenzie Wallace, *Russia*, vol. i (1877).

Chapter 7

Studies of the gloomy period of the 1850s include William A. Jenks, *Francis Joseph and the Italians, 1849–1859* (1978) and György Szabad, *Hungarian Political Trends between the Revolution and Compromise, 1849–67* (1977), which is the best possible guide to a difficult subject. Denis Mack Smith, *Victor Emanuel, Cavour and the Risorgimento* (1971) reveals the king's authoritarian penchants while the failure of reaction in Spain is documented by V. G. Kiernan, *The Revolution of 1854 in Spanish History* (1966). A scholarly synthesis of the Second Empire is available in Alain Plessis, *The Rise and Fall of the Second Empire, 1852–71* (1973, trans. 1984). W. H. C. Smith's *Napoléon III* (1982), in French, is a brilliant reassessment, and better than his *Napoleon III* (1972) in English. James McMillan's *Napoleon III* (1991) is extremely useful. On Great Britain, there is J. B. Conacher, *The Aberdeen Coalition, 1852–55* (1968).

On the Crimean War, there is David M. Goldfrank, *The Origins of the Crimean War* (1994), Paul W. Schroeder, *Austria, Great Britain and the Crimean War: The Destruction of the European Concert* (1972), John Shelton Curtiss, *Russia's Crimean War* (1979), Hugh Ragsdale (ed.), *Imperial Russian Foreign Policy* (1993), part III, William Echard, *Napoleon III and the Concert of Europe* (1983), J. B. Conacher, *Britain and the Crimea, 1855–6: Problems of War and Peace* (1987), and W. E. Mosse, *The Rise and Fall of the Crimean System, 1855–1871* (1963).

Winfried Baumgart's *The Peace of Paris: Studies in War, Diplomacy and Peace-Making* (1981) includes an analysis of the effects of the war on Russia. This issue may be pursued in Alan K. Wildman, *The End of the Russian Imperial Army* (1980), George L. Yaney, *The Systematization of Russian Government, 1711–1905* (1973),

Terence Emmons and Wayne S. Vucinich (eds.), *The Zemstvo in Russia* (1982) and W. Bruce Lincoln, *The Great Reforms* (1990). Rising discontent in Russian society is charted by Ronald Hingley, *The Nihilists* (1967), Daniel R. Brower, *Training the Nihilists* (1975) and Franco Venturi's monumental *Roots of Revolution* (1960), on Populism. Difficulties in the Empire with Finland are covered by J. Paasvirta, cited above, and with Poland by R. F. Leslie, *Reform and Insurrection in Russian Poland, 1856–65* (1963) and Stefan Kieniewicz, 'Polish society and the insurrection of 1863', *Past and Present* 37 (1967). Michael B. Petrovich, *The Emergence of Russian Panslavism, 1856–70* (1956) looks at Russian ambitions in the Balkans. On the Balkan states, there is Barbara Jelavich, *Russia and the Formation of the Romanian Nation State, 1821–78* (1984), C. E. Black, *The Establishment of Constitutional Government in Bulgaria* (1963), Douglas Dakin, *The Unification of Greece* and Michael Petrovich, *A History of Modern Serbia*, vol. i, already cited.

Beales, Coppa, and Stuart Woolf, cited, provide useful introductions to Italian unification. Arnold Blumberg, *A Carefully Planned Accident: The Italian War of 1859* (1990) is a good diplomatic history. Raymond Grew, 'How success spoiled the Risorgimento', *Journal of Modern History*, 34 (1962) and *A Sterner Plan for Italian Unity: The Italian National Society and the Risorgimento* (1963) examine a strategy that succeeded; Clara Maria Lovett, *Carlo Cattaneo and the Politics of the Risorgimento* (1972), and Frank J. Coppa, *Giacomo Antonio Antonelli and Papal Politics in European Affairs* (1990), two that failed. The elegant and scholarly contributions of Denis Mack Smith include *Cavour and Garibaldi 1860: A Study of Political Conflict* (1954, reissued 1985), *Victor Emanuel, Cavour and the Risorgimento* (1971), and *Cavour* (1985). The question of Piedmontese dominance is examined in Alberto Caracciolo, *Stato e Societa civile. Problemi dell' unificazione italiana* (1960), E. Passerin d'Entrèves, *L'Ultima battaglia politica di Cavour. I Problemi dell' unificazione italiana* (1956), and R. Romano and C. Vivanti, *Storia d'Italia*, vol. iv, no. 3, *Dall' unità a oggi* (1976). M. I. Finley, Denis Mack Smith, and Christopher Duggan (eds.), *A History of Sicily* (1986) and John A. Davis, *Conflict and Control, op. cit.*, ch. 11, offer insights into the origins of the Mafia.

Clear introductions to German unification are William Carr, *The Origins of the Wars of German Unification* (1991), Hagen Schulze, *The Course of German Nationalism* (1991), W. M. Simon, *Germany in the Age of Bismarck* (1968), and W. D. Medlicott, *Bismarck and Modern Germany* (1965). Helmut Böhme's majestic *Deutschlands Weg zur Grossmacht* (1966), which is particularly strong in the economic dimension of unification, has been made accessible as a collection of texts and summaries translated by Agatha Ramm, *The Foundation of the German Empire* (1971). The best biography of Bismarck is now Lothar Gall, *Bismarck, the White Revolutionary* (2 vols., 1986). W. E. Mosse, *The European Powers and the German Question*, already cited, surveys the international scene. The struggle of authoritarianism and liberalism is documented in Eugene N. Anderson, *The Social and Political Conflict in Prussia, 1858–64* (1954), Gordon A. Craig, *The Politics of the Prussian Army* (1955), James J. Sheehan, *German Liberalism in the Nineteenth Century* (1978) and K. Jarausch and L. E. Jones (eds.), *In Search of a Liberal Germany* (1990). Fritz Stern *Gold and Iron: Bismarck, Bleichröder and the Building of the German Empire* (1977) makes much of little. The debate on the parallels between Bismarck's system and Bonapartism is conducted in German and French in Karl Kammer and P. C. Hartmann (eds.), *Bonapartismus*

(1977). The view of unification from the side of the losers has merited attention. Richard B. Elrod, 'Bernhard von Rechberg and the Metternichian tradition: the dilemma of conservative statecraft', *Journal of Modern History* 56 (1984), is helpful on Austria. On Hanover there is Stewart A. Stehlin, *Bismarck and the Guelph Problem, 1866–90* (1973) and the beginning of Margaret Anderson, *Windthorst: A Political Biography* (1981), which is a major work of scholarship. On Central Germany, Nicholas Hope, *The Alternative to German Unification: The Anti-Prussian Party, Frankfurt, Nassau and the Two Hessen, 1859–67* (1973) and Dan S. White, *The Splintered Party: National Liberalism in Hessen and the Reich 1867–1918* (1976) compliment each other. The problem of South Germany is examined by George C. Windell, *The Catholics and German Unity, 1866–71* (1954) and Rolf Wilhelm, *Das Velhältnis der Süddeutschen Staaten zum Norddeutschen Bund, 1867–70* (1978). Two long-serving books on the outbreak of war with France are Lawrence D. Steefel, *Bismarck, the Hohenzollern Candidacy and the Origins of the Franco-German War of 1870* (1962) and Georges Bonnin, *Bismarck and the Hohenzollern Candidature for the Spanish Throne* (1957). Michael Howard, *The Franco-Prussian War* (1968) is the definitive military history. More recent contributions are Stéphane Audoin-Rouzeau, *1870: La France dans la Guerre* (1989), Philippe Levillain and Rainer Riemenschneider (eds.), *La Guerre de 1870–71 et ses conséquences* (1990), the proceedings of an excellent conference, François Roth, *La Guerre de 1870* (1990), a standard narrative, Brian Bond, *War and Society in Europe, 1870–1970* (1983), and Paul W. Schroeder, 'The lost intermediaries: the impact of 1870 on the European system', *International History Review* 6 (1984).

On the *Ausgleich*, György Szabad, *Hungarian Political Trends*, already cited, is very helpful, as are Jörg Hoensch, *A History of Modern Hungary, 1867–1986* (1988), Jean-Paul Bled, *Franz Joseph* (1992) and Lásló Peter, 'The dualist character of the 1867 Hungarian settlement' in G. Ranki (ed.), *Hungarian History, World History* (1984). F. R. Bridge, *From Sadowa to Sarajevo. The Foreign Policy of Austria-Hungary, 1866–1914* (1972) is thorough and reliable but his *The Habsburg Monarchy among the Great Powers* (1990) is more recent.

Chapter 8

Introductions to anarchism and socialism in the middle years of the century include George Woodcock, *Anarchism: A History of Libertarian Ideas and Movements* (1962), Milorad M. Drachkovitch (ed.), *The Revolutionary Internationals, 1864–1943* (1966), which puts the First International in context, and Dick Geary, *Labour and Socialist Movements before 1914* (1989). On the manifestation of revolutionary movements in different countries, John Breuilly, *Labour and Liberalism in Nineteenth-Century Europe* (1992), offers an excellent comparison of the strategies of labour movements in Great Britain and Germany. There is Henry Collins and Chimen Abransky, *Karl Marx and the British Labour Movement* (1965) and Royden Harrison, *Before the Socialists* (1965), on Great Britain; for France, Robert J. Hoffmann, *Revolutionary Justice: The Social and Political Theory of P.-J. Proudhon* (1972) and Jean Maitron, *Le Mouvement anarchiste en France*, vol. i (1975); on Germany, Roger Morgan, *German Social Democrats and the First International, 1864–72* (1965) and Vernon L. Lidtke, *The Outlawed Party: Social Democracy in Germany, 1878–1890* (1966); on Italy, Maurice F. Neufeld's unorthodox *Italy: School for Awakening*

Countries (1961), Richard Hostetter, *The Italian Socialist Movement*, vol. i, *Origins, 1860–82* (1958); on Spain, Gerald Brenan, already cited, Murrary Bookchin, *The Spanish Anarchists* (1977) and Temma Kaplan, *Anarchists of Andalusia, 1868–1903* (1977). Biographies of peripatetic anarchist leaders include E. H. Carr, *Michael Bakunin* (1937; reissued 1975), Caroline Cahm, *Kropotkin: The Rise of Revolutionary Anarchism, 1872–1886* (1989), and David Stafford, *From Anarchism to Reformism* (1971), on Paul Brousse. A fundamental work on the Paris Commune is Charles Rihs, *La Commune de Paris* (1955; 2nd edn., 1973), but some of its conclusions have been contested by Jaques Rougerie in *Paris libre* (1971), a useful collection of texts, and his essay in *Jalons pour une histoire de la Commune de Paris* (1973), and by Eugene Schulkind, *The Paris Commune of 1871* (Historical Association pamphlet, 1971) and another collection of texts, *The Paris Commune of 1871: The View from the Left* (1972). With these must be read J. M. Roberts, *The Paris Commune from the Right* (1973) and Robert Tombs, *The War against Paris, 1871* (1981). Karl Marx, *The Civil War in France*, in Marx and Engels, *Selected Works in One Volume* (1968) and elsewhere, is a familiar blend of polemic and history.

Introductions to the French Third Republic include R. D. Anderson, *France, 1870–1914* (1977) and Robert Gildea, *The Third Republic, 1870–1914* (1988). Also helpful on French politics in the 1870s are Samuel Osgood, *French Royalism since 1870* (1970), John Rothney, *Bonapartism after Sedan* (1969), and J. P. T. Bury, *Gambetta and the Making of the Third Republic* (1973). Christopher Seton-Watson, *Italy from Liberalism to Fascism*, cited above, provides a detailed guide to Italian politics. There are other useful perspectives in Denis Mack Smith, *Italy and its Monarchy* (1989), Clara M. Lovett, *The Democratic Movement in Italy, 1830–76* (1982) and Richard A. Webster, *Christian Democracy in Italy, 1860–1960* (1961). Writing on the Spanish Republic and Restoration has been of a high standard and includes C. A. M. Hennessy, *The Federal Republic in Spain* (1962). Earl R. Beck, *A Time of Triumph and Sorrow: Spanish Politics during the Reign of Alfonso XII, 1874–1885* (1979), Robert Kern (ed.), *The Caciques* (1973) and *Liberals, Reformers and Caciques in Restoration Spain, 1875–1909* (1974). Among accounts of the 1867 Reform Act in Great Britain are F. B. Smith, *The Making of the Second Reform Act* (1966), Gertrude Himmelfarb, 'The Politics of democracy: the English reform act of 1867', *Journal of British Studies*, 6 (1966), and Maurice Cowling, *1867. Disraeli, Gladstone and Revolution* (1967). The changing nature of party politics is examined by H. J. Hanham, *Elections and Party Management: Politics in the Time of Disraeli and Gladstone* (1959, 2nd edn., 1978). Other helpful works include H. C. G. Matthew, *Gladstone, 1809–1874* (1986), T. A. Jenkins, *The Liberal Ascendancy, 1830–1886* (1994), which is concise, John Parry, *The Rise and Fall of Liberal Government in Britain* (1993), which also goes up to 1886, Ian Machin, *Disraeli* (1995), and Richard Shannon, *The Age of Disraeli, 1868–81. The Rise of Tory Democracy* (1992).

German politics in the 1870s is discussed by James Sheehan, Gordon Craig, and W. M. Simon, already cited. Karl Rohe, *Elections, Parties and Political Traditions: Social Foundations of German Parties and Political Systems, 1867–1987* (1990), contains useful essays. The basic work in German is Michael Stürmer, *Regierung und Reichstag in Bismarckstaat, 1871–1880* (1974). Hans Rosenberg, *Grosse Depression und Bismarckzeit* (1967) analyses the economic and fiscal roots of policy. On the Centre party there is Margaret Anderson's *Windthorst* and John K. Zeender, *The*

German Centre Party, 1890–1906 (1976). Austrian liberalism is examined by Herbert Mathis, 'Sozioökonomische Aspekte des Liberalismus in Osterreich, 1848–1918', in H.-U. Wehler, *Sozialgeschichte Heute* (1974). On Taaffe's conservative era, William A. Jenks, *Austria under the Iron Ring, 1879–1893* (1965) is thorough. On Russian ambitions in the Balkans, B. H. Sumner, 'Russia and Panslavism in the Eighteen-Seventies', *Transactions of the Royal Historical Society*, 18 (1935) and *Russia and the Balkans, 1870–1880* (1937) may be supplemented by Mihailo Stojanović, *The Great Powers and the Balkans, 1875–78* (1939), W. N. Medlicott, *The Congress of Berlin and After* (1963), David Mackenzie, *The Serbs and Russian Pan-Slavism, 1875–78* (1967) and his essay 'Russian Balkan policies under Alexander II, 1855–61', in Hugh Ragsdale (ed.), *Imperial Russian Foreign Policy* (1993). The impact of diplomatic humiliation on domestic politics is the subject of Peter A. Zaionchkovsky's brilliant *The Russian Autocracy in Crisis, 1878–82* (1979).

Chapter 9

Questions of linguistic unification, popular education, and popular culture are dealt with by Tullio De Mauro, *Storia linguistica dell'Italia unita* (1963), Dina Bertoni Jovine, *Storia della scuola populare in Italia* (1954), Marjorie Lamberti, *State, Society and the Elementary School in Imperial Germany* (1989), Yvonne Turin, *L'Education et l'école en Espagne 1874–1902. Libéralisme et tradition* (1959), Esteban Medina, *La Lucha por la educación en Espagna, 1770–1970* (1977), Ben Eklof, *Russian Peasant Schools: Officialdom, Village Culture and Popular Pedagogy, 1861–1914* (1986), and Jeffrey Brooks, *When Russia Learned to Read: Literacy and Popular Literature, 1861–1917* (1985).

Matthew Arnold, *Essays in Criticism* (1865, repr. 1918) and *Culture and Anarchy* (1869) serve as introductions to the question of philistinism. Stefan Collini, *Matthew Arnold: A Critical Portrait* (1994) provides the background, but Janet Wolff and John Seeds (eds.), *The Culture of Capital: Art, Power and the Nineteenth-Century Middle Class* (1988) questions the philistinism of the British middle class. Useful works on the widening of the reading public include Alan J. Lee, *The Origins of the Popular Press in Britain, 1855–1914* (1978), Elger Blühm and Rolf Engelsing, *Die Zeitung* (1967), Claude Bellanger's *Histoire générale de la presse française*, vol. iii, *1871–1940* (1972), and, on a fading idiom, Jean-Jacques Darmon, *Le Colportage de librairie en France sous le Second Empire* (1972). On music, Florian Bruyas, *Histoire de l'opérette en France, 1855–1965* (1974) is scholarly and Elizabeth Bernard, 'Jules Pasdeloup et les concerts populaires', *Reveue de musicologie*, 56 (1970) very useful. Joseph Wechsberg, *The Waltz Emperors* (1973) and *The Lost World of the Great Spas* (1979) are more popular in style. Paul Gerbod, 'Les Fièvres thermiques en France au XXe siècle', *Revue historique* 277 (1987) looks at spas in France, John Pemble, *The Mediterranean Passion: Victorians and Edwardians in the South* at British tourism more generally. Holt, *Sport and Society* already mentioned, John Lowerson, *Sport and the English Middle Classes, 1870–1914* (1993), and Peter Bailey, *Leisure and Class in Victorian England* (1978), are full of interest, while Christiane Eisenberg, 'The middle classes and competition: some considerations of the beginning of modern sport in England and Germany', *Interdisciplinary Journal of the History of Sport* 7 (1990), offers a useful comparative perspective.

Issues of Church, state, and society in France and Germany are examined by Ralph

Gibson, *A Social History of French Catholicism, 1789–1914* (1989), Jonathan Sperber, *Popular Catholicism in Nineteenth-Century Germany* (1984), and David Blackbourn, *Marpingen: Apparitions of the Virgin Mary in Bismarckian Germany* (1993). A. C. Jemolo's first-rate *Church and State in Italy, 1850–1960* (1960) may be supplemented by many essays in the Atti del quarto Convegno di storia della Chiesa, *Chiesa e religiosità dopo l'unità, 1861–1878* (1973). On Spain, Frances Lannon, *Privilege, Persecution and Prophecy: The Catholic Church in Spain, 1875–1975* (1987) follows on from William J. Callahan, *Church, Politics and Society in Spain, 1750–1874* (1984). Quite excellent is Juan López-Morillas, *The Krausist Movement and Ideological Change in Spain, 1854–1874* (1981). Jewish emancipation and assimilation are examined by Jonathan Frankel and Steven J. Zipperstein, *Assimilation and Community: The Jews in Nineteenth-Century Europe* (1992), Peter Pulzer, *Jews and the German State* (1992), and Marsha L. Rozenblit, *The Jews of Vienna, 1867–1914: Assimilation and Identity* (1983). The best introduction to scientific movements and their challenge to the established Churches is J. W. Burrow, *Evolution and society: A Study in Victorian Social Theory* (1966). Andrew Cunningham and Perry Williams (eds.), *The Laboratory Revolution in Medicine* (1992) is excellent. D. G. Charlton, *Secular Religions in France, 1815–70* (1963) and W. M. Simon, *European Positivism in the Nineteenth Century* (1963) are extremely useful. Emile Durkheim, *Le Socialisme* (1928) translated as *Socialism and Saint Simon* (1959) is a penetrating analysis of the roots of positivism; Mary Pickering, *Auguste Comte: An Intellectual Biography I* (1993) begins to look at its father; Louis Legrand, *Le Positivisme dans l'œuvre scolaire de Jules Ferry* (1961) analyses its application to French education. On other thinkers see M. W. Taylor, *Man versus the State: Herbert Spencer and late Victorian Individualism* (1992), Michael Biddiss (ed.), *Gobineau: Selected Political Writings* (1970), and Jon Elster, *An Introduction to Karl Marx* (1986).

On Realism, there are useful introductions by Lilian Furst, *Realism* (1992), Linda Nochlin, *Realism* (1971) and *Realism and Tradition in Art, 1848–1900* (1966). F. W. J. Hemmings has edited *The Age of Realism* (1974), with contributions on the major European countries. On France, Hemmings, *Culture and Society in France, 1848–1898* (1971) and *Life and Times of Emile Zola* (1977) are indispensable. Gillian Beer, 'Plot and the analogy with science in later nineteenth century novelists', *Comparative Criticism*, 2 (1980) looks at the novel as experiment. Patricia Mainardi has contributed first-rate studies with *Art and Politics of the Second Empire: The Universal Expositions of 1855 and 1867* (1987) and *The End of the Salon: Art and the State in the Early Third Republic* (1993). Useful studies on other countries include Sherman H. Eoff, *The Novels of Pérez Galdós* (1954), Robin Lenman, 'Painters, patronage and the art market in Germany, 1850–1914', *Past and Present* 123 (1989), and Edna Sigarra, *Tradition and Revolution: German Literature and Society, 1830–1890* (1971). Aaron Scharf, *Art and Photography* (1968) is a good introduction to the subject.

Chapter 10

On demographic issues, Thomas McKeown, *The Modern Rise of Population* (1976) discusses falling mortality, while the falling birth-rate in western Europe, which is intimately bound up with family history and social mobility, is treated by John

R. Gillis, Louise Tilly, and David Levine (eds.), *The European Experience of Declining Fertility, 1850–1970* (1992), James Woycke, *Birth Control in Germany, 1871–1933* (1988), R. P. Neuman, 'Working-class birth control in Wilhelmine Germany', *Comparative Studies in Society and History*, 20 (1978), and André Armengaud, 'Mouvement ouvrier et néo-malthusianisme au début du XXe siècle', *Annales de démographie historique* (1966). Michael Mitterauer and Reinhard Sieder, *The European Family* (1982) and David L. Ransel (ed.), *The Family in Imperial Russia* (1978) are good examples of recent studies of the family. On urbanization, Waller, *Town, City and Nation*, Schmal (ed.), *Patterns of European Urbanization*, and Köllmann, *Bevölkerung*, already cited, together with Köllmann, 'The process of urbanization in Germany at the height of the industrialization period', *Journal of Contemporary History*, 4 (1969), are very useful. The question of urbanization and social mobility is debated by Hartmut Kaelble, *Social Mobility in the Nineteenth and Twentieth Centuries* (1985), and Andrew Miles and David Vincent (eds.), *Building European Society: Occupational Change and Social Mobility in Europe, 1840–1940* (1993). Richard Evans, *Death in Hamburg* (1987) is excellent. To Walter F. Willcox, *International Migrations*, vol. ii and *Les Migrations internationales de la fin du XVIIIe siècle à nos jours* may be added Dudley Baines, *Emigration from Europe, 1815–1930* (1991), Charlotte Erickson, *Emigration from Europe, 1815–1914* (1976) and François-Xavier Coquin, *La Sibérie. Peuplement et immigration paysanne au XIXe siècle* (1969).

A basic survey of European industrialization is Alan S. Milward and S. B. Saul, *The Development of the Economies of Continental Europe, 1850–1914* (1977). W. Arthur Lewis, *Growth and Fluctuations, 1870–1913* (1978) traces the ups and downs of economies on both sides of the Atlantic. S. B. Saul's succinct *The Myth of the Great Depression, 1873–1896* (1969) is limited to Great Britain. Wolfgang Mommsen, *Britain and Germany, 1800 to 1914: Two Developmental Paths towards Industrial Society* (1986) is succinct and suggestive. Lively work on national economies includes A. L. Levine, *Industrial Retardation in Britain, 1880–1914* (1967), Martin Wiener, *English Culture and the Decline of the Industrial Spirit* (1981), which is contradicted by W. D. Rubinstein, *Capitalism, Culture and Decline in Britain, 1750–1900* (1993), Maurice Lévy-Leboyer, 'La Décéleration de l'économie française dans la seconde moitié du XIXe siècle', *Revue d'histoire économique et sociale*, 49 (1971), Gustav Stolper, *The German Economy, 1870–1940* (1940), Lennart Jörberg, *Growth and Fluctuations of Swedish Industry, 1869–1912* (1961), Jon S. Cohen, 'Italy 1861–1914' in Rondo Cameron (ed.), *Banking and Economic Development* (1972), R. A. Webster, *Industrial Imperialism in Italy, 1908–1915* (1975), Theodore von Laue, *Sergei Witte and the Industrialization of Russia* (1963), Teodor Shanin, *Russia as a 'Developing Society'* (1985). I. T. Berend and G. Ránki, *Economic Developments in East-Central Europe* (1974) and their *The European Periphery and Industrialization, 1780–1914* (1982) are indispensable; they may be supplemented by David F. Good, *The Economic Rise of the Habsburg Empire, 1750–1914* (1984) and John Komlos (ed.), *Economic Development in the Habsburg Monarchy* (1983). Questions of free trade and protection are examined by Forrest H. Capie, *Tariffs and Growth: Some Illustrations from the World Economy, 1850–1940* (1994), P. J. Cain and A. G. Hopkins, 'The political economy of British expansion overseas, 1750–1914', *Economic History Review*, 33 (1980), Alan Sykes, *Tariff Reform in British Politics, 1903–13* (1979), Aaron L. Friedberg, *The Weary Titan. Britain and the Experience of Relative*

Decline, 1895–1905 (1988), Smith, *Tariff Reform in France*, already cited, and Kenneth D. Barkin, *The Controversy over German Industrialization, 1890–1902* (1970). Alongside David Landes, *The Unbound Prometheus*, Charles Singer (ed.), *A History of Technology*, vol. v, *1850–1900* (1958) and vols. vi and vii, *1900–1950* (1978), should be used for reference. On banking and industrialization Rudolf Hilferding, *Finance Capital* (1910; English edn., 1981) is a key text. J. J. van Helten and Y. Cassis (eds.), *Capitalism in a Mature Economy: Financial Institutions, Capital Exports and British Industry, 1870–1939* (1990) revises some long-held assumptions. Debate on German banking and industrialization between H. Neuburger and H. H. Stokes, and R. Freudling and Richard Tilly may be found in the *Journal of Economic History*, 34 (1974) and 36 (1976). Alexander Gerschenkron has contributed stimulating essays in *Continuity in History* (1968), *Europe in a Russian Mirror* (1970), and *An Economic Spurt that Failed: Four Lectures in Austrian History* (1977). Richard L. Rudolph, *Banking and Industrialization in Austria-Hungary* (1976) is an excellent monograph. Herbert Feis, *Europe, the World's Banker* (1930) is still worth reading. M. Falkus, 'Aspects of foreign investment in Tsarist Russia', *Journal of European Economic History*, 8 (1979) is a good overall survey and René Girault, *Emprunts russes et investissements en Russie 1887–1914* (1973) remains indispensable.

On the entrepreneur there are four useful collection of essays, in which the same writers tend to reappear: H. Daems and H. van der Wee, *The Rise of Managerial Capitalism* (1974); A. D. Chandler and H. Daems, *Managerial hierarchies* (1980); Lévy-Leboyer, *Le Patronat de la seconde industrialisation*, already cited; and N. Horn and J. Kocka, *Recht und Entwicklung der Grossunternehmen in 19. und frühen 20. Jahrhundert* (1979). Also useful are Payne, *British Entrepreneurship*, already cited, D. H. Aldcroft, 'The Entrepreneur and the British economy, 1870–1914', *Economic History Review*, 17 (1964), M. Lévy-Leboyer, 'Le patronat français a-t-il été malthusien', *Mouvement social*, 88 (1974), and John P. Mackay, *Pioneers for Profit: Foreign Entrepreneurship and Russian Industrialization, 1885–1913* (1970). There has been much interesting writing on the formation of the working class, including Peter Stearns, 'Adaptation to industrialization: German workers as a test case', *Central European History*, 3 (1970), David F. Crew, *Town in the Ruhr: A Social History of Bochum, 1860–1914* (1979), Christopher Klebmann, *Polnische Bergarbeiter im Ruhrgebiet, 1870–1945* (1978), S. H. F. Hickey, *Workers in Imperial Germany: The Miners of the Ruhr* (1985), Rolande Trempé, *Les Mineurs de Carmaux, 1848–1914* (1971), Michael P. Hanagan, *The Logic of Solidarity: Artisans and Industrial Workers in Three French Towns, 1871–1914* (1980) and Charles Wynn, *Workers, Strikes and Pogroms: The Donbass-Dnepr Bend in Late Imperial Russia, 1870–1905* (1992). Jürgen Kocka, 'The study of social mobility and the formation of the working class in the nineteenth century', *Mouvement social*, 3 (1980), is a valuable survey of the literature. The organization of labour is examined by Dick Geary, *European Labour Protest, 1848–1939* (1981), ch. 2, Geary (ed.), *Labour and Socialist Movements in Europe before 1914* (1989), H. A. Clegg, Alan Fox, and A. F. Thompson, *A History of British Trade Unions since 1889*, vol. i (1964), F. Ridley, *Revolutionary Syndicalism in France* (1970), Victoria Bonnell, *Roots of Rebellion: Workers' Politics and Organizations in St Petersburg and Moscow, 1900–1914* (1983), and Wolfgang J. Mommsen and H. G. Husing (eds.), *The Development of Trade Unionism in Great Britain and Germany, 1880–1914* (1985). The problems of the lower middle classes have also attracted interest, notably from Christian Baudelot *et al.*, *La Petite bourgeoisie en France* (1974), Philip G. Nord, *Paris Shopkeepers and the Politics of Resentment* (1986), Geoffrey Crossick, *The Lower Middle Class in Britain, 1870–1914* (1977), Geoffrey Crossick and Heinz-Gerhard Haupt (eds.), *Shopkeepers and Master-Artisans in Nineteenth-Century Europe* (1984), Robert Gellately, *The Politics of Economic Despair: Shopkeepers and German Politics, 1890–1914* (1974), Shulamit Volkov, *The Rise of Popular Antimodernism in Germany: The Urban Master Artisans, 1873–1896* (1978), and, in critical vein, David Blackbourn, 'The *Mittelstand* in German society and politics, 1871–1914', *Social History*, 4 (1977). Useful collections with a European perspective include Adolf Sturmthal, *White Collar Trade Unions* (1968) and especially Jürgen Kocka (ed.), *Angestellte im Europäischen Vergleich* (1981).

A first-class work on the landed interest in England is Avner Offer, *Property and Politics, 1870–1914* (1981). Georges Duby and Armand Wallon (eds.), *Histoire de la France rurale*, vol. iii (1976) is a useful introduction to French agriculture. Important aspects are studied by J. Harvey Smith, 'Agricultural workers and the French winegrowers' revolt of 1907', *Past and Present*, 79 (1978) and Laura Frader, *Peasants and Protest: Agricultural Workers, Politics and Unions in the Aude, 1850–1914* (1991). On Spain, Albert Balcells, *El problema agrari a Catalunya, 1890–1936. La questió rabassaire* (1968) examines Catalan land tenure and R. J. Harrison, 'The Spanish Famine of 1904–6', *Agricultural History*, 47 (1973) a late subsistence crisis. Paul Corner's *Fascism in Ferrara 1915–25* (1975) starts with the industrialization of agriculture in the Po valley. John A. Davis (ed.), *Gramsci and Italy's Passive Revolution* (1979) has useful contributions on the peasantry. Co-operatives are examined by Clemens Pederson (ed.), *The Danish Co-operative Movement* (1977) and Gavin Lewis, 'The peasantry, rural change and conservative agrarianism: Lower Austria at the turn of the century', *Past and Present*, 81 (1978). Ian F. D. Morrow explodes the myth of Prussian latifundia in *The Peace Settlement in the German–Polish Borderlands* (1936), but inequality in landed society in eastern Europe is highlighted by Philip Eidelberg, *The Great Rumanian Peasant Revolt of 1907* (1974), Geroid Tanquary Robinson, *Rural Russia under the Old Régime* (1949), Maureen Perrie, 'The Russian Peasant Movement of 1905–7', *Past and Present*, 57 (1972), Ben Eklof and Stephen P. Frank, *The World of the Russian Peasant: Post-Emancipation Culture and Society* (1990) and Esther Kingston-Mann (ed.), *Peasant Economy, Culture and Politics of European Russia, 1800–1921* (1991).

The German élite at the end of the nineteenth century has been intensively studied. Fundamental contributions include Lamar Cecil, *Albert Ballin: Business and Politics in Imperial Germany* (1967) and 'The creation of nobles in Prussia, 1871–1918', *American Historical Review*, 75 (1970), J. C. G. Röhl, 'Higher civil servants in Germany, 1890–1900', *Journal of Contemporary History*, 2 (1967), Daniel J. Hughes, *The King's Finest: A Social and Bureaucratic Profile of Prussia's General Officers, 1871–1914* (1987), Holger Herwig, *The German Naval Officer Corps: A Social and Political History, 1890–1918* (1973), K. Jarausch, 'The social transformation of the university: the case of Prussia, 1865–1914', *Journal of Social History*, 12 (1979), and Hartmut Kaelble, 'Long-term changes in the recruitment of the business élite', *Journal of Social History*, 13 (1980). There has been some very interesting writing on the position of the Jews in Germany by W. E. Mosse, *The German-Jewish Economic Elite, 1820–1935* (1989) and in Hungary by William O. McCagg, *Jewish Nobles and*

Geniuses in Modern Hungary (1972) and Victor Karady and István Kemeney, 'Les Juifs dans la structure des classes en Hongrie', *Actes de la recherche en sciences sociales*, 22 (1978). On Hungary and Russia, István Déak, *Beyond Nationalism: A Social and Political History of the Habsburg Officer Corps, 1848–1918* (1990) and Edith Clowes *et al.* (eds.), *Between Tsar and People: Educated Society and the Quest for Public Identity in Late Imperial Russia* (1991) are excellent contributions. On France, Christophe Charle, *A Social History of Modern France in the Nineteenth Century* (1994) is an excellent synthesis, while Gary Wray McDonogh, *Good Families of Barcelona: A Social History of Power in the Industrial Era* (1986) is an eloquent monograph. Older studies of Great Britain, such as Robert Nightingale, 'The personnel of the British Foreign Service and Diplomatic Service, 1851–1929', *American Political Science Review*, 24 (1930), C. B. Otley, 'The social origins of British army officers', *The Sociological Review*, 18 (1970), and Ralph Pumphrey, 'The introduction of industrialists into the British peerage', *American Historical Review*, 65 (1959), have been complemented by recent work such as W. D. Rubinstein's collection of articles, *Elites and Wealth in Modern British History* (1987), David Cannadine, *The Decline and Fall of the British Aristocracy* (1990), Maureen E. Montgomery, '*Gilded Prostitution': Status, Money and Transatlantic Marriages, 1870–1914* (1989) and Harold Perkin, *The Rise of Professional Society: England since 1880* (1989).

Chapter 11

Good introductions to international socialism are Dick Geary (ed.), *Labour and Socialist Movements in Europe before 1914* (1989), and his *European Labour Protest, 1848–1939* (1981), ch. 3, Julius Braunthal, *History of the International*, vol. i, *1864–1914* (1966) and James Joll, *The Second International, 1889–1914* (1955, 2nd edn., 1975). Leszek Kolakowski, *Main Currents of Marxism*, vol. i (1978) is far and away the best guide to theoretical issues. On Great Britain, Henry Pelling, *The Origins of the Labour Party* (1965) is standard and solid, C. Tsuzuki, *H. M. Hyndman and British Socialism* (1961) a useful monograph, and Paul Thompson, *Socialists, Liberals and Labour: The Struggle for London, 1885–1914* (1965) a first-class local study. Willard Wolfe, *From Radicalism to Socialism: Men and Ideas in the Formation of Fabian Socialist Doctrine, 1881–89* (1975) should be read alongside Edward Pease's 'inside' *History of the Fabian Society* (1916). On German social democracy, Vernon Lidtke, *The Outlawed Party* (1966), is now complemented by his *The Alternative Culture: Socialist Labour in Imperial Germany* (1990). W. L. Guttsman, *The German Social Democratic Party 1875–1933* (1981) is better than Guenther Roth, *The Social Democrats in Imperial Germany* (1963). German working-class mentalities are also investigated by Richard J. Evans, *Proletarians and Politics* (1990), while key texts of the reformist controversy are published by H. and J. M. Tudor, *Marxists and Social Democracy: The Revisionist Debate, 1896–1898* (1988). On individual figures there is William H. Maehl, *August Bebel* (1980), Dick Geary, *Karl Kautsky* (1987), and F. L. Carsten, 'Georg von Vollmar: a Bavarian Social Democrat', *Journal of Contemporary History* 25 (1990). Vincent J. Knapp, *Austrian Social Democracy 1889–1914* (1980) is slightly disappointing on a complex problem; Tibor Süle, *Sozialdemokratie in Ungarn* (1967) scholarly on a non-issue. Good writing on France includes Maitron and Stafford, already cited, Roger Magraw, *A History of the French Working Class II* (1992), chs. 1 and 2, Robert Stuart, *Marxism at Work: Class and French Socialism during the Third Republic*

(1992), on the Guesdists, Harvey Goldberg, *The Life of Jean Jaurès* (1962), Leslie Der-fler, *Alexander Millerand: The Socialist Years* (1977), and Jacques Julliard, *Fernand Pelloutier* (1971). Peter Schöttler, 'Politique syndicale ou lutte des classes: notes sur le syndicalisme "à politique" des Bourses du Travail', *Mouvement social*, 116 (1981) dis-pels ancient myths. On Italy there is Louise Tilly, *Politics and Class in Milan, 1881–1901* (1992), which is broader than its title suggests, Alexander De Grand, *The Italian Left in the Twentieth Century* (1989), chs. 1 and 2, James Edward Miller, *From Elite to Mass Politics: Italian Socialism in the Giolittian Era, 1900–1914* (1990) and Spencer Discala, *Dilemmas of Italian Socialism: The Politics of Filippo Turati* (1980). On Spain, Gerald Brenan and E. J. Hobsbawm, *Primitive Rebels* (1959) has been joined by Temma Kaplan's excellent *Anarchists of Andalusia, 1868–1903* (1977), Paul Heywood, *Marxism and the Failure of Organized Socialism in Spain, 1879–1936* (1990), ch. 1, George Richard Esenwein, *Anarchist Ideology and the Working-Class Movement in Spain, 1868–1898* (1989), and Angel Smith, 'Social conflict and trade-union organization in the Catalan cotton industry, 1890–1914', *International Review of Social History* 36 (1991). There is no shortage of works on Russian socialism. Arthur P. Mendel, *Dilemmas of Progress in Tsarist Russia* (1961) and Samuel H. Baron, *Plekhanov: The Father of Russian Marxism* (1963) examine problems of adapting Marxism to Russian conditions. Derek Offord, *The Russian Revolutionary Movement in the 1880s* (1986) examines a period of transition. Alan K. Wildman, *The Making of a Workers' Revolution* (1967) underlines spontaneous discontent. Richard Pipes, 'The origins of Bolshevism: the intellectual development of young Lenin' in his *Revolution-ary Russia* (1963), J. L. H. Keep's scholarly *The Rise of Social Democracy in Russia* (1968) and the early part of E. H. Carr, *The Bolshevik Revolution, 1917–1923*, vol. i (1950) examine Bolshevism and Menshevism. J. P. Nettl's biography of *Rosa Luxem-burg* (1966) is definitive. On revisionism and the non-socialist opposition, see Richard Pipes, *Struve, Liberal on the Left, 1870–1905* (1970) and Shmuel Galai, *The Liberation Movement in Russia, 1900–5* (1973).

On the Roman Catholic question, Pierre Vercauteren, 'La place de Paul Janson dans la vie politique belge de 1877 à 1884', *Res Publica*, 11 (1969), is a useful guide to Belgian problems. Katherine Auspitz, *The Radical Bourgeoisie: The Ligue de l'Enseignement and the Origins of the Third Republic, 1866–1885* (1982) is slightly insubstantial on French anticlericalism; Benjamin Martin, *Count Albert de Mun: Pal-adin of the Third Republic* (1978) better on the Catholic Right. Alexander Sedgwick, *The Ralliement in French Politics, 1890–98* (1965) is very useful; Jean Bruhat, 'Anti-cléricalisme et mouvement ouvrier en France avant 1914', *Mouvement social*, 57 (1966), very penetrating. On Italy, there is a lack of material in English apart from Jemolo and R. A. Webster, cited and the first chapter of John N. Molony, *The Emergence of Political Catholicism in Italy* (1977); Francesco Traniello, 'Nuove prospettive sul clerico-moderatismo' in Annali dell' istituto storico italo-germanico, *Il Cattolicesmo politico e sociale in Italia e Germania dal 1870 al 1914* (1977) looks at an episode in Italy's failed *Ralliement*. Frances Lannon, *Privilege, Persecution and Prophecy. The Catholic Church in Spain 1875–1975* (1987) is authoritative on Spain. On German Catholicism, Margaret Anderson's *Windthorst* and Zeender, *The Ger-man Centre Party*, already cited, should be supplemented by David Blackbourn's searching study of Württemberg, *Class, Religion and Local Politics in Wilhelmine Germany* (1980).

For Ireland, Emmet Larkin, *The Roman Catholic Church and the Creation of the Modern Irish State, 1878–1886* (1975) discusses the conversion of the hierarchy to Home Rule. Other useful contributions include Nicholas Mansergh, *The Irish Question, 1840–1921* (1965), which is strong on the British and imperial context, D. George Boyce, *Nationalism in Ireland* (1982), and Paul Bew, *Conflict and Conciliation in Ireland, 1890–1910. Parnellites and Radical Agrarians* (1987). On Wales, Kenneth O. Morgan, *Wales in British Politics, 1868–1922* (1980) will not easily be surpassed while H. J. Hanham, *Scottish Nationalism* (1969) still imposes itself. S. G. Payne, 'Catalan and Basque nationalism', *Journal of Contemporary History*, 6 (1971), may be supplemented by Marianne Heiberg, *The Making of the Basque Nation* (1989). Dan P. Silverman, *Reluctant Union: Alsace-Lorraine and Imperial Germany, 1871–1918* (1972) traces the decline of Alsatian reluctance under German rule while Maryon McDonald, *We are not French! Language, Culture and Identity in Brittany* (1989) looks at the rise of Breton national feeling. Raymond Pearson, *National Minorities in Eastern Europe, 1848–1945* (1983) is a helpful survey. William W. Hagen, *Germans, Poles and Jews: The Nationality Conflict in the Polish East, 1772–1914* (1980) illuminates thorny questions, while Alvin W. Fountain, *Roman Dmowski: Party, Tactics, Ideology, 1895–1907* (1980) is a welcome study of a major figure in Polish nationalism. Edward Thaden, *Russification in the Baltic Provinces and Finland, 1855–1914* (1981) and Andrejs Plakans, 'Peasants, intellectuals and nationalism in the Russian Baltic provinces, 1820–90', *Journal of Modern History* 46 (1974) are first-rate. The early part of John J. Reshetar, *The Ukrainian Revolution, 1917–20* (1952) looks at the emergence of the Ukrainian nationalism. Thoughtful works on Jewish assimilation are Michael Marrus, *The Politics of Assimilation* (1971), dealing with France, Gary B. Cohen, 'Jews in German Society: Prague, 1860–1914', *Central European History*, 10 (1977), Dennis B. Klein, 'Assimilation and the Demise of Liberal Political Tradition in Vienna, 1860–1914' in David Bronson (ed.), *Jews and Germans from 1860 to 1933* (1979), Steven Aschheim, *Brothers and Strangers: The east European Jew in German and German Jewish Consciousness, 1800–1923* (1982), on the *Ostjuden*, Marsha Rozenblit, 'The Jews of the dual monarchy', *Austrian History Yearbook* xxxiii (1992), Robert S. Wistrich, *The Jews of Vienna in the Age of Franz Josef* (1989), and Sanford Ragins, *Jewish Responses to Anti-Semitism in Germany, 1870–1914* (1980). The dilemma of Jews in the Russian Empire is examined by Jonathan Frankel, *Prophecy and Politics: Socialism, Nationalism and the Russian Jews, 1862–1917* (1981). The Zionist option is described by David Vital in *The Origins of Zionism* (1975); the socialist option by Henry Tobias, *The Jewish Bund in Russia from its Origins to 1905* (1972), Nora Levin, *Jewish Socialist Movements, 1871–1917* (1977), which is particularly good on the Jewish proletariat, Robert J. Brym, *The Jewish Intelligentsia and Russian Marxism* (1978), and Yoav Peled, *Class and Ethnicity in the Pale: The Political Economy of Jewish Workers' Nationalism in Late Imperial Russia* (1989). Recent work on the nationalities problem in the Austro-Hungarian Empire includes A. G. Whiteside, *The Socialism of Fools: Georg von Schönerer and Austrian Pan-Germanism* (1975), Bruce M. Garver, *The Young Czech Party 1874–1901* (1978), Gary B. Cohen, *The Politics of Ethnic Survival: Germans in Prague, 1861–1914* (1981), H. Gordon Skilling, *T. G. Masaryk: Against the Current, 1882–1914* (1994), Dennis I. Rusinow, *Italy's Austrian Heritage, 1919–46* (1969), the early part of which examines Italian irredentism, and Carol Roger, *The Slovenes and Yugoslavism,*

1890–1914 (1977). However, R. W. Seton-Watson's *Racial Problems in Hungary* (1908) and *The South Slav Question and the Habsburg Monarchy* (1911) are irreplaceable accounts of a contemporary observer and historian.

Overviews on the women question and feminism include Bonnie G. Smith, *Changing Lives: Women in European History since 1700* (1989), Richard J. Evans, *The Feminists: Women's Emancipation Movements in Europe, America and Australasia, 1840–1920* (1977), his *Comrades and Sisters: Feminism, Socialism and Pacifism in Europe, 1870–1945* (1987), and Georges Duby and Michelle Perrot (eds.), *A History of Women in the West IV. Emerging Feminism from the Revolution to the First World War* (1993). Works on Great Britain include Patricia Hollis, *Ladies Elect: Women in English Local Government, 1865–1914* (1987), Leah Leneman, *A Guid Cause: The Women's Suffrage Movement in Scotland* (1991) and Emmeline Pankhurst, *My Own Story* (1914). On France the pioneering French work is Lawrence Klejman and Florence Rochefort, *L'Egalité en marche: Le Feminisme sous la Troisième République* (1989) but there is much in English, such as Patricia Kay Bidelman, *Pariahs Stand Up! The Founding of the Liberal Feminist Movement in France, 1858–1889* (1982), Charles Sowerwine, *Sisters or Citizens? Women and Socialism in France since 1876* (1982), Patricia Hilden, *Working Women and Socialist Politics in France, 1880–1914. A Regional Study* (1986), Stephen Hause and Anne R. Kenney, *Women's Suffrage and Social Politics in the French Third Republic* (1984), Stephen Hause, *Hubertine Auclert: The French Suffagette* (1987), Felicia Gordon, *The Integral Feminist: Madeleine Pelletier, 1874–1939* (1990) and Karen Offen, 'Depopulation, nationalism and feminism in fin de siècle France', *American Historical Review* 89 (1984). On Germany Ute Frevert, *Women in German History: From Bourgeois Emancipation to Sexual Liberation* (1989) is excellent; there is also R. J. Evans, *The Feminist Movement in Germany, 1894–1933* (1976), Amy Hackett, 'Feminism and liberalism in Wilhelmine Germany' in Berenice Carroll (ed.), *Liberating Women's History* (1976), Ann Taylor Allen, *Feminism and Motherhood in Germany, 1800–1914* (1991), Jean H. Quataert, *Reluctant Feminists in German Social Democracy, 1885–1917* (1979) and Roger Chickering, 'Casting their gaze more broadly: women's patriotic activism in Imperial Germany', *Past and Present* 118 (1988). Important works on Russia include Richard Stites, *The Women's Liberation Movement in Russia: Feminism, Nihilism and Bolshevism, 1860–1930* (1978), Linda Edmondson, *Feminism in Russia, 1900–1917* (1984), Rose L. Glickman, *Russian Factory Women: Workplace and Society, 1880–1914* (1984) and William Wagner, 'The Trojan mare: women's rights and civil rights in late Imperial Russia', in Olga Crisp (ed.), *Civil Rights in Imperial Russia* (1989). On masculine identity, uncharted waters are opened up by J. A. Mangan and James Walvin (eds.), *Manliness and Morality: Middle-Class Masculinity in Britain and America, 1800–1940* (1987) and Robert A. Nye, *Masculinity and Male Codes of Honour in Modern France* (1993).

Chapter 12

On colonialism and imperialism in general, see D. K. Fieldhouse, *Colonialism, 1870–1945: An Introduction* (1981), Wolfgang Mommsen, *Theories of Imperialism* (1981), and Andrew Porter, *European Imperialism, 1860–1914* (1994). Daniel R. Headrick, *The Tools of Empire: Technology and European Imperialism in the Nineteenth Century* (1981) examines the technological underpinning of Western imperialism. J. M. Mackenzie, *The Partition of Africa* (1983) deals succinctly with a central issue. On the British Empire, Bernard Porter, *The Lion's Share: A Short History of British Imperialism, 1850–1983* (2nd edn., 1983), P. J. Cain and A. J. Hopkins, *British Imperialism: Innovation and Expansion, 1688–1914* (1993), and Ronald Hyam, *Britain's Imperial Century, 1815–1914: A Study of Empire and Expansion* (2nd edn., 1993) are excellent introductions. Judith M. Brown, *Modern India. The Origins of an Asian Democracy* (1985) is first-class on British–Indian relations. Robert Robinson and John Gallagher, *Africa and the Victorians* (1961; 2nd edn., 1981) is now a classic. C. J. Lowe, *The Reluctant Imperialists: British Foreign Policy, 1878–1902* (1967) sets a high standard. Other valuable works include Andrew Porter, *The Origins of the South African War: Joseph Chamberlain and the Diplomacy of Imperialism, 1895–99* (1980) and Ian Nish, *The Anglo-Japanese Alliance, 1894–1907* (1966). On the popular enthusiasm for Empire, John M. Mackenzie, *Propaganda and Empire: The Manipulation of British Public Opinion, 1880–1960* (1984) and Frans Coetzee, *For Party or Country: Nationalism and the Dilemmas of Popular Conservatism in Edwardian England* (1990) are indispensable. Different approaches to Anglo-French rivalry are Felix Ponteil, *La Méditerranée et les puissances depuis l'ouverture jusqu'à la nationalisation du Canal de Suez* (1964), Prosser Gifford and W. M. Roger Louis, *France and Britain in Africa* (1971), and Winfried Baumgart, *Imperialism: The Idea and Reality of British and French Colonial Expansion, 1880–1914* (1982). A very readable introduction is Henri Brunschwig, *French Colonialism, 1871–1914: Myths and Realities* (1966). Two exceptional articles are C. M. Andrew and A. J. Kanya-Forster, 'The French "colonial party": its composition, aims and influence, 1885–1914', *Historical Journal*, 14 (1971) and Jean Bouvier, 'Les Traits majeurs de l'impérialisme français avant 1914' in J. Bouvier and R. Girault (eds.), *L'impérialisme français d'avant 1914* (1976). George F. Kennan, *The Fateful Alliance: France, Russia and the Coming of the First World War* (1984) deals with the diplomacy of the Franco-Russian alliance while William H. Schneider, *An Empire for the Masses: The French Popular Image of Africa, 1880–1900* (1984) investigates the culture of jingoism. Roger Glenn Brown, *Fashoda reconsidered: The Impact of Domestic Politics on French Policy in Africa, 1893–98* (1970) has not been supplanted by Darrell Bates, *The Fashoda Incident of 1898: Encounter on the Nile* (1984). On Dutch and Belgian imperialism there is Maarten Kuitenbrouwer, *The Netherlands and the Rise of Modern Imperialism: Colonialism and Foreign Policy, 1870–1902* (1991) and Jean Stengers, 'Leopold II and the Association Internationale du Congo' in an excellent collection edited by Stig Förster, *Bismarck, Europe and Africa. The Berlin African Conference, 1884–1885 and the Onset of Partition* (1988). On Portuguese and Spanish imperialism see Gervase Clarence-Smith, *The Third Portuguese Empire, 1825–1975: A Study in Economic Imperialism* (1985) and James W. Cortada, *Spain in the Nineteenth-Century World: Essays in Spanish Diplomacy, 1789–1898* (1994). The basic introduction to Italian foreign policy is that of C. J. Lowe and F. Marzari, *Italian Foreign Policy, 1870–1940* (1975), which is clearer than R. J. B. Bosworth, *Italy, the Least of the Great Powers* (1979). John A. Thayer, *Italy and the Great War: Politics and Culture, 1870–1915* (1964) is colourful and suggestive on all aspects of the Post-Risorgimento. Immanuel Geiss, *German Foreign Policy, 1871–1914* (1976) is an excellent introduction; Paul Kennedy, *The Rise of Anglo-German Antagonism, 1860–1914* (1982) is bulky but masterly. The debate started by A. J. P. Taylor, *Germany's First Bid for Colonies 1884–85* (1938) has now been updated by Hartmut Pogge von Strandman, 'Domestic origins of Germany's colonial expansion under Bismarck', *Past and Present*, 42 (1969), Hans-Ulrich Wehler, 'Bismarck's imperialism, 1862–1890', *Past and Present*, 48 (1970), and Stig Förster *et al.*, cited above. George Kennan, *The Decline of Bismarck's European Order: Franco-Russian Relations 1875–90* (1979) traces the estrangement of Germany and Russia, notably over the Balkans. On German navalism the most accessible work is Jonathan Steinberg, *Tirpitz and the birth of the German Battle Fleet* (1968). Dietrich Geyer, *Russian Imperialism 1860–1914* (1987) analyses the burdens of backwardness.

Chapter 13

The problem of mass education is tackled for Great Britain by J. S. Hurt, *Elementary Schooling and the Working classes, 1860–1918* (1979). J. E. B. Munson, 'The Unionist coalition and education, 1895–1902', *Historical Journal*, 20 (1977), and John Lawson and Harold Silver, *A Social History of Education in England* (1973) are also useful. On France Prost and Françoise Mayeur, cited above, may be supplemented by Robert Gildea, *Education in Provincial France: A Study of Three Departments* (1983) and Barnett Singer, *Village Notables in Nineteenth-Century France: Priests, Mayors, Schoolmasters* (1983). A valuable essay on popular education in Germany is Eugene Anderson, 'The Prussian Volksschule in the nineteenth century' in G. Ritter (ed.), *Entstehung und Wandel der modernen Gesellschaft* (1970). While on Russia Ben Eklof, *Russian Peasant Schools* (1986), cited above, is fundamental. For secondary and higher education Fritz Ringer, cited above, and Detlef Müller, Fritz Ringer and Brian Simon, *The Rise of the Modern Education System, 1870–1920* (1987) cover Germany, France and Great Britain. Germany is covered also by James C. Albisetti, *Secondary School Reform in Imperial Germany* (1983). On Spain there is Yvonne Turin and P. Sola in Willem Frijoff (ed.), *The Supply of Schooling*, all cited above. Jósef Miaso, 'Education and social structures in the Kingdom of Poland in the second half of the nineteenth century', *History of Education*, 10 (1981) looks at clandestine schools. Arcadius Kahan, 'The development of education and the economy in Czarist Russia' in C. A. Anderson and M. J. Bowman (eds.), *Education and Economic Development* (1963) contains some useful statistics. James C. McClelland, *Autocrats and Academics: Education, Culture and Society in Tsarist Russia* (1978) is excellent on the higher reaches of education.

W. J. Mommsen (ed.), *The Emergence of the Welfare State in Britain and Germany, 1850–1950* (1981) and Gerhard Ritter, *Social Welfare in Germany and Britain* (1983) are admirable comparative studies. Joachim Umlauf, *Die Deutsche Arbeiterschutzgesetzgebung, 1880–1890* (1980) analyses the various pressures on the drafting of Bismarck's laws. Catholic welfare provisions are studied in Ronald J. Ross, *The Beleaguered Tower: The Dilemma of Political Catholicism in Wilhelmine Germany* (1976) and Mary Nolan, *Social Democracy and Society: Working-Class Radicalism in Düsseldorf, 1890–1920* (1981). William A. Jenks, *Austria under the Iron Ring, 1879–1893* (1965) has good material on social welfare, but an important recent work is Kurt Ebert, *Die Anfänge der modernen Sozialpolitik in Österreich* (1975). Italy remains a problem, but the collection *Il Cattolicesmo politico e sociale in Italia e Germania*, cited above, may be consulted. On Spain, Frances Lannon, already cited, comes to our aid. For France there is an excellent survey by Judith F. Stone, *The Search for Social Peace: Reform Legislation in France, 1890–1914* (1985); Jean-Marie

Mayeur, *Un Prêtre démocrate: L'abbé Lemire, 1853–1928* (1968) and Emile Poulat, 'Pour une nouvelle compréhension de la démocratie chrétienne', *Revue d'histoire ecclésiastique*, 70 (1975) cover Christian democracy there. On Great Britain, reliable contributions include J. R. Hay, *The Origins of Liberal Welfare Reforms, 1906–14* (1975), H. V. Evy, *Liberals, Radicals and Social Politics, 1892–1914* (1973), John Mason, 'Political economy and the response to socialism in Britain, 1870–1914', *Historical Journal*, 23 (1980), and E. P. Hennock, *British Social Reform and German Precedents: The Case of Social Insurance, 1880–1914* (1987).

The question of anti-Semitism has received a great deal of attention. The pogroms in Russia are studied by I. Michael Aronson, *Troubled Waters: The Origin of the 1881 Anti-Jewish Pogroms in Russia* (1990), John D. Klier and Shlomo Lambroza, *Pogroms: Anti-Jewish Violence in Modern Russian History* (1992), and Hans Rogger, *Jewish Policies and Right-Wing Politics in Imperial Russia* (1986). McCagg, *Jewish Nobles and Geniuses in Modern Hungary*, cited above, demonstrates the exception to the rule. An excellent guide to central Europe is Peter Pulzer, *The Rise of Political Anti-Semitism in Germany and Austria* (new edn. 1988). R. S. Levy, *The Downfall of Anti-Semitic Political Parties in Imperial Germany* (1975), James Retallack, *Notables of the Right: The Conservative Party and Political Mobilization in Germany, 1876–1918* (1988) and David Blackbourn, 'The politics of demagogy in Imperial Germany', *Past and Present* 113 (1986) examine anti-Semitism as device of right-wing parties. John W. Boyer, *Political Radicalism in Late Imperial Vienna: Origins of the Christian Social Movement, 1848–1897* (1981) and Richard S. Geehr, *Carl Lueger, Mayor of Fin de Siècle Vienna* (1990) deal with anti-Semitism in the Habsburg capital. Stephen Wilson, *Ideology and Experience: Anti-Semitism in France at the Time of the Dreyfus Affair* (1982) is equally long, but more stimulating. Peter Gay, *Freud, Jews and other Germans* (1978) and Norman Cohn, *Warrant for Genocide: The Myth of the Jewish World Conspiracy* (1967) go some way to explaining the virulence of anti-Semitism.

Authoritarianism in French political life after 1880 starts with Boulangism, on which Frederick H. Seager, *The Boulanger Affair* (1969) is very clear. Two useful older books by Raoul Girardet are *La Société militaire dans la France contemporaine, 1815–1939* (1953), and a collection of texts, *Le Nationalisme français 1871–1914* (1966). Two important ones, by Zeev Sternhell, are *Maurice Barrès et le nationalisme français* (1972) and *La Droite révolutionnaire, 1885–1914* (1978). The latter is a mine of valuable information, but distorted by its underlying thesis of a 'French fascism' which can be traced back to the nineteenth century. Robert Tombs (ed.), *Nationhood and Nationalism in France from Boulangism to the Great War* (1991) is an excellent collection. Douglas Johnson, *France and the Dreyfus Affair* (1966) leans more to narrative, Roderick Kedward, *The Dreyfus Affair* (1969), more to analysis; both are good. On Italy, Christopher Seton-Watson, *Italy from Liberalism to Fascism* (1967) and Candeloro, vols. vi (1970) and vii (1974) may be supplemented by Frank Coppa (ed.), *Studies in Modern Italian History from the Risorgimento to the Republic* (1986), Denis Mack Smith, *Italy and its Monarchy* (1989), A. W. Salomone, *Italy in the Giolittian Era: Italian Democracy in the Making, 1900–1914* (1960), and by John Whittam's rather thin *Politics of the Italian Army, 1861–1918* (1977). For Spain, works by Earl R. Beck and Robert W. Kern have already been cited. The impact of the defeat of 1898 is analysed by Frederick B. Pike, *Hispanismo, 1898–1936: Spanish Conservatives and Liberals and their Relations with Spanish America* (1971) and by Martin Blinkhorn and José Varela Ortega in *Journal of Contemporary History* 15 (1980). Raymond Carr, 'Spain: rule by generals' in Michael Howard (ed.), *Soldiers and Governments* (1957) and Stanley G. Payne, *Politics and the Military in Modern Spain* (1967) are thorough and full of ideas. Similar questions in Greece are treated by Gerasimus Augustinos, *Consciousness and History: Nationalist Critics of Greek Society, 1897–1914* (1977) and S. Victor Papacosma, *The Military in Greek Politics: The 1909 Coup d'état* (1977). The Unionist domination of British politics is analysed at the social level by James Cornford's essays, 'The transformation of Conservatism in the late nineteenth century', *Victorian Studies*, 7 (1963) and 'The parliamentary foundations of the Hotel Cecil' in Robert Robson (ed.), *Ideas and Institutions of Victorian Britain* (1967). W. S. Hamer, *The British Army: Civil-Military Relations 1885–1905* (1970) shows that civilians kept control. More recent studies include Richard Shannon, *The Age of Salisbury* (1995) and E. H. H. Green, *The Crisis of Conservatism: The Politics, Economics and Ideology of the Conservative Party, 1880–1914* (1995). J. L. Garvin's *Life of Joseph Chamberlain*, vol. iii, *1895–1900* (1934), covering his period at the Colonial Office, was completed by Julian Amery: vol. iv, *1901–3* (1951) and vol. v, *Joseph Chamberlain and the Tariff Reform Campaign* (1969). Popular conservatism and nationalism is considered by Robert McKenzie and Allan Silver, *Angels in Marble: Working Class Conservatism in Urban England* (1968) and Paul Kennedy and A. Nicholls (eds.), *Nationalist and racialist Movements in Britain and Germany before 1914* (1981). Responses to the challenge of imperialism are analysed by G. R. Searle, *The Quest for National Efficiency* (1971) and H. C. G. Matthew, *The Liberal Imperialists* (1973). A good introduction to the politics of Imperial Germany is J. C. G. Röhl, *Germany without Bismarck* (1965). Gordon Craig, *The Politics of the Prussian Army* (1955) and Martin Kitchen, *The German Officer Corps, 1890–1914* (1968) should be consulted on military affairs. Röhl and N. Sombart, *Kaiser Wilhelm II: New Interpretations* (1982), Lamar Cecil, *Wilhelm II: Prince and Emperor, 1859–1900* (1989) and Thomas Kohut, *Wilhelm II and the Germans: A Study in Leadership* (1991) focus on the mercurial Emperor, but the trail-blazing work on the interrelation of domestic and foreign politics is Fritz Fischer, *The War of Illusions: German Policies from 1911 to 1914* (1975, trans. from German edn., 1969) which has its roots in the nineteenth century. Geoff Eley has continued the scholarship with 'Defining social imperialism: use and abuse of an idea', *Social History* 3 (1976), his major *Reshaping the German Right, Radical Nationalism and Political Change after Bismarck* (1980) and his collection of essays, *From Unification to Nazism* (1986). On Austria, Macartney, Sked, Jászi, and R. W. Seton-Watson remain essential reading. On Russia Hans Rogger, *Russia in the Age of Modernization and Revolution, 1881–1917* (1983) is a standard text, Francis William Wcislo, *Reforming Rural Russia: State, Local Society and National Politics, 1855–1914* (1990) belies the sense of total rigidity, while Peter Zaionchkovsky, *The Russian Autocracy under Alexander III* (1976) is a brilliant and searching analysis.

Chapter 14

On the popular press and literature, Altick, Lee, Bellanger, Engelsing, and Schenda, cited above, may be supplemented by Kurt Kozyck, *Deutsche Presse im 19. Jahrhundert, teil II* (1966), Ronald Fullerton, 'Towards a popular culture in Germany: the development of pamphlet fiction 1871–1914', *Journal of Social History*, 12 (1979) and

G. S. Turner, *Boys will be Boys* (1948, rev. edn., 1957). Raymond Mander and Joe Mitchenson, *British Music Hall* (1965), Cecil W. Davies, *Theatre for the people: The Story of the Volksbühne* (1977), and David Fisher, 'The origins of the French popular theatre', *Journal of Contemporary History* 12 (1977) cover one form of popular entertainment. On another, Georges Sadoul, *Histoire générale du cinema*, vol. i, *1832–97*, vol. ii, *1897–1909* (1948) and vol. iii, *1909–20* (1951) is the most comprehensive. The early cinema in Germany is studied by Lynn Abrams and David A. Welch in *German History* 8 (1990). Sport in France and Britain is examined by Eugen Weber, 'Gymnastics and sport in fin de siècle France', *American Historical Review*, 76 (1971), and Holt, *Sport and Society* and *Sport and the British*, cited above. Tony Mason, *Association Football and English Society 1863–1915* (1980) is echoed for Germany by Siegfried Gehrmann's 'Football in an industrial region: the example of Schalke 04 Football Club', *International Review of the History of Sport* 6 (1989) and Christiane Eisenberg's 'Football in Germany: beginnings, 1890–1914' in the same review, 8 (1991), while the difficulties of workers' sport is analysed by Horst Verberhorst, *Frisch, frei, stark und treu. Die Arbeitersportbewegung in Deutschland, 1893–1933* (1973). Robert Wohl, *A Passion for Wings: Aviation and the Western Imagination* (1994) looks at flying as hero-worship and in art.

Hugh McLeod, *European Religion in the Age of the Great Cities, 1830–1930* (1995) is a valuable introduction to questions of religious life in this period. Robert L. Nichols and T. G. Stavrou (eds.), *Russian Orthodoxy under the Old Regime* (1978) and John Shelton Curtiss, *Church and State in Russia: The Last Years of the Empire* (1940) concentrate on organization; Leonid Sabaneeft, 'Religious and mystical trends in Russia at the turn of the century', *Russian Review*, 24 (1965), and Donald A. Lowrie, *Rebellious Prophet: A Life of Nicholas Berdyaev* (1960), deal with intellectuals. Jerzy Peterkiewicz, *The Third Adam* (1975), on the other hand, offers a fascinating picture of the dissident Mariavite sect in Catholic Poland. Gavin Lewis, *Kirche und Partei in Politischen Katholizmus* (1977) looks at the links between priests, peasants, and social Catholicism in Lower Austria while Germany is surveyed by W. R. Ward, *Theology, Sociology and Politics: The German Protestant Social Conscience, 1890–1933* (1979). Two biographies of prominent Christian democrats are Sergio Zoppi, *Romolo Murri e la prima democrazia cristiana* (1968) and Madeleine Barthélémy-Madaule, *Marc Sangnier, 1873–1950* (1973). Maurice Larkin, *Church and State after the Dreyfus Affair: The Separation Issue in France* (1974) is patient and scholarly; Richard Griffith, *The Reactionary Revolution: The Catholic Revival in French Literature, 1870–1914* (1966) studies the élite; Y.-M. Hilaire, 'Les ouvriers de la région du Nord devant l'Eglise Catholique, XIXe–XXe siècles', *Mouvement social*, 59 (1966) is of the best order of religious sociology. Gibson, cited above, and Gérard Cholvy and Y.-M. Hilaire, *Histoire religieuse de la France contemporaine II 1880–1930* (1986) offer more general accounts. On Great Britain, contemporary writing such as Ralph Mudie-Smith, *The Religious Life of London* (1904) is illuminating. Good recent studies include Hugh McLeod, *Class and Religion in the Late Victorian City* (1974) and D. W. Bebbington, *The Nonconformist Conscience* (1982).

Far and away the best introduction to social theory is H. Stuart Hughes, *Consciousness and Society: The Reorientation of European Social Thought, 1890–1930* (1979). More specific studies include Robert A. Nye, 'Heredity or milieu. The foundations of modern European criminological theory', *Isis*, 67 (1976), and *The Origins of Crowd Psychology: Gustav Le Bon and the Crisis of Mass Democracy in the Third Republic* (1976), Daniel Pick, *Faces of Degeneration: A European Disorder c.1848– c.1918* (1989), Steven Lukes, *Emile Durkheim: His Life and Work* (1973), J. P. Stern, *Nietzsche* (1978) and his lecture, *The Mind of Nietzsche* (1980), and Philip Rieff, *Freud, the Mind of the Moralist* (1959). Two interesting studies of the cultural life of European cities are Gerhard Masur, *Imperial Berlin* (1971) and Carl E. Schorske, *Fin de Siècle Vienna: Politics and Culture* (1979). Harold B. Segal, *Turn-of-the-Century Cabaret: Paris, Barcelona, Cracow, Moscow, St Petersburg, Zürich* (1987) studies the international avant-garde. Mikulás Teich and Roy Porter, *Fin de Siècle and its Legacy* (1990) is a wide-ranging collection of essays. The themes of Symbolism and Decadence are examined by Jean Pierrot, *The Decadent Imagination, 1860–1900* (1981), the editor's essay in Robert B. Pynsent, *Decadence and Innovation: Austro-Hungarian Life and Art at the Turn of the Century* (1989), Henri Peyre, *Qu'est-ce que le Symbolisme?* (1974) and the lavishly illustrated Pierre-Louis Mathieu, *The Symbolist Generation, 1870–1910* (1990). Specific studies include Ralph E. Shikes and Paula Harper, *Pissarro, His Life and Work* (1980), Mark Roskill, *Van Gogh, Gauguin and the Impressionist Circle* (1971), Maria Makela, *The Munich Secession: Art and Artists in Turn-of-the-Century Munich* (1990), and Camilla Gray, *The Russian Experiment in Art, 1863–1922* (new edn. 1986). Bernard S. Myers, *Expressionism: A Generation in Revolt* (1957) and John Golding, *Cubism: A History and an Analysis, 1907–14* (1968) are useful accounts of the schools. Literary themes are tackled by G. Michaud, *Mallarmé* (1971), Michael and Erika Metzger, *Stefan George* (1972), Steven P. Sondrup, *Hoffmannstahl and the French Symbolism Tradition* (1976), Michael Hamburger, *Hoffmannstahl: Three Essays* (1972), Maurice Valency, *The Flower and the Castle* (1963), or Raymond Williams, *Drama from Ibsen to Brecht* (1968), on Ibsen and Strindberg, Oliver M. Sayler, *Max Reinhardt and His Theatre* (1924), Bettina Knapp, *Maurice Maeterlinck* (1975), J. M. Cocking, *Proust* (1956), R. Shattuck, *Proust* (1974), George D. Painter, *Marcel Proust: A Biography* (2 vols., 1966–7), and Renato Poggioli, *The Poets of Russia, 1890–1930* (1960). To Eric Salzman, *Twentieth Century Music, An Introduction* (2nd edn., 1974) may be added Edward Lockspeiser, *Debussy* (5th edn., 1980), Igor Stravinsky, *Chronicle of My Life* (1936), Richard Buckle, *Diaghilev* (1979), and Willi Reich, *Schoenberg: A Critical Biography* (1971).

Chapter 15

On the Russian revolution, the standard study is now Abraham Ascher, *The Russian Revolution of 1905 I* (1988), *II* (1992). Richard Pipes, *The Russian Revolution, 1899–1919* (1990) goes back to this period. Wildman, Keep, Tobias, and Carr, already cited, should be supplemented for the SRs by Maureen Perrie, *The Agrarian Policy of the Russian Socialist Revolutionary Party from its Origins through the Revolution of 1905–1907* (1976) and Christopher Rice, *Russian Workers and the Socialist-Revolutionary Party through the Revolutions of 1905–1907* (1988). Important work from the perspective of the Tsarist state includes Geoffrey A. Hosking, *The Russian Constitutional Experiment* (1973), Marc Ferro, *Nicholas II* (1991), Dominic Lieven, *Russia's Rulers under the Old Regime* (1989), Sidney Harcave (trans. and ed.), *The Memoirs of Count Witte* (1990); Marc Szeftel, *The Russian Constitution of April 23, 1906* (1976), Terence Emmons, *The Formation of Political Parties and the First National Elections in Russia* (1983), Roberta T. Manning, *The Crisis of the Old Order in Russia: Gentry and Government, 1905–17* (1982), Robert Edelman, *Gentry Politics on the Eve of the Russian Revolution: The Nationalist Party, 1907–1917* (1980), and Alfred Levin, *The Third Duma: Election and Profile* (1973). On strikes and socialism in the west there is Carl E. Schorske's valuable *German Social Democracy, 1905–17* (1955), Nettl, *Rosa Luxemburg*, already cited, Richard J. Evans, 'Red Wednesday in Hamburg: social democrats, police and lumpenproletariat in the suffrage disturbances of 17 January 1906', *Social History* 4 (1979), Henry Pelling, *Popular Politics and Society in Late Victorian Britain* (1968), Ralph Miliband, *Parliamentary Socialism: A Study in the Politics of Labour* (2nd edn., 1973), F. Ridley, *Revolutionary Syndicalism in France* (1970), Jean-Jacques Fiechter, *Le Socialisme français de l'affaire Dreyfus à la grande guerre* (1965) and Jacques Julliard, *Clemenceau, briseur de grèves* (1965). For Italy, Christopher Seton-Watson and Maurice Neufeld, already cited, may be supplemented by the early pages of John M. Cammett, *Antonio Gramsci and the Origins of Italian Communism* (1967). J. Romero Maura, *La Rosa de Fuego* (1974) is the Spanish edition of his excellent Oxford thesis, 'Urban working-class politics in Catalonia 1899–1909' (1971). Joan C. Ullman, *The Tragic Week* (1968) is probably more accessible.

The First World War and its origins has given rise to literature of vast proportions. Any selection can only scratch the surface. Good general approaches include James Joll, *The Origins of the First World War* (2nd edn., 1992), Keith Wilson (ed.), *Decisions for War, 1914* (1995), R. J. W. Evans and H. Pogge von Strandmann (eds.), *The Coming of the First World War* (1988), L. C. F. Turner, *The Origins of the First World War* (1970), Lawrence Lafore's vigorous *The Long Fuse* (1971), and H. W. Koch (ed.), *Origins of the First World War* (1972). The causal responsibility of German ambitions has been argued by Fritz Fischer in *Germany's War Aims* (trans. 1967 from German edn., 1961) and *The War of Illusions* (1975), already cited. Debate has raged in the learned journals, such as the *Journal of Contemporary History* (1966), *Past and Present* (1966, 1967) and the *Journal of Modern History* (1971, 1972). Storm-tossed students may find refuge in V. R. Berghahn's excellent *Germany and the Approach of War in 1914* (1973). Since then, interpretations have become multipolar and responsibility shared between the contending powers. This is suggested by Paul Kennedy (ed.), *The War Plans of the Great Powers, 1880–1914* (1979). In this light Gregor Schöllgen (ed.), *Escape into War? The Foreign Policy of Imperial Germany* (1990) is fairer on Germany. Austria has been restored as a fully playing partner by Samuel Williamson, *Austria-Hungary and the Origins of the First World War* (1991). The internal difficulties of the Austro-Hungarian Empire should be studied in Paul Vsyšný, *Neo-Slavism and the Czechs, 1898–1914* (1977), Joachim Remak, 'The healthy invalid? How doomed was the Habsburg Empire?', *Journal of Modern History* 41 (1969), Alan Sked, 'Historians, the nationality question and the downfall of the Habsburg Empire', *Transactions of the Royal Historical Society* 31 (1981) and Mark Cornwall (ed.), *The Last Years of Austria-Hungary* (1990). Bridge, *From Sadowa to Sarajevo* and his *The Habsburg Monarchy among the Great Powers* (1990) are the best guides to its foreign policy. Anderson, *The Eastern Question*, is a starting point for the Ottoman Empire, together with Feroz Ahmad, *The Young Turks* (1969), Marian Kent (ed.), *The Great Powers and the End of the Ottoman Empire* (1984), Petrovich, *A History of Modern Serbia*, and Stavro Skendi, *The Albanian National Awakening, 1878–1912* (1967). In British foreign policy, rivalry with Germany

458   *Bibliography*

analysed by Paul Kennedy, *The Rise of Anglo-German Antagonism* (1987), Arthur J.
Marder, *From the Dreadnought to Scapa Flow*, vol. i (1961), Samuel R. Williamson,
The Politics of Grand Strategy: Britain and France prepare for War, 1904–14 (1969),
Avner Offer, *The First World War: An Agrarian Interpretation* (1989) did not fully
eclipse fear of Russia. C. J. Lowe and M. L. Dockrill, *The Mirage of Power*, vol. i,
British Foreign Policy 1902–14 (1972) and Zara Steiner, *Britain and the Origins of the
First World War* (1977) are first-class studies in this respect. French and Russian ambi-
tions are admirably treated in John F. Keiger, *France and the Origins of the First
World War* (1983), Gerd Krumeich, *Armaments and Politics in France on the Eve of
the First World War* (1984), D. C. B. Lieven, *Russia and the Origins of the First World
War* (1983), Dietrich Geyer, *Russian Imperialism, 1860–1914* (1987), part III, and
David M. McDonald, 'A lever without a fulcrum: domestic factors and Russian
foreign policy, 1905–1914' in Hugh Ragsdale (ed.), *Imperial Russian Foreign Policy*
(1993). On the internal problems of states, Peter Christian Witt, *Die Finanzpolitik des
Deutschen Reiches von 1903 bis 1913* (1970) tackles the thorny problem of German
finances, and Katherine Anne Lerman, *The Chancellor as Courtier: Bernhard von
Bülow and the Governance of Germany, 1900–1909* (1990), sets them in context while
Beverly Heckhart, *From Basserman to Bebel* (1974), Fischer and Ely, already cited
(above, p. 454), examine the failure of a bourgeois-labour coalition in Germany. Its
relative success in France and Great Britain may be seen from Jean-Denis Bredin,
Caillaux (1980) and Madeleine Reberioux's contribution to Jean-Marie Mayeur and
M. Rebérioux, *The Third Republic from its Origins to the Great War* (1984), Robert J.
Scally, *The Origins of the Lloyd George Coalition* (1975), Bruce K. Murray, *The People's Budget 1909–10: Lloyd George and Liberal Politics* (1980), and David Brooks,
The Age of Upheaval: Edwardian Politics, 1899–1914 (1995). On the capitulation of
the labour movement to the war effort there is useful material in William Maehl, 'The
triumph of nationalism in the German Social-Democratic party on the eve of the first
world war', *Journal of Modern History*, 24 (1952), Jacques Julliard, 'La C. G. T.
devant la guerre, 1900–1914', *Mouvement Social*, 49 (1964), Jolyon Howorth, 'French
workers and German workers: the impossibility of internationalism, 1900–1914',
European History Quarterly 15 (1985), Jean-Jacques Becker, *The Great War and
the French People* (1985), and Georges Haupt, *Socialism and the Great War: The
Collapse of the Second International* (1972).

BIOGRAPHICAL DICTIONARY OF
MAJOR FIGURES

Andrássy, Count Gyula (1823–90). A Magyar nationalist, radical ally of Kossuth, who fought in the unsuccessful war for Hungarian independence, 1848–9. Exiled in England and France till 1858, he returned to negotiate the *Ausgleich* with Austria 1867 and served as Hungarian Minister-President 1867–71. As Foreign Minister of the Empire in 1871–9 he sought good relations with Germany and an alliance of Austria, Germany, Italy, and Great Britain against Russia, which was never realized. Suspicious of Russian ambitions in the Balkans, he was ill at ease in the Three Emperors' League and was anxious to maintain the Ottoman Empire intact, or to secure Austria's position in the Balkans if Turkey had to be expelled from Europe.

Bakunin, Mikhail (1814–76). A Russian noble, who was dismissed from the artillery cadet school of St Petersburg in 1834 and then from the army in 1835. He conversed with intellectuals in Russia before travelling to Germany (1840), Switzerland (1843), and Paris (1844–7), where he met Marx and Proudhon. Meanwhile the Tsarist regime deprived him of his noble rank and property and ordered his banishment to Siberia. In 1848 he participated in the Pan-Slav Congress at Prague. Arrested after the Dresden rising of 1849, he was handed over to the Russian government and imprisoned. He escaped from Siberia in 1861 and returned to Europe to pursue anarchist conspiracy, founding the International Brotherhood at Naples (1865–7) and then the International Social-Democratic Alliance in a bid to take over the First International from Marx. In 1870 he tried to set up a revolutionary commune at Lyons. The final breach with Marx came in 1872. He died in Berne.

Bennigsen, Rudolf von (1824–1902). A Hanoverian noble, civil servant, and politician, who became the leader of the liberal opposition in Hanover's second chamber after 1855. He was founder and president of Nationalverein (1859), which attempted to unite all German liberals. He failed to keep Hanover neutral in the Prussio-Austrian War of 1866, as a result of which it was annexed by Prussia. In the Prussian Landtag and the Reichstag he fought for a constitutional regime and refused ministerial office in 1877. Opposed to the capitulation of the National Liberals to Bismarck he resigned his seats in the Landtag and Reichstag between 1883 and 1887. Between 1888 and 1897 he was *Oberpräsident* of the province of Hanover.

Bethmann Hollweg, Theobald von (1856–1921). A Prussian jurist and civil servant, *Oberpräsident* of Brandenburg province 1899–1905, who became Prussian Minister of the Interior 1905 and Secretary of State at the Reich Ministry of the Interior 1907. As German Chancellor in 1909, he tried to reconcile the Centre party and population of Alsace-Lorraine to the Reich. He was unable to tame the Prussian establishment, which rejected his plans for a more democratic Prussian constitution, or to control the military in internal and external affairs. Bethmann suffered rather than provoked the outbreak of war in 1914 and resigned in the face of the high-handedness of the military leadership in 1917.

Bismarck, Otto, Prince von (1815–98). A Brandenburg noble, who served in the Prussian civil service and briefly in a Guards regiment before retiring to his newly inherited estates in 1838. In the United Landtag of Prussia in 1847 and the Prussian lower chamber in 1849 he joined the conservatives and brought himself to the notice of Prince William, heir to the throne. He embarked on the diplomatic career he had coveted as Prussian minister at the Frankfurt Diet in 1851, and ambassador at St Petersburg in 1859–61. Appointed Minister-President of Prussia in 1862 to break a constitutional deadlock, he governed without a budget for four years until the defeat of Austria. He became chancellor of the North German Confederation in 1867 and of the new German Reich after the defeat of France in 1870. The right-hand man of King (then Emperor) William I, he was less appreciated by William II and resigned as Minister-President and Chancellor in 1890.

Bülow, Bernhard von (1849–1929). Son of representative of the Duchy of Holstein at the Federal Diet of Frankfurt, who became Bismarck's Foreign Minister in 1877–9, the young Bülow served in the Franco-Prussian War, entered the diplomatic service in 1874 and became ambassador in Rome in 1894. He was promoted Secretary of State for Foreign Affairs in 1897 and became Chancellor in 1900. A champion of *Weltpolitik*, his room to manœuvre was limited by Holstein at the Foreign Office, and above all by William II, who indulged in irresponsible personal diplomacy. He resigned in 1909 after failing to get a budget approved by the Reichstag. In 1914 he returned briefly to public life in a vain bid to bring Italy on to the side of Germany and Austria, and died in Rome.

Capodistrias, John, Count (1776–1831). An Ionian noble, who was born in Corfu under Venetian rule and studied at Padua University. He became Secretary of State (Foreign Affairs) of the Septinsular Republic (the Ionian Islands) in 1803 after their liberation from the French until their restoration to France after Tilsit (1807). In 1809 he entered Russian service as Councillor of State in the Foreign Ministry and went on diplomatic missions to Vienna and Bucharest. Russian plenipotentiary at the Congress of Vienna, he was made Secretary of State in 1815 and played a key role in Russian foreign policy until forced to resign, largely at the behest of Metternich, in 1822. Capodistria went into exile in Switzerland until he was elected President of the Greek Republic by the Greek National Assembly in 1827. He was assassinated in 1831.

Castlereagh, Robert Stewart, Viscount (1769–1822). Son of an Irish peer, he was elected member of the Irish parliament in 1790 and the English Parliament in 1794. As Chief Secretary for Ireland 1798–1801, he defended it against Irish revolutionaries and French invaders, and steered through the Act of Union in 1800, but resigned when George III refused to grant political rights to Catholics. He was Secretary of State for War and Colonies in 1805–6 and 1807–9, until the disastrous expedition to Walcheren at the mouth of the Scheldt. As Foreign Secretary between 1812 and 1822 he helped to form the final coalition to defeat Napoleon and then promoted the Concert of Europe to ensure peace. He committed suicide.

Cavour, Camillo di, Count (1810–61). A Piedmontese aristocrat, who served for a short period as an engineer army officer before retiring in 1831 to improve his father's estates and travel in England and France. In 1847 he founded the journal *Il Risorgimento* to press for constitutional reform and sat in the Piedmontese assembly in 1848 and again in 1849. He became Minister of Agriculture and Commerce in 1850, and Minister of Finance in 1851 under d'Azeglio, and formed his own ministry in 1852. Cavour prevailed on King Victor Emmanuel II to bring Piedmont into the Crimean War and to launch war on Austria with French support in 1859. When the king concluded an armistice with Austria he resigned. He returned to power at the end of 1859 to bring all of Italy, except Venetia and the Papal States, into a united state before his death.

Chamberlain, Joseph (1836–1914). The son of a London boot and shoe manufacturer, he went into business in Birmingham as a screw manufacturer. He was elected mayor of Birmingham in 1873, 1874, and 1875 and MP for Birmingham (with John Bright) in 1876. Chamberlain helped to organize the Liberal victory of 1880 and became Gladstone's President of the Board of Trade, but disagreed with Gladstone over Home Rule and resigned in 1886. His Liberal Unionists supported the Conservatives and he became Colonial Secretary in Salisbury's government in 1895 at the height of Great Britain's imperial expansion. However, the Conservatives disagreed with his strategy of an imperial customs area protected by high tariffs and he resigned his post in 1903. He suffered a stroke in 1906 and withdrew from public life.

Cobden, Richard (1804–65). The son of a yeoman farmer who set up as a calico-printer near Blackburn in 1831. He founded the Anti-Corn Law League in 1838 and was elected MP for Stockport in 1841. His campaign was crowned with success with the repeal of the Corn Laws in 1846, and a European tour of 1846–7 met with widespread acclaim. Cobden's opposition to the Crimean War cost him his parliamentary seat in 1857. Re-elected in 1858 he was offered the presidency of the Board of Trade by Palmerston but declined it, on account of Palmerston's warlike tendencies. He negotiated an important free trade treaty with France on the behalf of the Chancellor of the Exchequer, Gladstone, in 1860.

Crispi, Francesco (1819–1901). A Sicilian lawyer who was one of the leaders of the revolution in Palermo against Bourbon rule in 1848. He fled to Piedmont and conspired with Mazzini for a unitary republic, but was expelled in 1853 for involvement in a rising in Milan. Crispi returned to Italy in 1859 and organized Garibaldi's expedition to Sicily, becoming Minister of Finance in the Sicilian provisional government. Elected a republican Deputy for Sicily in 1861, he converted to monarchism three years later and became President of the Italian Chamber in 1876. Crispi served as Minister of the Interior under Depretis in 1877–8. As Prime Minister in 1887–91 he tightened Italy's alliance with Bismarck's Germany. He returned to power in 1893 as a strong man who could crush rebellion in Sicily, but his imperialist ambitions came to grief in 1895 when the Italian army was defeated by the Ethiopians. This finished his political career.

Czartoryski, Adam, Prince (1770–1861). A Polish-Lithuanian noble, who fought for Poland against Russia on behalf of the Constitution of 1791 and went into exile in 1793, before the final partition of Poland in 1795, but became a friend and principal adviser of Tsar Alexander I. As Russian Minister of Foreign Affairs in 1804 he helped to build the third coalition against Napoleon, but was dismissed after Russia's defeat in 1806. From 1812 he campaigned for a separate kingdom of Poland which would nevertheless be united to Russia, and this was approved by the Congress of Vienna in

1815. Czartoryski did not get on with Nicholas I and during the Polish revolt of 1831 became President of the Polish national government. After the Polish leaders fled to Paris, he became the effective head of a government in exile, but lost influence to the radicals, who were bent on insurrection in 1846 and 1848, and was unable to rely on Napoleon III to wage a determined war against Russia.

Disraeli, Benjamin, 1st Earl of Beaconsfield (1804–81). Born into a family of Spanish-Jewish origin which converted to Christianity in 1817, he studied for the Bar but took to writing and travelling in the Mediterranean in 1828–31 before being elected to Parliament in 1837. With the 'Young England' movement he defended land, the Church and the Crown against what he saw as Peel's betrayal, but was concerned also for the people. In 1848 he became leader of the Conservative party, and served as Chancellor of the Exchequer in 1852, 1858, and 1866. As Leader of the Commons he was responsible for the Reform Bill of 1867, became Prime Minister in 1868 but lost the election that year to Gladstone. His ministry of 1874–80 was characterized by imperialism and social reform. Disraeli was made Earl of Beaconsfield in 1876.

Garibaldi, Giuseppe (1807–82). A native of Nice, of a sea-going family, he became involved with the revolutionary activities of Mazzini and fled to Brazil after the failure of an insurrection in Genoa in 1834. Most of his life was spent as a guerilla leader, fighting for Uruguay against Argentina, for Charles Albert of Piedmont against the Austrians in 1848, in defence of the Roman Republic against the French in 1849, in the Alps for Victor Emmanuel of Piedmont in 1859, against the Bourbons in Sicily and Naples in 1860, attempting to liberate Rome in 1862, returning to the Alps for Victor Emmanuel in 1866, and fighting for France against Prussia in 1870. He was elected Deputy to the French National Assembly in 1871 and to the Italian parliament for Rome in 1874, but he was no politician.

Giolitti, Giovanni (1842–1928). The archetypal lawyer and liberal politician of post-Risorgimento Italy, he served as a magistrate and administrative official in the Ministry of Finance before his appointment as Councillor of State and election as Deputy for his native province of Cuneo in Piedmont in 1882. Giolitti was Finance Minister under Crispi in 1889–90 and became Prime Minister in 1892–3, but fell over a bank scandal. Returning as Interior Minister under Zanardelli in 1902, he was Prime Minister in 1903–5, 1906–9 and 1911–14, during which Italy went to war against the Turks in Libya. He opposed Italy's intervention in the First World War and was ill-suited to the violence of Italian politics after the war, although his last ministry was in 1920–1.

Gladstone, William Ewart (1809–98). The son of a rich Liverpool merchant and landowner, educated at Eton and Oxford, Gladstone was elected to Parliament in 1832 under the aegis of an aristocratic patron. For twenty years he was a Peelite, holding office under Peel in 1834 and 1841–5, and was Chancellor of the Exchequer in the Aberdeen coalition of 1852–5 until the Peelites withdrew. Gladstone's chancellorship under Palmerston in 1859–65 and Lord John Russell in 1865–6 marked his passage to the Liberal party, of which he became leader in 1868. He was Prime Minister four times, in 1868–74, 1880–5, 1886, and 1892–4. Unable to prevent the split of the Liberal party over his policy of Home Rule for Ireland, he resigned the premiership in 1894 and was succeeded by Lord Rosebery.

Hardenberg, Carl August, Prince von (1750–1822). A Hanoverian by birth, he entered the Hanoverian civil service, then that of Brunswick (1783), before becoming the administrator of the principalities of Ansbach and Bayreuth, which had just fallen to Prussia (1790). In 1795 he was Prussian plenipotentiary at Basle, and entered the Prussian cabinet in 1797. His career as Foreign Minister in 1804–6 and 1807 was dogged by the antipathy to him of Napoleon, who defeated Prussia in 1806. Hardenberg became State Chancellor in 1810 and was made a prince in 1814, but was outmanœuvred by Metternich at the Congress of Vienna and in the German Confederation.

Hohenlohe-Schillingfürst, Chlodwig Karl Victor, Prince zu (1819–1901). A Bavarian noble of mixed Catholic–Protestant parentage, he served in the Prussian civil service in 1844–6, sat in the Bavarian Reichsrat and after the defeat of Bavaria in 1866 became President of the Bavarian Council of Ministers and Minister for Foreign Affairs. He tried to navigate between Bavarian particularists and Prussian hegemony and was forced to resign early in 1870. As a member of the German Reichstag in 1871 he founded the *Liberale Reichspartei* and became Prussian ambassador in Paris in 1873. He headed the German Foreign Office temporarily in 1880, during an illness of Bismarck, and became Governor of Alsace-Lorraine in 1885. Between 1894 and 1900 Hohenlohe was Chancellor of Germany, and a moderating influence on the Kaiser and his circle.

Karageorgević. One of the ruling dynasties of Serbia. Its founder, Karageorge or Black George (*c.*1766–1817), waged irregular warfare against the Turks culminating in a rising in 1804, and was elected that year supreme leader by the Serbs. After his position was made impossible by the Russo-Turkish treaty of 1812 he fled to Hungary and was later murdered. Alexander, his son (1806–85), was elected Prince of the Serbs in 1843 and ruled until 1858. His son, Peter (1844–1921), became king in 1903 and took a strong line against Austrian ambitions in the Balkans. He entrusted the regency to Crown Prince Alexander in 1914 and took a passive role in the First World War but after the war was elected 'King of the Serbs, Croats, and Slovenes'.

Kossuth, Lajos (1802–94). A Hungarian leader from a poor noble family, Slovak in origin but Magyarized. He made his name as a deputy for an absentee count at the Hungarian Diet in Pressburg in 1832–6, was imprisoned for high treason in 1837–40, and launched *Pest News* in 1841. In the Hungarian Diet of 1847 he led the extreme liberals and became Minister of Finance in the 'responsible' Hungarian ministry of March 1848. When Hungary went to war with Austria in 1848–9 he was elected President of the Committee of National Defence and then Governor-President of Hungary. After Hungary's defeat in 1849 he fled to Turkey, where he was interned till 1851. He travelled to England and the United States, and played with revolutionary nationalist projects. Though elected to the Hungarian Diet in 1867 he was never reconciled to Hungary of the *Ausgleich* and lived in Italy until his death.

Lenin, Vladimir Ilyich, family name Ulyanov (1870–1924). Russian revolutionary, the son of school inspector. His elder brother was hanged for terrorism in 1887. He studied law at Kazan and St Petersburg universities till 1891, then discovered Marx, went to Geneva to meet the Liberation of Labour group, was arrested for propaganda activities in St Petersburg in 1895 and exiled to Siberia from 1897 to 1900. In 1900 Lenin returned to Switzerland, published *Iskra* (*The Spark*) newspaper, and after

1903 became the leader of the Bolshevik wing of the Russian Social Democrats. His attempt to exploit the revolution of 1905 was a failure, and he left Russia in 1907, not to return until 1917. In October 1917 Lenin became head of the new revolutionary government, the Council of People's Commissars.

Lloyd George, David (1863–1945). The son of a Welsh schoolmaster, born in Manchester, he qualified as a solicitor in 1884 and was elected to Parliament for Carnarvon Boroughs in 1890. Lloyd George was a champion of Nonconformity and Welsh nationalism, and opposed the Boer War, but was made President of the Board of Trade by Campbell-Bannerman in 1905. As Chancellor of the Exchequer after 1908 he was responsible for the 'People's Budget' of 1909. In the Asquith–Bonar Law coalition he was Minister of Munitions (1915), but helped to overthrow Asquith in 1916 and became Prime Minister of a coalition government which lasted until 1922. In opposition, he presided over the decline of the Liberal party.

Marx, Karl (1818–83). Born at Trier, in the Prussian Rhineland, the son of a Jewish lawyer who converted to Christianity in 1824, Marx studied at the universities of Bonn and Berlin and collaborated on the staff of the radical newspaper, *Rheinische Zeitung*, in 1842–3. He moved to Paris in 1843, where he co-edited the *Deutsch-französische Jahrbücher* and parted company with the content, if not the form, of Hegel's ideas. Expelled and moving to Brussels in 1845, he became involved with a secret society, the League of the Just, which became the Communist League in 1847. Marx was involved in the events of 1848 in Cologne, until he was expelled by the Prussian authorities. After 1849 he and his family were based in London, where he wrote *Capital* (the first volume was published in 1867) and helped to build the International Working Men's Association, the First International.

Mazzini, Giuseppe (1805–72). A Genoan, the son of a doctor, and university professor, Mazzini studied law there and joined the Carbonari. He was imprisoned for revolutionary activities in 1830 and forced to leave for Marseilles on his release in 1831. Mazzini founded the Young Italy movement to struggle for an independent, united Italy, and led a fruitless invasion from Switzerland into the (then Piedmontese) province of Savoy in 1834. Expelled by the Swiss Diet in 1836, he went to London. During 1848–9 he was involved in revolutionary movements in Milan, Florence, and Rome, where he became a triumvir. In 1853 Mazzini staged an insurrection in Milan, which was brutally suppressed. He was marginalized by the unification of Italy under the Piedmontese monarchy and was arrested and imprisoned in 1870, on his way to organize a rising in Sicily. He died in Pisa.

Metternich, Clemens von (1773–1859). An Austrian statesman, but born a Rhinelander in Coblenz. He was the son of a representative at Vienna of the Elector of Trier who became the Minister of the Austrian Emperor to the Rhineland bishops and (in 1790) Minister of the Austrian Netherlands. Clemens von Metternich was educated at the universities of Strasbourg and Mainz, but when the French Revolutionary armies invaded the Rhineland in 1794 he was forced to flee with his family to London and then Vienna. He became Austrian ambassador at Dresden (1801–3), Berlin (1803–6), and Paris (1806–9). As Minister of Foreign Affairs after the defeat of Austria by France in 1809 he negotiated the marriage of the Emperor's daughter Marie Louise to Napoleon, then brought Austria into the coalition against Napoleon at the last moment and put the stamp of Austria on the post-war European settlement. From 1821 until 1848 he was Austrian Court Chancellor and Chancellor of State. He was forced into exile in the Netherlands and England by the revolution of 1848 but returned to Vienna in 1851.

Napoleon I (1769–1821). Born at Ajaccio, Corsica, the year after its reunion to France, Napoleon Bonaparte made a career as an artillery officer, recapturing Toulon from royalists supported by the British fleet in 1793 and suppressing a royalist rising in Paris in 1795. On behalf of the Directory he commanded the army of Italy against the Austrians in 1796–7 and led an expedition to Egypt in 1798. In 1799 he overthrew the Directory by a *coup d'état* and was endorsed as First Consul (1800), Consul for life (1802), and hereditary Emperor of the French (1804) by successive plebiscites. In 1805–7 he defeated the third coalition of European powers against France since the Revolution, but his power waned after 1808 as a result of the Peninsular War, defeat in Russia, and the triumph of a fourth coalition of European powers. In 1814 he was obliged to abdicate and exiled to Elba, where he had sovereign authority, but returned to France where he ruled as Emperor again for a Hundred Days in 1815. After his final defeat at Waterloo he was sent as a prisoner of war to the island of St Helena in the Atlantic.

Napoleon III (1808–73). Louis-Napoleon Bonaparte was the third son of Louis Bonaparte, brother of the first Emperor, and King of Holland. After the fall of the Empire he was brought up in exile in Switzerland and Italy, where he took part in the rising against the Papacy in the Romagna (1831). In 1836 he staged a mutiny in the garrison of Strasbourg, after which he was deported to the United States. Captured after a landing at Boulogne in 1840, he was imprisoned in France until his escape in 1846. In June 1848 he was elected to the National Assembly, where he took his seat after a decree banishing the Bonapartes from French territory was abrogated. In December 1848 he was elected President of the Republic by direct suffrage but, hemmed in by a royalist assembly, dissolved it by a *coup d' état* in 1851 and proclaimed himself Emperor of the French in 1852, with the approval of plebiscites. Napoleon III was Emperor until the defeat of France by Prussia in 1870. He died in exile in England.

Obrenović. The second ruling dynasty of Serbia, rival to the family of Karageorgević. Miloš Obrenović I (1780–1860) was elected Prince of the Serbs in 1817, supported by the Turks as the only guarantee against disorder. He was forced to abdicate in 1839, recalled twenty years later but died soon afterwards. His son, Milan Obrenović II, succeeded him in 1839 but died the following year. Another son, Michael Obrenović III (1823–68), who ruled 1840–2 and 1860–8 was Serbia's ablest modern ruler. He reorganized the army and built a Balkan alliance against Turkey before his untimely assassination. His son, Milan Obrenović IV (1854–1901), became prince in 1868 at the age of fourteen. The regent he had for the first four years of his reign subsequently became Prime Minister, and drove him into supporting the Bosnian insurrection of 1875. Milan did not trust the Russians to protect Serbia, and turned Serbia into a satellite of Austria, in return for which Austria recognized him as king in 1882. In 1889 he was forced to abdicate in favour of his child, Alexander, aged thirteen. Alexander recalled his father from exile in 1894 and appointed him Commander-in-Chief of the

Serb army in 1897. Alexander's marriage to his mistress in 1900 alienated both his father, who left for Vienna, and his subjects, who assassinated him in 1903.

Palacký, František (1798–1876). Born in Moravia of a Protestant family, the son of a schoolteacher, Palacký studied at Pressburg, and moved to Prague, which was dominated by Germans, in 1823. Under the patronage of a Bohemian noble, Count Franz Sternberg, he edited the *Journal of the Bohemian Museum* after 1827. His *History of Bohemia* was published first in German (1836–67), then in Czech, as the *History of the Czech Nation* (1848–67). In 1848 he refused an invitation to the Pre-Parliament of the German Confederation of Frankfurt, and instead chaired the Congress of Austrian Slavs at Prague. In the imperial Constituent Assembly of 1848–9 he sat on a committee to draft a constitution for the Empire. After the period of reaction in the 1850s he became a life member of the House of Lords of the Imperial Diet (1861–5) and led the National party or Old Czechs in the Bohemian Diet. After the consecration of German–Magyar dualism in 1867 he attended the All-Slav Ethnographic Exhibition in Moscow and withdrew from public life in the 1870s.

Palmerston, Henry John Temple, 3rd Viscount (1784–1865). The son of an Irish peer, who succeeded to the title in 1802, which did not prevent him sitting in the House of Commons, to which he was elected in 1807. Between 1809–28 he occupied the modest post of Secretary-at-War at the War Office, preferring the life of a *beau* to more demanding tasks. He entered Wellington's cabinet with the Canningites in 1827, and left with them the same year, unable to get on with die-hard Tories. In opposition he became interested in foreign affairs, especially after the French Revolution of 1830, and became Foreign Minister in Whig cabinets (though he claimed not to be a proper Whig) in 1830–41 and 1846–51, when he was dismissed for supporting Louis-Napoleon's *coup d'état*. In the Aberdeen cabinet of 1852–5 he was Secretary of State for Home Affairs. He became Prime Minister of a Whig–Peelite administration during the Crimean War and held the office till his death in 1865.

Peel, Robert (1788–1850). The son of a rich Lancashire cotton-spinner, educated at Harrow and Oxford, he was elected to Parliament in 1807. He rose under the patronage of Lord Liverpool to become Secretary for Ireland (1812–18), a wearisome post which he resigned, and Home Secretary in the Liverpool cabinet (1822–7). He was Home Secretary under Wellington in 1828–30 and supported Catholic emancipation, but opposed the Reform Bill. He was Prime Minister briefly in 1834–5 and again in 1841–6, when he was forced to resign by protectionist Tories. In opposition he lent his support to the Whig administration. He died after a riding accident.

Pius IX, Giovanni Maria Mastai-Ferretti (1792–1878). Of Italian noble family, he became Bishop of Imola in 1832 and was elected Pope as Pius IX in 1846. Between 1846 and 1848 he undertook fundamental reforms in the Papal States, but refused to join the Piedmontese war against Austria. After the assassination of his Prime Minister and the establishment of a republic in Rome, which forced him to flee to Gaeta in the Kingdom of Naples, he declared undying war on the nineteenth century. He returned to Rome in 1850 under the protection of a French garrison, affirmed the Immaculate Conception of the Virgin Mary in 1854 and issued the *Syllabus of Errors* in 1864. The Vatican Council proclaimed the infallibility of the Pope in doctrinal matters in 1870, shortly before the French garrison withdrew to fight against Prussia. Piedmontese troops entered the city of Rome and for the last eight years of his pontificate Pius IX refused to recognize the Italian state and considered himself a prisoner in the Vatican.

Poincaré, Raymond (1860–1934). A Lorrainer, born to a civil service family, he studied law at the University of Paris, became a successful barrister, and was elected Deputy for the Meuse in 1887. He served as Minister of Education in 1893 and 1895–6, and Minister of Finance in 1894–5 and 1906. His great rivals were Caillaux and Clemenceau, who dominated the political scene between 1906 and 1909. After the fall of Caillaux over the Morocco crisis of 1911, Poincaré became Prime Minister (1912) and President of the Republic (1913). He restored vigour to the presidency, improved relations with Russia, and (despite personal animosity) put Clemenceau in power in 1917 to win the war. He was Prime Minister again in 1922–4 and 1926–9.

Proudhon, Pierre-Joseph (1809–65). Of humble peasant-artisan stock, Proudhon received some education at the College of Besançon but had to leave early to take up work as a printer. In 1838 he won a three-year scholarship from the Academy of Besançon and went to Paris, where he wrote *What is Property?* (1840), a tract which resulted in his trial by the assize court of Besançon, and acquittal. In June 1848 he was elected to the National Assembly and took to journalism, but was condemned to three years' prison (1849–52) for attacking the President of the Republic, Louis-Napoleon. A further three-year condemnation for anticlerical writing followed in 1858. Proudhon fled to Brussels and did not return to France till 1862. His last work developed the idea of federalism.

Rothschild. A Jewish banking family based at Frankfurt. Meyer Amschel Rothschild (1743–1812), who raised funds after 1801 for the landgrave (then elector) of Hesse-Cassel, had five sons. These were Amschel Meyer (1773–1855), who became Bavarian court banker in 1820; Nathan (1777–1836) who settled in London in 1804; James (1792–1860), who set up in Paris in 1811; Solomon (1774–1855), established in Vienna in 1820, and Carl Meyer (1788–1855), who arrived in Naples in 1821. Nathan's son Lionel (1808–79) was elected MP for the City of London in 1847, 1849, 1852, and 1857, but barred because he refused to take the Christian oath; he eventually took his seat in 1858. His son, Nathan Meyer (1840–1915), became a peer in 1885.

Salisbury, Robert Cecil, 3rd Marquis of (1830–1903). Educated at Eton and Oxford, elected to Parliament in 1853, he dabbled in the journalism of the *Quarterly Review*. He was Secretary of State for India in Lord Derby's cabinet of 1866–7, but resigned over the Reform Bill and disliked Disraeli. On the death of his father in 1868 he entered the House of Lords, attacked Gladstone's reforms, and became Secretary of State for India again in 1874. He made his mark at the Congress of Berlin in 1878 and was promoted to be Foreign Secretary. Lord Salisbury was Prime Minister and Foreign Secretary in three separate administrations, 1885–6, 1886–92, and 1895–1902. He resigned as Foreign Secretary in 1900, as Prime Minister in 1902, for reasons of ill-health.

Stein, Karl, Baron vom (1757–1831). Born to a family of imperial knights near Nassau, entered the Prussian service in 1780 and made his mark administering Prussia's western possessions, as Director of the Board of War and Domains west of the Weser (1787) and President of the Westphalian Chambers of Commerce and Mines (1796).

In 1804 he moved to Berlin as Minister of State for Trade. Following the defeat of Prussia by France and the dismissal of Hardenberg, Stein became Chief Minister and executed a series of fundamental reforms in anticipation of a national insurrection (1807–8). After his fall he went to Austria, but was invited to St Petersburg in 1812 and master-minded the Russian–Prussian offensive of 1813–14 against Napoleon. He became Superintendant for the Administration of Liberated Territories on behalf of the Allies, but his plans for a united Germany under Prussian leadership were frustrated by Metternich.

Talleyrand-Périgord, Charles Maurice de (1754–1838). A French aristocrat, the son of a general, destined for the Church, he became Bishop of Autun in 1789 but approved of the Revolutionary church settlement and was excommunicated by the Pope 1791–1802. He emigrated to England in 1792 and to the United States in 1793–5, then became Foreign Minister under the Directory (1797–9). He was close to Napoleon Bonaparte and became his Foreign Minister in 1799–1807, but did not always agree with his ambitions and quarrelled with him in 1814. After the fall of Paris in 1814 he turned against Napoleon with the rest of the French Senate and declared his crown forfeit. Having persuaded the Allies to restore the Bourbon monarchy he fought to end France's isolation by concluding a secret alliance with Austria and Great Britain against Russia and Prussia. In 1815 he was briefly Foreign Minister and President of the Council, then High Chamberlain, but played no further public role until 1830, when he accepted an embassy in London.

Thiers, Adolphe (1797–1877). A French politician, born in Marseilles, who studied law at Aix and made a career in Paris after 1821 as a liberal journalist. A firm supporter of the July Monarchy, he was elected Deputy for Aix in 1830 and became Minister of the Interior in 1832 and 1834–6. He was President of the Council of Ministers for short spells in 1836 and 1840. In June 1848 he was elected to the National Assembly and became leader of the 'party of order'. An opponent of Louis-Napoleon's *coup d'état*, he was expelled from France until the summer of 1852. Thiers re-entered political life in 1863 as a Deputy for Paris, and led the Orleanist opposition to the Empire in the Chamber of Deputies. After the defeat of France by Prussia, the National Assembly elected in 1871 made him Chief of the Executive Power, to finalize peace terms with Germany and restore order in Paris. He was President of the Republic between 1871 and 1873.

INDEX

Entries marked by an asterisk (*) are enlarged in the Biographical Dictionary of major figures. Kings of Serbia are to be found there under the ruling family (Karageorgević, Obrenović).

The end of a reign is the same as the death of the ruler, unless otherwise stated.

Index